France 1789–1815

France 1789–1815
Revolution and Counterrevolution

D. M. G. SUTHERLAND

New York   Oxford
OXFORD UNIVERSITY PRESS
1986

Oxford University Press

Copyright © 1985 D. M. G. Sutherland

Originally published in Great Britain by William Collins Sons & Co Ltd.
in 1985

First published in the United States in paperback in 1986 by
Oxford University Press, 200 Madison Avenue, New York, New York 10016

Oxford is a registered trademark of Oxford University Press

Library of Congress Cataloging-in-Publication Data
Sutherland, Donald (Donald M. G.)
France 1789–1815.
Bibliography: p.
Includes index.
1. France—History—Revolution, 1789–1815.
I. Title.
DC148.S855   1986   944.04   86-719
ISBN 0-19-520512-X
ISBN 0-19-520513-8

Printing (last digit): 9 8 7 6 5

Printed in the United States of America

For my parents

Preface

For anyone trying to make sense of the enormously complicated and confusing events of the history of France between 1789 and 1815, the theory of the bourgeois revolution comes to mind most easily. It is not much of a caricature to say that this view portrays the French Revolution of 1789 as a product of a bourgeoisie nourished on several centuries of developing capitalism; that its aspirations were frustrated by the aristocracy's monopoly of power; that the financial crisis of the Old Regime monarchy and the eventual calling of the Estates-General provided the occasion for the bourgeoisie to seize power and reshape social, legal and political institutions according to its own interests; that the resistance of the aristocracy to its own menacing demise explains both why the Revolution had to be violent and why the revolutionary era was so long; that the most dramatic challenge to the bourgeoisie's hegemony came from the urban *sans-culottes*, an autonomous movement of artisans and miscellaneous terrorists whose idea of direct democracy, total political commitment and limitations on the rights of property were too much even for Jacobins on the Committee of Public Safety; that once the alliance of Jacobin and *sans-culotte* collapsed in 1794, the bourgeoisie reasserted control but could not consolidate itself through representative institutions; that it then surrendered to the military in 1799 but Bonaparte, ever the adventurer, usurped power so that the bourgeoisie had to await the defeat in Russia in 1812 to consign the imperial despotism to the rubbish heap; and finally that with the Restoration in 1814–15 with its limited electorate and constitutional government, the bourgeoisie found the regime which most suited it. To compress this description of the period still further, the history of the French Revolution is the history of the consolidation of the bourgeoisie.

This encapsulates the classical theory of the Revolution. Despite its obvious Marxist overtones, most historians have accepted its basic framework in greater or lesser degree. This is because the notion that the Revolution had to occur to adjust legal institutions to changed property relations goes back to such diverse authors as Barnave, Tocqueville and Aulard. With such illustrious support, it has simply become embedded in our way of viewing the entire period. Alfred Cobban began the process of undermining classical historiography on many issues, and although subsequent research has not always supported his formulations, nonetheless it has continued the tendency towards disintegration. Much of this investigation has concentrated on the origins of the Revolution and, as we shall see in chapter one, the whole idea of the class origins of the Revolution with a distinct, ambitious, frustrated, capitalist bourgeoisie has collapsed, probably forever. At the other end of the period, and with a good deal less fanfare, researchers are quietly showing that the kind of ruling class that emerged from the revolutionary maelstrom was one of landed proprietors and officials, not of capitalist bourgeoisie. Moreover, the Old Regime nobility had such a prominent role among the post-revolutionary 'notables', as they are called, that it is hardly possible to depict the period as the definitive overthrow of one class by another.

This research on the elite origins of the Revolution and nature of the ruling class at its aftermath has implications for the general narrative of the revolutionary era. If the role of class is less important than was once thought, the theme of bourgeoisie consolidating its power fades considerably. If the bourgeois-aristocratic conflict is fuzzy, then aristocratic resistance to bourgeois hegemony cannot be the sole reason for resistance to the reforms of 1789–90. The class basis of the various revolutionary regimes, particularly the thermidorean, the Directory and the Consulate, is consequently also in doubt. Finally, the ultimate significance of the relationship between supposedly 'bourgeois' Jacobin dictatorship and 'popular' *sans-culotte* democracy becomes hazy.

The thrust of much of the revisionist writing on the Revolution has been negative, and for many general readers who have delved into the subject the result must have been extraordinarily frustrating. For many academic historians who immerse themselves in damp and dusty documents and who have gathered immense intellectual rewards from the experience – and I count myself among them – these ambiguities at the heart of the subject probably do not matter much. For many of us it is enough to show that the Revolution looked quite different from the point of view of 'our' townsmen or 'our' peasants from that given in the standard histories; that for many Frenchmen, the Revolution was a genuinely liberating experience while for others it had a less publicized underside in the form of loss of employment, higher taxes, increased rents and religious dislocation; that from the point of view of provincials, its chronological rhythms were different in that, for example, many may have been stunned by the enforced removal of their priest, scarcely affected at all by the Terror but rendered utterly miserable by bad harvests and criminal gangs after 1794. The effect of much provincial and local history which has enjoyed such a vogue in the last twenty years has thus been much the same as revisionist history. It too dissolved time-honoured interpretations because the Revolution begins to look quite different depending upon the locale, regional social structures and regime economies. Indeed, the gap between the Parisian and provincial revolutions is sometimes so great that some reviewers have wondered whether they are dealing with the same phenomenon.

With so many familiar signposts knocked down and so much information to process, general readers are badly in need of a new chart to guide them through the era. One possibility is to abandon single-minded class-based theories of the Revolution and accept a number of propositions: that the conflict between privileged and non-privileged was real enough even if it was not based on class; that force of circumstance in the summer of 1789 brought to power men who had a fairly clear idea of what they wanted but no clear mandate from the nation to implement it; that the combination of fear of the privileged orders and the collapse of government converted many other leaders to this vision; that roughly the same factors radicalized many ordinary people, particularly in the towns and in some country districts, who then went on to formulate demands their leaders could hardly accept; that many other people, largely but not entirely peasants, never did go beyond the demands they made in 1789; that the reforms of 1789–91, which were far beyond anything anticipated in the spring of 1789, offered extraordinary gains to some people, nothing to others and possibly less than they had had before to still others. In other words, general readers will see that the destruction of the privileges of the first two orders, the Church and the aristocracy, did not necessarily benefit everyone, even roughly, in the Third Estate. The Revolution imposed certain ideas of individual liberty, unrestricted rights of property, political power derived from consent, religious toleration and ecclesiastical independence which were incompatible with regional privileges enjoyed by the Third Estate, with corporate and communal rights and with ancient cultural norms. This was profoundly upsetting to many people and where these abrupt changes occurred in combination, and where critical groups in the population received little or no material compensation, then there was massive discontent which could erupt into counter-revolutionary disturbances.

The history of the entire period can be understood as the struggle against a counterrevolution that was not so much aristocratic as massive, extensive, durable and popular. This theme explains why the revolutionaries violated their own ideal of the rule of law with scarcely a qualm. It helps explain the early recourse to repression, the foreign war (undertaken paradoxically to cope with the interior enemy), the Terror, the failure of constitutional government between 1794 and 1797 and the necessity of a dictatorship in 1799–1801. In the meantime, the revolutionaries tore themselves apart through incessant purges, put immense demands on the national economy and required extraordinary sacrifices from ordinary people. All of this merely added to the discontent against them. Despite some attempts to reform itself, a disintegrating government succumbed to another coup in 1799, a coup whose sponsors cared little for popular consultation and who were determined to protect men of property. The dictatorship ended up favouring the rich and so prepared the way for many of the struggles of the nineteenth century.

In writing a book aimed at general readers, I am especially aware of the great influence of my own teachers, Alfred Cobban, Douglas Johnson who is also general editor of this series, and Maurice Hutt. I owe them much for showing me how exciting the revolutionary era can be and for trying to show me how to control flights of imagination with common sense. I would also like to thank D. J. Goodspeed, T. J. A. Le Goff, C. Lucas and M. J. Sydenham for giving up so much of their time to offer so many valuable comments on parts of the manuscript. Carolyn Green, Jennie Gurski and Mary Warner were also more patient typists than anyone could have reasonably expected. Naturally, I am responsible for the remaining errors.

St Catharines, Ontario
November 1984

Contents

France 1789–1815

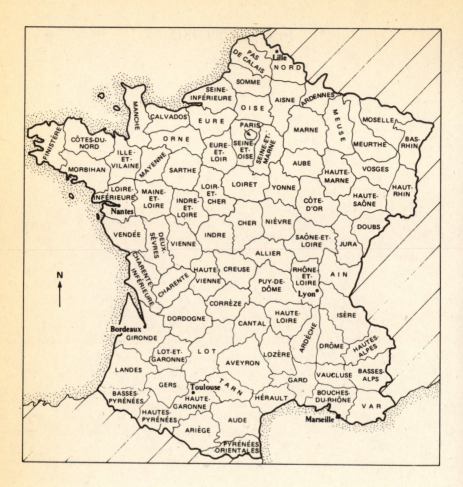

Chapter 1

The Revolution of the Notables

The Classic Theory of the Bourgeois Revolution

There was a time when historians could be fairly confident in describing the origins of the French Revolution. The operative concept was 'aristocratic reaction'. It meant several things at once. Politically, it referred to the undermining of the absolutism of Louis XIV which was thought to have subverted the independence and privileges of the aristocracy. The parlements, the regional sovereign and appeal courts of which that of Paris was by far the most important, were the driving forces behind the noble offensive. They were able to transform their right of registering laws and edicts into a veto on progressive royal legislation. The Crown was consequently much weaker. This had implications in the social sphere as well. In the course of the eighteenth century, the aristocracy ended up monopolizing the highest offices in government, the military, the Church and judiciary. This in turn had its effects on the bourgeoisie. No longer able to advance to the top of the major social and political institutions of the day, the bourgeoisie became increasingly alienated from the state and from respectable society. Frustrated from achieving its highest ambitions, its loyalties strained, ever open to suggestive criticisms of the system, it was well placed to take advantage of the political crisis of 1788–9 to overthrow the old order altogether. One of the many crises of the Old Regime was a crisis of social mobility.

The argument was irresistibly attractive, partly because of its internal elegance and partly because it explained so much. It made sense of the reign of Louis XIV, the eighteenth century and the Revolution too. The struggle between revolution and counterrevolution could be reduced to two actors, the bourgeoisie and the aristocracy, who had first come to blows in the closing years of the reign of Louis XIV. The aristocracy lost, of course, and specialists of the nineteenth century could move on to the next round, the struggle between the bourgeoisie and the working class.

Unfortunately, research and reflective criticism over the past twenty years have rendered the classical view of the origins of the Revolution utterly untenable. In the first place, it assumes rather than demonstrates the aristocracy's progressive monopoly of high posts. It assumes, too, that the society of the seventeenth century was more open than its successor but relies on incomplete evidence and a limited range of contemporary complaints. The Duc de Saint-Simon's famous observation that Louis XIV raised up the 'vile bourgeoisie' turns out to be untrue in the case of the episcopate, partially true but grossly misleading of the ministry and unknown in the case of the officer corps of the army. More refined methodologies have turned up some odd anomalies. All the intendants (the immensely powerful representatives of the king in the provinces) of Louis XV and Louis XVI were nobles, but the trend in appointments, such as it was, was increasingly to prefer nobles of more recent creation. Closer examination of some of the major signs of noble exclusivism shows that restrictions were often aimed at excluding the rich parvenu nobles not a rising bourgeoisie. The famous Ségur ordinance of 1781, for instance, limited the recruitment of army officers to men with 'four quarterings' of nobility, that is, four generations on the father's side had to be noble. Oddly enough, the aim was part of an ongoing process of professionalizing the army by excluding nobles who had recently amassed a fortune in commerce or finance and consequently whose values of cupidity and self-interest were thought to be antithetical to genuine military values of self-sacrifice and discipline, thought to be the preserve of staid, landed families. Even the few parlements which took similar four quarterings decrees had much the same object in mind. The Parlement of Rennes, for instance, most of whose magistrates could trace their noble lineages back two centuries, managed to maintain its caste-like character against all comers, noble and roturier, until the very end. The Parlement of Paris, whose jurisdiction covered one third of the country, never bothered to restrict its entry and remained amazingly open to the rich men of banking, high finance and government service most of whom were nobles already. To be sure, exclusivist tendencies were worrying to many bourgeois, even though they were not affected directly, because they feared an even greater tightening in the future.

It was always possible for many to acquire noble status. The Crown always granted nobility directly, and after 1760 or so began to broaden the basis of selection considerably. The annual number of direct grants more than tripled to nearly a dozen per year and, while outstanding service in the military and judiciary continued to be rewarded as before, so now were contributions in government service, commerce, industry, culture and science. The Old Regime monarchy, in fact, rewarded a broader range of talents than did Napoleon.

By far the most important device for creating new nobles was venal ofice. There were roughly 50,000 offices in the royal bureaucracy which could be bought, sold and inherited just like any other piece of property. Of these, roughly 3750 in the civil, criminal and financial courts and some municipalities conferred hereditary nobility on the owner or his family mostly after one or two generations. No one is certain how many families were ennobled by the process of venal office during the reigns of Louis XV and Louis XVI, but one conservative estimate suggests 2200. Creations by direct grant, through the military and via the 900 *secrétaires du roi*, a very expensive sinecure which conferred immediate hereditary nobility, account for another 4300 creations. In other words, the century witnessed the birth of 6500 new noble families. These comprised somewhere between one quarter and one third of all noble families in 1789. The Old Regime aristocracy was thus comparatively young and was in a constant process of renewal.

The doors of the Second Estate were well oiled to men of talent but above all to those with money. Society was therefore capable of absorbing the most thrusting, entrepreneurial and ambitious men of the plutocracy. An ennobling office was far from cheap. In 1791, they were commonly priced well above 50,000 *livres*, enough to keep up to two hundred families of rural weavers alive for a year. The owner of an ennobling office was therefore a very wealthy man indeed. The classic source of these nobles is usually thought to have been an aspiring merchant family which gradually withdrew from trade over a generation or two, and bought land, offices and a title instead. Such families were certainly very numerous and the temptation to follow this route may well have increased for many merchant families along the Atlantic coast because the successes of British privateering made investment in the overseas trade more risky. But this was not the only pattern. Many other families rose to the top through tax-farming or the fiscal system generally. This route could lead to some dizzying ascents with rises from the artisanate or even the peasantry in one or two generations. Still other families had been primarily landowners and rentiers for some time, content to build up the family's status through the patient acquisition of ever more prestigious offices until it slid almost imperceptibly into the Second Estate.

Since the aristocracy was so open to money, there were few qualitative economic differences between it and the bourgeoisie. Approximately 80 per cent of the private wealth of the country was in land, urban real estate, bonds and so on and both groups invested heavily in them. Although the proportions varied greatly from place to place, the nobility and the bourgeoisie together were everywhere important landowners. In some of the rich agricultural areas of the country, like maritime Flanders, around Versailles, parts of Burgundy, the river valleys of Provence and so on, they owned land out of all proportion to their numbers. Nobles were also heavily involved in industrial activities closely related to land and its resources like forest products, mining and metallurgy, not to mention the marketing of grain and wine. Although there remained a strong prejudice against direct participation in trade, nobles were major investors in colonial trading companies, land-clearing and speculation companies, and banking, industrial and tax-collection enterprises of all sorts. The prominent contributions of nobles to capitalist ventures and the strong presence of bourgeois on the land show that from the point of view of economic function, the two groups were a single class. At the very least, the bourgeois-noble split of 1789 did not have economic origins.

The effect of the revisionist critique of the classical interpretation has been to reassert the importance of the political origins of the Revolution. If the nobility had always been a dominant class, if whatever trends there were towards exclusivism are problematic to interpret, if opportunities for advancement were far greater than was ever suspected, and if nobles and bourgeois shared similar economic functions and interests, the notion that the Revolution originated in a struggle between two distinct classes has to be abandoned. Politics remains. Both groups could agree to unite to overthrow absolutism in favour of a liberal constitution but, according to which revisionist historian one follows, they fell out either over means or because of a failure of political leadership or the form the political crisis took, or even over something as amorphous as 'style'.

Another view is possible, however. Circumstances mattered largely because the good will of moderate leaders of both sides was

not able to overcome fundamental differences over the nature of
the liberal constitution to be imposed on the monarchy. This in turn
arose because of critical differences in the social position of the two
groups, that is over the related questions of wealth and privilege.
Nobles were the wealthiest single group and were among the most
privileged. Although many nobles were willing to surrender all or
most of their privileges and maintain their leading social position
simply through their massive ownership of property, the majority
of the elected representatives of the Second Estate were not. Pure
selfishness apart, they retained an older view that privilege was a
useful defence against unbridled absolutism. All that was needed
was a constitution to supplement these privileges. In the event,
many bourgeois agreed on the necessity to reinforce privilege. It
was the role of the liberal leadership, both noble and bourgeois, to
convince their constituencies that group privileges were no longer
adequate. They failed, and since privilege was removed by violence
and chicanery in August 1789, they created one of the strands of
the counterrevolution.

Aristocrats and Bourgeois

It is hard to imagine how wealthy the eighteenth-century
aristocracy was. Of course, there were many poor nobles. To cite
only one example, Sublieutenant Bonaparte earned only 1000 *livres*
per year in the artillery, which was less than the court aristocrats,
the La Tremoilles, spent on their boxes at the *Comédie Française*
and the *Théâtre Italien*, let alone the 44,000 *livres* they spent on
dinner parties. Other court families like the Orléans, with their
revenues of two million per year, or the Contis with their 3.7
million, were among the wealthiest people in the country. There
were similarly breathtaking bourgeois fortunes. The Luynes family,
merchants at Nantes, had a fortune of over four million *livres* in
1788. On the whole, however, the nobility's fortunes were greater
than those of most others. Even in Lyon, the largest industrial city
in the country, the average noble fortune, much of it in the hands
of office-holders, was three times that of the silk wholesalers, the
wealthiest single group in the bourgeoisie. In Troyes, another
manufacturing city, noble fortunes were more than double those of
the wholesale merchants. Of the sixteen wealthiest people in the
little port of Vannes, twelve were nobles. Of the marriage contracts

signed at the administrative centre of Dijon in 1748, all those of the nobility but not one of those of the bourgeoisie were worth more than 50,000 *livres*. Finally, in the administrative centre of Toulouse, nobles held over 60 per cent of the private wealth in the city and two thirds of that noble wealth belonged to the magistrates in the *parlement*. Despite the overlappings these figures reveal, the overwhelming tendency was for the aristocracy to be wealthier than anyone else.

Wealth, status and professional ties also made nobles a fairly closed group. Although much work remains to be done on the question of marriage alliances, what evidence there is suggests a considerable endogamy. Eight out of ten marriages of the magistrates of the Parlement of Brittany took place within the circle of fully fledged aristocrats. Marriages with merchants and financiers were very rare for the magistrates of the Parlement of Paris, who had close family relationships among themselves and with some of the most illustrious names at court.

The revolutionaries defined nobles with some justification as a wealthy group. They also claimed they were excessively privileged. Although this charge is harder to assess, there was considerable truth to it. One of the difficulties is that there were few privileges common to the aristocracy throughout the realm and many varied in their impact. Their honorific rights defined in heraldic and sumptuary legislation marked them out without harming anyone else materially. Others could have real but intangible consequences: exemption from the jurisdiction of the bankruptcy courts, exemption from hanging or flogging except in cases unworthy of their station like treason or perjury, the privilege of *committimus* by which some nobles (and some clerics, among others) could demand a trial in civil cases before a higher jurisdiction, and so on. Still others could have a direct material benefit for individuals or their families. Nobles alone could own seigneuries or fiefs outright. Roturier owners had to pay a tax known as *franc-fief*. In regions of customary law, they enjoyed a different testamentary code which could permit primogeniture, thus preserving their estates from the disintegration which threatened those of roturiers every generation.

Above all nobles benefited from tax exemptions. It is not true that nobles paid no direct taxes in the Old Regime. In 1695, Louis XIV subjected them to the *capitation*, a tax on overall revenues, and in 1749 his successor imposed the *vingtième*, a 5 per cent tax on net landed revenues. But nobles were exempt from compulsory billeting, militia service, the *corvée* or compulsory road work, and the *gabelle*, or salt tax. They were exempt too from the *taille personnelle* which covered three quarters of the country. In practice, this meant they could cultivate a home farm directly and pay no tax. Turgot, who as finance minister and a former intendant was in a position to know, estimated that this exemption was worth up to 2000 *livres*, and the reduced taxes on the farms of tenants allowed the noble landlords to demand higher rents. They also paid less than they ought to have done on the taxes they owed. The richest noble families around Toulouse paid an average rate of less than 15 per cent while a typical peasant family paid considerably more. The princes of the blood ought to have paid 2.4 million *livres* in *vingtième* but actually paid only 188,000 *livres*, while one of them, the Duc d'Orléans, bragged that he paid whatever he wanted. In Brittany the noble-dominated provincial estates collected taxes on behalf of the Crown on separate rolls for the nobility. They assessed themselves at half the per capita *capitation* of roturiers. The result was that the Marquis de Piré who had a gross fortune of 2.5 million *livres* paid only 27 *livres* in taxes, less than a prosperous baker paid. Privilege then was worth having. So too was ennobling office despite the low formal return on investment.

Many non-nobles thought privilege was worth having too. In fact, the most privileged corporation in the kingdom was the Church which paid no taxes at all and instead negotiated a *don gratuit* or 'free gift' with the Crown every five years. In return, it received a monopoly of public worship, education and public charity. Many roturiers were privileged as well. No Bretons paid the *taille* or *gabelle* with the result that their tax load was less than one fifth that of their counterparts in the Ile-de-France. Indeed, as Necker, the Director-General of Finances, revealed in 1784, the regional disparities in the incidence of taxation were immense. Within the provinces too, various towns had bought or acquired exemption from the *taille*, as had various individuals, office-holders and occupations. Given the primitive fiscal machinery of the time, it is likely too that towns in general paid less than the countryside, although the system tried to compensate for this by elaborate indirect taxes on articles of consumption such as alcohol, soap, legal documents and playing cards.

The Crisis of the Old Regime

Aside from obvious self-interest, one of the reasons Frenchmen of
whatever rank clung to privilege so much was that it protected them
from a fiscal system which was both a mystery and accountable to
no one. Indeed, the government itself had no idea what its resources
or what its expenditures were. Although there were considerable
efforts to adopt a more responsible system of internal accounting
under the reign of Louis XVI, the Old Regime monarchy never
thought of opening the books to outside scrutiny, or even to a
centralized internal audit, let alone of justifying its fiscal policies to
the public. Yet the monarchy did expect its subjects to pay and its
officials were astonished when other bodies questioned them.

The first great crisis of this sort occurred in the wake of the Seven
Years War (1756–63). To raise money for this disastrous war, the
government doubled the *vingtième* in 1756, and tripled it in 1760.
Some exemptions from the *taille* were suspended, those remaining
exempt had their *capitation* doubled, indirect taxes were raised and
surtaxes were created. No one questioned that everyone had to
make sacrifices in wartime but these measures were so drastic that
they raised the question of the government's right to tax as it saw
fit. Since the government proposed to continue these measures into
the peace for reasons that were clear to no one, the question quickly
arose of the limits of the monarchy's fiscal powers and of the proper
relation beween the Crown and its subjects. The men best placed
to pose these questions were the magistrates in the parlements, not
only because the fiscal expedients of the war directly affected their
pocket books but because venality of office offered them a measure
of protection against reprisals. But they also spoke for everyone
else who was affected, privileged or not, or for all those haunted
by the nightmare of unchecked fiscality devouring the wealth of the
nation.

Although the parlements lost in the struggle against the
monarchy, they did habituate the politically conscious public to the
idea that the solution to royal voracity was the rule of law. In 1763–
4, the Parlement of Paris argued that the king held his throne and
legitimacy from the fundamental laws of the realm which were
immutable. The parlement had the right to determine whether
ordinary legislation conformed to the principles of the ancient
constitution. In fiscal matters, the magistrates claimed, 'the

infraction of the sacred right of verification simultaneously violates the rights of the Nation and the rights of legislation; it follows that the collection of a tax which has not been verified is a crime against the Constitution . . .' The purpose of government was to 'maintain the citizens in the enjoyment of rights which the laws assure them', those rights being liberty and honour. Provincial parlements went even further with strikes, collective resignations and orders to arrest local governors for enforcing the edicts. The most agonizing and dramatic conflict came with the Parlement of Brittany. This struggle lasted until 1770 with arrests, counterarrests, suspension of the parlement, resignations and arrest of magistrates. When the Parlement of Paris refused orders to cease its intervention, the Chancellor Maupeou in effect abolished it in February 1771. Subsequent protests from provincial parlements led to their 'remodelling'.

It was utterly typical of the ways of the Old Regime monarchy that the Controller-General, Terray, did nothing to profit from these circumstances and reform the government's finances. Force had shown that the monarchy could push its critics aside and stumble from one expedient to another as it always had. Thus when Louis XVI, who ascended the throne in 1774, immediately restored the parlements in an attempt to win popularity and govern by consensus, men drew a number of conclusions from Maupeou's 'revolution', as it was called at the time. The parlements issued a number of declarations which showed they were unrepentant and protested Turgot's attempt in 1776 to transform the *corvée* into a money tax, but in practice the judges showed an extreme reluctance to risk provoking the monarchy again. Other commentators were simply dismayed. The timid Paris bookseller Hardy accused Maupeou of destroying 'the ancient constitution of the French government' but could think of nothing better than to look to the princes of the blood on whose protests 'depends perhaps the salvation of the French and the conservation of the true rights of the nation'. Others were more imaginative. Malesherbes, the magistrate of the *cour des aides* who later defended Louis XVI at his trial, remonstrated on behalf of his colleagues that the courts 'supplemented' the role of Estates in consenting to taxes and, in 1775, demanded the king hear 'the nation assembled. . . . The unanimous wish of the nation is to obtain the Estates-General or at least, provincial estates.' Some of the provincial parlements like Grenoble, Bordeaux and Besançon demanded provincial estates as well, bodies which would give their provinces a bargaining power over taxes and a lever against the intendants such as the Bretons had and which they alone could not provide. In fact, the parlements had a strong sense of their own fragility which was only reinforced by the docility of the Paris parlement. It registered a double *vingtième* in 1780, a triple *vingtième* in 1782 and loans of 125 million *livres* in 1784 and 80 million *livres* in 1785, with only perfunctory demands for further economies in the royal household and finances. The long-term effect of Maupeou's revelation of the parlements' weakness and their subsequent docility was thus to discredit the parlements as a defence against despotism. Rabaut-Saint-Etienne, the Protestant minister and deputy to the Constituent Assembly, wrote that part of the nation regarded the parlements as a 'barrier to despotism of which everyone was weary'. Clearly, he had his doubts while others explained the absence of heroics as obsequiousness, ambition or corruption. The abbé Morellet, a minor writer, accused the parlement 'of letting us be overwhelmed [with taxes] for over a century, [of permitting the government] all its waste and its loans which it knew all about . . .' Necker's first ministry (1776–81) had an even more sinister lesson. He was extraordinarily popular for financing France's intervention in the War of American Independence by loans instead of taxes, but thoughtful observers also realized that he had pointed the way towards bypassing the parlements altogether.

Many Frenchmen of the 1780s had concluded that the risks of the monarchy degenerating into a despotism were very real and that the solution was not to reinforce the powers of the parlements but to revive the provincial estates or the Estates-General. So far as one can tell, the question of privileges had not yet arisen. Indeed, the parlementaires who demanded the revival of representative institutions clearly thought of them as augmenting their constitutional powers and consequently protecting their privileges, not supplanting or suppressing them.

The government's freedom of manoeuvre in this general crisis of confidence in existing institutions was consequently limited. Nor had the two important finance ministers of the period, Necker and Calonne, raised the level of confidence. When a powerful coalition of tax-farmers, resentful courtiers and spiteful ministers pushed him out of office in 1781, Necker claimed in his famous *Comte rendu au roi* that there was a surplus on hand of 10 million *livres*. Whether this was misleading, as his detractors later suggested, is less

important than the fact that, as the first public declaration of royal
finances, it created a sensation and established Necker's reputation
as a miracle worker. The triple *vingtième* and the huge loans after
his fall only reinforced this impression and Calonne underlined it
by heaping huge pensions on avid courtiers and authorizing the
Crown's acquisition of the lovely châteaux of Saint-Cloud and
Rambouillet. By contrast, Necker had tried to impose greater
internal accountability, closer surveillance of the tax-farmers and
economies on the royal household: the very programme the
parlements over a generation had educated the public to believe
was the solution to the Crown's financial woes.

Calonne's strategy, however, was not to maintain himself in
office with unrelieved prodigality as his enemies insisted. The
purpose of the intense borrowing was to repay some creditors to
increase government credit still further. A great deal of money thus
sprung from the rentiers and foreign bankers was invested in public
works such as ports, roads and canals. But if the investments were
intended to stimulate the economy which in turn would increase
government revenues, they also touched off a stock market boom,
particularly in shares which were known to have government
backing or ministerial protection. In addition, the boom fed, and
was fed by, a mammoth speculation in urban real estate in which
the court was directly involved. The Duc d'Orléans, for example,
developed his properties around the Palais Royal, the Comte de
Provence financed a great deal of building in the Vaugirard quarter
of Paris and the Comte d'Artois ran up debts of 28 million, a victim
of his own speculative appetites and peculation in his own
household. A mountain of paper and credit surrounded the houses
of the great and the ministry. By 1787, the government found itself
subsidizing inflated shares in the New India Company, the Paris
Water Company (which delivered no water), and in fire and life
insurance companies (which ensured no lives). Nor was this as
foolish as it appears, since much of the tax-gathering machinery was
let out to men who were at one and the same time private
businessmen and public officials with interests in myriad private and
public enterprises. The government had to support such
speculation to a point, lest its own credit suffer. Yet the financiers
were in serious trouble by late 1786. Wine prices had been low since
1783 and the country was entering a manufacturing depression. The
financiers' revenues from taxation were consequently declining and
so, indirectly, were those of the government. With share prices in

the India Company, Water Company and Discount Bank falling in the wake of the speculative boom, many financiers were hard-pressed and Calonne had reached the limit of his ability to support them. In the first half of 1787, five went bankrupt, further shaking the government's credit, amid charges of fraud and embezzlement. At the very least, all this demonstrated the financial incompetence of the old monarchy.

Calonne proposed to deal with this gathering crisis once and for all, not by revamping the system of collection, but by tapping into the nation's resources in a new way. In August 1786, he announced to Louis XVI that the Crown no longer had any money. The third *vingtième* was due to expire the next year, the government had borrowed 1.25 billion since 1776, debt service alone would cost 50 million a year by 1790 and short-term loans were already too high at 280 million. Further taxes were politically impossible, would not yield enough anyway, and further economies would be insufficient. The only solution was a revamping of the entire fiscal and administrative structure of the state and a reform of its relationship to the economy.

There was nothing new about Calonne's proposals but they were entirely appropriate to a former intendant who had begun his career in Maupeou's entourage, for underlying them all was the attempt to free the Crown's finances from constitutional control.

At the heart of his proposals was the replacement of the *vingtièmes* by a 'territorial subvention', a tax collected in kind on the basis of the landed income of all proprietors irrespective of their privileged status. The new tax would be apportioned by local assemblies representing all proprietors, again irrespective of their privileged status. Other fiscal measures included reforms in the royal domain, extension of the stamp tax, rescheduling the national debt, commuting the royal *corvée* into a money tax, and reducing the salt tax. There were a number of proposals designed to stimulate the economy as well. Uniform tariffs, abolition of internal customs and freedom of the grain trade would all liberate the economy from administrative tutelage.

Whatever the merits of Calonne's plan, he knew that his reputation with the magistrates and the reluctance of the Parlement of Paris to register the huge loans earlier in his ministry would be bound to evoke resistance in that quarter. He also needed a ringing statement of confidence from outside the government which would shore up the monarchy's credit. Since public and parlementary opinion claimed that only an Estates-General could consent to taxation, this expedient was out of the question. Another, an Assembly of Notables, which had last met in 1626, would give him the needed endorsement. By tradition, this body was composed of the princes of the blood, prelates, great nobles, magistrates and representatives of the *pays d'états* and some cities. Calonne could certainly expect some questions to be asked about how Necker's surplus had so rapidly become his deficit and some rancour about the attack on privilege entailed in the territorial subvention, but he hoped he could pack the assembly with enough sympathizers to get the reform package through. He also hoped that acquiescence from the notables would dampen the hostility of the parlements but he was always prepared to force the reforms on them by a *lit de justice*, a perfectly legal constitutional device which required a parlement to accept a government law or decree. He also needed the full support of Louis XVI. In the end, none of these assumptions worked out. Of the princes who owed him so much, only the Comte d'Artois was loyal. Provence and Orléans were in open opposition while the others remained quiet; the clergy was outraged by the attack on its privileges; the parlements were encouraged to believe once again that they represented public opinion; and Louis XVI, stung by the extent of the opposition and timid as always, allowed the situation to drift.

The Collapse of Absolutism

The Assembly of Notables met at Versailles from 22 February to 25 May 1787. By sheer bad luck, the period coincided with the bankruptcies of several major financiers and the subsequent charges of graft, so the government's reputation sunk still lower. Opposition to the reform package itself was vociferous from the start. Much of it came from the clergy and the representatives of the *pays d'états* who were afraid of losing their privileges. But not all of the criticism was completely self-interested. A tax collected in kind would not only attack the privileged but would be immensely expensive to collect and remove what little external control on revenue and expenditure remained. The provincial assemblies would not only confound the three orders but could be simple adjuncts of the intendants because they would have no authority to determine the level of taxation or expenditure in their regions. Nor could the representatives of the privileged provinces agree to the abolition of their rights to import freely certain colonial products, the extension of the state's tobacco monopoly and the generalizing of the salt tax even at a reduced rate.

Calonne undermined his own position by his high-handed refusal to lay the royal accounts before the notables and his self-serving attacks on the ever popular Necker. Once opposition began to grow, he published a pamphlet attacking the notables' unwillingness to make sacrifices and presenting himself as the defender of the non-privileged. This was a demagogic and fraudulent appeal to the Third Estate, particularly so since Calonne proposed to exempt the nobility from the *capitation*, maintain the *taille*, albeit at a reduced rate, and retain the distinction between *taillable* and *non-taillable* when assessing the commuted *corvée*. The government's attack on the privileged, in other words, had always had its limits but this mattered little to the outraged notables whose motives had been so unjustifiably impugned. Louis XVI, equally angered, promptly sacked Calonne and called in one of his bitterest critics, the Archbishop of Toulouse, Loménie de Brienne. Brienne made a number of important, if futile, concessions. The territorial subvention would no longer be collected in kind, would have a fixed term and would be limited to government needs. The stamp tax was revised, economies promised, government accounts opened and the distinctions of the privileged in the provincial assemblies were to be recognized. But Brienne fared no better with the notables than Calonne. They had no desire to compromise themselves with an aroused public opinion and refused to vote any taxes, which they claimed they had no mandate to do. Brienne had no choice but to dismiss the notables and take his proposals to the Parlement of Paris which was now thoroughly aroused.

The government had calculated that the prestige of the notables would overawe the parlements. Yet articulate opinion which had first seen the notables as mere tools of the ministry was delighted at their show of independence. This reaction only encouraged the magistrates to believe that they represented the entire nation's distrust of royal fiscality. No doubt much of the parlement's action in the ensuing crisis was motivated by self-interest. Fiscal reform would certainly hurt them as landowners. But the parlement operated under other pressures as well. The magistrates' defiance was popular. As in the previous reign, the public saw the parlements as a defence against ravenous fiscality. As Rabaut-

Saint-Etienne recognized, 'In demanding the convocation of the Estates-General, the Parlement of Paris gave in to public opinion. No one knew it better because it studied it incessantly in order to rest upon it.' Pasquier, then a young magistrate, said the same thing and recalled that 'from the moment our interest was clearly at stake, we saw nothing more beautiful than to sacrifice it to what we considered the public good. Generous sentiments overwhelmed us and there was no way of holding us back.' Such idealism centred around the young councillors in the parlement, Adrien Duport and Hérault de Séchelles, who were working towards a constitution which would make ministers truly accountable. Although it was hardly apparent at the time, other magistrates were more conservative. Duval d'Eprémesnil and Saint-Vincent, for example, saw the great enemy as 'ministerial despotism' and tried to exploit the crisis to enhance the prerogatives of the parlements and protect the corporate structure of French society of which the aristocracy was, of course, a vital part. Not only was the parlement internally divided on motives which were only partially articulated, it also suffered from the scepticism resulting from its behaviour earlier in the decade. Moreover, it had no real interest in precipitating a general crisis of confidence since many magistrates and their families were close to the world of public and private finance. In a real crisis, it could be induced to compromise.

The parlement, sitting as a Court of Peers, composed of the usual magistrates as well as the dukes and peers of the realm, accepted the least controversial of the government's proposals easily. The declarations freeing the grain trade, commuting the *corvée* into a surtax on the *taille* and establishing the provincial assemblies in principle were all registered by the end of June 1787. The major fiscal measures were another matter. Both the stamp tax and the territorial subvention were rejected on the grounds that only an Estates-General could consent to new taxes. Most of the peers and magistrates were aware that this was a revolutionary demand. Some recalled that the American Revolution had begun with resistance to a similar stamp tax. Others feared that an Estates-General would amount to a revolution, although many were probably consoled with the idea that it was the traditional Estates that were being demanded, not a National Assembly. The recourse to a very old French parliamentary tradition was also a result of rumours which began to circulate from the summer of 1787 onwards that the parlements would be emasculated or abolished as punishment for their resistance, as in 1771. The Estates-General would protect the parlements who knew from experience that the government had the means, and, if sufficiently provoked, the will, to repeat the Maupeou experience.

How much esteem the government had lost, and how much support the parlements had, was shown in the reaction to the attempt to enforce registration of the fiscal edicts. On 6 August, they were registered by a *lit de justice* and when a defiant parlement declared this null and opened an enquiry into Calonne's conduct for abuse of authority, the government struck. On 15 August, the magistrates were exiled to Troyes, but this only raised an unprecedented clamour throughout the country. Dozens of lower courts protested, some echoing the parlement's call for an Estates-General. Opinion at large followed, especially in Paris where crowds of young law clerks and porters roamed the streets stoning officials' houses and shouting antigovernment threats in the markets. Neither Brienne nor the magistrates desired such an outright confrontation, however, and by mid-September a compromise had been worked out whereby the government withdrew the controversial land and stamp taxes in return for a continuation of the *vingtièmes* which would be more vigorously collected.

At first sight, the compromise appears to have favoured the parlement, but by withdrawing the new taxes Brienne undercut the magistrates' rationale for demanding the Estates-General. The crowds which welcomed the return of the judges to Paris did not understand this, but some acute observers did. The abbé Morellet, for example, wrote, 'On whom would you have the nation rely today? The parlements, which defended it so badly, have again deserted it. . . . We need some bar to the repetition of abuses: we need the Estates-General or the equivalent. That is what people everywhere are saying.' The bookseller Hardy who heard much of the gossip emanating from the law courts, reported that 'all the young jurists . . . exploded in anger at the parlement's moderation, which they regarded as sheer cowardice'. Disappointment was sharp. Earlier both Lafayette and Mirabeau had hoped the crisis would lead to genuine representative institutions but by September it appeared that the government had avoided any such commitments.

This was certainly Brienne's intention. He had decided to abandon fiscal reform in favour of an ambitious programme of retrenchment, rescheduling debts and pruning the military. Recovery was planned for 1792. In the meantime, however, a series of loans of 120 million would have to be authorized by the parlement. Since there was likely to be some resistance from magistrates disgruntled over the September compromise, the government was willing to grant civil status to non-Catholics, a move popular in enlightened circles, and to promise an Estates-General before 1792, which, with recovery accomplished, would only be in a position to applaud the government's reforms. The Crown might have received a majority for the loans in the royal session of 19 November if it had not bungled its own case. Lamoignon, the Keeper of the Seals, promised the magistrates their opinions would be heard, but after the edicts were read out Louis XVI ordered their immediate registration. The Duc d'Orléans protested that this was illegal and a nonplussed king replied, 'That is of no importance to me. . . . You're indeed the minister. . . . Yes, of course . . . it is legal because I will it.' The next day, the parlement, maintaining the procedures had been illegal, and outraged at the contention that it only had a consultative voice in financial matters, refused to transcribe the loan. Angered by this defiance of authority, the government exiled the Duc d'Orléans and imprisoned two leading magistrates. Remonstrances against the detentions and finally a general condemnation of arbitrary arrests through *lettres de cachet* and demands for individual liberty as a natural right on 4 January and 13 March 1788 produced no result. On the contrary, the government had decided to have done with the parlements. Rumours along these lines had long been rampant and, in anticipation, the parlement published, on 3 May 1788, a declaration of the fundamental laws of the kingdom, a crystallization of the parlements' views of the constitution which had been formulated clearly in the crisis of the 1760s. These included the descent of the Crown by male primogeniture, a regularly convoked Estates-General freely consenting to taxes, respect for provincial customs (which included local parlementary review of royal edicts), judicial tenure, and a right to a prompt trial. As a revolutionary statement this was not new but its challenge to royal sovereignty would have transformed France, as Louis XVI had said earlier, into 'an aristocracy of magistrates'.

The parlement's fears were justified. On 8 May, Lamoignon forced the registration of Six Edicts which emasculated the parlements. Registration of new edicts was transferred to a new

Plenary Court, composed of princes of the blood and royal officials; lower courts, known as 'présidial' courts, received wider jurisdiction and were placed under new 'superior bailiwick' courts, thus reducing the competence of the parlements. Seigneurial jurisdictions were further reduced; and judicial torture was finally abolished. There was a promise of thoroughgoing judicial reform in the future.

Lamoignon's coup initiated the final crisis which brought about the collapse of the old monarchy and it did so by exhausting the government's capacity to borrow. This was difficult to foresee. Investors quickly took up the advantageous loans in the November edicts, and government stocks, buoyed along by a promising *compte rendu* published in April, climbed in the immediate aftermath of the coup. But the aristocratic revolt which followed helped to sap investor confidence. While Paris remained calm, there were violent riots in Rennes, Grenoble and Pau. The intendant of Brittany, Bertrand de Molleville, had to flee the province in July, while in Grenoble troops were showered with roof tiles by the outraged citizenry, four people were killed and scores injured in the subsequent repression. The Assembly of the Clergy, dominated by aristocratic prelates, gave the government a miserable 1.8 million *livres* in *don gratuit* instead of the requested 8 million and published a strident denunciation of Lamoignon's 'revolutions', as they called it. Elsewhere provincial parlements and présidiaux protested, lawyers promised to boycott the superior bailiwicks and in Brittany aristocrats formed 'correspondence committees' with the towns to stir up public opinion. The government might have mastered this unprecedented wave of discontent because, in the end, the army, for all the discontent among some junior officers, remained loyal. In any case, the opposition was far from united. The new provincial assemblies were on the whole cooperative, not all the parlements protested, and some présidial magistrates and some towns were delighted to have their status raised or to become the site of a new court.

But a divide and rule tactic was no longer possible in the summer of 1788 because the political crisis finally ruined government credit. By early August, Brienne found the treasury empty. A sure sign of trouble had come earlier in July when, in an attempt to bolster confidence, he moved forward the meeting of the Estates-General to May 1789. Thus the confident assumption that the 1792 assembly would simply congratulate the government for restoring public finances had already disappeared, and the Crown for the first time admitted it could not govern without a representative assembly of some sort. The final blow came on 8 August when the government suspended treasury payments, which many panicked investors interpreted as a partial bankruptcy. Defeated by a credit crisis and the aristocratic revolt, Brienne could only resign. With great reluctance but with no alternative, Louis XVI turned to Necker as the only man who could salvage the situation. Finally the parlements were restored and the May edicts withdrawn. Absolutism had collapsed.

The Men of Liberty

The Parlement of Paris saw itself as the great victor in this triumph over despotism and declared on 25 September that the Estates-General would meet according to the form of the last one in 1614. This is usually taken as the moment when the aristocracy threw off its mask, determined to preserve its privileges at any price since adherence to the forms of 1614 required each estate to vote separately and each would have a veto over the actions of the other two. Thus the aristocracy would be able to control the pace of reform. This was undoubtedly a revelation for many, as the scores of municipal deliberations and outraged pamphlets testify. But the situation was less clear. The magistrates could not have thought through the implications of their action, since adherence to the 'forms of 1614' would have put them in the Third Estate. The declaration was also a reflex action from a body which had always based its defiance of government innovation on the ancient unwritten constitution. To the magistrates, the Estates of 1614 had been constitutionally correct. Clumsy as it was, the parlement's attempt to anticipate the structure of the Estates-General sparked a new campaign among those whose support for the aristocratic revolution had always been tactical or tepid. Barnave, Target and Sieyès, all future leaders of the Third Estate, supported the parlements in the crisis as the only way of opposing the despotic plans of the ministry. Lafayette and Mirabeau stayed aloof from the struggle altogether, despite their hostility to Lamoignon's coup and their hope, frequently enunciated since 1787, that the crisis of the monarchy would result in a constitution which would effectively check absolutism. Some, like Condorcet, supported Brienne to the end, partly out of hatred of the parlements and partly because, in their estimation, Brienne's provincial assemblies offered a better route to an eventual national representative government. Whatever their attitude in the crisis following Lamoignon's coup, the ultimate aim was a 'National Assembly', presumably modelled on something like the English parliament or some American state legislatures, an aim which was quite at variance with the 'forms of 1614'. For them, the parlements were a weak reed against despotism, as the compromise of September 1787 had shown. The magistrates had opposed enlightened reformers like Turgot in 1776 or had long before ruined their reputation with the Protestant community. For men like these, support for the parlements or enlightened ministers had always been contingent upon reform. With the meeting of the Estates-General now certain, their agenda switched towards securing a National Assembly which offered a better hope than any other institution.

They called themselves 'patriots' which at the time meant 'a lover of liberty'. Who were they? In fact, the composition of the group is not well known at least in part because the patriots constantly represented themselves as the entire nation. Since they won the propaganda battle of 1788–9 so decisively, it is easy to read the history of the period as that of the nation against despotism. From what little is known about them, however, they were certainly not 'the nation', nor were their followers entirely bourgeois. In fact, the Paris leadership was hardly bourgeois at all. The most influential body which took upon itself the task of educating the nation in its rights was the Society of Thirty, a hastily formed club drawn from the various salons of the capital. Of the fifty-five identifiable members, fifty were nobles, split roughly evenly beween courtiers and the younger magistrates. Almost all of them came from families which had been ennobled for generations, and among the courtiers, all but one had been ennobled before 1500, making them among the most ancient and illustrious families in the entire aristocracy. Paradoxically, many had been alienated because of Louis XVI's policy of professionalizing his councillors, intendants and army officers by recruiting them from the provincial squirearchy, and all of them despised Marie-Antoinette for spitefully freezing their families out of lucrative court honours and sinecures. A few, like Lafayette, were veterans of the war in America where they had picked up notions of individual rights, contract theories of government and the rhetoric of popular sovereignty. None expected these notions would shake their own position in society. As Lafayette put it, the purpose of a reform in France would be to establish 'the executive power of the monarchy, the predominance of the nobles, and the rights of property [on the basis of] a free constitution that would permit all citizens to participate in the advantages which nature had accorded to all men . . .' Finally, some were connected with Turgot and fell from court favour when he fell from the ministry. That great disappointment must have prepared many to look outside the existing order for a genuine reform.

The connection with Turgot was a direct connection with the Enlightenment for it was men like the members of the Society of Thirty whom the *philosophes* influenced most. The *philosophes* did not have a particularly wide impact. Professional, religious and historical themes dominated provincial reading culture and the bestseller of the century was not one of the 'enlightened' classics but a justly forgotten but endlessly reprinted book of devotions called *The Guiding Angel*. Although literacy rates were climbing dramatically, particularly for women and southerners, popular reading tastes scarcely changed at all. These remained mired in a culture of the marvellous, the supernatural and the fantastic. Not so that of the nobility. In so far as it is possible to attach ideas to a class, enlightened culture was practically the culture of the cultivated nobility. It was they who patronized writers, corresponded with them, and publicized them through the salons of the capital, out of all proportion to their numbers. In the provinces, the parlementary magistrates encouraged the spread of reason and light through the provincial academies they dominated. Nobles were also prominent among the buyers of the great enlightened work of the century, Diderot's huge, expensive and enormously popular *Encyclopédie méthodique*, to which many nobles including d'Alembert and Jaucourt contributed. Of course, only a minority of the bourgeoisie was affected by the advanced ideas of the century. Moreover, much enlightened thought dealt with themes like man's place in the universe, original sin and the nature of sense impressions which had little to do with the issues of the 1780s. There was also an extensive and well-argued Catholic counterpolemic which meant that the *philosophes* did not carry all before them. Nonetheless, in a general sense, the Enlightenment taught its followers to judge institutions by reason and utility, not by their antiquity or sacredness. This provided the justification of the reforms of 1789–90. In particular, its desacralization of life required religious toleration and the suppression of many privileges of the Church. For those associated with Turgot, it also meant a society dominated by landowners, not privileged persons, a more rational fiscal system, freedom of the grain trade, the end of immunities in taxation, the suppression of monopolies like guilds, and the creation of representative assemblies. In short, the Enlightenment was enormously influential on a small group of men who were themselves enormously influential in the winter of 1788–9 and in the Estates-General.

It is difficult to be more precise about the impact of the propaganda of the Society of Thirty on the provinces. As wealthy men, its members were able to flood the country with pamphlets and broadsides attacking privilege and suggesting the form the Estates-General ought to take. Their immediate demand was for vote by head; that is, a single chamber, and double representation for the Third Estate. Both devices would counterbalance the defences of the orders of the clergy and the nobility. As an appeal to the relatively non-privileged, this was enormously successful but the provinces had their own reasons, aside from this propaganda or the Enlightenment, for responding as massively as they did. People feared there was no limit to the government's ability to tax the nation and the Estates-General would stop that. People also accepted the government's analysis that the deficits existed because of the exemptions of the privileged classes. There was little or no discussion of the similar privileges of the Third Estate, partly because of self-interest but partly because neither Calonne nor Brienne had laid much emphasis on them as causes of the state's financial problems.

On the whole, the 'patriots' in the provinces were the relatively non-privileged but this was not an invariable rule nor were the patriots exclusively bourgeois. In Dauphiné in the summer of 1788, nobles and clerics associated themselves with a movement led by the lawyers Barnave and Mounier to have the provincial estates organized on the basis of the doubling of the Third, vote by head and elected representatives, not *ex-officio* ones. This culminated in a meeting of all three orders on 21 July at Vizille which promulgated these demands and which agreed to have all taxes assessed on the basis of fiscal equality. The union of the three orders in Dauphiné made a great impact on public opinion in the country but it was rare elsewhere. In Burgundy, for example, the barristers of Dijon and a handful of doctors led the patriot movement from early December against the parlementary magistrates. They were able to draw in related guilds like the notaries, procurators and scribes and through them reached out to others like the tanners, apothecaries, clockmakers and wigmakers. The appeal seems to have been limited to the fairly wealthy guilds, however, since only thirteen of the more than fifty adhered, and in the smaller towns of the province sometimes only the lawyers were prominent patriots. One of the reasons for this rather disappointing response was that the parlement removed the barristers' propaganda of a uniquely overtaxed Third Estate by formally abandoning the nobility's fiscal privileges within a few weeks of the guilds' adhering to the patriot movement. They drew the line, however, at vote by head and double representation in either the provincial estates or the Estates-General. This only encouraged the patriots to appeal to the reluctant guilds, the municipalities, the village assemblies and the parish clergy, claiming that privileged dominance of the Estates was responsible for the heavy taxes of the Third. Once this sort of talk reached the countryside, peasants began to mistreat tax collectors. It was the first sign of the popular revolution that would overwhelm that of the patriots.

In Brittany, similar events took a more violent course because the parlement and the noble-dominated provincial estates had a long history of resistance to reform. As early as 1768, the issue of noble tax privileges had arisen in the Estates and continued for every session thereafter. It provoked the young law professor Lanjuinais to advocate a wider and more effective voice for the Third Estate. When the final crisis broke, the parlement encouraged violent demonstrations against Lamoignon's Edicts, and the Comte de Botherel, the procurator of the Estates, toured the province's law courts in the summer claiming new taxes violated the terms of union between Brittany and the Crown. The Paris parlement's demand for the 'forms of 1614' would have nullified the Third's hope for tax relief, however, since ancient usage would have permitted the local estates to choose the deputies to the Estates-General. The reform of the Estates thus became an urgent priority. The patriots used the same techniques as their counterparts in Burgundy of working through traditional institutions like guilds, municipalities and parish councils to create the impression of an overwhelming wave in favour of reform. Perhaps because Brittany had a more active political life in the Old Regime, they were much more successful even though they too appealed to specific groups. In Rennes, the legal professions, merchants and wholesalers and master-craftsmen (particularly in the building and clothing trades) adhered to the patriot movement far out of proportion to their numbers in the population, while the journeymen, labourers and domestic servants were considerably underrepresented. As early as December 1788, the revolutionary coalition which was to dominate the political life of the city for the next six years, and indeed the nation, had emerged. Moreover, the patriots were well off. The poor were singularly underrepresented. The average patriot paid four times the city average while the really wealthy who formed one third of the patriots paid 80 per cent of the group's taxes. Not all the wealthy, not every lawyer and not all the trades were as enthusiastic as others and why this should be so is not clear. In faraway Toulouse, it was impossible to distinguish patriot from non-patriot barristers on the basis of age or wealth. One clue comes from the little Breton port of Vannes where the patriot municipal councillors tended to be those who were more zealous participants in local affairs than non-patriots and whose political education had been primed by trying to cope with the obstruction of the privileged in town affairs for a half-century. For them, eliminating privilege at the local level could only come with undermining it in the provincial constitution. But for others the choices were less clear. Clientage, family relations, professional interests and fear of disorder kept them with the privileged. In Rennes, the barristers as an order, as opposed to enthusiastic individuals, tried to mediate the pretensions of both groups. Their leader, Le Chapelier, who had just inherited noble status from his father, stayed aloof from the demagogues of the dominant aristocratic faction and the exalted law students. It took the parlement's refusal to open an enquiry into the activities of aristocratic thugs who had engineered a riot on 26 January 1789 to commit the barristers to the 'Third Estate'. The fact that aristocrats were prepared to send their servants and lackeys into the streets to do battle with the law students and the parlement's condoning of violence explains much of the Breton delegation's intransigence in the Estates-General.

Elections and Issues

Throughout the gathering agitation in the provinces, the government remained cautious to a fault. Necker, who had no great liking for the Estates-General anyway, was preoccupied initially with negotiating new loans and reestablishing controls on the grain trade in response to the catastrophic harvest of 1788. Once he had time to consider it, and with no better idea than anyone else about what the 'forms of 1614' would mean in detail, he summoned a second Assembly of Notables to decide how the Estates-General should be constituted. But if the idea was to undermine the Parlement of Paris, or curry favour with patriotic opinion, the second Assembly of Notables proved no more pliable than the first. Five out of six subcommittees rejected doubling the Third by a total vote of 111 to 33. Fifty members rejected vote by head outright as unconstitutional while the others left the matter either to the Estates-General itself or to each order individually. In other words, the notables were closer to the 'forms of 1614' formula than to those of the patriots. Meanwhile, Necker persuaded the Parlement of Paris to clarify its 25 September declaration and the magistrates, attempting to restore a lost popularity, explained on 5 December that they had only meant that the judicial bailiwicks, not fiscal districts, should be the electoral units. They also refused to take a definite position on the question of doubling and passed over the question of vote by head. As a response to an aroused Third Estate, this meant very little but in the implicit refusal to support the opinions of the notables, it did give Necker a kind of support for the authorization of the doubling of the Third which was granted on 27 December. Equally important were the electoral regulations of 24 January which stipulated that deputies would be chosen by bailiwicks, even in most of the *pays d'états*. This was a great victory for the patriots in these regions. At a stroke, the government made it nearly impossible for the two privileged orders through the Estates, or for itself through the intendants for that matter, to influence the outcome of the elections to the Third Estate. Bailiwicks were presided over by présidial magistrates whose venal offices made them difficult to control.

The mode of elections to the Third Estate contributed to a latent unity among the deputies. In the countryside, the inhabitants met in March and early April to choose delegates who met at the seat of the bailiwick to choose deputies to the Estates-General. In the towns, the guilds, corporations and town councils chose deputies to the bailiwick assembly in a two-, three- or even four-stage process. At each stage the assemblies drafted *cahiers de doléances*, or statements of grievances, which the general bailiwick assembly consolidated into a general *cahier* while at the same time it chose deputies to the Estates-General. The elections were among the most free of the entire revolutionary period and deputies were chosen on a wide franchise, but the system of indirect elections favoured men of substance, particularly the legal professions, at every step of the way. This was because lawyers were used to public speaking anyway and because the deputies to the bailiwick assemblies and to the Estates-General were generally expected to pay their own expenses. The conditions of election produced a remarkably homogeneous group. Counts vary but on the whole the legal professions were overwhelmingly represented among the deputies to the Third Estate. Nearly two thirds had legal training. Over 200 were qualified advocates who were at the peak of their careers and who were to be very active speakers and committee men, while 127 were bailiwick magistrates who tended to be spectators. Over 40 per cent of the deputies were venal office-holders while businessmen and landowners totalled only about one fifth of the delegations. Nearly three quarters of the deputies came from towns with a population greater than 2000 at a time when 80 per cent of Frenchmen lived in smaller agglomerations. No less than one quarter of the deputies came from the larger towns and cities which were inhabited by only 10 per cent of the population. The strong urban representation was particularly significant because the general *cahiers* of urban regions were more critical of noble privileges and seigneurial rights, and more demanding of representative institutions, than the *cahiers* of parish and guild assemblies. Northern deputies also outnumbered southern by over two to one and since northern France tended to be more heavily urban, there was a strong contingent of deputies who were highly critical of existing institutions. The system of indirect elections then produced an embryonic political elite with remarkably similar ideas.

The elections to the privileged orders also produced some unpredictable results. The government allowed the parish clergy a direct role in choosing delegates to the First Estate, and in the diocesan assemblies they took advantage of it. Only fifty-one bishops were elected while nearly two hundred parish priests were. These were highly professional men, disproportionately recruited from urban bourgeois families and highly dedicated to pastoral work. The 'liberal' curés also had a more extensive education than their conservative counterparts. Most had grievances. They were critical of the opulence of the upper clergy, worried that the Church was losing its sense of vocation, and anxious about the increasing secularization of the country represented by the spread of impious, 'philosophic' writings. Most were unhappy at the granting of partial civil status to Protestants and resentful at being excluded from high office and the deliberative bodies of the Church. The solution for many was greater control of the Church from below and greater clerical influence over national life. Although there was a significant party of 'patriots' led by the abbé Grégoire, most never envisaged the Church losing its corporate identity. On secular matters the clerical *cahiers* were in broad agreement with those of the general bailiwicks. They too saw regular constitutional government and the abolition of fiscal privileges, including those of the Church, as the route to national regeneration.

The elections to the Second Estate also produced some surprises. For all their visions of themselves as defenders of the nation against despotism, the parlementaires fared badly. Only twenty-two were ever elected, revenge no doubt for the disdain in which parlementaires had long held country gentlemen, and a reflection too of the gentry's determination to defend their interests themselves. The court and Parisian aristocracy did better than might have been expected considering the provincials' dislike of high living in the capital but, contrary to what was once thought, political divisions did not align court liberals against provincial reactionaries. Such a split scarcely existed. Instead, the 90 (out of 282 noble deputies) liberals were younger. One half were under forty in 1789 whereas three quarters of the conservatives were over forty. Liberals were also more likely to have an urban background. Nearly 90 per cent of them lived in a town of more than 2000 inhabitants while less than three quarters of the conservatives did. Liberals too were more likely to have travelled to England or even America, and more likely to belong to a local academy or learned society and therefore to have participated in the vibrant cultural life of the century. In other words, the liberal nobles, whose influence in the design of the constitution was to be disproportionate, had much in common with the activists in the Third Estate and perhaps even the lower clergy: youth, an urban background and hostility to privilege.

There was a broad consensus too on constitutional questions. The aristocracy believed that absolutism had to be checked and that concessions had to be made on the fiscal issue. In its 5 December declaration, the Parlement of Paris envisaged an Estates-General which would meet regularly, which would consent to taxation and to which ministers would be responsible. Individual liberty, the rule of law and freedom of the press were also essential features of a regenerated nation. The parlement, the second Assembly of Notables and the famous Memoir of the Princes submitted to the king on 12 December all claimed that nobles were willing to sacrifice their pecuniary privileges. An impressive 89 per cent of the noble *cahiers* also favoured the surrender of fiscal immunities. Nobles were less certain than the larger cities on some other constitutional issues. Just half of the nobles' grievances demanded a constitution while three quarters of the cities did, and 60 per cent of the noble *cahiers* demanded individual liberties while over 80 per cent of the cities did. While neither foresaw the complete overthrowing of traditional institutions as yet, the nobility was much more likely to want to limit the role of the Estates-General to the defence of those institutions, whereas the cities were more likely to want to fix the relationship between individuals and state institutions.

These differences on constitutional questions derived from the differences between the nobility as a wealthy privileged ruling class and the relatively non-privileged bourgeoisie. The nobles trusted the institutions they controlled to curb the arbitrariness of the monarch; whereas scepticism was greater among the patriots. The social differences produced even more marked differences of opinion on issues of civil equality. Where a mere 5 per cent of noble *cahiers* demanded equality of opportunity regardless of birth, 73 per cent of the cities did. Where less than one fifth of the noble *cahiers* demanded the abolition of the *franc-fief*, the tax roturiers paid to own seigneuries or fiefs, nearly two thirds of the cities did. Where less than one third of the noble *cahiers* demanded abolition of venality in office, 82 per cent of the cities did – an indication incidentally of how little influence office-holders had in drafting general urban *cahiers*. The nobility and the bourgeoisie did share similar economic functions and interests but differences of power, wealth and privilege produced conflicting outlooks on the nature of the constitution, on how open the elite was to be and on the role of birth, property and talent in the composition of that elite.

This is why the issue of vote by head was so important in the Estates-General. The nobility was almost evenly divided on the issue. About 40 per cent of their *cahiers* demanded vote by order, roughly another 40 per cent vote by head, and the rest would have permitted vote by head depending upon the issue. Some nobles clung to vote by order so tenaciously because it was a way of defending what d'Eprémesnil called 'the just prerogatives of the nobility and the clergy', by which he meant the monopolies in the army, education, the Church, state and judiciary. The Memoir of the Princes (signed by all but the 'liberals', Provence and Orléans) threatened a noble boycott of the Estates-General if vote by head were conceded. On the other hand, a substantial minority of nobles, and a majority on fiscal issues, were willing to take the risk that vote by head would not undermine their eminent social position or their property.

The bulk of Third Estate opinion did not aim at a total subversion of the existing order either. It was mainly in the larger cities that there were clearly articulated demands for change, numerous grievances and a strong sense of the importance of individual rights as a device for regulating the relationships between the state and the citizen. This was important since the larger cities were overrepresented in the Estates-General but their radicalism did not go so far as to undermine urban privileges and provincial rights. Indeed the universal demand for provincial estates, the absence of any thorough anticlericalism or hostility to the nobility as an institution, the respect for the authority of the king, and the very infrequent references to national or popular sovereignty all suggest that opinion within even the upper Third Estate was still poised between the defence or revival of traditional institutions and the newer doctrines. Needless to say, opinion in the smaller towns, guilds and village assemblies was even more conservative. Nothing could be more misleading, therefore, than to take the abbé Sieyès's famous pamphlet *What is the Third Estate?* as typical of opinion in the nation. He argued that the two privileged orders were parasites on the nation, their privileges usurpations to be removed, not generously surrendered. It would be some time before this view acquired much popularity.

The Revolution of the Lawyers

When the Estates-General opened at Versailles on 5 May 1789, all observers agreed that the government wasted an opportunity to give a lead on the major questions of the day. A programme of broad reform based on the common elements in the *cahiers*, and a decision on the vote by head issue, might have satisfied some expectant deputies. Instead, Barentin, the Keeper of the Seals, announced that the Estates-General would itself decide how to solve the vote by head controversy. Necker, in a somnolent three-hour speech mostly devoted to the financial crisis, suggested that orders met separately pending a decision from the nobility and the clergy to surrender their fiscal privileges. This was already a precedent, and in order to counter it, the Third raised the issue of the verification of election returns which was to dominate the political scene for the next seven weeks. In itself the issue was trivial but if a committee composed of delegates of all three orders verified the returns, a precedent would be set for vote by head. From this, a single-chamber legislature would follow which would be dominated by the Third Estate, whose doubled representation aided by the liberal nobles and clerics would shape a regenerated France according to its own wishes. Separate verification of powers would ultimately allow the nobility to retain its privileges.

The Third Estate, therefore, refused to verify its powers or declare itself constituted which, since it was not a formal body, led to the anomalous result that curious sightseers from Versailles and Paris were allowed to wander among the deputies on the floor of the Salle des Menus Plaisirs where they met, shouting encouragement to their favourites. The deputies were not diverted, however, and after the failure of conciliatory conferences in mid-May sponsored by the clergy, a delegation led by Target, a former member of the Society of Thirty, invited them on 26 May, 'in the name of the God of peace . . . and in the name of the nation, to join with them in the general assembly's chamber . . . [to] seek means to establish peace and concord'. This was a skilful appeal to the lower clergy and only the eloquence of Boisgelin, Archbishop of Aix, arguing that the invitation was only a prelude to the disappearance of the clerical order, prevented many curés from responding. Meanwhile, the nobility declared itself constituted by a vote of 185 to 46 and verified its powers on 11 May. The interorder conferences which followed did not have much chance and were scuttled altogether when the nobility, angered at the Third's appeal to the lower clergy, declared on 28 May that vote by order and mutual veto were fundamental to the monarchial constitution and were the only way to preserve the throne and liberty. This passed by a vote of 202 to 16. As the Marquis de Ferrières explained, 'It's

not right to let ourselves be led by the nose by all these advocates.'
But the nobility's refusal to consider vote by head was a challenge
to the government as well, and Necker, who had kept in touch
privately with many deputies, sponsored a new round of negotiations which failed again because of the nobility's intransigence.

The increasing polarization between the Second and Third
Estates dismayed moderates on both sides but drew both to the
militants in each order. The Comte d'Artois and the appalling
Polignacs kept an open table for the provincial nobles while
d'Eprémesnil and Cazales took the most combative defence of
noble interests in the Assembly. Among the Third Estate the
Breton delegation, under the informal leadership of Le Chapelier,
gained greater ascendancy. Finally, the abbé Sieyès persuaded the
Third that the way out of the impasse was to 'cut the cable'. On 10
June, on Sieyès's motion, the Third by a vote of 246 to 51
announced it would begin the verification of powers of all deputies
to the Estates-General with or without the cooperation of the other
two orders. A very similar motion by Le Chapelier had failed a
month earlier. On the 17th, again on a motion by Sieyès, the Third
took the title 'National Assembly' by a vote of 491 to 90. On a
motion by Le Chapelier and Target, they guaranteed existing taxes
for the existing session only and invited a tax strike should the
Assembly be dissolved by force. The deputies were under no
illusion: ever since the deadlock among the orders had manifested
itself in mid-May, there had been rumours that the Estates would
be dismissed and the financial crisis resolved by new loans. The
assumption of national sovereignty and constituent power implied
in the decrees of 10 and 17 June gave a new fillip to these rumours
and Le Chapelier's motion represented an invitation to open
rebellion as a defence. The lawyers in the Third Estate had become
revolutionaries.

Meanwhile, the clergy were still torn by the problem of common
verification of powers. They had voted against it on 6 May but after
the failure of Necker's attempts at compromise, an increasing
number became anxious to take an initiative on their own. Already
twenty had responded to the Third's roll call after 10 June and on
the 19th, by a narrow majority of about a dozen, they voted to verify
powers in common. In the minds of many, this was not meant to
prejudice the question of vote by order or the clergy's separate
status, but, whether they knew it or not, the clergy had in effect
voted to join the National Assembly.

All three orders had in their way defied Necker's suggestions of 5 May, the First by its vote on 19 June, the Second by its declaration of 28 May and the Third by its constant insistence on vote by head. With the situation disintegrating all around him, Necker finally persuaded Louis XVI to try to take the matter in hand by holding a royal session of all three orders. Yet the king, with only his good will to guide him, was irresolute. Numbed for a time by the death of the dauphin on 4 June, he was pressured by the queen, Artois and the leaders of the noble deputies to take a strong stand. The ministry too was divided with Necker, Montmorin and Saint-Priest urging conciliation, while Barentin demanded firmness. The resulting royal programme reflected these conflicts, offering at once a broad programme of reforms without satisfying the liberal deputies on the main issues. The royal programme was nonetheless important because it represented the transformation of absolute into constitutional monarchy, which Louis later said was his last free act. It also represented a reference point for the counterrevolution without, however, being the central policy of the counterrevolution. Louis XVIII agreed to accept a constitution only in his Declaration of Saint-Ouen in 1814 and the Restoration Charter differed from it on several important points.

The bungling of the preparations for the royal session only reinforced the National Assembly's resolution to stand firm. The Salle des Menus Plaisirs where the Third Estate met was closed to prepare for the session, but no one officially informed Bailly, the president of the Third. When the deputies arrived on the morning of the 20th to find placards closing the assembly hall and two hundred soldiers standing guard, many immediately concluded that a formal dissolution was imminent. Angered at the contempt for their rights and fearful of intrigue, they went to a nearby enclosed tennis court and there took an oath not to separate from the National Assembly, and to reassemble wherever necessary if it was dissolved, until they had established a constitution for the kingdom. The Tennis Court Oath was one of the great days of the Revolution which was immortalized in David's magnificent painting. It was a symbol of national unity (only one deputy formally refused and two others timidly absented themselves) and it reaffirmed the assumption of sovereignty taken on the 10th and the 17th. Equally important, it helped undermine the king's solution even before it was offered.

The *séance royale* of 23 June was hardly designed to satisfy men who had shown such hard resolution. It is true that Louis promised a regular Estates-General which would have a wide measure of financial control over government operations including the sanctioning of taxes. He also promised to establish provincial estates in every province, which would have considerable local autonomy. But this was only what the parlementaires and noble publicists had announced was part of the historic constitution in the autumn of 1788. He also invited proposals on the abolition of *lettres de cachet* consistent with state security and on press freedom consistent with morals and religion. But this was only what the Parlement of Paris had demanded on 3 May and 5 December 1788. He also proposed a reform of the civil and criminal administration, of indirect taxes, of militia service and the abolition of internal customs, of the *corvée* and of the *taille*. But this was consistent with many of the noble *cahiers* in 1789. In other words, the king offered nothing which would flaunt the desires of the privileged. On the major issues, he aligned himself completely with the privileged orders. He said he would sanction fiscal equality only if the privileged orders first agreed, that all property, including the seigneurial system and the tithe, would be respected and that privileged exemptions from such things as compulsory billeting and militia service would remain unless the Estates-General commuted them into a money tax. Vote by head in the Estates-General would be permitted on issues of common utility but specifically excluded from this rubric were affairs 'concerning the ancient and constitutional rights of the three orders . . . feudal and seigneurial property and the useful rights and honorific prerogatives of the first two orders'. This was a fleshing out of the formula which had been suggested in Necker's opening speech on 5 May and which the Third had immediately and consistently rejected. If the Third persisted, Louis continued, 'if you abandon me in such a worthy enterprise, I alone will achieve the welfare of my people'.

Not surprisingly, the nobles were exultant and many even welcomed the threat to dissolve the Estates. The nobility and many clerics filed out of the hall but the Third refused, reaffirmed the Tennis Court Oath and carried on as before. Within hours, the royal initiative had collapsed.

There was no alternative now before the king except a military solution. On or about 25 June, the decision was taken to resign the state to bankruptcy and dissolve the Estates-General by force. The King's Guard was recalled from its march to its garrison, Marshal de Broglie was summoned to Versailles and orders went out to the commanders of the garrisons on the northern and eastern frontiers to march to Paris and Versailles. The troop movements were disguised on the pretext of keeping order. Partly as a ruse and partly to protect them from daily mob attack for remaining separate, Louis ordered the remaining nobles and clerics to join the National Assembly on the 27th.

The revolution of the lawyers appeared doomed. It was saved by the people.

Chapter 2

The Revolution of the People

Up to the early summer of 1789, the conflict between 'aristocrats' and 'patriots' in the National Assembly had resembled the kind of struggles over a constitution which had racked most western European countries from mid-century on. What popular violence that had taken place was more or less peripheral to the struggle, flashes of summer lightning on the horizon. When the common people did intervene in July and August 1789, they transformed conflict among the elites into something quite different. Not only did the urban risings and attacks on the châteaux in the countryside save the patriots from the king's counterrevolution, they inaugurated a feature which distinguished the rest of the period: from now on, both revolutionary and counterrevolutionary elites had to take account of the common people and few hesitated to mobilize them in their interest. Yet ordinary people were not docile followers; in 1789 and after, they had their own interests to promote, interests which were quite often different from and at variance with those of the politicians.

The Crisis of Daily Life

For all the patriots' talk about 'the nation', there was little in the social and economic life of that nation that bound it together. Life experience was remarkably limited. It was more than likely that a person would marry and die within ten kilometres of where he was born. A river, a small range of hills or more subtle changes of landscape could mark off one *pays* from another and people could tell a 'stranger' from even a short distance away by their distinctive dress or from different voice inflexions or accents. Indeed a substantial number of the subjects of the King of France did not even speak French. Breton, Flemish, German and Provençal were foreign languages but the innumerable local dialects rendered people incomprehensible to each other as well. Not surprisingly, all but the very rich or the very poor stayed close to home. Even the large cities drew on their hinterlands. In Lyon, for example, over half of the silk-workers were born in the city or the Lyonnais. Paris fitted into this pattern as well. Although the legendary stonemasons from Limousin were long-distance migrants and although roughly two thirds of the working people of the city were born in the provinces, over 80 per cent of the migrants came from nearby provinces, rarely from south of the Loire. It was likely too that a man married a woman whose family's social status, wealth and even trade were roughly the same as his own. In a society where so much wealth was in precious land or tools, parents could not permit the young a random choice of partner.

Work routines were also unvarying. The classic agricultural system based on nuclear villages practising a bi- or triennial rotation of crops divided among large fields broken into innumerable long strips can be traced back to the Middle Ages. Even the exceptions to this pattern were very old. The scattered settlements whose tiny fields were surrounded by high hedgerows which were found west of a line drawn from Le Mans to Poitiers date from no later than the sixteenth century. The transhumance of the Alps, Massif Central and Pyrenees and the viticulture of the Gironde and Rhône valleys and Mediterranean littoral can be found in Roman documents.

Yet important changes had taken place in the rural world over the past two centuries. One of the original characteristics, to use Marc Bloch's phrase, of rural society in France was the extensive amount of property peasants owned. This had come about between the thirteenth and fifteenth centuries as seigneurs, battered by demographic collapse and war, saw their jurisdictional rights weaken and their domains fragment. The subsequent period witnessed a slow reconquest of the land on the part of the lords and newly enriched urban bourgeois, most recently in the seventeenth century. Agrarian historians of Burgundy, the Ile-de-France, Languedoc and Poitou have been able to show in detail how the large landed estate reemerged at the expense of a peasantry weakened by war, excessive taxation and demographic crisis. Yet the reconquest was never complete, and by the eighteenth century it had lost its impetus with the peasantry being able here and there to increase its holdings relative to those of the Church, the nobles and the bourgeois. Thus on the eve of the Revolution all classes owned land. There were, of course, extreme variations. Nonpeasant property was more extensive in the north than the south. Around the capital and the parlementaire towns, it could drop to very small proportions. Thus around Versailles, peasants owned less than 2 per cent of the land while around Toulouse and Aix nobles owned 40–50 per cent and 25 per cent respectively. The land was also very unequally divided. In the Limousin, where peasant property was extensive, nearly 60 per cent of the landowners cultivated less than two hectares. In the Orléanais, over 80 per cent of the landowners cultivated less than four hectares which was more or less the cut-off between bare subsistence and poverty. In general, it has been estimated that the upper 10 per cent of the population owned half the land, the rest having to make do with the other half. The maldistribution was least extensive in the west where it was rare to find more than one fifth of the heads of households paying half the taxes, while on the northern plains, around 10 per cent of the household heads paid half the taxes. The inequality was most extreme in the viticultural districts of the Midi simply because grape cultivation requires less land to live on. Not surprisingly, the nobility were the major beneficiaries of this inequality because the rich found it so easy to acquire noble status. Thus in Provence, nobles, clergy and bourgeois comprised 10 per cent of the population but owned 50–55 per cent of the land, while around Montpellier nobles who comprised 3 per cent of the proprietors owned nearly 20 per cent of the land. Relatively large estates owned by the nobility and the clergy for the most part, with a few owned by bourgeois here and there, surrounded by a mass of peasant property with infinite gradations but with a very large base of small and inadequate holdings – these too were original characteristics of the French rural scene.

The typical rural community then, if there was such a thing, was a hierarchy, not an unrelieved lump of destitute cultivators. Invariably well represented among the village elite were the larger peasants, 'gros laboureurs' as they were known in some places, the 'rural bourgeoisie' according to some historians. In the west, they were men of fairly modest means and there were many of them, but on the northern plains they were rare and well off indeed. They may have owned land in their own right but more often they made their living as tenants of the larger farms, sometimes of more than one which was a cause of resentment. Sometimes, as in the Brie region south of Paris, they lived apart from the village proper in large farmsteads, the entire building complex surrounded by high walls.

As many as fifty people worked there. At times, they resembled a caste, marrying into each other's families, assuring good places for their sons in the legal professions and the Church. They controlled parish and municipal government both before and after 1790 and probably had a disproportionate influence on the parish *cahiers* in 1789. Through their influence and position in the rural community, they could nearly determine how the entire region would react to the Revolution.

Few of their neighbours were so fortunate and it was the scourge of poverty which impressed outside observers of French villages. Depending upon the region, somewhere between half and three quarters of country folk had no land at all or not enough upon which to survive. Families thus had to live by a whole range of expedients to derive a second source of income. One of the most important of these was rural industry. Housewives were spinners almost everywhere but each region specialized, with sailcloth-making in Upper Brittany, cotton in Upper Normandy where whole villages were given over to it, silk-spinning in the Vivarais, woollens in Languedoc and, in parts of the Massif Central, knife-making. There is no doubt that a substantial proportion of French industrial production was generated in the countryside. Helping with the harvest was an expedient everywhere but there were truly massive migrations in the viticultural districts when grapes had to be picked quickly. Thousands came from the Charollais and Bresse to help out in the Mâconnais and almost whole villages in the southern Massif migrated to the coast and worked their way north again. Other regions exported people. The Limousin was famous for its wandering masons but many trinket merchants came from there as well. The Alps even exported teachers who wandered the country offering to show people how to read and, for a slightly larger fee, how to read and write.

Life was almost indescribably difficult for the destitute. Comprising perhaps an unbelievable 40 per cent of the national population, they made their living, such as it was, by public and private charity for the most part. They squatted on wastelands and forests, huddled by church doors, slept under bridges or in dosshouses, their only possessions a few miserable rags. A large proportion were women, ruined by the death of their husbands and incapable of remarrying because they were encumbered with children. People like this were a problem only to overstretched charitable institutions but the more daring could be more of a nuisance to the better off. The line between poverty and petty crime was easily crossed. The criminal dossiers of the Old Regime are full of prosecutions for theft of bread or drying laundry or of pennies from charity boxes in parish churches. Bands of beggars wandering a countryside which was nearly unpoliced posed an even greater threat. A group of able-bodied paupers who menaced isolated farmers for food and lodging could easily grow into a vast criminal gang. The bande Hulan which was the scourge of the Beauce and the Ile-de-France at mid-century was succeeded by the bande d'Orgères, a floating group of several hundred men, women and children who spoke their own specialized slang and who were responsible for countless thefts, murders and maimings until the army finally rounded them up in 1798. No other gang's activities were so sensational but every part of the country suffered from brigandage in one form or another, whether it was the legendary smuggler Mandrin who amassed forty murders over his bloody career in the Dauphiné, to the part-time toughs with their trained dogs and subterranean hideouts who smuggled salt over the Brittany-Maine border. Smugglers were often popular heroes but the wandering poor were potential thieves. The pauper, who was still regarded as an object of Christian charity, was becoming more and more ominous as the century wore on.

The poor as such played almost no role in 1789 or after. Fear of them was one of the complex elements in the Great Fear and the peasant revolts of the summer of 1789, and many paupers turned to brigandage of the most appalling sort following the collapse of the economy after 1794. But poor people generally fended for themselves throughout the period as they always had. On the other hand, declining living standards did play a role in the coming of the Revolution. This was because the economy could not keep pace with a growing population and this in turn reverberated through the structure of society, both town and country.

According to the most recent estimates, the population of France grew from 22.4 million to 27.9 million between 1705 and 1790. Yet there was no concomitant increase in the food supply. The balance between population and subsistence had always floated delicately between more or less fixed limits from the fifteenth to the seventeenth century, but after 1730 or so the population began a gentle swing upwards which only slowed but did not stop after 1770. Probably several factors at once contributed to this 'demographic revolution'. The absence of plague after the outbreak in Marseille in 1720, the absence of prolonged wars and invasion, the more frequent garrisoning rather than billeting of troops were all preconditions of population growth. A genuine change in climate is still being debated although it is certain that there were no meteorological calamities between 1709–10 and 1788, so that the food supply was reasonably certain most of the time. Another factor whose impact is difficult to measure was the elaborate controls imposed on the grain trade by government, the parlements and the seigneuries. Their overall purpose was to assure supply to local people at a reasonable price. Whether the reasons lay in a decline in the incidence of disease or in a healthier or more abundant diet, the fact remains that in the second quarter of the century more infants and children survived into adulthood.

Yet there was no agricultural revolution to parallel the demographic. The country remained tied to yields and production plateaux which undulated within limits which had been common since the fourteenth century. Eighteenth-century yield and production figures show no upward tilt except in very fortunate areas like Normandy which may have witnessed a genuine breakthrough. The imbalance between population and subsistence could only have had as its result a decline in living standards for consumers and marginal poor producers. This does not mean there were no alternatives. The west appears to have escaped this crisis altogether possibly because typhoid and typhus outbreaks kept the population down. In regions where the subsistence-population gap was great, like the Toulousain, people took to cultivating maize, and in northern regions the potato. Almost everywhere, too, people cultivated wastes and scrubs as they always had in times of population pressure and, as the Revolution showed, both rich and poor tried to usurp the village common lands for their own use and some even dreamed of dividing them. Yet these were expedients. So long as farmers' profits were snuffed out by high rents and their security was reduced by short leases, and so long as landlords retained their mania for offices and lavish consumption, the countryside would see needed investment drained to the towns. And since the towns and the rich, noble or not, were relatively undertaxed, privilege would hamper agricultural improvement, just as it blocked government financial reform.

Prices were influenced by this long-term economic crisis and by a money supply increasing more quickly than production. Between 1726–41 and 1785–9, wheat prices increased by 66 per cent, rye, a common staple, by 71 per cent, meat by 58 per cent, firewood by 91 per cent. Over the same period, wages lagged behind. Agricultural wages increased by only 16 per cent, construction wages by only 24 per cent. A model budget suggests that the cost of living increased by 62 per cent for a working man over the century. Attempts to get behind these rather abstract figures produce ambiguous results but suggest regional and trade differences could be important. A contemporary estimated that a family of day-labourers around Arles just held its own between 1750 and 1788 while an analysis of a budget of a family of weavers in Abbeville shows they spent about the same proportion of their income on bread in the 1780s as they had in the 1760s. The only attempts to measure the fortunes of large groups over time do suggest serious difficulty, however. A comparison of levels of fortune of journeymen and master silk-weavers in Lyon between mid-century and the Revolution shows no general impoverishment, rather the contrary, but this was accomplished, at least in part, by drawing more wives and therefore more dowries from outside the trade and outside the city. In the countryside around Vannes in Lower Brittany, a declining town in a declining region, the better-off peasants held their own or even improved themselves over the century but the proportion of the very poor increased significantly. In the town, no group escaped impoverishment but it was particularly marked in the food, clothing and building trades as well as among ordinary labourers. In Paris, for working people in both skilled and unskilled trades, incomes lagged well behind food prices and far behind a truly staggering rise in rents which exceeded 140 per cent. There were a few expedients by which people could cope: accept poorer quality food, work more if at all possible, rent cheaper accommodation, have fewer children or not marry at all. All of these things occurred over the century but with limited success for many people. On the eve of the Revolution, the number of poor and marginal folk, always high in the best of times, had reached crisis proportions.

The decline in living standards, where it took place, was a slow process, probably not even perceptible to most people. What counted for them was a short-term harvest shortage. These hit the last generation of the Old Regime with increased frequency – in 1769–71, 1778–9, 1781–2, 1785–6, 1788–9 – and such a crisis reverberated throughout the entire economic system. In normal years, working people could spend anywhere between 45 per cent and 60 per cent of their incomes on bread, but a harvest shortage which could double or triple prices in a few months could push this figure beyond 90 per cent. As if this was not bad enough, the contraction in purchase of non-food items could cause a crisis in the manufacturing sectors with falling orders and increased unemployment. In the country, there was less work in harvesting and rural industry and poor peasants were forced to market grain they would need the next spring to pay taxes, rents, dues and tithes. A harvest shortage too was often accompanied by disease, and convalescence of either breadwinner could wipe out modest savings and capital. A reasonable security could be transformed overnight into destitution. During any crisis, the folklore of dearth told of people dying of hunger, of desperate suicides and of people being forced to eat rotten food or grass.

But people rarely believed they were the passive victims of inclement weather. Hard times provided wonderful opportunities to speculators of all sorts, from grain dealers and bakers to wealthy peasants who, in popular opinion anyway, withheld grain from the markets to drive prices still higher, bought low in one market to sell high in another and engaged in all sorts of sharp practices like adulterating bread and cheating on weights and measures. And since in time of shortage there was likely to be more grain than usual on the road because speculators were unusually active, popular opinion that a shortage was man-made appeared to be confirmed. The result was that any shortage was usually accompanied by grain or bread 'riots', a misnomer since the violence involved was rarely wanton and rarely went beyond roughing up or threatening the local grain dealers, farmers or bakers. After the grain was prevented from leaving a threatened area or pillaged on the market square or sold at a price the crowd considered fair and the proceeds given to the dealer, people usually went home. Nonetheless, the hundreds of disturbances and demonstrations over grain in the last two decades of the Old Regime reveal the mentality of ordinary working people fearful of being pushed over the edge. They reveal too a pre-capitalist mentality which assumed that people had a right to a decent subsistence and that the private interests of those in the food trades could not override community interests. Authority was also expected to enforce these assumptions and on the whole up to the 1760s, government and courts did so with elaborate controls on the grain trade. When the government relaxed or abolished these controls as in 1764–70, 1774–5 and 1787–8, in an attempt to stimulate production, crowds attempted to enforce the controls on their own or created a situation in which the police would be forced to control prices and supply. In other words, people were protesting about the commercialization of food which was vital to life and against the decline of paternalistic monarchy which the adoption of free trade implied. In the capital anyway, this protest was direct. The belief in hoarding was inherent in grain disturbances and belief in famine plots was not new but these opinions were given a great fillip when in the 1760s Leprévost de Beaumont published a pamphlet purporting to uncover a vast plot on the part of ministers and perhaps even the king to solve the government's deficit by forcing up grain prices under the guise of liberalism. As a characterization of government policy towards provisioning Paris, this was a grotesque distortion but it reflected a deep unease people were beginning to feel about government generally. In September 1770, the bookseller Hardy reported the appearance of a seditious wall poster threatening 'if you don't lower the price of bread and put order into the affairs of state, we'll know what to do'. It was also said that Louis XV was criminally indifferent to the sufferings of his people. Later, Hardy reported that a drunk was arrested on the Place Maubert for accusing the king of 'letting his people die of hunger while he's just given the Comtesse du Barry, his mistress, a carriage which they say cost 60,000 *livres*'. The Parlement of Paris was popular in these circumstances because not only did it protest against rising taxes, it was also a consistent critic of liberalization. Thus, after the parlement was remodelled in 1771, a wall poster appeared demanding 'Bread at two *sols,* chancellor hanged or revolt at Paris'. One wonders how much popular support the parlement lost when it reversed its traditional policy and meekly registered Brienne's edict freeing the grain trade in July 1787. In any case, when the old debauched king died in 1774, he was universally loathed because in some people's minds grain and fiscal policies were linked and because the parlements were no longer able to defend people against them. Louis XVI acquired instant popularity by restoring the parlements and with them paternalistic monarchy. Indeed, the rioters in the so-called Flour War which broke out in Paris and its region in May 1775 believed they had the well-meaning king's authorization to lower bread prices to 'just' levels, no matter what his ministers may have ordered. The belief in Louis's benevolence lasted to 1789 and beyond, but throughout the period there remained dark suspicions that ministers might also be speculators.

It is doubtful whether fears of a government-sponsored famine plot penetrated far beyond Paris but provincials had problems of their own. In the Midi particularly, the reign of Louis XVI coincided with a disastrous crisis in viticulture. The overextension of vineyards and a series of abundant crops in the 1770s and 80s resulted in falling prices. Between 1726–41 and 1785–9, the price of wine increased by only 14 per cent. Squeezed by higher food prices, many small viticulturalists were ruined, along with industries which depended on them such as barrel-making and transport. Elsewhere, landlords, banking on a volatile grain market, jacked up rents, which were behind prices in the 60s, more or less matched them in the 70s and went beyond them in the 80s. Depending upon the region, they may have doubled or tripled over what they had been a generation before. On top of all this, the constitutional crisis coincided with economic calamity. Two dry summers in a row in 1785 and 1786 ruined forage crops and forced peasants to sell cattle, horses and sheep at low prices. In 1787, the silk harvest failed throwing thousands of Lyon workers on to charity. Continual rains in the autumn delayed the sowing of wheat and a mild winter, which is always conducive to weeds and pests, was followed by heavy rains in June and a hot summer drought which shrivelled the ripening grains. The harvest of 1788 would be poor anyway and was ruined by a hailstorm on 13 July which devastated crops on a mile-wide path through Burgundy, the Ile-de-France and Picardy. Some hailstones were so large that grazing horses were killed. The price of bread began to rise almost immediately and by the spring of 1789 it has been estimated that 88 per cent of a Parisian working man's income was being spent on bread. Bankruptcies increased dramatically. The 199 bankruptcies in Rouen in 1789 were among the highest of the century and the size of debts left by bankrupts in 1788 and 1789 was more than double what they had been in 1787. Unemployment increased as well. In one parish in Lyon, half the working population was living off charity. In Rennes, one of the sailcloth factories was only kept going through the generosity of its owner, a priest. The textile trade in Normandy was particularly hard hit. In Bayeux one fifth of the population was receiving charity, in Elbeuf half the workforce was unemployed, while in Rouen, the figure reached 10,000. Unemployment in the countryside was less severe but, even so, it averaged 12 per cent of the workforce in Upper Normandy. Those who did find work in town and country had their wages drastically reduced. Charitable institutions, already overburdened by financial problems of their own, were swamped. The army and the *maréchaussée,* or mounted police, were scattered throughout the country in innumerable patrols to police markets and grain convoys. Significantly, the underpaid soldiers and policemen sometimes showed sympathy for the rioters. The response in the towns to the government's obvious inability to maintain police services was the formation of citizen committees to handle it for themselves. In March 1789 a committee representing all three orders took over the municipality of Marseille and established a citizens' militia. Similar militias, forerunners of the National Guard, were later established at Montpellier, Caen, Etampes and Orléans. The Old Regime, already paralysed by the constitutional crisis, was beginning to crumble from below.

The Politics of the People

It was in this atmosphere of protracted economic crisis and disintegrating authority that ordinary people met to choose delegates for the bailiwick assemblies and to draw up preliminary *cahiers de doléances.* The very act of participating in the political process transformed people's expectations and gave them a hope that they would not otherwise have had that their plight could be solved by political means. After all, their reasoning went, if the king was asking them to state their grievances, he intended to do something about them. Thus was born the almost millenarian hope that was so characteristic of 1789: that the Estates-General, the king or 'the great ones' would alleviate the sufferings of the common people. Yet the process of drafting *cahiers* did not excite everyone. Although the *cahiers* were often vague on the subject and although there was great variation even within one region, it appears that turnout in the parish meetings was often fairly low. In Upper Brittany, it was less than one third, in the Vexin region west of Paris, it averaged only 22 per cent, and around Rouen only 23 per cent. On the other hand, substantial majorities appeared at the rural meetings in the bailiwick of Sémur-en-Auxois in Burgundy and in Upper Normandy. In all cases, however, the assemblies elected the wealthiest men of the parish, generally the 'gros laboureurs', notaries and merchants, to carry the local *cahier* to the bailiwick assembly.

This would help explain the intriguing phenomenon of *cahiers* becoming more critical of the Old Regime as they were consolidated. Thus while three quarters of the rural *cahiers* demanded an end to the fiscal privileges of the nobles and clergy, all of the cities and bailiwicks with a sizeable urban population did. The phenomenon also occurred with other demands as well. While it has always been known that urban *cahiers* were more articulate on the subject of the form and role of the Estates-General, they were also much more likely to demand the abolition of serfdom, seigneurial courts, seigneurial monopolies on winepresses and mills, hunting rights and so on. Although hostility to the Church was rare in the *cahiers* no matter what the type, it was also much more likely that urban *cahiers* would demand the abolition of monasticism or the tithe.

It is not true, therefore, to say that the urban bourgeoisie was forced to abolish 'feudalism' in the countryside against its will. In Brittany, for example, patriots in Nantes drew up a model *cahier* following the break with the aristocracy which denounced the seigneurial regime as a total usurpation and demanded its outright abolition. Patriots in Rennes then distributed the model to the countryside where almost every parish adopted entire clauses or modified them to suit their particular situation. The abbé Sieyès collaborated on another similar model *cahier* for distribution around the domains of the Duc d'Orléans. Sieyès's hostility to the seigneurial regime was based on an old tradition common to both the Crown and the Parlement of Paris that a seigneur's powers were a devolution of public authority that properly belonged to the sovereign. No doubt this explains why many patriot lawyers felt the same way. The deputies from the parishes probably had fewer legalistic reasons. As reasonably wealthy men, they suffered from unlimited hunting rights, from the costs of the requirement to use the lord's mill or press or from the chicanery of justice exercised in private hands, not to mention the various dues themselves. Men like these were often behind the rural rebellions of the summer of 1789. For the moment, however, the well-off in the countryside and the urban elites found themselves allies.

The elections were remarkably peaceful in most places but there were indications that many ordinary people were not going to limit their activities to the formal legal process. Throughout the period, a great deal of popular political activity would occur in a much wider arena than the ballot box. Thus in Toulon, Marseille, Mâcon and

Reims, journeymen and apprentices, who had been excluded because they paid too little in taxes to qualify as electors, disrupted electoral meetings. The most dramatic example of the growing political awareness of some of the common people occurred in Paris in the so-called Reveillon riot which broke out at the end of April.

It was said that Reveillon, a wealthy wallpaper manufacturer, and Henriot, a saltpetre maker, had advocated a reduction in wages during the electoral meetings in their districts. Coming at a time when bread prices were high and many resented being excluded from the electoral meetings, such remarks were highly inflammatory. The disturbances which followed were not particularly serious – in the end, the crowds looted a few foodshops and devastated Henriot's and Reveillon's houses. In fact, the forces of order unleashed far more violence as angry and frightened infantry and artillery opened up on an unarmed population which had pelted them with roof tiles and chimney pots when the soldiers tried to manoeuvre through the narrow streets of the faubourg Saint-Antoine. There was a traditional ritual element too in the riots as Henriot and Reveillon were burned in effigy and people paraded through the streets to the sound of drums. But the slogans they shouted showed that popular consciousness had begun to change. Besides the usual cries for cheap bread, and loyalty to the king, they fêted the Duc d'Orléans and Necker, both of them heroes of patriots. They stopped the carriages of sightseers to ask the startled occupants if they were for the Third Estate. Obviously the 'Third Estate' did not include Reveillon. Indeed, some rioters cried out, '. . . if we don't rise up against the rich, we should all be done for.' A war on the rich in the name of the Third Estate was far from the minds of the deputies who at that very moment were gathering in Versailles.

If people expected great things from the deputies, they also feared the aristocracy and clergy would stop at nothing to retain their privileges. In one form, the idea of a noble plot was a revival of the idea of a 'famine plot' which was so popular during the reign of Louis XV but it acquired a quite different political content in the circumstances. In February, Hardy noted that 'some say that the princes have been hoarding grain the better to overthrow M. Necker. . . . Others said that the Director-General of Finances was himself the chief and the first of all the hoarders, with the consent of the king, and that he only favoured and supported such an enterprise to get money more promptly for his majesty . . .' Once

the deputies met and became stalemated over the issue of
verification of powers, people began to fear the Estates-General
would be dissolved. In early July, Hardy noted that people were
certain that the government was hoarding grain because, if the
Estates-General came to nothing, its financial problems could be
solved by profiteering. An observer reported to the government in
mid-June that he had discovered a plot in which the clergy, the
nobility and the parlement had combined to bring about the fall of
Necker, by accusing him of being a grain speculator in the
government's interest. Such a rumour terrified holders of
government bonds who linked his fall with their own and the
nation's bankruptcy. He also reported the existence of a false letter
going the rounds which 'announced that the deputies of the Third
Estate who, threatened with assassination by the nobles, were
asking for help'. People were talking of arming themselves and
marching to Versailles. Nor was the idea of a noble plot to starve
the people and serve themselves and government confined to Paris.
A curé in the province of Maine later noted that 'many great
seigneurs and others holding high office . . . undertook secretly to
ship all the grain from the kingdom to foreign countries, thus
starving the kingdom, force it to revolt against the Estates-General,
disunite the assembly and prevent its success'. The age-old fantasy
of a famine plot had clearly been combined with the hope of
regeneration and the fear of the aristocracy. There were further
additions as well. One was the ubiquitous fear of brigands. No
doubt there were more vagabonds on the roads in the spring and
summer of 1789, and fewer means to control them as the
maréchaussée and the army were preoccupied with protecting
markets and grain convoys. Wandering beggars had often posed
threats in the past but they now became assimilated to the
aristocratic plot. As the situation became increasingly critical
throughout June and July, there were more and more rumours of
secret armies moving through forests at night, of roving bands
maliciously destroying growing crops, of plots nipped in the bud to
blow up towns and of landings on the coasts. And the fear of
brigands easily slid into fears of foreign intervention. There were
dozens of stories of the queen having written to her brother, Joseph
II of Austria, for help, of the Comte d'Artois fleeing to Spain or
Piedmont to seek support from his relatives, of pirates landing on
the Mediterranean coast, and so on. The notion of such vast
conspiracies linking food problems, aristocratic machinations,

hired criminals and foreign invasions was to appear not only in 1789 but in every subsequent crisis in one form or another down to 1815.

The Fall of the Bastille

In this frenzied atmosphere, the government decided to try once again to control the National Assembly. There probably was no firm plan of how to accomplish it but there was talk of issuing paper money or of arranging new loans. Some undoubtedly wanted to dismiss the National Assembly but more likely, Louis XVI intended to have another royal session in mid-July to impose his earlier programme. If there was resistance this time, he might do what the Crown had always done with the parlements: move the Estates-General to another city, suspend it, or arrest, exile or imprison some of the more outrageous deputies. In other words, the government operated on an *ad hoc* basis. Moreover, it felt strong enough to do so. After the recall of the King's Bodyguard from its march to its home garrison, orders went out to the garrison towns of the north and east to mass troops around Paris and Versailles. It was expected there would be 20,000 infantry, cavalry and artillery in the region by 18 July. This was an immense increase in the number of available security forces. In ordinary times, Paris was policed by only 1500 men scattered in forty-odd detachments, a very low figure despite the opinion of contemporaries, to which were added about 3600 men from the French Guards regiment. After the Reveillon riots and the growing restiveness in the capital in May and June, the Baron de Besenval, in effect the military governor of the city, brought up thousands more troops to keep order. With the additional frontier troops in place by mid-July, a veritable army under the command of the aged Marshal de Broglie would ring Paris and Versailles. Yet the government did not expect an insurrection or expect to have to attack the capital. Broglie's orders to Besenval were to secure the arsenals at the Invalides and the Bastille, guard the approach roads to Versailles from an attack by a Parisian mob, protect the royal treasury and government bonds and, above all, not to provoke the population.

But these basically defence measures served only to inflame opinion, not intimidate it. From late June onwards, the most fantastic rumours began to circulate in Paris: that the deputies would be held as hostages in the Bastille, others would be executed, that four thousand troops would be coming from Spain, another nine thousand from Switzerland, that the Salle des Menus Plaisirs had been mined, that Paris would be shelled from the heights of Montmartre, that the city would be laid waste and pillaged. The deputies themselves were equally alarmed. When Mirabeau made a violent speech denouncing the troop movements as a dangerous provocation, he was ignored. An address by the National Assembly on 8 July requesting withdrawal of the troops was met with the blithe reply that order had to be kept. Several deputies feared for their lives and began to sleep in the assembly hall or at the homes of friends.

Whatever the government ultimately intended to do, all might have gone well if serious problems of morale and discipline had not developed among the troops. This showed itself first among the French Guards, a police unit permanently established in Paris who, contrary to their reputation, were an increasingly professional and militarized force, composed increasingly of non-Parisians, cut off from their fellow citizens in disciplined garrisons. Their defection was, therefore, all the more significant and disastrous for the government. The French Guards had been fully loyal in the repression of the Reveillon riots, but in the aftermath of disturbances at Versailles on the evening of 23 June, and during the mobbing of the Archbishop of Paris on the 24th, they refused their police duties. Four days later, a group of them told an apprehensive crowd at the Palais Royal they would never march on them. When their colonel had the ringleaders arrested, a crowd of four thousand besieged the Abbaye prison, forced their release and carried them in triumph to the Palais Royal. By 14 July, five out of six battalions of the French Guards had deserted and many were prominent in the attack on the Bastille. Desertion and fraternization with civilians plagued other regiments as well. Soldiers quick-marched to Paris, and bivouacked in makeshift conditions along the way, arrived to inadequately prepared quarters which were low on food supplies. All were tired and many were ill. Yet the populations in the little towns around Paris – Saint-Denis, Vanves, Issy, and so on – received the soldiers well, fed them, lodged them and, above all, shared their fears with them. There were also direct attempts to incite soldiers to disobedience. At least two itinerant booksellers were arrested at the Champ de Mars parade ground for selling seditious pamphlets, and orators at the Palais Royal urged the troops not to use their weapons against the people. Other regiments too began to suffer from desertions, sometimes in company strength and sometimes from even the German-speaking regiments. In the end, only a small proportion of all the troops encamped around Paris deserted before 14 July but this, and the fraternization, and the incitement from civilians, unnerved their officers who became convinced they could no longer be sure of their men. The defection of the French Guards also caused a sensation. Because of it, the Marquis de Ferrières was convinced that the government was on the verge of a catastrophe.

Yet neither the king nor those who now had his ear – the queen, his brothers, the Polignacs – saw it this way. Preparations went ahead. An essential first step was to unload Necker as part of an overall plan to create a stronger ministry under the Baron de Breteuil. Necker had never been popular at court and had incensed the king (but delighted Parisians) by absenting himself from the royal session on 23 June. He was dismissed on 11 July and told to leave the country quietly. Yet the news leaked out and arrived in Paris on the morning of Sunday the 12th. Morning strollers immediately concluded that the departure of Necker, the patriot, the financial genius, the enemy of speculators, meant the dissolution of the National Assembly, bankruptcy and high bread prices. The famine plot was unfolding. Thousands now rushed to the Palais Royal, the town house of the Duc d'Orléans whose courtyards had for months been an oasis of free speech and a centre for distributing pamphlets because the duke's property was outside the jurisdiction of the Paris police. Dozens of orators standing on tables urged resistance. Alas, the story of one of them, Camille Desmoulins, the later associate of Danton, who said that he urged people to arm themselves against an impending massacre, cannot be believed. But others, whose names are unknown, urged action. Crowds then fanned out to close the theatres as a sign of mourning while another group took the busts of Necker and the Duc d'Orléans from a waxworks museum and paraded them through the streets before black banners. They clashed with the Royal-Allemand cavalry on the Place Louis XV, and when they were driven into the nearby Tuileries gardens they pelted the soldiers with stones and debris. According to the English traveller, Dr Rigby, this incident was decisive. Up until then, the orators at the Palais Royal had urged the crowds not to give the military a pretext to intervene but as soon as the clash was known, the cry went up for the crowds to arm themselves for their own defence. The French

Guards, thus alerted that a massacre had taken place, then entered the square and charged the Royal-Allemand. Swiss regiments stationed on the left bank crossed the Seine but too late after darkness to have any effect. Shortly after midnight, the Place Louis XV was evacuated. Meanwhile, crowds had begun pillaging gunshops, and the guards at the Hôtel de Ville were disarmed. With the exception of a tiny detachment at the Bastille, the right bank was now in the hands of the insurgents. Around midnight, crowds began setting fire to the customs posts around the gates of the city because these were held responsible for the high price of wine and many consumer goods. French Guards, supposedly protecting the posts, instead took part in the pillage. Throughout the night and well into the next day, huge bonfires ringed the city. Thirty-one of the forty posts were destroyed. Early on the morning of the 13th, other crowds sacked the monastery of Saint Lazare and carried off not only huge quantities of grain, flour and wine but almost anything they could find. And while crowds were loading foodstuffs from Saint Lazare on to carts, other crowds released the inmates of the debtors' prisons which in turn sparked a prison riot at Le Châtelet where dangerous criminals were held.

The city appeared to be collapsing into anarchy. The electors of Paris took it upon themselves to try to control the situation. This was an overwhelmingly bourgeois body – 180 out of 407 were lawyers – and so they were probably less concerned about famine plots than ordinary working people. Nonetheless, since it presaged state bankruptcy, the fall of Necker was as alarming as the mounting disorder in the city. Consequently, they decided on the 13th to form a 'Permanent Committee', which effectively displaced the old municipality, and a citizens' militia to keep order and perhaps defend Paris against attack. By early evening, rudimentary patrols wearing cockades of red and blue, the city's colours, had restored some kind of order. Yet they were desperately short of arms – pillaging the gunshops, getting others from old stores or stopping barges laden with powder yielded little. Only the royal armouries at the Invalides and the Bastille had arms in sufficient quantity.

Immense crowds easily overran the Invalides on the morning of the 14th and some 32,000 muskets were distributed pell-mell to whomever wanted them. But 10,000 pounds of powder and cartridges were stored in the Bastille, an ancient fortress normally used as a state prison, whose ninety-foot walls towered over the faubourg Saint-Antoine. A crowd had been there too from early morning, and crackling gunfire between the besiegers and the small garrison had broken out from noon onwards. During poorly observed truces, the Permanent Committee, meeting at the Hôtel de Ville, sent four separate delegations in the course of the day to ask the governor, the Marquis de Launay, to surrender but he refused. During one assault in which the crowd lowered a drawbridge leading to an inner courtyard, the defenders fired on the assailants killing ninety-eight and wounding seventy-three. The decisive moment came in the mid-afternoon when the French Guards, hidden in the smokescreen of burning straw brought up in carts, breached the outer defences and trained cannon on one of the drawbridges leading to the inner courtyards. De Launay threatened to blow up the powder magazines and with them half the neighbourhood but wiser counsels prevailed and he ordered the main drawbridge lowered. The fortress had surrendered. Six of the garrison were later murdered in retaliation for the earlier shootings. De Launay, whom the crowd suspected of treachery in the earlier negotiations, was dragged through the streets, beaten, stabbed and shot; his head was hacked off with a pocketknife and paraded through the streets on the end of a pitchfork because, as the man who did it later claimed, 'in his job as a cook, he knew how to work on meat'. The same happened to Jacques de Flesselles, the acting head of the Permanent Committee, whom the crowd suspected of withholding arms on the 13th and 14th. On 22 July, the intendant of Paris, Bertier de Sauvigny, and his father-in-law, Foulon de Doue, who were suspected of food hoarding, were also murdered and decapitated, and their heads and hearts paraded through the streets. The Old Regime had sometimes displayed the remains of executed criminals; the crowds were now exacting justice for themselves.

The Fall of the Bastille is rightly celebrated as a symbol of triumph over despotism. Despite the popular mythology at the time, however, there were only seven prisoners inside, only one of them political, a reflection of the reluctance of governments under Louis XVI to use *lettres de cachet*. Nonetheless, in a wider sense, the fall of the Bastille destroyed the king's plans and saved the National Assembly. It took some time to realize this at Versailles. After the withdrawal of troops from the Place Louis XV on the 12th, Besenval had done nothing to support the small garrisons at the

Invalides and the Bastille. On the evening of the 14th, he withdrew troops from the Champ de Mars to secure the approaches to Versailles. In other words, he abandoned Paris to the insurgents but he did not disperse his troops. The king informed the deputies when he appeared at the Assembly the next day that no dispersal was contemplated. Later, Barnave and Mirabeau demanded the dismissal of Breteuil's government and the recall of Necker but there was no guarantee as yet that Louis would accede. It was only at a council meeting on the morning of the 16th that the king learned that the situation was hopeless. Marshal de Broglie informed him that the loyalty of the troops was in doubt and flight was out of the question. Louis had to capitulate. The troops were sent back to their garrisons and Necker recalled. The next day, caving in to a popular clamour, Louis made his way to Paris where, on the steps of the Hôtel de Ville before a cheering crowd armed to the teeth, he donned the tricolour cockade (white was the Bourbon family colour, blue and red those of Paris) and confirmed the appointment of Bailly as mayor of Paris and of Lafayette as commander of its National Guard, the new name of the citizens' militia. In short, the fall of the Bastille was less important than the slow realization that the troops were potentially unreliable.

Revolution in the Provinces

Whether the government simply lost its nerve during the crisis following the dismissal of Necker and misread the soldiers' morale is one of the most interesting speculations of the period. Part of the answer to it can be obtained by examining the reaction to the crisis in the provinces.

Municipalities, local electoral committees, literary societies and people avid for news followed events in Versailles and Paris closely. From late June onwards, addresses inundated authorities protesting the closure of the assembly hall on 20 June, protesting the king's having been misled on 23 June, expressing their joy and their suspicions at the reunion of the orders on 27 June and complaining of the build-up of troops around the capital in early July. But the provinces did not await the dismissal of Necker to take action on their own. There was no relationship between the formation of permanent committees in the largest provincial towns and distance from the capital. Instead, provincials reacted to more local pressures. A town was much more likely to have a municipal revolution where a large body of working people in manufacturing, military or naval construction were disturbed by sharply rising prices and/or where local administrations were particularly oligarchic and had been reluctant to show themselves 'patriotic'. Thus municipal revolutions were more common in the north than the south where price rises were less steep and where local institutions had not succumbed to royal absolutism, and more common in the interior than in the ports which could rely on shipments by sea. The form the collapse of government took varied considerably from place to place. Thus, at Rennes, crowds seized weapons from the armoury and the troops threw down their weapons. There were similar incidents at Auxonne and Strasbourg. At Nantes, Dijon, Marseille, Bordeaux and Le Havre, the citadels were seized by crowds or were freely surrendered by the troops; at Nantes, Château-Gontier and Bourg, tax offices were invaded and people in Lyon threatened a tax strike. The king's visit to Paris, a symbol of the victory of the Third Estate, did little to calm provincial opinion for people still believed the aristocrats capable of anything. So permanent committees spread. In some cities they took over the municipality, while in others power was shared. Some of them even took over the government of the countryside. Thus the Nantes committee instructed the priests to have strangers disarmed and arrested. National Guards were also established and despite attempts of the committees to control it, the militia was enrolled and armed in the same haphazard fashion as their Parisian counterparts. The subsistence crisis, which had reached terrible proportions in the provinces, also played a role in the establishment of committees and militias. There were innumerable riots to stop the transport of grain, or to fix prices, or simply pillage, and in the Paris region and Touraine some grain dealers were killed. Some municipalities like Dijon and Cherbourg collapsed before riots. As in Paris, the committees and militias were not only conceived as a defence against royal attack but as protection against popular disorder. Indeed, Barnave recommended that Grenoble follow the Paris model because it was 'bonne bourgeoise'. Almost everywhere, royal authority collapsed. The intendants, who for 150 years had done so much to create that authority, were powerless. Some simply closed their offices and went home.

Authority collapsed in the countryside too. The peasant revolution was one of the most distinct features of 1789 and the lurid spectacle of Jacques Bonhomme murdering seigneurs and firing châteaux horrified contemporaries and has fascinated historians ever since. The risings are far from easy to understand, but for nearly a century the explanation has revolved around the concept of 'seigneurial reaction'. It is generally believed that in the latter half of the century seigneurs avid for profit, or fearful of economic decline, restarted the process of tightening the bonds of dependence over their peasants. This took the form of revising the 'terriers' or register books in which the various seigneurial dues were inscribed. The result was either raising dues, reviving others which had fallen into disuse or being less tolerant of arrears. It is generally believed also that seigneuries were most vigorous in the 'backward' regions of the country or where seigneurs depended on dues for a considerable proportion of their income. The result was that peasants resented the increased vigour of the seigneurie, complained about it in their *cahiers* and revolted against it in 1789, were dissatisfied at the arrangements made for its 'abolition' after 4 August and continued to struggle against it until its final abolition in July 1793.

This explanation of the peasant rising in 1789 needs considerable revision. Although it is difficult to be precise because so many papers went up in smoke during the risings themselves, the weight of seigneurial dues varied considerably from one insurgent region to another. This was because there was nothing new about revising terriers in the eighteenth century. It was inherent in the seigneurial regime since periodic revisions were necessary to keep abreast of changes in landholding patterns brought about through sales, inheritances and clearings. This could be a costly operation and peasants could take advantage of the seigneur's inability to keep track of their holdings to escape or reduce payments. Nor was the revision of a terrier very frequent. Within the jurisdiction of the Parlement of Paris which covered one third of the country, a terrier could only be revised every thirty years. Once royal permission had been obtained, the process of revision itself could take as much as ten or twenty years. Nor did the revision of a terrier invariably lead to raising dues. In Upper Britanny, reputedly a backward area where some seigneurs depended on their fiefs for half or even more of their income, the rate and level of income generated by dues scarcely changed for 150 years before the Revolution. Yet there are signs of a 'reaction' here and there. The Saulx-Tavannes family, in order to 'celebrate' the erection of their Burgundian marquisate into a dukedom, forced their vassals to pay a fee which had not been collected since the thirteenth century. In Flanders, there are a handful of examples of seigneurs attempting to impose rights which the peasant communities claimed had never been collected. Attempts to invent rights were rare, however. Far more common was the attempt to collect arrears, some of which had not been collected for such a long time that contemporaries assumed the dues had fallen into disuse. Especially after a terrier had been remade, seigneurs were in a position to claim arrears which had not been collected for thirty and forty years. This could become an object of business speculation. In Burgundy and the Toulousain, there are examples of seigneurs farming out the right to collect arrears. Yet up to the end of the Old Regime, many fiefs were just so many bad debts, because of the difficulty of keeping track of all the land transactions within a seigneurial jurisdiction. Thus in Flanders the rate at which some dues were collected had dropped on some seigneuries without anyone knowing why, and in Brittany and the Toulousain seigneurs proved unable to collect the full amount owing on some fiefs. In other words, peasants could refuse to pay. In Burgundy there were periodic and localized efforts at defiance organized by disgruntled wealthy peasants and country notaries. In Normandy, seigneurial agents who went too far were mugged, while in the wild mountains of Auvergne seigneurs lived in fear of the peasants' clubs. In the Lodève where almost everyone was armed, an overzealous seigneur could find himself being shot at from a hedgerow on his way to church. These were isolated or poor regions where the village community scarcely existed as an institution, but where it did, and where it had resources in the form of revenues from common lands, it was always possible to take the seigneur to court and peasants did not always lose.

Just because it is difficult to demonstrate that peasants were experiencing unprecedented rigours from the seigneurial regime before 1789, it does not follow that they felt they were receiving value for money. There were immense variations in what peasants paid in seigneurial dues. There were still 1.5 million serfs or *mainmortables* in France in 1789 living in a crescent-shaped pattern running through Lorraine, Franche-Comté, Burgundy and Berry. The claims on their land and persons could be considerable. All the medieval panoply of rights ranging from marriage, death and exit fees, to restrictions on the right of movement and sale of property, persisted. The *mainmortables* were heavily burdened. In one village in the Franche-Comté, the average annual payment per household was 62 *livres*, which would have represented something more than half of an agricultural labourer's annual income. Few regions were as badly off, however. In Lower Languedoc, the burden of seigneurial dues was derisory, and in northern regions it was generally light. As a general rule of thumb, the seigneurial system probably skimmed off between 5 and 10 per cent of agricultural production in most regions of the country. But it did not distribute this burden evenly. Poor peasants and labourers with only a garden to cultivate normally paid only token quitrents and perhaps a mutation fee as part of a transfer of inheritances. In addition to this, wealthier peasants in the land market paid the private taxes on land sales and necessarily paid the monopoly costs of the constraint to have grain milled at the seigneurial mill or grapes and olives crushed at the seigneurial press. That is, peasants involved in larger scale production and seeking to reinvest their profits in land probably paid a disproportionate share of the burdens of the seigneurial system. Where the seigneurs had the right, better-off peasants were constrained to make up what their poorer neighbours could not. As poverty increased in the villages, this must have been increasingly common, and if villages were more restive under Louis XVI, as they apparently were in Burgundy, it was the wealthy who were restive.

The same phenomenon operated with taxes. Controlling for wealth and population growth, the real incidence of taxation changed little between 1725 and the 1780s but whether this was true of the tax distribution among various social groups is more problematic. The increase in poverty threatened to put more of the burden of direct taxation on village notables, and since the weight of indirect taxation remained the same the poor were hard-pressed to buy necessities like salt, wine or cider. Where better-off villagers were also tenants, they also suffered from rapidly increasing rents. The blame for these calamities could be laid on the seigneurs, for were the seigneurs not also exempt or partially exempt from taxes and were they not also landlords?

The château also made life difficult for the village poor as well. All the regional monographs insist that in open-field country at least, the seigneurs and their agents were extremely aggressive at exploiting their strong market position at the expense of common rights. With wood prices rising dramatically, they tried to curtail foraging in private forests, either to sell wood directly or for their forges or to enlarge roads without compensation at the expense of peasant property and plant trees alongside. They tried to usurp or enclose common lands, or insist on water rights for their mills, or restrict access to mountain meadows, or monopolize common pasture for their herds or authorize the clearing of wastelands or marshes. No one has ever been able to measure the incidence of such activities but complaints in the *cahiers* are so common that even where the attack was relatively feeble, peasant communities sensed the danger of the threat and their inability to stop it.

In short, a powerful coalition embracing most villagers was building up. People resented not only the seigneurial system as such but the whole range of economic and fiscal activities of the great estate as it had functioned for centuries. It did not matter that some of these estates were owned by bourgeois – the peasant revolution of 1789 and after did not make the distinction.

The economic crisis of 1789 made all of these problems more acute because the great estate was not only a source of age-old vexations, it was also a storehouse of grain. The estates, lay or ecclesiastical, were the most vital institutions for transferring grain received in the form of rents, dues and tithes to the towns and, by the spring and early summer of 1789, they were almost the only places where grain was held in bulk. To view the estate owners as food hoarders was therefore a natural step. Country people began to combat them first indirectly by the countless attacks on grain shipments and then directly, particularly in the Midi, by refusing to pay taxes, dues and tithes. This had happened in earlier times of troubles but what transformed resistance born of desperation into overt attacks were the fall of the Bastille and the visit of Louis XVI to Paris on 17 July. Country people knew the Third Estate had achieved a great victory and assumed they had the king's sanction to take matters into their own hands.

There were five regions of peasant rebellion which lasted from 19 July to 3 August: the wooded region northwest of Alençon in Normandy and in the Lower Maine; the Hainault region of Flanders; and Upper Alsace–Franche-Comté, the Mâconnais and Dauphiné which were set off in a chain reaction one after the other. The risings themselves took different forms depending upon the local system of property holding under feudal law. Thus in Flanders and, to a lesser extent, in Normandy and Maine, bands of peasants forced lay and ecclesiastical lords to sign renunciations of dues and titles which were sometimes later notarized because the law presumed land to be subject to seigneurial jurisdiction, unless the vassal could produce legal proof to the contrary. In eastern and southeastern France, by contrast, the law presumed land to be allodial (i.e., free of seigneurial claims) unless the seigneur could produce a title, and so peasants in these regions rarely bothered with renunciations but burned charters and terriers instead.

The peasant risings were thus far from the explosions of blind furies contemporaries tended to think they were. They were also occasions for celebration and opportunities to settle old scores. Almost everywhere people believed they had the king's sanction. In Franche-Comté, a contemporary chronicler wrote, 'For several weeks, news went from village to village. They announced that the Estates-General was going to abolish tithes, quitrents and dues, that the King agreed but that the peasants had to support the public authorities by going themselves to demand the destruction of titles. Some produced declarations of the King's Council authorizing violence.' But the violence involved was rarely wanton. The attack on the château of Lignou in Normandy, for instance, was led by a wealthy 'gros laboureur' named Louis Gibault, who, it was said, owed the seigneur the impressive sum of 40 écus in dues. Gibault sent his farmhands around the region to spread stories of a false royal declaration.

After three hundred villagers burnt the feudal papers in the courtyard, destroyed the hedges around the seigneur's meadow and pastured their animals on it, and fished in the seigneurial millpond, Gibault forced the seigneur to serve him wine. Nearby, other leaders included an iron merchant and his barrister son, and a postmaster-landowner. All of them incited poorer villagers to demand restitution of fines, some of which went back twenty and thirty years. In Flanders, there were similar acts of popular justice. In one case, the villagers demanded that the monks of Château return every penny collected in tithe since 1709, while in another case the abbot had to produce the original titles and agree to reduce the rate of collection. In this region, arson only occurred when the seigneurs tried to resist. Almost everywhere the risings were clearly another way of carrying out lawsuits which the villagers had lost or which were pending.

If the Norman risings show most sharply the coalition in the villages which carried out the peasant revolution of 1789, those of the Mâconnais show most clearly the atmosphere of fear, hope and celebration. The townspeople of Mâcon, Chalon-sur-Saône and Pont-de-Vaux gave the signal by attacking the municipal customs barriers and grain merchants on 20 July. A few days later, a rumour began to circulate that the postmaster at Saint-Albain had received a letter to the effect that Louis XVI had said that no one would be punished if the people destroyed the châteaux within three days. A judicial holiday was common enough in the charivaris of the Old Regime but this was not the only folkloric element to the risings. Peasants armed with farm tools trooped to the courtyards of the châteaux, mounted the towers and tore down weather vanes (a seigneurial monopoly), destroyed pigeon coops (another monopoly), and compelled the seigneurial agents to lay a table and give everyone food and drink. Masons were forced to climb roofs and towers and literally began to demolish the châteaux by removing tiles and bricks. Only later did someone think to head to the archive rooms and toss the charters out of the windows where others made a gleeful bonfire. Grain bins were pillaged, wine cellars were sacked and the contents consumed on the spot, and furniture and curtains were taken. Nor were the châteaux the only enemies. Seigneurial agents apart, country notaries, rentiers and curés were forced to give the rebels food and drink and sometimes money. In the middle of the spreading insurrection, a rumour, probably an echo of the risings in Franche-Comté, that brigands were about to cross the Saône, put dozens of villages on the alert, and bands of partially armed men who went down to the banks to fight them off were taken for brigands by others. It may well be that this panic was blamed on the monks of Cluny, for on 29 July thousands of peasants attacked the town. They were repulsed by the citizens' militia. This put an end to the insurrection but dozens of châteaux had been sacked and a few burned, possibly in some cases by accident. Summary courts eventually sentenced twenty-six leaders to death by hanging.

The complicated relations of fear and reprisal were also evident in Dauphiné. The troubles started here when rumours that brigands were invading from Franche-Comté put everyone on the alert. When the rumours proved false, people began to mutter, 'Was it the seigneurs who were the cause and who wished to do harm to us?' Others were less rhetorical. 'It was the seigneurs who caused this alarm because they wished to destroy the Third Estate and they sent brigands to do it.' The attacks on the châteaux began on 29 July, but seigneurial archives were not always the principal object. Instead, as in the Mâconnais, wine cellars were broken into, or bedclothes, tapestries and money were taken by bands marching in military order behind beating drums. Many of the country people believed the king had ordered the sacking of the châteaux. Later, notaries were dragged in, forced to stand on tables with a little wine to fortify them, and compelled to read out titles of papers which were then burned amid gunshots fired in celebration. The repression from the towns began almost immediately. The National Guard from Lyon along with regular troops were most prominent, and in various encounters about a dozen 'rebels' were killed and about fifty were arrested.

No other region of the country was quite so agitated as these five regions but disturbances were still widespread. There were threats against seigneurs and widespread killings of game birds in the Ile-de-France, and attacks on tax offices and tobacco bureaux (a state monopoly) especially after the burning of the barriers in Paris, which provincials interpreted as a sign that Parisians no longer had to pay taxes; and there were grain riots in Lower Normandy and a refusal to pay direct taxes, dues and tithes almost everywhere. Most alarming because it was so irrational was the Great Fear, a vast panic which spread over almost the entire country from six original centres between 20 July and 6 August. It was invariably linked with a fear of brigands who were seen as capable of anything, particularly of destroying the crops whose harvest was vital because of the shortage and the unnaturally wet July. At times the fear of brigands was joined to stories of an invasion of foreign troops from almost any country in Europe and it was occasionally coupled with dark fears of the aristocratic plot. The Great Fear further envenomed relations with the aristocracy and encouraged the formation of more citizens' militias and permanent committees. Yet it reinforced the solidarity of society as well because in some regions priests, nobles and magistrates joined the emergency committees, and towns which had eyed each other with dark suspicion over food supply now sent each other offers of help.

The 4 August and the Patriots' Revolution

The greatest effect of the Great Fear and agrarian revolts, however, was on the deputies in Versailles, the fear because it convinced them that malevolent forces were at work, and the revolts because there was no indication as yet that they had reached a natural limit. Yet for all their horror of violence, the deputies' attitude was ambiguous. When Lolly-Tollendal proposed a motion condemning the murders of Bertier de Sauvigny and Foulon, Barnave replied with his famous apostrophe, 'Is this blood then so pure that one should so regret to spill it?' A motion on 3 August calling on people to pay their taxes and dues was referred to a committee for consideration. Yet no one wanted the seigneurial regime and fiscal systems reformed from below. It was not so much a question of the deputies being reluctant to 'abolish feudalism' – the bailiwick *cahiers* were more hostile to it than most parish *cahiers* – as one of containing mounting disorder, the risk of an attack on all forms of property and the catastrophe for state finances of a continuing tax strike. Yet the Assembly had no means to enforce its writ as desertion in the army had increased dramatically since 14 July and an appeal to the king would put them back in the hands of the court party.

The solution to this dilemma was found in the Breton Club, originally a café society of Breton deputies, attractive to other like-minded deputies for its intransigent hostility to the nobility. By early August, it had about 150–200 members. The Bretons persuaded their colleagues that the disturbances were the result of a popular 'desire for liberty' and that the moment had come to throw off 'slavery and tyranny', as one of them, Coroller du Moustier, explained. A caucus of deputies agreed that they would support a proclamation exhorting calm only if it also contained a renunciation of fiscal privilege. In other words, the Bretons were prepared to use popular violence as a lever against the First and Second Estates. They persuaded the Duc d'Aiguillon, one of the richest men in the country, a patriot and former member of the Society of Thirty, to propose a motion suppressing tax exemptions. Yet the caucus clearly anticipated resistance even from their fellow deputies in the Third Estate. Otherwise, it would not have been necessary to use 'a kind of magic', as the deputy Parisot put it; that is, manoeuvre the nobility into renouncing its fiscal and seigneurial privileges voluntarily at a night session when fewer of those not privy to the secret would be present.

For all that it was planned, the 'Night of 4 August' was an astonishing patriot victory. It began with the Comte de Noailles and Aiguillon demanding fiscal equality among the orders, the suppression of provincial and urban privileges, and compensation for the abolition of seigneurial rights. These were generous offers, as were all the other renunciations of rights and privileges which deputies from all three orders rushed to make in the next eight hours. But the session was not quite a delirium of unrelieved generosity punctuated by thunderous applause after each renunciation. Aiguillon's estates in the southwest brought in considerable sums in dues, and his proposal that compensation be set at 7½ per cent of the value of the fiefs over thirty years was a very high rate of return and probably more than the seigneuries were worth. Noailles and Aiguillon were also court nobles, less dependent on dues than many provincials, and it was not long before an obscure noble deputy from Périgord proposed the abolition of useless and excessive pensions which did so much to support courtiers. If the rich looked after themselves, there were also hesitations. No cleric proposed abolishing the tithe and when the Third Estate deputies got up to surrender the rights and privileges of their provinces and towns, many did so on the understanding that they would have to seek the concurrence of their constituents. A certain bloody-mindedness and an exaggerated respect for imperative mandates (which the king had abolished) underlay the attitudes of many. Yet there were genuine sacrifices too. The Vicomte de Beauharnais's proposal to open high posts in Church and state to commoners and to establish equality of judicial punishments was one example. Many deputies, privileged and roturier, also had something to lose by the abolition of seigneurial justice and venality of offices. Moreover, the renunciations came so quickly that no one could have thought out the full implications of what they had done, no matter how much subsequent legislation tried to clarify the principles sketched on the night of the 4th. As we shall see, the abolition of everyone's fiscal privileges meant that many members of the Third Estate also had to pay more taxes.

Afterwards, many breathless deputies justified what they had done by claiming it was necessary to appease popular clamour and to restore order. This was true only to a point. Such claims were useful to persuade constituents, who had shown a great attachment to the privileges of their own towns, provinces and corporations in the spring, that a renunciation of their liberties was necessary. As far as many deputies were concerned, the Night of 4 August was a way of escaping from a parliamentary impasse, as well as a device to appease the peasantry. Ever since 9 July when they declared themselves the 'Constituent Assembly', the deputies had been debating the form and necessity of a declaration of rights as a preamble to the constitution. The privileged orders had been resisting this and had even gone so far as to propose that a two thirds majority be required on constitutional questions. This would have reintroduced all the disadvantages of vote by order. By early August, the patriots had concluded that the legal underpinnings of privilege had to go before any progress could be made on the constitution. As the Breton deputy Boullé put it: after the decisions of 4 August, 'all interests finding themselves blending together, and from now on being the same, the rest of the work on the constitution will be much easier and quicker'. Parisot was even more explicit. He made no reference to the risings or to seigneurial rights but explained to his constituents that the delaying tactics employed by the nobility and clergy to a declaration of rights convinced the patriots that 'so long as the two privileged classes had any privileges whatever, the particular interest would override the general good . . .' and that 'to fulfil our views . . . while making a truce on the Constitution, it was a question of destroying all the privileges of classes, provinces, towns and corporations'. This required some effort at persuasion, especially to sceptical provincials who were still attached to their own privileges. Boullé exhorted his particularist constituents, 'When the intimate union of all the provinces under the dominion of law and liberty presents such a great and majestic idea, what interest could one have in isolating oneself . . . ?' The Night of 4 August thus went far beyond the mere abolition of seigneurialism and introduced changes into people's lives which few had anticipated five months before. It remained to be seen whether they would cede to sentimental appeals like Boullé's.

The deputies' accommodation of the peasant revolution also raised hopes in the countryside. These had been mounting for some time in some regions since the parish meetings in the spring, when the first timid criticisms against the seigneuries had been aired. By the summer, some peasants, impelled by fear, hope and distress, went beyond their own earlier demands. Thus the legislation of 11 August which 'abolished feudalism' is less of a fraud on country people than is often supposed. Abolishing mortmain and other marks of personal servitude like seigneurial *corvées* was a genuine gain. Retaining other dues until the seigneurs were compensated at a rate to be determined was also to be expected from an assembly concerned to protect the rights of property. On the other hand, the fact that the Assembly was willing to go so far encouraged peasants in some regions to expect still more. These expectations made a mockery of the attempt to distinguish between usurped and contractual seigneurial rights because peasants soon found they could refuse to pay any. They could get away with it because local authorities were increasingly reluctant to enforce the law. Thus seigneurialism abolished itself 'from below' in any case.

The enabling legislation had great implications for the Church as well. The abolition of the tithe was not a common demand in the spring and when the Duc du Châtelet proposed it (in retaliation for the Bishop of Chartres's motion to abolish hunting monopolies), he seems to have had in mind a substitute money tax with compensation to the Church. No compensation was allowed for in the law of 11 August but already the idea was abroad that the Church's wealth could be used to pay the state's debts. Clerics would be supported 'by other means', according to the law. Implicit in this was the disastrous Civil Constitution of the Clergy which would turn the priesthood into salaried officials. The deputies also forgot their qualms about consulting their constituents about the abolition of provincial rights. The law of 11 August also abolished provincial, urban and corporate rights because, as the law explained, 'a constitution and public liberty are more advantageous to the provinces than the privileges which some of them enjoy . . .' This was the sum total of the political experience of the entire generation. Privilege had not been able to resist a rapacious state whenever the monarchs exercised their will and in the autumn of 1788, the patriot party had successfully complained that the balance of privilege was inequitable. By the summer of 1789 a majority of deputies had come to the same conclusion. But it was all the more necessary to define the relationship between the state and society, in other words to promulgate a declaration of rights.

The Declaration of the Rights of Man and Citizen, which was adopted on 26 August, was intended to be an educational device to enhance the nation's love of liberty and a statement of principles against which the institutions and performance of government could be measured. Despite the rioting which no one could be sure was over, the Assembly resisted the recommendations of three of its own committees headed by Mounier, Mirabeau and the archbishop Champion de Cicé which laid great stress on duties and obedience. A mutual respect for rights implied a recognition of reciprocal obligations. Instead, the final Declaration closely followed Lafayette's drafts which had been in the making since the previous January and which in turn owed much to the Virginia Declaration of Rights and the Declaration of Independence (Thomas Jefferson, then American Resident in Paris, annotated Lafayette's second draft). These in turn can be traced back to the political theories of Locke, Montesquieu and, to a lesser extent, Rousseau, and, through them, to the whole European tradition of natural law. Although the deputies acknowledged their debt to America, the Declaration of the Rights of Man addressed itself to specifically French problems. The statements that men are inherently free and equal in rights, that social distinctions are based only on utility (Art. I), that virtue and talent are the only requirements for public office and equality of taxation (Art. XIII) confirmed the destruction of aristocratic privileges. The power of the monarchy was severely restricted. Sovereignty rested with the nation (Art. III), not the king (but, unlike America, not with the people either); all citizens had the right to take part in the legislative process (Art. VI); arbitrary arrests and punishments were illegal (Arts. VII and VIII); consent to taxation and accountability of public officials were essential rights (Arts. XV and XVI); as was freedom of speech and the press (Art. XI). All these clauses were directed against the practices of government under absolute monarchy. Nor was the Church spared. Freedom of opinion 'even in religion' (Art. X) and the invocation of the 'Supreme Being' (preamble) rather than God, eliminated the Church's monopoly of public worship as well as its claim to special status. The Declaration was more than an attempt to exorcize the Old Regime, however. The purpose of all political association was to preserve 'the natural and imprescriptible rights of man. These rights are liberty, property, security and resistance to oppression' (Art. II). (This last was drafted during the military build-up in early July, while Lafayette's addition, to preserve 'the common good', was later deleted.) The right of property was left undefined possibly because to have tried to do so would have reopened the question of seigneurial property and the tithe. Liberty was defined to mean any activity which does not harm another, a common-sense formulation which had nothing to do with the more positive Rousseau-Robespierrist exercise of civic virtue. The specific protection given to property (Art. XVII) was understandable

enough in a country where there were so many people who owned
land, but it did raise the question of the role in the polity of those
with little or none. Journeymen, town and country labourers,
tenants and sharecroppers all had claims which were not compatible
with a strict defence of the rights of property. As had the guilds.
The resolutions of the 4–5 August, consistent with the *cahiers*, only
promised to reform them. The Declaration of Rights implicitly
subverted them.

October Days

The concern for order manifested in the debates on the Declaration
of Rights among the hitherto unified patriot politicians reappeared
in September during discussions of specific features of the
constitution. Mounier emerged as leader of the 'monarchiens' or
'Anglophiles', who, as admirers of the English constitution, wanted
a bicameral legislature and an absolute royal veto on legislative
enactments. The patriots under Barnave, Duport and Alexandre de
Lameth, with a distrust of the potential of an aristocratic upper
house and strong executive, argued for a unicameral legislature and
a 'suspensive veto', that is, one which could be overridden by
successive legislatures. The monarchiens lost these votes in the
Assembly massively (single chamber: 490–89, 122 abstentions;
suspensive veto: 673–352, 11 abstentions; which incidentally
illustrates the very large number of absent deputies). But the
divisions among the patriots encouraged manoeuvres among their
enemies. One of these may have been a hazy plot to have the Duc
d'Orléans declared regent or even king, although in Jefferson's
view the duke was 'a man of moderate understanding, of no
principle, absorbed in low vice, and incapable of abstracting himself
from the filth of that to direct anything else'. More serious were the
machinations of the court. Louis XVI, consistent with the policy
outlined at the royal session, had refused to promulgate the
constitutional decrees – on the abolition of feudalism, the
Declaration of Rights, the unicameral legislature and the
suspensive veto – and when the Assembly insisted on 18 September,
the king temporized. At the same time, the 1100-strong Flanders
Regiment, which was noted for its discipline, was ordered to march
to Versailles by 25 September from its garrison at Douai. In the
king's mind, this was probably only supposed to offer him

increased protection in the deteriorating political situation brought on by his refusal to sanction the constitutional decrees. There were shrill denunciations by Mirabeau and Le Chapelier of his policy in the Assembly, and a rag-tag band of three hundred under the Palais Royal agitator, the Marquis de Saint-Huruge, had tried to march to Versailles at the end of August. On 17 September, Lafayette warned that the attempt might be renewed. But others around the king had grander ideas. The queen was involved in obscure plots; Montmorin, the Foreign Minister, and Mounier, who ever since the monarchiens' parliamentary defeat was in alliance with the right and whose friends were talking of moving the Assembly to safer quarters at Compiègne or Soissons, both tried to purchase the neutrality of the Paris National Guard by offering Lafayette the lieutenant-generalship of the kingdom; and some aristocratic adventurers were trying to form a corps with the sinister name of the 'Guards of the French Regeneration' to protect the king or perhaps even kidnap him.

Few of these plots were known in Paris but the Palais Royal, the districts and the flourishing press had kept the city in an extreme agitation ever since the debates over the veto. The feeling gradually grew that the king and the Assembly were surrounded by nefarious aristocratic influences and that Louis would be safer in Paris. Lafayette even came to accept the idea although, unlike the orators in the Palais Royal and the increasingly active politicians of the districts like Danton and Desmoulins, he would never have dreamed of forcing a transfer. A new form of the economic crisis also kept tempers high. There were demonstrations by journeymen tailors, journeymen wigmakers and the inmates of the charity workshops in Montmartre over employment and wages. Worse still was the problem of bread. Although the harvest in the Paris region had been good, hoarding of specie due to imminent fears of state bankruptcy (another loan floated by Necker in August was poorly subscribed) dislocated the food-supply system. Furthermore, a mild drought and lack of wind delayed milling the harvest. Thus bread prices remained high and, to stop disturbances, the city ordered dealers to sell grain only at the central markets and posted National Guardsmen in front of bakers' shops. But as in July, people attributed the shortage of supply somehow to the manoeuvres at Versailles. Women stall-keepers at the central market were especially restive and began to murmur at the inaction of their men. Desmoulins even feared that the queen would ask her brother, Joseph II of Austria, to attack and that the royal family would flee the country. As in July, an aristocratic-foreign-famine plot was aggravated by the military build-up. Several Paris districts expressed alarms about its significance and when the municipality itself asked for clarifications, the ministry replied evasively. Later, the district of Cordeliers where Danton had great influence, demanded that Lafayette secure the return of the Flanders Regiment to its base. In short, the source of everyone's political and economic troubles was at Versailles and the solution was to bring the king to Paris.

The famous banquet held by the officers of the King's Bodyguard to welcome their counterparts of the Flanders Regiment on the evening of 1 October determined the Parisians to act. The king's health was drunk but, conspicuously, there were no toasts to the nation. The king, just returned from hunting, and the royal family were received with elation. As the banquet wore on, a few inebriated stragglers shouted 'Down with the Assembly!' outside the queen's apartments. By the time these stories got back to Paris, it was being said that the tricolour cockade had been trampled underfoot and that officers were wearing white on black (the Hapsburg colours) cockades. There was no better proof of the evil designs around the king. Parisians were determined to avenge the insult. On 3 October, the municipality had to disperse a crowd outside the Ecole Militaire which probably wanted arms, and the next day, a Sunday, a woman at the Palais Royal began to talk of going to Versailles. On Monday, a crowd of several thousand women accompanied by many men set out for Versailles in the afternoon after having broken into the Hôtel de Ville to demand bread and procure arms. The municipality, faced with a near-mutiny among the ranks of the National Guard who wanted to follow, finally authorized Lafayette to lead a 20,000-strong contingent to Versailles to keep order and to request the king to come to Paris. The military procession set out in a torrential downpour in the late afternoon and arrived around midnight. Meanwhile, the wet and exasperated women milled about the château and joined the disconcerted deputies on their benches. The patriots, some of whom almost certainly knew of and perhaps even had encouraged the Parisians' intentions, demanded that the king accept the constitutional decrees 'pure and simple'. Louis, refusing the dishonour of flight, immediately agreed but temporized when Lafayette presented the municipality's request to move to Paris.

The Parisians then forced the issue. Just after daybreak on the 6th, a crowd, intent on avenging the insult of the infamous banquet, broke into the palace grounds and one of them was shot by the King's Bodyguard. In retaliation, two bodyguards were killed, their heads later displayed on the ends of pikes on the gardens of the Palais Royal. In order to calm the situation, the royal family appeared with Lafayette on a balcony of the château where the king announced his intention of moving to Paris. Later that afternoon, a huge procession, accompanied by heavy wagons of flour from the palace reserves, made its way to the capital amid shouts from spectators and burly market-porters that they were bringing back 'the baker, the baker's wife and the baker's boy'.

That night as the royal family settled into the Tuileries palace, the city was illuminated in celebration but nothing could disguise the fact that political authority had shifted decisively. Unlike July when Parisians' actions had been essentially defensive, the October Days represented the first and hardly the last occasion when direct Parisian intervention decisively affected national politics. The first victim was, of course, the king, who was intimidated into accepting the constitutional decrees and into moving. Louis never sincerely accepted this and so became increasingly attracted to the idea of flight. The Constituent Assembly too was in a sense a victim of October and when the deputies installed themselves in a converted riding school near the Tuileries in early November, they too had had their actions dictated to them by a Paris crowd. Although the monarchiens' influence had been broken in the votes on the legislature and the veto in September, Mounier was convinced the Assembly was no longer free and tried to rouse his native Dauphiné against the intimidation of Paris. The attempt to raise the provinces against the capital failed but was nonetheless a significant prefiguration of the federalist crisis of 1793.

Most significant, Parisians had begun to learn the lessons of insurrectionary politics. The people who understood that the constitutional deadlock could be broken by a show of force had gone some distance in increasing their political understanding from the rather abstract identification with the Third Estate they had shown less than six months earlier. This can be attributed to the effervescent revolutionary press and the orators of the Palais Royal but already the sixty district assemblies were beginning to play the active role in political education they were to assume the next year, pretending to a status partially independent of the commune.

Furthermore, the acquiescence of the provinces in the October Days planted the idea that Paris had a special role within the country to protect the Revolution. Finally, Parisians were acquiring organizations which would permit the imposition of their ideas. The district assemblies were one, the National Guard was another. In theory, the National Guard was supposed to have been purged of unreliable propertyless elements in July and the requirement that militiamen buy their own uniforms ought to have kept it solid. The few surviving lists with their inordinate numbers of merchants, clerks, functionaries and artisans from the skilled and luxury trades suggest that this may well have been so. It was all the more significant, therefore, that Lafayette could barely control them. As the October Days and subsequent experience showed, in any genuinely perceived emergency, the line between 'bonne bourgeoisie' and 'unreliable' elements collapsed.

But this was for the future. Looking backward over that turbulent summer and out from Paris, a number of features which were to mark the entire period were already evident. One was the universal hostility to the peasant movement. The conquerors of the Bastille were national heroes, recognized as such by distinct medals and uniforms; the peasant insurgents were hanged, convicted by the summary courts whose procedures the revolutionaries normally found so appalling. The Constituent Assembly refused to entertain any appeals for clemency and even Marat's *L'Ami du Peuple* had nothing to say. The day had not yet arrived when the revolutionaries denounced the country people as priest-ridden knaves or food hoarders or both, but already the gap in appreciating rural aspirations was clear.

The Revolution was the work of townspeople and reflected their desires, but in order to understand it a number of distinctions must be made. The violent groups in 1789 were not particularly bourgeois. This can only be known for Paris, the only city whose crowds have been subject to minute study, but the example is instructive. Among the officially recognized conquerors of the Bastille, not one was a lawyer or other professional, there was only a handful of businessmen and in a city with so many of them, wage-earners, domestic servants and members of the luxury trades were almost certainly underrepresented. Instead, the cutting edge of the 'violent classes' came from the building, clothing and furnishing trades, men who were far from representing the urban poor, and men who were to be dominating forces in neighbourhood politics down to 1795. It is customary to cite Santerre, the wealthy brewer with an international reputation, as an example of this, but it should also be noted that the three largest trades represented on the lists were locksmiths, cabinet-makers and joiners, all skilled artisans and therefore, presumably, moderately well off. They were also a more settled group in the sense that just over half had been born in the provinces, while in the faubourg Saint-Antoine generally just over two thirds were provincials. But men used to working with their hands, often with a skilled apprenticeship behind them (and therefore presumably with families wealthy enough to finance it) and with long-standing ties to their neighbourhoods, did not necessarily see economic individualism and freedom as the solution to their problems. Regulation of the food trade was only the most dramatic example of their demands but an examination of the *cahiers* of the trades shows that regulation of most aspects of economic life was a natural reflex. Like their counterparts in Lyon, where the social struggles between master-weavers and merchants are much better known, no one embraced the world of free trade which was opening up before them.

Even more remarkable was the shift in power at the provincial level. With the collapse of the royal bureaucracy in the summer, the towns acquired an unprecedented autonomy which they only surrendered in the emergency of 1793–4. Thousands of addresses poured into Paris adhering to the decrees of the Constituent Assembly but experience soon showed that the tutelage of the deputies was only moral. The decree of 29 August freeing the internal grain trade, for example, proved to be very difficult to enforce. The northern Burgundian towns freely interfered with grain shipments intended for Lyon, and as late as October units of the Paris National Guard were authorized by the commune to fan out into the countryside to buy wheat at fixed prices. In Anjou, and no doubt elsewhere, people simply refused to obey the decree of 23 September provisionally reestablishing the salt tax. An assembly of towns and parishes convoked by the Angers committee voted to substitute a money tax for it. But provincial autonomy did not necessarily bring with it a complete revolution of institutions or personnel. The wave of agitation throughout the summer led to assaults on local institutions, but the panic which soon followed led to a rallying together of the wealthy orders. The men who took power in the provinces were far from poor. In Montpellier, Reims and Troyes, the members of the permanent committees were at least twice as wealthy as the average townsman and often the transfer of power from one class to another was curiously incomplete. Of the major provincial centres, the administrations of Aix, Grenoble and Toulouse survived more or less intact and, while in most other places the old local administrations were restructured, elements of the Old Regime persisted. In Berry, power was generally exercised by nobles, priests and judges along with the old municipalities. The permanent committee at Lyon, born of fears of agitation among the master-weavers, was representative of all three orders, while at Marseille the local revolution succumbed to a bloody military countercoup which lasted until the end of the year. Even at Dijon where the authority of the committee was not contested, the lawyers and skilled artisans had to share power, at least nominally, with representatives of the nobility and clergy. Committees which held the nobility at arm's length, as at Rennes or Montauban, were, therefore, fairly rare. The same appears to have been true of the provincial National Guards. Dijon's exclusively bourgeois officer corps was exceptional, while even in Rennes there were nobles among the officer corps, as well as at Nancy, and in Lorraine generally where it was deliberate policy to recruit them. Fear of brigands and of popular violence thus tended to reinforce ties among the elites who temporarily forgot their differences.

Chapter 3

Consolidation and Challenge

By the end of 1789, men were beginning to use the word 'revolution' in a new way. Until then, its connotations suggested any sudden or unexpected change in the state, as in Maupeou's 'revolution' in 1771. The new meaning extended the old by adding the associations of a mass uprising and the overthrow of social groups. In the spring of 1789, men could not foresee a revolution in this modern sense because they did not have the concept. Once they began to try to explain to themselves what had happened in that extraordinary summer, they invented the concept and with it the exhilarating, intoxicating sense of humanity reborn. The collapse of the Old Regime had been so sudden and so complete that many journalists and pamphleteers thought it possible to put an end to history and build the heavenly city. Although many deputies in the Constituent Assembly were almost as enthusiastic about the work of reconstruction, they faced the more prosaic task of designing new, more effective and fairer institutions. Yet in their determination to solve the state's financial problems as quickly as possible, and in their rather inflexible definition of absolute property rights, they could not satisfy everyone. By the end of 1790 and early into 1791 blood had been spilled in some regions over the liquidation of the seigneurial system, the granting of civil rights to Protestants, and the role of the Church in the new order. There was widespread discontent over food-distribution policy, high taxes and the cost of living. Whether violent outbursts or mere grumbling, not all of these discontents were counterrevolutionary, and even where they were the popular visions of a successful counterrevolution often differed greatly from those of the aristocratic reactionaries. Whatever the degree of commitment, the disturbances did offer an opening to the émigré armies slowly forming on the frontiers and to conspirators inside the country. Yet even as protests against the Constituent Assembly's work spread, the very idealism of '89 was drawing men into institutions like the clubs and the National Guards which took an instransigent defence of the Revolution's achievements. These men had their grievances too and wanted to enlarge the political nation by democratizing institutions. Unless the politicians could master these various currents of opposition, they would contribute to adding another connotation to 'revolution': civil war.

Reform and the Bourgeois Revolution

To understand this process, it is necessary to describe the new institutions of government, and the kinds of people who ran them.

The basis of local government was the department. Unlike the Old Regime whose institutions operated on a functional basis with little regard for each other, the departments had a strict geographical basis which contained all the operations of government. Thus, the fiscal, administrative, judicial and ecclesiastical institutions all operated within the territory of the department. At first, the penchant for a rational system of local government was itself carried to extreme lengths. Some deputies, for example, proposed that department boundaries be established on a strict grid, but in drawing boundaries, the deputies showed more common sense by recognizing historic and economic associations. Thus the five new departments of Brittany closely approximated the boundaries of the five largest dioceses which were also the administrative subdivisions of the old Estates. The core of the department of the Ardèche was the old Vivarais region to which other communes were added to make it viable. Inevitably, however, such a vast reorganization could not satisfy everyone. For every town whose civic pride swelled by being chosen as the site of a new governmental organ, there were dozens who felt slighted. Marseille, for example, felt so outraged that Aix was chosen as the capital of the Bouches-du-Rhône that in August 1792 its National Guard literally kidnapped the department administrators and installed them where the Marseillais felt they should have been in the first place.

Like Brienne's provincial assemblies whose attributions and composition they curiously resembled, the departments were at the head of a hierarchy of local government. Below them were the districts whose number varied with the size and topography of the department, and below them were the communes, one for each parish in the countryside. The cantons had no administrative role except to group communes into primary assemblies for electoral purposes and to mark the jurisdictions of the justices of the peace. In the towns, a role similar to the cantons was allocated to the sections, of which there were forty-eight in Paris, thirty-two each in Marseille and Lyon, and so on. The departments and districts had similar structures. Qualified electors chose a council which in turn chose a directory which was responsible for handling business on a day-to-day basis. Each directory also had an elected procurator or executive officer who was supposed to represent the king's interests, while each commune, which had a single council, had an elected mayor. This was not, however, a federal system, in the sense of each body having exclusive jurisdiction over designated operations of government. Rather, central and local government were divisions of labour, all of its officers theoretically responsible to the Crown which could dismiss them. However, the departments, districts and municipalities had, in fact, a good deal of freedom to manoeuvre. As elected and modestly paid officials whose careers in no sense depended on the royal bureaucracy, local politicians were able to defy and circumvent the wishes of the national government. It was through the liberal use of their police powers that they steered the country through the first manifestations of popular counterrevolution and the military crisis of 1792.

On the whole and except for many rural communes whose members were often illiterate and which were short on talent, the new system of government worked remarkably well. This was because men whose Old Regime careers brought them into close contact with government administered the departments, districts and urban communes. This in turn was because of the system and practice of elections. The electorate was divided into three groups: passive citizens who paid less than the equivalent of three days' labour in taxes, active citizens who paid more and who had to meet age and residence qualifications, and eligible electors who paid more than the equivalent of ten days' labour in taxes. Active citizens chose a slate of electors from a list of eligibles. The electors in turn chose most govermental officials ranging from deputies, civil administrators, judges and priests. The division of the electorate into active and passive citizens was widely denounced at the time as a violation of the Declaration of the Rights of Man and it is undoubtedly true that the deputies feared the levelling tendencies of the poor. It is unlikely, however, that many of the skilled artisans, let alone the bourgeois, who made the Revolution were disqualified as active citizens by the fiscal limitations of the electoral law, and probably very rarely by the age and residence qualifications. The active citizen electorate was very large – one estimate puts it at 4.3 million which would encompass two thirds of the adult males and make it proportionately larger than that of England and many American states. The result was that in Dijon, for example, every trade was well represented among the corps of active citizens, and people in the manual occupations, who made up just over half the corps, were certainly numerous enough to make their presence felt in any election. But by basing the electoral system so heavily on taxes, the Constituent Assembly favoured the countryside over the towns because the electoral rolls were still based on the fiscal rolls of the Old Regime whose per capita direct taxes weighed more heavily on the countryside. Thus in the rural communes of the Sarthe over 90 per cent of the adult males were active citizens while in the towns roughly 70 per cent could vote. In the eastern Ille-et-Vilaine, three quarters of the rural male population was enfranchised while roughly two thirds of the overall population was. In one village in the Toulousain, 96 per cent of the men were active citizens but only 40 per cent were in Toulouse itself. In Paris half, and sometimes considerably more depending on the section, of the adult males were disenfranchised. The rural bias in the electorate ought to have been corrected at the level of eligibles since so many more rich people lived in the towns, but by how much is unknown. In any case, the social bias introduced at this level was dramatic. Although the ten days' labour qualification did not eliminate the peasantry and skilled artisans entirely, it did put direct electoral power disproportionately into the hands of the rich, that is, the bourgeoisie and the aristocracy. The corps of electors was consequently very small.

By law then the elections to the departmental and district councils and directories brought to power men who were much better off than their fellow citizens. They also represented the triumph of the bourgeoisie. Nobles were clearly eligible but, either because the electorate mistrusted them or because they chose not to stand, there were very few elected. In the Calvados, Morbihan, Ille-et-Vilaine, Tarn and Rhône-et-Loire, there were none at all, while in many other departments they were a mere handful. The shift of power these elections represented, therefore, was enormous. Unlike the Old Regime, and unlike the makeshift arrangements of 1789, the privileged orders were singularly absent from local government. Not surprisingly, given the structure of the bourgeoisie of the Old Regime, the legal professions were overwhelmingly represented, although the Cher and the Indre appear to have been exceptional in electing so many former office-holders and subdelegates. Elsewhere, the victors were more often small-town lawyers of various types. They were men of some experience all the same. If the departments of Lower Normandy were typical, they were often men who had received an apprenticeship in local government in the provincial assemblies after 1787, and who had been prominent patriots in the electoral campaign of 1789. Almost everywhere, however, it is possible to detect a reaction against the imperious rule of the permanent committees. In some municipal elections – Dijon, Nîmes and Montauban, among others – the advanced revolutionary party was actually defeated. The electorate and the adminstrators clearly wanted order and an end to adventures. It was all the more significant, therefore, that such conservatively minded men were to contribute to the radicalization of the Revolution when it was challenged in 1791/2.

A decentralized government run by local citizens was an ideal common to almost everyone in the early Revolution. Whether it would be accepted in the longer term depended on how the lawyers used the power the electorate conferred on them, and this in turn depended a great deal on the other reforms of the Constituent Assembly.

Finance and the Civil Constitution of the Clergy

The Constituent Assembly was dominated by questions of finance. It had been called into being by the state's deficit and it had kept itself in being in the critical months of 1789 by guaranteeing the national debt. The crisis shaped its reforms of taxation and ecclesiastical affairs. Moreover, the crisis grew worse every day. The royal bureaucracy crumbled, the nation took a tax-holiday and investors showed little confidence in the loans authorized in 1789. One solution, adopted on 2 November 1789 on an earlier proposal by Talleyrand, Bishop of Autun, was to sequester the property of the Church. This was a very rare demand in the spring and only the gravity of the crisis drew the deputies to it. Even so, the financial situation worsened. In March 1790, Necker, whose popularity was sinking with every failed loan and alarming financial statement, forecast a staggering deficit of 294 million, far more than Calonne's which had begun the final crisis of the Old Regime in the first place. Consequently, the deputies decided on 17 March that Church property would be sold to the public. In the meantime, the state would emit 400 million *livres* of treasury bills or 'assignats' at 3 per cent interest, which would be guaranteed by the newly nationalized property or 'biens nationaux'. The early assignats were, therefore, bonds based on solid collateral and the slight fall in their value can probably be explained as an effect of discounting. However, because of the great interest in *biens nationaux*, and because of the debt, the Assembly authorized a new emission of 800 million of assignats in September in denominations as low as 50 *livres* and this time they would bear no interest. In other words, the deputies had authorized the creation of paper money. This in itself was no bad thing because the 1200 million assignats in circulation at the end of 1790 was well below the value of the *biens nationaux*. The assignats would raise their price at auction and accelerate their sale. But the appearance of the assignats coincided with a shortage of specie which was itself due to hoarding, and with a balance of payments deficit brought on by the emigration of many aristocrats and the necessity to pay for grain imports. Without money, therefore, the economy was grinding to a halt as peasants held on to their grain and working people were not being paid. The solution to this was the creation, mainly by the Jacobin clubs, of 'billets de confiance' or notes of small denominations which in combination could be exchanged against the larger-denomination assignats. In other words, the state was losing control of the money supply. It also contributed to its expansion by authorizing the issue of 21 million in small coins which soon disappeared, and by issuing 100 million in assignats in denominations of 5 *livres*. This simply led to further hoarding of specie and a dreadful spiral of printing more assignats in ever smaller denominations, price inflation, a fall in the value of the assignat, quicker circulation of money and still further inflation. By the end of December 1791, assignats had depreciated by 25 per cent; on the eve of the war, by 40 per cent. Living standards of the poor and artisans invariably fell with immense consequences for labour relations, for the marketing mechanism of grain and for the continuation of disturbances in both town and country. A difficult and complex financial operation therefore eventually led to a challenge to the rule of the bourgeois citizens.

More important, because it was more visible and easier to

establish blame, was the Civil Constitution of the Clergy, as the reorganization of the Church was called. The financial situation affected this too. The decision to abolish the tithe and the nationalization of Church property stripped the Church of its resources. The idea that the clergy would be paid was implicit in the decree of 11 August 1789 and many of the deputies pointed out in debate that this was the obverse of nationalizing the Church's property. Thus, the Constituents claimed a right to have a voice in the organization of the Church and how much of it they would support. They would not support 'useless' religious orders and 'superfluous' dioceses. On 28 October 1789 they suppressed religious vows and dissolved contemplative orders, retaining only those involved in education, hospitals and charity. Later they decided that there would be just one diocese in each of the 83 departments, thus eliminating 52 others. Financial considerations were not the only factors affecting the reorganization of the Church. By guaranteeing religious toleration and freedom of thought and expression, Articles X and XI of the Declaration of the Rights of Man undermined the Church's rationale for its existence as a separate, organized order. Protestants received full civil rights on 24 December 1789, although Jews had to wait until 27 September 1791. Equal treatment of religious sects and their followers did not imply separation of Church and state. However many freemasons, deists or tepid Catholics there were among the deputies, all of them shared the Voltairean assumption that without religion the popular classes would have no morals. If only in the interests of public order, the protection of property and the defence of the Revolution, they intended to tie the Church even more closely to the state than it had been under the Old Regime. Many of them, including many of the curés both in the Assembly and in the country, also dreamed of restoring the Church to the less opulent, purer existence of the first and second centuries when clergy and laity were a simple association of the faithful. The vision of a primitive Church was powerful even among those who eventually rejected the religious settlement, and explains why there were so few protests over the sequestration of Church property despite the arguments of reactionaries like the abbé Maury in the Assembly. Idealism and empirical solutions to practical problems were equally powerful impulses.

The most controversial element of the Civil Constitution was the election of new curés and bishops by the active citizens and electors.

As its opponents pointed out, this allowed non-Catholics to help choose priests. Elections would also violate long-established tradition by undermining episcopal discipline as well as the doctrine of apostolic succession. But it is difficult to see how the Constituents could have acted otherwise. Both the theory of sovereign government and the political circumstances of 1790 propelled the deputies towards what many clerics felt was a high-handed and imperious attitude to the Church. The apologists of the Civil Constitution were determined to claim ultimate jurisdiction over the Church whether as a civil or a religious institution, a power which French kings had exercised ever since the Counter-Reformation. They insisted that the Civil Constitution in no way affected dogma or the Church's spiritual rights, that suppressing certain ecclesiastical institutions, altering diocesan boundaries or electing priests was within the rights of the sovereign. Archbishop Boisgelin of Aix, the most articulate opponent of the Civil Constitution, admitted there were precedents for most of these reforms but insisted that ecclesiastical discipline had been broken and that, in any case, however desirable reform was, it had to be undertaken after the consultation and consent of the Church. Gallicanism was so pervasive that neither side laid much emphasis on securing the consent of the Pope. Anyway, the deputies thought this might be easy to get since an antipapal revolution at Avignon had voted for union with France. This allowed the Constituent Assembly a good deal of leverage against Rome. With the papacy of little concern, the deputies could push ahead and ignore the protests of clerical spokesmen. Aside from a desire to make all officials responsible to the electorate – and the clergy had become civil servants – the bishops of 1790 were aristocrats. Some bishops had already emigrated and others, beginning with Le Mintier of Tréguier in Brittany in November 1789, had denounced the Declaration of Rights. Could anyone trust the bishops to choose patriotic curés? Moreover, by the time the Civil Constitution was finally voted, on 12 July 1790, riots had broken out in some of the cities of the Midi whose slogans were not only anti-Protestant but counterrevolutionary. Religion could not be permitted to become the stalking horse of counterrevolution. Thus, the Constituents refused to consider the convocation of a national council of the Church to discuss the Civil Constitution, because a sovereign body could not tolerate the rebirth of an old order which in the past, most recently in 1788, had defied the Crown. Would such a council not also become a focus for counterrevolutionaries? Once the question was posed with such clarity, compromise of any sort was very difficult. There was a slim hope that the Pope could mediate and 94 clerical deputies, still not a majority of the old order, declared that reforms were acceptable only with his approbation. But France was represented at Rome by the reactionary cardinal Bernis who was violently hostile to the Civil Constitution, and Pius VI temporized. In any case, an appeal to the Pope looked like a delaying tactic from a clergy which was normally proud of its Gallicanism. Finally tired of apparently sterile debates which had continued since May, and uneasy at a swell of religious troubles, the exasperated Constituents imposed an oath of loyalty to the entire constitution. This received royal sanction on 26 December. Those who refused it, bishops, curés and vicaires, would be expected to leave their posts with a pension as soon as a replacement was elected.

The oath to the Civil Constitution is rightly considered one of the great crises of the Revolution because it gave the counterrevolution a popular base. In order to understand why this was so, it is necessary to make a distinction between the reasons some clerics rejected it and why certain regions of the country supported that decision. There were many elements in the Civil Constitution which made the decision to take or reject the oath very difficult. The residence requirements for bishops, the reduction of scandalous incomes to respectable salaries, the prerequisite of pastoral experience which opened the episcopate to the lower clergy, and the assurance of a decent income for themselves, not to mention the welcome secular reforms, were close to many of the demands expressed in the clerical *cahiers* of 1789. Yet the clergy had dreamed that the national regeneration inaugurated by the calling of the Estates-General would have a religious gloss, which in some cases came close to advocating theocracy. Could this be done without the security of an established, self-governing order, the sacrifice of which was far greater than that asked of the nobility? Many of the curés who took the oath, soon to be called constitutionals, were convinced not only that it could, but that the Civil Constitution was the voice of God. Those who refused, the refractories, were not so sure and could point to the Declaration of Rights, the dissolution of religious vows, the defeat of a motion by the reformer Dom Gerle in April declaring Catholicism the state religion, and the talk of permitting divorce as indications that the laity had no intention of being led by the clergy.

By midsummer 1791, about 60 per cent of the curés and a little more than half the vicaires had taken the oath. Only seven bishops, including Talleyrand and Loménie de Brienne, did. The split between upper and lower clergy which was manifest in the elections of 1789 was now in the open. But more went into the decision than ideology or continuity with previous attitudes. The curés were subject to a great deal of pressure, not least from the Pope whose long-awaited condemnations on 10 March and 13 April 1791 sparked a flurry of retractions. Family, friends, fellow priests, seminary professors, bishops, officials and Jacobin clubs inundated the curés with advice, threats and fulminations. Thus no single or even multiple explanation can be found which would explain why some curés took or refused the oath. In Brittany, for example, there is a strong correlation between a priest on his own and oath-taking, and a priest with assistants and refusal. Whatever this means – a little clerical society offering each member support or a deeper lay piety or both – the correlation is weak elsewhere. Broadly speaking, one of the most important factors affecting the decision was pressure from the laity. The geography of oath-taking was not random. Instead, a broad belt beginning in Picardy and running through northern Burgundy on the east and the frontier of Maine on the west, and finishing in Berry and Lower Poitou, represented an area of massive oath-taking. So did another belt beginning in the Ain which ran east of the Rhône through the Alps to the Mediterranean. By contrast, a zone beginning in Upper Languedoc and continuing in a northern crescent through the southern Massif Central and ending in the Lyonnais, another in Alsace and still another in the Nord and Pas-de-Calais represented regions of massive refusals. Most impressive of all was the refractory region roughly west of a line drawn through Caen, Le Mans and Poitiers. In very general terms, the map of oath-taking and refusals is also the map of popular attitudes to the Revolution and of left-right voting in the Second and Third Republics.

The revolutionaries at the time explained the popular support for the refractories as the result of their preaching on an ignorant, servile population, and all of the punitive legislation against the refractories down to the deportations of 1792 and 1797 was ultimately directed at controlling a hostile laity. Historians are not so naive and a great deal of effort has gone into exploring the hypothesis that the map of oath-taking also correlates with the map of literacy, higher circulation of books, better communications, and

pre-revolutionary dechristianization. While this research continues
– and much of it is built upon the old assumption that the
constitutional church was somehow not truly Catholic, or that it
represented a decline in religious fervour – another explanation is
possible. The Civil Constitution of the Clergy altered no
fundamental dogma and did not touch the liturgy which was a more
vital element in popular culture than belief, of which most ordinary
people were astonishingly ignorant. The constitutional priests were
as capable and as qualified to perform the rites of passage and
invoke the deity against the evils of a malevolent and capricious
spiritual world as the refractories. In some regions of the country,
people allowed them to perform this role; in others, they did not.
Whatever else it was, the Civil Constitution of the Clergy was also
a kind of plebiscite for and against a Church that was associated
with the Revolution, which was expected to proselytize for it and
to keep order for it. In other words, to reject the Revolution was
to reject the rule of the citizen-lawyers who had come to power in
1790.

Discontent and the Distribution of Benefits

Part of the explanation for the challenge was the overall land
settlement which had to do with the liquidation of the seigneurial
regime, the new fiscal system and the sale of *biens nationaux*.
Where this was favourable, particularly to the important groups in
village society, the Revolution found support. Where it was not,
there could be trouble, ranging from continuing disturbances to
open counterrevolution.

   In providing for the disappearance of the seigneurial regime, the
law of 15 March 1790, the work primarily of Merlin de Douai, a
specialist in the arcane workings of feudal law, distinguished
between rights bearing on persons or whose origins were thought
to be usurpations which were abolished, and those bearing on land
which were brought under the law of contract until they could be
redeemed. The law was unworkable. In practice Merlin's
distinction was often impossible to make. The high redemption
payments – twenty-five times the value for dues and twenty for
transfer fees – encouraged few and securing an assessment of the
land was a long and cumbersome process. In the end, redemption
payments were very rare. The few who did exercise their rights

under the law were the occasional urban bourgeois or wealthy peasant who took advantage of the falling assignat early in 1792 to redeem their land at much less than the rate envisaged in 1790. In this context, the laws of July and August 1792, which required seigneurs to produce the original titles, let alone that of 15 July 1793 which abolished feudalism without compensation, were virtually meaningless.

Peasants soon found they could not only avoid redemption but refuse to pay even the dues. The refusal to pay, which had begun in 1789, continued and became more general. In the region north of Rouen, which had been quiet in 1789, seigneurs received much less than half what was owing them in 1790, and still less as time went on. In Flanders, where peasants soon got control of the municipalities, there was a concerted effort to contest rates, harass seigneurial agents and demand titles. One of the communes even forbade its inhabitants to pay 'under pain of death'. In northern Burgundy, the coalition of village notaries and wealthy farmers who controlled the municipalities undertook a similar campaign which eventually wore down seigneurial resistance. As one of the segneurial agents put it, 'People tell me that they are exempt from all types of *dîmes* and will not pay them in the future.' What made evasion possible was the final abolition of seigneurial courts in August 1790. A seigneur wishing to enforce his claims no longer went to his own court but to the district tribunals whose judges were elected by the active citzens and electors. Not surprisingly, judgements in the seigneurs' favour were not to be hoped for and cases of this sort were extremely rare.

But the seigneurial regime did not crumble from below everywhere. Between the end of 1789 and mid-1792 there were over 150 incidents in well over one third of the departments involving demonstrations, protests and mass violence by country people who refused to accept the Constituent Assembly's settlement as final. The seigneurs' attempts to claim their rights kept the countryside even more effervescent. In Upper Brittany and in Quercy-Périgord-Limousin, there were dramatic insurrections. In February 1790, in Upper Brittany between Rennes and Ploermel, peasants rose up against the seigneurs' still legal attempts to collect arrears of dues and forced many to sign renunciations of their titles. At the end of January 1790 in Lower Limousin, peasants were convinced that 'the rich' were suppressing the decrees of the National Assembly. A band of eight or nine hundred in marching order headed by a billiard master, devastated a handful of châteaux between Brive and Tulle and opened the sluice-gates of a number of seigneurial ponds. More significantly, they took the benches reserved for the seigneurial judges (presumably local lawyers) from the churches and gleefully burned them on the public square. Since the bourgeoisie in this region also owned fiefs, peasants attacked them too. They took receipts and reconnaissances and pillaged their houses. Disturbances continued throughout the year. In March and April in the Bourbonnais, Berry, Limousin and Nivernais where peasant microproperty was very extensive, there were rumours that the National Assembly had reduced the price of bread. In June, these regions were racked by a wave of popular price-fixing and demands that seigneurs surrender usurped wastelands.

The most intractable rebellions were those which broke out in the departments of the Dordogne and Lot at the end of 1789. These continued with few interruptions until the spring of 1792. They began around Sarlat in the Dordogne in late November 1789, with attacks on seigneurial agents and demands that seigneurs remit dues which had already been collected, sometimes as much as twenty years before, and return guns, some of which had been confiscated from the insurgents' fathers. Like their counterparts elsewhere in the summer of 1789, peasants clearly had long memories for grievances and took advantage of the unsettled conditions to right old wrongs. This was not the only parallel. The folkloric element was prominent, although here it took the distinctive feature of planting what were called 'May trees'. These were trees planted in the village square decorated with flowers, laurel leaves, and blue, white and red ribbons and topped with a crown. They did not differ from the thousands of 'liberty trees' which were springing up all over the country. But, like any powerful symbol, May trees had more ancient levels of meaning in the south-west. They certainly came to symbolize regeneration and deliverance and may have related to a customary belief that if they were kept standing for a year and a day, vassals would be free of seigneurial dues. They also symbolized the joy of spring and rebirth, and villagers traditionally marched them throughout the countryside and planted them in the lord's courtyard. By suspending measures, small sacks of grain, chicken feathers or weather vanes from them, the villagers informed the lord symbolically that they considered his collection of dues abusive.

Planting May trees, therefore, was a symbol of freedom and a provocation to the lords. The practice of planting them to celebrate the union of the three orders in June 1789, or the anniversary of the fall of the Bastille in 1790, also shows how villagers blended traditional and new symbolism to express their aspirations to be rid of the seigneurial regime entirely.

People began to plant May trees along the valleys of the Dordogne, the Corrèze and the Vezère in the spring of 1790. Bands of peasants, sometimes in National Guard uniform, marched to the sound of flute and drum to the lord's château where the lord had to give everyone food and drink, promise restitution of dues and guns, surrender his weather vane (a symbol of high justice, retained, despite the Crown's having taken it over long before) and watch his pigeons put to death. These demonstrations were quite peaceful, even joyful, indeed in one case, handshakes with the seigneur were spurned in favour of hugs because 'they were all equal'. As in the Limousin, pews were removed from the churches and burned in the village square and, as elsewhere, feelings against the bourgeois ran as high as against the nobles. When the lawyers of Saint Pierre-de-Chignac came to vote in the municipal elections, people cried out, 'We don't want any of these P. . . messieurs in the assembly . . . they were thrown out, *tutoyés*, vilified and threatened with death.' When authorities tried to tear down the May trees, women and children prevented it. The attempt of the Department of the Lot in September to use the army and the *maréchaussée* to do this systematically, as a prelude to enforcing the laws on feudal dues, provoked a rising of nearly five hundred peasants, many of whom were National Guards armed with old hunting weapons and farm tools. Convinced that the laws of feudalism were the works of aristocrats, not the National Assembly, they invested the town of Gourdon, destroyed the houses of the administrators of the district, the former subdelegate and the rich, as well as a number of outlying country houses.

Nobles took up arms to defend their property. They roamed the countryside on horseback and fired on crowds of demonstrators. This provoked a wave of violent attacks on châteaux which lasted until January 1791. As in the Mâconnais, people set about literally demolishing the châteaux by destroying towers and tearing off roofs or setting fire to them. Eventually, a band of rural National Guardsmen killed the leader of the noble horsemen, the Marquis d'Escayrac-Montratier, by shooting into a subterranean dugout in which he had been forced to take refuge. The troubles died down after this but only in degree, for throughout 1791 and into 1792 there were sporadic attacks on châteaux, firings of granges, demonstrations demanding the restitution of dues, destruction of pigeon coops and so on.

These risings were highly significant, because, as in 1789, peasants made little distinction between so-called revolutionary bourgeois and reactionary aristocrats. They had their own aspirations, and in these regions they meant to impose them. Equally significant was the geographical distribution of resistance. In open-field country, where there was a long tradition of communal organization and where the rural elite acquired control of the communes, there was little the departments and districts could do to enforce the law even if they had been so inclined. In the isolated hill farms of the Massif Central, where bourgeois penetration into the seigneurial regime was extensive, or in the lonely scrublands of the west where the only common focus was simply the parish and the new communes were a genuine innovation, rebellion was the only alternative.

In some regions then, country people expected more than the Constituent Assembly and its local allies were able to deliver. The same was true of taxes. The end of fiscal privilege did not bring the relief that people had hoped for, although the situation was complicated by region and circumstances. The new fiscal system depended a good deal less on indirect taxes than the old, which meant that the incidence of taxation shifted from consumers to producers and, to a lesser extent, from the towns to the countryside. Furthermore, until the country could be surveyed entirely, a process that was not completed until the 1830s, the old tax rolls formed the basis of the new so that the massive regional disparities in taxation remained – disparities so great that the inhabitants of the Seine-et-Marne paid five times more per capita than those of the Ariège. It is also likely that income from capital, dividends and interest were as relatively undertaxed as they had been in the Old Regime, largely because the bureaucracy, whose personnel was mainly recruited from that of the monarchy, was incapable of making an inventory of all forms of private wealth. Yet to estimate more precisely whether the citizen paid more than the subject is extremely difficult because each fiscal system was so different and because Old Regime fiscality was so chaotic. On the whole, it appears that people paid more, especially once the war began in

1792. The revolutionaries claimed otherwise and put the net gain of the abolition of fiscal privilege and cheaper forms of collection at about the equivalent of eight days' labour. But there was some sleight of hand in this since official figures rarely included the additional surtaxes necessary to finance local government and assumed that the tithe had been abolished, which was only a half-truth. When the mass of figures is sorted out, it is certain that taxes did not go down, and in some cases may even have risen, sometimes by over 20 per cent. Furthermore, since the new fiscal system was in no sense progressive, the reasonably well-off gained proportionately more than the poor. Local studies bear out these generalizations. In the Nord for example, per capita taxation increased by about one eighth and, after hostilities began, by nearly one half over what it had been during the Old Regime. In Upper Brittany, per capita direct taxes doubled, although they still remained considerably less than those of the Nord. In the Puy-de-Dôme, the majority of cantons witnessed no real change in per capita taxation, although the very rich, including the former nobility, paid considerably more from the start and more still in forced loans and revolutionary taxes once the war began, while the very poor were given a welcome relief. The Constituent Assembly, in short, had taken a major step towards fiscal justice but for all those who hoped that the suppression of privilege would lighten their burdens, there had been little change. People were as reluctant as ever to pay, therefore, and the system of collection did little to encourage them. The administrators of the departments and districts were elected officials with no first-hand experience in fiscal questions and no career interest in efficient collection. Furthermore, the revolutionaries, even under the Terror, found constraint repugnant in a free society. This could only have discouraged civic-minded taxpayers. The continuation of the system of allowing private businessmen to collect taxes for an auctioned fee was an incentive to the dishonest and the inept. The lack of talent and enthusiasm in the rural municipalities completed the chaotic system of collection. For all these reasons, payments to the national treasury were extremely slow and so the fiscal crisis continued.

Whether peasants paid more overall is another issue, and the Constituent Assembly introduced an automatic social distinction in its handling of the ecclesiastical tithe. With almost no debate, an assembly of lawyers and landowners by the law of 2 December 1790 turned the tithe over to landowners and authorized proprietors to add the equivalent of the former tithe to their leases. For a peasant proprietor, the *de facto* abolition of seigneurial dues and the gift of the former tithe more than compensated for whatever increased taxes there were. In regions like northern Burgundy, where feudal dues were high, both owner-occupiers and farmers probably gained, but in most other regions feudal dues were considerably lower. For farmers and sharecroppers, especially in regions where feudal dues were light in relation to taxes and tithes, there was no gain at all and perhaps even a loss. What this could mean was shown when the rents on the estates of the Duc de Cossé-Brissac in the Deux-Sèvres were raised by nearly 25 per cent in 1791 because the tenants no longer had to pay the *taille,* tithes, salt tax and indirect taxes. No matter that tenants could eventually pay rents in devalued assignats, no matter that in devastated war zones like the Nord rents were no higher in 1799 than they had been a decade earlier, the intention of the Constituent Assembly was clear: the revolution in the countryside was to be one of landowners, not of tenants and sharecroppers, let alone labourers. One month after the law on tithes was passed, the parish clergy began to take the oath to the Civil Constitution of the Clergy. Many laymen now had an interest in the outcome of the oath.

The abolition of seigneurial dues and the tithe represented a far greater transfer of wealth than the sales of *biens nationaux* but these were important because they created, as was intended, a constituency of thousands who had a material stake in the success of the Revolution. They did not, however, contribute much to solving the problem of insufficient land for the poor peasantry because there was too little ecclesiastical property and because the lands were sold at auction which invariably favoured the highest bidder. All social classes were represented among the buyers including some of the future leaders of the counterrevolutionary rebellion in the Vendée. In many regions of the country, a surprising number of newcomers, who somehow managed to float enough credit, acquired property for the first time. Nonetheless, given the conditions of sale, the rich, particularly the urban bourgeoisie, were disproportionately successful. A considerable amount of money was mobilized for what amounted to a profitable way of showing one's patriotism. Bids were usually well beyond the original estimates and payment so assiduous that many buyers did not even profit much from the depreciation of the assignat (thus rendering the operation a financial success for the state). One of the most successful groups were the former office-holders who used the assignats given in payment for their suppressed offices to buy *biens nationaux*. From about one fifth to one half of the former bailiwick magistrates, for example, bought national property, and an impressive minority invested not only their indemnities but part of their personal fortunes as well. In other words, the Revolution rearranged the investment patterns of many of the old landed bourgeoisie and made their presence in the countryside more prominent than ever. The land settlement, therefore, favoured those who already had some wealth, or at least access to credit, and probably enhanced the importance of the urban grip on the countryside.

The reforms of the Constituent Assembly benefited certain groups more than others. That the deputies had gone beyond their mandates probably mattered less than that the package of reforms did create large reservoirs of support in the countryside. Although few had anticipated the reforms themselves or how they would work out, no doubt many proprietors were grateful that the abolition of the tithe and dues compensated for the disappointing effect of the abolition of fiscal privilege. A whole range of landowners from the wealthy bourgeoise to the small independent proprietor were all net beneficiaries. So too were townsmen and the fairly poor everywhere who gained from the abolition of most of the regressive indirect taxes. On the other hand, some groups gained little and may even have lost. The Church is the most obvious institution but so too were nobles, particularly where, as in Brittany, Burgundy, Auvergne and Upper Languedoc, they were heavily dependent on seigneurial dues for important portions of their income. Among the Third Estate, farmers and sharecroppers, who continued to pay the tithe in the form of rent, and rentiers, whose land had once been privileged or its owners had been, had no reason to support a regime of landowners. If they could carry the landless, the artisans, labourers and hired hands with them, and if enough pressure was put on them from the outside, whether in the form of a constitutional priest or requisitions of men and supplies, the counterrevolution could have an opening.

The Contours of Counterrevolution

The first phase of the counterrevolution was much more a conspiracy or a series of conspiracies than a mass uprising, however. The counterrevolution may be said to have begun with the emigration of the courtiers most compromised in bringing about the dismissal of Necker in July 1789, that is of the Comte d'Artois, the Condés, the Polignacs, and so on. By September, Artois had established a committee in Turin whose purpose was to plan 'une contre-révolution'. Other courtiers joined the émigrés after the October Days and groups of officers followed in the aftermath of the many mutinies among the troops in 1790. At first, there was no plan of organizing the émigrés militarily, at least partly because the Turin committee had no money and the new arrivals, convinced the national delirium would soon pass, brought little with them. In any case, all that apparently had to be done was to rescue Louis XVI and appeal to the foreign powers in the name of monarchial solidarity. This turned out to be impracticable. The king, true to his policy of not wanting to provoke a civil war, refused to be rescued, and the queen did not want to be rescued by the émigrés because, in the curious way that she combined personal spite and political acumen, she disliked Artois and realized that a successful émigré-sponsored counterrevolution would enslave the monarchy to the courtiers. Rescue was also dangerous, as the Marquis de Favras, in an apparently lone attempt, possibly encouraged, possibly betrayed by the Comte de Provence, found, as he was hanged for trying to kidnap the royal family in February 1790. The monarchy had its own strategy anyway. One element was to buy influence. The most notable catch was Mirabeau who went on the secret payroll in early 1790 and, among the club leaders in Paris, possibly Danton. The more important element was Marie-Antoinette's brothers. But Joseph II, embroiled with a rebellion in the Low Countries and a war with Turkey, and a believer in popular sovereignty outside his own lands, refused any help. When Joseph died in February, Leopold II contented himself with sonorous epistles to the queen and the émigrés which amounted to nothing. Of the other powers placed to intervene, none was willing to help. George III considered the Revolution a divine visitation on the French for meddling with the American colonies. Spain had no money and soon got itself involved in an obscure dispute with Britain over Nootka Sound near

Vancouver Island, which required an appeal to Louis XVI and the Constituent Assembly which was eventually refused. The German princes and Swiss cantons would do nothing without money or great power support. Of the foreign powers, only Artois's diminutive and bellicose father-in-law, Victor-Amedeus III of Sardinia, was willing to translate his hospitality into active intervention, at the price, of course, of some territory. The probability that all the powers might exact compensation for intervention did not worry the Turin committee overmuch, although it did bother others. Nor were its members anxious that its activities or rescue plans imperilled the royal family. Artois soon veered towards the idea, later developed by the vicious counterrevolutionary spymaster, the Comte d'Antraigues, that the monarchy was more important than the king, which in Antraigues's case meant that if Louis XVI had to martyr himself for aristocratic honour and privilege, so be it.

But by itself the counterrevolution of the émigrés could not amount to much. With no money and minimal foreign support, its helplessness was only underlined by the Prince de Condé's quixotic plan to invade the country at the head of a column of gentlemen. Domestic support was obviously crucial but it was not obvious where this might come from. Many aristocrats had wanted a constitution, and the end of privilege and the equality of talents would certainly help men who resented the influence of the court on military appointments in the Old Regime. The Constituent Assembly helped along the process of noble alienation by abolishing hereditary nobility and titles on 19 June 1790. This did not bother the Marquis de Ferrières, who considered the essence of nobility to have disappeared already, and who was more disgusted that the desultory debate had been preceded by a ludicrous salute to the deputies by people in national costumes representing the 'entire universe' led by the fatuous Prussian baron, Anacharsis Cloots. Ferrières worried that his constituents in Poitou might not take the symbolic destruction so lightly, however, and rightly so, for almost immediately, the Baron de Lezardière began to form a 'coalition' which would act as a fifth column in the event of a foreign invasion. No doubt other provincial nobles began to think along the same lines, although similar conspiracies in Normandy and Brittany did not get organized until the next year.

The most promising base of domestic counterrevolution had to come from roturiers, however, and the first offer came from a former accountant of the cathedral chapter of Nîmes and of the royal domain, François Froment, whose unemployment and fanatical Catholicism were matched only by his bitter desire to avenge his father's removal as municipal tax assessor for fraud by Protestant textile interests. In January 1790, Froment visited Turin and argued that 'one cannot snuff out a strong passion except by a stronger one . . . that religious zeal alone could stifle the revolutionary delirium'. The plan was to organize a simultaneous insurrection throughout the cities of the Midi; the means, to capture the municipalities and infiltrate the National Guard, or use Catholic companies which had already been organized against 'patriot' authorities or 'Protestant' guards at the right moment. Artois was enchanted, and with the light-hearted promise that the princes could take care of foreign support and procure arms, Froment's agents fanned out to recruit adepts throughout the cities. Whether it can all be attributed to Froment's conspiracy is unknown, but by the spring there were reactionary companies or volunteer organizations in Toulouse, Uzès, Montauban, Nîmes and other cities. After a barrage of propaganda claiming among other things that Protestants were plotting a massacre of Catholics, the Catholic party swept most of the municipal elections. Throughout the spring, handbills circulated in Toulouse, Montauban, Castres, Uzès and Nîmes that the decrees of the Assembly had annihilated religion. At the end of April, in Toulouse, Montauban, Uzès and Nîmes, there were mass meetings in the assembly halls of local monasteries demanding the passage of Dom Gerle's motion proclaiming Catholicism the state religion and the suspension of the inventories of religious property. But the anti-Protestant crusade once begun could not be easily controlled. At Toulouse on 29 April, a patriot crowd attacked another group signing a petition, and in the ensuing disturbances, during which shots were fired, the municipality arrested the Comte de Toulouse-Lautrec, the commander of the reactionary National Guard companies. At Montauban on 10 May, some four to five thousand women, some of them with pistols stuffed in their belts, prevented the municipal officers from making inventories of the religious houses. While a black man named Balthazar harangued crowds in the Cordelier monastery, the men threatened to burn the houses of leading Protestants. The Protestant National Guard, some of whom incidentally had helped in the repression of the peasant risings in Quercy a few months before, fled to the hôtel de ville. After five guardsmen were killed in a short siege of the courtyard, they surrendered. Thousands of Protestants fled, including the pastor and future member of the Committee of Public Safety, Jeanbon Saint-André, while the counterrevolutionary municipality disarmed and imprisoned leading patriots. But this only provoked the National Guard of Bordeaux, followed later by that of Toulouse, which marched to the outskirts of Montauban demanding the release of the prisoners. Unable to fight, the municipality conceded. The election of a patriot department in June effectively neutralized them.

This left the conspirators with the Department of the Gard where their inability to focus on the task at hand led to an appalling massacre at Nîmes. On 3 May, some members of Froment's unofficial companies, known variously as 'cébets' (onion eaters) or 'poufs rouges' for their red pompoms, quarrelled with soldiers and a soldier was killed. This only alienated the garrison and encouraged the Protestants, who had been shut out of the municipal elections, to make a strong showing in those of the department. While the electors were gathering on 13 June, a Protestant National Guardsman arrested one of Froment's followers for creating a disturbance. A crowd gathered to demand his release, the guards panicked and fired into the crowd. Throughout the night, each side called on its coreligionists from the countryside – much the same had happened earlier at Montauban to no effect – and the next day, rural and urban Protestant guardsmen assailed the Catholics. Once Froment's forces were defeated, an orgy of murder of Catholic monks and laity continued for the next two days. In the end, about two to three hundred were slaughtered. Not surprisingly, Catholic electors fled and the department was in the hands of the Protestants.

As vengeance for age-old persecutions and hatreds, the *bagarre de Nîmes* may have given some satisfaction but it also unleashed an ever-widening circle of support for counterrevolution throughout the Midi. The first response was a gathering of 20,000 Catholic National Guards with crosses sewn into their hats who met at Jalès in the Ardèche in August. Some of them broke off to protest the massacre at Nîmes and to demand a prompt trial of the 'poufs rouges' outside the department. This was tame stuff, but later in October someone, perhaps the organizing committee, issued a virulent manifesto accusing the National Assembly of treason against God and the king and demanding an end to 'oppression' of Catholics. With the first *camp de Jalès*, religious sectarianism leapt beyond the town walls to the countryside. It also encouraged plots in other cities. In Lyon, the former *échevin*, Imbert-Colomès, had already had an attempt to form separate National Guard legions foiled by a popular uprising. The new plan was to rely on the troops of the Comte de la Chapelle who would seize the city pending the arrival of the king, an army of the princes and a corps of nobles from the Forez and Auvergne. But one of the initiates denounced the plot to the municipality which arrested three of the leading conspirators on 12 December, while Imbert-Colomès and others fled to the country or abroad. Meanwhile, another conspiracy based in Provence, led by the barrister Pascalis in Aix and the former commander of the National Guard of Marseille, Lieutaud, was preparing to facilitate the invasion of the Prince de Condé. But some members of Pascalis's newly formed club, the *Amis du Roi, de la Paix et de la Religion*, got into a pistol fight with some local patriots who were soon joined by a hastily formed expedition of National Guards from Marseille. Pascalis and two others were imprisoned, when, on 14 December, the guardsmen and their hangers-on broke into the prison, held a mock trial in the courtyard and hanged the prisoners. The Marseillais marched home with the grisly trophy of Pascalis's head on the end of a pike. It was the first prison massacre of the Revolution.

The discovery of the Lyon conspiracy, the lynchings at Aix and the king's continuing refusal to be rescued, temporarily destroyed the prospects of the counterrevolution. The princes soon decamped to Coblenz on the Rhine and began to solicit help even more earnestly from the great powers. But the internal disorders, once unleashed, could not be so easily contained. At Uzès on 13 February 1791, a fight in a cabaret was followed by demonstrations in which people shouted 'A bas la nation! Vivent les Aristocrats!' Far from controlling the situation, Catholics in the National Guard rebelled and began sounding the cathedral bells, which authorities feared was a signal to call in rural Catholics to avenge the *bagarre de Nîmes*. Loyal troops and National Guards from Nîmes soon appeared, however, dispersed the crowd and closed down the 'Club monarchique ou la liberté'. Several hundred Catholics immediately fled to Jalès, killing a Protestant farmer along the way. The 'federal committee' of Jalès, which had remained in being, sent out letters of convocation to the Catholic rural legions. About ten thousand men, fearing an impending Protestant massacre or believing they were about to avenge their coreligionists at Uzès, responded. But it is doubtful whether the leaders had such aggressive plans, and after great confusion and futile debate the men dispersed. Thus when troops and patriot National Guards from as far away as Lyon and Marseille converged on the plains of Jalès, they found no army to oppose them. One of the leaders of the Jalès committee, Bastide de Malbosc, was arrested and imprisoned at Pont Saint-Esprit. A few weeks later, his body was found on the banks of the Rhône.

The first phase of the counterrevolution was over but its permanent strategy was already in place – an alliance of foreign powers and internal conspiracy and insurrection, a strategy which was eventually to work in 1814 and again in 1815. It is easy, of course, to mock the émigrés' and the conspirators' conceited assumption that they represented the true France which had temporarily fallen under the yoke of a self-seeking cabal, a cabal which Antraigues believed was a secret committee of Orléanists controlling the entire network of Jacobin clubs. Such fantasies aside, they were not wrong in believing they had considerable support. From the vicar-general and former procurator of the parlement who incited the petition campaign at Toulouse, to the canon-counts of Lyon, to the country squires who organized the *camps de Jalès*, through to disgruntled army officers and rural gentry whose 'coalitions' would only 'explode' if someone else lit the fuse, it was not surprising that the counterrevolution acquired some consistency from the former privileged orders. The combination of hurt pride, ancient loyalties, fear of disorder, loss of income, and the prospect of unemployment propelled many of these men into careers of conspiracy and exile. More interesting is the problem of roturier counterrevolution. One element was the counterrevolutionary bourgeoisie. Many of them clearly had close professional or emotional ties with the institutions of the Old Regime. The Froment clan and the Trinquelaques of Uzès, lawyers, tax assessors and church officials; Imbert-Colomès, one of the richest wholesalers of Lyon only recently ennobled; Pascalis, a defender of Provençal liberties in 1788 who made a notorious speech defending the parlements in September 1790, are all examples. Craftsmen and peasants were clearly drawn into counterrevolutionary politics by religion which split the unanimity of the old Third Estate as clearly as shattered quartz. Whatever conflict the continuing economic slump engendered in the silk-weaving towns of the Midi between weavers and spinners on the one side, and Protestant and petty Catholic merchants on the other, was subsumed in confessional strife. Ancestral memories blended with the active role of the church in daily life. The suppression of the many religious houses and cathedral chapters which offered employment to laymen, from musicians to gardeners, and whose charity was vital in a region where population pressed on resources more than it did elsewhere, raised unprecedented anxieties. It was easy to blame and to fear Protestants whose newly acquired civil rights suddenly gave them the political power and military force to avenge past wrongs, as in the *bagarre de Nîmes*. Popular religiosity and folklore also played a role in mobilizing opposition. Possibly in Languedoc, certainly in Provence, the demonstrative baroque Christianity of the common man suffered no decline, unlike that of the elite. It was surely no coincidence that the disturbances at Montauban began after a procession marking the first day of Rogations, that Froment worked through the lay penitent funeral confraternities, that the Catholic guardsmen set out for the first *camp de Jalès* just after Assumption, or that the demonstrations at Uzès took the form of the *farandole* or long snake-like dance through the streets. The old 'society of orders', cemented by religion, no longer by deference, survived. It was encapsulated in the social composition of the counterrevolutionary National Guard battalion of Montauban which was quite different from the battalions of the patriots. Whereas the officer corps of the latter was almost entirely dominated by wholesalers and the liberal professions, that of the former was dominated by retired army officers. As for the rank and file, artisans, of which there were only twelve masters, outnumbered all the other groups combined in the counterrevolutionary battalion. Textile artisans alone made up nearly half the artisan contingent. Religious conflicts clearly overlay trade disputes between 'patriot' merchants and 'counterrevolutionary' wage-earners, but not entirely since artisans and the liberal professions were represented on both sides while petty merchants and retailers opted for the patriots on the whole.

The same complex disputes between and among trades can be seen in the long and bitter conflict in Avignon. Because the Comtat was papal territory until France incorporated it in September 1791, and because the territories were in a state of more or less continuous civil war from early 1791 onwards with the pro-French town of Avignon leading the way against the pro-papal towns of Carpentras and Cavaillon, the situation was not quite comparable to that in France proper but the social conflicts the war engendered illustrate how complex the battles in the towns of the Midi could be. The list of those massacred at La Glacière on 15–16 October 1791 – in which sixty-five people were thrown from the top of a tower of the Palais des Papes into the latrines below by a pro-French committee headed by Pierre Jourdan, former grain and wine merchant, rumoured smuggler and commander of the Avignon army, who deserved his nickname of Coupe-Tête – were mostly artisans of various types, while Jourdan's committee were mostly but not entirely in the liberal professions. The majority of Jourdan's followers, however, were mostly artisans, particularly the volatile silk-workers, so that the world of work and to a lesser extent the professions split along occupational lines, with the main distinguishing factors being that the extreme revolutionaries were younger and relative newcomers to the city.

Looking at the Midi as a whole, it is evident that neither the Revolution nor the counterrevolution had a natural constituency among ordinary people. Depending upon the city, the silk- or textile-workers or artisans in general can be found on either side of the political divide, and as later experience would show more clearly, so could peasants. Much depended upon the political loyalties of the various urban elites and the kinds of conflicts within trades. This is another way of saying that ordinary people could not be manipulated at will by anyone and that they had aims which were often different from those of their leaders. Thus, the guardsmen on the way to the second *camp de Jalès* took the opportunity to rough up the patriots of the small towns and wreck their houses. These victims were evidently the men who had combined seigneurial judgeships, crooked legal practice and usury in the Old Regime. Peasant delegates in the primary assemblies in 1790 had spoken against these men when they argued against the introduction of cantons because 'they are persuaded that they are to be given three or four judges and many procurators and since they have been vexed enough, they don't want them any more'. The participants in the antiseigneurial risings in Upper Brittany, the Limousin and Quercy-Périgord had not wanted them either and so, in a curious way, both antiseigneurial and pro-Catholic peasants shared similar aims. The lesson for historians is to be cautious in transposing political labels which had some validity in the towns to the countryside where they could take on different meanings.

Religious Dissidence

By the turn of the year, large areas of the country had already shown their dissatisfaction with the political, fiscal and land settlement the Constituent Assembly had designed. Apart from the regions of sectarian conflict, many people had gained little or nothing from the new arrangements and while their loyalties were clearly fluid at such an early date, more self-interested groups were in a position to bid for their allegiance with some hope of success. It was in this shifting situation that the parish clergy began to take the oath to the Civil Constitution of the Clergy. It was not that there was a direct relationship between the oath and earlier troubles. There appears to be no correlation either in Upper Brittany or in Quercy between oath-taking and subsequent religious troubles on the one side, and antiseigneurial demonstrations on the other. Undoubtedly, religious questions realigned local politics in these regions in ways that are still poorly understood. But both in the Nord and parts of the west, there does appear to be a relationship between religious troubles and regions where tenants who had gained little were numerous enough or powerful enough to carry their neighbours. Certainly, people tried to influence the curé's decision. Thus a curé in the Calvados claimed, 'I would have taken the oath if there had not been obstacles from my parishioners which a false zeal misleads or rather who let themselves be persuaded by the seditious speeches of some self-interested fanatics.' The municipal officers of Thieix in the Morbihan wrote, 'We consider . . . priests who are cowardly enough to take the oath as unworthy of our confidence.' At Aubenas in the Ardèche, a general assembly of the women decided to prevent the priests from taking the oath, 'to throw stones at those who replace them and then require the receiver of the district to pay the refractories'.

In these regions where the refractory had considerable support, particularly in the west and the north, the country people went to extraordinary lengths to make the life of the constitutionals miserable. Services and sacraments were boycotted, masses were drowned out by chants outside the churches, shots were fired outside the presbyteries in the middle of the night, dead animals were hung on the doors of their homes, threats were made to bury them alive, children hooted them as they passed by, and so on. In many places, municipal officers resigned rather than have anything to do with them, and electors absented themselves from the primary assemblies called to choose them. Often the only people present at the installation ceremony were a handful of officials from the district, perhaps a few members of a Jacobin society and a corps of urban National Guards in their resplendent blue uniforms. Nothing could better dramatize the urban origins of the Revolution and on whom the constitutional curé depended. If the new curé tried to weather the constant harassment, the National Guards could always march in to deal with troublemakers. To oppose the constitutional was also to oppose men like these, the local bourgeoisie of the urban administrations, clubs and guards, men who supported a land settlement which offered little or nothing to many country people.

Loyalty to the refractories was a way of demonstrating hostility to the Revolution as well, and their very presence rendered the ecclesiastical settlement unworkable. They had rights of access to their old churches and there were unedifying struggles over keys, ornaments, parish registers, hours of rival masses, and so on. Often refractories retired to outlying chapels where they baptized, confirmed and married parishioners loyal to them. Many of them did no more than this, but there were others who denounced the constitutional bishops and clergy and even lay officials as heretics and schismatics, and claimed that religion was abandoned or that the National Assembly would soon impose Protestantism. A few came close to preaching civil war. Yet the refractories reflected opinion as much as they instigated it, for resistance to the Civil Constitution soon took on the characteristics of a mass movement. In Strasbourg, the women rioted in January 1791 when a rumour got round that authorities were going to suppress parishes and close down the cathedral chapter. A few weeks later, German-speaking Catholics led by a few lawyers and small merchants organized a society based on the lay confraternities to defend religion and prevent Lutherans from taking over their churches. When adherents tried to involve the garrison, the municipality closed the society down. A month later, there was a riot in Colmar in which people shouted, 'Vive le Roi! Vive le Comte d'Artois!' But the most dramatic examples of mass resistance took place in the west. In the summer and autumn of 1791 in the Côtes-du-Nord, Loire-Inférieure and Maine-et-Loire, there was a series of eerie torchlight processions of entire villages, with everyone barefoot, silently winding their way to local shrines. At the same time in the Maine-et-Loire, there were stories of the Virgin and Child appearing to the faithful in venerated oak trees at night, and of formerly simple-minded children who no longer needed food prophesying the future of the Church. Much of this was simply an old tradition in Anjou but authorities understood that in the changed political context it was intolerable. In what must have been the first act of revolutionary dechristianization, the deputy La Révellière-Lepeaux, on mission to enquire into local religious troubles, had a statue of the Virgin and her chapel destroyed. But soon there were stories that she had reappeared. On occasion, there could be far more serious violence. In January 1791 hundreds of country people around Vannes became convinced that their refractory bishop was being held prisoner and invaded the town. It took an expedition of troops and National Guards from Lorient to bring the situation under control. In February, three or four hundred people tried to invade Maulévrier in the Maine-et-Loire in order to defend 'religion' and, as they said, 'destroy the district', an interesting indication of whom they blamed for their troubles. In early May, at Saint-Christophe-du-Ligneron in the Vendée, a handful of sharecroppers destroyed the pews of the 'bourgeois', barricaded themselves in the church and withstood for a few days a siege by the local Jacobins and National Guard, most of whom were lawyers. But violence was not all on one side. In June, the women of a local patriotic society approached the prioress of the Carmelite convent just outside Nantes and demanded the nuns take the civic oath because they knew that 'there were secret meetings at the convent which tended nothing less than to plan the slaughter of their husbands' in the National Guard. Their men, armed with sabres and pistols, arrived later and when the prioress continued to refuse, the crowd broke into the convent, destroyed some furniture and punched a few nuns.

Jacobins and Democrats

By mid-1791, whether it was in the form of the violent outbursts and demonstrations of the Midi, the hundreds of smaller incidents of the west, Flanders and Alsace, or the antiseigneurial risings of the centre, opposition to the revolutionary settlement had reached extensive proportions. Yet it should not be exaggerated. In many areas of the country, where the clergy took the oath, life carried on much as before. Even where, as in the Corrèze, many of them refused, there were few incidents. At the same time, the patriots had built up a series of organizations and acquired a consciousness which would stand them in good stead in the trying times to come.

One of these organizations was the National Guard. Unlike the Jacobin clubs these are not well known, but in the disturbances of 1790 and beyond they were a vital arm of repression. The myriad military expeditions of the towns of the Midi to dangerous spots and the lesser police actions in the west gave an opportunity to local militants everywhere to test their oaths of sacrifice for the Revolution. An examination of their social origins illustrates who was willing to make these sacrifices. At Montauban, despite the formal restriction of service to active citizens, nearly three quarters of the guardsmen were petty merchants and artisans but almost all the officers who, by law, were elected, were bourgeois. The same deference in elections to the officer corps was shown at Rennes but, interestingly enough, almost all groups, except merchants and wholesalers, were underrepresented in relation to the population as a whole. This was particularly true of artisans, labourers and the former privileged orders. In a city where the parlement, estates and charitable institutions had contributed so much to the local economy, revolutionary militants were bound to be in a more or less isolated minority. Consequently, almost the entire Jacobin club were also members of the Guard.

At this stage, the Jacobins were spectators of local and national events but, unlike the National Guards, they had a national network of affiliated clubs which were frequently in contact with each other. The system had begun as a café society of the radical Breton deputies in 1789 and, with other like-minded deputies, had been instrumental in preparing the Night of 4 August. After the *journées* of October, it installed itself in the former Jacobin convent in Paris. Although everyone could belong if they were good patriots and could afford the stiff entrance fee, the Paris club functioned as a caucus of radical deputies under the aegis of Barnave, Duport, the Lameth brothers, and, to a lesser extent, Robespierre and Pétion. The provincial societies had a different role. The early ones evolved out of masonic lodges or reading societies, or were founded in direct imitation of the Paris club which offered them affiliate status. Members came together to discuss events of the day. From the start, they developed an extensive correspondence network which was used to gain adherents to addresses and to petition the 'mother society' and the National Assembly. Since their membership fees were generally much lower than the Paris club, the potential existed for a more popular recruitment but, on the whole, their members represented the elite of local society. Many future deputies honed their political and oratorical skills in the frequent local meetings. Yet the influence of the clubs should not be exaggerated. There were too few of them in the early stages to have much influence on the major legislative achievements of the Constituent Assembly. Although there were over nine hundred of them by the late spring of 1791, their local influence was spotty. Curiously, their greatest electoral successes may have come in regions where electors were so alienated by the Civil Constitution of the Clergy that they refused to vote. Although it cannot be entirely attributed to local Jacobins, the most radical departments were often those where rural hostility was greatest.

There was always a substantial element of artisans and tradesmen in the Jacobin clubs, in part at least because some clubs only required active citizen status, if that, to become a member. In some of the larger cities, however, there were popular societies which emerged in response to aristocratic propaganda and the early agitation over the Civil Constitution of the Clergy. Their minimal entrance requirements attracted a great popular following. In Lyon, for example, from September 1790 onwards, there were clubs in each of the 32 sections which sent delegates to a 'central club', whose purpose was to agitate against the presence of nearby troops and to oppose counterrevolutionary propaganda, including Froment's writings. The popular societies soon boasted of a membership of three thousand, as opposed to the forty-odd in the atrophied Jacobin club. They soon attracted the notice of ambitious local politicians like the Rolands. In Bordeaux, there was a much smaller 'Patriotic Society', distinct from the Jacobins, composed almost entirely of artisans and petty merchants, almost all of them active citizens, whose purpose was to enlighten its members, and defend citizens against the arbitrary acts of authority. Although there were popular societies in other cities as well, Paris had the most flourishing movement. Sometimes it was based on the 48 section assemblies into which the city had been divided in July 1790, sometimes on the handful of fraternal societies based on sections or trades. Some affiliated with the famous Cordeliers club. From its founding in April 1790, the Cordeliers and the fraternal societies, along with radical journalists like Marat and Fréron, took the lead in criticizing Bailly's conduct as mayor, the accumulation of power in Lafayette's hands and the distinction between active and passive citizens. Since the institutions governing the capital were so new, conflicts of jurisdiction quickly broke out between the commune and the sections and between Lafayette's National Guard headquarters and its paid companies and the volunteer section battalions over where the ultimate locus of authority lay. In terms of principle, the conflict was one between representative theories of government and doctrines of direct democracy, and in the course of their feverish activities the Cordeliers leaders developed democratic theories which soon spread to the fraternal societies, and later to the sectional movement as a whole. The sovereignty of the section, the recall of deputies, the sections' mutual support, the right of insurrection, the right of referendum, the responsibility to prevent deputies and municipal officers from usurping popular sovereignty, and even some of the symbolism like the eye of surveillance enclosed in the masonic triangle – all the important doctrines associated with the *sans-culottisme* of the Year II – can be found in the writings and speeches of the Cordeliers leaders and radical journalists of 1790–1. No doubt these ideas found a ready audience among artisans and working people in the city because they articulated many aspects of their aspirations and daily experience, but they were not generally developed by men of the popular classes. Unlike the faubourg Saint-Antoine, with its heavy concentration of construction, building and furniture trades, the Théâtre-Français section on the left bank where the Cordeliers was located was home to an inordinate number of journalists, printers and book dealers. The leaders, who caucused regularly at the café Procops, were hardly ordinary working men either. Danton and Desmoulins were lawyers who had been rather indifferent to their practices in the Old Regime. Some, like the coarse Hébert, or Fréron, had been scribblers forced by printing and censorship regulations to combine semiserious writings with pornography and now were starting a journalistic career thanks to freedom of the press. Brissot had been forced to even more desperate measures when he spied on his friends for the police to feed his numerous family, and was now combining journalism with a place on the Paris commune. Marat, always a lonely tortured soul, was a failed doctor and bankrupt, who had considered himself a persecuted medical Newton and who had dabbled in mesmerism, then considered by its adepts as a cure-all if magnetism manipulated invisible fluids properly. Men of this sort had retained their idealism but their travails had envenomed their hatred of power and privilege and made them quick to denounce, in the most violent and personal terms, those in authority whose celebrity and wealth had apparently come so easily. Few societies could boast as many creative and energetic talents as the Cordeliers but both the members of the smaller clubs and the section militants were no more plebeian in origin. The rare membership lists indicate that the genuinely committed were a mix of those in the liberal professions and officials along with a respectable proportion of more or less skilled artisans and shopkeepers. Despite the societies' democratic basis, labourers and the very poor were very rare, undoubtedly because few had spare time for politics. In any case, the radicals distrusted them. The destitute, the transients, the vagabonds, and so on, while deserving of the greatest sympathy, were all too easily corrupted by the rich and the aristocrats. The ideal citizen was an independent, settled, working man with a family. Thus, while it is possible to find some daring schemes for a progressive income tax or price controls or general denunciations of the rich as sources of corruption or of low pay in the radical literature of 1790, the amount of space devoted to social questions in the radical press was minimal. A hatred of oppression in all its forms, however, would soon take the Cordeliers further.

By the late spring of 1791, opposition to the solutions of the Constituent Assembly had begun to develop on a wide front. The continuing difficulties in collecting taxes, the refusal to pay the still legal seigneurial dues let alone the rarity of redemptions, the sectarian violence in the Midi linked to the gradual appearance of counterrevolution, the mobilization of the country people of the west against the Civil Constitution of the Clergy, the slow rise in the cost of living brought on by the still gentle inflation of the assignat, and the development of the club movement and the popular societies, were all serious indicators of opposition to the bourgeois liquidation of the Old Regime. Yet, although it could not have been apparent to them, the deputies and their supporters in the provinces could be forgiven a certain complacency. The opposition was hardly unified, organizationally or ideologically; indeed much of it was working at cross-purposes. Moreover, the continuing loyalty of the rank and file and many of the officers of the army, as well as the vast majority of the National Guard, gave the bourgeois revolutionaries and their allies an immense superiority to deploy against anyone from counterrevolutionary conspirators to outraged peasants. The deputies themselves also shared much of the broad consensus of 1789 which had not yet run its course. The basic mistrust of the common people and the horror of violence, especially after the October Days, went along with a respect for orderly parliamentary change. The Civil Constitution of the Clergy had, of course, permanently alienated many of the clerical deputies which was a significant break of the general consensus. But it held because the politicians still trusted the king. The Flight to Varennes broke the consensus and with it the unity of the bourgeois politicians which was vital if the smooth transition from the Old Regime was to be made.

Chapter 4

The Fall of the Monarchy

Louis XVI fled the Tuileries at dawn on 21 June 1791; he returned in the evening of the 25th a prisoner, the fate of the dynasty in the hands of men unknown two years before. For an adventure so long expected and so long prepared, it had been bungled from the start. His insistence on taking his wife and children and their governess for their own safety required a huge carriage which moved at a walk and which necessarily was bound to arouse suspicions that some wealthy émigré was leaving the country. The slow pace and inevitable delays along the way were misinterpreted by the soldiers organizing the changes of horses who believed the king's departure had been unaccountably postponed so that the relay and escort system was broken. Louis was finally recognized by the postmaster of Sainte-Menehoud who alerted the municipality of Varennes whose National Guard blocked the route. The king might have been able to save himself by appealing to troops waiting nearby but, abhorring bloodshed and fearing for his family, he surrendered. As he was escorted back to Paris by special commissioners of the Constituent Assembly, he was heard to mutter, 'There is no longer a king in France.' By contrast, there was a new irritation. With none of his brother's scruples for his family and position, the Comte de Provence sped to Brussels, where he added another voice, and hardly a moderate voice, to the councils of the emigration.

It is not clear what Louis XVI had hoped to achieve by the Flight to Varennes. Part of the plan was certainly to flee to the frontier town of Montmédy in Lorraine and put himself under the protection of the troops of the Marquis de Bouillé, the military commander of the region. There, backed by some threatening troop movements promised by the Emperor, he might be able to renegotiate the parts of the constitution he found objectionable with the National Assembly from a position of strength. Instead, as he knew both before and after the flight, he might have caused a civil war. He had always been reluctant to go because of the risks involved, but he had finally given in to the urgings of a host of advisors from the queen to Mirabeau. The occasion was determined by his knowledge that he would have to force a renegotiation of the constitution before its imminent completion, by his distress at having authorized the Civil Constitution of the Clergy and by his disgust at having been prevented by an unruly crowd of National Guardsmen from hearing Mass performed by a refractory priest at Saint-Cloud at Easter. Yet his objections to the work of the Constituent Assembly had been long-standing. As early as 15 July 1789 he drafted a letter to Charles IV of Spain (finally sent after the October Days) disclaiming everything he might be forced to do. He left behind at the Tuileries a long memorandum which mixed peevish complaints about the state of the Tuileries on the royal family's arrival with relevant criticisms of the new constitution. A comparison of the memorandum with his speech at the *séance royale* is an interesting exercise since it shows the evolution of Louis's thinking over the two years of revolution. There was no longer any question of defending the prerogatives of the privileged orders. Instead, he specifically endorsed promotion by merit in the army. But he was quite consistent in his insistence on the necessity of a strong executive. He complained of the limitations of his power of appointment, dismissed the suspensive veto as practically meaningless and deplored the restrictions of his power to conduct diplomacy and war which he had to share with the legislature. He pointed out that the Constituent had done little to solve the financial problem and above all lamented the extreme decentralization and confusion of power at the local level, and the growing influence and pretensions of the Jacobin clubs. Contemporaries might have labelled the assumptions behind the memorandum 'ministerial despotism'; Bonaparte might have had a clearer idea of what the king was groping for.

It is rare that a single episode such as the Flight to Varennes has such momentous and extensive consequences both short- and long-term. By breaking the fragile accords among the patriots in the Assembly, it created a situation where some politicians were willing to go beyond the parliamentary arena for support, first to the clubs and then to the popular movement itself against the legislature. The very success of the repression of the popular protests following Varennes, and the compromises other politicians were willing to make with a tarnished monarchy, tempted others to the extremist solution of demanding a war to smoke out what Brissot called the 'great treasons'. More subtle but equally important, the flight taught provincials, whether they were Jacobins or not, that neither the executive nor the Assembly itself could entirely be trusted. More and more, they adopted their own solutions for handling local disturbances, particularly if it was 'counterrevolutionary'. Dissidence in the provinces was increasingly met with repression which authority in Paris could do little about. The Flight to Varennes, in other words, also weakened the moral force by which the National Assembly had governed since 1789.

The most immediate consequence was precipitate decline in the popularity of the king. This had always been dependent on the general perception that Louis supported the Revolution. When the English traveller Dr Rigby watched the king pass from his vantage point on a balcony overlooking the rue Saint-Honoré on 17 July 1789, he was surprised at the silence of the crowd, undoubtedly suspicious of the monarch's role in the previous weeks. It was only when Louis donned the tricolour cockade on the steps of the Hôtel de Ville that the crowds erupted in joy. The October Days too, of course, were an example of the extent to which the ancient notion of the king misled by his advisors remained in the minds of ordinary people. The king was also popular among provincials. At the federation of 1790 in Paris to celebrate the anniversary of the fall of the Bastille which was attended by thousands of provincial National Guard units, he was cheered hoarsely and, during an illness in the spring of 1791, dozens of clubs wished him well. The flight and the fatal memorandum showed that he could no longer be trusted. As he returned to Paris through the Champs-Elysées, he was met with glacial silence. But the episode did not convert the country to republicanism overnight. Only two Jacobin clubs, Montpellier and Strasbourg, specifically demanded a republic and less than one fifth of the affiliated clubs petitioned that the king be put on trial. If many of the local elites remained in a stupor, they soon learned to ignore the monarchy altogether. Equally important, a significant number of deputies, who up to June had expressed trust in the king and wished to calm the masses, now began to express distrust of the monarch and to talk of mobilizing the common people, while their opponents responded by strong demands for restraint of popular activity. Varennes introduced a new, sharper division among the politicians.

Troubles and the Massacre of the Champ de Mars

During the immediate crisis, however, the National Assembly
acted with calm and remarkable unity. Disputes between
Lafayette's and the Barnave-Lameth-Duport factions were
smoothed over and the politicians put out the story that the king,
the victim of evil councillors, had been kidnapped – a fiction they
maintained even after the discovery of the memorandum. The king
was suspended and the Assembly assumed complete legislative and
executive sovereignty, forming joint committees with the
ministries, ordering suspicious movements within the kingdom to
be watched, sending special commissioners to the provinces,
suspending the elections to the new Legislative Assembly and
forbidding the export of arms and money. Although more severe
proposals, such as arming the people, mobilizing the National
Guard or suspending suspect officers from the army, were defeated,
the Constituent's actions prefigured those of the Convention – and
for the same reason. As in any national emergency, the politicians
resorted to exceptional measures.

   Yet neither the capital nor the provinces had to wait on the
Assembly for direction. In Paris there were rumours of an
army of aristocrats and refractory priests gathering north of
the city, of sewers being mined with bombs and of prison plots, the
latest version of the fear of brigands of 1789. Citizens spontaneously
closed the city gates and some small arms depots were pillaged. In
the provinces, already distressed over the activities of refractory
priests and, as always, edgy over the state of the harvest, reactions
were more vigorous still. Almost everywhere, local authorities
formed 'permanent committees' merging the administrative and
military hierarchies. The Department of the Nord helped put the
fortresses on the frontier in a state of readiness. Around
Strasbourg, the army and National Guard secured the bridges on
the Rhine. Near the frontiers, there were rumours of imminent or
actual invasion. Along the Pyrenees it was the Spanish; in the Nord,
the émigré armies dressed in black priests' costumes and wearing
death's-heads. Repression against the refractory priests was
immediate. In Lyon, the authorities closed twenty-five churches
used by the refractories; their counterparts in the Nord ordered the
closure of all refractory churches in the entire department. In the

Ariège, a handful of refractories were arrested trying to leave the country. In Picardy and the Lyonnais, there was a wave of château-burning and some aristocrats were killed. The most famous was the murder near Sainte-Menehoud of the Comte de Dampierre, known as a harsh seigneur and feared as a counterrevolutionary. Almost simultaneously a very similar incident took place at the outskirts of Lyon, when the domiciliary visit of some rural National Guards at the château of Guillen du Montet, who brought his habits of the captain of a slaving ship to the administration of his estates, degenerated into a siege. When shots broke out, the seigneur fired back with bullets and a bizarre assortment of African weaponry. He finally surrendered but was stabbed and beaten to death, his body dismembered.

The parallels with 1789 are obvious, but equally important was that the crisis of 1791 did not engender anything like the same conflagration. Undoubtedly, this was because of a more general confidence in local administrations and the National Guard as well as the reasonable supplies remaining from the harvest of 1790 and the prospects for a good one in 1791. There would have been no crisis at all, of course, if there had been no fear that the king's flight did not also presage a counterrevolution. But the émigré armies on the frontier, the conspiracies and disturbances in the Midi and the agitations surrounding the refractory priests almost everywhere showed that the risk of counterrevolution was all too real. The other difference was that the radical movement, particularly in Paris, was much more articulate and organized. And unlike 1789, its agitation was directed against the Assembly.

The precipitate for this new round of agitation was the decision, mainly by the Triumvirs and their friends, to ignore the demands that the king be dethroned or put on trial. They balked at the idea of remaking a constitution into which they had poured so much emotional energy in the previous two years. They were also convinced that republics were only suitable for small states and that a monarchy was a better defence of property and order than a republic which classical precedents indicated could degenerate into a democracy. But these considerations required an accommodation with the king and Barnave began a secret correspondence with Marie-Antoinette to try to reach an understanding. Publicly, the Assembly revealed its intentions by only suspending the king on 25 June and on 15–16 July made Bouillé, who had conveniently emigrated, the scapegoat for the whole Varennes affair.

The radical movement in Paris was appalled by these unseemly manoeuvres. In the Jacobins, Robespierre claimed the National Assembly had ceased to represent the people. The Jacobins came close to associating themselves with the Cordeliers' project of demanding a national plebiscite on the fate of the king but balked when the Assembly made its decision to forgive Louis. Robespierre and Pétion even advised calming the agitation lest the radicals fall into the trap which was being prepared for them. Even Danton, Desmoulins, Fréron and Santerre, now commander of the National Guard of the Enfants-Trouvés section, went to ground. Other Cordeliers were willing to take the risk. On 22 June, they had taken a bloodcurdling oath of tyrannicide and Danton claimed to a crowd in the Tuileries gardens that their leaders were traitors. Along with the fraternal societies, they began an agitation demanding the trial of the king and a referendum. The decrees of 15–16 July provoked a hastily organized series of petitions which were supposed to be signed on the *autel de la patrie* on the Champ de Mars, the military parade ground and site of the anniversary celebrations of 14 July 1789. Besides calling Louis a perjurer and a traitor, one of the petitions argued that he had formally abdicated. Another demanded 'the organization of a new executive power', the very vagueness of the phrase suggesting that if a republic was intended, no one had a very clear idea of what was involved.

For their part, the authorities intended to have done with the incessant agitation, particularly since their moral position was so weak. But their determination went back further than the Flight to Varennes. In May, the Assembly forbade clubs to present collective petitions and required that members sign them individually. This only stimulated the popular societies to protest the restrictions on the right of petition while their agitation against the restrictive electoral laws and on the right of referendum and recall of deputies continued. In fact, they intended to campaign for a revision of the Constitution in a democratic direction in the approaching elections. Besides this agitation in the clubs and the press, a movement of journeymen, carpenters, hatters, typographers and building workers for higher wages continued throughout the spring. This was probably linked to the scarcity of specie and inflation but the Cordeliers had links to the fraternal societies of these workers, and sympathetic journalists like Marat, true to the policy of aiding the oppressed everywhere, offered them a forum for airing their grievances. The result was the passage by the Constituent Assembly of the Le Chapelier law outlawing workers' 'coalitions' on 14 June, a law which finally completed the process of abolishing the guilds but which evoked little protest all the same. The Cordeliers also had links with the agitation against the successive closures of public workshops which threw thousands out of work. There were three large demonstrations of the unemployed after 24 June and, on 3 July, Desmoulins presented a petition demanding, in effect, that the state guarantee the subsistence of its citizens. A demonstration of twenty thousand followed the next day. The stonecutters protested that the Revolution could not permit 'a few to gorge themselves with gold instead of giving bread to everyone'. Thus, although the petitions at the Champ de Mars were strictly political, the context in which they were signed indicated that the change to the 'new executive power' would have social consequences.

Authorities were determined to prevent this. The decision to declare martial law against the petitioners on 17 July was taken five or six hours after it was known at the Hôtel de Ville that the crowd had murdered two unfortunates who had crawled under the *autel de la patrie* to gape at the women's legs and despite reassurances from its own commissioners that all was peaceful at the Champ de Mars. The pretext was a minor, unrelated incident in which someone had thrown stones at a National Guard patrol. No doubt some of the crowds at the Champ de Mars were armed, and there had been talk among hotheads of bringing sand and pebbles to use against cavalry horses and knives to cut the harnesses, but at no point had there been a call to arms. The repression, however, degenerated into a riot by the National Guard. Neither Lafayette nor Bailly deployed the red flag signifying the declaration of martial law nor did they summon the crowd to disperse. Instead, someone in the crowd fired a shot, the National Guard panicked, let loose a fusillade and charged the petitioners. As many as fifty may have been killed; the number of wounded is unknown.

The Assembly immediately announced that it had saved society from anarchy and arrested a few foreigners to demonstrate the nefarious origins of the democrats. More to the point, there were domiciliary visits at the homes and workshops of the radical leaders, while Hébert, Momoro, Desmoulins and Santerre were arrested, the presses of the *Ami du Peuple* were confiscated, Marat went underground, Danton fled to England and the Cordeliers was closed until 7 August. Authorities also profited from the occasion to suppress a few royalist newspapers as well.

The Champ de Mars Affair was another branch in the genealogy of Parisian *journées*. The democratic movement had acquired martyrs, and from now on to be charged with associating with Lafayette was the worst of insults. The fact that the Cordeliers also gathered some six thousand signatures for a change in the executive also showed that many Parisians had been weaned from their visceral loyalty to the king which had been so prominent in 1789 and in the federation of 1790. The political education of Parisians had advanced considerably and the events of June and July had shown that a subsistence crisis was no longer necessary to mobilize working people behind a radical programme. From the Champ de Mars Affair onwards, subsistence questions faded into the background as a major factor in the future *journées*, and in the petitions of 1792 they were rarely mentioned. This was an obvious advantage to the democrats but up to this point it was not yet clear even then that a republic was the only alternative. Throughout 1790, the monarchy had been seen as the mandatory of the people, and Varennes only confirmed the growing criticism of Louis's personal and political vices which had been apparent for the previous six months. It would take another crisis 'to force' the radicals to see monarchy as an institution incompatible with democracy. Furthermore, the probability that the Assembly's quick action did much to stifle a gathering movement among the provincial clubs for a change in government showed how much prestige the deputies retained, despite the unpopularity of many of its 'undemocratic' reforms with the clubs. The new crisis of 1792 was also necessary to push the provinces towards the Republic. Finally the repression in Paris was a success. In so far as provincial opinion commented, it sided with the Assembly, showing the extent of Paris's political isolation in the country. Despite the quick release of many democratic leaders and the revival of the radical press, the popular movement took nearly a year to recover. The greatest crisis the Revolution had traversed, in other words, did not have the momentous consequences that might have been feared.

The crisis did split the Jacobin club. Barnave and his friends were appalled at the flirtation with republicanism and split off to form a new club, the Feuillants, taking over half the Jacobins with them. They lost the Jacobin network, however. Only seventy-two (of nearly five hundred) affiliated clubs adhered to the Feuillants. Thanks to the vigorous campaigning of Pétion and Robespierre, whose popularity had been growing in the provinces for the past year, and to the fact that some of the newspapers most popular with provincial Jacobins also condemned the Feuillants, most of these societies drifted back to the fold in the next few months.

This loss was less significant to the Feuillants than their failure to appease the king, and most significant of all was their isolation in the Assembly. Although they were able to persuade the Assembly to restore the prerogative of mercy to the king and give him more authority over military appointments, these hardly met the basic objections of Louis's memorandum. In any case, Marie-Antoinette considered the Feuillants her dupes and, to Barnave's dismay, even refused the charade of public displays of support for the Revolution. More ominous was the inability to rally the Assembly. The right was furious at the suspension of the king and dissociated itself from the Assembly's work. The Feuillants did manage to revise the electoral law. The *marc d'argent* qualification to sit as a deputy (the equivalent of 50 days' labour), against which Robespierre had campaigned so vigorously and to which he owed much of his popularity, was eliminated. Instead, deputies could be chosen from the list of active citizens by electors paying anywhere between 150 and 400 days' labour. This would have restricted direct suffrage to the very wealthy bourgeoisie and former nobility. It was never applied. But the Feuillants failed to revive Mounier's old project of a second chamber against which they had campaigned two years before, or to get the elimination of the prohibition of deputies becoming ministers. A press law failed and a law on clubs was considerably diluted. In short, however, much as they distrusted democracy and popular radicalism, the deputies distrusted the king more.

Undermining the Constitution

The Feuillants thus failed in their natural constituency and they, like everyone else, looked forward to the meeting of the Legislative Assembly which held its first session on 1 October. All of the deputies were new because the Constituent had excluded its members from standing for election on a motion by Robespierre on 16 May. In origins, the new deputies ought to have been fairly conservative because in theory they had to meet the electoral qualifications. There was a handful of clerics and ex-nobles, lawyers were the largest single group, there were even fewer businessmen than there had been in the Constituent, and there was a sizeable contingent of military men, including Carnot and Prieur de la Côte-d'Or, both future members of the Committee of Public Safety. Their inexperience in national politics is often deplored but a significant proportion of them did have experience at the local level as department or district administrators of all sorts. This meant that many of them had dealt with the manifestations of counter-revolution in the Midi the year before, or with the continuing frustration of applying the Civil Constitution of the Clergy.

Yet few were committed to the Jacobin-Feuillant quarrel since roughly two thirds of them did not join either club, while the Feuillants began a slow decline in January since the club's sessions were persistently interrupted by boisterous cat-calls from the galleries. The Jacobins did not necessarily reap the benefits directly but they did receive a tacit support because even the uncommitted deputies were searching for a solution to the problem of domestic and foreign counterrevolution.

If the deputies' opinions are hard to categorize, those of the public are even more so. Less than one quarter of the active citizens actually voted, about the same as in the elections to the Estates-General or in the local elections of 1790. Undoubtedly this was due to an inability to see how national bodies could affect local affairs but in some regions like the west, active citizens hostile to the Civil Constitution abstained, with the result that the deputies were disproportionately Jacobin. But the election everywhere represented both the inability to mobilize voters and the comparative weakness of the clubs. Even in Paris where there was a furious campaign in the press, turnout was only 10 per cent. The Legislative Assembly thus represented the minority of the nation that was politically active, a minority loyal to the Constitution, on the whole moderate, but willing to defend the gains of 1789 as well.

The necessity to defend these gains undermined their moderation, a phenomenon first remarked in the provinces. One of the subtle effects of the Flight to Varennes was that the central government lost its tenuous hold on the provinces, and local bodies in turn became increasingly repressive of refractory priests. Repression itself was not new. The clubs had clamoured for it in the spring and a handful of departments had petitioned for, or actually took, harsher measures against the refractories. But after Varennes, such demands became much more general. Thus, between Varennes and the general amnesty of September 1791, at least twenty-one departments either petitioned for a general law exiling refractory priests or anticipated such a law by interning or exiling individuals or whole groups of refractories to various distances from their former parishes without a hearing or a trial. Many cited the influence of the confessional, especially on women, or the general conspiracy of silence to justify going beyond the law. The Rhône-et-Loire, for example, claimed that its decree of internal exile was necessary because of the progress of fanaticism, the latent 'state of insurrection' and the complicity of the municipalities. Others developed it into a general philosophy. The Sarthe adopted its decree in the name of 'the most imperious of laws, the safety of the people'. The Haute-Garonne justified its exile decrees by claiming that 'it's in vain that they claim liberty of religious opinions here; let this liberty only apply to the honest citizen who . . . does not seek to propagate his principles and reconciles the exercise of his rights with respect for public order.' Naturally enough, in a case of latent civil war, one had the right to defend oneself but at the price in many cases of the due process of law. The bourgeois moderates elected in 1790 to consolidate and administer were edging towards the mentality of the Terror.

Sometimes private citizens took these matters into their own hands. In the Ille-et-Vilaine, National Guards from the towns and 'patriotic' villages arrested supporters of refractory priests, closed down refractory churches and pillaged their enemies' homes for good measure in two waves in the late summer of 1791 and around Easter in 1792. There were similar incidents in the Ardèche as at Villeneuve-de-Berg: when patriots hooted a refractory at Mass, his supporters started a fight in which someone was killed. In the Nord, the villagers of Berlaimont who supported the refractory were assailed by the National Guards of fifteen neighbouring communes who eventually sacked the local convent. In March 1792, National Guards in the Sarthe roamed the countryside trying to force the refractories to take the oath because they were convinced that 'the moment of the counterrevolution was near, that the Constitution is on the point of being overthrown, that the constitutional priests are going to be chased out . . .' Elsewhere, refractories were insulted, shot at or forced to emigrate. But such incidents only underlined what was often clear from the beginning: that the constitutional church was the church of the regime. Violence against the constitutionals also became more common as more refractories were replaced during the summer of 1791 and after. Consequently, the threats, boycotts, stonings, petty harassments, beatings and nocturnal processions which had been present from the beginning also became more common, and with them the departments' resort to extra-legal measures. Even so, the constitutionals were often in an impossible position and many fled their charges. The few who remained and their dwindling number of friends could only be supported by armed force. Behind the isolated constitutionals were thus the districts and departments, supported by National Guards they could hardly control. From the rural point of view the bourgeois townsmen were attempting to impose an alien priest and everyone involved in the process was a heretic. For the patriots in the towns, they were dealing with a benighted, ignorant and superstitious peasantry, with people who were easily misled by the self-interested refractories. The solution was to get rid of the refractories. Yet there was no support from Paris.

The problem of the clergy was easily linked in the minds of the patriots with that of the émigrés. It is only in retrospect that the émigré armies appeared so pathetic. The three separate armies which were established in 1790 and 1791, of which Condé's, based at Coblenz, was the largest, were poorly financed and organized and demoralized by the failure of the great powers to recognize the court of the princes. In fact, most émigrés led a penurious existence relying on hand-to-mouth jobs and the generosity of foreigners when they were not engaging in unseemly intrigues for commissions in the princes' armies. A small army of a few thousand in which nobody wanted to be a soldier was not much of a threat to anyone but this is not how it appeared at the time. Artois, with his ebullient optimism, glossed over the problems and patriots were stunned by the mass of desertions of the officers of the regular army after Varennes. By the end of the year, over six thousand officers had emigrated, frustrated by two years of insubordination, disgusted that the new oath of loyalty contained no mention of the king and convinced that there was no loss of honour in emigration because the king had tried to give the example. This, of course, only reinforced the impression among the patriots that the officers who remained were not to be trusted. Civilians emigrated in great numbers too: almost the entire corps of Old Regime bishops and many of the great court and parlementaire families, taking with them what appeared to be vast amounts of much-needed money and valuables. Could anyone doubt that such people were not plotting a vengeful return? In fact, conspiracies did exist. Calonne, who had become in effect the prime minister of counterrevolution, hoped to cover the entire country with a network of 'coalitions' which would act as a fifth column in the event of a war which the émigrés were confident they would win. By the turn of the year the network was filling out. Active as ever, Froment had established committees in Arles, Carpentras and Avignon, had received 100,000 *livres* from the émigré court to purchase arms, and plans were unfolding to establish a redoubt at Bannes in the Jalès valley which in turn would draw on royalist support in the Vaucluse, Drôme, Gard, Ardèche and Loire. There was another conspiracy being organized in Normandy under the Comte de Oilliamson who was negotiating for foreign support, and still another in Brittany headed by the Marquis de La Rouerie who had established cells in most of the major towns of the old province by the spring of 1792. Local authorities never knew the details of these conspiracies, of course, but it was impossible to conceal all the recruiting and the massing of arms. The fear of internal and external conspiracy was hardly a figment of the Jacobin imagination.

Great power politics also contributed to the mounting apprehension. Artois finally persuaded Leopold II to make some show of support, and by the Declaration of Pilnitz of 27 August 1791 he and Frederick-William of Prussia promised to use force to affirm 'the basis of a monarchial government equally suitable to the rights of the Sovereigns and the well-being of the French nation'. Neither country intended to act without the other powers, and since the British were indifferent and Catherine II was urging an antirevolutionary crusade to distract the other powers while Russia grabbed more of Poland, the Declaration meant little. But such qualifications were dimly perceived, particularly in the patriot press in Paris which saw only the threat of war.

The Debate on War

The solution to these problems of refractory priests, of émigré armies, internal conspiracies and foreign threats was a preventive war. Fears of war never quite died down after Varennes but more and more groups in France began to see it as a positive benefit, each for their own reasons. Brissot, who is usually given so much credit for the successful war agitation, first came to the idea from an idealistic and practical direction. Citing America as an example, he believed a free people invincible against despots. In his first speech to the Legislative Assembly, he advocated a war against the German princes who were harbouring the émigrés as a measure of self-defence only if the princes refused to disperse the émigré armies. After the king vetoed the law of 9 November demanding the émigrés disperse before 1 January on pain of death and seizure of the revenues of their property, he came out for an immediate declaration of war, deploying an argument that Madame Roland had developed earlier, that armed struggle tempered the character of a free people and purged the vices of despotism. The cathartic effect of war was closely linked to the notion of a romantic crusade against the despots. As the demagogic deputy Isnard put it, '. . . if, in spite of their [the French] people's might and courage, they should be vanquished in defence of liberty, their enemies will reign only over corpses.' Louvet was even more extravagant: 'with the swiftness of lightning let thousands of our citizen soldiers precipitate themselves upon the domains of feudalism. Let them stop only where servitude ends; let the palace be surrounded by bayonets, let the declaration of rights be deposited in the cottage.'

The notion of revolutionary liberation lent an unreal air to the diplomacy leading up to the war. As always, Leopold II realized war would endanger the royal family, but was sympathetic to the cries of support from the German princes who refused all offers of compensation from the French for the loss of their feudal rights in Alsace. He was also determined to stop the incursions of National Guards on to German territory. Yet these issues could have been settled through diplomatic channels and he showed his willingness to be pliable by agreeing to have the émigré armies dispersed (which did not occur), but destroyed the effect by ordering troops to the Alsatian frontier. A note protesting the violence of the republicans in February 1792 was denounced as an unpardonable interference in French affairs. All along, he believed that intimidation alone would protect the royal family. When he died in March, his successor, Francis II, had no such inhibitions.

Groupings within France, however, wanted a more aggressive policy. Still distrusting the émigrés, Louis and Marie-Antoinette wanted at the very least an armed congress of the European powers to restore the rights of the monarchy. Louis, who privately thought war would be disastrous, nonetheless appeared before the Assembly on 14 December to announce that war would be the consequence of the refusal to disperse the émigrés. The Lafayette group in the Legislative Assembly also converted to a war policy, because a successful war would bring their leader to power who would then crush the Jacobins. Finally, the new War Minister, Narbonne, who claimed to be the illegitimate son of Louis XV, gave a series of optimistic reports of military preparations.

The conversion of so many groups to a war policy undermined the Feuillants whose policy required peace, which in turn required Austria's unconditional recognition of the Constitution, the return of the Comte de Provence and the Crown's willingness to accept its constitutional role. Yet Provence, who had fled to Brussels at the time of Varennes, refused to return despite a decree ordering him to do so or lose his rights to the succession. Barnave's influence on the queen was also minimal. He thought Louis's summons to the émigrés on 27 November equivocal, and was dismayed that the King's Guard was not recruited from patriots. Frustrated, Barnave and the Lameths withdrew from the political scene. Aside from Duport who stayed on as a journalist, the Feuillant leadership had disintegrated.

As the Jacobins saw it, the Crown used its constitutional rights to undermine the Revolution. Not only did Louis veto the law on émigrés, he vetoed the law of 29 November on refractory priests. This required the clergy to take an oath of loyalty to the Constitution from which the Civil Constitution had been detached. Refusal would entail losing their pensions and risking being considered 'suspects of revolt against the law and of evil intentions against *la patrie*' and being held responsible for religious troubles in their communes. The Assembly had taken a hesitant step towards undermining due process but the law did go some way to meet the demands of the departments which had been demanding action against the refractories. Naturally, the two vetoes provoked a storm of protest that the king was using the Constitution to undermine the Constitution. Local authorities defied the veto anyway. By the end of April, forty-two departments had taken measures to exile or intern refractories, and by the end of June at least four others had done the same. The Maine-et-Loire justified its internment measures most succinctly: 'This measure is not in the law but the safety of the people is the supreme law.'

The struggle between the legislature and the executive also revived the popular movement in Paris. Thirteen sections including the old Cordeliers stronghold, Théâtre-Français, whose petition was presented by Desmoulins, protested against the use of the veto.

Enfants-Rouges saw the law on refractory priests as a necessary measure of self-defence against 'the frightful troubles excited by fanaticism which are only the prelude to a counterrevolution', while Observatoire spoke of the 'unpatriotic usage of the veto by he to whom it was perhaps too lightly given'. Mauconseil declared that 'once the people has explained itself, the King is no longer free to refuse his sanction'. At least twenty-eight provincial clubs joined the chorus and although none was quite as democratic in tone as the sections of Paris, the challenge to the veto was all the same leading towards the undermining of the Constitution itself. Indeed the club of Pontoise declared it would ignore the veto while at least one department (Ille-et-Vilaine) imposed an oath of loyalty on the refractories anyway, while two others (Finistère and Loire-Inférieure) interned priests suspect of 'incivisme'. Defence against the internal and external enemy, the willingness to go to war to defend the Revolution and protests against the veto were all linked. Sixty-six provincial clubs sent addresses to the Legislative Assembly along these lines – almost as many as had demanded the king be put on trial after Varennes. Some clubs went even further. Nantes, for example, demanded an immediate war: 'Let the warrior's trumpet give the signal to combat; around the flame of liberty, certain guarantee of victory, will gather so many unfortunate peoples who suffer under the most atrocious slavery and who will aid us give the final blows to expiring tyranny.' The National Guard volunteers of the Corrèze agreed: 'The time has come when war will no longer be the scourge of the human race but the surest means of freeing oppressed peoples and of raising new altars to liberty.' Whatever else it was – and it is often asserted that the patriot war party had business connections who wanted war, Brissot through his friend, the financier Clavière, the Gironde deputies Vergniaud, Gensonné and Guadet via Bordeaux shipping interests – a vigorous defence against internal and external enemies and, for some, a war of liberation, was also popular. But it was a war of a new kind, no longer for territory or commercial advantage, but for the defence of liberty which would not only undermine the Old Regime in Europe but the Constitution as well.

The war issue also split the Jacobins. Marat was against it because the court so obviously wanted it. After flirting with the idea of a defensive war, Robespierre too became suspicious and went on to develop some prescient arguments pointing out that the officer corps of the army was not reliable, that foreign countries were not ripe for liberation, that conditions in Europe and America were different and that a war could increase the powers of the king and counterrevolutionary generals, such as Lafayette. Yet Robespierre was virtually a voice in the wilderness: his policy of peace had almost no constituency in the country. The increasingly bitter debates fought out in the Paris Jacobin club, which was fast becoming a rival power to the Legislative Assembly, are chiefly interesting because Robespierre managed to acquire support from some relatively unknown deputies who later formed part of the corps of the Montagnards in the Convention. Yet the Brissotins, or the Girondins as they are known after the split with Robespierre became manifest, faced a greater challenge from below, which would completely alter their conceptions of a popular war against internal and external enemies.

A Popular Mobilization

Throughout the country, the harvest of 1791 had been mediocre and a warm summer was followed by heavy autumn rains. Local hailstorms had delayed the sowing of winter grains. Heavy flooding, due perhaps to the melting of Alpine glaciers which fed the Rhône, and heavy rains in the Massif Central, washed away bridges and hills and inundated low-lying fields. Olives, mulberries and vines were still suffering from the excessive frosts of the winter of 1788–9. At the same time, the revolt in the West Indies had disrupted the colonial trade, causing shortages of sugar and coffee to which people in the large cities, particularly Paris, had become greatly attached. On top of this, the assignat began its truly precipitate fall. From 82 per cent of its nominal value in November 1791, it fell to 57 per cent by the following June, aided by continuing emissions and massive counterfeiting. The result was the slow collapse of industry, which was particularly marked in places like Lyon. Grain imports through Marseille which had always been vital in the Midi were also disrupted. Grain prices rose between 25 per cent and 50 per cent depending on the region, so that the real income of consumers in both town and country declined each time the assignat took another plunge, while speculators took advantage of the opportunities opening before them. Ordinary peasants also refused to sell their grain in exchange for increasingly worthless assignats and billets de confiance which had become the money of the poor, and which were rarely accepted outside the towns where they had been issued. Thus the whole system of foreign and domestic trade was slowly unravelling and with it, the system of production.

The mounting speculation and shortages brought waves of riots throughout much of the country from the autumn of 1791 onwards. There was a wave of popular price-fixing in the Pas-de-Calais and the Haute-Marne in November, which was renewed at Dunkirk and in the market towns of the Nord in February. At the same time, poor artisans in the textile and building trades in the river ports along the Aisne and the Oise stopped barges loaded with grain and moved it to secure locations or sold it at a fixed price. In January and February in Paris, crowds of women, later joined by the men, forced grocers and wholesalers to sell sugar at a fair price. This was followed almost immediately by a wave of riots throughout the Beauce region, and beyond to the north and west of Paris. Those most affected by the progressive breakdown of the marketing mechanism were the poorer regions and the marginal elements of rural society living on the edges of many forests dotted throughout the region: pin-makers, nail-makers, spinners, weavers, day-labourers, charcoal burners and so on. Thus, in several waves from late February until April, bands of these people sometimes numbering in the thousands marched behind their mayors who wore their sashes of office, from one market town to another. They fixed the prices not only of grain and bread but also of eggs, butter, textiles, iron and wood. They also stopped grain shipments and searched the farms of wealthy peasants for hidden stores. But the movement was not entirely one of the country against town or poor against rich. Urban workers, particularly women, also participated, and among the leaders there were forest stewards, forge-masters, master glassmakers, millers and even the occasional man with legal training. Most remarkable was the participation of a dozen or so constitutional priests, of which the most famous was Dolivier, curé of Mauchamp, who denounced the principle of private property itself in the name of the prior claims of the community in the columns of Robespierre's newspaper and to the Paris Jacobin club and the Legislative Assembly. But such ideas were less 'socialistic' than the articulation of much older traditions. The chiliastic calls for a massive bloodletting which would precede the division of property by Petit-Jean, curé of Epineuil in the Cher, was more reminiscent of medieval notions of the end of days than of the red dawn of the future. In any case, his parishioners had the altogether practical aim of knocking down the fences of the recently enclosed village commons, while the waves of rioting in the Beauce can be interpreted as a desperate attempt on the part of hundreds of rural communities to reestablish proper relationships among their members and assure a fair distribution of resources. This would explain why there were also demands for fair wages and rents, why the greed of the rich was so widely denounced and why those rich who were sympathetic to the popular cause were also accepted as leaders. But the wealthy farmers who continued to try to ship grain were sometimes beaten up and it was widely claimed that the shortages 'were used to provoke a counterrevolution because the Vexin [a Norman region] is full of wheat'. Thus the belief in famine plots continued and the struggle against the great estate was revived.

An even more impressive example of popular mobilization took place in the Midi. The obvious preparations of the counter-revolutionaries in cities like Arles and Avignon and the comings and goings of the old Jalès leadership stimulated the Jacobins, particularly in Marseille, to found daughter societies in the countryside. The organization of agriculture around large peasant towns and the close contacts between local bourgeois societies, and the tendency of the lower classes to imitate their example, had given the region a flourishing collective life before the Revolution which made the spread of local Jacobin clubs easy. With mounting war fever and the concomitant fear of counterrevolution, the club movement leapt beyond the town walls so that from the spring of 1792 onwards somewhere between 50 and 90 per cent of the villages in the plains of the Ardèche, Drôme, Gard, Vaucluse, Bouches-du-Rhône and Var had Jacobin societies. Within Marseille itself, the numbers attending section meetings quadrupled between the spring and the crisis of August 1792. The Marseillais also gave the example of the value of a preemptive strike by marching to Arles to disarm the clerical-royalist 'chiffonistes' in March, and there was a widespread feeling that the government's unwillingness to disarm known counterrevolutionaries while the external enemy was at the gates justified citizens acting on their own. Rural mobilization began with a small jacquerie in the Ardèche on 18 March which spread like brushfire with the propaganda the Jacobins were able to make out of a suspicious-looking accident in which 69 National Guards were drowned near Pont Saint-Esprit on 25 March. From late March until early June, ignoring for the most part Catholic and

Protestant boundaries, the movement spread south into the Gard and east into Provence and, in a second branch, west through the Cantal to the Charente and south to the Haute-Garonne, emphasizing different forms along the way. There were strong fears that authorities were too indulgent towards counterrevolutionaries and everyone felt the necessity to avenge the drownings. The belief that the National Assembly had ordered the destruction of towers on châteaux, but that these orders had been suppressed by aristocrats, was also widespread and people set about demolishing not only towers, but roofs, moats, crests and coats-of-arms (especially those the owners had merely plastered over in hopes of better days) and removing weather vanes. Furniture was often destroyed, there were searches for arms and occasionally the insurgents helped themselves to the contents of the wine cellar. The property of known counterrevolutionaries was particularly singled out while that of 'patriotic' aristocrats was spared. No less than twenty-five châteaux went up in flames in two days in the Gard alone, and all four châteaux belonging to the Comte d'Antraigues in the Ardèche were burned. Particularly in the district of Uzès, seigneurs or their agents were forced to renounce formally all titles, and people made a joyous bonfire of old papers in the courtyards. There were forced price-fixings on grain here and there, usurped commons were reclaimed as fences and walls were knocked down, seigneurs were forced to return fines which had been collected in the Old Regime, and, along the Rhône near Beaucaire, inhabitants began to divide up the flood plains which until then had been claimed as seigneurial property.

In terms of the size of the movement or the extent of damage, the jacquerie of the Midi of 1792 was as important as any of the risings of 1789 and was comparable also to the riots of the Beauce and the risings of Upper Brittany and Quercy-Périgord of 1790 both in its form and personnel. As in these regions, rural labourers and village artisans suffering from low wages due to the imbalance of population and subsistence, and from widespread unemployment due to the agricultural disasters of the previous four years, were heavily implicated. But so too were rural National Guard units, including their officers, as well as a number of municipal officers. Nor were suspect aristocrats and priests the only enemies. The National Guards of the communes around Aurillac in the Cantal marched in military order to the châteaux and planted their flags under the towers before beginning the work of demolition. They also fixed grain prices, and they and their counterparts in the Ardèche threatened refractory priests and their followers. Grain dealers, notaries, tenants of noble or bourgeois property, whose houses were often sacked, were also among the victims. The departmental administrators of the Ardèche were accused of taking 'the part of the former seigneurs . . . and [the rioters said that] we were opposed to their projects because we had fiefs [censives], that the department lied to them, that it printed whatever it liked at Privas [the capital] and that it suppressed a decree which ordered the demolition of the châteaux'. Yet behind the outbreak, it is possible to detect broader elements of support for the rioters. In Provence, at any rate, riots broke out in regions where noble and ecclesiastical property was most extensive and, since economic inequality here had reached scandalous proportions, this suggests a strong protest element against a revolution which as yet had only a narrow base in the countryside. Significant too was the fact that in the Ardèche several communes which had sent their National Guards to the two camps de Jalès earlier were also among those which revolted in 1792. Was it simply a coincidence that one of the leaders of 1792 was a former municipal officer of Uzès and a notorious 'cébet' in 1790? At any rate, the country people had their own hopes to which either counterrevolutionary or revolutionary elites could appeal, but neither elite could count on unswerving support.

Both the price-fixing riots of the north and the antiseigneurial risings of the Midi had curiously muted repercussions at the national level. It was difficult to take a stand after all, because if the grain riots had been successful the food supply of Paris would have been threatened. Robespierre did denounce Simonneau, mayor of Etampes and a prominent Jacobin, killed in one of the grain riots, as a food hoarder. The Gobelins section in Paris did denounce the 'vile hoarders and their infamous financiers' who invoked the principle of economic liberty which, they said, was a liberty to do harm and therefore a violation of the Declaration of the Rights of Man. Sympathy for the oppressed could therefore evoke some reaction but on the whole even the Jacobin press said nothing about Dolivier's famous petition while affairs in the Midi were passed over in virtual silence. The rioters who declared that 'the substance of all men cannot be the property of one alone' were also enunciating a principle which no politician or journalist was yet prepared seriously to espouse. Some aspirations were never taken up. The troubles at Bretheuil in the Eure in March had taken the form of a demonstration to limit the price of grain 'as it had been in 1789 . . . by the officials of the Old Regime' but behind it lay the anxieties of the smaller forge-masters for their supplies of wood and iron when larger partnerships had taken all the leases of the forests for themselves and bid up the price on all available supplies of iron. Such protests against concentration of enterprise both in industry and agriculture had been heard in the *cahiers* in 1789 and would be heard again but the implicit demand to share work and resources was always ignored. In any case, the rioters met with about as much repression as local authorities dared exercise when even the National Guard was occasionally unreliable, but this was still enough to imprison hundreds of people both north and south of the Loire who were not released until the amnesty in September. No wonder one rioter was heard to say, 'Ah! damn, we'll soon cut the neck of the National Assembly, because it doesn't do anything.'

The country therefore was badly divided when it entered the war, with opposition not only from counterrevolutionaries and refractory priests – this had been expected and was even desired – but also from a series of popular movements dissatisfied over the land settlement and the question of food supply.

War and Revolutionary Defence

With only ten votes against, the Legislative Assembly declared war on the 'King of Bohemia and Hungary' on 20 April, and not on the German princes against whom the war agitation had been directed in the first place. But the German Empire lent support from the start and in fact Prussia was the first to take the offensive. The king had finally resigned himself to war and after a violent press campaign against his 'Feuillant' ministers, he called in Brissot's friends: Roland at the Interior, Clavière at Finance, Servan at War and the military adventurer who had made himself a reputation as a patriot general in the Vendée, Dumouriez at Foreign Affairs. From the beginning the war went badly belying the calculations of all those who hoped to profit from a short conflict. Claiming the army was short of supplies and seasoned officers, the generals along the northern frontier, of whom Lafayette was the most prominent, undertook only desultory operations and were forced to retreat after engagements at Mons and Tournai. This was only too easily interpreted as treason and the Brissotins fanned the agitation by claiming the existence of an 'Austrian Committee' which was betraying the country. They had a point since Marie-Antoinette did alert the Austrians to the overall French strategy although no one knew this for certain. But the lurid accusations of a secret directory composed of the queen, former ministers and the Austrian ambassador who were conspiring to organize a blood bath of patriots invited the same kind of defensive reactions which earlier crises had provoked. The Paris sections became increasingly alarmed, accentuating their popular character by referring to themselves as 'sans-culottes' (literally without knee breeches), and dropping 'aristocratic' forms of address like 'monsieur' in favour of the egalitarian 'citoyen'. There were several armed demonstrations before the Assembly, replete with the symbolic pikes and red caps of liberty.

The Girondin ministry, riding the crest of this mounting agitation but also fearful of it, got the Assembly to pass a law on 27 May requiring the deportation of refractory priests after twenty active citizens denounced them. Another dissolved the King's Guard and replaced it with a camp of 20,000 volunteer National Guards or 'fédérés' who were to defend the capital against invasion, check the Paris sections and protect the government from a coup by the generals, particularly Lafayette. When Louis refused to sanction either law, Roland, in a widely publicized letter to the king drafted by his wife, protested. Louis promptly sacked Roland, Servan and Clavière on 13 June and Dumouriez resigned a few days later. On the 19th, Louis formally vetoed the laws on refractory priests and on the camp of 20,000 fédérés. The day before, the Assembly had heard a violent letter from Lafayette denouncing the Jacobin clubs as a state within a state. Could there be any doubt that the military dictatorship so long denounced by Marat was unfolding? (Although Lafayette's intentions were merely to reinforce royal authority, he had undertaken secret negotiations for an armistice with the Austrians.) Such alarms redoubled the intentions of the section leaders to hold an armed demonstration on 20 June, the anniversary of the Tennis Court Oath and the Flight to Varennes. Yet the Jacobins stayed aloof and the organizers were mostly Cordeliers leaders who had been involved in the petitions of the Champ de Mars: Legendre, Rossignol and Fournier l'Américain.

The journée of 20 June was a failure all the same. Thousands of demonstrators, many of them National Guards, poured into the

Tuileries while the king, seated on a chair before a large window, donned the cap of liberty and passively listened to endless and threatening harangues laced with crude insults demanding the sanctioning of the decrees on refractory priests and the fédérés and for the recall of the patriot ministers. Teams of deputies flocked to the château to pacify the crowds, and finally Pétion, mayor of Paris since November, arrived and persuaded the demonstrators to disperse. Yet the king was not intimidated and advisors close to him began to plan the military defence of the Tuileries. An assault, almost certain as the foreign armies advanced, was bound to be a bloody affair. Moreover, Pétion was suspended from his post so that patriot influence in government actually declined further. The provinces also flooded the Assembly with addresses protesting the outrage to the king but, significantly enough, only two departments in the west (Manche and Calvados), most of whose counterparts had adopted exceptional measures against the refractory priests, joined the chorus. The local struggle against counterrevolution was weaning even the conservative lawyers on the departmental directories from their loyalty to the monarchy. In general terms, however, the country was divided, even in Paris where a protest petition signed by over seven thousand people was submitted on 1 July. Yet despite demands for it, there was no repression as there had been after the Champ de Mars, possibly because such an operation would have been directed to a large extent against the Paris National Guard, an essential force given the alarming situation on the frontiers. The crowds were also demanding the implementation of laws the Assembly had passed. As always, some politicians were not averse to profiting from the violence they deplored in public.

In any case, the hostility to the sectional movement gave Lafayette a second chance. On 28 June, he appeared before the bar of the Assembly to denounce the instigators of 20 June and to demand the destruction of the Jacobins. The next day, he tried to raise the National Guard to march on the Jacobins but failed completely, a significant rebuke even from the kinds of groups which deplored 20 June, and an indication that the forces of order in the city were broadly sympathetic to the Jacobins. Lafayette's intervention also had the effect of unifying temporarily all the revolutionary forces. Brissotins and Robespierrists both condemned him in the Jacobin club while at least twenty-two sections, including Place-Royale and Fontaine-la-Grenelle normally thought to be 'bourgeois', denounced him as an aspiring dictator and demanded the reinstatement of Pétion. So too did the fédérés. Some of them had set out before the veto had been applied and continued the march afterwards in defiance of it, while others began to march to Paris after Louis XVI agreed on 3 July to authorize them to come to celebrate 14 July, on condition they depart for a camp at Soissons. Yet the fédérés were hardly mere citizen volunteers. Many of them were highly politicized. The Marseille fédérés had to have served in the National Guard since 1790 and members were required to have a 'certificat de civisme' signed by the officers, many of whom were active Jacobins, while the fédérés of Finistère were recruited by the Jacobin club of Brest. Those of the Midi had been involved in the repression of counterrevolution from 1790 onwards, while those from the west had much the same experience in propping up the constitutional curés. For many, the march to Paris was simply another expedition in defence of the Revolution. As soon as they began to arrive in the capital, several submitted addresses along the lines of those of the Paris sections, while on 17 July a delegation representing all the provincial battalions then in the city demanded the suspension of the king, the trial of Lafayette, a purge of aristocrats in the army and the civil administration because 'we know that without the treason of the enemies of the interior, the others were not to be feared or rather they would not exist'. The first rampart to breach was thus at home, but it is doubtful whether the leaders of the fédérés' coordinating committee, composed of obscure provincials and some of the Cordeliers, were as yet seriously planning an armed assault, because another address on 23 July reiterated earlier demands and invited the Assembly to hold what amounted to a referendum on the monarch's constitutional rights. In any case, action had to be coordinated with the sections which took time to catch up to the fédérés' lead. Only two sections, Fontaine-la-Grenelle and Mauconseil, adhered to the deposition movement before the end of the month. This was a reflection of the limitations of the fédérés' committee and it would take the commune to bring the sections along. In the meantime, the Assembly, now more or less paralysed in its debates, took two steps which made an insurrection more likely. The first was the declaration on 11 July of 'la patrie en danger' which ordered the departments, districts and communes into permanent session and mobilized the National Guard. Besides the electric effect of the phrase, *la patrie en danger*, it created the impression that the Revolution could be saved only by bypassing the Constitution. This was certainly how Robespierre took it when he said that in the present situation, with corruption and treason everywhere, only the people could save themselves, while Mauconseil put it more directly in demanding 'the right to forget the law to save *la patrie*'. The second step was the order on 25 July that the sections go into permanent session and these responded, one after the other, by admitting passive citizens to their meetings. The revolutionaries on the commune also used the law to create a central correspondence bureau, composed of a delegate from each section, to coordinate action. The initiative was passing from the fédérés to the Paris sections. On 1 August, the Assembly ordered the municipalities to arm every able-bodied man with a pike if he had no other weapon and, two days later, decreed that any volunteer for the army would become an active citizen. Before the national mobilization, property franchises and the Constitution itself were crumbling.

But these concessions were no longer enough. Provincials, because they faced the problems of refractory priests and counterrevolution more directly than Parisians, began to demand more radical steps. As early as 19 June, an address on behalf of the central club representing the popular societies of Lyon called Louis a perjurer, and demanded the Assembly take bold steps to seek out conspirators everywhere to 'prevent . . . an insurrection which your indifference would render legitimate'. Shortly after, the municipality of Marseille denounced hereditary monarchy as a violation of the Rights of Man and on 18 July a mass petition from Angers demanded Louis's deposition. These were followed by petitions from eleven other towns demanding the trial of the king or deposition, while protests against the court and the use of vetoes continued to pour in from departments, towns and clubs. Meanwhile, more contingents of fédérés were arriving, the largest from Marseille singing the battle hymn which made them famous and already known throughout the country for their revolutionary extremism and the awesome poetry of their language: 'La liberté française est en peril: les hommes libres du Midi sont tous levés pour la défendre. Le jour de la colère du people est arrivé.' The mentality of inexorable struggle they brought with them was joined to the mounting agitation in the sections. On 3 August, the reinstated Pétion, representing all but one of the forty-eight Paris sections, appeared before the Assembly to demand the elimination of the dynasty and the calling of a National Convention. Yet almost immediately fissures began to open within the sectional movement. Sixteen sections disavowed this petition and the Mauconseil address of 31 July, and there were charges that signatures on a monster petition demanding deposition presented by the Jacobin club on 6 August were forged. Clearly different groups were fighting for power within the sections. The basis of the struggle is largely unknown except for the National Guard battalion of Filles Saint-Thomas located in the financial quarter. Its officers defended the monarchy up to the last minute. They were bankers, wholesalers and skilled artisans by profession. Yet one of the sections opposing the deposition movement was Temple, in the heart of the faubourg Saint-Antoine. This is not much but it does suggest that royalists and republicans were not sharply split along lines of class or wealth.

More divisive still was the defection of the Brissotins who began to argue that the national emergency was no time to change the executive and condemned the deposition movement. In fact, Vergniaud, Gensonné and Guadet had entered into secret negotiations with the court with a view to persuading the king to accept new patriot ministers, presumably themselves, and an unofficial council of advisors, including Pétion. Private intrigues using the popular movement to gain office, and public harangues, like those of Condorcet expressing fear of unknown consequences 'when the foreign enemy is at the gates', were certainly inept and naive since Girondin propaganda had done so much to instil the idea of a treacherous Austrian Committee in the public mind. Failure to act looked like calculated treason as the effects of the appalling Brunswick Manifesto began to sink in after its publication on 3 August. Issued in the name of the commander of the allied armies, the Duke of Brunswick, but in fact written by the émigrés, it promised that National Guards captured fighting would be punished as 'rebels to their king', that civilians defending their homes against troops would have their houses razed and be punished 'according to the rigour of the law of war' and declared all Parisians collectively responsible for the safety of the royal family. Otherwise the allies would execute 'an exemplary vengeance and forever memorable, by delivering the city of Paris to a military execution and a total subversion . . .' As a declaration of war on an entire city this was unprecedented, but far from intimidating the sections, it only made them bolder. Gravilliers, for example, in demanding deposition and a National Convention elected by direct universal suffrage on 5 August, took it as proof that the king was the centre of a vast conspiracy linking foreign tyrants, émigrés, counterrevolutionary generals and corrupt politicians. Unless the Assembly saved 'la patrie', 'we will do it ourselves'. Yet the Assembly refused deposition and proved their corruption in the eyes of the radicals when in a roll call vote of 406 to 224 on 8 August it defeated a motion to put Lafayette on trial. This convinced many Jacobins of the necessity of an insurrection, although Robespierre felt completely paralysed by events and the Girondins were against it.

Fall of the Monarchy and Popular Vengeance

With the Assembly defiant and the Jacobins divided, lesser known revolutionaries took the initiative. On the night of 9 August, an insurrectionary committee, many of whom were active in the Cordeliers agitation of the previous year and who had strong links with the sections and the fédérés – Rossignol, Robert, Hébert, etc. – installed itself at the Hôtel de Ville and overthrew the old municipality. Pétion, under house arrest, appointed Santerre commander of the National Guard and ordered the mobilization of the Guard through their officials in the sections. Yet the Guard itself, both the battalions helping to guard the Tuileries and those in the sections, remained extremely hesitant. There were several reasons for this. The Paris National Guard had no formal links with the sections but instead was divided into sixty separate battalions theoretically responsible to general headquarters, which is usually assumed to have been pro-Lafayette, and to the commune which had just been overthrown. As the events of 9 thermidor were to show two years later, the National Guard would not necessarily respond to the orders of an illegal authority. It was also in the process of being reorganized to make it more responsible to the sections. Thus, not only were lines of command exceptionally confused, so too were officers' loyalties. Also, of the major leaders of the revolt whose names are known, only a handful, Santerre and Alexandre notably, were also Guard officers. Finally, as the events of the previous week had shown, a significant minority of royalists in the sections was strong enough to overturn the petitions in favour of deposition. These considerations thus explain why the Parisian radicals put so much effort into recruiting the fédérés and why an alliance with them was so essential. The overthrow of the monarchy was thus an immense gamble. Whether Parisians or provincials, the citizen soldiers who had been won to the side of insurrection faced a formidable enemy. The château was defended by no less than 4000 men, some of whom, like the Swiss regiments and bodyguards composed of aristocrats, were certain to resist. On the other side were 2000 fédérés and a theoretical complement of 25,000 Parisian guardsmen, who would have to assail defensive positions prepared during the previous six weeks.

In the early morning of the 10th, the king, seeking to protect his family, sought refuge in the Assembly where they were lodged in an adjoining printing room. This flight had been provoked by the defection of the Guard artillery companies to the insurgents but it affected the morale of the other defenders. The National Guards and the mounted gendarmes fraternized with the insurgents approaching from the right bank. Meanwhile, the defences of the bridges, preventing the crossing of the forces from the left bank, collapsed. Somehow, the insurgents got into the courtyards of the château and, believing the battle over, began to fraternize, yet some Swiss fired from the upper windows and attacked. The crowd fled, crying treason, but the Marseillais counterattacked with devastating grapeshot. Louis then ordered a cease-fire but this did not save the Swiss, some 600 of whom were massacred. Among the insurgents, about 90 fédérés and nearly 300 Parisians were killed or wounded. It was the most bloody *journée* of the Revolution.

The consequences of the insurrection did much to satisfy patriot demands. The Assembly's liberation of itself from the veto of the law of 27 May against refractory priests, the calling of the primary assemblies to elect a National Convention by universal suffrage and the return of the patriot ministers – Roland, Clavière, and Servan with Danton at Justice to keep the sections in line – were all in the broad spectrum of the demands made since June. So, too, was the deportation of refractory priests. On 26 August the Legislative ordered the deportation of all priests who refused a new oath to liberty and equality, unless they were over sixty and in poor health, in which case they were to be interned. Including previous émigrés, about 30,000 to 40,000 priests and monks, about 40 per cent of the Old Regime corps, were scattered through Europe, the United States and Lower Canada. Since some regions had so many refractories who had never been replaced, this required the laicization of the birth, marriage and death registers which now became the responsibility of the communes. Thus civil existence was defined by the state, no longer by the Church. Yet the application of these measures introduced a new element of uncertainty. The deportation law was undoubtedly popular since local authorities had been demanding something like it for a long time. Indeed they anticipated it. On 5 August, the municipality of Lyon expelled all non-native refractories from the city and interned any others denounced by twenty active citizens. As soon as they heard of the revolution of 10 August, authorities in the Ille-et-Vilaine began rounding up priests who had refused an oath the department had designed the previous spring. Their counterparts in the Cher and Charente did much the same, while in the Doubs all refractories were arrested. As early as 1 July, authorities in the Finistère ordered internment at Brest or expulsion to Spain or Portugal, while three weeks later, the Corrèze arrested all refractories. Other departments had already imprisoned refractories as much as six months before. Yet despite the very large number of priests who were deported, many others went into hiding, protected by a sympathetic laity. This helped nullify the law on the laicization of the vital statistics registers, for the refractories who stayed behind kept their own records or ordinary people simply refused to make the proper declarations before the mayors. Thus even a baptism could become a way of demonstrating hostility to the regime.

The hostility to the laicization of the vital statistics registers was only a small example of how measures of revolutionary defence provoked demonstrations of dissent. There were royalist risings in several regions of the west against the law of 20–22 July mobilizing the National Guard and requesting volunteers. The troubles began with the sacking of a country house belonging to an administrator of the Deux-Sèvres on 19 August and on the 22nd, a crowd estimated at 10,000, believing the enemy was in Paris 'to protect religion', invaded Châtillon-sur-Sèvre and destroyed the papers of the district and municipality. On three occasions equally large bands of peasants attacked Bressuire which had to be defended by National Guards from Poitiers, Niort and Cholet. A band of several thousand was dissipated around Carhaix in the Finistère, there was a pitched battle outside Josselin in the Morbihan and there were demonstrations demanding the release of interned refractories around La Roche-sur-Yon in the Vendée. There were antirecruiting riots throughout the Mayenne in which insurgents shouted, 'The democrats have been masters long enough. We don't recognize the National Assembly or its laws. We'll never consent to send soldiers against the king and the priests . . .' One of the leaders of the Mayenne riots was a former salt-smuggler named Jean Cottereau, alias 'chouan', who was to give his nickname to a counterrevolutionary peasant movement as extensive as *sans-culottisme*. Cottereau had links with the conspiracy of the Marquis de La Rouerie in Brittany which was supposed to act as a fifth column once the allies reached Paris, but fortunately for the patriots local authorities discovered one of the cells in Rennes. Some good detective work rooted up other cells in the Morbihan and Loire-Inférieure and the conspiracy gradually disintegrated. The antirecruiting riots were quickly mastered as well but it was clear that the commitments the Revolution had to ask people to make risked a powerful countermobilization.

The troubles in the west were handled with minimal direction from Paris because a dangerous power vacuum had opened in the capital. Immediately after the overthrow of the monarchy, the rivalry between the Legislative Assembly and the revolutionary commune developed into a dangerous and paralysing conflict. The suspension rather than the deposition of the king, the appointment of a governor for Louis's son, the refusal to order the arrest of Lafayette and the begrudging acceptance of a special tribunal to try those accused of treason raised questions about the Assembly's intentions. Both Assembly and commune struggled for authority over the country and each sent out special commissioners to explain and justify the events of 10 August, those from the Assembly with wide powers to arrest suspect civilian and military authorities, which anticipated the representatives on mission of the Year II. Whatever their hesitations, the politicians also were willing to suspend civil rights, as in every national emergency.

With the national government working at cross-purposes and peasant counterrevolution spreading in the west, the situation on the frontiers seemed on the verge of collapse. Lafayette, dragging in a few civilian administrators, tried to march his army against Paris. The troops failed to support him, however, and he had to flee to Belgium on 17 August. Two days later the Prussians crossed the frontier with a small army of joyous émigrés in their train, in some consternation that they had been assigned the ignominious duty of minor siege warfare and reconnaissance, but so convinced of impending victory that already disputes had begun over who was to get which ministerial portfolios. On 23 August, the fort of Longwy surrendered, under suspicious circumstances, after a desultory bombardment. On 2 September, Parisians learned that Verdun was under siege. Danton's bullying helped keep his fellow ministers from abandoning the capital, and his magnificent speeches to the Assembly called for courage and audacity while the entire human and material resources of the nation were mobilized for war. After Lafayette's treason and the fall of Longwy, everyone was convinced that treason was ubiquitous and the Brunswick Manifesto left no one in doubt what the consequences of defeat would be. Fear and repression therefore intensified. On 26 August, the commune ordered the disarming of suspects and house-to-house searches for weapons. It was in this atmosphere of counterrevolution, treason and defeat that the September Massacres began.

The belief in prison plots and subsequent massacre to prevent treasonous criminals from escaping to inflict who knew what atrocities was hardly new and hardly unique to Paris. In some ways it was the transference to prisoners, whether they were priests or ordinary criminals, of the fear of brigands of 1789. Indeed, the mentality which saw Louis XVI as the centre of a vast conspiracy, which had to be attacked before it unfolded, was the same which saw prisoners as fifth columnists only awaiting the appropriate signal from their aristocratic paymasters to break out and massacre patriots. A prison massacre, therefore, was a way of preventing the domestic and foreign plot from coalescing. Thus, for example, in June, a crowd of people in Dijon, including many National Guards, threw over one hundred refractory priests and nuns into prison as soon as they heard that refractories were with the Austrian troops killed on the northern frontier. A month later, a crowd at Bordeaux murdered two refractories when a rumour got around that six hundred nobles and priests were plotting to turn Saint-Malo over to the English. Priests were not the only victims. At Lyon, where an attack of Swiss and Piedmontese was expected at any moment, the municipality ordered domiciliary visits, disarming of suspects, the suppression of royalist newspapers, and the expulsion of dangerous foreigners. In the surrounding countryside, volunteers talked of cutting off the heads 'of all the aristocrats' before leaving, in order not to leave their families at the mercy of these malevolents. In all, there were at least thirty-four separate incidents of lynchings and murders of priests, officials or counterrevolutionaries in the provinces before the massacres at Paris broke out, and a total of sixty-five between July and September. In many of them there was an air of celebration as the victims' heads were carried about on the end of pikes.

All of these elements – the fear of foreign invasion and of fifth columns, fears for defenceless civilians, the paralysis of government and the courts, and the necessity of a preventive attack – puts the Parisian massacres into their context. Fréron, Marat and the vigilance committee of the commune may have incited and encouraged the murders, the Legislative's attempt to dissolve the commune may have stifled government in the city, Roland and Danton may have shown a surprising torpor or a callous indifference to the victims until the slaughter had begun to peter out – all of these elements may have made the massacres worse than they might otherwise have been, but they did not cause them. Panic, self-defence and vengeance were enough. The grisly slaughters began in the afternoon of 2 September and for the next five days, mobs, including National Guards and perhaps some fédérés, went from prison to prison and to monasteries and seminaries, killing some in cold blood or holding tumultuous 'trials' here and there, illustrative of a sense of popular sovereignty expressing its own justice. In the end, between 1100 and 1400, about half the prison population, were killed, nearly three quarters of them non-political prisoners.

Although the massacres were widely denounced at home and abroad, the 'septembriseurs' considered themselves patriots, their contribution as important as the assault on the Tuileries on 10 August. More decisive in fact was Kellermann's and Dumouriez's victory over the Prussians at Valmy on 20 September. With the Prussians in retreat, the successful invasion of Savoy and Nice and the occupation of the left bank of the Rhine up to Mainz, the Revolution was saved. On 21 September, the Convention abolished the monarchy and proclaimed the Republic.

Revolutionary Democracy and Popular Countermobilization

The theme of the period between 1789 and 1792 is usually considered to be the movement from bourgeois monarchy to egalitarian republic and, in social terms, the displacement of the bourgeois notables by *sans-culotte* people. In broad terms, this has some justification. Excluding the poor from active citizenship, the attempt to appease seigneurs with generous compensation payments, the Le Chapelier law, the repression after the Champ de Mars Affair and the constant upholding of the freedom of the grain trade all made it clear that the bulk of opinion in the Constituent and Legislative Assemblies, and among the men who assumed power in the provinces, intended the regime to be favourable to the men of wealth. The failure to introduce any progressive element into the tax system – the same could be said of the Convention and the Directory, both of which only went so far as to require forced loans from the rich – the failure to do anything about the education system and the slowness of the Assemblies to alter inheritance systems, all suggest that the much-vaunted career open to talents would be limited to families which could finance careers for their sons. For people like this, the overthrow of the monarchy was the defeat of a certain conception of society which restricted political power to a fairly narrow elite of educated and wealthy notables, who represented the whole nation in a kind of metaphysical sense but who never meant to allow ordinary people a direct voice over their destinies. By contrast, the 10 August brought the radical democrats to power. They advocated a form of government in which every (male) citizen exercised his share of sovereignty collectively and directly. Of course, there were limitations on the kind of democracy actually instituted. The mandating and recall of deputies and the referendum (with one exception) never became part of revolutionary practice and even universal suffrage elections to the Convention were vitiated by having the citizens choose electors who alone chose the deputies directly. But 10 August was a victory for the democrats all the same. A sizeable number of veterans of the Cordeliers and the fraternal societies became members of the revolutionary commune and about one third of its members, not much less than the commune of 1793–4, were artisans and shopkeepers. Most of the rest were lawyers, professionals and men of letters, men with backgrounds similar to that of the original Cordeliers leadership. The contrast with the elected commune of notables of 1789 was massive.

The example of the commune suggests some displacement of notables by *sans-culottes*, but it also suggests a radicalization of many of the social groups who were recognized participants in the political system. The directors of the departments and districts, whose actions against the refractory priests either in defiance of the vetoes or in spite of them, did so much to undermine the rule of law and, therefore, the Constitution, were bourgeois, mostly lawyers, who had to meet the eligibility requirements of the electoral law and therefore commanded an amount of wealth well beyond that of the vast majority of their fellow citizens. The Jacobin clubs too, which alternately acclaimed, deplored, protested and mobilized throughout the crisis of 1791–2, were composed mostly of professional and commercial bourgeois allied with a significant representation of urban artisans. There was a wide range of wealth among the club members, most of whom must have been active citizens, at least in theory. As for the National Guards, it is evident from the rare studies that once again the revolutionary coalition was represented by an officer corps of bourgeois and men with military experience, sometimes even nobles, elected by artisans and occasionally peasants in the ranks.

It is too easy in other words to equate the growing radicalism of the period with growing 'plebeianization'. Of course, the Revolution did democratize itself and, under pressure of the war crisis, recognized and encouraged it, so that ordinary people became drawn into the political process. Thus, for example, the Jacobin club at Strasbourg, one of two which demanded a republic in July 1791, had three times as many artisans among its members after 1792 as before, and the proportion of commercial and manufacturing bourgeois, many of whom also joined the local Feuillant club, dropped. But the bourgeoisie as a whole did not defect to the Feuillants. The numbers of those in the liberal professions and the clergy in the post-schism Jacobins also increased. If this example is typical, what appears to have happened in 1792 is that, as the crisis deepened, more and more people became drawn into the political process, on either the left or the right, some original Jacobins defected but the new members reinforced a solid corps of professionals and artisans who had been present from the beginning. The experience of the club in the little Norman town of Vire was different from that of Strasbourg but pointed in the same direction. After Varennes, it wanted the king punished and the primary assemblies consulted on his fate and, after he applied the veto on the laws against refractory priests, it called him an accomplice of rebels. The authors of these petitions, so typical of hundreds of others, were a barrister who was also a member of the local 'National Committee' of 1789 and founder of the club, and another barrister who was also a National Guard officer and administrator of the district.

It is possible to see the process of radicalization of the existing revolutionary class and concomitant democratization in comparing the voluntary levies of National Guards in 1791 and 1792. Both groups were remarkably young, on average at least three quarters were less than twenty-five. Urban recruits, particularly from the smaller towns, were always overrepresented but whereas 15 per cent of the volunteers of 1791 came from the countryside, 69 per cent of those of 1792 did. Nobles virtually disappeared from the elected officer corps in 1792 but in both levies, nearly half the officers were bourgeois of one sort or another and about one third had had some previous military experience. Moreover, it was the battalions of 1791, theoretically all active citizens, who had the opportunity to prove their revolutionary mettle, from the petitions and expeditions of the fédérés to the massacres and lynchings in the provinces in the summer, not to mention the march on the frontiers later.

But not everyone was mobilized in 1792 and not everyone was able to use what democratization there was to make their voices heard. Contemporaries were struck by the magnificent enthusiasm of Parisians throughout the crisis of August and September, as endless streams of delegations appeared before the Assembly to make patriotic gifts, as women made clothes and bandages, as volunteers went to the outskirts to make ramparts, and men, some of them without weapons even, marched to the frontiers. But not everyone was so enthusiastic. One example is voting turnout where, in contrast to the next significant universal suffrage elections in April 1848, the degree of apathy was staggering. The elections of August 1792 have not been well studied but it appears that turnout ranged between about 10 per cent in four departments in the west to a little over 50 at Colmar in Alsace. Furthermore, the poor recruiting due to religious troubles in Alsace, where the army was traditionally popular, was significant while the riots at recruiting meetings in the west were ominous. In this region, thousands of young men were being mobilized in the counterrevolutionary cause, made all the more sacred by the deportation of the refractory priests. The failure of the Jacobins and the Assembly to appreciate the religious issue had done much to bring this mobilization about, just as the use of the vetoes had done much to turn provincial revolutionaries into republicans. The historiography of 1792 which emphasizes a rising of the entire French people culminating in the 'revolution of equality' consistently underplays the fact that the mobilization of 'the people' evoked a powerful counter-mobilization of quite ordinary people too who were headed in exactly the opposite direction. It was no coincidence that the communes in the Ille-et-Vilaine which contributed the fewest volunteers to the army were also those where hostility to the Civil Constitution was greatest. The revolutionaries' dangerously simple analysis that these troubles could be blamed solely on the refractory priests, and that the problem could be solved by deporting them, was storing up massive problems for the future.

Popular demands were ignored or rejected outside the west as well. The food riots of the late winter and spring brought no concrete result and even the sympathy of some Jacobins for such popular causes can be overstated. It is a long way from Dolivier's questioning of the principle of private property in the famous number four of *Le Défenseur de la Constitution* to Robespierre's moralizing commentary about the greed of the rich which accompanied it. Furthermore, it is doubtful whether a direct connection can be made between the antiseigneurial riots in the Midi in the spring and the laws of July and August which required seigneurs to produce original titles to collect transfer fees and dues. Thus none of the deputies who spoke on the law of July represented a region affected by the riots, and none referred to expediency or popular pressure as a reason for passing the law. Only one of the nine deputies who spoke was hostile to the proposed law but five of the nine voted 'no' on the 8 August motion on whether Lafayette should be put on trial. In other words, on an issue vital to the countryside, social and political conservatism did not overlap. Nor was the Girondin-Montagnard split evident. The 'Montagnard' Couthon merely wanted to make redemption easier and would have allowed both original titles and receipts as proof of legitimacy, while the 'Montagnards' Maihe and Delacroix joined the 'Girondin' Louvet in denouncing the whole seigneurial system as a usurpation.

Of course, it takes time for people to learn how voting, local affairs and national politics interact, and politicians often do things for expediency while pretending to high principle. But in broad terms, the political system from 1789 to 1792 had not been as responsive as many had hoped. Fiscal equality had not brought much relief, the seigneurial system was abolished in spite of the politicians, urban and rural consumers' standards of living were dropping with each fall in the assignat, the religious settlement had alienated large members of people in Flanders, Alsace, the Midi and the west, and demonstration by grain riot had brought some expressions of sympathy but no action beyond repression. It remained to be seen whether the exigencies of war and the bourgeoisie's near monopoly of political power could be adapted to so many conflicting popular aspirations. This was the agenda which lay before the Convention.

Chapter 5

Republic, War and Civil War

The Convention and the King's Trial

In the 1830s, when they were old men, a cult grew up around the surviving *conventionnels*, as men who had changed the course of European history. Our generation, brought up to believe that history consists of the nearly imperceptible movement of production and population and that methodology consists of applying a set of mental callipers to measure subtle changes in the price of grain or birth rates, would be more sceptical. Yet the *conventionnels* did govern France until November 1795 and, by law, assured themselves an important influence in the legislatures down to 1798, while a majority of the directors, the executive government, had sat in the Convention. During its lifetime, the Convention mastered the greatest crises the Revolution faced, devised the machinery which contained the counterrevolution at home, which split the coalition of foreign powers arrayed against France and which laid the groundwork for the subsequent French expansion into Europe. It was a remarkable achievement but there was a negative side that is often less appreciated. The Convention's violent methods, its failure to solve the economic and financial problems and its deliberate amputation of the club and *sans-culotte* movement left a legacy of problems which overwhelmed their successors.

The *conventionnels* were experienced men. Of 730 elected in September 1792, 269 were former deputies of the Constituent or Legislative Assemblies and 357 others had held some kind of elective office at the local level. Within broad limits they resembled the deputies to the old Third Estate, the only other legislative body which has been subject to such minute analysis. The Convention was somewhat younger – two thirds were less than forty-four while roughly half of the Constituents were. There was the same relative overrepresentation of the towns and cities. In each case, roughly one quarter came from towns with a population of over fifteen thousand at a time when these were home to only 10 per cent of the population as a whole. In so far as it is possible to make the comparison, the overall composition of the social backgrounds of the Third Estate and Convention were broadly similar. The proportion of lawyers in private practice was almost identical (about 29 per cent) and although the number of office-holders declined by half, and the proportion of men whose occupations required some legal training declined considerably, just about half the *conventionnels* were lawyers of one kind or another. The proportion of businessmen and artisans remained about the same, while those in agriculture and from the academic, literary and medical worlds declined slightly. In social terms, the Convention represented a shift away from the serene world of the office-holders, law courts and academies which had characterized the public life of the provinces of the Old Regime towards the boisterous world of the clubs, guards and administrations of the Revolution. Put another way, the lawyer-activists of local political life came into their own in the Convention. But they were no more of a new or thrusting group than were the Constituents; in each case, roughly half the lawyer-politicians also came from legal families. Finally, the second-degree electors of 1792 were not particularly hostile to the former privileged orders. There were 55 clerics elected; so were a fair number of ex-nobles, some of them quite prominent on the 'left': the Duc d'Orléans (rebaptized Philippe Egalité), Hérault de Séchelles who became a member of the Committee of Public Safety, and Lepelletier de Saint-Fargeau, who later joined Marat and Chalier as 'martyrs of liberty'.

In its first phase down to 2 June 1793, the history of the Convention is the history of the struggle beween the Girondins – the Brissotins and Rolandists of the Legislative Assembly – and the Montagnards – strongly but not exclusively based on the Paris delegation led by Robespierre, Danton and Marat – and so called because they occupied the upper benches of the Assembly to the left of the chair. Neither group was a party in the sense that they accepted a common discipline to implement an agreed programme: the ethos of the day, which equated party with faction and exalted the independence of the individual member, was too strong for that. Because of this, counts of how many deputies belonged to which group vary considerably. Much depends on how deputies are classified according to a prearranged scheme. In fact it is extremely difficult to identify who belonged to which group in a very fluid situation, because not even contemporaries knew. Marat produced a list of 102 'Girondins' but it is not at all clear what criteria he used. The Paris sections and the commune, who more than anyone else were responsible for the later purge of the Convention on 2 June 1793, produced five lists of deputies they wanted expelled between 10 March and 1 June 1793, but only six names out of a total of forty are common to all five lists, and nine deputies were expelled on 2 June whose names appear on none of the lists. The lists of proscribed deputies produced during the rest of the year fluctuated considerably. The common element in them is that they contain a disproportionate number of deputies who voted for a referendum on the king's fate (83 per cent in favour in the composite Parisian list as opposed to 40 per cent in the Convention as a whole, for example) but this does not mean that these splits were present from the beginning, far from it. The fate of individual deputies evolved considerably. One might class Barbaroux as an extremist for his support of the fédérés of Marseille in the summer of 1792 but he ended as an antiterrorist, while Fouché's views on the religious question became more and more radical over the same period. Isnard, normally thought to be a typical Girondin, voted consistently against Louis XVI and introduced the legislation establishing the Committee of Public Safety, but ended up on the list of 1 June probably because of a famous speech threatening Paris with destruction if the radicals attacked the Convention. This does not mean that all was chaos in the Convention or that voting blocs did not emerge which acquired some consistency over time. Most historians would agree that neither Girondins nor Montagnards had a reliable majority in the Convention and that both small general staffs competed for the allegiance of a third group, the supposedly uncommitted Plain. Yet neither set of leaders was itself united. The Montagnards were much more coherent in their voting, perhaps because they dominated the Jacobin club, particularly after Brissot's expulsion on 10 October, and so the club acted as a sort of caucus. Yet there were important differences of opinion between Robespierre and most of his colleagues over the claim of private property to complete legal protection, with Robespierre admitting some limitations; and Marat's earthy violence embarrassed almost everyone. The Girondins were even less united, in part because their loose grouping around a number of salons, particularly Mme Roland's, was more conducive to relaxed discussion and gossip than to planning concerted action.

Most deputies, including those of the Plain, shared a number of common concerns or policies. One was an aggressive foreign policy. After Dumouriez's victory over the Austrians at Jémappes which permitted the occupation of Belgium, the Convention adopted a series of measures which were bound to expand the war: opening the Scheldt to international commerce which alienated the British and Dutch, offering 'fraternity and assistance' to oppressed peoples, annexing Savoy and bringing the Revolution to conquered territories by introducing the assignat, by abolishing feudalism and by sequestering noble and ecclesiastical property. The French clearly intended to use the war to destroy the entire Old Regime of Europe and the Convention accepted the implications of implanting the Revolution abroad with little demur. Finally recognizing the inevitable fissures in international relations these expansionary measures caused, it declared war on Britain and Holland in February 1793 and on Spain in March almost unanimously.

The deputies also shared a broad consensus on economic policy in that most firmly believed in private property and freedom of the grain trade. Their reaction to the popular disturbances of the winter of 1792–3 shows this well. In November–December 1792, a series of grain riots as extensive as those of the previous spring swept over the Beauce, spreading as far south as Tours and as far west as Le Mans. From September to mid-October, a wave of château-burning rolled over Provence. Neither the Girondin nor the Montagnard deputies or journalists had much to say about these troubles except to accuse their opponents of having instigated them. Even the Cordeliers group among the Montagnards, men like Danton, Desmoulins, Fréron, Fabre d'Eglantine and so on, who had struggled against economic and political oppression in 1790–1, did not take up the popular cause. Indeed Robespierre, Danton, Roland and Buzot leapt over factional considerations by all agreeing on the necessity of putting them down. On a more abstract basis, Robespierre made a famous speech on 2 December recognizing limits on property rights, and Marat reiterated what he had been saying for years that the poor had gained nothing from the Revolution, but when it came to appreciating popular aspirations the politicians did not adjust. As in the previous spring, sympathy for economic hardship took second place to more pressing political considerations.

On the other issues, however, many new or uncommitted

deputies were drawn into violent disputes arising from earlier debates in which the Montagnards had become convinced that the Girondins were unduly and stupidly tolerant of royalism and counterrevolution, and in which the Girondins were convinced that their opponents would permit or encourage any massacre or any insurrection in order to institute a personal dictatorship, or to establish Parisian hegemony over the provinces. Thus, many debates in the Convention aimed at reducing the respective factions to an insignificant minority so that it was often difficult to deal with the issue at hand entirely on its merits. This was particularly clear in the case of the king's trial, which began in late December. Almost everyone was convinced of Louis's treason and scarcely anyone was prepared to defend him on the grounds of constitutional inviolability when the debates began. Nor was the Convention willing to accept the argument that Robespierre had taken from the hitherto unknown deputy Saint-Just, that the people had given its verdict on 10 August and that the only course was outright condemnation. But the overwhelming 683 votes against Louis led in the direction of declaring him guilty. In these circumstances, the proposal of some Girondins to subject the verdict to a popular referendum could be easily represented as an attempt to save the king. Although the *appelants*, as they were called, could thus flaunt their democratic credentials, the Convention agreed with Robespierre that the measure would give counterrevolutionaries an opportunity to infiltrate the primary assemblies. In plain language, he feared the chaos that might result if a popular vote should go in the king's favour. Almost as dangerous was the proposal to grant Louis a reprieve from the death penalty on the grounds of the incalculable effects on foreign opinion. As the Montagnards pointed out, Brissot among others had cared little about foreign opinion during the 'Austrian Committee' agitation six months earlier. Thus, the charge of inconsistency could be added to that of equivocation. In the event, the Convention voted against a reprieve by 387 to 334, and when Louis was guillotined on 21 January 1793 his death symbolized not only an irrevocable break with the Old Regime but left the factions more hostile to each other than ever.

The execution of the king was a victory for the Montagnards in several ways. By forcing the Convention to come out for the most uncompromising possible outcome of the king's trial – death without a referendum or a reprieve – they acquired an ascendancy which they rarely lost afterwards. The trial shook much of the anti-

Montagnard opposition. The debates and the voting showed a fatal disunity among Brissot's friends with only a handful of them consistently voting in a moderate direction. Moreover, Brissot, Buzot and Vergniaud, among others, spoke rarely after the trial and the Montagnards and their supporters increasingly came to dominate the committees. The Montagnards also consolidated their political base both in Paris and in the provinces because many of the clubs and popular societies came to identify the *appelants* as either dangerous moderates or as crypto-royalists. Yet the victory was far from total. The voting in the trial had revealed for all to see a solid bloc of moderates which under certain conditions could perhaps become a majority. What made this all the more dangerous was a series of separate but simultaneous crises: the outbreak of violent counterrevolution in the west, Dumouriez's treason, and a new cycle of popular disturbances brought on by the deteriorating economy. The linkage of these disasters in the minds of the Paris radicals eventually brought the expulsion of the Girondins from the Convention.

The Crises of '93

By the winter of 1792–3, the counterrevolution had begun to ebb. Two of the émigré armies had been dissolved for lack of money, while the third, that of the Prince de Condé, appeared to be about to share the same fate. The internal counterrevolution had virtually collapsed as well. La Rouerie's conspiracy, which was supposed to turn Brittany over to the princes, had been broken, La Rouerie was dead (from natural causes), and his subordinates either executed, arrested, driven underground, or fled abroad. The only other conspiracy of significance, that of the Comte de Saillans in the Midi, had also disintegrated. This was an attempt to form another fifth column based on Jalès, but as early as February 1792 associates in the Lozère rose too soon and to no purpose. Meanwhile, as the allied campaign got underway in the summer, Saillans quarrelled with Thomas Conway, the general commander of the Midi, over when to start the rising. Revolutionary authorities invested Jalès yet again, Saillans was eventually murdered and piles of compromising papers fell into the hands of the government. Finally, the popular counterrevolution had also been checked. The deportation of the refractory priests, or their going into hiding, had reduced the number of incidents against the constitutional clergy considerably. The enforced reduction in the rivalry of the two clergies changed no one's mind, of course, but superficially at least, the countryside was quieter than it had been in nearly two years.

The expansion of the war revived the counterrevolution and drew vastly more people into it. In order to fight the impending campaign and support the war on almost every frontier, the Convention decreed the levying of 300,000 men on 24 February. This was the first time the young Republic asked the nation to make sacrifices and the result was disturbing. The response to the levy was an unprecedented wave of riots whose extent remains to be investigated but which was almost certainly greater than the subsistence and antiseigneurial riots of the previous year. And unlike the previous troubles, these forced the Convention to take the first tentative steps towards centralizing authority and systematic repression. Some of the troubles of 1793, such as the hostility of the young men at the recruiting meetings in Besançon, Autun, Alençon and elsewhere, were probably no more than an attempt to avoid conscription. In the countryside of the west, where the young men's dislike of conscription could be easily linked to the stock of grievances accumulated over the religious issue, the risings quickly involved entire communities in Normandy, Brittany, Maine, Anjou and Poitou. Young men tore down liberty trees, burned draft lists, beat up mayors or National Guardsmen or constitutional curés and donned white royalist cockades. North of the Loire, in the second and third weeks of March, people armed with hunting weapons and farm tools marched on the towns behind white flags demanding the abolition of the districts, which were thought to be the source of every evil from the Civil Constitution to arbitrary taxes. In Brittany, almost every district capital was attacked, and Rochefort and La Roche-Bernard in the Morbihan, and Savenay and Guérande in the Loire-Inférieure, fell into rebel hands. Here and there refractory priests joined the bands, but more often than not the country people sought out local nobles and demanded they take the lead. Authorities reestablished control by early April but south of the Loire in the four departments which came to be known as the *Vendée militaire*, or simply 'the Vendée', where there were fewer troops and National Guards available and where communications were more difficult, government collapsed. By the end of March, in a region bounded roughly by the Loire on the north and Fontenay-le-Comte in the south, the rebels had taken all the towns and were responsible for some appalling massacres of republicans. Nantes, Angers and Saumur were under constant threat. By early April, the regional leaders, mostly local nobles but also priests, estate stewards and peasants as well, announced the formation of the Catholic and Royal Army with its own insignia of a cross mounted on a Sacred Heart, and sent off emissaries to seek English help.

The risings in the west, with their demands for a return of the priests and the Old Regime and their vengeance against the bourgeois revolutionaries for the wrongs done ever since 1791, occurred almost at the same time as defeat and treason on the northern frontiers. The armies encamped in Belgium were badly paid and clothed and their poor discipline alienated the civilian population. The imposition of the assignat at artificially high levels and the implementation of the entire package of religious reforms completed it. Disorganized ministries and quarrelling generals and authorities on the spot and in Paris also wasted precious time which could have been better spent consolidating the victory. Dumouriez's offensive into Holland in February had to be abandoned after the Austrians drove a wedge between the French armies in Belgium and the troops fell back from Aix-la-Chapelle and Liège. On 18 March, Dumouriez was badly defeated at Neerwinden. But he made the same mistake as Lafayette the year before in trying to impose his own political solution at a time of military defeat. He ordered the restoration of plate to the Belgian churches, he closed the local Jacobin clubs, and in a letter to the Convention he blamed the War Department for the defeats. The step to treason came with the conclusion of an armistice with the Austrians, the surrender of a number of forts and the attempt to turn his army on Paris to support 'the sane part of the Convention' and to restore the Constitution of 1791, including the monarchy in the person of Louis XVII. The whole adventure collapsed ignominiously as the army failed to respond to his overtures, and Dumouriez and some of his staff had to flee to the Austrian lines under fire from his own troops.

The third major crisis was financial and economic. Dilatory payment of taxes continued to plague the government. By the end of 1792, just over half the anticipated tax revenues had been paid; over one in ten communes had not yet drawn up their tax rolls; and tax revenues constituted a diminishing fraction of expenditure. The only way the war could be financed, therefore, was by printing more assignats. These continued to decline in value partly because of the quantities issued and partly because of the 50 per cent decline in foreign trade. The fall also reflected the minimal investor confidence in *biens nationaux* as the prospects of the counterrevolution rose. Although the harvest of 1792 was reasonably good in northern parts of the country, and although most of the large towns subsidized the price of bread, the price of grain and other commodities shot up because of monetary inflation, and shortages became increasingly acute.

As a result, the popular movement in Paris began to concentrate on subsistence questions for the first time in over a year. In January, there was a wave of protests when the commune proposed to raise the price of bread. On 12 February a delegation of commissioners from the forty-eight sections and some of the remaining fédérés denounced the principle of freedom of trade, so recently defended by all sides in the Convention, as a licence for speculators to oppress the poor. It demanded a fixed price, or 'Maximum', for grain throughout the country. Two weeks later, a delegation of washerwomen demanded the death penalty for hoarders. This hostility to absolute property rights and the demand for a controlled economy can be traced back to 1790, or even to the food riots of the Old Regime, but it was expanded more forcefully in the difficult months of 1793 by the disparate group known as the 'enragés', of which the radical priest Jacques Roux and a well-educated postal clerk, Jean Varlet, were the best-known spokesmen. Roux encouraged the riots against grocers and wholesalers which broke out in Paris on 25 and 26 February. The poor and the economically vulnerable – water-carriers, market-women, domestics, etc. – were particularly prominent and when they did not fix prices on such products as soap, sugar and candles, they simply pillaged. The commune mobilized the National Guard as a show of force and so handled the riots easily. But the commune itself shared the preoccupations of the rioters if not their methods, for the next day, its procurator, Chaumette, demanded a law against hoarding, a reduction in the number of assignats and a programme of public works. Chaumette's justification was significant: it was the only way to attach the poor to the Revolution. It was a theme more and more Jacobins began to espouse.

These economic difficulties, as well as the civil war in the west, military defeat and treason abroad, had an obvious explanation for patriots both inside the Convention and out: they were the result of plots. The belief in sinister forces manipulating disparate events had been present from the beginning but the very scale of the crisis in 1793 fuelled sensitive imaginations for some dizzying flights. Taken to its extremes, it led in the direction of terror and justified it. In the early phases of the crisis, some of the manifestations of the plot mentality were banal enough. Thus the Montagnards, notably Robespierre, claimed counterrevolutionaries incited the subsistence rioters in February. There was a little more plausibility to the Girondins' accusation that Marat incited the riots, even though it was only a coincidence that *L'Ami du Peuple* published a call to hang a few grocers on the very day the riots broke out. Some of these charges were simply the stuff of political debate in this period, a rhetorical device intended to offer the grossest of insults. Other conspiracy theories were more sincerely held and more dangerous. Thus, the risings in the west were quite wrongly attributed to the La Rouerie conspiracy or to returned émigrés. The risings were also linked to Dumouriez's treason and occasionally all of these troubles were attributed to an even deeper conspiracy masterminded from London.

Fanciful as some of these notions were, they all affected the way people responded to the crisis. The predilection to believe in conspiracies led them to the simple analysis that the economic difficulties were the fault of hoarders. Despite the petition of the section commissioners and fédérés demanding controlled prices, agitation in the sections and from Roux and the other enragés concentrated less on the question of national price controls than on securing a law against hoarders. These limited aims could not push the Convention far off its adherence to the orthodoxy of free trade – Marat called the petition for a national maximum 'subversive of all good order'. With the politicians anyway believing the agitation was directed by sinister forces for partisan ends, pressure from the streets on subsistence questions had few chances of success.

If plot theories blinkered the vision of the radicals and hampered an alliance with sympathetic groups in the Convention, they did affect the measures taken to deal with the deteriorating military situation. The Convention decided to establish the Revolutionary Tribunal on 10 March to exercise summary justice in cases involving state security, because they believed that the early defeats in Belgium involved more than simply the incompetence of the generals and the Executive Council. Similarly, beliefs that traitors were everywhere lay behind the establishment of elected revolutionary committees on 21 March in each section or commune. Their original purpose was to intern foreigners and suspects without passports, but they acquired or took on considerably greater police powers over the course of the summer. Suspicion of the executive lay behind the establishment of the Committee of Public Safety on 6 April which, from the beginning, was an embryonic government. It could oversee the Executive Council and even suspend its decrees, while it was empowered to take whatever measures were necessary for internal and external defence, the only limitations being the requirement to inform the Convention of its activities and certain qualifications of its powers of arrest.

The deputies were well aware that these measures went beyond the ordinary rule of law, and as the crisis deepened they went even further. The law of 19 March, providing for the trial and execution of armed rebels within twenty-four hours without a jury or an appeal by a military commission, was a direct response to the risings in the west. Scared by the scale of domestic resistance and suspicious of all the generals after Dumouriez's treason, the Convention granted increased powers to the representatives on mission. Eighty-two of these deputies had been sent to the provinces in early March to encourage recruiting for the levy of 300,000. In April, they were granted additional and almost unlimited powers over the army and the activities of the departmental administrations. In fact, many of the earlier representatives on mission had taken independent initiatives, partly because they felt that weak local administration had been responsible for the crisis in the first place, and partly that the departments on their own could not coordinate repression in the civil war zones. By extraordinary measures, both judicial and administrative, the central government reasserted its authority. Administrators who disobeyed could now be punished with dismissal or even arrest.

The notion that the public safety was the supreme law was hardly new. The departments had used it to justify their exceptional measures against the refractory priests and it was the rationale behind their deportation. But the extraordinary dangers and the mentality of 1793 enhanced the corollary that moderation was more dangerous to the Republic than extremism, that evil, self-serving elements had taken advantage of the muddled tolerance of those who tried to take an even-handed approach. The results of such policies were the ominous disasters of March. The deputy Fouché, who was gradually moving to an uncompromising radicalism as a result of the crisis, expressed a typical view when he blamed the risings in the west on the 'softness of the [local] administrations [which] have lost everything. . . . By a false system of moderation and tolerance, they have betrayed their country.'

Girondins and the Crisis

This developing attitude put the Girondins in an invidious position. Ever since the king's trial, they had taken a moderate line on most issues. They were not against exceptional measures on principle. They had fought a long and successful campaign to lift the parliamentary immunity of Philippe Egalité and have him arrested; they had not opposed the law of 25 March authorizing the disarming of nobles, priests and suspects. More importantly, Lanjuinais and his Girondin friends proposed the law of 19 March which put rebels under the jurisdiction of military commissions. They had opposed the much less severe powers granted to the Revolutionary Tribunal a few days before (unlike the commissions, it had a jury). Lanjuinais later defended the idea of a forced loan on the rich when it was introduced in May. The problem for the Girondin leaders was less the principle of revolutionary government than the risk that these institutions would fall into the hands of their political enemies. That this risk was real was evident when Robespierre demanded on 14 April that Brissot be brought before the Revolutionary Tribunal. Yet no one had initially envisaged that it would be used against deputies. The Girondin leaders' opposition to the granting of more extensive powers to the representatives on mission is also comprehensible in that most of them were Montagnards who, it was charged, used their position to spread their own propaganda and support the clubs. The Montagnards could make the same accusations. In any case, the Girondins were less hostile to the principle of increasing the powers of the representatives on mission than to a clause in the bill establishing a central committee of authorities and clubs. The clause was defeated and, when they were in power, the Montagnards banned the practice. Thus the issue of what historians call 'revolutionary government' – the right to take extraordinary measures to save the Republic – became indistinguishable from the usual faction fights.

If some Girondins drifted towards moderation because of the fear of how the exceptional institutions would be used, their attitude towards popular involvement in revolutionary defence also began to divide them from the Montagnards. It was not that the Girondins were against prosecuting the war or levying men and requisitioning supplies. Rather, they assumed that the people would accept their role passively while the Montagnards revived the policy of popular mobilization. Brissot and his friends had demanded this in near-demagogic terms the year before but in the interval popular radicals had defined them as enemies. Instead, Barère, Danton, Robespierre and Jeanbon Saint-André spoke or wrote of the necessity of an alliance with the people which would win over popular support by making economic concessions, such as subsidizing bread by a tax on the rich or selling émigré property in small lots to make it available to the poor. Such considerations were also linked to the nightmare of another Vendée. In so far as the revolutionaries had a sociology of counterrevolution, it was the belief that its origins lay in poverty and that the rich, who had abandoned the Republic, had stirred it up. Thus the sympathies for economic hardship which they had always held became harnessed to the political aim of saving the Revolution.

The Girondins did not block all the exceptional measures. Nor, despite their revolutionary rhetoric, did the Montagnards and their allies initiate them all. In fact the construction of 'revolutionary government' was a chaotic process with a whole series of movements, authorities and circumstances contributing. The commune of Paris and the sections were one such lobby group. They had campaigned for some time for a war tax on the rich whose proceeds would subsidize bread prices. Although it was never systematically applied, the Convention voted the principle on 5 April. The commune had also demanded the demonetization of gold and silver which would render the assignat the only legal tender. The Convention voted this on 11 April. Subsistence questions lay behind much of the agitation in the capital but contrary to a widespread belief among historians, the demand for a maximum was not particularly common in the sections and clubs. Since the municipality subsidized bread prices, the problem was one of supply. From the end of March onwards, there were reports of bread queues, disturbances in front of shops, bakers' apprentices threatening strikes and so on. The sections were therefore vociferous in demanding a law on hoarding. To implement such a law and to fight the interior enemy, they also demanded a revolutionary army – a vigilante force recruited solely from the ranks of proven *sans-culottes*. On top of this, they demanded a progressive tax on the rich which could rise to a marginal rate of 100 per cent and a purge of former nobles in the army. As the Gravilliers section, where Roux was influential, pointed out, the object was laws which would be 'to the advantage . . . not of the rich but to the labouring and virtuous class of society'. The Convention ignored all of these demands, which shows that even in a great moment of peril, it was able to resist pressure from the streets. Instead, it passed a partial maximum on 4 May which pegged grain prices at the average price of the first four months of the year, limited sales to market places only and permitted inventories of supplies and requisitioning. This was at the urging of some provincial authorities as well as the Department of Paris, which could not prevent outlying communes from provisioning themselves on the Paris markets. They wanted a general maximum on prices applicable to the entire Republic. The Convention was not willing to go as far. Yet, as framed, the law did help solve a problem which had worried the Committee of Agriculture since the previous autumn: how to prevent public authorities, including army suppliers, from competing with each other. As a return to Old Regime practices the maximum was impressive but without constraints on hoarding it meant little. More importantly, as the Girondin Barbaroux pointed out, to the extent that legalized prices were lower than the market price – and they would be so long as inflation continued – they could discourage production and so contribute little to solving the problem of supply. The *sans-culottes* would soon express their disappointment.

The special tribunals, the revolutionary committees, the special taxes, the maximum and the wide-ranging powers granted to the representatives on mission were all vital elements of the Terror. Its development was a chaotic process with the commune and sections, Convention committees and ordinary deputies on the floor all contributing, its various authors responding in their own way to the pressures of the March crisis. The very circumstances of its origins show that it was not intended to be a system, nor was it, since most of the legislation was applied half-heartedly, if at all, especially outside the civil war zone in the Vendée. Yet the way the legislation was perceived in the provinces and the way it filtered through the particular character of local Jacobinism in some regions contributed to the very process of disintegration the Convention was trying to stop.

Federalism and Extremism

In so far as it is possible to characterize patriot provincial opinion up until March, most of it did not take sides in the Girondin-Montagnard struggle. An overwhelming number of clubs approved of the execution of Louis XVI but this did not in itself imply acceptance of the Montagnard line. In fact, many of them spent immense amounts of energy on non-partisan activities like collecting patriotic gifts in the form of money and military equipment, and many simply deplored the unedifying and baffling faction fights in Paris. Several clubs had their own way of viewing things which cannot be characterized in Parisian terms. That of Villefranche-sur-Saône, for example, demanded the arrest of Marat, 'the vile instrument of a disastrous faction' in December 1792, while three months later it petitioned that the Republic declare food supplies to be 'national property' and distribute it free, the costs to be borne by the rich – a line far more radical than most of the proposals emanating from Paris. There were many other clubs which had earlier protested the apparent sway of Parisian 'anarchists' over the Convention but later swung behind the emergency laws. In terms of national politics, such clubs were switching from the Girondins to the Montagnards, but from their point of view they were evolving in response to the national crisis in the same way the mother society in Paris had. In any case, there were always the Montagnard deputies on mission who were eager to enlighten the provincials on the significance of the war, treasons and rebellions.

But not everyone was willing to be brought 'à la hauteur des circonstances', as the phrase went. The explanation for the rebellion against the terrorist legislation of the spring of 1793, which is known as federalism, has much to do with the workings of local politics and particularly with the strength and character of the local Jacobin movement. This was overlaid with intense regional rivalries, usually involving a 'federalist' department capital and one or two district administrations which remained loyal to the Convention. Alençon versus Domfront in the Orne, Lons-le-Saunier versus Dôle in the Jura are examples. So it is only partially correct to describe the federalist movement as 'provincial' since Paris did retain large islands of loyalty throughout the Republic which were later used as bases for repression.

In addition, though federalism certainly attracted royalists, it was not on the whole counterrevolutionary or decentralizing. The federalist manifestos proclaimed their loyalty to the principle of the indivisibility of the nation and, in most places, to the Republic. Royalists and émigré officers certainly flocked to the federalist armies, but in Lyon, for example, many of the leaders who were royalists were constitutional monarchists who had to hide their intentions from the rank and file. Even the Comte de Précy, whose appointment as commander of the Lyon army was a public relations disaster for the federalists because he had fought on the side of the defenders of the Tuileries on 10 August, was probably a liberal monarchist. Précy and his staff were by no means agents of the émigrés; they had no formal or regular relations with the princes throughout the siege. The Comte de Provence, self-proclaimed regent since the execution of his brother, actually set out for Toulon when the federalists there proclaimed the monarchy, but it was the Constitution of 1791 that had been restored, not the 'constitution' of the Old Regime. In fact, federalism was much more negative than reactionary. None of the manifestos adhered to the proclamation the Comte de Provence issued on 28 January when he assumed the regency. This promised a root-and-branch restoration of the Old Regime minus undefined abuses, but the federalists concentrated much more on a fear of the intentions of the Jacobins. One Jura federalist summed up these fears well when he claimed that the Montagnards had preached murder and pillage and 'put peaceful citizens whose only crime is to be rich on the index but whose fortune in truth has become their prey'.

The possessing classes' fear of lower elements gave federalism a wide appeal, particularly in Bordeaux, Lyon, Marseille and Toulon. So too did the maximum which was particularly inappropriate to the circumstances of the Midi. Both the grain and wine harvests of 1792 south of the Loire had been poor and heavy rains in the autumn and consequent flooding caused fears for the winter grain harvest in 1793. The coastal cities had always been dependent upon imports, but with the entry of England into the war shipments from Italy or North Africa through the Mediterranean, and from Holland or southern Brittany along the Atlantic seaboard, were at risk. This made the cities more dependent than ever upon hinterlands which had never been adequate sources of supply, while Lyon had to compete with the Army of the Alps for supplies in one of its traditional breadbaskets in the Isère. Payment for foreign imports was rendered difficult anyway by the inflation of the assignat and the decline in shipping. Furthermore, since the maximum set prices on the basis of departmental averages and since all the major cities of the Midi drew their supplies from a hard-pressed hinterland extending over several departments, the grain trade was bound to be disrupted and supplies threatened. The maximum was unpopular even in the countryside of the Midi. Unlike the northern plains where the numerous rural poor, the landless, the day-labourers and the petty artisans could see it as assuring their subsistence at a fair price, in the Midi where landownership was more widely diffused it squeezed the profits of small cultivators at a time when conscription was causing a labour shortage. In this region, no less than fifty-three primary assemblies spread over twenty-seven departments demanded its abrogation. Because the conditions of production and trade in the Midi were considerably different, it was easy to present the maximum as a plot which suited Parisian interests to the exclusion of everyone else's.

Jacobinism in the Midi was also particularly extreme because of the long history of struggle against royalist conspiracies and this in turn contributed towards alienating part of a constituency which in Paris would be classed as 'sans-culotte'. In Toulon, for example, the local Jacobins seized control of the municipality after a massacre of a dozen people including some departmental administrators in the summer of 1792 and then proceeded to mismanage their relations with the truculent dock workers by imposing stricter labour discipline and paying them in deteriorating assignats. The basis of the anti-Jacobin coup in July 1793 was the artisan- and shopkeeper-dominated National Guard and the city's sections, goaded into action by fears that the Jacobins were contemplating another massacre to retain power. In Bordeaux, local authorities closed the Club National after an ominous food riot in March because extremists had demanded a 'supplement' to the September Massacres.

The fear of uncontrolled Jacobinism and the rapid isolation of the militants was also evident at Lyon. Here, the Jacobins, who controlled the municipality and Central Club, worked together to impose their own version of the Terror. They had been struggling against counterrevolution ever since 1790 and, because of the crisis of March–April, they reacted quickly and emotionally. They formed a local Committee of Public Safety, appointed revolutionary committees composed of their own followers, created a revolutionary army, instituted a forced loan on the rich, and undertook a long campaign to obtain a revolutionary tribunal. The Montagnard deputies on mission did little or nothing to prevent these steps, which were often illegal, but even so they might have been acceptable if they had been limited to defence and police functions. But the leaders of the Central Club made it clear that they were directed against the internal enemy which could include not just the aristocrats and the rich but some quite humble people as well. Ever since the local massacres of the previous September, there had been talk of using the guillotine against merchants who frequently refused work to militant silk-workers, or of bringing food hoarders before a revolutionary tribunal or arresting the entire corps of bakers because they made a vile 'dog's bread'. The Jacobin club of the Croix-Rousse section posted in its meeting halls the names of all those refusing to sign petitions demanding the execution of Louis XVI. This was clearly an open invitation to intimidate moderates. A crazy demagogue, Joseph Chalier, issued a poster threatening them in lurid terms: they would 'stain with their blood the waters of the Rhône which will carry their corpses to terrifying seas'. Worse still, the Central Club appeared to be on the verge of acting on such bloodcurdling sentiments. On 5 February, the municipality, with the help of agents designated by the club, undertook a day-long series of arrests of 'dubious' elements. On the 6th, at a closed night session, Chalier swore everyone present to keep the discussion that night secret on pain of death and then proposed creating a revolutionary tribunal to judge 'all the enemies of equality' starting with the moderate members of the municipality. Nothing came of this but rumours of what had been said set off a complicated struggle within the municipality and in the streets, which culminated in the sacking of the club on the 18th by a crowd of over one thousand people. The Jacobins replied by jailing their opponent in the imminent mayoral election (he won anyway), and then winning a subsequent election, with the help of the representatives on mission, who clearly understood little of the situation. They persuaded the anti-Jacobin candidate to resign. The fears such behaviour aroused were given more substance by illegally constituted revolutionary committees which were authorized to disarm 'all suspect individuals, whether attornies, men of law, store clerks, etc.', and to make lists of all 'hoarders, rich capitalists and the indifferent'. The committees, too, were empowered to designate those subject to the forced loan destined to finance the revolutionary army, which itself was supposed to be composed of only the purest *sans-culottes*. The municipality also tried to disarm or dissolve the elite companies of the National Guard which were automatically suspect because they contained better-off elements. The local Terror in Lyon, then, was the instrument of a party which defined itself in exclusive and increasingly antidemocratic terms. Yet the Jacobin dictatorship was not as solid as its potential victims feared. Just before their downfall, the truly exalted formed a 'Society of Jacobins' which coopted only the purest as opposed to the Central Club, which, being composed of merely elected delegates from the neighbourhood popular societies, was potentially unreliable. This provoked howls of protest from some of the societies and the resulting fissure within the popular movement gave the moderates their chance. They forced the municipality to recall the dormant sections and elect revolutionary committees in accordance with the law of 21 March. The new committees were generally anti-Jacobin and immediately suspended the collection of the forced loan – an interesting sign of who dominated both them and the sections. But the municipality refused to disband the old committees and, as at Toulon, street violence gave rise to rumours that the Jacobins were planning a fresh round of massacres. This was untrue but they did express hopes in public for a purge of the Convention which would permit them to establish their revolutionary tribunal (refused on 15 May) and made intemperate threats about 'exterminating the slanderers'. This did nothing to defuse the coming trial of strength between sections and municipality. The Convention section, located in a merchant quarter, undoubtedly spoke for many others when it denounced the agitators who demanded a 'tribunal of blood' and who spoke of 'despoiling the proprietors'. Chalier, in turn, demanded the arrest of the officials of the sections after which patriots would 'wash their hands in their blood'. Amid cries for Chalier's arrest, the sections began to express their lack of confidence in the municipality and when the irresolute representatives on mission refused petitions to suspend city government, sections formed a central committee to plan the anti-Jacobin insurrection. The town hall fell to an armed assault on 29 May. Arrests of prominent Jacobins followed and a provisional municipality composed, among others, of two merchants, a landowner and a printer-journalist, assumed power although the *éminence grise* of the sections remained the royalist lawyer Fréminville. While protesting their loyalty to the Republic and the Convention, the insurgents sent off commissioners to Bordeaux and Marseille 'to fraternize with them so that the Holy Coalition of the *gens de bien* could overawe the horde which wishes to exist only by pillage and . . . blood'.

The *gens de bien* triumphed at Marseille for similar reasons and in similar ways. The continuing economic crisis, the collapse of shipping, the high price of bread (double that of Paris, even with subsidies), the widespread belief that the government was neglecting the needs of the fleet at Toulon and the pervasive fear of royalist plots were the local variants of the crisis of the spring of 1793. They evoked an identical response: authorities and the club instituted a revolutionary tribunal, tried to raise conscripts, levied forced loans and revolutionary taxes on the rich, disarmed all manner of suspect people and formed a special army of *sans-culottes*. The sections had no objection to these measures in themselves but the club's general behaviour did much to alienate the support of ordinary people both within the city and without. It denounced indiscriminately any manifestation of wealth, it pretended to be the arbiter of everyone's revolutionary pedigree and it sponsored practically lawless punitive expeditions to any real or imagined royalist disturbance within reach – in one of them, two people were hanged at Auriol and a 4000 *livres* tax imposed on the unfortunate village. There was also a general atmosphere of rising lawlessness, exemplified by the five separate prison massacres which occurred at Aix in February. It was easy to blame the club for all of this. Finally, its influence over all levels of local administration, its sponsorship of a quite illegal central committee of the revolutionary committees of the sections and the support it received from the representatives on mission widened the split with the sections. By the end of April, some Jacobins had split off and led denunciations of 'anarchy', 'despotism' and the 'men of blood'. Some sections were questioning the need of terrorist measures at all or even the legality of the club's existence. The sections also defied the representatives' order to dissolve their Popular Tribunal until it had condemned to death two of the most extravagant 'anarchists'. On 18–19 May, the most prominent Jacobins were arrested while the club itself was closed two weeks later. The collapse of the Jacobins was greeted with profound relief by groups well beyond the small circle of rich men whom the Convention affected to believe were behind the revolt. As at Lyon, the Jacobins had denounced too many people, rigged too many elections, defied public opinion too often and put out of business too many employers upon whom many ordinary people depended for a living. Federalism was popular because it seemed to be a way of stopping a cabal of uncontrollable fanatics. Thus the Jacobins' self-definition as an exclusive band of revolutionary saints hardly enhanced their appeal. But not all the Jacobins were mentally unbalanced extremists like Chalier. Most had come to the belief in an uncompromising and pitiless defence of the Republic because of the unfolding of local politics. It is surely no coincidence that extreme Jacobinism emerged close to those parts of the Midi where the counterrevolution had long been active. Lyon had been a focus of counterrevolutionary designs since mid-1790 and the inability or unwillingness of local or national authorities to control the activities of nobles and priests was a constant source of complaint. Further south, the struggles in Avignon and Arles, the risings in the Lozère and Ardèche and the appalling sectarian strife in and around the Protestant areas made the struggle against counterrevolution a more or less constant reality. One can only speculate why Jacobinism in the west was never so extreme, but here the enemy was comparatively poorly armed and easier to define as the refractory priests and their followers. The tragedy of Jacobinism in the Midi in 1793, and nationally a year later, was that it drove many ordinary people in directions they obviously did not want to go.

The Montagnards were not entirely wrong in seeing their opponents as representative of wealthy and privileged men, but they were not entirely right either, for disquieting numbers of more humble elements were federalist as well. Thus at Marseille, just over half the members of the Jacobin club and nearly three quarters of the victims of the federalists were artisans, shopkeepers or wage-earners. Yet, more than 50 per cent of those accused of federalism were also working people while over one third were officials, 'bourgeois' or wholesalers. This certainly suggests an overrepresentation in federalism of the better-off groups relative to the population as a whole, but the extent of popular support was so large that it could not be ignored. The same phenomenon occurred at Lyon. Although the social composition of the Central Club is not well known (the leaders were almost all in the professions, however), that of the federalists has been carefully examined. Of those who held sectional office during the siege, nearly three quarters were bourgeois of one sort or another. The merchants, officials, rentiers, professionals and clerks were clearly committed to the anti-Jacobin offensive. But so, too, were many working people. Over a third of the officer corps of the Lyon army was composed of artisans, shopkeepers and even silk weavers, and proportions among the ranks were even higher. If the examples of Marseille and Lyon are typical, federalism broke, or rather realigned, the revolutionary coalition of politically committed bourgeois and urban artisans in ways that were quite different from those where federalist revolts did not occur, ways which are still poorly understood.

The Purge of the Girondins

One of the most important elements in federalism was the widespread refusal to make the sacrifices the Convention demanded after the crisis broke in March. The crisis also led in another direction: to the purging of the Girondins from the Convention.

Large currents of opinion among the Jacobins, Cordeliers and militants in Paris felt the Convention had to be cleansed but, initially, few felt this had to be done by force. The so-called 'insurrection' of 9–10 March which tried to expel the 'traitors' got no support from the Jacobins, the Cordeliers and the commune, let alone from within the Convention. Instead, Varlet, Fournier l'Américain and a few other obscure agitators tried to take advantage of the first reports of the defeats in Belgium to spark a rebellion whose purpose was the punishment of traitorous generals, perfidious ministers and the elimination of the deputies who voted for 'the life of the tyrant and the appeal to the people'. Aside from arousing a single section which hurriedly retracted and a few hundred soldiers and some remaining fédérés and inciting them to smash the presses of Gorsas's and Brissot's newspapers, the attempt got nowhere as soon as Santerre mobilized the National Guard. But the abortive *journée* was significant in that it showed that radical opinion was convinced that the Girondins shared some responsibility for the March crisis and so should be removed from the Convention. After all, the reasoning went, since a free people was invincible, only treason could defeat it. Thus the Girondins and their friends in the ministry became victims of the doctrine of the internal enemy, as others had in earlier crises.

Other sectors of radical opinion agreed with the analysis but not the solution. Before the federalists overthrew them, for example, the Jacobins, sections, clubs and municipality of Marseille, always ahead of everyone else in the nation, were among the first to demand the recall of the *appelants*. As soon as news of Dumouriez's treason filtered to an increasingly panicky opinion, section after section demanded that his accomplices, whoever they were, be tried, that traitors, wherever they were, be punished. Sometimes the conspirators were named but no one could agree on who all of them were, even though everyone was sure that the disasters had to be someone's responsibility. The movement reached a climax on 15 April when the commune and thirty-five sections added various lists of deputies who would be recalled as soon as a majority of departments agreed. Dumouriez's treason also convinced the Jacobins that a purge was needed. At the club, Augustin Robespierre invited the sections to force the Convention to arrest the 'unfaithful' deputies, while Maximilien made two speeches in the Convention linking the Girondins with the rising in the Vendée and with Dumouriez's treason. This probably convinced only those who wanted to be convinced since both he and Marat had made laudatory speeches in Dumouriez's favour a month before and the Girondins were able to score a number of hits against Danton's mysterious business deals while on mission in Belgium.

The Jacobins, sections and commune clearly hoped the *appelants* could be expelled peacefully either by a vote in the Convention or by persuading their constituents to recall them. The Girondin response made this impossible. As part of the recall campaign, the Jacobins sent out a violently worded circular to the sister societies which Marat had signed as temporary president of the club. The Girondins persuaded the Convention to lift his immunity and send him before the Revolutionary Tribunal. As an attempt to defend themselves and intimidate the Jacobins, the move was a failure since Marat was acquitted, although the incident is interesting since it showed once again that no one was above using exceptional measures and institutions for partisan purposes. A more direct attack came with the formation of a Commission of Twelve which was supposed to investigate the situation of the commune and sections. This was composed almost entirely of moderates who immediately ordered the arrest of Varlet, Hébert, the popular journalist and member of the commune, and some section leaders. But the commune had its own defences. Since early April, municipal authorities had been meeting with commissioners of the sections to discuss problems of recruitment and taxes and these meetings became more or less regular from mid-May. Thus was born the *Comité de l'Evêché* which soon acquired an existence of its own and whose executive committee, composed of obscure radicals, planned the *journées* of 31 May–2 June.

Ever since the failed insurrection of 9–10 March, there had been talk from hotheads of taking violent measures against the *appelants* although nothing was done until the Commission of Twelve ordered the arrests of popular leaders. While relays of sections protested against this at the bar of the Convention, the Committee convoked a meeting of electors and militants on 28 May which decided on the necessity of a rising. On the 30th and 31st delegates from twenty-eight sections declared Paris in a state of insurrection, fused with municipal authorities to become the Central Revolutionary Committee, named Hanriot, a customs clerk, to replace Santerre who had gone off to the Vendée, as commander of the National Guard and decided to raise an army of 20,000 *sans-culottes*. Yet on the 31st, the Convention treated the petition demanding the arrest of the Girondins the way it had all the others by passing it to the Committee of Public Safety. The Central Revolutionary Committee was not to be duped, however, and on Sunday 2 June, surrounded the Convention with Hanriot's troops and forced it to decree the arrest of twenty-nine deputies and two ministers.

Like all the Parisian *journées*, the 31 May–2 June was a military affair in which the balance of force was decisive. Like 10 August too, it was an affair in which the leading Jacobins played a secondary role. Although the Montagnards probably had some idea of what the *Comité de l'Evêché* was doing and possibly even attended some meetings, they kept their distance. On the eve of the insurrection, Robespierre made a speech of such despairing ambiguity as to disqualify him from any claims of active leadership while Danton was clearly embarrassed throughout the decisive weekend. Legalistic qualms and a realization that the provinces would likely carry out threats to protect the integrity of the Convention which they had repeated the week before explain the hesitations. But from another point of view, the expulsion of the

Girondins was not necessary because the Montagnards generally got what they wanted from the Convention. The Girondins had only been able to reverse this situation in unusual circumstances. Only 312 were present to vote on the impeachment of Marat. Although 507 voted on the reinstatement of the Commission of Twelve, the motion passed by only 41 votes. Some of these men must have voted for the exceptional legislation earlier so that in their minds taking measures to defend the Republic did not require protecting rabble-rousers like Varlet and Hébert. In any case, this vote was something of a fluke since on the major issues since the king's trial, the Girondins had been in a minority. The exceptional pieces of legislation supported by Montagnard speakers rallied sufficient votes, even when the Girondins opposed them, which did not happen in every case. That the special repressive and economic legislation passed after the March crisis was not significantly altered until the following August–mid-September also suggests that there was no pent-up Montagnard frustration which could only be released by calling on outside support.

Of course, the Girondins were victims of their own moderation even if the Montagnards railed uselessly against it. This can be dated from the previous summer when some of them tried to stifle the insurrection against the monarchy and when they subsequently undertook a series of demagogic attacks on Paris. Their endorsement of a referendum on the king's fate reinforced popular suspicion against them. By appearing to try to save the king, the *appelants* became victims of a mentality which had been present from the beginning of the Revolution, a mentality in which internal conspiracies were the major explanation of the nation's troubles. Once the early reverses in Belgium were known, considerations of this sort lay behind the demands from the sections both for a purge and the Revolutionary Tribunal. As civil war and treason deepened the crisis, the movement acquired more consistency, involving the Jacobins and the commune both of whom joined the movement after it had begun.

The purge meant little in terms of social policy, which again suggests that the notion that the handful of Girondins represented the interests of a conservative bourgeoisie resisting popular government is either untrue or irrelevant. The commune, the sections and the National Guard were able to impose some concessions on the Montagnards who were themselves reluctant to implement them. The Convention decreed the arrest of suspects but never defined a suspect so the decree got nowhere. It voted the establishment in principle of a revolutionary army but was able to profit from differences of opinion among the *sans-culottes* themselves over the desirability of this institution to do nothing. It also voted the sale of émigré property in small lots but local authorities were too preoccupied with other affairs to do much about this. The decision to permit villages to divide their common lands at their initiative was discussed before the purge to no one's great objection. Everyone agreed with the now common argument that extending ownership as widely as possible was in the Republic's interest, although in practice it tended to set poorer villagers against their neighbours. In any case it was not relevant to the *sans-culottes*. The law of 17 July which abolished feudalism outright without compensation irrespective of titles was scarcely even relevant to the peasants, although it did give legal recognition to existing practice. In all, the social consequences of 31 May–2 June were meagre. Part of the reason was that the Jacobins were preoccupied with the federalist rebellion.

The Crisis Generalized

Many departmental officials had long expressed their dismay, often fuelled by the reports of their own deputies, at the apparent influence of Paris over the Convention and at the favourable financial subsidies the commune received merely by threatening insurrection. Addresses viewing Parisians as savage *septembriseurs* and threats to form departmental armies to protect the deputies from them had been common since the Convention first met. As the atmosphere in the capital deteriorated, several departments began to take action. They had already become accustomed to taking independent actions and, like the anti-Jacobin movements in the Midi, had no objection to exceptional measures as such. Thus the federalist department of the Calvados approved of the maximum, the tax on the rich and the Revolutionary Tribunal, the Orne set up its own Committees of Public Safety in March with extensive powers over suspects and domiciliary visits while the Loire-Inférieure applied the laws on émigrés to the Vendean rebels to expedite their trials. Departments in the west had long been used to taking their own initiatives against refractory priests and one suspects the Convention would not have objected to the police measures they took in the spring. Other independent steps were more ambiguous. The Calvados tolerated the formation of a semi-official army which some administrators joined. In March, the Jura sponsored directly a special corps of volunteers from each district. So long as these semiofficial forces were to be used in the war effort, no one could object but they also gave the departments involved in forming them a certain leverage in domestic politics. From the Montagnard point of view, it was even more objectionable when several departments adhered to the project of convoking a new Convention at Bourges. Thus, as in Bordeaux, Lyon and Marseille, the anti-Montagnard movement preceded the fall of the Girondins. Yet the 31 May–2 June gave these movements a national significance they might not otherwise have had: firstly because the Paris rising broke the chain of legality and the federalists were able to make great propaganda by claiming they would adhere to all laws passed by the Convention up to the end of May, although practice proved to be considerably different; and secondly, because the fall of the Girondins widened the movement. Some sixty departments and a number of clubs protested against the expulsions but the movement rarely acquired any consistency, fragmenting in a shower of retractions and very often disintegrating in the face of local hostility or indifference. Federalism in the western and eastern departments proved to be a pathetic affair. Despite the inspiration provided by the presence at Caen of a number of Girondin deputies – Barbaroux, Pétion, Buzot and Salle, among others – and despite securing General Wimpffen, commander of the Army of the Coasts of Cherbourg, as leader, a tiny army of Normans and Bretons under the Comte Joseph de Puisaye panicked when an equally poorly equipped 'Montagnard' army fired a few cannonades into the trees by their encampment at Brécourt near Pacy-sur-Eure on 13 July. Similarly the National Guards of Dôle easily defeated the departmental army of the Jura at Tassenières on 2 August in a farcical skirmish. A tiny army from Bordeaux disintegrated a mere fifty kilometres from its home base. In fact, the federalist leaders were remarkably naive. The Breton and Norman departments were indulging themselves if they believed they could raise armies which they were in no position to finance or equip when the levy of 300,000 men had gone so badly throughout the west. Other departments quickly dissociated themselves. Sarthe refused to join because of quite understandable fears of exposing themselves to a Vendean invasion, while Manche and Seine-Inférieure were appalled by the federalists' arrest of the deputies on mission, Romme and Prieur de la Côte-d'Or. The authorities in the Orne found themselves quite isolated when an assembly of local authorities showed itself much more interested in petitioning the Convention to abolish the maximum than in undertaking hopeless expeditions to the capital. Departmental authorities in the Eure also got practically no support from lower administrators. The federalists in the Jura did much to undermine the moral authority of their case when they ignored the sacking of the club at Lons-le-Saunier and the mugging of leading Jacobins by one hundred specially outfitted gendarmes, part of the department's volunteer forces known as the 'plumets rouges'. The federalist Popular Commission in Bordeaux showed its own partisan conception of legality when it held the representatives on mission under virtual house arrest and seized monies in the local mint.

The federalists' incompetent leadership, the lacklustre military performance and their dwindling and patchy support gave the Convention an opportunity to seize the initiative. The publication of a constitution in June did much to undermine the federalists' position because it announced the Convention's adherence to a regime of law. The clauses of the Constitution of 1793 and the circumstances of its acceptance mattered less than the invitation it contained to rally to the Convention. The limitations on property rights, recognition of the right to work and subsistence and the right of referendum were hardly compatible with the federalists' conception of government. The Constitution was also approved by an overwhelming majority (with the usual dismal turnout) in a hastily organized referendum but was immediately shelved for the duration of the war and was never, in fact, applied. Nonetheless, the Constitution was popular even in some federalist areas and in Marseille, for example, people were punished for expressing approval of it. The Constitution thus added another fissure to the already rickety federalist apparatus. The Convention also intimidated federalist authorities into surrender. On 27 July, it gave them three days to retract and when they did, as at Caen and Alençon, the pacification which followed was reasonable and selective. Where there were hesitations or flickering defiance, as at Bordeaux or Lons-le-Saunier, repression was more severe but, even so, fairly restrained, because the representatives on mission realized that federalism had had limited popular support.

The rebellion continued, however. In Lyon, there were further arrests of Jacobins and the federalists threw down the gauntlet by executing Chalier, who immediately became a popular martyr. There were over a dozen similar executions at Marseille and authorities opened negotiations with Lord Hood, commander of the British fleet, with a view to guaranteeing the free passage of food supplies. The General Committee of Toulon, which was dominated by the pre-revolutionary merchant oligarchy, set up its own tribunal which condemned some thirty dock workers and artisans convicted for participation in the local massacres of the previous year. But the General Committee in Toulon went much further than it had originally anticipated because of the desperate subsistence crisis. The representatives Fréron and Barras cut off food supplies from the land and attempted to break the lifeline by sea from Genoa and Leghorn. The Toulon authorities vainly raised the price of bread by 25 per cent, issued ration cards and began negotiations with the British to assure supplies. Hood demanded they proclaim the monarchy and so, in return for rations of sea-biscuits, the federalists recognized Louis XVII. On 27–28 August, British and Spanish troops entered the town and the Mediterranean fleet fell into allied hands.

But it did not take Toulon's treason or the appointment of the royalist Comte de Précy and the émigré Villeneuve as commanders of the Lyon and Marseille armies to render federalism counterrevolutionary in the eyes of the Convention. Because of the running sore of the Vendée and further deterioration on the frontiers, continued defiance could only be interpreted as treason. Despite occasional victories, the war in the Vendée was going badly. In May, the Vendeans took Bressuire, Thouars and Parthenay in the Deux-Sèvres and Fontenay in the Vendée. The royalists also acquired a greater consistency by forming a general council, and in June they took Saumur and Machecoul. This forced the evacuation of Angers, and on 24 June the Vendeans moved on Nantes. The siege was short-lived and royalists lost their general-in-chief, Cathelineau, but, even so, they destroyed General Westermann's army at Châtillon. Worse still, the republicans had fallen out among themselves with the representatives on mission quarrelling among themselves and launching extravagant denunciations of the generals who naturally replied in kind. By the autumn, the war in the Vendée would be carried to the floor of the Convention and several deputies would be its victims.

Meanwhile, the nightmare of a second Vendée in the south was being realized. In the Ariège at the end of August an attempt to round up deserters provoked a rising of six hundred people who roamed the countryside around Pamiers shouting that everyone had to declare for the Spanish and to kill or disarm the democrats and the Protestants. Or they simply cried out, 'This won't go on any longer! ['Ça n'ira pas!'] Down with the nation! Long live Louis XVII whom we are going to put on the throne!' The National Guard of Mirepoix soon brought the situation under control. In the Lozère, the notary and former Constituent, Charrier, and the Allier brothers, who had been involved in Froment's conspiracies, formed a 'Christian Army of the Midi' which took Marvéjols and Mende in May. Significantly, the people of both towns welcomed the small army of fifteen hundred rebels but they were soon dispersed by the timely arrival of the National Guards from several neighbouring departments and Charrier was guillotined in July. Despite this, troubles in the Lozère continued for the rest of the year. However insignificant these risings, there could be no doubt that popular royalism was spreading.

This coincided with disaster on the frontiers. After Dumouriez's treason, the Austrians crossed the frontier and laid siege to the fortresses of Condé and Valenciennes while the Prussians surrounded a French army at Mainz. The sieges might have lasted for some time but the offensive of the Vendeans in June forced the government to transfer troops to the west so that one fort after the other fell to the allies in July, amid the usual cries in Paris that the generals were traitors. Further south, the Sardinians were poised to attack Nice and the Spanish were crossing the Pyrenees.

As was predictable, the expulsion of the Girondins did nothing to contribute to the war effort. To try to reduce the number of its enemies, the government adopted a conciliatory line towards the foreign powers. As early as April, Danton persuaded the Convention virtually to negate its offer of 'fraternité et secours' to oppressed peoples. He undertook negotiations with some of the smaller states and tried to split Britain and Prussia from Austria. These moves failed because the allies were convinced of the Republic's imminent collapse. The only alternative was to fight on and the Convention showed it recognized this by putting Robespierre on the Committee of Public Safety on 27 July. On the eve of the fall of the Girondins he had written of the necessity of a single will, by which he meant not a personal dictatorship, but a rallying point for national energies. He had also come to see the bourgeois as the great enemy. Other Jacobins had come to similar conclusions. The Terror was about to be applied in earnest.

Yet the circumstances of that terrible summer of 1793 ensured that it would be difficult to control the application of the Terror. There was no single will and little agreement about how the Republic was to be saved. There was an equal ambiguity about the use of the instruments of repression. So long as they were used against an identifiable enemy, whether that was a foreign army or a refractory priest, the Terror could be conceived as a series of police measures. The federalist and Vendean revolts changed this in several ways. As convinced democrats, the Jacobins had always expressed sympathy with popular economic problems, even if they remained as hostile as they had always been to insurrection as a solution. Federalism and the Vendée convinced them of what the extremists had been saying for a long time that only 'the people' could save the Revolution and that 'the rich' were the enemy. Allying with the *sans-culottes* was both necessary and desirable. The tragedy of 1793 was that it dragged many ordinary people into the federalist and counterrevolutionary armies so that it was impossible to tell who the enemies really were. The lesson was only confirmed by the murder of Marat, in his medicinal bath, by Charlotte Corday, a noble and friend of the Caen federalists, on 13 July. If treason and assassins were everywhere, moderation was counterrevolutionary and unremitting suspicion and vigilance were patriotic duties.

Chapter 6

Terror and Dictatorship

Terrorists

'A man will never be free so long as he believes that his and his family's existence depend on the caprice of another man', proclaimed the *Instruction* of the *Commission Temporaire* of Lyon. Soboul called this a manifesto of the *sans-culottes* and from it can be derived most of the basic aspirations of the urban working people of the Terror. Thus, in contrast to the Jacobins who believed in representative institutions, the *sans-culottes* believed in the direct and daily practice of popular sovereignty. In the course of their struggles, the section militants, drawing on their political education in 1790, hedged representative institutions of all levels with such checks as the popular initiative, referendum and recall of deputies and the right to bear arms. The people could choose to exercise their sovereignty at any time by withdrawing their mandates from representatives and by dictating their wishes to deputies through petitions and demonstrations, or by choosing to exercise justice and its punishments whenever and wherever necessary. The experience of the Revolution taught the *sans-culottes* that no popular leader could be trusted entirely, and should representatives betray the people the ultimate resort was the right of insurrection, which could mean anything from an armed attack, as on 10 August, to mass demonstrations as on 2 June and 5 September. Again, as experience showed, the people could be easily duped and so instruction, both through formal schooling and self-education, was vital. Their fierce anticlericalism derived in part from a constantly reiterated theme that priests had spent centuries inculcating a set of beliefs which permitted the aristocrats and the rich to usurp the wealth created by ordinary people. An awareness of one's rights, the willingness to exercise them, and the requirement to effect a revolution in one's conscience and morals were therefore part of the struggle against oppressors. Yet for all the strict egalitarianism, the *sans-culottes* remained attached to a society of small property-holders.

Economic and social dependence was the enemy, the right to a decent existence and a modest comfort was the aspiration. The ideal could mean many things in practice: depriving the countryside of its 'surplus' in order to feed the towns because the fruits of the earth belonged ultimately to the entire community; revolutionary taxes on the rich, not only to finance the war which the greed of the rich had provoked in the first place, but to deprive them of their most ostentatious possessions; an organized system of public relief; measures to reduce the scandalous gap between rich and poor and measures to put produce of first necessity within the reach of everyone, were all aspects of their social ideas. All of this would take place within the context of ceaseless struggle. As the *Instruction* put it, 'So long as there is an unhappy being on the face of the earth, there will still be great strides to make in the conquest of liberty.'

If the stirring idealism of the *Instruction* illustrates much of the radical thinking of the entire Revolution, so too is there a lesson in the social background of its authors. Of the thirteen people who signed it whose occupations are known, only one, who worked in the highly skilled trade of joinery, worked with his hands. Among the others there were three 'men of law', two former priests and two clerks, these latter two having worked in the hated tax adminstration of the Old Regime. Indeed, it is an error to equate the *sans-culottes* or the terrorists with working people, simple artisans, the poor or even the relatively deprived. Of 293 known terrorists at Toulouse, for example, 90 were merchants or in the liberal professions and 133 were artisans, the majority of them masters and small employers. Not only did most of these people own their own houses, 73 per cent of the Jacobin leaders could be classed as 'well off'. Similarly at Montbrison in the Loire, medium-sized fortunes predominated among the terrorists while the wealthier members of the club who could more easily spare the time, staffed the leading terrorist institutions of the revolutionary army and the municipality. A more general study of the Jacobin clubs in over a dozen towns and cities shows that the average member after 1792 paid over one third more in taxes than non-members and that the handful of men labelled 'terrorists' later on, paid nearly double the taxes of the average male. There were, of course, many working people among the *sans-culottes*, as in the revolutionary committees of Paris two thirds of whose members were either artisans working on their own or who also owned a small shop. But the examples of the *Commission Temporaire* and the provincial Jacobins and terrorists show the immense diversity within *sans-culotterie*, that even if it was a popular movement, there were many honorary members who often described themselves in more humble terms than their social position actually justified and that many of them were by no means as destitute as their own self-image would suggest. From what fragmentary information there is, many, undoubtedly a majority on the section committees, were literate which, in an age where parents usually had to sacrifice the labour of their children to send them to school, is almost as good an indicator of social standing as occupation or wealth. The *sans-culottes*, in other words, were a heterogeneous social group, who were often the elite of their neighbourhoods and trades. Nor were they necessarily new men. In the Luxembourg section of Paris, for example, eleven of the eighteen who served on the revolutionary committee paid the equivalent of ten days' labour in taxes in 1791 which put them in the top quarter of the population of the city, and although the section's fraternal society witnessed a significant influx of new members from more humble social groups in the course of 1793, the club's officers had long been active members. A similar phenomenon – enlargement and plebeianization of membership which did not, however, overwhelm the more established professional and better-off artisan members – occurred in the provincial Jacobin clubs. In other words, the terrorists of 1793–4 were sometimes new men recruited from below but, depending on the time and place, were as likely to be the men who had been active in local politics since 1790.

Because of the tremendous efforts their ideology demanded, the *sans-culottes*, or the Jacobins for that matter, were a minority. One estimate puts the number of Jacobin clubs at about three thousand, which even if it is a gross underestimate suggests that there was less than one club for every ten communes. They were very unevenly distributed. In the southeast usually over half the communes of the plains, river valleys and coasts had a club (at least on paper: one rural club rarely met even at the height of the Terror because of lack of news to discuss) while they were a good deal more rare in the rugged mountains or where the religious issue had already alienated opinion. The size of the membership is unknown but rarely exceeded a few hundred even in the large cities. The same dominance by a political elite was evident in Paris. There in the referendum on the Constitution of 1793, it was rare indeed for even one quarter of the population of a section to vote. In the June election, which amounted to a confirmation of Hanriot's position as commander of the National Guard, only 15,000 voted out of an electorate of approximately 165,000. Since Hanriot won by some three thousand votes, an election marked by massive malpractice showed the existence of a smaller minority of moderates whose expulsion from the sections, often through a few well-aimed chairs and fists, was only completed in September. Attendance at section assemblies was no better. Before and after the abolition of the distinction between active and passive citizens, it was rare for the turnout to elections for sectional office to exceed 10 per cent.

Being a militant required immense sacrifices of time and energy. Some of these efforts had to be directed at organizing the less active or less interested. How this was done illustrates much of the mechanics of organizing demonstrations or insurrections. Contrary to the myth which the militants themselves liked to propagate, one did not simply launch the call to arms or announce that 'the people' had 'risen' or was 'in insurrection'. Rather, if the three sections of the faubourg Saint-Antoine were typical, an insurrectionary movement depended on a handful of men, of mature years, owners of medium-sized firms in the furniture, building and textile trades, long established in the city, who already had family, commercial and credit relations with lesser master artisans and their workers. The visceral hatred of such men for big financiers, bankers and bureaucrats was quite compatible with ideas of economic equality which never went much beyond demands for limitations on 'excessive' wealth and actions against hoarders and monopolists in town or country. But just as their ideas were shaped by their social position, so the scope of their political action was limited. Power which operated through preexisting familial and corporate hierarchies in neighbourhoods was limited to the section and even a handful of them could only with difficulty influence the others. Thus, when Roux presented an address which is often taken as typical of much of *sans-culotte* thinking to the Convention on 25 June, he gained the support of only one section besides his own and even then he was quickly disavowed by both. A natural fractiousness apart, the sections had no coordinating body outside the commune and the experience of the failed insurrection of 10 March 1793 and events down to the expulsion of the Girondins showed how difficult it was to create a body which could substitute for it. Only the commune was really capable of taking the military and political steps necessary to organize an effective demonstration. But, in the end, neither commune nor sections could dictate to the Convention because, even in the chaotic days of the summer of 1793, the politicians retained enough authority to channel the militants. An examination of how and why economic controls were reinforced illustrates the limitations of popular pressure, and the experience of the controls themselves shows how even the Convention was constrained to take account of the social structure of an overwhelmingly agricultural country.

War and the Economy of Terror

Although it considered the first maximum a temporary measure, circumstances drew the Convention further and further towards a controlled economy. The law of 4 May had never worked well. Since prices were set by departments on the basis of local averages, those who set their prices high or those who only made a show of enforcing the law drew supplies from departments where the law was rigorously applied. This set one department against another, as when the Pas-de-Calais tried to prevent its grain from being shipped to the Nord. Several departments around Paris did much the same either refusing to ship the grain or showing the utmost bad faith in dealing with the commune's grain commissioners. Requisitions for the towns set off panics or even riots in the countryside while a census of existing stocks had to depend upon the dubious good will of the village notables. Naturally enough, grain dealers or peasants with a surplus were extremely reluctant to bring grain to controlled markets when they could do better elsewhere. The civil war also contributed to shortages in the cities, particularly in Paris where federalism in Normandy rendered shipments along the Seine valley precarious.

Attempts to deal with this situation were only partially successful. The Convention finally conceded a law on hoarding on 26 July, after a long campaign which had begun in the spring. The law established special commissioners ('commissaires aux accaparements') with extensive powers to examine merchants' books and verify stocks. These men became essential cogs in the controlled economy later on, but initially the law probably did more harm than good. It recognized no difference between hoarding and stocking, was applicable to a whole range of products including many whose prices were uncontrolled and recognized only the death penalty for violators. Juries were understandably reluctant to convict. Some panicky retailers sold their entire inventory as quickly as they could and did not restock, which in turn threatened to drive wholesalers out of business. Thus the law against hoarding which the *sans-culottes* were convinced would bring to light a whole range of hidden supplies actually contributed to aggravating shortages.

This was only one of several pressures which drove the state into filling the void. At first, this happened at the municipal level. Many towns had subsidized bread prices out of their own revenues, from grants, public subscriptions and even from the pockets of the councillors themselves. But as inflation wreaked havoc with the market mechanism, they took more drastic steps. As early as August 1792, the Department of the Haute-Garonne established a 'subsistence bureau' in Toulouse which had the power to discourage speculators, to require dealers to sell, to forbid 'exports' and to sign special contracts with food commissioners who scoured Upper Languedoc for supplies. The economic ideas of the bureau were entirely subordinated to the interests of Toulouse: they lectured surrounding communes on the virtues of free circulation while maintaining the most rigorous controls within the city. These men welcomed the new maximum laws of September because they would assure lower prices and guarantee supplies. Much the same occurred at Bordeaux. The federalists repudiated the maximum because it hampered supplies, but since the situation did not improve they instituted a system of domiciliary visits and requisitions. After the Montagnard reconquest of the city, authorities rationed grain to bakers who, if they managed to acquire their own on the market, had to record their transactions in special registers. The maximum was also unpopular at Marseille, but when fifteen local bakers went bankrupt in the spring the municipality opened four ovens of its own. After the collapse of federalism, the food commissioners of the city's subsistence bureau on mission in Languedoc were obliged to buy grain well above the controlled price and pay for one third of it in hard cash. Authorities also had to compete with the military in traditional sources of supply, so that they welcomed greater government control in September as a way of easing their difficulties.

Both Montagnard and federalist authorities, then, responded to the subsistence crisis less by a sense of class interest than by the

imperatives of regional and urban interests. State control of the
economy was popular all the same. All those who had rioted in the
spring and autumn of 1792 were animated by an implicit hostility
to the logic of the free market, notions which increasingly saw the
controlled economy as a way of correcting social inequality and
consolidating the Republic. Nor was this entirely a movement of
urban consumers. In the winter and spring around Compiègne, for
example, rural municipalities, acting under the pressure of
labourers and poor artisans, established illegal markets where
farmers were forced to sell their produce at fixed prices and, in a
practice the revolutionary armies were to make common later on,
the inhabitants of one small market town forayed out to the
countryside to force farmers to bring grain to their market. In the
Calvados, locals beat up bakers from Vire who tried to provision
themselves on 'their' markets. With large towns exercising their
own pressures on their hinterlands and villages attempting to resist
or impose their own solutions upon farmers and bakers and with
departments eyeing each other suspiciously, the country was sliding
into an economic federalism every bit as dangerous as the political.
One either had to return to a free market, with few guarantees it
would solve the problem of subsistence, or exercise greater central
control.

Pressure from the streets in Paris also helped propel the
government in this direction. In May, the actress Claire Lacombe's
society of revolutionary women, the *Républicaines révolutionnaires*, demonstrated before the Jacobins to demand harsh
measures against 'the mercantile aristocracy', a cry which Roux
revived after 2 June. The movement culminated on 25 June when
Roux led a delegation of his own, another section and the
Cordeliers to the Convention to condemn the politicians for doing
nothing for the poor and to criticize the Constitution for not
prescribing the death penalty for hoarders. The Convention
eventually voted the law on hoarding after a long press campaign
but such talk was extremely dangerous, for not only did Roux's
insolent language undermine Montagnard attempts to use the
Constitution to acquire a patina of legitimacy against the
federalists, it clearly had a resonance among the *sans-culottes* of
Paris. With all the difficulties surrounding the supply of the capital
and in the agonizing wait for the new harvest to come in, bread
queues were forming again. There were complaints of shortages
and high prices of uncontrolled goods, and on the very day Roux

spoke a series of disturbances broke out in the streets and along the docks of the Seine in which crowds of washerwomen stopped shipments of soap and sold them at 'fair' prices.

After a vicious campaign by the commune and Hébert and Marat in their newspapers, Roux was dismissed as editor of the commune's news sheet. The Cordeliers club and Bonne-Nouvelle and Gravilliers sections were persuaded to disown him. Nonetheless, the problem which Roux posed remained. One or two sections began to issue ration cards and instituted public bakeries. A particularly dry summer hampered milling and grain shipments by water and ruined the vegetable crop in the environs of Paris, while the wine harvest in Burgundy and Touraine was poor for the sixth year in a row. It will probably never be possible to measure the success of the grain harvest itself. Journalists and politicians insisted it was abundant while local authorities claimed it was poor. Each had obvious interests and policies to defend and the most extensive harvest survey of the century cannot be trusted because the peasants feared it was only a prelude to requisitions. But the expedients authorities were forced to take the following spring would suggest the harvest was at best average and possibly worse. As the situation became more acute, section militants proposed that the districts throughout the country impose price-ceilings, take inventories of stocks, impose sales or even that the state manage stocks and distribution. By August, there were similar proposals in the Jacobin club which petitioned for a uniform price for bread and a 'general measure' regarding other necessities on the 20th. Hébert, though he still detested Roux, became a convert and lent all the crude language of the *Père Duchesne* to the movement. The justification that the right to grow food was a trust and property rights were subordinate to the overriding claims of the community had been heard in the Cordeliers in 1790 and during the similar crisis of the spring of 1792 but the solutions proposed were now more concrete. The Convention also gave in but only after a final push.

Popular orators and journalists in the summer of 1793 tended to emphasize the problem of hoarding rather than a maximum – Roux in his famous speech of 25 June clearly had monopolists and currency speculators in mind and never once demanded price controls – a successful policy against 'the mercantile and bourgeois aristocracy' after all would render the maximum unnecessary. But the war crisis and the measures taken to solve it required state

tutelage of the entire economy. With Danton's peace initiatives a
failure, conciliation with the federalists only a partial success, with
progressive defeats in the Vendée and along the frontiers and
spurred on by Marat's campaign (continued by Hébert and Roux
after his death) against 'endormeurs' on the Committee of Public
Safety, the Convention itself became caught up in the war fever. In
late July and early August, it passed a rapid series of measures:
impeachment of the Girondins remaining in Paris and outlawry for
those involved in the federalist revolt, a vague law against suspects
and a declaration that Pitt was 'the enemy of the human race'.
Following a report by Barère on behalf of the Committee of Public
Safety, it declared that the Vendée would be systematically
devastated, and ordered Marie-Antoinette to the Revolutionary
Tribunal and the demolition of the royal tombs at Saint-Denis.
Some of these measures had been anticipated by the militants but
just because the demand preceded their enaction does not mean
that the Convention was always forced to take measures it
regretted. It never gave in to demands for the arrest of the
appelants, for a general purge of nobles and priests from the armed
forces and the civilian administrations, and for confiscatory taxes
on the rich. Conversely, it is difficult to see why the Convention
maintained so many measures anticipated by the militants long
after any danger from the streets had passed. This is how the *levée
en masse* should be seen: a measure popular among the *sans-culottes*
but which had an obvious utility in a national crisis. In so far as the
idea has a paternity, it can be traced back curiously enough to the
Brissotins in 1791–2 then to the enthusiasm of the volunteers of
1792 which Danton later articulated, and its principles were revived
by the Montagnard leaders in the spring. Roux demanded a mass
rising to crush interior and exterior enemies on 23 July, a few
section militants followed suit and on 16 August, a deputation
representing all forty-eight sections petitioned for 'a spontaneous
movement of a great people who will throw itself *en masse* on its
enemies to exterminate them'. The militants clearly envisaged a
sort of vast national *journée* which would rid the country of its
enemies at a stroke. No doubt this is why Robespierre dismissed the
idea as useless but the Committee of Public Safety was already
preparing a project which would channel such magnificent energies.
A 'guerre des masses' had been envisaged by the best minds of the
army general staff of the Old Regime and the Committee's military
advisor, General Grimoard, was an enthusiastic supporter. The

Committee recalled Lazarre Carnot and Prieur de la Côte-d'Or, both military engineers, from their missions on 6 August and both became members on the 14th. The *levée en masse* – the draft is in Carnot's hand – was voted on the 23rd.

In principle, it mobilized the entire nation for the war. All bachelors or childless widowers between the ages of eighteen and twenty-five were conscripted, older and married men were to devote themselves to war work, women were to serve in hospitals and make clothing and tents, and old men were to engage in propaganda. Even children could make themselves useful. The entire economy was to be mobilized for the war. As Barère put it, '. . . all the French, both sexes, all ages are called by the nation to defend liberty.'

More than any other measure, the *levée en masse* turned the Committee of Public Safety into a government since it was given the authority to implement the decree. It also required the maximum. Throughout the summer, representatives on mission complained of the peasants' refusal to sell grain at maximum prices and where this was compounded by support for the refractory priests, as it was along the dangerous northern frontiers, requisitions were the only method of supplying the armies. Not even this had worked well as peasants did everything they could to defraud government agents. To return to a free market in such a situation was impossible because with the assignat having fallen to less than 40 per cent of its value by the end of August, the government would have had to finance the feeding of the cities and the equipment of the vast new armies required by the *levée en masse* with a deteriorating currency. The consequent enormous expenditure would have created a situation in which the Revolution would have immolated itself with paper money. The alternative was either punitive taxes on wealth, for which there was no time and little inclination, or a more rigorous application of controls. In other words, the maximum had the financial objective of avoiding bankruptcy and the military one of supplying the armies, both of which were quite compatible with *sans-culotte* concerns about subsistence. Although no one framed the problem this way, it is possible to follow the logic in the debates in the Convention. After an inconclusive discussion at the end of July in which all the grievances against the maximum of 4 May were aired, the Convention took a harder line in favour of controls. On 15 August, it ordered special requisitions for the Paris markets, but since the preamble to the decree made it clear that the motive was one of public order, these would presumably be unnecessary once the harvest was fully gathered. The *levée en masse* made controls permanent. The decree itself authorized public storehouses to be stocked by payments in kind from taxpayers and farmers of *biens nationaux*, the rate, according to Barère's accompanying report, to be calculated on the basis of the maximum. That is, price controls would last as long as the war did. But it took longer for the implications of this to be realized. On 25 August, after a report by Barère, the Executive Council was authorized to requisition for departments threatened with shortages, at the maximum price. An *ad hoc* committee of the Convention recommended allowing local authorities to requisition not only grain but harvest workers and sell grain at a uniform price throughout the country. The deputies accepted this in principle on 3 September. On 11 September, uniform price-ceilings were decreed on grain and flour, and on 29 September the Convention decreed the General Maximum. This limited the price of thirty-nine essential commodities to one third of what they had been in 1790 with transportation costs and wholesale and retail profits added on later, while wages could not exceed one half. In some cases, this meant a reduction in wages, notably for dockyard workers in the naval ports and in Paris so that the maximum on wages was not applied until July 1794 in the capital.

The Convention had thus committed itself to a wholesale reduction in the cost of living, partly as a result of pressure from local authorities and from the *sans-culottes* of Paris, but largely because the solutions to the national emergency drove the deputies to it. The *sans-culottes* could be satisfied but even on so limited a number of products, the general maximum and the maximum on grain were enormously ambitious. The government proposed to regulate an extremely decentralized economy in which almost everyone was a producer or a trader or both, at a time when there was no formal bureaucracy and little administrative expertise for enforcing it. Almost every revolutionary authority had a hand in applying the regulations including representatives on mission, revolutionary committees, revolutionary armies, local subsistence bureaux, municipalities, districts and clubs. Conflicts of the sort which had different representatives on mission requisitioning the same stock of grain, or districts trying to use representatives to avoid fulfilling requisitions to other districts, were inevitable. They were eased considerably once the Subsistence Commission, established on 22 October, made its presence felt. This soon acquired a staff of over five hundred which not only oversaw the coordination of distribution but launched vast enquiries into the production of grain and livestock and attempted to stimulate the draining of marshes, the clearing of wastelands and the search for improved breeds of animals. The intendants of the Old Regime had tried to do the same but no earlier government had worked on so vast and frenetic a scale. The intendants were also grappling with intractable problems of near starvation and public order. The Subsistence Commission and other authorities had a different object: military success. They gave the armies priority over the cities and even in Paris, which was supposed to be treated on the same level as the army, the *commissaires aux accaparements* became little bureaucrats in the vast machinery of military requisitions, focusing less on subsistence problems *per se* than on rounding up useful equipment.

The paradox of the maximum laws is that while everyone complained about them, they worked tolerably well. They said little about qualities and varieties of goods so that there tended to be a deterioration in qualities. There were general accusations that bakers adulterated bread with inferior flour or worse throughout the period, while butchers sold cooked pork which was not controlled rather than raw which was. Attempts to deal with such problems after the revision of the maximum in February produced dozens of printed tables each with microscopic columns containing hundreds of figures – an administrative nightmare both for the ballooning bureaucracy which produced them, as well as for a baffled population which was supposed to verify them in the shops. The difficulty of translating the maximum into the thousands of local weights and measures always offered plenty of scope for cheating. Evasion, black marketeering and bartering were common. Restaurateurs in Paris sent agents into the countryside to buy supplies at prices above the legal limit and communes just outside the gates connived at illegal sales of wood and meat. Even in the city where the maximum on grain was generally respected, meat, eggs, butter and vegetables were constantly sold above it. If housewives complained, the burly market-women of the central markets drove them away empty-handed with a barrage of colourful insults. Thus the maximum divided the common people against each other even before the application of the maximum on wages.

Attempts to deal with these problems drew authorities towards greater public control. At Toulouse, peasants and dealers ceased to bring grain to market in October and the city was fed by requisitions, grants from the Subsistence Commission and what the subsistence bureau could buy on its own account. There were constant alarms about shortages, and at one time agents had to go as far as Toulon to acquire cooking oil and soap. Most cities introduced rationing and public bakeries as a way of handling shortages and limiting fraud. All of this was accompanied by bloodcurdling threats from the militants of what would happen to hoarders and black marketeers and, although the courts punished few offenders, the revolutionary committees did intern a number of people for 'négociantisme'. By such expedients as these, local authorities did manage to keep the urban populations fed. Even Marseille, which was under a constant menace until the spring from the British navy cruising off the coasts, never faced an actual shortage.

But the countryside paid the price even outside the special case of the war zones. Fraud in the cities was as tempting as it was because the maximum set agricultural prices below the cost of production. As controls revived the assignat to nearly 50 per cent of its value in December, the agricultural sector received some compensation but paper money began its final decline in January. To the extent that the overworked districts delayed payment for requisitions, the falling assignat hurt suppliers even more. Consequently, there was less and less incentive to obey the law, to the point that by February in the district of Mâcon and undoubtedly elsewhere, the maximum was described as 'an illusory law'. At the same time, the various levies from 1791 onwards drained the countryside of young farmhands and casual labour which created irresistible temptations for those who remained to demand higher wages. Since the maximum on wages was set at the communal level, there was immense variation from place to place and attempts to enforce it were not only unworkable, they too were resisted. By the spring, the representatives on mission had created a new category of economic crime, stigmatizing those who demanded higher wages as 'royalists and conspirators . . . excited by the agents of Pitt'. The Committee of Public Safety ordered their punishment but in vain.

The revision of prices upwards in favour of producers in February 1794 illustrates how the Committee of Public Safety had to balance competing economic interests. The sans-culottes would have preferred 'grandes mesures' against the countryside but antirural economics was impossible to practise for very long. The classic inequality of French rural society put local government in the hands of wealthy peasants who controlled a disproportionate share of the harvest but whose cooperation was crucial to make the Terror work. Such people were municipal councillors and tax collectors who were also expected to oversee requisitions, make lists of economic resources, compile lists of the poor, inventory émigré property and distribute money to the indigent. Unless the government proposed to break into the family networks of these men and undertake a generalized attack on private property – and no one did – then people like these would have to be mollified. Thus the maximum which was supposed to rectify inequality in the cities depended for its execution upon the rich in the countryside.

Jacobins and *Sans-culottes*

The history of the maximum laws encapsulates the general lesson of the relation between Jacobins and *sans-culottes* in other areas: in order to govern and conduct the war, the Committee of Public Safety had to make compromises with other social groups whose aspirations and interests often conflicted with those of the *sans-culottes* themselves. The fate of the achievements of the *journées* of 4–5 September illustrates the essential divergence within the revolutionary forces.

The *journées* themselves were a curious affair. In many aspects, the complaints of the demonstrators reflected the anxieties which had been common coin in Paris for the previous month: the failure to put Marie-Antoinette and Brissot and his friends on trial, the creaking pace of the Revolutionary Tribunal, the necessity of a purge of aristocrats, the intractable problem of food supplies, the failure to arrest 'all' suspects and, especially, demands for a revolutionary army whose organization the Convention had shelved, doubtless with some relief, thanks, in part, to quarrelling in the sections about the desirability of a 'Praetorian guard'. The fall of Toulon, officially announced on the 4th but known for the previous two days, also stimulated the zeal to seek out traitors, just as the fall of Mainz had provoked a new round of arrests five weeks earlier. The initiative to approach the Convention originated with the Jacobin club, many of whose members had been expressing

identical anxieties, and which decided on 23 August to hold a mass
demonstration before the Convention to demand a purge of
aristocrats and a revolutionary army. The club activists also invited
the sections and popular societies to adhere to the movement on 28
August and their approach appears to have been reasonably
successful since commissioners from twenty-nine of the former and
five of the latter are named in the collective petition of 5 September.
The commune also gave the *journée* a last-minute, opportunistic
push. It was clearly caught off guard by large demonstrations of
people working in the building and furniture trades for bread and
higher wages on the 4th. It gave orders to arrest those causing
trouble in the bread queues and to disperse other demonstrators but
too late or too ineffectively to prevent crowds from tumbling into
the Hôtel de Ville. Chaumette, the procurator, welcomed them
with a demagogic speech about the rich oppressing the poor and
pointed out that a revolutionary army was designed, in part, to
assure subsistence and that the recently voted maximum would
assuage their fears over the cost of living. Hébert then invited the
crowds to march to the Convention the next day. In other words,
a demonstration about subsistence was being hooked to the Jacobin
project of a mass petition and, to make sure of it, the commune
invited masters to close their shops the next day. On the 5th, a joint
delegation from the commune, Jacobins and sections accompanied
by immense banner-carrying crowds mingled with the disconcerted
deputies. After some stirring speeches by Pache, the mayor,
Chaumette, the Jacobins, a handful of sections separately and some
oratory from its own spellbinders, the Convention decreed the
institution of the revolutionary army and the arrest of suspects, and
put 'the terror on the order of the day'.

Soboul saw the *journées* as a 'mouvement [qui] sortait des masses
profondes du peuple . . . une victoire populaire: les sans-culottes
se sont imposés par leur manifestation . . .' In a sense this is true
for not only were the major decrees instituted, measures were also
taken to speed up the Revolutionary Tribunal, to ease constraints
on the revolutionary committees and to bring the Girondins and
Marie-Antoinette to trial. A largely unarmed demonstration had
imposed demands which had reverberated around the capital
throughout the summer. Yet it was the Jacobins, not the sections
or the fraternal societies, which took the initiative to organize a
mass petition, because the club had been as affected as the militants
by the collapse of the frontier fortresses, the disasters in the

Vendée, the break with Lyon and the deployment here and there of the federalist armies. Since early August, the club too had heard orators propose a general purge of nobles, denounce phoney food shortages, and demand an intensification of repression and limitations on prices. In this sense the Jacobins were no different from the *sans-culottes* but they clearly did not intend to be governed by extremists. Thus, Billaud-Varennes who had proposed the wholesale arrest of suspects, and Collot d'Herbois, another firebrand, were coopted on to the Committee of Public Safety. But, some demands were not met at all or were severely altered. The demands for the arrest of all nobles as suspects or their purge from the army were both ignored. The only specific task the revolutionary army was given was to assure the arrival of subsistence, whereas all the petitions which demanded it envisaged a little itinerant cohort of armed *sans-culottes* equipped with its own revolutionary tribunal and guillotine which would terrorize country people into disgorging their hoards as well as exercise summary justice on the malevolent enemies of the interior. Nor were the revolutionary committees to be allowed a free hand with suspects. Their members were to be paid (and hence controlled) by the government and they were to undergo a purge by the commune. This was a considerable step backward from the law of 21 March which provided for their election by the assembly of the section. The commune used its new authority extensively since, of the officials in place towards the end of the year in sixteen sections, nearly 60 per cent had been appointed since 1 September. Already, the popular movement was being bureaucratized, a process which was continued by having the revolutionary committees correspond directly with the Committee of General Security by the law of 17 September and completed by subjecting them to it exclusively by the law of 14 frimaire (4 December). In fact, it is hard to believe that the deputies were taken completely by surprise by a demonstration which had been in preparation for over two weeks and which Robespierre, Danton and Chaumette had all supported. Danton, who moved the adoption of the revolutionary army on the 5th because, he said, it was necessary to channel the revolutionary energy of the people – an old theme with him – in the same breath persuaded the Convention to limit section meetings to two a week and pay 40 *sols* per session to those who attended. This was almost certainly directed against Roux. Danton, who from his Cordeliers days knew better than most how to pack a small assembly, was trying to encourage poorer *sans-culottes* to attend. Clearly, he hoped to dilute the influence of the militants. When Barère denounced counterrevolutionaries who were stirring up the women over the subsistence question, he almost certainly had in mind a letter the police seized from Roux in which he counselled something like this tactic. Roux was arrested that very night, Varlet two weeks later and Leclerc, sensing the wind, disappeared. The high-water mark of the *sans-culottes*, therefore, dissolves into a blur on closer scrutiny. The Jacobins and the commune may have become the spokesmen of the *sans-culottes* on 5 September, they were also fast becoming their masters.

These divisions between the Convention's desire to control the revolutionary movement and the *sans-culottes'* conceptions of direct democracy were covered in a flood of rhetoric against enemies of all sorts. As it turned out, divisions between the politicians and the popular movement first manifested themselves, not over police functions or subsistence questions, but over the dechristianization campaign.

Dechristianization

Revolutionary dechristianization was a complex phenomenon whose origins are difficult to trace. At a bare minimum, it involved stripping the churches of their valuables and economically useful materials and funnelling them into the war machine. There had been a wave of this in the crisis of 1792 and it returned in force in the autumn of 1793 with an added emphasis on iconoclasm and anticlericalism. The churches themselves were often turned into barracks, arsenals or stables. Where there was also a formal ceremony in which statues, relics, roadside crosses and other sacred objects were burned or otherwise destroyed, it is clear that dechristianization went beyond the war effort. The climax of the negative side of dechristianization came with the forced or voluntary resignation of the parish priest, perhaps his renunciation of the priesthood altogether and, occasionally, his marriage to a suitable patriotic spinster. The eradication of the old religious order was accompanied by attempts to create a new one in the form of revolutionary cults, cults of Reason and the Supreme Being, the desacralization of everyday life – so thorough that it included purging the names of streets, public squares, tavern signs, cities and towns of all reference to the Christian or feudal past. Parents named their babies after appropriate republican heroes or in accordance with 'nature' and adults even changed their names in 'debaptism' ceremonies. The introduction of the revolutionary calendar in October 1793 by Danton's friend, the poet Fabre d'Eglantine, symbolized the anti-Christian and 'rational' nature of the entire movement. The most important date in history became the founding of the Republic on 22 September 1792. Each of the twelve months had thirty days each, with five 'sans-culottides' or public holidays tacked on to the end of each year. Each of the months was renamed to reflect the seasons (the so-called universal calendar mirrored the northern French climate all the same). Sundays and feast days were replaced by a 'week' of ten days, called a 'décade', which meant that there were only three official days of rest per month instead of four or five.

The attempt to remake all of man's references to time and place could not have been more complete. Yet, how had such a situation come about when just three years before the association of the Church and the new regime had been so intimate? The Civil Constitution of the Clergy had symbolized this, as did the Masses at the federation of 1790, the blessings of the colours of the National Guards, the Te Deums for the new constitution and so on. An old Catholic tradition saw dechristianization as the logical outcome of the Enlightenment, but whatever the obvious borrowings from the philosophies in the Year II, 'écrasez l'infâme' was meant to be a long educative process, not a wholesale destruction. An interpretation in vogue at the moment sees Old Regime 'dechristianization' as a necessary prelude for that of the Year II. Apart from the fact that the correlation has never been statistically demonstrated, it is hard to see how declines in demands for Masses after death, charitable donations and the establishment of foundations which manifested themselves in Provence, Anjou and Paris from 1750 onwards, are connected to the revolutionary cults. How does the apparent indifference of the one phenomenon connect with the profound imprint of the Catholic religiosity of the other? In any case, eighteenth-century dechristianization is measured through those wealthy enough to draw up wills, while the revolutionary variety was often the work of people of lower social groups which are underrepresented in the sample of wills and which other sources indicate were on the whole practising Catholics. This is not to deny there were no Old Regime roots. The misogynist elements of dechristianization are probably related to age-old male resentments at the priests' apparent influence over women through the confessional. Nor is this to deny that from the beginning the Revolution showed religious characteristics. The habit of dating 1789 as the 'first year of liberty', the propensity to speak of the 'Law', 'Constitution' or 'Liberty' in mystical terms, the dedication of infants to 'la patrie', the spread, especially during 1792, of revolutionary symbols such as pikes, red caps or liberty trees, tricolour cockades and so on, as well as the missionary zeal of the National Guards and fédérés, are only some examples. But all of this was compatible with the constitutional church. Up until 1793, the litmus test of revolutionary commitment was going to the Mass of the constitutional curés whose doctrine and liturgy were certainly Christian and Catholic, despite the disavowals of the Pope and the old bishops. Dechristianization was a break with the constitutional church first and foremost, and to explain this break is to understand much of the origins of dechristianization.

Dechristianization came about because of the failure of the constitutional church. Whatever the reasons for establishing it, the constitutional church became the church of the regime and was expected to proselytize for it. Many curés fulfilled this role with enthusiasm, not only through their preaching but through their activities in clubs, popular societies and the administration. In return, the authorities did everything they could to support them. The constitutional curés were the first line of defence against 'fanatisme', that is, against the supporters of the refractories and the popular counterrevolution, but by the summer of 1793 was not 'fanatisme' on the point of triumphing? In this sense, the constitutional church was a victim of the royalist risings, particularly those in the west. It is possible to follow this evolution in Joseph Fouché, perhaps the most famous dechristianizing deputy of all. Whatever his private beliefs, he had spoken in 1792 of 'the necessity' of religious sentiments and had foreseen a role for the teaching orders in the new system of public education. It was only after his mission to Nantes in March 1793, in which he helped organize the defence of the city against the 'religious fanatics' of the Vendée, that he denounced the clergy wholesale. He attributed the risings to 'ignorance and fanaticism [which have become] the blind instruments of the aristocracy which work with it to annihilate the cities . . .' Shortly after, he advocated a system of 'public instruction . . . inspired by the revolutionary and clearly philosophical spirit [which alone] can offset the odious influence of religion'. Georges Couthon, the paralytic deputy from the Puy-de-Dôme and member of the Committee of Public Safety, was a Rousseauist believer in the natural goodness of man, a deist, a believer in the afterlife and an anticlerical, but until the autumn of 1793, he advised 'giving Philosophy the care of delivering us' from priests and Catholicism. He only proposed bypassing philosophy's role in his native department, however, after a local constituency anxious 'to throw off the yoke of religious prejudice' had shown itself in October and after he was able to observe at first hand the involvement of many constitutional curés in the Lyon rebellion. Jacobins like Fouché and Couthon had always insisted that there was no difference in doctrine or liturgy between constitutionals and refractories so that if religion was the device by which self-interested nobles and priests manipulated popular credulity, then these machinations could be defeated by undermining religion itself. As one official around Mâcon put it, 'Since the beginning of the Revolution, the Catholic cult has been the cause of many troubles. Under the cloak of religion, the progress of civic-mindedness has been much hampered. Disastrous wars have taken place. Would it not be appropriate to authorize only the cult of the Revolution?' Dechristianization was thus another strategy in the struggle against popular counterrevolution, just as the persecution and deportation of the refractory priests had been.

Dechristianization was not entirely or even consciously manipulative, however. Dechristianizing deputies usually associated it with an extreme democratic egalitarianism. Claude Javogues in the Loire, for example, believed the democratic republic to be the only form of government which would permit the poor and the miserable to achieve their happiness, and that its natural enemies were the rich, the aristocrats, the priests, the dishonest lawyers, the hoarders; in a word, the inherently selfish. His revolutionary taxes were justified in part as restitution for the *sans-culottes* of the wealth which the rich had usurped. Javogues was an extravagant man given to intemperate verbal bombast and physical abuse, but cooler heads among such deputies shared similar ideas. On his mission to the Nièvre and Allier in September–October, Fouché, true to the principles of the Constitution of 1793, believed that the Republic owed subsistence and work to the people, organized some schemes to assure this and ordered that 'unfortunate citizens be clothed, fed and housed at the expense of the excess of the rich' because 'the wealth in the hands of individuals is only a deposit which the nation has the right to dispose of'. Other deputies such as André Dumont on mission in the Somme and Oise or Joseph Le Bon in the Pas-de-Calais and the Nord expressed almost identical beliefs. Although none of them was a proponent of the 'loi-agraire', that is, the equal division of all fortunes, they were all committed to the concept of the moral equality of all men. Everyone had a right to understand 'philosophy', therefore, and so dechristianization was inseparable from the effort to construct the new republican man, an individual purged of the slavish vices and prejudices of the old order, a man of austere moral virtues, unselfish, modest, honest and patient, but invincible when provoked.

The presence of a dechristianizing representative could be vital, in part because, as with Dumont in the Oise or Couthon in the Puy-de-Dôme, they set the movement in motion, and in part because only they were powerful enough to organize it systematically over a wide area. Fouché's celebrated *arrêté* of 10 October, desacralizing cemeteries, prescribing purely secular funerals, and ordering the slogan 'Death is an eternal sleep' inscribed at the gates of every cemetery, even had a national impact. Its influence has been found at the foothills of the Pyrenees and on the plains of Picardy. Often the departure of such deputies led to a considerable decline in the zeal of local authorities.

Aside from the patronage of some deputies, almost every sector of the revolutionary coalition was involved in the dechristianizing movement, often for its own reasons. In the Cher, the representative Laplanche did no more than apply the laws on the clergy, but his agents, two of whom were former college professors (like Fouché), aided half-heartedly by the revolutionary committee of Bourges, were the activists. They were not very effective until the signal came from Paris in mid-brumaire (early November) and only then did priests begin to resign in significant numbers. Paradoxically, former constitutional priests, often with a background in teaching in the Old Regime, were noted for their extravagant and violent spoliation of churches. They became apostles of liberty because of their conviction that religion and the Revolution were compatible, that is, for the same reason many had taken the oath to the Civil Constitution. Now, in a blinding flash along their own roads to Damascus, they became missionaries for Reason, Liberty and Equality or Natural Religion, never ceasing to be preachers and often throwing themselves into the war effort as petty bureaucrats. Another agent was the revolutionary army of Paris which in one of its forays stimulated acts of destruction along the entire highway from the capital to Lyon, themselves taking part in the closing of churches, ripping out crosses, destroying holy images and burning statues in Auxerre and Cluny. Other departmental armies were involved in similar incidents, but so, too, were conscripts of the *levée en masse* while regular soldiers set fire to churches in the Vendée in a spirit of joyful revenge. Certain clubs were also prominent, and in the Nord and Pas-de-Calais they were able to use their influence over soldiers and the local revolutionary armies to despoil and close churches and organize civic fêtes. There can be no doubt that dechristianization was popular. Even in Paris, where the iconoclasm followed initiatives in the provinces and had to be given a stimulus, societies and sections gave it a life of its own. On the night of 16 brumaire (6 November), the deputies Bourdon, a friend of Danton, and Cloots, the friend of humanity, rousted Gobel, Bishop of Paris, from his bed and persuaded him to renounce his functions. The next day, Gobel and his vicars-general resigned before the Convention. On 20 brumaire, Notre Dame, converted to a Temple of Reason, was the scene of a civic festival, presided over by an opera singer dressed as Liberty. The involvement of ambitious characters like Chaumette or Momoro in these manoeuvres took place against the backdrop of a rising enthusiasm in the sections for the cult of martyrs of liberty and, from the end of brumaire, section after section trumpeted its renunciation of Catholicism. Dechristianization was thus capable of involving most terrorists under the right circumstances. The march of a revolutionary army through a country district to seize church bells and confiscate valuable plate often encouraged village atheists to come to the fore, with murderous consequences for them when the revolutionary tide ebbed in the Year III. It could also offer great scope for individuals, as with Charles Lanteirès, national agent of the district of Alès in the Gard, whose expeditions at the head of a little column of gendarmes against 'fanatic' communes were the terror of the region. But aside from the limitless opportunities for eccentric behaviour which this period of 'anarchic terror' offered to extravagant individuals, most dechristianizing fell into one of several patterns. The apparent connection between abdications of priests and civil war zones is striking. True, there were few in the Var where Augustin Robespierre, who shared his brother's suspicions of the movement, was supervising the siege of Toulon – which once again underlines the importance of a sympathetic deputy. But the proportions in the departments around Lyon were very high, as if the representatives, popular societies, revolutionary armies and *Commission Temporaire* were trying to build a *cordon sanitaire* around the 'ville infâme'. Further afield, in fourteen districts in Normandy for which complete information exists, almost all the constitutional clergy abdicated after the Vendean invasion of the province. These examples cast a slightly different light on the old assertion that dechristianization was a minority movement. It is true that not all revolutionaries were violent dechristianizers but such activists were quite representative of those who sponsored the Terror and became so out of fear of counterrevolution which they attempted to combat.

It is also said that dechristianization was superficial and undoubtedly it was. The cult of martyrs of liberty scarcely survived the boring officially sponsored cult of the Supreme Being which in turn did not survive the fall of Robespierre, while the civic fêtes of the Directory never caught on. Although the revolutionary calendar was in use until 1806, Sunday work was resisted wherever possible. But there were exceptions. In Beauvais, over half the children born in the Year II were given revolutionary names and there were few legal rectifications even in the Restoration – a reflection of political commitments being passed through the generations.

Most disastrous was the effect on the constitutional church. It is not easy to estimate how effective the abdications of the Year II were. Most of them were forced, as Parent of Boissie-le-Bertrand in the Seine-et-Marne who wrote, 'I am a priest, I am a curé, that is, a charlatan. Until now, a charlatan in good faith . . .' Such typically quivering honesty raises the question of how permanent such abdications were. Many curés did take up their functions again but others made their peace with the refractory church in the Years III and IV. Roughly six thousand or about one in ten of the constitutionals may have married from late 1792 on. Some were executed, others were later murdered by the chouans of the west or the 'brigands royaux' of the Midi. After such travails, some were still willing to reconcile themselves to the Concordat church but the biases of the new bishops kept many unemployed and probably no more than one quarter of the former constitutionals became parish priests again. At first glance, the emigration and clandestine activities ought to have saved the refractories, so that to a certain extent dechristianization had exactly the opposite effect of what was intended in that circumstances saved the 'fanatic' clergy. But not entirely. Executions, natural deaths, the inability of the seminaries to produce sufficient new priests for nearly fifteen years and a certain loss of vocation while abroad affected the refractories too. The Concordat church was much smaller than that of the Old Regime. The number of curés fell by over 35 per cent, the number of vicaires by over 70 per cent. In some regions, it was even worse. In the Isère, the number of clerics dropped by over 200 per cent, in the Seine-Inférieure, the number of parishes by 135 per cent. One can only speculate over what this meant for the laity. From 1791 when the departments took their first exile decrees against the clergy until well into the Empire, large areas of the country lived without priests. The effect could not have been negligible.

The notion that dechristianization was superficial also tends to focus attention away from the extent to which it was resisted. In some areas, this was a continuation of struggles which had begun in 1791 but resistance often spread to regions which up to this point had been fairly quiescent. The most common and the least dangerous were disturbances, often spearheaded by women, over authorities' attempts to remove church bells. But resistance became more general after the publication of the law of 12 frimaire (16 December) recalling earlier legislation on freedom of religion which country people naively interpreted as authorizing the reopening of churches. Every adult male of the commune of Plessis-Biron in the Oise petitioned the Convention for the reopening of its church on 'Sundays and feast days as in the past' to no avail. When the women of Beaubourg in the Nord did the same, the revolutionary committee arrested the vicaire for having put them up to it. In practice, with the inevitable exceptions, the law of 12 frimaire was a dead letter. For roughing up a few startled Jacobins of La Ferté-Gaucher in the Seine-et-Marne on 15 December when they came to retrieve confiscated religious objects, no less than eight hundred country people were arrested and twenty were sent for trial to the Revolutionary Tribunal of Paris. Interestingly enough, about half the accused would be classed as rural sans-culottes. In the Nièvre, where Fouché's dechristianization had been very thorough, resistance was dramatic. On 6 nivôse (25 December), crowds of country women invaded the district headquarters at Corbigny and declared that they 'intended to exercise their religion again, that they wished to live and die for it, that they demanded right away the return of their church bells and ornaments as well as the free use of the church . . .' In the Sancerrois region of the Nièvre, conscripts marched from village to village forcing municipal officers to ring bells and restore crosses and emblems and compelling priests who had resigned to say Mass. This was a region which later had a chouannerie of its own. Local militants tried to ignore the law, in some cases successfully. The military revolutionary tribunal of the Indre-et-Loire and Loir-et-Cher, for example, condemned René Guérin of Cussai to death for shooting at a band of outside Jacobins who came to keep the commune's church closed despite the law of 12 frimaire. The constitutional vicaire was arrested on the pretext he was not authorized to read out the law on toleration to the public. But resistance did not have to be violent to be alarming. In messidor (June 1794), about one thousand faithful gathered in the fields outside Mortain in the Manche to hear a nocturnal Mass recited by a priest whom people believed was a direct agent of God. In the Cornouailles region of the Côtes-du-Nord, around St John the Baptist's Day (24 June), the Virgin began appearing to announce the end of the world and St Michael to warn of God's vengeance. To forestall divine wrath, crowds of barefooted people journeyed great distances to pray at local shrines and sanctuaries. At Cébazan in the Hérault there were only about twenty people inside the church on 20 prairial (29 May) to practise the official cult, while outside everyone else 'was crying that they wanted the religion which they had before'. Sometimes a priest was not even necessary. In the canton of Buxy in the Saône-et-Loire, later a stronghold of the 'Petite Eglise', people seized the churches, recited prayers 'in Latin' and laymen performed 'white Masses'. There were similar practices in the countryside around Auxerre, as burly men with muskets guarded the churches while the faithful inside practised their own version of Mass. This region had accepted overwhelmingly the Civil Constitution and was massively non-practising in the next century but attempts to remove the priests or close the churches were a constant source of disturbance and riot throughout the Year II all the same. The extent to which refractories practised at the height of the Terror cannot be known but a number of diocesan archives still contain the little notebooks in which some recorded baptisms and marriages. They were occasionally caught and executed, every guillotining providing an extensive martyrology for the faithful in the next century.

More than any other aspect, dechristianization was the face of the Terror for ordinary people in both town and country. Outside the civil war zones, repression did not affect large numbers of people. It was always possible to live outside the controlled economy. Hiding a few sacks of grain or disguising one's wealth from the sporadic control of amateurs in the towns was comparatively easy for a peasantry that had defrauded tax collectors for centuries. With the complicity of neighbours, it was even possible to avoid conscription. But it was impossible to avoid dechristianization and many people resented it. It is not difficult to see why. Since one aim of popular religion was an attempt to control and manipulate the caprices of an omnipresent and potentially malevolent supernatural world through ceremony and liturgy, efforts to substitute different beliefs and practices were not only meaningless but harmful. What could the government do faced with peasants in northern Burgundy who attributed a hailstorm which destroyed two thirds of their vines to 'the disappearance of their priests and their stone saints'? Thus, like the controlled economy, dechristianization contributed to the crisis of the terrorist regime, a crisis which could only be solved by repression, which in turn brought the regime to an end.

Victory and Vengeance

Before the repression came the victories. By early August, all thoughts of a federalist offensive were out of the question. Communications between Lyon and Marseille were slowly cut throughout July, neighbouring departments which had joined the chorus against 2 June accepted the Constitution and federalism in Normandy, Brittany and Bordeaux collapsed. Within the remaining anti-Jacobin cities, the poor response to the military levies, the indecision and quarrelling among the leaders and the unwillingness, whether through remaining pro-Jacobin sentiment or simply indifference, of large pockets of the urban populations to respond to increasingly authoritarian measures, threw the intransigent federalists into desperation. Although the Marseille army did occupy Avignon, it failed to take Orange and was defeated by a small army under General Carteaux on 11 and 19 August. On the 25th Carteaux entered the city, many of the most compromised fleeing to Toulon. Detachments of the Lyon army were forced to withdraw from Saint-Etienne three days later while Montbrison was occupied on 9 September. Lyon itself took longer. Although the siege had begun on 8 August, the Convention's forces were divided because of fears of a Piedmontese attack over the Alps. The terrible bombardment did not begin for another three weeks and the exhausted city finally surrendered on 9 October. This left Toulon, which finally succumbed on 18 December once republican forces captured the forts overlooking the city and the artillery under Captain Bonaparte could threaten the allied fleets in the port below.

There were significant victories along the northern frontiers as well. The Battle of Hondschoote on 8 September forced the British forces to lift the siege of Dunkirk and the Battle of Wattignies on 16 October forced the Austrians to lift that of Mauberge. Although neither battle was entirely decisive, they did compel the allied armies to begin a slow retreat. By the end of the year, the Austrians and Prussians had also been pushed out of Alsace. Thus, as the respective combatants settled into their winter quarters, the Republic could carry on its internal struggles safe from the foreign enemy.

The most dangerous internal enemy, the Vendean armies, remained. After their massive defeat at Cholet in mid-October, the Vendean generals finally decided to cross the Loire to stir up Brittany, Maine and Normandy and to receive arms from the British fleet at one of the coastal ports. The crossing of perhaps 30,000 fighting men, their families, priests and noble officers was accomplished on 17 October and victories at Château-Gontier, Laval and Mayenne against a republican army one third their size were fairly easy. But communications with the British were extraordinarily difficult to maintain and at one time the Vendeans appeared to be making for Saint-Malo until they headed north again to Granville. Desperately short of ammunition, they had to break off a twenty-six-hour siege of Granville on 13–14 November. This failure was the beginning of the end. The British expedition could not be readied in time and only sailed to the coast weeks later. Only a few hundred Bretons and Normans, who began to call themselves 'chouans', even joined the Vendeans. Now, after Granville, tired and defeated, the rank-and-file royalists only wanted to go home and so were increasingly unresponsive to their leaders. But the republicans were strong enough to prevent the re-crossing of the Loire and inflicted a progressive series of defeats at

Pontorson, Dol, Antrain, Angers and Le Mans on a wandering and visibly disintegrating army. The royalists had to abandon their dead and wounded, camp-followers straggled behind, food and munitions were desperately low and many were suffering from dysentery. Finally, a republican army under General Westermann smashed the Vendeans at Savenay on 23 December. Thousands of royalist soldiers and civilians were killed in the battle itself or shot in subsequent mopping-up operations, thousands of others died in the forests and bogs and thousands more were jammed into makeshift prisons in nearby Nantes. The 'great war' of the Vendée was over. The repression could begin.

The repression of the Year II is the most notorious aspect of the period and no historian has ever been neutral on the subject. Georges Lefebvre's immense common sense did much to cut through the welter of special pleadings and distortions surrounding it by pointing out that the terrorist mentality was inherent in the Revolution from the start, a function of fear and danger, and a desire to punish counterrevolutionaries or prevent them from doing their worst. The Terror as repression was thus an episode of the dialectic of revolution-counterrevolution which was a theme of the entire period. People were executed before the Terror for counterrevolution and exceptional jurisdictions were used after, most notably courts martial in the west up to the Year IV or military commissions against so-called brigands in the Midi in the Year IX. In all cases, these special courts were supposed to operate quickly and without appeal and so have a greater deterrent effect than ordinary courts. As for the Terror *per se*, the Revolutionary Tribunal in Paris and the five others established in imitation in the provinces were most like regular courts in structure and proceedings until the law of 22 prairial (10 June) allowed the jury to convict on the basis of moral certainty of guilt. The sixty-odd military commissions, or the dozen or so revolutionary commissions, differed only in that the military or civilian judges also acted as juries (as in the Old Regime). All gathered evidence and execution was supposed to take place within twenty-four hours of conviction. Most of the convictions took place under the law of 19 March 1793 which specified death if the accused were found armed in a counterrevolutionary assembly. Thousands of Vendeans met their deaths because of this law which, as we have seen, was proposed by the Girondin Lanjuinais. Louis XVIII made him a peer.

Outlining their legal powers is a rather arid way of describing the informal functioning and operational context of the revolutionary courts. From the infamous Revolutionary Tribunal in Paris to the most humble and short-lived, they were all supposed to settle scores and strike fear into the hearts of enemies. As the representative Maignet put it when requesting the establishment of the infamous Popular Commission of Orange, 'we have to terrify and the blow is frightening only so long as it falls before the eyes of those who have lived among the guilty'. In a sense, therefore, all the trials before the revolutionary tribunals were political in that they were supposed to impress the communities in which they took place with the inflexible power of the Montagnards. Thus the political trials in Paris – of Marie-Antoinette and the Girondins in October, and the Hébertists and Dantonists the following March–April where the government expected and got convictions – were exceptional only because of the fame of their victims. With such widely defined powers and with such extraordinary results expected of them, internal procedures protecting elementary justice in some of the courts quickly broke down. One judge on the Commission of Orange complained of another that he 'is worthless, absolutely worthless, at his job; sometimes his opinion is to save counterrevolutionary priests; he has to have proofs, as with the ordinary courts of the Old Regime'. It is hard to believe, too, that the rapid interrogation of batches of ten, twenty and thirty people at a time at Angers, Nantes, Rennes, Lyon and elsewhere assured anything like a fair trial. But then the law itself only required establishing the presence of the accused at a counterrevolutionary assembly. Every good Montagnard knew what that was.

Not all of the courts functioned with such a shocking disregard for elementary justice even within the civil war zones. Despite the impressive range of powers they had, two of the three revolutionary courts in the Loire showed a maddening attachment to ordinary rules of evidence while the third was active for less than a week. The same thing occurred at Marseille. This was because many courts were dominated by regular judges and lawyers whose professional scruples could not be shed overnight. This also meant that using the judicial system to overawe enemies did not always succeed – a phenomenon which must have been a good deal more common than is usually thought since only five departments were responsible for nearly 70 per cent of all death sentences, while only thirteen were responsible for 90 per cent. Not too surprisingly, these areas of heavy repression were the *Vendée militaire*, the western departments north of the Loire through which the Vendeans marched, the federalist cities of the Midi, particularly Lyon, Marseille and Toulon, and finally Paris. These regions, too, witnessed great atrocities on top of 'official' repression. The march of General Turreau's 'infernal columns' through the Vendée apart, among these atrocities were the representative Francastel's orders to shoot two thousand people without trial near Angers and the shooting of eight hundred people immediately after the fall of Toulon upon simple identification by local Jacobins. Thus the cycle of reprisal and counterreprisal which began earlier continued under the Terror and would continue afterwards. Terror, repression and 'popular government' were all closely linked. This, at any rate, is the lesson of the Terror at Lyon and Nantes.

After its fall on 9 October, Lyon became a proving ground for a whole range of radical and *sans-culotte* ideas which were only implemented sporadically elsewhere. Couthon, who had helped direct the siege, believed that a moderate policy of repression, rather than wholesale punishment, was all that was required. The Jacobins imprisoned by the federalists were released and the club reopened. Revolutionary committees in each of the thirty-two sections were formed under the overall supervision of a city-wide surveillance committee who together were to seek out suspects and counterrevolutionaries. These in turn were to be judged and dispatched by two special tribunals. Between 12 October and 1 December, the two tribunals passed death sentences on 209 people, no small number but nothing in comparison to what was to come. But moderation was not popular in Paris. Ever since the conspiracies in Lyon in 1790, radical circles had seen the city as infested with counterrevolutionaries, and after the conquest they were determined to set an example. Robespierre himself supported a policy of pitiless vengeance, and on 10 October Saint-Just gave a famous speech declaring there could be no quarter between the Revolution and its enemies. Two days later the Convention ordered the houses of the rich destroyed, the sequestration of the property of the rich and the counterrevolutionaries (the income to be used to aid the poor), the change of the city's name to Ville-Affranchie (Liberated City) and the construction of a monument for posterity bearing the inscription: 'Lyon fit la guerre à la Liberté; Lyon n'est Plus'. The destruction which followed thus took place within an overall framework provided by the Convention. Collot d'Herbois and Fouché, both thought to be more ruthless, replaced Couthon who was recalled. Since Collot had been an actor and playwright and Fouché had already considerable experience in the Nièvre, they organized a dechristianization ceremony which as a single event illustrates the mockery and sentimental religiosity of the movement as a whole. On 10 November Chalier's body was exposed to 'public veneration' while, as Collot reported, 'Tears flowed from every eye at the sight of the dove which accompanied and consoled him in his frightful prison and which seemed to lament before his image.' The head was shipped off to the Convention as a relic but not before an ass dressed in a bishop's mitre and staff was paraded around the square while assistants sprinkled incense. Holy objects were then smashed on Chalier's tomb. Criticism of the great and the powerful through burlesque was a very old European tradition while the use of donkeys in public ceremonies often symbolized humiliation or even death. But traditional folklore was only a temporary release and generally acted to reinforce regular authority. Despite the obvious borrowing of religious vocabulary and ceremony, Collot's staging was clearly blasphemous, not titillating, and was meant to have a far more liberating effect. Indeed there was a great deal of theatre in the joint mission as a whole. Gruesome as it sounds, this is ultimately what lay behind the mass shootings. As the *Commission Temporaire* – a revolutionary body composed exclusively of non-Lyonnais instituted by the representatives to support and stimulate the regular administration and whose members showed an unrepublican doggedness for elaborate uniforms when they were not inventing vexatious regulations for prisoners – expressed it, as it gave the direct order for the shootings, the object was 'the complete and entire execution of the judgement [of the Revolutionary Commission] which will be accomplished in a manner to imprint terror without exciting pity'. Or, as Fouché and the other representatives said, 'we are sceptical of the tears of repentance, nothing can disarm our severity . . . indulgence is a dangerous weakness, liable to rekindle criminal hopes . . . devouring flames alone can express the total power of the people'.

On 14 frimaire (4 December), 60 people bound to a rope before already dug graves on the meadow of Les Brotteaux were mowed down by cannon balls and grapeshot and then finished off with musket fire. The next day, 208 met a similar fate. Of the 1667 actual victims of the representatives' Revolutionary Commission which shortly assumed responsibility from Couthon's slower courts, 935 people were shot and 732 guillotined over its 130-day existence. Revolutionary justice was preceded by some radical social reforms. In comformity with the famous *Instruction* of the *Commission Temporaire*, Fouché imposed punitive taxes on the rich and graded their weight to political opinions, guaranteed state aid to the poor, the old and the infirm, ordered full employment for every trade, commanded the baking of a single type of bread, requisitioned 'surplus' clothing and ordered everyone to wear wooden shoes at home. It would be be interesting to know how devastating this garrison equality was to the upper classes of Lyon. Certainly, the confiscation of all the property of the condemned must have been disastrous, even if many were aristocrats whose property was outside the city. Yet there were limits. For all the bombast about blowing up or burning down buildings because the ordinary work of demolition was going too slowly, only the façades of a number of town houses, a hundred or so buildings and the fortifications were destroyed. Furthermore, the attempt to intimidate the population had the opposite effect. From the Year III onwards, Lyon was the headquarters of the vicious counterterrorist murder gangs. There was a lesson too for the popular militants. The revolutionary committees of Lyon were among the most '*sans-culotte*' in the country, with almost all of their members shopkeepers and artisans; one third, no less, were silk weavers. But what kind of power was it to arrest neighbours when overall authority was exercised by men including the representatives, the detachments of the Paris revolutionary army and the *Commission Temporaire* who bore themselves as foreign conquerors and who distrusted even the friendly natives because they were not 'à la hauteur'? The *sans-culottes* in Paris, too, would find the same disillusioning experience of exercising power in a dictatorship.

At Nantes, it is customary to blame the representative Carrier for the gruesome *noyades* in which barges loaded with prisoners were floated out to the mouth of the Loire and sunk. Some two thousand people may have died in these horrible drownings and many more were shot. Carrier appears to have been under the impression that the seven *noyades* which can be documented were of those Vendean prisoners who had been condemned by the military tribunal. But the revolutionary committee and members of the revolutionary army which were more directly responsible for organizing the *noyades*, did not make the distinction between the

condemned and those awaiting trial. They emptied the prisons not
only of the miserable Vendeans but of priests who may or may not
also have been rebels, and of common criminals. Many of these
local Jacobins were brutal men but the city itself had been terrified
by Vendean atrocities ever since the massacres at Machecoul in
March and the siege in June. Moreover, after the battle of Savenay
on 23 December, the city's makeshift, stinking, wretched prisons
were full of half-starved and sick Vendean soldiers who could, it
was feared, break out and who were also a threat to public health
and the food supply. Outside was the wily Charette, the most able
of the Vendean generals, and until his army was pushed off the
peninsula of Noirmoutier on 2 January, there was always the
additional threat of a British landing. In short, the *noyades* and
illegal shootings at Nantes were a variant of the foreign plot/internal
plot mentality which had produced the vigilante justice of 1792 and
the September Massacres. It should also be noted that Carrier was
recalled to Paris on 20 pluviôse (8 February), not because of the
noyades which had been public knowledge since 2 nivôse (23
December) but because he requested it and because local
extremists claimed he was not pursuing the war vigorously enough.
Moreover, the Paris Jacobin club gave him a hero's welcome.

The experience at Nantes and perhaps also at Angers and Lyon
suggests a situation in which the terrorists were overwhelmed by
their own institutions. Some of the speeches made in Paris in the
winter of the Year II also suggest that the government was losing
control of repression. Certainly there was a loss of perspective.
Robespierre, but also Saint-Just, Billaud-Varennes and Couthon,
talked of using the Terror to assure virtue and purge the corrupt,
of making it a device towards building the new society, which meant
that all external standards of guilt would evaporate. But whatever
the pontiffs in the Convention said, repression was generally
directed against counterrevolution. There is another tradition,
however, which claims that it was part of a class struggle and at first
glance the social breakdown of the death sentences might lead to
this conclusion: roughly 6.5 per cent of the death sentences were
pronounced on the clergy, 8 per cent on the nobility, 14 per cent
'upper middle class', 10.5 per cent 'lower middle class', 31 per cent
'working class' and 28 per cent peasants, which in the case of the
clergy and nobility is an overrepresentation of at least three times
their number in the population as a whole, while the 'middle class'
was certainly overrepresented as well. Yet, aside from some

terminological problems (e.g., the clergy and the nobility were legal entities not classes), a breakdown of these figures into their regional components permits a more nuanced appraisal. For part of the *Vendeé militaire* where there are independent lists of rebels, the social breakdown of the victims of the revolutionary tribunals mirrors almost exactly the participants in the rebellion as a whole with no one social group being more counterrevolutionary than another. That is, the Terror was aimed at guilty individuals, not classes as such. In the longer perspective, the Terror in the west was the brutal culmination of a struggle which began before the Year II and which continued, sporadically, until 1832. The corroborative check provided by the independent lists does not exist for the victims of the repression in the federalist cities but there is some evidence that the conquerors did go through the available lists rather carefully. At Lyon, where the nobles, clergy and upper bourgeoisie dominated the federalist army and civilian administrations, punishment of these groups was exceptionally severe. Of the 1734 people whose occupations are known who were executed after the reconquest, close to half were clerics, nobles, merchants, professionals and rentiers, that is from the well-off non-manual minority in the largest industrial city in the country. But the Convention's vengeance descended into the world of work as well. The luxury, highly skilled and food and drink trades, all of them well remunerated in the Old Regime and long denounced by the Jacobin Central Club before the revolt, were overrepresented relative to other working groups; the non-silk textile and construction groups were about even; while the near absence of silk-workers, almost all of whom were too poor to qualify as active citizens in 1790, is remarkable. The example of Lyon again illustrates the selectivity of repression and suggests that the struggle between merchants and master-weavers, which had begun a half-century before, broadened into one between the rich and the poor.

The role of the representatives on mission and the exceptional tribunals are the most sensational aspects of the Terror but their work would not have been possible without the lesser organs of repression, the revolutionary committees and the revolutionary armies. Of the two, the revolutionary committees were by far the most effective. These had been organized in March–April 1793 but except for those established by representatives on mission or other authorities, they lapsed into torpor in the summer after an initial flurry of activity. Outside the large cities, there were few foreigners to arrest and despite the laws of 2 June and 12 August which ordered the arrest of all suspects, the remaining committees were hampered by the lack of a definition of what a suspect was. The Law of Suspects voted on 17 September filled the gap. Among other categories, it defined suspects as those who had shown themselves to be partisans 'of tyranny, of federalism and enemies of liberty'. They were to be imprisoned or held under house arrest by the revolutionary committees. With this terrible power, the committees acquired a new lease of life, particularly after the arrival of an energetic representative on mission who was often responsible for stimulating their foundation or renewed activity. Either because the power was delegated to them, or because they took it on themselves, the committees also involved themselves in purging the administration, collecting revolutionary taxes and valuables from churches and private individuals, searching out deserters, censoring mail, stamping passports, enforcing the maximum, delivering 'certificats de civisme' without which no one could occupy an official post, closing churches and imposing the décadi, and even enforcing local police regulations like those on cheese production or gambling. In short, the committees were administrative bodies which supplemented or usurped the work of the regular organs of government, and since they had close relations with the club, which often named its own members to staff them, the committees brought to local power the uninhibited and the zealous which revolutionary government required in order to function.

The committees were undoubtedly effective instruments of revolutionary government but there were limitations on their activities. There were comparatively few of them. Local studies of the Loire and the districts of Le Mans in the Sarthe, Mâcon in the Saône-et-Loire and Saint-Pol in the Pas-de-Calais indicate a rather uneven implantation, with committees usually only in the principal centres, in larger villages along main roads or rivers or at important crossroads. The few rural committees were not very active because they were hampered, as the municipalities had been earlier, by the lack of literate talent and because country people still preferred to settle disputes among themselves. One rural committee in Normandy actually protected the refractory priest and not many cooperated in implementing the maximum. Even the urban committees showed varying degrees of zeal. That of Saint-Pol arrested 1460, Toulouse close to 1000, Dijon around 400, Nancy

334, Dax around 300 and so on. As with dechristianization, waves of arrests depended on the stimulus of a representative on mission as when Saint-Just and Lebon ordered the arrest of all nobles and wives of suspects in the Pas-de-Calais. Since the more sincere revolutionaries were aware of the terrific power the Law of Suspects gave them, the committees and representatives often reviewed suspects' cases even before the Convention ordered this in ventôse (February) and so there were numerous releases throughout the period. This makes it very difficult to estimate how many suspects there were but it seems that Louis Jacob's estimate of seventy thousand is about right. If it is, it means that less than 0.5 per cent of the population was arrested as suspects.

It was not the relatively few arrested but their essential arbitrariness and the fact there was no formal appeal against arrest that made the committees such effective agents of the Jacobin dictatorship. Who would ever have expected, for example, the arrest of one unfortunate individual at Draguignan in the Var because he was 'suspect of suspicion'? The committees also had a long reach. Thanks to the enthusiasm of the committee of Saint-Pol, 85 per cent of the communes in the entire district witnessed at least one arrest. This example too shows another characteristic of the committees: their urban base. They were keen dechristianizers and zealous enforcers of the maximum. They thus became instruments of urban control over the countryside, another solution, like the National Guards earlier, to the problem of disciplining the peasantry.

For all that, the committees reflected local concerns. That of Narbonne in the Aude, for example, was so remote from national rhythms that it tried to find a confessor for the soldiers in the hospital. Nancy was so illiberal as to demand the expulsion of Jews from the Republic. Every committee tended to arrest people whom it thought backed the local version of the counterrevolution. All prisons housed their fair share of suspect nobles, wives and daughters of émigrés, nuns who refused the civic oath and so on, but in Toulouse well over two thirds of the suspects were from the two former privileged orders while at Dijon about half were. In these cities, where aristocratic power had focused greatly on the parlements, the committees contributed more than any other revolutionary institution to visibly overturning the old social order. Elsewhere, however, counterrevolution wore a different mask and so the victims came from different social categories. Almost all the suspects at Fontenay-le-Comte on the very edge of the *Vendée militaire* were artisans or labourers who were thought to be sympathetic to the rebels. Further away from the civil war zones, 'fanatisme' was often one of the most important reasons for arrest. Thus at Montauban in the Lot, nearly half the suspects were country people and 'complicity with the refractories' was the third largest category. For the committee of Sainte-Foy-la-Grande in the Gironde, 'fanatics' were the second largest category, while at Sainte-Geniez-d'Olt in the Aveyron 25 of 44 rural suspects, who comprised once again over half the total, were arrested for trying to protect a refractory priest or for insulting the constitutional. Indeed, in some country districts of the Calvados, Côtes-du-Nord, Pas-de-Calais and Nord, a suspect was automatically someone who refused to go to the Mass of the constitutional priest. In short, for all the bombast against the rich in the Year II, the committees were less instruments of the class war than new institutions for the continuation of the local struggle against counterrevolution. The Civil Constitution of the Clergy may have been a dead letter by the Year II; the struggle against its enemies continued, as, of course, it did afterwards.

In the eyes of the *sans-culottes*, the revolutionary armies were supposed to represent the quintessence of the Revolution, a mobile society of the most pure, striking fear into the hearts of the rich, the counterrevolutionaries and the backward peasants. What a disappointment they must have been! Aside from the Paris army, there were only fifty-six local ones, many of them remarkably small and remarkably short-lived. Conditions of pay and service were better than those of the regular army, and so a few attracted an embarrassing number of young men of military age, to the consternation, naturally, of the older *sans-culottes*. Most of the soldiers were quite ordinary people, married men of humble origin, mostly, but not entirely townsmen, with no impressive pedigree in revolutionary politics, so that unlike the Paris army, and a handful of others, whose members passed through the white-hot scrutiny of the revolutionary committees and popular societies, there was considerable reluctance to undertake the great punitive expeditions which were the armies' theoretical *raison d'être*. Most of the armies' activities involved seconding local authorities in searching out suspects, guarding jails, escorting prisoners, acquiring precious metals, and so on. The bulk of the Parisian army was scattered throughout the customary supply zone of the capital along the Seine valley and into the Beauce, guaranteeing grain shipments against the bad faith of farmers, millers, grain dealers and ordinary people who were always terrified of departures in times of shortage. Thus the revolutionary army acted against the interests and aspirations of many of those who had rioted in these same regions in 1792 and illlustrate the very narrow social base the extreme institutions had. For the radical townsmen, however, these activities were not great operations but the daily experience of thousands of petty details and frustrations. The atrocities which can be pinned on the revolutionary armies – in the Morbihan, Aveyron and Ariège – were far from typical. Rare too were the civil commissioners, men of heterogeneous but scarcely plebeian backgrounds, united in their close links with the clubs and their instinctive devotion to the egalitarian Republic and their hatred of the rich. For many of the military officers, whether they had previous experience or whether they were recruited from the National Guard, the revolutionary armies were often simply stepping stones in their careers.

The Politics and Bureaucracy of Terror

Despite many problems remaining, by the end of 1793 the Montagnards had gone a long way towards saving the Republic. No one could have underestimated the remaining dangers. The allies were at bay but the war was hardly over. The armed counterrevolution was defeated, yet no one could be sure of that and there was still punishment to be inflicted. The value of the assignat had risen but the subsistence question remained in all its myriad complexity. Still, it was time to take stock. Some Montagnards of hitherto impeccable political records began to question whether the Terror still needed to be so intense. Since many of these men were also involved in questionable financial operations the debate over principle became impossibly confused in shady dealings. The result was to stifle debate within the Montagnards and push the country further towards dictatorship. Another process 'from below' worked in the same direction. It was obvious that the Terror was hardly a system of government. It was intended to be an expedient and showed it in everyday activities. For all that the Jacobins, *sans-culottes* and terrorists saw themselves as belonging to a single movement dedicated to liberty and happiness, there was too much local control, too much local definition of priorities and too much scope for bizarre or zealous or fanatical individuals to go their own way. There was not yet the 'single will' that Robespierre had called for earlier that summer. Yet bureaucratic tendencies within the revolutionary movement were already working towards making administration more uniform. The bureaucratic spirit was implicit in the *levée en masse* and the attempt to mobilize the nation's resources for war. It had already coopted the revolutionary committees and so subverted democratic local control of police. The tendency continued throughout the winter and spring. Moreover, the resistance which had begun to crop up here and there – to dechristianization, to controlled prices and requisitions and to conscription in parts of the west and the Massif Central – invited greater control and repression. Thus the Terror was becoming more and more a system. But since it could not accommodate dissident Montagnards, the atmosphere of crisis at the top continued.

For all its intractability, the reform of the controlled economy in ventôse–germinal (February–March) was the easiest to decide in principle. By allowing higher prices and margins, the government admitted its evident inability to constrain the economy completely and attempted to bind private interest more closely to overall state direction. It was also a concession, especially in the food trades, to producers, dealers and retailers, no small constituency in themselves, at the expense of consumers. Needless to say, there was considerable murmuring in Paris, although no one defended them in the Convention.

The politics of dechristianization was a good deal more complicated. Robespierre, Saint-Just and the Committee of General Security had received mutual denunciations from Danton's friends, Fabre d'Eglantine and Chabot, implicating each other as well as Hébert in corrupt dealings in the winding up of the India Company. This incredibly complicated intrigue was supposed to involve cosmopolitan revolutionaries like Cloots, the English bankers Boyd and Rutledge, the German bankers Frei, and its mastermind, the counterrevolutionary adventurer the Baron de Batz who had tried to save Louis XVI on the very day of his execution. Thus was born the Foreign Plot, a supposedly vast international conspiracy to bring the Revolution down, which in a sense it did since it began a process which contributed not only to the fall of Hébert and Danton but of Robespierre as well. Much, but not all of the plot was a figment, but through it Robespierre had an additional reason to condemn the extremism he had always distrusted, because some of the most active dechristianizers had also been denounced as conspirators. Even without the plot, he was offended by the movement's apparent atheism because, like many of his contemporaries, he believed it socially corrosive and morally offensive and he saw it as a useless provocation of the religious sensibilities of ordinary people. To denounce it required some courage as well, since the dechristianizing deputies were an important lobby who might have expected support from Couthon and Collot d'Herbois in the Committee. To attack dechristianization was thus both brave and realistic but the Foreign Plot did provide the framework. On 1 frimaire (21 November), at the Jacobins, Robespierre argued that dechristianization would only inflame religious zeal, that priests should be prosecuted only for infractions of the law and that the dechristianizers were agents of foreign powers whose purpose was to discredit the Revolution by exaggerating patriotism. He demanded and got the instant expulsion of a few extremists from the Jacobins. It was a measure, too, of Robespierre's personal ascendancy that Chaumette scuttled for cover and Hébert showered himself with protestations of loyalty. But the Convention's confirmation of religious liberty on 18 frimaire (8 December) was not intended to undo what the dechristianization campaign had accomplished. The churches often remained closed, valuables were still sequestered and the government did nothing to halt priests resigning. In some parts of the southeast their numbers reached a climax in pluviôse (January–February). The declaration of 18 frimaire was a weapon against the government's political enemies; from the point of view of the faithful, even if they were followers of the constitutional curés, let alone the outlawed refractories, it was meaningless. Nor did the government fundamentally object to the dechristianizers' ultimate objective of creating a civil religion eventually to replace Catholicism, so long as it was theistic. This was shown at the festival of the Supreme Being of 20 prairial (8 June), a ceremony intended to inaugurate a series of arid and rationalistic quasi-religious civic ceremonies in honour of deism and virtue. Parisians received the ritual well enough but the deputies who were dragooned into participating grumbled and made crude jokes. Many took it as proof that Robespierre aspired to a personal dictatorship.

The debate over repression also involved corruption and ended by similarly reinforcing fears of a personal dictatorship. The selective destruction of documents, the panic-stricken lying of most of the principals to save their necks, the framing of indictments to achieve maximum publicity and conceal facts the government found inconvenient all make the intrigue extremely difficult to disentangle. Nor can it be assumed that the public utterances of the accused were always a cloak for sordid motives. Danton is a good example. He had never been averse to taking bribes from anyone who offered them but, as Lefebvre pointed out, handsome sums did not always guarantee his conduct. His demands for a relaxation in the Terror in the autumn of 1793 coinciding with the fall of Lyon, the defeat of the Vendeans at Granville and victory on the frontiers were also quite consistent with a man whose public speeches had usually indicated he accepted the Terror only as an expedient. A debate over where legitimate defence stopped and pitiless war to the death of the last enemy began could be conducted on the level of principle alone. Yet things were not so simple. As in the Old Regime, private profit in the public business of equipping the armies was a common and legitimate enterprise and, as always, war contractors and financiers needed patrons and found them among the deputies. One of them, the abbé d'Espagnac, was strongly suspected of having given kickbacks to deputies. Some deputies, particularly those on the Committee of General Security, Amar, Chabot, Julien de Toulouse and possibly the painter David, may also have taken bribes for certificates of non-emigration or for releasing prisoners, while the alteration of the decree liquidating the India Company, in which Chabot and Fabre had implicated each other, seems to have been part of a general scheme to bilk other bankers and financiers, including the Baron de Batz who had extensive shares in water and insurance companies. From mid-October on, Robespierre received increasing amounts of information from interrogations and denunciations and ever since his speech of 1 frimaire denouncing the Foreign Plot and dechristianization, no one knew what the Incorruptible would do. In fact the committees were not inclined to do much: General Security, because a partial purge left Amar still on and he had no interest in pursuing matters, and Public Safety possibly because, with a charge of corruption hanging over his head, Hébert well knew from the political trials then taking place that questions of guilt or innocence were of secondary importance. With the newspaper popular in Paris and distributed through the *sans-culotte* stronghold in the War Office to the armies, having the *Père*

Duchesne on a string was a useful way of restraining *sans-culotte* opinion. Yet the longer the charges of corruption and counterrevolution festered, the more the poisonous Montagnard habit of seeking hidden motives in the utterances of political opponents was reinforced. No debate could be conducted on its merits.

Yet the balance could not be easily maintained. The Indulgents, as those who wanted a relaxation of the Terror were called, began their campaign as early as 10 November when Danton's friend Thuriot denounced the bloodlust of unnamed individuals and Chabot denounced the tyranny of the committees. The next day, Philippeaux, just returned from his mission in the Vendée, began a long campaign against Ronsin, the commander of the revolutionary army, and the incompetent *sans-culotte* general, Rossignol, for their disastrous interference with the operations of the professional officers in the west. With the revelation by Amar of the general contours of the Foreign Plot a week later, the return of Danton from a rest in the country shortly after and Robespierre's 1 frimaire speech, extremism was on the run. In the famous third number of his *Vieux Cordelier* published on 25 frimaire (15 December), Desmoulins drew an audacious parallel between the tyranny of the Caesars and the bloodletting of the present and attacked the Committee of Public Safety directly. Two days later, the Indulgents persuaded the Convention to arrest Ronsin and Vincent, Hébert's protégé at the War Office. The Indulgents had gone too far. Collot d'Herbois, fresh from regenerating Lyon, alarmed no doubt that attacks on Ronsin's revolutionary army would compromise his own activities, returned to Paris on 1 nivôse (21 December), raised Hébert from his lethargy and the two rounded on the Indulgents in the Jacobin club. This in turn threatened to divide the Committee itself, so on 5 nivôse (25 December), Robespierre tried to recall the factions to first principles by defining revolutionary government as one with exceptional powers but not capricious in practice. After revolutionary government had saved the country, a regular constitution could be implemented. This speech was very important because he added to these platitudes his own sinister gloss equating the struggle to one between virtue and vice, with vice a weapon of foreign spies. Revolutionary government was thus also moral government, an interpretation no one had foreseen the previous March when most of the exceptional laws were passed.

But the truce Robespierre hoped for did not last. Fabre was finally arrested which must have alarmed the Indulgents, while the Cordeliers began an agitation which resulted in the release of Ronsin and Vincent on 14 pluviôse (2 February). They were looking for revenge and Hébert joined both them and Carrier in a cry for a new 'holy insurrection' against an oppressive faction worse than Brissot's, a faction they so carelessly and widely defined that it included the entire revolutionary government. Since this came at a time when the common people of Paris were distressed over shortages and the revision of the maximum, and since the militants remained attached to the idea of a mass assault on rural hoarders by the revolutionary army equipped with a mobile guillotine, the situation was extremely dangerous. When the Cordeliers covered the Declaration of Rights with a black funeral cloth as a symbol of oppression, the Committee of Public Safety had to act. The 'conspirators' thus played straight into the government's hands. Hébert forgot, if he ever knew, that contrary to the myth of merely launching a call to arms, the sections would have to be organized. In the end only one section showed a halting sympathy and the commune stood aside. Hanriot, commander of the National Guard, was overtly hostile. Ronsin, far from organizing the revolutionary army for a coup, ordered artillery and cavalry detachments to missions further from the capital. But the volubility of this political general and the ultras in the Cordeliers allowed Fouquier-Tinville, prosecutor of the Revolutionary Tribunal, to construct an elaborate indictment charging the Hébertists with planning a military coup to be followed by a horrible series of prison massacres and famine plots to prepare the return of the monarchy. It was a diabolically clever method of turning the subsistence question to the government's advantage. On 4 germinal (24 March), the Hébertists – Hébert, Vincent, Momoro and Ronsin, as well as Cloots, tossed into the dock to prove the Foreign Plot – were guillotined.

The fall of the Hébertists also led to the fall of the Dantonists. Amar produced a report on the corruption of Chabot and Fabre but Desmoulins brought out another issue of the *Vieux Cordelier* renewing the attacks on the committees and the continuing violations of civil rights. In the Convention, the Indulgents secured the arrest of one of the Committee of General Security's chief agents. This challenge in the Convention was a threat to the committees who therefore decided to arrest Danton himself. He had remained prudently silent for the previous month but the

Committee of Public Safety probably feared he would become a rallying point for the Indulgents and so a preemptive strike was necessary. After a travesty of a trial, Danton and his leading associates – including Delacroix, Desmoulins, Philippeaux, Fabre – were executed on 16 germinal (5 April).

The fall of the factions was supposed to put an end to the great political trials but this was impossible so long as men associated with the factions were still active. Among the Dantonists, Bourdon had survived, and among the radicals, deputies like Carrier and Fouché, not to mention Collot himself, if they were not Hébertists, were still closely associated with the ultrarevolutionaries. So survivors of both factions remained to be denounced and perhaps, in their turn, to be purged. Men like these had everything to fear from the dictatorship of the committees. The trials also had a decisive effect on the *sans-culotte* movement. When Ronsin and the Cordeliers raised the cry of insurrection, they implicitly raised the question of what had happened to the old maxim that moderation was dangerous and counterrevolutionary. But, however useful the Committee of Public Safety found the support of the Indulgents, it had not become their prisoner. Instead, it had become a government. There was nothing new in this. From the beginning, the *Actes* of the Committee of Public Safety are full of the mundane things to be expected of a war government – directing representatives or its agents to requisition grain, saltpetre, cavalry horses and so on, or overseeing the movement of armies on the frontiers or in the interior. This aspect of its work was symbolized by Carnot buried in mountains of directives and campaign strategies for eighteen hours a day. The organizing and bureaucratic spirit behind the law of 14 frimaire (4 December) was therefore not new. It did represent a fundamental shift of tactics. Instead of representatives, special commissioners and local revolutionary bodies interpreting decrees as they saw fit, in the hope that their collective efforts would act as a hidden hand guiding the nation to victory, all was now to be subordinated to the Convention and its committees. The role of the departments in local government was much downgraded in favour of the districts which were put under the effective control of 'national agents' appointed by and responsible to the government. Unlike the 1790 arrangement, therefore, local bodies, elected or not, could not claim to be emanations of the sovereign which was now formally at the centre. It is a prerogative that no French government since has surrendered. The powers of the representatives on mission were also circumscribed since no tax, loan or armed force could be raised without official sanction. All provincial authorities were to correspond at least every *décade* with the committee. Parallel authorities like regional revolutionary committees and local revolutionary armies were suppressed, and others, like local revolutionary committees, were made more responsible to the government or, like the revolutionary courts, reminded that they existed on sufferance.

Although it proved far from easy to implement, the law of 14 frimaire was a major step in bureaucratizing the Terror and it can be shown that by the spring, in police matters at least, the revolutionary committees were increasingly responsive to the central government. The committees of government, therefore, had acquired immense power. What turned them into a genuine dictatorship were the laws of 8 and 13 ventôse (26 February, 3 March). These are usually seen in a different light. The proposal to sequester the property of suspects and use it as a basis to indemnify poor patriots has been interpreted as a manoeuvre to pacify the *sans-culottes* during the struggle against the Hébertists or as a poorly conceived and inadequate measure to solve the problem of rural poverty. It was hardly that, since Saint-Just's speeches justifying the laws made it clear they were another measure to undermine the internal enemy. Moreover, it was applied in intended partisan fashion in the Puy-de-Dôme at least, where small property-holders found their way on to the lists while some of the genuinely destitute were omitted for political reasons. But the ventôse laws also transformed an emergency government into a dictatorship whose results would be permanent. On 10 October, the government had been declared revolutionary until the peace, underlining the transitory nature of the regime, but the confiscation of the property of suspects and their perpetual banishment even after the conclusion of peace implied that revolutionary government would have lasting social consequences. The Committee of General Security was given the power to release or detain suspects after reviewing tables forwarded by local revolutionary committees. In other words, the laws introduced an administrative system of arrests and punishments whose results went far beyond the temporary deprivation of liberty envisaged by the Law of Suspects. One measure of the effectiveness of the terrorist bureaucracy is that by early May the Committee of

General Security had received dossiers on about half the suspects.

The Jacobin dictatorship, like all dictatorships, began at the top and seeped down, absorbing or crushing any resistance. The *sans-culotte* movement was a major victim. The strength of the section movement was progressively weakened in the course of the Year II. It has been estimated that no less than twenty-three thousand Parisians were absorbed into the army by the *levée en masse* alone, while large numbers of older militants found their way into the swelling civilian bureaucracy as clerks, commissioners, procurement agents, and so on. The War Office was a notorious *sans-culotte* fief thanks to Vincent, and the Committee of Public Safety alone employed hu ndreds of people. For all their predilection for local squabbles, the rev olutionary committees were also part of the police bureaucracy. In short, *sans-culottisme*, whether as individuals or institutions, was simply grafted on to the Jacobin bureaucracy. Where this did not happen, as in the case of the sections and popular societies, they were ploughed under. The response to limiting section meetings to two per *décade* was the formation of a large number of clubs or popular societies whose militants, acting either as a caucus or through the revolutionary committees, influenced section meetings, arranged nominations to sectional offices, controlled certificats de civisme and attempted to dominate women's and young people's organizations. The government naturally looked on the societies with some suspicion and first the Jacobins, then the Cordeliers, refused affiliation to any society founded after 31 May. It is probably no coincidence that this harder line came at the same time as Robespierre's denunciation of the Foreign Plot and the extremists, a warning to which the societies were sensitive as well since they had always believed in the doctrine of an interior enemy working in the shadows on naive patriots. The result was an orgy of self-purgings, which excluded anyone whose revolutionary pedigree did not stretch back to 1789 or else which eliminated the cowardly, the weak or the lazy. In many cases, these were impossibly high standards which only served to set militants in the societies and the revolutionary committees against each other and isolate all of them from ordinary people who quite naturally resented the arrogance of such men. Moreover, the militants were less and less responsible to their fellow citizens. By an abusive interpretation of the law of 14 frimaire, the Paris commune began to fill empty seats on its council by cooptation rather than election, or simply left the seats of purged members empty. It also successfully claimed the power to review the membership of the revolutionary and civil committees of the sections. General meetings of the entire section became increasingly meaningless and reverted to activities which had been prominent since the beginning of the war such as collecting saltpetre, gathering militarily useful equipment or denouncing hoarders and big merchants. Thus, even before the fall of the Hébertists, much of the spontaneity had evaporated from neighbourhood political life and many militants had become willing agents of the committees or the now self-perpetuating commune. But the law of 14 frimaire subjected the commune even more to the government, and the all-important revolutionary committees were made directly subordinate to the Committee of General Security, bypassing the commune altogether. This gradual cooptation probably had some influence in cauterizing the militants against any temptation to join the Cordeliers in their cry for an insurrection in ventôse. After the arrests of both Hébert and Danton, the stupor, confusion, even anger of many militants must have been tempered by the knowledge that they had joined the rogues' gallery of popular politicians who, from the Duc d'Orléans and Lafayette in 1789 onwards, had always been false patriots and secret intriguers and who were now unmasked. In the final analysis, for all the wild talk about there being only fifteen patriots in it or replacing it with a 'grand juge', the militants trusted the Convention. But the trust was hardly reciprocal, for as Soboul so justly remarked, what was on trial in germinal was *sans-culotterie* itself and the government men profited from it. Marat's reputation in popular opinion went into eclipse on the grounds that if Hébert was guilty, the *Ami du Peuple* must have been too. In the provinces, there was a minor wave of denunciation against ultra-revolutionaries, while some sections in Paris began purging 'partisans of Hébert', and the Committee of General Security ordered a minor sweep of officials of the revolutionary committees who were suspected of Hébertist sympathies. It was the first time since the repression following the Champ de Mars Affair in 1791 that extremism was not an asset. The sweep was fairly limited, however, a warning to those who remained to adhere to the government line. More serious was the rapid dissolution of the Paris revolutionary army, the suppression of the *commissaires aux accaparements*, the replacement of the War Office by a number of commissions and the scattering of the *sans-culotte* officials throughout the bureaucracy and, with the arrest and execution first of Chaumette and then the mayor, Pache, the appointment of Jacobin loyalists to the commune. Finally, at the urging and intimidation of the Jacobins, the fraternal and popular societies began to dissolve themselves. By early prairial (late May), thirty-nine had disappeared, their former members directed to rally round the 'sainte Montagne'. It was the end of the *sans-culottes* as an autonomous movement.

The Tragedy of Terror

It would be comforting indeed to conclude that there was a direct connection between the fall of Robespierre and the disciplining of the *sans-culottes*, the collapse of the dictatorship being the ironic dénouement of the repression of the *sans-culottes*. The situation was a good deal more complex, for there is every reason to think that the Jacobin dictatorship had become largely independent of the popular movement which had contributed so much to its rise. After one had the Subsistence Commission, for example, one no longer needed the revolutionary armies. Once one had the national agents, one was less dependent on the clubs and revolutionary committees for reliable personnel. And so on. The completeness of the process of bureaucratization should not be exaggerated, but, with time, it might have become still more reliable and solid. That it did not, had less to do with popular disaffection than with the inability of the Montagnards to put an end to their fatal quarrels.

With the fall of the factions, the Committee of Public Safety had imposed a political settlement on the Convention. But there was no consensus. Many Indulgents remained, cowed for the moment but with a fallen hero to avenge. Some of the extremist deputies also had reason to fear. Carrier, who had compromised himself with the Cordeliers in ventôse, had also been denounced by the Committee's special agent, the odious young fanatic, Marc-Antoine Jullien, for 'oppressing patriots', an extraordinary confusion since the patriots in question were responsible for the *noyades* at Nantes and for shooting a handful of peasants emerging from church at Noyal-Muzillac in the Morbihan. There was also a more or less permanent lobby of Jacobins from Lyon in the capital steadily denouncing Collot d'Herbois and Fouché for abuses of power. At Marseille and Toulon, Fréron and Barras had been extremist enough by anyone's standards, attributing the 'unexpected successes' of their mission to 'inflexible severity', presumably their own, lambasting their predecessor Albitte for his repugnance for 'grandes mesures', and claiming the dockers, sailors and port workers of Toulon were as counterrevolutionary and as selfish as the wholesalers and merchants. All this undoubtedly went down rather well with native Jacobins but the two deputies went too far when they ran foul of the officials of the Revolutionary Tribunal of Marseille whom they accused of moderation. Also they changed the name of Marseille to 'Sans-nom', thus apparently punishing all the inhabitants for the transgressions of the federalist cabal. The Marseille Jacobins too joined the chorus denouncing representatives to the Convention. In general terms then, these struggles were not so much between a Committee of Public Safety anxious to moderate the Terror and a group of extremist deputies determined to go their own way, often in defiance of the law of 14 frimaire or the declarations of religious liberty, although in the cases of Javogues and Fouché there was an element of this. Rather, they were often disputes between terrorist deputies and local Jacobins whose exaggerations had done so much to bring on the federalist crisis in the first place and whose intense communalism quickly led them to resent the tutelage of outsiders. In Lyon, for example, where the representatives had never allowed local Jacobins much scope, Fouché considered Chalier's friends so extreme and so disrespectful of authority that he closed the club. His suspicions were not entirely groundless either since they and the national agent had criticized the dreaded *Commission Temporaire* for releasing too many suspects. Yet Robespierre took the side of the 'oppressed patriots' in the Convention on 1 germinal (21 March), secured orders they be pursued no longer and got Fouché recalled to explain his conduct. Similarly, when Marc-Antoine Jullien denounced Tallien and Ysabeau at Bordeaux, he did so on the basis of their not pursuing a policy of economic levelling directed against the merchant class. Thus when deputies like this were recalled to Paris, the disputes were over the scope and direction of the Terror, not its principles, differences of opinion which could be mortal all the same.

An indication of the Committee of Public Safety's thinking was policy towards the pacification of the Vendée. One of its members, Prieur de la Marne, was present when General Turreau presented his infamous plan of destruction. He undoubtedly knew, as the Committee of Public Safety undoubtedly knew, of Turreau's general orders to his subordinates commanding the 'infernal columns' when they began operations in January: 'You will employ every means to discover the rebels, everyone will be bayoneted; the villages, farms, woods, wastelands, scrub and generally all which can be burned, will be put to the torch.' In any case, the representatives Garrau and Hentz were sent out to supervise Turreau and 'to coordinate the means of exterminating the Vendeans'. In February Prieur approved a plan creating what a later generation wold call a 'free-fire zone', after the evacuation of 'patriots'. Turreau himself was relieved of his command in floréal (May), less because of the savagery of his troops, which had been denounced to the government for at least two months, than because wholesale destruction had reignited resistance. Even so, some of his subordinates still managed to lead marauding expeditions into the interior of the *Vendée militaire* burning all before them without control or reprimand from higher authority. Adding to the policy of rigour was the ubiquitous Jullien who denounced the generals to Robespierre for not winning the war in weeks because they were corrupt secret royalists. After all, they had to have been royalists since they were not winning. In fact, what brought this phase of self-destructive repression in the Vendée to an end was less a new-found humanitarianism than the necessity to remove troops from the region to reinforce the army on the frontiers for the summer campaign. With an offensive policy no longer possible, it might have been logical to offer an amnesty but the Committee of Public Safety explicitly denied that it was considering one. Even 'unarmed rebels', however such a category was to be defined, were to be brought before the military commissions while the 'misled', another undefined category, were only promised 'generous' treatment. Policy towards the 'interior enemy' had thus reached the point of utter sterility. Its lasting results consisted of exterminating up to one third of the population of some communes and so reducing the region's productive capacity that some market towns were still uninhabited in 1800.

The fact is that the government meant to have sole control of the apparatus of repression and often relied upon extremist local groups to wrest it from the representatives. As experience in the Vendée showed, it did not necessarily mean to moderate it. The law of 19 floréal (8 May) suppressed the provincial revolutionary tribunals and commissions outside the capital and gave exclusive jurisdiction to try counterrevolutionary crimes to the Paris

Revolutionary Tribunal. The law of 22 prairial (10 June) deprived the accused of counsel and the right to call defence witnesses and allowed the jury to convict on the basis of moral certainty. This notorious law thus created a murder machine. It was envisaged that a good proportion of the accused were to be sent up by the six special commissions (only two were ever established) which, by Saint-Just's ventôse laws, were to process the dossiers of suspects. They were now to funnel unfortunate individuals, accused of the vaguest of crimes and convicted simply by administrative fiat, to a tribunal which could only acquit or punish with death. This inaugurated the Great Terror in Paris where 57 per cent of all the victims of the Revolutionary Tribunal were convicted in June and July alone, amid tales of prison plots, Baron de Batz plots, and other fantasies.

The law of 22 prairial itself was passed because the Committee of Public Safety were afraid for their own lives after assassination attempts on Robespierre and Collot d'Herbois. It is an interesting commentary on the pervasive atmosphere of black suspicion that this law was seen as a solution when, in more normal times, the committee men might have hired some alert bodyguards. In fact, no deputy could feel safe after Robespierre's denunciation of Danton which was an interminable litany of personal vices and political errors, a useful rhetorical weapon when directed against the Girondins and when the only penalty was intended to be expulsion from the Convention, but deadly a year later. Worse still, the law of 22 prairial quietly removed the deputies' already frayed right to parliamentary immunity and, as in earlier crises in 1789 and the spring of 1793, even ordinary deputies had taken to carrying arms and sleeping at different addresses. However, the swirling discontent might have been mastered had the governing committees not fallen out. The Committee of General Security interpreted the Committee of Public Safety's creation of its own police bureau as the beginning of a usurpation of its functions and there were rumours that the bureau was Robespierre's personal agency. Amidst innumerable petty rivalries, some members of the Committee of General Security took the fête of the Supreme Being on 20 prairial (8 June, Pentecost in the old calendar) not only as an occasion for clever wisecracks but also as a prefiguration of an appeasement with Catholicism. They thus became a focus of support for the dechristianizing deputies. One of its own members, Vadier, was able to turn a report on Catherine Théot, a self-styled

'Mère de Dieu' and harmless visionary whose prophecies of the end of days included the identification of Robespierre with the Messiah, into a sarcastic diatribe against religion and counterrevolution. In fact, much of the opposition to Robespierre in general came from rabid anticlericals and dechristianizers who represented the Midi and the west, regions in which defence of the Revolution and vigorous measures against the clergy had always been synonymous. If the two governing committees were snarling at each other over both personal and policy matters such as these, so too were individual members of the Committee of Public Safety. The loose triumvirate of Robespierre, Couthon and Saint-Just did less and less of the daily administrative work which undoubtedly peeved the workhorses, Carnot, Lindet and Prieur de la Côte-d'Or. Billaud-Varennes and Collot d'Herbois were hostile to Robespierre's attempt to delay the Théot case and were probably sympathetic to Vadier on policy matters anyway. Robespierre also insisted on handling the Théot case personally because he thought Vadier's report minimized connections with bigger conspiracies which manipulated the credulous, and this could hardly have aided relations between the committees. Finally, Saint-Just resented the general lack of interest in implementing certain provisions of his ventôse laws.

Most of the threads thus led to the Incorruptible but his position was greatly undermined by victory at the Battle of Fleurus on 8 messidor (26 June). With the Austrian armies in retreat, the Prussians more interested in gobbling more of Poland and with the armies of Pichegru and Jourdan in Brussels and Antwerp just over a week later, the case for the Terror as an emergency government was much weaker. But on 17 ventôse (5 February) Robespierre had defined the purpose of the Republic as regenerating private and public morals, and so in his mind there was no connection between military success which was the original purpose of the legislation of March–April 1793 and relaxation of the Terror. Yet Robespierre had ceased to attend either the Convention or the Committee after mid-June probably because of a dispute with his colleagues over how many people to kill under the provisions of the prairial law. He continued to work on his dossiers at home, which only increased suspicions against him among almost everyone in and out of the Committee. He undoubtedly planned to purge at least four deputies, including Fouché who turned to outright conspiracy soon after Robespierre persuaded the Jacobins to expel him. The practised intriguer retaliated by simply spreading rumours about who was next on the list of those to be purged. Right up to the last minute, however, there was a possibility of an accommodation between the two governing committees and on 4–5 thermidor (22–23 July), a truce involving promises to reduce the power of the police bureau and to speed the reviewing of suspects' dossiers was reached. The price of reconciliation in other words was to be hundreds more executions. No one had any qualms about this but Robespierre broke the truce because he suspected the sincerity of his colleagues. On 8 thermidor he appealed over their heads to the Convention. In a rambling and maudlin speech, he attacked the Indulgents and, as a way of unmasking a 'criminal coalition' in the Convention, he called for a purge of unnamed individuals in the two governing committees. Some of the more moderate deputies might have been only too happy to support this since the issue the speech raised overrode the tortuous delivery. Robespierre also received rousing support in the Jacobin club which met that evening. When he repeated his speech and Billaud and Collot tried to reply, they were chased from the society with cries of 'Les conspirateurs à la guillotine' ringing in their ears. This, however, shattered the public façade of the Committee. They could only turn to the other conspirators. When Saint-Just tried the next day to read what he intended to be a conciliatory speech in the Convention, Tallien interrupted. Collot, who was in the chair, then allowed Billaud and Vadier to launch direct attacks on Robespierre. Each time he in turn tried to defend himself, a prearranged hubbub drowned him out. Finally, the Convention decreed the arrest of Robespierre, his brother Augustin, Couthon, Saint-Just and Le Bas, their friend on the Committee of General Security. Less than an hour later, the commune intervened. Armed force, not parliamentary manoeuvres, would decide the *journée* of 9 thermidor.

It is common to explain the tepid support the commune received from the sections by referring to the maximum on wages which was finally announced on 5 thermidor. The drastic reductions envisaged were extremely unpopular, and since the commune had been applying the Le Chapelier law forbidding workers' associations since the previous April to stop strikes for higher pay, it 'lost the support of the Parisian *sans-culottes*'. This assumes, of course, that the *sans-culottes* were all wage-earners which was far from being the case. In fact, the social composition of the commune which applied these measures was itself '*sans-culotte*': the usual mix of artisans, small manufacturers, officials and professionals who were the cutting edge of the Revolution. In the holocaust that was visited on the general council on 10–12 thermidor – 84 members were executed for supporting the Robespierrists – a minimum of 40 would have to be classed as artisans of varying skills. The maximum on wages undoubtedly counted but the judgement has to be tempered with the suspicion that *sans-culotte* employers of labour might have welcomed it, just as they might have welcomed the revision of the maximum. As always, questions of economic policy could divide as much as unite.

The outcome of the *journée* depended above all on leadership and organization. The Convention moved quickly. In the early afternoon, Barère had a proclamation printed up warning the sections against the agitation of a handful of intriguers. By 9 p.m., this was in the hands of all the sections and nineteen either refused the commune's call to assemble or quickly drafted addresses of loyalty to the Convention. (These were not particularly moderate sections since fifteen of them had adhered to the Halle-au-Blé petition of 15 April 1793 demanding the removal of the Girondins from the Convention.) The Committee of General Security similarly put the revolutionary committees on guard and only ten of these sent delegates to the commune, mostly as observers who, after being forced to take an anodyne oath to 'la patrie', returned to inform their sections of the seditious actions of the commune. This was extremely important, for the fundamental police agencies of Paris thus remained loyal to the Convention. Because these bodies had had a strong influence over the sections since the autumn and were staffed with a high percentage of artisans and small shopkeepers, a significant proportion of *sans-culottes* also opted for the Convention. Equally important was the attitude of the armed forces. The Convention ordered the arrest of Hanriot, commander of the National Guard, and with his influence removed four of the six legion commanders consequently remained loyal to the government. The other two, more out of confusion and negligence, complied with the commune's order to send troops to the Hôtel de Ville. Thus, about two thirds of the city's National Guard remained lost to the supporters of Robespierre. All of this left the commune in considerable difficulty. Where every *journée* since 10 August had taken at least a week to organize, this crisis had broken so quickly that there were only a few hours. The 9 thermidor was not a regular meeting day and members of the commune and sections had to be found and summoned, often in conditions of incredible confusion. When the extraordinary session of the commune opened at 5.30 p.m., no more than thirty (of 140) councillors were present, while others drifted in over the next few hours largely ignorant of the situation and of decisions which had already been taken. The Jacobins were also thrown into disarray. Although some members did comprise themselves, the club itself did not send a delegation to the commune until after 1 a.m., when the whole enterprise was on the verge of collapse. Many sections were torn. Bonconseil (formerly Mauconseil), the first section to demand the overthrow of the monarchy two years before, sent off deputations to both commune and Convention and militants returned to the assembly to quarrel for hours about what to do and finally recalled its artillery. Popincourt, in the faubourg Saint-Antoine, at first believed the trouble had to do with workers' grievances over the maximum or with plots to assassinate Robespierre, then, when the clouds cleared a bit, its civil commissioners and general assembly opted for the Convention, its artillery for the commune.

The commune's one success led directly to its undoing. Throughout the night, small units liberated Hanriot and the five deputies from their various places of confinement and escorted them to the Hôtel de Ville. None of the deputies exercised much leadership once they arrived but this was probably less important than is usually thought, since none of them had ever been good revolutionary tacticians and the commune had already formed a 'Committee of Execution' which was planning an armed assault on the Convention the next day. The progressive liberations, however, provoked the Convention to declare Robespierre and his colleagues, as well as the commune, outside the law. This meant that any one of them could be executed within twenty-four hours, without trial, once a criminal or revolutionary court had simply verified their identity. The vicious law had first been introduced by Saint-Just against the Girondin deputies at Caen in July 1793 and was now being turned against him. The declaration of outlawry wasted the commune's only asset. Although the response of the National Guard had been relatively poor, this still left 3400 of them to gather on the Place de Grève before the Hôtel de Ville, more than enough to undertake a serious military operation, especially since seventeen section artillery companies with a total of thirty-two highly mobile pieces obeyed the orders of Hanriot's artillery commander. But the outlawry decree decided many sections. As soon as they heard of it, special commissioners or officials of the revolutionary committees made their way to the Place de Grève and persuaded their detachments to go home. Seeing this, other sectional forces just drifted away. By 1.30 a.m., the Place de Grève was empty.

The Convention had triumphed and it triumphed because its own prestige was greater than any popular loyalty to individual deputies. This had always been true and after the trial of the Hébertists and Dantonists in germinal, the Convention had shown how foolish defiance was. From the point of view of the exercise of political power, the Convention worked through the hierarchies of *sans-culotte* institutions, through National Guard command structures and the revolutionary committees. Unlike the *journée* of 5 September, neither the commune nor the Jacobin club could mobilize the militants, the former because the Committee of General Security controlled the revolutionary committees and the law of 14 frimaire had stripped the commune of much of its power, the latter because, after the self-destruction of the popular and fraternal societies, it no longer had any affiliates in the city. Like 5 September, however, the 9 thermidor was a popular *journée* even if, this time, it was directed against militants.

The dénouement was swift and pathetic. When they heard that the section companies had disappeared, the deputies in the Hôtel de Ville despaired. Le Bas killed himself with a pistol, Robespierre tried to do the same but only broke his jaw, Augustin threw himself from a window but survived even though he landed head first, Couthon fell down a flight of stairs while trying to manoeuvre his wheelchair, Hanriot flung himself into a small courtyard where he lay undiscovered for twelve hours. Only Saint-Just remained unperturbed. Thus, when the Convention's forces, composed for the most part of companies from the sections led by the deputies Barras and Léonard Bourdon, finally invested the Hôtel de Ville around 2 a.m., there was no one to fight, only dispirited and disfigured bodies to carry off. Later that same afternoon, 10 thermidor, after identification by the Revolutionary Tribunal, Robespierre, his brother and his friends were executed.

Although no one knew it, the Terror was over.

Chapter 7

Thermidor and Counterterror

Contours of Thermidor

Everyone has a theory about when the Revolution 'went wrong'.
For out-and-out reactionaries at the time with selective memories,
it was the decision of the feeble Louis XVI to call the Estates-
General in 1788. For liberal monarchists like Mme de Staël, it was
the failure to stem the rising tide of Jacobinism in 1792. Such views
have been out of favour for over a century and the profession has
settled on thermidor as a convenient date. If the Revolution was a
genuinely popular revolution, the argument goes, then the
destruction of a popular government on 9–10 thermidor or,
alternatively, the defeat of the *sans-culottes* in germinal–prairial An
III, marked the end of the Revolution. The aftermath was a
depressing downhill slide into reaction, mindless violence, failed
bourgeois consolidation, shocking corruption, heartless
indifference to the poor and political instability until finally the
ruthless man on horseback put an end to the experiment and
launched the nation on ultimately fruitless and endless wars of
conquest.

No one can deny that something did go horribly wrong after
thermidor but winding up revolutionary government was not the
sole reason for the gathering catastrophe that befell the country
between 1794 and 1801. In the first place, not even the Montagnards
had ever had a clear and consistent definition of what they meant
by 'revolutionary government' and unless one is to follow Mathiez
and erect Robespierre into the arbiter of orthodoxy, one has to
admit that many Montagnards were thoroughly sick or thoroughly
frightened of the policy of unrestricted repression. It was after all
a cabal of ultraterrorists in the Convention who engineered
Robespierre's fall and the critical agents of the revolutionary
committees of Paris who let it happen on the night of 9–10
thermidor. One of the most remarkable aspects of the immediate
post-thermidor period is the extent of the discredit of repression.

From ultraegalitarians and democrats like the journalist Babeuf, to the dozens of provincial clubs who profited from the occasion to denounce home-grown Marats who had made themselves thoroughly obnoxious, to the hundreds of suspects or their relatives, a national consensus rapidly emerged against the revolutionary dictatorship. Within a month, this current of public opinion had become powerful enough to affect debates in the Convention and some of the more unscrupulous politicians began to use it against their opponents. This in turn only discredited the democrats who had been the most prominent defenders of revolutionary government. 'Stage two' of the thermidorean reaction, which can be dated from the winter of the Year III, thus involved the persecution, and often murder, of Jacobins and *sans-culottes* in the name of a new settling of accounts.

With no support for 'grandes mesures', the thermidorean Convention had to face problems which had begun to manifest themselves under the Terror and which a combination of circumstances aggravated afterwards. The original purpose of revolutionary government was to defeat internal counterrevolution and the foreign invaders but the process required economic, religious and human sacrifices which many Frenchmen, particularly in the countryside, were not prepared to make. A weaker government therefore had to deal with spreading discontent. Not only did counterrevolution seep into new areas, so too did a whole series of resentments arrayed under royalist banners and slogans. If the Year II was the year of the *sans-culottes*, the Years III–V were the years of the popular counterrevolution. For that reason alone, the Revolution itself was not over.

The thermidoreans might have been able to surmount the problem of counterrevolution if they had been able to end the foreign war, if the economy had not nearly collapsed and if they had been able to manage the government's finances. One of the reasons this proved impossible was the removal of much of the terrorist personnel from government. It is not possible to quantify the size of the political nation in this period but the electoral turnout and the relatively limited numbers in the clubs suggest that the pool of talent willing to devote itself to public service was fairly small. Purging such men often left no other local talent but incompetents, or worse, federalists with their own scores to settle. On top of this, such men were expected to implement remnants of revolutionary legislation on controlling the clergy or managing the economy with which they had no sympathy. The result was an administrative paralysis. The thermidorean reaction began with the best of intentions of restoring the rule of law; it ended by producing an extraordinarily weak government, incapable of defending itself against counterrevolution.

The Rejection of Legality

The overthrow of Robespierre and his friends was largely the work of committed terrorists but renegade terrorists like Tallien and Fréron, Indulgents like Thuriot and Lecointre and hitherto little-known moderates profited most from it. Many of these men had accepted the revolutionary legislation of March–May and September–October 1793 only as an expedient and were dismayed at Robespierre's accretion that it could also be used to construct a moral and just society. They felt too that they had had a narrow escape from a horrifying despotism and they were determined to prevent all possibility of its recurrence. Thus the lack of response to Barère's bland reassurance in the Convention on 10 thermidor that revolutionary government would carry on as before. Tallien persuaded the Convention to accept the principle of rotation on the governing committees; six new members were appointed to the Committee of Public Safety which lost its primordial role of supervising the overall business of government; and by September, five of the still-living members of the Great Committee of the Year II had been removed. The Committee of General Security was similarly purged, while the Paris Revolutionary Tribunal lost its obsequious prosecutor, Fouquier-Tinville, who was impeached. The law of 22 prairial was repealed and arrests could only be made on specific charges which the accused could dispute. Convictions in counterrevolutionary crimes had to take account of the accused's motives as well as his actions. Similarly, the law of 7 fructidor (24 August) suppressed the revolutionary committees in all but the district capitals and in communes with a population of over eight thousand. Those remaining would have jurisdiction over the surrounding countryside and six new members would be appointed every three months by a representative on mission or the Committee of General Security. In Paris, there was to be one committee for each of the twelve new 'arrondissements' into which the sections were grouped and the principle of rotation was imposed on them as well.

In themselves, these reforms removed abuses without severely hampering the operations of government. Furthermore, the law of 19 March 1793 which was the legal basis for repression, the Law of Suspects, the law of 14 frimaire on revolutionary government and the laws requiring the death penalty for returned refractories and émigrés all remained in force. The thermidoreans were clearly trying to make government more effective while restoring the collegial structure of the Convention which the Montagnards had undermined.

Accompanying the reforms was a dramatic decline in the use of repression. The number of death sentences fell suddenly from the summer of the Year II while the bloody revolutionary tribunals of the west became mere police agencies until their cases were transferred to military courts martial or the criminal courts the following winter and spring. The revolutionary committees, often against their own better judgement, began to release suspects under the widest possible interpretation of the law of 21 messidor (9 July 1794). This authorized the release of harvest labourers and small-town artisans, and after 29 thermidor (16 August) it was extended to middle-class people who had been ruined and therefore had to work with their hands. There were outside pressures demanding the release of suspects too. In Paris, for example, it came from the families of moderates who slowly began to return to the section assemblies and from the ordinary *sans-culottes* who had long resented the high-handedness of the revolutionary committees. In the provinces, the pressure sometimes came from the representatives on mission. In the Côte-d'Or, the representative Calès began releasing suspects wholesale in vendémiaire (October) and the last were gone the following pluviôse (January). In the Ille-et-Vilaine, the representative Boursault established a 'Philanthropic Commission' to review suspects' cases. He also released them outright as part of a wider policy of conciliating a disaffected countryside. At Uzès in the Gard, it was the municipality, still largely composed of 'terrorists', which pressured the committee, so successfully that of the three hundred suspects held in the local prison on 1 thermidor (19 July), only a handful remained three months later. With opinion moving against them and little or no support from the Committee of General Security or the representatives, the committees lost heart. Even where the terrorist personnel was retained in the post-fructidor reorganizations, there were very few new arrests. The Law of Suspects merely withered away.

The released suspects and the relatives and friends of the victims of the tribunals soon formed a powerful coalition demanding a settling of accounts with the terrorists. More diffuse but equally debilitating to authority was the continued resistance to dechristianization and the Convention's religious policy generally. In a phenomenon that was to be extremely common for the next five years, many country people interpreted 9 thermidor as a reversal of official anticlericalism. In its overblown rhetoric, the popular society of Pernes in the Pas-de-Calais observed, 'Fanaticism whose hideous head has been crushed by the revolutionary chariot, is a monster which like Robespierre has left a tail which visibly agitates . . . Sundays continue to be a day of rest . . . and solemnity such that there only lacks . . . the ancient and ridiculous antics of the Roman Mass.' But far from being a remnant, such manifestations became more and more common. Around Neufchâtel in the Seine-Inférieure, for instance, 'a village doctor . . . imitates all the superstitious ceremonies of the Catholic cult' since there were no priests to hand. Elsewhere, there were innumerable stories of priests emerging from hiding or returning from abroad to say Mass to hundreds of people, or of people forcing infirm monks newly released from prison to perform baptisms and marriages. As under the Terror, women were in the forefront of demanding the reopening of churches, harassing officials to turn over keys and urging the men to avoid the *fêtes décadaires*. Such demonstrations did not always have a direct political overtone, but occasionally the link with antiterrorism was explicit. On All Saints Day 1794, for instance, five to six thousand people went to the mass graves of the victims of the popular revolutionary commission of Orange. In the event, the local committee arrested the 'poor farm worker [who] . . . recited the litanies of the saints' and issued a stern warning against 'the poisoned breath of fanaticism'. Stern measures of this sort were rare, however. Elsewhere, committees were more inclined than they had been just a few months earlier to leave 'fanatics' alone.

The comparatively sudden relaxation of political repression and the continuing protests over the Convention's religious policy showed that the alienation of town and country was still deep. Economic policy made it worse still. As in so many other areas, the source of the problem can be traced to some of the limitations of the Terror. The financial and economic policies of the revolutionary government did much to keep the towns fed and the armies supplied but the government continued to help finance itself with further emissions of assignats and it did little to improve the system of tax collection. Consequently, the money supply was greater than it ever had been. So long as the government paid for requisitioned materials at fixed prices, this probably did not matter but the amount of paper in private hands must have increased, since the maximum on wages was often more difficult to apply than that on prices. Conscription and the war economy probably also reduced the productive capacity of the civilian sector. After all, this was the price of mobilizing the nation for war. This situation, as well as the persistent shortages, ought to have increased the amount of black marketeering but by definition this is immeasurable and, in any case, the evidence is that the terrorist authorities were able to cope reasonably well throughout the spring and summer thanks to the usual *ad hoc* methods and by introducing more strict rations. The harvest of 1794 completely overwhelmed the system. After a most promising growing season, severe drought in the late summer destroyed much of the crop and rendered the harvest very poor. It was perhaps one third less than that of 1793. The conscription of young farmhands and the requisition of horses and carts for the military also delayed the gathering of the harvest. An intensely cold winter followed. The weather disrupted the transportation system and caused shortages which were unheard of a year before. Huge chunks of ice threatened ships at Le Havre, barges carrying grain and wood were frozen in the canals, the Seine froze all the way up to Paris, and wolves, driven out of the forests by hunger, were seen scavenging at the outskirts of many towns. The controlled economy was therefore subject to enormous pressures and began to crack almost as soon as the harvest was in. Peasants' attempts at fraud and outright defiance were consequently more daring than ever, and even after the harvest was fully gathered urban authorities complained of shortages, complaints which became more shrill as the winter approached. There were reports in Paris that transport workers did nothing else but black marketeering as well as widespread complaints from the common people that they were no better off than in Robespierre's day because the official markets were empty.

The Convention's attempts to meet this situation were desperate and ineffective. On 19 brumaire An III (9 November) the

Convention eliminated the national system of prices and allowed the districts to set prices at two thirds above the 1790 level. The consequent rise in prices over those of the general maximum did little to attract grain to market, however, and on 4 nivôse (24 December) it abolished price controls altogether. The reasons for doing so were unbelievably frivolous and beside the point. There was much criticism of the sizeable bureaucracy which administered the controls, of the blockages and shortages such a system created, of possible corruption among its officials and even extraneous charges that they were all Robespierrists. Some even claimed the abolition of controls would save the government money although it would be impossible to make any serious economies until the war was over. Only one or two deputies argued that abolition would lead to a painful rise in prices but would also give peasants an incentive to provision urban markets.

No one foresaw that in the context of large amounts of unspent currency, a poor harvest and no possible government commitment to reduce its expenditures, the problem of urban supply was bound to be aggravated terribly. With no new sources of revenue and the state acquiring its war materials at market prices from private contractors, the only recourse was to print more assignats. Even before the abolition of the maximum, the assignat had fallen from 34 per cent of its 1790 value in thermidor to 20 per cent the following nivôse. After abolition, it dropped to 8 per cent in germinal and 4 per cent in prairial. At the same time, consumers and traders were bidding up prices while farmers and grain merchants were holding on to their stocks in the hope that prices would rise still higher. Bread prices on the free market in Paris rose by 1300 per cent between March and May 1795, beef more than sextupled and pork and eggs more than doubled. Overall, the cost of living climbed by over 900 per cent between 1790 and 1795, and, needless to say, wages lagged far behind. Even so, Paris was relatively privileged since subsidized prices and diminishing rations were maintained for the poor at the expense of cities in the hinterland. In the Nord, for example, a free market ceased to exist in the late winter of the Year III and the towns could only be fed by requisitions again because farmers insisted on payment in hard cash which had disappeared. Amiens and Abbeville in the Somme managed to feed their poor by cutting rations and reducing the subsidies on bread prices, but by spring peasant defiance had reached the point where requisitions brought in only one tenth of what they had the year before. The two cities then had to purchase grain on foreign markets but paid extortionate prices to greedy middlemen.

The economic collapse of the Year III and the appalling cold produced indescribable misery. The number of deaths recorded at the hospital of Bicêtre in Paris climbed after ventôse and there were the usual stories, always a sure sign of shortage and misery, of suicides of young mothers and their children, and of people eating grass. Whether these were rumours or not, the number of deaths increased dramatically. Deaths in Rouen in the Year III were nearly double those of a normal year, while those of the Year IV were higher still, the killer season being the spring between harvests in both years and the victims being the very old, the very young and the working poor. In effect, the country had reverted to a situation it had escaped nearly a century before, of a more or less direct correlation between prices, supplies and death rates. As always in time of dearth, criminality born of misery also increased. In the Nord there were more and more reports of petty amounts of grain being stolen from farmers. Around Amiens there were huge bands of vagabonds roaming from farm to farm. The national agent of Mâcon reported the appearance of brigand bands in the countryside for the first time. Interestingly, the only way he could fulfil the town's grain quota was to imprison the mayors and national agents of the communes – a measure unprecedented even in the Year II. With increasing misery, inflation and brigandage, government was beginning to collapse.

Sociology of Counterrevolution

The Mâconnais was a quiet place where the *de facto* abolition of heavy seigneurialism after the risings of 1789 gave the countryside a powerful incentive to support the Revolution. Dissidence here never went further than going to clandestine Masses and observing Sundays. Elsewhere the requisitions, arrests of local officials, house-to-house searches, unprecedented rationing in the countryside, forbidding beer production to save on grain and so on, snapped the remaining links between the big farmers and landowners and the urban revolutionaries. In the Nord, this united whole rural communities which had once been divided between rich and poor over wages, disposition of the commons, accumulation of leases and so on, against all outside authority. The result was nearly

complete impunity for Belgian missionary preachers, resistance to
requisitions, protection for deserters and draft-dodgers, and
brigandage. Where still other regions contained substantial
numbers of men who had received no reason to support the land
settlement, the result was liable to be an outbreak of
counterrevolution. One example of this process was the Gers which
already had a long history of tithe strikes in the Old Regime and
which was sharply disappointed when the Constituent Assembly
decided to allow proprietors to add the equivalent of the former
tithe to the leases. The peasants never accepted this and a meeting
of three hundred at Mirande in July 1793 demanded half the tithe
for the sharecroppers. The department responded by arresting five
ringleaders and issuing a stirring proclamation in patois warning the
country people of false patriots and aristocrats who 'lead you like
animals'. The representative on mission, Dartigoyete, tried to
reverse this and claimed the sharecroppers 'will only abandon the
aristocrats when they find advantages in taxes and the tithe'. It is
doubtful whether he found many rural friends, however, since he
was also an uninhibited dechristianizer, and in any case the law of
1 brumaire An II (22 October 1793), which turned the tithe over
to lessees, was a dead letter. In the summer of 1794, proprietors
were still trying to collect 'their' tithe but to mounting resistance.
With its usual insensitivity, the thermidorean Convention not only
confirmed the 1790 law but decreed the law of 2 thermidor An III
(20 July 1795), permitting proprietors to receive half their rents in
kind – a wonderful boon in time of heavy inflation which allowed
owners to participate in a frenzied speculation in foodstuffs. In the
Gers and elsewhere in the Midi, the result was a mounting number
of demonstrations over refractory priests, church bells and
conscription until the region joined the overtly royalist insurrection
of the Year VII.

    The sharecropping communities of the Midi tended to be pulled
in several different ways because of the counterbalancing presence
of masses of small proprietors and day-labourers who were often
landowners too, so the spread of popular counterrevolution was a
slow and confusing process. On the other hand, the communities
of the west tended to be divided more sharply between owners and
tenants and the divisions between rich and poor were less
noticeable than on the northern plains or in the viticultural regions.
Labourers and hired hands were often tied to tenants through stable
employment or kinship and the better-off tenants had a common

experience of reasonable security, limited geographical mobility and, before 1789, of sharply rising rents. The Constituent Assembly, obsessed with protecting landowners, offered no fiscal or financial relief. This won the bourgeois revolutionaries, who took power in 1790, many friends in the property-owning regions of the west, which received the tithe and seigneurial dues outright. This alliance was put to good use when they tried to implement the Civil Constitution of the Clergy. The price, however, was the hostility of all those who received nothing and who resented the claims of outsiders to regulate ancestral religious practices in the name of a revolutionary legitimacy no one accepted. In Lower Brittany where ownership of land and buildings was divided between landlords and tenants in a unique system known as *domaine congéable*, the process of alienation was similar. At the very least, tenants wanted more security if not a greater share of ownership, but after much vacillation and confused attempts at reform, they received much less than they expected. In March 1793, large regions of Brittany, Normandy, Maine and northern Anjou rebelled against the levy of 300,000 and later in the year, hundreds of daring young men joined the Vendeans in their march across the Loire. When the representatives on mission arrived in the autumn and winter of the Year II to supervise the *levée en masse*, many more took to the woods rather than submit. There they began to organize themselves into bands to overthrow the persecutors of their religion. The result was 'chouannerie' – the most extensive, persistent and durable peasant movement of the Revolution.

Chouannerie represented the armed wing of a rural community outraged at the shattering it had undergone since 1790 and nostalgic for an Old Regime in which people settled their problems on their own with little interference from government. The Civil Constitution split the ideal community and people dreamed of the day they could invert the existing order of things and expel the local republicans who had illegitimately imposed themselves. Popular counterrevolution was therefore of a different order than that of the émigrés but the chouans often accepted their leadership because they too were a part of the ideal community and because they knew they were weak. Above all, they lacked arms and munitions. Attempts by their leaders – Cadoudal in the Morbihan, Boishardy in the Côtes-du-Nord, Frotté in Normandy and Puisaye, the commander for all Brittany – to secure them from the incompetent British were generally failures. Chouannerie was therefore reduced to guerrilla tactics involving murders of republican officials and constitutional priests, stopping grain convoys, forbidding the payment of rents to landowners, collecting rents on *biens nationaux* and ambushing republican patrols. Although the chouans were never more than loose confederations of impermanent bands, by the late summer of the Year II their tactics had brought government in the countryside to a halt. The war had also begun to spread to ten departments north of the Loire on a line west of Caen, Le Mans and Angers.

There is a persistent republican tradition that thermidorean weaknesses and incompetence were responsible for the spread of royalist insurgency. In fact, terrorist policies towards the Vendée had first reignited resistance and then offered no hope to rank-and-file insurgents because of the refusal of an amnesty. The inability of both the Montagnard and thermidorean Committee of Public Safety to reinforce the armies in the west because of the necessity of exploiting successes in the Low Countries therefore created a temptation for the new representatives on mission to try other devices. Boursault's Philanthropic Commission was one, so was the amnesty of 3, 26 vendémiaire An III (24 September, 17 October 1794) to draft-dodgers and chouan soldiers. The amnesty was not particularly successful, however, because it did not guarantee immunity from conscription and some refractories denounced it. This only made another tactic more imperative. Boursault had long been an advocate of wider religious freedom, as was the new commander in Brittany, General Hoche, and on 24 nivôse (13 January) the representatives Guesno and Guermeur in the Morbihan removed priests who obeyed the laws from the lists of suspects without requiring an oath of loyalty. The Convention followed up by the law of 3 ventôse An III (21 February 1795) which proclaimed religious liberty once again and reopened the churches. Refractories could profit from those dispositions too, provided they were not émigrés and provided they took the oaths of submission required by the laws of 11 prairial An III (30 May 1795) and 7 vendémiaire An IV (29 September 1795). Unsatisfactory as some of these divide-and-rule measures proved to be, they did produce a serious crisis of morale among the chouan leadership. At the same time, the government moved troops against Charette and Stofflet in the Vendée so Charette signed the Treaty of La Jaunaye on 29 pluviôse (17 February). The chouans had already signed a truce, and were as despairing as Charette was

of receiving British aid. They signed the comparable Treaty of La
Mabilais on 15 germinal (20 April). Although a majority of chouan
band chiefs refused to sign the treaty and the leaders were only
buying time, the republicans were able to use the occasion to
reinforce their troops and increase pressure on the unpacified areas.

At best, the treaties were merely the beginning of a restoration
of authority since the chouans were to remain armed and police
their own areas. Still, the Republic might have been able to profit
from the demoralization and disorganization the treaties produced
among the chouans and Vendeans, had not government begun to
collapse elsewhere. The signal for this came from within the
Convention itself.

Politics of Anti-Terror

Aside from gradually removing the most notorious terrorists from
the Committees of Public Safety and General Security, most
members of the Convention initially showed no wish to investigate
the past. The deputies rejected a denunciation by the Dantonist
Lecointre of the members of the terrorist committees as a calumny
and on 26 fructidor (12 September) even voted to transfer Marat's
remains to the Panthéon. After Carrier counterattacked the
Indulgents in a furious speech, the Jacobins voted to expel
Lecointre, Fréron and Tallien. Yet this was the high-water mark of
Jacobin influence. Barère's proposal to distribute *biens nationaux*
to soldiers was defeated and Lindet's attempt to hold the factions
together by promising protection to members of the old
revolutionary committees while restoring 'liberty to all who have
been useful' fell on deaf ears. Denunciations of the clubs in the
Convention continued while the Committee of General Security,
now in the hands of Indulgents and moderates, continued to arrest
petty terrorists in Paris. The most important setback, however, was
the arrest, trial and, on 26 frimaire (16 December), execution of
Carrier. This broke the thermidor coalition because the trial before
the Revolutionary Tribunal of 94 Nantes federalists revealed the
noyades in grisly detail. This caused a sensation among
pamphleteers, including Babeuf who satirically depicted Carrier as
Robespierre's instrument in a heinous plot to depopulate the
country and redistribute wealth among the survivors. Babeuf's
intent was to criticize the granting of arbitrary powers, but other

journalists were able to indict the Terror as a whole. The revelations so disconcerted the Montagnards that Billaud-Varennes moved the arrest of Turreau for his use of the 'infernal columns' in the Vendée. With such an outcry from democrats and antiterrorists, the Convention ordered Carrier's arrest. The trial was a farce since Carrier and two of his accomplices were convicted on the improvised and ironic charge of 'favouring counter-revolution' while most of the members of the revolutionary committee who were more directly responsible for the *noyades* and the brutal soldiers of the 'Compagnie Marat', the local revolutionary army, were all released. Meanwhile, the Jacobins' feeble attempts to defend the vigorous measures required in the Year II, if not Carrier himself who symbolized them, incited crowds to attack the club. On the pretext of keeping order, the Convention closed the mother society on 22 brumaire (12 November), and later forbade affiliation and collective petitions. This was a sign for many representatives on mission to close or purge the provincial clubs.

Carrier's trial was only one example of the deputies' predilection for raking up the past. Already there had been insults over their mutual behaviour while on mission, or their actions at the time of the September Massacres and, above all, a continuing debate over the legitimacy of 31 May. Carrier's trial not only discredited repression still further but raised questions about how much the governing committees knew of the *noyades* and the atrocities of Lyon. So far had the atmosphere changed that on 18 frimaire (8 December) the Convention unanimously reinstated the seventy-eight deputies who had been imprisoned for the *journée* of 31 May–2 June. On 7 nivôse (27 December) it voted to impeach Barère, Billaud-Varennes, Collot d'Herbois and Vadier. Finally, on 18 ventôse (8 March) with only one dissenting voice, it recalled the Girondins who had participated in the federalist risings. Although the return of the proscribed deputies could be justified as a return to legality, it definitively altered the balance of forces in the Convention. The outlawed deputies had faced immediate execution upon mere indentification in the Year II, those imprisoned had heard constant cries for their trial while those who had voted for the *appel au peuple* during the king's trial had had to suffer periodic demands for a new purge. Not all of them demanded vengeance. But they were fearful enough of any popular disturbance that they overwhelmed even the Indulgents in their antiterrorism. This showed both in the Convention's handling of the last Parisian *journées* and in the policies of some while on mission.

Risings of Misery or Democracy?

The Parisian risings occurred against the background of the most extensive disturbances since 1792. From the winter of the Year III onwards, there were troubles and riots in Rennes, Rouen, Amiens, Dieppe, Honfleur, Caen, Chartres, Melun and Saint-Germain-en-Laye, as well as characteristic attacks on large farms, mills and grain convoys in the districts north of Paris along the Seine valley, and throughout the coastal regions of Flanders. As always in grain troubles, women were prominent in the disturbances, either directly or as instigators of the men. Unlike 1792, price-fixing was less important than generalized protests against the favourable treatment of Paris, and at the meagre rations the municipalities allotted the poor. People also demanded that local prices be as low as those of the controlled prices in the capital. At Rouen and Amiens, there were also cries for the return of the monarchy and elsewhere for the implementation of the Constitution of 1793 – any slogan, in other words, that would shock the authorities into action.

The Parisian risings were more complicated because they occurred in the context of the declining sectional movement. Despite the liberalization after thermidor, few popular societies revived and within a few months most of the sections had passed into the hands of moderates or their officers bent to the new wind. Those who still had a taste for politics concentrated their efforts towards democratizing sectional and municipal institutions, so there were few protests against the small waves of arrests of the unpopular officials of the revolutionary committees and the vexatious *commissaires aux accaparements*. But this struggle for democracy was definitively lost when the new arrondissement revolutionary committees were appointed. Not a single former militant was continued. By the autumn, the *sans-culottes* had to defend themselves too from the *jeunesse dorée*, the coiffed young vandals known for their extravagant dress, affected language and arrogant manners. Although these thugs were not the private armies of Fréron and Tallien as was once thought, they certainly did enjoy protection from on high since many were petty civil servants and many were draft-dodgers or deserters. Nor were they a particularly important group. They did make such a nuisance of themselves that they forced the Convention to remove Marat's corpse from the Panthéon on 20 pluviôse (8 February) and they were among the crowds which mobbed the Jacobin club the previous brumaire. Ordinarily though, their activities were simply demeaning: destroying or defacing statues of martyrs of liberty, howling down 'Jacobin' theatre performances, beating up former terrorists, and so on.

Galling as the *jeunesse dorée* was, hostility to them played a minor part in the *journées* of 12 germinal (1 April) and 1 prairial (20 May). Instead, the risings showed that many ordinary people had altered their thinking and that the antiterrorist upsurge immediately following thermidor did have lasting consequences. In both cases, the cry for bread was not accompanied by the bloodcurdling threats against hoarders and speculators or demands for 'great measures' against the big farmers, dealers and millers. The nostalgia for Robespierre and the observation that food was available when the guillotine functioned daily went hand in hand with observations that the king provided food too, and such remarks should be taken less as a revival of the terrorist reflex than as a useful way of making police spies and the government nervous. The demand by some militants and sections for the implementation of the Constitution of 1793 signified a general desire for direct democracy, for the release of patriot prisoners and those who had been arrested in disturbances in bread queues and for the restoration of an independent municipality.

Indeed the 'insurrection' of 12 germinal was not properly a rising at all but a demonstration, analogous to that of 5 September 1793, in which the people, who were carrying no arms, intended to read a series of petitions and addresses drawn up in the general assemblies of the sections to its representatives who were then expected to implement them. The situation got out of hand because the government, despite expecting a rising for days and despite distributing arms to 'honest' citizens, only provided the Convention with about one hundred guards who were quickly swept aside by crowds estimated at over ten thousand. As people poured on to the Convention floor and commissioners read the petitions in great tumult and confusion for four hours, even the Montagnards eventually tried to persuade them to leave. As it happened, the demonstration presented an opportunity that was too good to miss. Barère, Collot d'Herbois, Billaud-Varennes and Vadier were ordered immediately to be deported to Cayenne and fourteen other Montagnards were arrested over the next few days. Among them were not only such notorious terrorists as Hentz, Amar and Maignet but Danton's friends Lecointre and Léonard Bourdon. The reaction had bypassed the Indulgents. Furthermore, Paris was declared to be in a state of siege which put it under military government and a disarming of 'terrorists', including those who had taken no part in the demonstration, began. The repression was not very severe. Only about 1600 were disarmed but it was a sign to others of where power really lay.

At one level, the *journée* of 1 prairial was a hunger riot, a protest against appallingly low rations which had dipped to a mere two ounces of bread during the previous month, while a free market in flour for pastry shops was allowed to continue. Many of the demonstrators who descended on the Convention had the slogan 'Bread or Death!' pinned to their hats. The day began with women from the eastern quarters of the city invading shops and apartments persuading other women and the men to join their march. But unlike 12 germinal, there was a real attempt to employ armed force whether by suborning the artillery companies or persuading National Guard battalions to join. Several did, including three from the faubourg Saint-Antoine, despite their officers' attempts to prevent it. Furthermore, an influential pamphlet which appeared on the eve of the insurrection called for the arrest of some deputies and for a new legislative assembly under the Constitution of 1793. The precedent this time was to be 2 June 1793 or even 10 August. Loyal National Guards and the *jeunesse dorée* beat back a series of crowds from the Tuileries, but finally the demonstrators, aided by the National Guard of the faubourg Saint-Antoine, burst on to the floor of the Convention. One deputy, the unknown Feraud, was shot dead trying to hold them back. The confusion and tumult lasted for hours until a few Montagnards persuaded the Convention to vote decrees releasing patriots and establishing an emergency Food Council. Loyal National Guards led by moderate deputies then arrived in the early evening and cleared the hall. Before retiring, the Convention ordered the arrest of the most compromised Montagnards. The next day, huge crowds, led by battalions from the faubourg Saint-Antoine and from the central sections, surrounded the Convention. With cannon trained on the Tuileries, they demanded bread and the Constitution of 1793. No one wanted to fire a shot, however, and, after the president of the

Assembly made some vague promises, the crowds dispersed. The Convention could now go over to the offensive. On 3 prairial, several thousand troops of the line and regular cavalry units surrounded the faubourg and the next day invested it, forcing the rebels to dismantle their barricades and to surrender their arms and cannon. The repression this time was swift. A military commission condemned seventy-three to death, deportation or imprisonment. About 1700 militants were disarmed and close to 1200 were imprisoned, many without trial, whether or not they had participated in the rising. Forty Montagnards including Lindet and Jeanbon Saint-André of the Great Committee of Public Safety were arrested and six were condemned to death. It was the definitive end of the *sans-culotte* movement, the remaining militants now turning to conspiracy more or less as a career, impaled on general police lists to be arrested as a matter of course whenever a regime – Directory, Consulate, Empire – felt jittery.

The repression following the insurrection of 1–2 prairial An III ended the cycle of insurrections in Paris which had opened the Revolution. Compared to other risings the weaknesses were obvious. With at most ten sections behind them in germinal, with very uneven support in the National Guard (because its officers had been made responsible to a central command once again shortly after thermidor), with no coordinating body to play the role of the Paris commune in 1792 of holding the National Assembly to its promises, and with many of the experienced militants trying to avoid commitments, the demonstrations and risings showed the limits of unorganized and spontaneous popular action. Babeuf drew the conclusion the next year. In the end, as in every *journée*, force decided the issue. The declaration of the state of siege after germinal, the order to move the army into Paris a few days before prairial and its use in the repression showed the dependence of the regime on the military. Most tragically of all perhaps, the deterioration of the economy after prairial completed the ruin of many former *sans-culottes*. Conditions in the Year IV were almost as bad as the year before. There was no insurrection. There was no hope.

The White Terror

The risings in Paris had a disastrous effect on provincial militants. The law of 21 germinal An III (10 April), prescribing the disarming of terrorists and thus depriving them of civic employment, often marked them out for innumerable vexations. In some places, this was relatively mild. There were only thirty-seven disarmed in Rouen, ten in Rennes, thirty-three in Bourges, eight in Uzès, and so on. The municipality of Melun, half of whom were former suspects, disarmed six 'terrorists' and instituted some imaginative legal proceedings against them which dragged on until the amnesty of the Year IV. Elsewhere, in regions where the Terror had been exceptionally bloody against the federalists, the reaction was much more severe. The role of the representatives on mission was often critical. At Marseille, for example, the representatives Auguis who had voted for a reprieve and Serres whose attacks on the Montagnards in 1793 were virtually unbalanced, instituted a policy of releasing suspects and imprisoning notorious terrorists at Aix, Avignon and Salon. When the Jacobins rescued one of the leading Marseille clubbists from prison, the deputies used the incident to purge the entire municipality and revolutionary committee and most of the administrators of the department and district. They also closed the club and released nearly half the city's suspects. This in turn produced a riot on 5 vendémiaire An III (26 September 1794) which only led to further arrests.

The new representatives' policies also encouraged the 'White Terror' which, whatever its form, was a vigilante justice, every bit as ghastly as that of 1792–3. In the spring and summer of the Year III, there were prison massacres at Bourg, Lons-le-Saunier, Montbrison, Saint-Etienne, Tarascon, Aix and Marseille. Their overall pattern was much the same as those of the earlier period even if the victims were on the other side of the political divide. The massacres at Lyon of 15–17 floréal (4–6 May 1795), which have been most thoroughly investigated, illustrate how antiterrorist legislation, administrative incompetence, complicity and incitement all worked together to produce an appalling disaster. After the purges of the terrorist administrations which continued from the summer of the Year II until their completion on the eve of the massacres, the terrorists were increasingly marked out, first by the law of 5 ventôse An III (23 February 1795) which ordered all those purged to return to their domiciles under the surveillance of their municipalities, and second, by the publication in Lausanne of a ninety-page widely diffused book listing the names and professions of 'dénonciateurs'. This suggests that its authors had access to the registers of the revolutionary committees. Meanwhile, the laws of 25 brumaire (15 November) and 12 floréal (1 May) prescribing death for returned émigrés and ordering the redeportation of refractory priests who had returned illegally were scarcely applied. In fact, false papers were remarkably easy to get and the flow of returned émigrés and priests scarcely halted. The representatives on mission in the city also ignored the signs of approaching disaster. They were unable to capture the perpetrators of isolated assaults and murders which began in pluviôse (February) because they were concentrating on the terrible subsistence crisis of that winter. They also tolerated the selection of officers in the resuscitated National Guard whose role in the anti-Jacobin coup of 29 May 1793 or during the subsequent siege was at best equivocal. In any case, the Guard was not yet armed. After the replacement of one notoriously 'Jacobin' battalion by others which had suffered terribly from desertion, there was no force remaining which could be trusted entirely to keep order. The incitement to vengeance was provided by the rabid *Journal de Lyon* whose masthead called for the extermination of those who 'spill the blood of men'. The occasion for the massacre was the application of the decree prescribing the disarming of terrorists, which locally served as the pretext to arrest all those terrorists still at liberty, while the immediate cause was the mob's dissatisfaction at the possibility that the trial of one terrorist would not result in execution. Finally, the grouping of so many Jacobins in a few prisons gave rise to rumours of an armed breakout followed by a generalized slaughter with multibladed guillotines. Like the fears preceding earlier massacres, this provoked a defensive reaction and so preventive murders. Unlike the September Massacres, the frenzy had its limits because the crowds, estimated at an unbelievable thirty thousand, allowed counterfeiters and criminals to escape while they set fire to the prisons to force the Jacobins on to the roofs where they were hacked to death. About one hundred people were killed.

The cycle of mob violence continued further south. When a rumour got round that the tribunal at Aix was going to acquit the Marseille Jacobins arrested by Auguis and Serres, a murder gang marched to the prison, released ordinary criminals, and massacred thirty Jacobins on 22 floréal (11 May). The troubles in Marseille provoked a 'Jacobin' rising in Toulon. Already, the militants had been exasperated by Auguis's and Serres's purging of the local administrations and the tolerance for returned émigrés. On 20 ventôse (10 March), a crowd of Jacobins and soldiers murdered seven émigrés. The news of the massacre at Aix stirred the arsenal workers who broke into the local hospital to try to murder more émigrés and into the town hall to get arms on 17–18 floréal (16–17 May). They shouted 'Vive la Montagne! . . . Vive la République démocratique!' and released arrested patriots. News of persecution of fellow militants at Arles and murders at Marseille provoked a rescue effort. A crowd of soldiers, sailors and working people estimated at between 3000 and 8000 armed with cannon set out to relieve Marseille. But loyal troops and National Guards from Marseille met them outside the village of Beausset on 5 prairial (25 May) where 40 to 50 Toulonnais were killed and 300 were taken prisoner. Relative to the number of participants, the repression was even more severe than that following the prairial risings in Paris. Aided by the local federalists, a military commission arrested 250 people, some of whom had taken no part in the expedition, condemned 52 to death and sentenced 14 to imprisonment or deportation. Meanwhile, in reprisal, crowds broke into the prison of Fort Saint-Jean in Marseille on 17 prairial (5 June) and murdered a further 97 Jacobins. Many of the victims were unrecognizable because they had been hacked to death and clumsy attempts made to burn the bodies. Finally, 23 prisoners were murdered at Tarascon on 1 messidor (19 June).

This brought to an end the round of large prison massacres but hardly an end to mob attacks which began before the massacres and continued for years afterwards. As early as pluviôse (February), for example, a furious crowd at Avignon clubbed one of the judges of the infamous Orange tribunal, threw him into the Rhône and finally killed him with a harpoon. There were several cases in the Gard where the National Guard itself killed the prisoners it was escorting. There are countless examples of judges and local officials simply letting it be known when a transfer between prisons was going to take place and letting the mob do its grisly work.

The thermidorean representatives also shared a responsibility for the emergence of the white terrorist murder gangs known as the Companies of Jesus around Lyon or the Companies of the Sun around Marseille. Cadray who had voted for a reprieve did nothing to investigate the prison massacres at Lyon and was accused of letting those of Marseille occur. The demagogic Isnard, a once-outlawed Girondin, was accused of incorporating assassins into the National Guard which marched on Toulon and urging them to dig up their fathers' bones if they had no other weapons. In fact, however, information on the origins, personnel and intercity organization of the gangs is very shadowy. Republican investigators did agree that they were usually composed of young men who preferred to murder terrorists rather than fight on the frontiers and that the fear, extreme weakness or complicity of local authorities permitted them to operate with impunity. Vengeance against the Jacobins for having shaken the traditional social order, and for having tried to involve ordinary people in politics, was almost the sole motivation. Their royalism was vague and derivative when it was even conscious or articulate. As a group of young men accused of being members of the gangs around Arles explained, after 9 thermidor, 'there remained to punish the assassins who covered the surface of the Republic with blood . . . the agents of royalism . . . put in motion sentiments of vengeance by perfidious and atrocious insinuations . . .' that the 'justice' of the Convention was not moving fast enough. But it is doubtful whether they were quite the passive mannequins they depicted since many of the murders were obviously premeditated. They were greatly aided by the inability of cities like Lyon and Arles to afford street lighting and so the grisly stabbings and shootings in the narrow streets of the old towns could continue anonymously, the bodies dumped quietly over the bridges into the Saône or the Rhône, or simply abandoned. These atrocities could happen in broad daylight before witnesses as well. In Lyon, five murderers stabbed a minor terrorist to death in his hospital bed where he had been taken after the same men had mugged him on the streets the day before. In Lyon too, the gangs broke into prisons before the actual massacres and murdered the terrorists in their cells, the frequency of this occurrence illustrating the complete breakdown of elementary government in the city. At L'Isle in the Vaucluse, the local gang murdered a gendarme on the altar of *la patrie*. The impunity of these attacks is shown in the case of one Magnien, a printer, who, despite a military escort, was murdered by a dozen mounted young men outside Montbrison in the Loire who mutilated his body and then repaired to a nearby inn to boast and refresh themselves. By the end of the Year III, local authorities often had a good idea of who the murderers were but were powerless because witnesses were terrified and courts almost invariably acquitted the accused. The young men thus took to wearing outlandish dress as uniforms including buttons decorated with fleurs-de-lis or to distributing cards inscribed with crosses or with the Virgin to young children. In Lyon, they lounged about the Hôtel du Parc on the Place des Terreaux; at Montbrison, they strutted about, their secret handshakes hardly necessary, armed with sharp-pointed canes, long swords, pistols stuffed in their pockets, stiletto knives – a favourite weapon everywhere – and long sticks known as 'juges de paix'. From the police sources, it would appear that the murderers were often the same kind of people who supported the federalists in 1793, that is, professionals, skilled artisans, and occasionally those in the food trades. Of the nineteen accused of belonging to the gang at Arles, all but four were reasonably skilled artisans. The gangs of the Loire were composed of young men who were related to some of the wealthiest families of the region, which had drifted back to local politics in the Year III to offer the gangs encouragement and protection. They were almost invariably men of military age, if not actual deserters, sometimes former suspects, or even militant federalists or men whose families had been victims of the Terror by the handful. Their victims, besides being former terrorist officials, were much more likely to have been working people and artisans, constitutional priests, and professionals, including Protestants in the Gard and Lozère or Jews at Avignon. At the beginning of the Year IV, the deputy Chenier claimed there were murder gangs operating in thirty towns and cities in ten departments, mostly in the southeast. The best estimate suggests the gangs may have murdered several hundred people, far below the number executed in the same region in the Year II but enough to paralyse government altogether.

The Verona Declaration and Counterrevolutionary Strategy

The spread of royalism throughout the southeast and the west and the destruction of militant Jacobinism created an opportunity for a compromise among the various political elites. This would have involved a restoration based on a constitutional monarchy under 'Louis XVII' and would have required a regrouping of 'monarchiens', Fayettists and conservative thermidoreans. Whether the chouans and white terrorists could have been induced to accept the moratorium on violence this would have also required will always be an open question, because when the young son of Louis XVI died in the Temple prison in June, his uncle, the Comte de Provence, proclaimed himself Louis XVIII. His Verona

Declaration on ascending 'the throne' was deplorable and inept, a more reactionary document in every way than Louis XVI's *séance royale* programme of 23 June 1789. The promise of a complete restoration of the 'ancient constitution' of the realm including the Church and parlements with a promise to investigate abuses without ever mentioning even the Estates-General by name could not have been palatable even to the authors of the noble *cahiers* of 1789, while the promise to restore all 'stolen properties' would have alienated a huge constituency of owners of *biens nationaux* and all those who benefited from the abolition of the tithe and seigneurial dues. The fact that the Pretender considered this a moderate document because it promised punishment only for the regicides in the Convention merely underlined his immense distance from reality. After this, only the Convention could defend the land settlement and civil equality. Thus, however unpopular the politicians had become, they were the lesser evil. Moreover, the Verona Declaration committed the royalist leaders to civil war because the inflexible defence of reaction rendered any kind of meaningful regrouping of conservatives impossible. As the events of the next two years would show, it was not possible to harness the pure and constitutional royalists to the same chariot.

'Louis XVIII' could be so intransigent because of the near certainty that the Republic was on the verge of internal collapse. On the frontiers, however, events had taken a favourable turn. After the successes of the previous summer, the armies poured into the Palatinate and into Catalonia. Once the rivers froze in that terrible winter, Holland was occupied with ease and Dutch 'patriots' proclaimed the 'Batavian Republic', the first of the sister republics. Prussia, hoping for great things from the last partition of Poland, abandoned the Coalition and by the Treaty of Bâle (5 April 1795) recognized French claims on the left bank of the Rhine in return for the neutralization of north Germany. This in turn permitted the French to impose the Treaty of the The Hague on the Dutch (16 May) whereby the Batavian Republic had to cede its forts in Flanders, support an army of occupation and pay an indemnity of 100 million florins. This implied of course the permanence of the annexation of Belgium which meant that peace with Britain was problematic. Finally, Spain made peace on 22 July by ceding its half of Saint-Domingo.

Despite the peace treaties with Prussia, Holland and Spain, the British were determined to open another front in Brittany following the collapse in Flanders. This was to be a long campaign in which the republicans were eventually to be expelled from the peninsula while the Austrians and internal insurrections further east pinned down possible reinforcements. In the event, Lyon did not explode, despite the murder gangs, Franche-Comté remained quiet and the Austrians showed no signs of shaking their lethargy. The British pressed on, however, buoyed by Puisaye's and their agents' assurances that a landing would spark a vast insurrection. Yet the royalists remained divided and weak. South of the Loire, Charette took to the field, massacring a few hundred republican prisoners, but Stofflet kept the peace. North of the Loire, the republicans resumed operations at the end of May when captured correspondence proved the chouans' perfidy. The death of Boishardy in a minor engagement shortly after dampened chouan morale and activity considerably in the Côtes-du-Nord while elsewhere the chouans' lack of arms prevented them from undertaking operations of strategic importance to cover the landing, whose other purpose, incidentally, was to provide them with just the arms they needed. Thus, within a few days of landing on the coast at Carnac in the Morbihan on 27 June, it was obvious that the expedition was in great danger. Very quickly, Hoche was able to assemble 10,000 troops against the 3000-odd émigré troops in British pay as well as the thousands of chouans and ordinary civilians who had flocked to the beaches to greet their liberators. Hoche then pushed them into the Quiberon peninsula, sealing them off, 'as well as the rats', as he reported. Meanwhile, quarrelling had broken out between Puisaye, the overall commander and his supposed advisor, D'Hervilly and the émigrés' disdain for the peasants and their hogging the best rations alienated the chouans. Unfortunately, contrary winds held up the first of two waves of reinforcements by British soldiers although another batch of émigrés did manage to land. Hoche was determined to act before further reinforcements arrived, however. By a combination of shrewd tactics and guile, he captured Fort Penthièvre on 21 July thus opening the approaches to the peninsula. Quiberon was the greatest single disaster the emigration suffered. According to the law of 25 brumaire An III (15 November 1794), among others, the officers and soldiers of the émigré regiments were returned émigrés and were punishable by death. Twenty-one military commissions passed sentences on 630 of them, including the Bishop of Dol, while the judges affected to believe the stories of the civilians that they had been drunk or were intimidated. All but 108 of the most compromised chouans were also released.

Quiberon had few direct effects on the national scene. It provided a voluminous martyrology to royalist apologists of the next century who saw it as a British plot to destroy the officer corps of the Old Regime navy. It probably created the antiaristocratic sentiments of chouannerie in the Morbihan. It ruined Puisaye's reputation among many chouan leaders and thus compromised the chances of transforming the chouans into armies on the Vendean pattern. But it did not destroy chouannerie. So the assassinations and ambushes continued to eat away at the social fabric of the rural world and at the threads between town and country. The failure of the peace treaties too convinced the politicians and the generals that the chouans would have to be crushed and so, as in the Vendée the year before, the west would be treated as an occupied country.

Constitution and the Last Insurrection in Paris

Otherwise, relative peace abroad and the victory at Quiberon allowed the politicians to concentrate on the original purpose of the Convention, drafting a constitution. The result was the Constitution of the Year III. This had begun slowly as an attempt to add 'organic laws' to the Constitution of 1793 but after germinal and prairial this procedure fell into complete discredit and by fructidor (August) the Convention had produced an entirely new constitution. Anyone could vote who paid a direct tax or who had fought in the armies. The number of voters therefore was certainly greater than the number of active citizens of 1790–1, and with a similar bias against townsmen. But the direct power of choosing deputies was in the hands of men whom the voters selected. The electors had to pay taxes equivalent to 150–200 days of labour depending on the size of the locality. This was so high that many who had been electors in 1790–2 were excluded since their number fell from roughly 50,000 to 30,000. It also excluded the middle-income groups who had led the revolutionary coalition from the beginning and, given the structure of wealth in the country at the end of the century, limited direct electoral power to the rich rentier bourgeoisie, rich tenant farmers and former nobility who were eligible, if none of their direct relatives was an émigré. Thus, the exclusion, by law, of émigrés and refractory priests could not have done much to counter the fact that the second-degree electorate was composed of men who had suffered directly or had been constantly threatened in the Year II, who had also suffered from the inflation of the Year III and who were the primary targets of the forced loans the Directory would soon impose. The consequences of giving the 'droit de cité' to these groups would show in every election down to the coup of fructidor An V.

The nature of the electorate, therefore, was a major cause of instability for the new regime. So too were the arrangements for the national government. The constitution-makers of the Year III were obsessed with preventing a dictatorship, whether from what they thought of as a Jacobin cabal manipulating a fickle populace or from a single individual. The solution was a rigorous separation of powers. To prevent a legislative dictatorship such as the Convention had exercised, the legislative branch was divided into two chambers, a 'Council of Five Hundred', composed of any citizen older than thirty, which initiated bills and passed them after three readings; and a 'Council of Ancients', composed of 250 citizens older than forty which approved bills but could not initiate them or amend those sent up from the Five Hundred. There were no property qualifications to sit in either house. The executive branch was confined to a Directory of five members, one of whom was to retire by lot every year, the Directors themselves being chosen for all practical purposes by the Five Hundred. The Directory could neither initiate, make, or veto laws but could only suggest the legislature discuss certain matters. Although it had no control over the treasury and could not declare war, the Directory's constitutional authority to conduct diplomacy, to supervise the military, to execute the laws and to make appointments gave it an enormous power. Seven ministers were responsible to it alone as were the thousands of commissioners attached to the civilian and military wings of government. They were supposed to supervise the execution of policy and so succeeded the representatives on mission and national agents and prefigured the Napoleonic prefectoral administration. The system of centralization thus continued. In practice, the commissioners acquired a great power over the elected department and cantonal administrations – the districts disappeared and the communes were grouped into a single municipality per canton – because they took initiatives when elected officials did not and because they targeted the feckless or the subversive whom the Directory, quite legally, could sack. Many of these men were former Jacobins whose records were not overly tainted and so the process of coopting proven patriots into the administration which was initiated by the law of 14 frimaire continued.

The Constitution of the Year III is often criticized for the rigorous separation of powers and for the system of elections in which one third of the Five Hundred retired each year. But the British system of the 1790s got round the formal separation of powers by building royal clienteles in the legislature and the Directors might have tried to do the same. Unfortunately, they could not. The financial situation meant that any patronage was meaningless. The Directory did influence public opinion by subsidizing the press but going further would have meant reviving the clubs. Apart from anything else, the Constitution tried to shackle a recurrence of Jacobinism by forbidding clubs to affiliate or present collective petitions. The Directory could try to influence elections but its attempts to subvert the electoral process in the Year VI brought mixed results. If the Directory could not build a party in the legislature, the legislature could not alter the composition of the Directory except by waiting for one Director to retire each year and replacing him with one of their own – a slow process for an impatient legislature.

The Convention itself knew that it was unpopular and by the decrees of 5, 13 fructidor (22, 30 August) declared that two thirds of the new representatives must be chosen from the corps of existing deputies, excluding sixty-seven Montagnards who had been arrested or suspended. Anyone who was eligible to vote in the 1793 referendum was invited to approve the new constitution and by a vote of 1,057,390 to 49,979 they did so. The decline of 40 per cent in turnout between the two plebiscites, while real, can be exaggerated. By the Year III, the civil war had spread so much that many primary assemblies in the west and the Midi never met at all. The law governing the plebiscite on the two-thirds decrees was so confusing that most primary assemblies just did not bother to vote on it. These decrees were approved by only 205,498 to 108,754. Nonetheless, the increase in abstentions was a poor omen for representative government, rendered all the worse because local authorities often attributed it to a vague royalism or to disgust with the Convention's religious policies. Nor was the positive vote in the plebiscite an endorsement of the Republic. In the Vaucluse and undoubtedly elsewhere, the royalist counterterrorists dominated the primary assemblies and voted for the Constitution as a way of getting rid of the Convention.

Most speeches in the primary assemblies showed that the electorate that did participate desired a return to regular government, internal peace and prosperity. The results of the elections to the legislature showed they thought that moderates were best able to achieve these goals. All but one of the deputies who protested on 31 May and who were recalled on 18 frimaire An III and all of the outlawed Girondins who were recalled on 18 ventôse were reelected. Of the 511 *conventionnels* reelected, only 157 were regicides. Of the 234 members of the 'new third', only 4 were *conventionnels* while 171 had never sat in a revolutionary legislature before. In other words, the electorate was not only anti-Montagnard but also hostile to politicians in general. This was another poor omen.

From their promulgation, the two-thirds decrees raised a storm of protest which reached a climax in the insurrection of 13 vendémiaire An IV (5 October 1795). This was easily the strangest of all the Paris insurrections. If it was royalist, it was never avowed in the insurgents' declarations and petitions. If it was simply against the two-thirds decrees or the Convention generally, its success would have aided the royalists yet the Pretender's agents in the city disavowed it as the work of constitutional royalists. If the protest was antiterrorist, the sections were adept at using the language of popular sovereignty and the right of insurrection in an antipopular cause. If the insurrection is rightly conceived to be 'bourgeois', the largest single trade category was composed of artisans and apprentices. Men who worked with their hands formed nearly one third of those arrested whose occupations are known.

The referendum in Paris had been marked by massive malpractice by both sides which only added bitterness to each side. Government supporters were ousted from at least a dozen sections while the government annulled the result on the referendum in thirty-three sections which had rejected the two-thirds decrees 'unanimously' on the pretext that the number of voters was not indicated. When partial national results were announced on 1 vendémiaire (23 September), a dozen sections refused to recognize them and, amid mounting disturbances involving the *jeunesse dorée* and the soldiers and campaigns in the 'antiterrorist' press, the Lepelletier section in the heart of the financial district began an agitation to dissolve the Convention and convoke the new legislature without the two-thirds decrees. On 11 vendémiaire (3 October), an assembly of electors from fifteen sections, including, ironically, Danton's old fief of Théâtre-Français, met to protest the decrees and that evening seven sections declared themselves in a state of insurrection. The Convention responded by forming an extraordinary Commission of Five to keep order and, since there were too few troops in the city, rearmed many of the victims of prairial and formed them into a special unit. The military command was given to General Menou, who, enthusiastic enough in the operations in prairial, had no heart for this. An irresolute general could have been disastrous because the rearming of the terrorists set off a panic among people who had been nourished on anti-Jacobin propaganda for a year. Undoubtedly this aligned many people behind the sections. Yet the sections were almost as indecisive as General Menou. When he was ordered to lead a column to disarm the Lepelletier section which had been among those declaring itself in insurrection, he contented himself with a useless promise that the rebels would retire. The Convention could hardly tolerate anything less than a retraction from the sections, however. Menou was promptly arrested and overall command was given to Barras who had also led the Convention's forces on 9–10 thermidor. Among the generals appointed to assist him was Bonaparte. Barras, whose previous experience had taught him something about street-fighting, ordered Major Murat to seize the cannon at Les Sablons on the outskirts of the city. This proved decisive. Meanwhile, the sections formed a central commission and a military committee, and after appointing the cashiered general Danican as their general moved off in several columns to attack the Convention. Government forces, considerably outnumbered with only 7800 men, had the advantage of cannon, and after a fruitless siege of several hours dispersed one column with grapeshot. Later, another column trying to advance from the south over the Pont Royal was similarly dispersed. By the next morning the city was in complete calm. The revolution of the 'honnêtes gens' was over.

Unlike prairial and Quiberon, the repression which followed was remarkably light. There were only two executions and although there was a considerable wave of arrests hundreds were soon released. Among them or tried *in absentia* were Suard, the literary toady of the Old Regime, the abbé Morellet, the friend of the Brienne ministry of 1788, and a handful of Louis XVI's exbodyguards. In part, vendémiaire was the insurrection of those who had lost something. About three hundred clerks were dismissed, which put an effective end to the *jeunesse dorée*, and draft-dodgers were forced to the front. Most important, over 35,000 guns were seized from the National Guard whether the section had participated in the rising or not and the Guard itself put under effective control of the new general of the Army of the Interior, Bonaparte. Once a protégé of the representatives Salicetti and Augustin Robespierre at Toulon, now of Barras, the twenty-six-year-old general would soon show he was his own master. For the third time in six months, the army had saved the thermidorean Republic.

Vendémiaire was important because it was part of an uncoordinated but real royalist offensive in the Year III. If the thermidoreans hoped that the nation would bury its differences in Robespierre's grave, they soon found that the language of reconciliation and antiterrorism meant something quite different in the mouths of the rabid anti-Jacobins and counterterrorists who by vendémiaire were calling the entire Convention to account. For those who wished to defend civil equality, the land settlement and representative government, the previous year had witnessed the royalists in the west using the pacification treaties as a cloak to reorganize themselves; the émigré landings at Quiberon backed by mercenary regiments supported by the navy of a foreign power; prison massacres; the emergence of murder gangs and innumerable acts of private vengeance in the Midi; the continuing ulcer of the chouannerie in the west; a religious revival which was still gathering momentum; and much of this in the name of Louis XVIII whose Verona Declaration promised that one of the first acts of a restoration would be the execution of the regicides and the reversal of everything men had fought for since 1789. Even as the Convention prepared to implement the Constitution of the Year III, the British were on the point of landing arms to Charette off the coast of Poitou, and the Comte d'Artois might have landed with them with incalculable effects on the Vendeans' sagging morale, if Charette had been able to fight his way to the coast sooner.

It was thus understandable that the expiring Convention should have passed the draconian law of 3 brumaire An IV (25 October 1795) reviving the earlier penalties against the refractories and the émigrés and ordering a new round of deportations. It was understandable too that the ex-*conventionnels* used their majority in the new legislature to elect La Révellière-Lepeaux, Reubell, Le Tourneur, Barras and Carnot, all of them regicides, as Directors. Their past would be a guarantee of their future. The constitutional regime would be revolutionary, in spite of its innermost longings, because the counterrevolution would not surrender.

Chapter 8

The Directory and Final Collapse

Like most contemporary analysts on both sides of the Atlantic, apologists for the Directory believed that social prominence should translate naturally into political power. This meant that the regime intended to draw the support of the men of property and substantial professionals. It also meant that the lower orders should not contest the system. In reality, the governments of the period received astonishingly little support from the notables. The small ginger group of Jacobins and, above all, the masses of plebeian royalists were also a constant source of turmoil. The Constitution assumed a fair degree of citizen participation in government which it rarely got and, as in the Year IV, the secondary electors repudiated the ruling clique whenever possible. The solution was the coup of fructidor An V. Even the Directory's undoubted successes – repression of the Vendeans and chouans and the Treaty of Campo Formio with Austria, notably – did not win it much support because the successes were not definitive. Moreover, the measures taken to try to cope with the financial chaos which continued for much of the period threatened the very notables the regime tried to curry. By the Year VII, the Directory had alienated most of the important constituencies in the political nation, including the army, and thus opened the way for Bonaparte.

Religious 'Revival'

The Directory has a totally justified reputation as one of the most chaotic periods in modern French history. The Convention's religious policies which the Directory inherited and vainly tried to apply explain much of the disturbances. The fundamental law governing religious observance, that of 3 ventôse An III (21 February 1795), permitted freedom of conscience but restricted freedom of religious expression. Churches, and presbyteries remained state property and communes could not in their collective

name buy or rent a building to be used for religious purposes nor
tax their inhabitants to build one. Religious collectivities could not
accept perpetual donations. Several restrictions on actual practice
paralleled the desire to debilitate the Church financially. Priests
could not wear their costumes in public and outdoor processions,
bell-ringing and statues, crosses and inscriptions which could be
seen by the general public were all forbidden, while the *décade* was
reserved for public worship. In short, aspects of the iconoclasm of
the Year II were maintained.

The law was unenforceable. Many priests who returned from
abroad or emerged from hiding never bothered either to take the
new oaths of submission required by the laws of 11 prairial An III
and 7 vendémiaire An IV or remove themselves from the émigré
lists, so they could still be arrested. Much religious activity
therefore retained a clandestine character. The law of 3 ventôse
itself was also bound to keep many of the faithful as alienated as
they had been in the Year II. Since the parishes had often
contributed a great deal towards building the churches, their
confiscation could only be considered governmental theft and since
popular religion contained elaborate ceremonial and liturgical
aspects, the forbidding of outdoor worship also alienated large
numbers of people.

The laity especially continued to defy the law. This was
particularly easy in regions where geography rendered government
weak. Thus in the wild and isolated mountains of the Massif
Central, with its impenetrable forests, daunting gorges and
appalling roads, supporters of the refractories lived almost entirely
outside the apparatus of government. In this region many
refractories had never been deported and conducted clandestine
worship from 1792 on, moving from one safe house to another,
conducting Mass in barns, private homes or simply outdoors at
night. While light from the torches danced eerily over the faces of
the faithful and under the tall pines above, shepherdesses kept
watch, crying 'Wolves! Wolves!' if any army patrol got too near.
The constitutional church was as despised as ever. In the Lozère the
constitutional bishop claimed that he was almost alone against
public opinion, while the department wrote that in the north there
were cantons which were 'entirely sold to the priests, where people
are totally ignorant of the republican regime; no official does his
duty; people sing publicly in the churches; processions and other
ceremonies take place outdoors'. At Blesle in the Haute-Loire in

the Year V, people were so anxious for religious ceremonies that they rescued two old and infirm refractories from house arrest and forced them to say Mass. In the same department, officials reported that 'several priests conspired to go in a procession according to the ancient usages to a hamlet called La Trinité, a place formerly so venerated that people came from far off to offer the priests living there offerings as considerable as they were multiplied'. There were also installation ceremonies once the priests came out of hiding or returned from abroad. The entire commune of Belpech in the Aude participated in such a ceremony with men carrying a large cross, women a smaller one, followed by the chanting priest in vestments, the rest of the inhabitants trailing behind, everyone making the tour of the parish while the church bells rang. There were similar processions at Lauzerte and Miramon in the Hérault in which people also danced the *farandole* and shouted 'Vive la République! A bas les Jacobins!' When gendarmes tried to arrest a refractory who was saying Mass in a hayloft to two hundred people at Marie in the Haut-Rhin, they received no help from the municipal officer who said he had a letter to write instead, while his wife cried out, 'Yes, we want the Mass and we'll have it and . . . know that you'll be the victim [of our religion] for everybody detests you.' Manifestations of religious fervour were not simply limited to the isolated hill country. By the Year V in the Nord and Pas-de-Calais, armed peasants were guarding refractories or missionaries from Belgium who regularly said Mass in the open to hundreds and sometimes thousands of people. In practices which were common enough throughout the country, liberty trees were torn down or defaced or replaced with calvaries. Nor was a priest always necessary. At Pecquencourt in the Nord, the women fell on the unfortunate buyer of a chapel, took the keys from him and then marched around the commune carrying a statue of the Virgin and singing vespers and litanies. In the canton of Moyaux in the Calvados, it was common for laymen to perform religious services and in Moyaux itself, the lay 'priest' was a cobbler. At Sette in the Hérault, about thirty women and a few men carried a corpse from its home to the cemetery, singing funeral psalms along the way.

Such anecdotes could be multiplied over and over again but these are enough to show that the desire for religious ceremonies was very extensive and that the movement should not be seen simply in terms of the government's supposed laxity towards refractory priests or returned émigrés. A priest, while desirable, was not always necessary. Unfortunately, the sociology and geography of the 'revival' of religion in the mid-1790s is very poorly understood. Several elements are clear enough. One is the importance of women. They were almost always in the forefront of the enforced reopening of churches and almost always had a role in rescuing refractories when the gendarmes were fortunate enough to capture them, whether by falling on the hapless gendarmes themselves or by acting as scouts for the men who were masked and armed. Women taught morality within the family in the Old Regime and persecuted other women who violated it, but they had always needed the priests to elaborate and reinforce their authority. The removal of the clergy disoriented their role considerably and much of women's religious activity in this period aimed to restore it. There was also a considerable continuity between these incidents and similar ones in 1791-2. The geography appears to have been much the same and so, often, were the forms. People continued to harass constitutionals in the same way, whether by boycotts or by interrupting their services. The difference was that in the later period, constitutionals were much more likely to be murdered in reprisal for the execution of refractories and so the constitutional church continued its sad decline.

From composing a majority of the parish clergy in 1791, the constitutional church was in its death throes by the Year III. Its priests in the west found refuge in the towns and garrisoned bourgs, not daring to emerge even in daylight, otherwise the chouans and Vendeans would have killed them. Here and in the centre and north of France, where dechristianization had removed them in one way or another, the parish network scarcely existed. Elsewhere, there are glimpses of occasional individuals trying to carry on but as often demoralized by the indifference or hostility of their parishioners. In these circumstances, the brave attempt of the abbé Grégoire, regicide bishop of the Cher, and a handful of constitutional bishops to revive the constitutional church, and with it the old ideals of a regenerated church in a Christian country, was a failure. Only thirty-two of the bishops elected in 1791 were at the head of their dioceses ten years later. Twenty-eight sees were vacant.

Although this had never been consciously intended, the revolutionaries had shamelessly used the constitutionals and after thermidor threw them away. Throughout the Years III and IV, many – how many is impossible to say – curés made their peace with the refractory church, the humiliating retractions imposed and accepted a sign of their disillusionment and bitterness. For the resurgence of religion in this period was that of the refractories, who were slowly rebuilding their parish organization from the ground up, often with the cooperation of a devoted laity. In several dioceses – Le Mans, Rouen, Le Puy and Lyon among them – the émigré bishops sent in vicars-general to reorganize the church. How successful this was is impossible to estimate but there is no doubt that many refractories were extremely active. Moreover, the refractory church was for all intents and purposes a royalist church. However much some Catholic journalists and seminarians in the capital were searching for a formula which would permit an accommodation with the Republic, others were totally committed to its overthrow. A majority of the émigré bishops pronounced against the oaths of submission because they violated the 'loyalty due our legitimate sovereign' and a few equated those who took these oaths with the schismatics of 1791. One parish priest from the old diocese of Dol in Brittany judged those who took the new oath as 'scandalous, suspects, very dangerous for religion, abetters of republicanism and dishonouring their ministry by their shameful conduct'. Other priests acted on their royalist sentiments. The abbé Bernier, later one of the negotiators of the Concordat, was an important advisor to the Vendean general, Stofflet, and other priests served on the royalist councils in Brittany. In the Midi, several were actually military chiefs of the royalist brigand bands. But it was their pastoral work which was most subversive. At Champagnat in the Saône-et-Loire, the refractory preached that the Constitution was the work of 'the wicked and the impious . . . [against] the usurpation of the property of the clergy and the émigrés . . . [and for the] return of the monarchy, seigneurial rights and the tithe'. In the Côtes-du-Nord, it was said that the priests 'inspired the greatest contempt for the patriots and promised heaven as a reward for those who assassinate them'. Around Orres in the Hautes-Alpes, an unidentified refractory was preaching 'to the credulous inhabitants of the countryside that the payment of taxes, that the call to the young men to fly to the defence of *la patrie* are not obligatory, that religion condemns it'. At Rosières in the Haute-Loire, the abbé Bernard 'forbade those who followed him from seeing or having any relation with the schismatics, that is, the republicans'. Such anathemas had been heard earlier in 1791–2 as well, but by the Year IV (summer of 1796) they were much more common for the quite understandable reason that so many of their colleagues had gone to the scaffold. For men like these, an accommodation with the godless Republic was inconceivable.

Administrative Collapse

The refractory church was able to make its resurgence because popular culture could not do without it, because the constitutionals had irrevocably sullied themselves by their association with the Jacobins and because it had allies in the government apparatus. Indeed, it is hard to imagine governments which had such a tenuous grip over their own officials and territory as the thermidorean Convention or the Directory down to fructidor An V. There were several reasons for this. The price of an aggressive foreign policy was that few troops were available for repression at home. In the thirteen departments which made up most of the old province of Languedoc, there were only 4200 troops in the spring of 1796, many of the others having been drained off for the campaigns in Germany and Italy. Not one of the departments ravaged by royalist guerrillas had more than eight hundred soldiers in their garrisons. The result of leaving the departments more or less to themselves was that, unlike the prewar days, what remained of the National Guard and the gendarmerie handled most of the dissidence. Yet both of these institutions had been purged of Jacobins and many of their most enthusiastic elements had volunteered earlier for the army. Where the National Guard had not been taken over by royalists or was not the Companies of the Sun or Jesus under another name, it was disorganized, apathetic and poorly armed. Like the old *maréchaussée* whom they succeeded, the gendarmes too were few, and large areas of the countryside remained more or less unpoliced. The appalling state of the government's finances made this even worse. There were constant reports of gendarmes having to patrol on foot either because they had no horses or no forage. Pay was constantly in arrears and many had to take on second jobs or ask ordinary citizens for food. The picture of policeman as vagabond was equalled only by their lack of zeal, which was quite understandable since they were obviously no match for either the royalist or the criminal brigand bands. When the brigands raided the tax office at Evans in the Creuse, two gendarmes tried to save their lives by falling to their knees and crying, 'Vive Louis XVIII!' The gendarmes might have been more zealous if the

administration had supported them but conditions were appalling
here as well. Almost everywhere, the Directory's commissioners
had to beg notable citizens to stand for office and on occasion even
threatened them with prison if their refusal continued. Suitable
candidates for office in the Côte-d'Or developed such an epidemic
of medical problems and business commitments that it took four
months to fill positions in the department's central administration.
Apathy and the inability of the government to pay promptly even
worthless stipends were only part of the problem. Politics had
shown itself to be too unrewarding or too dangerous for the men
who so zealously assumed local office in 1790. In the Var, for
instance, 105 men were department administrators between 1790
and 1795, not one of them for the entire period. At the district level,
there were nearly five hundred administrators, procurators or
national agents and only two served throughout. Similarly, not one
of the sixty-odd individuals who served on the district of Narbonne
had a continuous record of service. With the Jacobin administrators
gone, this often left only the feckless, the indifferent or the
downright hostile to manage local affairs. There are many well-
documented cases of provincial officials refusing to obey directives,
protecting and even encouraging murder gangs, deserters and
draft-dodgers or, especially in rural areas, not investigating or even
reporting assaults on constitutional curés or murders of owners or
farmers of *biens nationaux*. Municipal officers in the countryside
connived at the massive evasion of the laws on religious observance.
Judges and juries were extraordinarily lax in applying the law and
witnesses were intimidated either by friends of the accused or by
those already acquitted so that building a case became next to
impossible. After the royalist victories in the local elections of the
Year V, defiance had reached such a point that officials even
trumpeted their attitudes. In the Lozère, where the president of the
central administration no longer did any official work and another
administrator spent all his time on a private lawsuit and where taxes
were not collected and émigrés threatened buyers of *biens
nationaux*, refractories had been allowed to take over all the
churches including the cathedral at Mende, because, the remaining
administrators claimed disingenuously, 'we do not understand by
fanaticism the religious sentiment which nature has engraved so
profoundly on the heart of man and which is for him . . . the
inexhaustible source of the most gentle consolation'. The
administrators of the canton of L'Etre in the Manche were more

honest when they said that enforcing the laws on religious observance would cause an insurrection 'which could have the most disastrous consequences'. Officials in the Cantal reported that municipal officers 'are in such a state of stagnation that, out of fear of being murdered or having their properties set on fire, they do not dare denounce them [the refractory priests] or demand the execution of the law'.

Brigands, Bandits and Chouans

One of the consequences of the administrative collapse of the period was brigandage. Like their counterparts in the Old Regime, many of the criminal gangs reflected the distressing misery of the countryside which was aggravated terribly by the economic crisis of the Years III and IV. Over one third of those indicted for their activities in the infamous bande d'Orgères which ravaged the Beauce joined after the Year II, men and women pushed to the edge by unemployment and near starvation, made desperate by the suppression of most public charities and the inadequacy of private philanthropy. Aside from the permanently rootless, many of them were of the same social groups which had rioted in the same region in 1792: agricultural labourers and artisans, some of whom had left a desperate situation in the towns to beg or to look for work in the countryside. Such bands could have a very wide area of operations. One band of *chauffeurs* – so called because they roasted the feet of farmers to extort money from them or to discover where the proverbial sack of coins was hidden – roamed the entire countryside between Rouen and Gand in Belgium. It was strongly suspected that they used the military and gendarmerie as fences. The entire village of Bollène in the Vaucluse apparently lived from robbing travellers, and when their chief was arrested in the Year VIII two hundred of his followers disarmed the soldiers at Valréas and released him, crying, 'Vive le Roi! Victory is ours!' Nor was such village support for brigands a unique case. The frequency of reports of the murder and robbery of isolated soldiers returning home through the Alpine passes from service in Italy, and the inability of authorities to stop it, suggests a widespread complicity on the part of the local population who, of course, also protected refractory priests. It is difficult, in fact, to distinguish activities of this sort from royalism. Highway robbers, disguised as National Guards, took only government tax money from the stagecoach between Coutances and Saint-Lô in the Manche and left ordinary passengers alone in messidor An V. Their counterparts dressed in green carmagnoles and speaking an unintelligible slang to each other who robbed the Paris–Amiens–Gand stage, near Chantilly outside Paris, said they were part of the 'armée de Condé' and wished to 'idemnify themselves for the losses which *la nation* had forced on them'. Those who robbed the Brest–Paris coach near Mayenne were nicknamed 'Bourbon', 'Condé' and 'Artois'. Bands of young draft-dodgers who lived in the faraway hills of the Var by robbing passing merchants and owners of *biens nationaux* called themselves 'chouans'. In the Year IX, police spies tossed a bomb into a cave in which the brigands of Aups in the Var were sleeping, killing eleven. Among the victims' effects was a 'letter' dictated by Christ Himself through a wise child of seven, in 'golden letters and in Languedocien', promising safe delivery for pregnant women and protection against the ravages of fire, pestilence and war. Much of the 'brigandage' of this period thus turns out on closer examination to have a counterrevolutionary intent.

The distinction between genuine criminals speaking the chic argot of royalism and the 'brigands royaux' proper is not easy to make because of the habit of republican authorities of labelling all clandestine attacks on their supporters as 'brigandage'. The distinction was often real enough in practice, however, because anti-Jacobin brigandage grew out of the resistance of many villagers throughout the Midi to Protestant ascendancy, to the Civil Constitution of the Clergy and to the Terror. As if these disturbances to the proper order of things were not bad enough in themselves, many village and small-town Jacobins had also violated community norms of settling disputes, political or otherwise, by an overwhelming use of force as in the *bagarre de Nîmes* in 1790, or by enforcing the laws on refractory priests or by welcoming the various expeditions of the urban National Guards. Of course, some Jacobins had scarcely compromised themselves at all, establishing their revolutionary committees but arresting nobody or busying themselves with tedious lectures to their uncomprehending neighbours or collecting saltpetre. Some popular societies even tried to mediate between the Protestant and Catholic clergies. But others had done great damage. The Protestant-Jacobin merchants of the Drôme who landed contracts to make uniforms refused work to Catholics on the pretext that they would not work on the *décadi*.

Others had thrown themselves unhesitatingly into the dechristianization campaign and denounced anyone who persisted in the older forms of worship. Still others had been all too willing to denounce people who had compromised themselves when the federalist armies marched through to the dreaded revolutionary commissions. There had always been resistance to these activities but the Jacobins were safe so long as they could rely on a vigorous representative on mission or their urban counterparts, but with the winding down of repression and the White Terror in the cities they were dangerously exposed. The lists of disarmed terrorists show how few such ultras were – too few to defend themselves against outraged communities.

Like chouannerie, popular royalism in the Midi had broad community support. As in the west, there are countless examples of communities forcing humiliations on local Jacobins by compelling them to replace liberty trees with calvaries or forcing them to abjure their errors by throwing them to their knees and requiring them to kiss the cross. Women had an important role in these ceremonies restoring proper relations in the community in both the west and the Midi. In both regions, nostalgia for an idealized community dominated. As one was accused of saying, 'Were we not really happy then? . . . We were free then; we hunted when we wanted.'

Like the chouans, the 'brigands royaux' took upon themselves the responsibility for harassing, mugging or murdering local republicans who had gone too far. They were often young men of military age who had taken to the hills rather than be incorporated. Draft-dodging had begun in the Year II and the terrorist authorities could scarcely contain it. After thermidor, it reached amazing proportions. It was said that there were 1000 draft-dodgers in the district of Villefranche in the Rhône alone in the Year III and 5000–6000 in the Vaucluse who could survive, thanks to the complicity of neighbours and municipal officers, with some ease. In the Haute-Loire, Tarn and Allier there were communes in which almost all of the young men managed to evade the draft and about one fifth and more later deserted their battalions. Neither the amnesty of 10–23 thermidor An III (28 July–10 August 1795) nor the recourse to military tribunals for evaders in the law of 4 nivôse An IV (25 December 1795) had much effect. Officials in the Landes had not arrested a single draft-evader or deserter in the Year IX despite all their efforts for the previous several months. Attempts to round up refractory priests and draft-dodgers led to outright insurrections. At Beaupuy in the Gers a patrol of only fifteen was disarmed by a furious crowd of 1500 shouting, 'To hell with the Republic and *la nation*! . . . We want our priests and a king!' This in turn sparked the men of Encausse, Monbrun and Cassemartin to invade L'Isle-Jourdain, the departmental capital, to retrieve the church bells which had been confiscated in 1793 while bands of young men began roaming the district mugging owners of *biens nationaux*. Efforts to arrest the members of these bands were completely ineffective. The four bands which operated around Saint-Palais in the Basses-Pyrénées, which specialized in the murder and pillage of the former terrorist personnel, were strongly supported by the local Basque population who had been forcibly removed from their homes by the representatives on mission, Cavaignac and Pinet, as part of the war effort in the Year II. Of the twenty-six brigands eventually captured, twelve were deserters. As these examples show, the bands grew out of the counterrevolutionary sentiments of the local population and so they were grafted willingly to the wider designs of the royalist leaders. The band of the émigré Goty-Roquebrune which operated in the Haute-Garonne was a part of one of these royalist networks in the southwest. He was shot in a gun battle in ventôse An IV, but his men were able to survive by fleeing into the Ariège or Aude, or at worst, into Spain. In some regions there was a direct continuity between the bands and earlier counterrevolutionary risings. The band of Jean-Louis Solier, alias Sans-Peur, began operations in late 1794 in the forest of Ballènes near Montpellier in the Hérault but Solier himself was involved in the planning of the third *camp de Jalès* in 1792 and possibly with the Charrier affair in the Lozère the following year. Solier, who was always armed with a double-barrelled musket and two pistols stuffed in his belt, was the former prior of Colognac in the Gard while his chief lieutenant, Raynal alias Belle-rose, was a former curé. The continuity with the refusal of the oath to the Civil Constitution was thus direct. His band of about four hundred carried on a guerrilla war against republican garrisons and extorted money from merchants on their way to the fair at Beaucaire until Solier's execution in 1801. The heavy-smoking, gross-mannered, smallpox-ravaged Dominique Allier, leader of a band which operated in the Haute-Loire and Ardèche until his capture near Le Puy in fructidor An VI (August 1798), could trace his counterrevolutionary pedigree through almost every conspiracy in the Midi beginning with Froment's in 1790.

Since the brigand bands were composed of clandestine warriors, it is difficult to know much about the nature of their local support or who their members were. The geography of their operations can be known in a general way from various police reports. Thus, it was concentrated in the departments of the Rhône valley beginning around Lyon and continuing south to the Mediterranean and branching west through the Aveyron and Hérault to the mid-Pyrenees and east through the Bouches-du-Rhône, Var and Alpes-Maritimes. Some districts were affected less than others but by now much is unknown. The social composition of the bands can be better known thanks to an analysis of some of those convicted by the special tribunals which operated over most of these regions in the Years IX and X. Thus, among the sixty convicted of being members of the bande d'Aubagne which operated in the Bouches-du-Rhône between the Years III and IX, there were four émigrés, two priests, four in the professions, eight in the food trades and, except for a single ploughman, the rest were in assorted other clothing and building trades. In other circumstances, and with the exception of the émigrés, this could have been the social composition of almost any small-town revolutionary committee of the Year II. Without an occupational breakdown of the population as a whole it is difficult to be sure, but this band may have been unique. Thus, of fifty-three people condemned by the special tribunals in the Basses-Alpes, Bouches-du-Rhône, Var and Vaucluse whose occupations are known, twenty-six were peasants, only six were in non-manual occupations and the rest were scattered throughout various artisanal trades. Since villages close to the Mediterranean were highly urbanized and therefore had a higher artisan component than elsewhere, it looks as if the social composition of the royalist brigand bands closely approximated that of the population as a whole. Whatever the case, the figures do show that 'brigandage' was a popular movement, dependent on refractory priests and émigré officers only to the extent that ordinary people wanted to be dominated or led. Nor was it brigandage of the rootless sort found in the bande d'Orgères. Where in this case only about half the mendicant brigands had been born in the region where the band operated, in the case of fifty-three royalist brigands where information is available, thirty were living in the same town or village where they had been born and only eight were domiciled outside their native departments. The lists of those condemned also confirm the importance of conscription. Of forty-three whose ages are known, twenty-eight would have been subject to it in 1793.

One of the reasons the Midi occupied so little of the Directory's attention was that the 'brigands royaux' were not able to accomplish much militarily. An attempt by Lamothe-Piquet's men to take Saint-Etienne in the winter of the Year IV failed. So did an attempt to take simultaneously Nîmes, Montpellier, Le Puy and Privas a few months later. The Vendeans and the chouans, on the other hand, were potentially much more dangerous because of the possibility the British would be able to arm them. Several such landings did take place – to Charette in December 1795 after the Comte d'Artois left the Ile-d'Yeu, to Cadoudal in the Morbihan and to the chouans near Fougères. These shipments were disappointingly meagre to the royalists but the Directory still had to prevent the rural populations of the west from being properly armed. Failure risked repeating the nightmare of another Vendée in 1793.

To crush the west, the Directory took measures which were as drastic as any attempted in the Year II. On 7 nivôse (28 December), they turned the western departments over to military control, amalgamated the three armies into a single Army of the Coasts of the Ocean and entrusted command of the new army and the entire region to General Hoche. Thanks to the release of troops from the Spanish front, the Army rose to about 100,000 men by spring, about half of whom were in the fields at any one time – more men in other words than were given to General Bonaparte who began his much more famous Italian campaign at the same time. The results were almost as spectacular. With such large numbers of men, Hoche employed what was called the 'flying columns' technique of counterinsurgency whereby troops criss-crossed a designated area, pursuing band chiefs, disarming the local population and preventing bands from coalescing into important assemblies. Moreover, the troops were concentrated on particular regions so that the impression was created of an overwhelming force. The method had already shown itself brutally effective against Charette in the early autumn of 1795. He found himself hunted down, safe only in the marshes of Poitou or the most impenetrable forests, shunned by the civilian population, his irregulars slipping away and his lieutenants prudently making accommodations with republican generals. When Stofflet finally broke the peace in late January, he was only able to gather a few hundred stalwarts. He was captured and shot a month later. Charette was captured too and before his execution on 9 germinal (29 March), he was paraded through the streets of Nantes in chains like a criminal to mark the contrast with the arrogant general who had negotiated a peace among equals with the representatives just a year before. Meanwhile, the areas north of the Loire had been stripped of troops. Yet the chouans were able to accomplish very little because they had so few arms and even less powder. Hundreds of them stalled before tiny garrisons of sixty men and were incapable of protecting properly the few landings of arms and émigré officers. They could hardly withstand the assault Hoche launched after the victories in the Vendée. Demoralized by the execution of the popular Charette and terrified of the thousands of troops marching through their areas, one by one the regional leaders began to surrender. The war in the west was over. On 28 messidor (16 July), the Directory decreed the Army of the Coasts of the Ocean 'worthy of *la patrie*'.

Yet the west was not pacified in the sense of being won over. It was crushed. Although Hoche advocated the greatest respect for freedom of religion and was willing to make accommodations with refractories at the local level, the law forbade genuine freedom of religious expression. Nothing at all was done to mollify grievances over higher taxes, requisition of foodstuffs or security of tenure. Hoche also attempted to impose greater discipline on his troops. Yet there were too many instances of marauding for this to have been effective, and in some areas the troops' very excesses secured the chouans' surrender. Moreover, the Army of the Coasts of the Ocean was authorized to supply itself locally – a reflection of the inability of the Directory to support an army even within the frontiers of 'la grande nation' and a measure which obliterated the line between requisition and pillage. What good was payment for requisitions in worthless assignats anyway? The path was prepared for the renewal of chouannerie in the Year VII . . . and for the region's enduring preference for right-wing voting ever since.

Victory in Italy

Hoche's victories against the Vendeans and chouans was a major step towards the stabilizing of the Republic. Yet the Directory could not really consolidate itself until it had completed the successes of the Year III against Spain, Holland and Prussia. This meant that the Austrians would have to be knocked out of the war which in turn might compel the British to come to terms. For the campaign of 1796, Carnot planned for Jourdan's Army of Sambre-et-Meuse to advance into Franconia while Moreau's Army of Rhin-et-Moselle would invest Swabia. At first, the Army of Italy was to play a diversionary role but its newly appointed commander, General Bonaparte, pestered the Directory into giving him a free hand and he was to meet Moreau at Vienna. In the event, the Army of Italy decided the campaign. No doubt the Directors cared little about Bonaparte's vague instructions because the material situation of the Army of Italy constrained it to a secondary role. Under a twenty-seven-year-old general with no field experience, the Army rarely had more than 30,000 effectives until the end of the campaign when reinforcements from the Vendée and Brittany raised it to over 40,000. The Austrians often arrayed twice that many against Bonaparte. Jourdan and Moreau had roughly 140,000 altogether. The soldiers had no uniforms as such, pay (in assignats) was years in arrears, military contractors supplied inadequate food and material, and the cavalry and artillery were lamentable. It resembled nothing so much as a horde, was often close to mutiny and could not be prevented from looting. The pillage of this army of liberators regularly provoked insurrections from exasperated populations.

Nonetheless, Bonaparte was determined to do great things with this depressing material. He promised his men 'honour, glory and riches' in return for their courage and endurance. By the end of April, a month after assuming command, he had knocked Piedmont out of the war, secured his flank and rear and opened the Po valley to his starving men. By taking the bridge at Lodi (7–10 May), he cleared the way to Milan which was made to pay an indemnity of twenty million. Much of the countryside revolted against these exactions but the soldiers were delighted to receive half their pay in cash. Carnot reinforced this growing personal attachment of the soldiers to their commander when he ordered Bonaparte to break off the drive to the Tyrol and head south. A respite in Italy was necessary because Jourdan and Moreau had not yet begun their offensives and this only helped consolidate Bonaparte. Because of the failures in Germany and his successes, he was able to force the Directory to rescind its order to divide his command with Kellermann. Further, the invasions of Modena,

Tuscany and the northern papal states in June which netted millions
in cash and precious manuscripts and art were extraordinarily
lucrative both for the government and the generals, including
Bonaparte himself. When the offensives beyond the Rhine finally
started, Bonaparte was able to resume the advance across the
Lombard plain. The rest of the campaign involved a baffling series
of marches and countermarches but they all had as their object
French attempts to capture the fortress of Mantua and Austrian
attempts to lift the siege. The major battles, Castiglione on 5
August, Arcola on 15–17 November (where Bonaparte had to be
prevented from leading his men over the bridge) and Rivoli on 15–
16 January, were all French successes, however, and Mantua finally
fell on 2 February 1797. The Austrians thus had their backs against
the Tyrol but in the meantime the Archduke Charles had driven
Moreau back to the Rhine so that Bonaparte was in no position to
advance through the treacherous passes to Vienna. In fact, the
Austrians might have taken the risk of transferring troops to Italy
but fearful of an attack from Moreau and from Hoche who had
replaced Jourdan, they agreed to the Preliminaries of Leoben, an
armistice and the basis of the peace signed later in the year.

The Italian campaign had immense consequences for Bonaparte
and consequently for the Directory. In the first place, it laid the
basis of his legend. The incident at Arcola, for instance, captured
the imagination of dozens of sketch artists, where for dramatic
effect the general was invariably presented as leading his troops
straight over the bridge to glittering victory. Bonaparte helped this
along by the stirring bulletins of the Army of Italy and by his own
newspaper, the *Courrier de l'Armée d'Italie*, where he was
presented as one of those men 'whose power has no other limits
than when the most sublime virtue supports an unlimited
brilliance'. The apotheosis of Bonaparte as the republican of
uncorrupted, stern genius came with David's famous unfinished
portrait which was painted about this time. By now, the war looked
eternal to the public and the quarrelling politicians appeared
incapable of ending it. Here was a republican general who could.

In the second place, Bonaparte successfully invaded the civilian
sphere as well. To consolidate his conquests, he organized a series
of Italian republics of which the Cisalpine, based on Milan-
Modena, was the most important. The Cisalpine Republic's
constitution was moderate enough and, as a sign of things to come,
its major positions were appointive, not elected. But the Directory

would have sacrificed all the Italian conquests to secure Belgium and the Rhine frontier. Bonaparte had other ideas. He proposed the Preliminaries of Leoben himself and the Directory had to accept the *fait accompli*. With the republicans having badly lost the recent elections to resurgent royalists, it might need the Army of Italy. For his part, as he said later, after Lodi, Bonaparte knew he was a truly extraordinary man.

The Conspiracy of the Equals

The government's policy of stabilizing itself also meant an offensive against the slowly rebuilding Jacobins. The ease with which this was done shows how weak the Jacobins were and how much they underestimated the unscrupulousness of the government. Babeuf's 'Conspiracy of the Equals' provided the occasion to strike not only at a shaky conspiracy but against the democratic opposition as a whole.

François-Noël Babeuf, known as Gracchus, had always been on the fringes of mainstream revolutionary thought, possibly because his poverty, brutalized childhood, the necessity to educate himself and his experience as an estate surveyor in Picardy were as remote as they could be from the background of most Jacobin leaders. His agonized sympathy for human suffering and his passion for equality had made him a village agitator in the peasant troubles of 1790 and his apparent orthodoxy got him a job in the Paris food administration in 1793 where he had to face the gigantic problems of provisioning the capital during the Terror. His ideas evolved with his experiences. At first an enemy of big property, he advocated a generalized welfarism in subsistence, education and medical services along with making property available to the poor; later he proposed an equal division of land and finally in 1795 an attack on the principle of private property itself. Like most revolutionaries he attributed scarcity to monopolists and hoarders whose control of the market gave them an incentive to manipulate prices, but unlike Roux, who demanded only dramatic punishment to deal with them, Babeuf proposed to eliminate the market altogether. His communism involved popularly elected magistrates linked together in a lateral and hierarchical national network allocating workloads, gathering produce and manufactures and distributing them on an absolutely equal basis. All state property would be organized immediately on this basis, the state would seize private property at the death of their owners and, in the meantime, individuals would be given an incentive to surrender their property to the community because only private property would be taxed. Within a generation at most, private property and misery would no longer exist. Babeuf would have denied the underlying bureaucratic authoritarianism of his utopia because he remained a Cordeliers democrat in his belief in popular education, recall, referendum and demonstrations throughout his life. At first, he believed such methods alone could achieve the just society, and for a time even toyed with the idea of establishing a utopian community which would spread by example and armed revolution. But just as his aims evolved with experience, so too did his proposed tactics. By early in the Year IV he had developed the doctrine for which he is best known, the leading role of the inner circle of the revolutionary vanguard. For this the Directory's policies towards the clubs were directly responsible .

The Directory's strategy of capturing the support of the 'honnêtes gens' required that it present itself as the only alternative to the threat of disorder from the royalists and Jacobins. With such a mentality, the era of reasonable hope and cooperation between the Directory and the Jacobins after the vendémiaire rising was bound to be short. The newly established neo-Jacobin Panthéon club was formally loyal to the Constitution of the Year III but hoped to push it in a more democratic direction. Several excited orators even raised the question of implementing Saint-Just's ventôse decrees and distributing land among veterans. With the Panthéon's membership approaching three thousand, and the spread of other clubs in the capital and in at least two dozen cities and towns in the country, Carnot, who was the architect of the policy of attaching the 'honnêtes gens' to the Republic, persuaded his fellow Directors to act. When the Panthéon protested the arrest of Babeuf's wife and appealed to the army, General Bonaparte closed it down on 8 ventôse (27 February). Closure of several provincial clubs followed. On 27 germinal (16 April), the government made advocacy of the Constitution of 1793 a capital crime and began purging the administration of Jacobins.

Babeuf's reaction played straight into the government's hands. From the beginning, Babeuf, who was in hiding, scorned the Jacobin policy of loyal opposition in his *Tribun du Peuple* and was scathingly critical of the Directory. He had also long been dismayed at the tendency of 'the people' to follow demagogues. With the

apathy after the prairial rising and the repression in the winter of
the Year IV, he formed an 'Insurrectionary Committee' to organize
the 'final' revolution, assume sole executive power for three months
to handle the problems of transition and finally to implement the
Constitution of 1793 and the communist utopia. Yet the
conspirators only had hatred of the Directory in common. Babeuf,
Buonarotti whose book established the legend of his mentor thirty
years later, and Lepelletier, brother of the 'martyr of liberty',
certainly shared the great ideal but others like Rossignol, the
'scourge of the Vendée' and Darthe, erstwhile prosecutor of the
Revolutionary Tribunal of Arras and Cambrai, could not see
beyond a mighty bloodbath of enemies of all sorts. For the
Montagnards who got involved at the last moment, the insurrection
would restore themselves and the revolutionary government of the
Year II. The *sans-culottes* who were recruited or who were
inscribed on Babeuf's lists as 'worthy of command' for the police
to find could have had little idea of the ultimate purpose. Few,
incidentally, had a militant past which indicates how thorough the
thermidorean repression had been. In any case, despite a serious
effort to recruit the critical artillery companies of the National
Guard and subvert the Police Legion which guarded the Councils,
the Day of the People never occurred. After an abortive mutiny,
the Police Legion was disbanded on 10 floréal (29 April). Betrayed
by a double agent on the eve of the rising, Babeuf and the
Committee were arrested on 21 floréal (10 May).

There is a tendency among some Anglo-Saxon historians to
minimize Babeuf's conspiracy just as there is a tendency among
continental Marxists to find in it the precursor of a great tradition.
The affair had quite another importance to contemporaries. The
government was determined to use the conspiracy to crush Jacobin
democracy once and for all. Hundreds of former militants or even
hapless subscribers to the *Tribun du Peuple* in the provinces who
admired Babeuf only as a persecuted patriot whose high principles
repeatedly landed him in prison, were arrested or otherwise
harassed for their part in a 'monstrous conspiracy'. Since the deputy
Drouet, the former Varennes postmaster who recognized Louis
XVI, was part of the conspiracy and deputies could not be tried in
ordinary courts, the government established a special High Court
at Vendôme to hear the case against all the defendants. This was
more a political decision than a constitutional one, however,
because Drouet mysteriously escaped and later surfaced as a

subprefect under Bonaparte. In fact, the special court offered a forum for maximum publicity designed to scare the 'honnêtes gens' into the arms of the Directory in the approaching elections of the Year V. Yet the overzealous prosecution bungled its case badly despite the support of a biased chief judge. In the end, only Babeuf and a colleague went to the guillotine on 8 prairial An V (27 May 1797), convicted not of conspiracy but of the improvised charge of advocating the Constitution of 1793. Most of the sixty-four defendants had to be acquitted. It is very unlikely that the trial won the Directory any support in the elections and it even comforted the Jacobins. Throughout the interminable preparations and during the trial itself, the democratic press was able to expose the arrest of obviously innocent militants, the shabby use of *agents provocateurs* and the high-handed moulding and intimidation of witnesses. Even some moderate journalists were appalled and so the affair ended with the Directory tasting ashes.

Misery and Monetary Collapse

One of the reasons Babeuf received the support he did was the continuing misery of the urban working population. Unlike the crisis of the Year III, the contours of the crisis of the Year IV are not well known but everything indicates that its effects were severe. The government compounded it by a truly disastrous monetary policy and alienated the rich by trying to impose a forced loan. In its defence, the Directory did inherit a chaotic currency. In June 1795, a *louis d'or* of 24 *livres* had risen to 1000 in assignats; on 30 October to 2600; and in February 1796 to 5000. At the same time, the Convention had ordered peasants to pay half their taxes in kind or hard cash but since they received assignats for marketing their produce, hardly anyone did so. Some districts had troops billeted on them to collect taxes which was bound to be unfair because it was ineffective. Furthermore, prices on the free market soared astronomically and the controlled subsistence economy teetered on collapse. In Paris in the winter of the Year IV, rations had to be reduced, controlled prices raised and unpopular substitutes found. In their search for Babeuf's accomplices, the police were able to turn up dozens of former militants who had sold even their beds and sheets – usually a poor man's most valuable possessions – and who were sleeping on straw. Many of these people were able to survive somehow but thousands of others could not. Deaths in Rouen and Dieppe were far more numerous than in the Year III and higher than the average for the decade in Nancy and Strasbourg. Overall, from the beginning of the crisis in 1793 to 1796, the deaths in the large towns were nearly 95 per cent higher than the average of the previous decade while those in the medium-sized towns were 53 per cent higher. It was probably in this period too that the urban population fell most. In 1790 there were 110,000 people living in Bordeaux; in 1806, only 92,986. In 1790 in Toulouse, 52,863; in 1814, 50,904. In 1789 in Strasbourg, 49,948; in 1805, 49,816. In 1789, more than 650,000 in Paris; in 1806, 580,609.

The government's attempts to deal with the catastrophe were a monumental failure. Since its own revenues were almost worthless when it received any at all, it tried to increase them and reduce the number of assignats in circulation by imposing a forced loan on the rich on 19 frimaire An IV (10 December 1795). It was hoped to raise 600 million in cash but the administrative chaos was so great and charges of political bias in assessments so loud that the attempt had to be abandoned in the summer of the Year IV. The forced loan was also intended to be a prelude to retiring the assignat but the new 'mandats territoriaux', created on 28 ventôse An IV (18 March 1796) were grossly overvalued relative to the assignat. They too began to depreciate rapidly, so much so that *biens nationaux* could be acquired at only two and three times their annual rental value. A month after their emission in March 1796, the *mandats* were worth 20 per cent of their face value; by July, less than 5 per cent. Until the government decided to accept only cash for *biens nationaux* months later, anyone with money could legally strip the state of its one valuable asset. The Directory finally recognized the failure of its policy by demonetizing the *mandats* on 16 pluviôse (4 February 1797). Of course, this did nothing to improve its financial situation, and following the elections of germinal An V it faced a vigorous royalist minority in the legislature determined to wreck any financial reform the Directory proposed. In short, financial policy, by threatening the rich, once again gave the counterrevolution an opening. It was one to which its leaders and backers were moving anyway.

Spies, Subversion, a New Coup

The pacification of the west and Bonaparte's continuing victories forced the royalists, émigrés and the British to emphasize another aspect of their strategy, subversion of the Directory from within. There was nothing new in this. From his arrival in Berne under diplomatic cover in the autumn of 1794, the British spymaster, William Wickham, had been trying to cobble an Austrian-Piedmontese-émigré invasion through the Franche-Comté and the Alps together with the royalist networks centred on Lyon. This was part of the broad strategy of which the disastrous expedition to Quiberon was a part. The plan fell far short of expectations. No Austrian invasion ever materialized, Imbert-Colomès, head of the conspiracy in 1790 and Précy, commander of the federalist forces in 1793, could never quite put Lyon in a position to revolt again. Some of Wickham's funds were used to smuggle émigrés into the southeast, to subsidize refractory priests around Mâcon and to form 'a party in the Forez'. In other words, British money was being used to support the white terrorist murder gangs. One of Wickham's agents was none other than Dominique Allier who had graduated from the Froment school of conspiracy in 1790 to become a brigand chief in the Year IV. Wickham's most notable catch was General Pichegru who succumbed in the autumn of 1795 to the blandishments of the Prince de Condé and to British gold because of the deplorable state of his army, the demands of a greedy mistress and the pleasures of high living for himself. Pichegru's reasons for treason were so light-headed and the man so timid that the royalists could scarcely get him to do anything, although a great deal of hope and effort were expended on him. When the Directory removed him from his command in March 1796 for failing to carry out offensives, his effectiveness evaporated.

By mid-1796, it was obvious that an equivocating general, stifled insurrections, low-grade assassinations and unrealized invasions were hardly the stuff of counterrevolution. Consequently, Wickham and the British reoriented their efforts towards getting royalist sympathizers elected to the legislature. This threw them on to the royalist spy organization, known as the *Agence de Paris*, which had pretended for years to have conduits to deputies who were secret monarchists. In fact, most of the Agency's reports were gathered from the newspapers or from the street gossip by a half-dozen 'spies' who mostly hated each other. The reports in turn were doctored with fantastic stories by the Agency's foreign head, the Comte d'Antraigues, who passed the quasi-fabrications on to foreign governments. With Antraigues, one enters the murky underbelly of fanatical royalism beside which the Pretender's intransigence and Condé's refusal to deal with constitutionalists until they repented appeared moderate. Before the Revolution, he hated Marie-Antoinette and despised Calonne. His friendship with Rousseau and his attacks on ministerial despotism in the name of provincial rights gave him a reputation as a patriot in 1788–9 but for Antraigues the ideal polity was dominance by the provincial squirearchy. As soon as he emigrated his dark obsessions overwhelmed him. He specifically aimed to be the Marat of the counterrevolution, was convinced that Jacobinism was part of a vast Orléanist plot and welcomed the execution of Louis XVI because it undermined the moderates. With a mentality like this, the arrest of many of the leading members of the Agency in January 1797 was something of a blessing in disguise.

The strategy of subverting the Directory from within also brought the British into contact with the Philanthropic Institutes and with the moderate deputies around d'André. The Institutes were royalist electoral organizations appealing to the fears and resentments of the 'honnêtes gens' under the guise of public charities and antiterrorist activities while keeping their true reactionary aims hidden. In the southwest at least, they also had a clandestine military organization. Around Bordeaux, one corps was recruited from draft-dodgers and deserters while another was composed of ordinary citizens. Around Toulouse, the local Institute was simply grafted on to a preexisting 'Society of the Friends of Order' run by a secret committee of royalists called the 'fils légitimes' which also had links with the demagogic *Anti-Terroriste* newspaper and the *Agence de Paris*. The Institutes were well placed to contact the 'brigands royaux' and the refractory priests and thus attract some popular support. In Toulouse, many of their members came from the hard-hit food trades. Wickham was so impressed with their potential that he allocated at least £10,000 to them; more, in other words, than the Directory itself spent on subverting the elections of the Year VI. Although both royalist and police sources had their own interests to promote in exaggerating their number, there were claims that there were Institutes in fifty-

eight to seventy departments in the summer of the Year V.
D'André, who had been elected to represent the nobility of
Provence in the Estates-General, was the major link between
Wickham, the Institutes, the Pretender's court at Verona and the
moderate deputies centred around the Clichy club. No one can be
certain how many *clichyens* there were since they included sincere
advocates of the rule of law under the Republic, men for whom a
restoration was a possible option, former Feuillants and Fayettists,
constitutional monarchists and outright reactionaries. D'André
himself wanted no more than improvements to the Constitution of
1791 but eschewed theoretical debates to concentrate on welding
the reactionaries to the constitutionalists of various hues. His great
problem was Louis XVIII who remained stubbornly wedded to the
Verona Declaration.. Although the Pretender finally issued a
proclamation on the eve of the elections promising clemency and
moderation, there was no backing down and no assurances for the
owners of *biens nationaux*. Some of his followers even hoped the
restored parlements would quash any amnesty and the vast settling
of accounts could begin. Undoubtedly because they were so
fundamentally at odds, the royalist campaign was vague and shrill:
peace at almost any price, promises of prosperity, denunciations of
anticlericalism, financial policy and of Jacobinism. The Directory
retaliated by publishing lurid details from the trials of the Agency
and of Babeuf but to little effect.

A negative strategy was good politics for the royalists since the
electorate continued to reject the men of the Convention as it had
in the Year IV. Of 216 *conventionnels* up for election in germinal
An V (March 1797), only 11 were returned and the proportion of
regicides in the new legislature dropped to less than one in five. Of
the 260 seats being contested, royalists of one sort or another won
180 bringing their total strength in the Five Hundred and the
Ancients to roughly 330, a sizeable enough group to swing a
wavering centre to their side on some issues. Wickham was
naturally exultant and credited d'André but it is doubtful whether
the royalists were correct in seeing a vast electoral wave rolling in
their direction. As usual, turnout was very low: 10.6 per cent in the
Meurthe, less than 10 per cent in the Eure-et-Loir, 22 per cent in
the Côtes-du-Nord, 25 per cent in the Côte-d'Or, 28 per cent in the
Sarthe, while Toulouse at 71 per cent appears to have been
genuinely exceptional. Furthermore, there was no correlation
between the reported existence of a Philanthropic Institute and

departmental election results. The results themselves were hardly a guide to national opinion. Rather, they showed an antipolitical attitude on the part of the rich secondary electors. Aside from the wholesale rejection of *conventionnels per se*, nearly half the deputies in the legislature of the Year V had never sat in a national legislature before and of the rightists, roughly two thirds were newcomers. Among these were General Willot who had protected the counterterrorist murder gangs in Marseille, Pichegru and Imbert-Colomès. It was a particular electorate that was profoundly alienated as well. The northern, wealthy, populous and urban departments returned the greatest proportion of royalists. These same regions also had been the most progressive in their *cahiers* of 1789. Thus the Directory had clearly lost the support of the wealthy landowners, rentiers and bourgeois. The regime floated in a social vacuum, hated by the elites whose favour it so desperately wanted, yet spurning any attempts to revive the politics of movement.

The Directory was not so weak that it could not fight back while the violence of the pures, worries about the Pretender's ultimate aims and differences over tactics exposed the falsity of the royalist coalition. They could agree on some issues. On 7 prairial (26 May), they elected Barthélemy, the ambassador to Switzerland, to replace Le Tourneur who drew the unlucky ballot, to the Directory. The new Director was a timid opportunist and an intriguer rather than a royalist but he could be influenced. Along with Carnot who was trying to reconcile the differences among the political elites of the nation and who believed the way to end constitutional deadlocks was to cede to the legislature, Barthélemy's election was a major step towards weakening the Republic. Barras's loyalty was vacillating. This left only the eternally squabbling Reubell and La Révellière to man the defences. If this was not hope enough, the royalists could reasonably count on having a majority in the legislature and the Directory in the Year VI. In the meantime they continued to flex their legislative muscle by admitting the deputies proscribed after the vendémiaire risings but invalidating the election of Barère, and by electing Pichegru to the presidency of the Five Hundred. In the name of the rule of law, the legislature repealed the law of 3 brumaire An IV on 21 prairial (9 June) thus removing the electoral penalties on the relatives of émigrés and much of the legislation on refractory priests. The Five Hundred also adopted a fundamentally unconstructive attitude on the agonizing question of finances, and refused to grant any new sources of revenue. This risked compromising the peace negotiations with Austria since the preliminaries had only been signed at Leoben on 27 April. Without the Italian treasuries Bonaparte was shipping home, the Directory faced bankruptcy. On 27 messidor (15 July), the Five Hundred voted to repeal all the laws on refractory priests and subject them to a weak oath of adhesion to the laws. On 6–7 thermidor (24–25 July) the legislature voted in effect to abolish all political clubs which led not only to the closure of the Jacobins' 'constitutional circle' but to that of the Clichy club as well.

If the royalists were willing to play fast and loose with electoral results and the already feeble guarantees on freedom of association, the Directory was equally prepared to violate the Constitution. In messidor (July), General Bernadotte captured Antraigues at Trieste and his superior, General Bonaparte, forwarded a mass of correspondence and interrogations to Paris, after carefully editing out all references to the royalists' attempts to recruit him. Mysteriously he then let Antraigues escape. After further investigations, the extent of Pichegru's treason and Wickham's involvement in internal subversion with the deputies was reasonably clear. It was enough to bring Barras on to the side of Reubell and La Révellière. The 'triumvirate' which was to dominate the national scene until the spring of the Year VII took an increasingly aggressive attitude towards the Councils. They ordered troops from Hoche's Army of Sambre-et-Meuse to Paris which were used as a demonstration of force while the government arranged a shuffle of ministers in a more 'republican' direction. This was a violation of the Constitution which forbade the presence of troops within the perimeter of Paris and a slap in the face to the moderate constitutionalists who were urging the appointment of ministers more to their liking. The royalist deputies were morose but in the end did nothing.

The episode revealed the inherent weaknesses of the royalist coalition. These had always been present. Legislative debates had shown an uncertainty of purpose. Many moderates, for example, deplored the mean speeches and vicious press attacks on Bonaparte's successes in Italy. These only resulted in lusty proclamations of loyalty to the Directory and the Republic from the officers and soldiers of the Armies of Italy and Sambre-et-Meuse. Creeping royalism at home convinced many in the military that the army was the last bastion of pure republicanism, and virtually invited them to intervene in politics. The menace to the royalists was thus obvious from midsummer onwards but differences of motive were also paralysing them. Some were convinced that removing the disabilities on refractory priests and émigrés was merely a return to legality and so were willing to work with the Directory in the short term. Others were convinced that these measures were part of the process of building the party which would topple the Republic altogether. Some therefore believed there was no threat, but d'André did, and began to try to build up the royalists' military forces. Significantly, a bill to arm the wealthy elite companies of the National Guard (a return to the tactics of 1790) was not promulgated but d'André claimed to have subverted part of the garrison of Paris. Dozens of chouan officers also began to move quietly into the capital. Another royalist rising was clearly being prepared but forceful measures only tended to alienate the constitutionalists.

The blow fell on the hopelessly divided *clichyens* on the morning of 18 fructidor (4 September) and continued to roll through the country for the next six months. With loyal troops under General Augereau whom Bonaparte had sent to Paris to support the government, the triumvirate purged Carnot and Barthélemy and ordered the deportation of fifty-three deputies. It annulled the elections in forty-nine departments, arrested thirty-two journalists and banned forty-two Parisian and provincial newspapers. The purge reached out into the provincial administrations as well. These had long tolerated all manner of questionable disturbances. During the summer as the legislature debated the anticlerical laws, the country people of the Midi who believed that full freedom of worship was imminent demonstrated massively in favour of the refractories and attacked buyers of *biens nationaux* and republicans generally. The brigand bands and murder gangs were extraordinarily active. It is no wonder that republicans felt that cries in the legislature for a return to legality were merely pretexts for violent counterrevolution. Local administrations which permitted these activities were purged far more systematically than in the Year II. In the Sarthe, 599 of 807 elected officials were replaced; in the Pas-de-Calais, 73 of 87 cantonal municipalities were purged; in the Haute-Loire, all six judges in the civil court, and 22 of 34 cantonal commissioners were dismissed and 29 of 34 municipalities purged. Of 509 municipalities in the fairly peaceful central and western regions of the country covering 10 departments, 241 were reorganized or purged. To judge from the rare studies on the new

terror of the Year VI, such a massive upheaval often brought local
Jacobins back to power, but if the Eure-et-Loir and Var were at all
typical, these men often had considerable administrative
experience dating back to the early Revolution as well. The 'Second
Directory', as it is called, was clearly trying to bureaucratize local
administration without being dependent on the clubs. The
Consulate merely consolidated the process.

The new terror tended to limit itself to the government machine
and to well-defined groups. The law of 19 fructidor An V (5
September 1797), wrested from a stupefied legislature, reinstated
the law of 3 brumaire An IV against émigrés and refractory priests.
It also imposed a new oath of *haine à la royauté* on the clergy and
officials. About 1800 French priests were ordered deported to
Guyana but since the British controlled the seas, most were held
in great hardship on the islands of Ré and Oléron. Acting on
Sieyès's suggestion, the deputy Boulay de la Meurthe also got the
legislature to deprive all ex-nobles of their citizenship. In legal
terms, the Third Estate became the nation and in combination with
the electoral law, the bourgeois revolution reached its apogee.
Never was the bourgeoisie less interested in playing the role the
politicians wanted to assign to it. The law was virtually ignored.

The number of executions following 18 fructidor numbered in the
hundreds rather than the thousands but a reinvigorated
administration was able to impose some peace on the country. The
brigand leaders, Dominique Allier and the Marquis de Surville,
were captured and executed at the end of the Year VI and protests
against the coup, like that of Saint-Christol in the Ardèche and
others in the Var, were lamentable failures. When brigandage
broke out again in the Year VII, administrators in the Ardèche,
Vaucluse, Lozère and Haute-Loire spoke wistfully of the previous
year as peaceful. The restoration of order was relative of course.
A band of around forty robbed the government's treasury wagon
near Lodève in the Hérault in frimaire An VI (November 1797) and
the brigand-priest Solier was extorting money from merchants on
their way to Beaucaire the following messidor (June). In the west,
the calm hardly meant acquiescence. Cadoudal, who had become
de facto commander of the chouan bands, was trying to put his men
on a war footing. He had even gone so far as to order the refractory
priests still in hiding not to marry young 'conscripts'.

Despite the obvious collapse of the Constitution of the Year III,
the Directory could govern without a hostile legislature. With a lull

in the fighting abroad and a semblance of peace at home, the Second Directory, quickly at its full complement with the addition of Merlin de Douai and François de Neufchâteau, was able to entrench itself considerably. The government's finances were consolidated by what amounted to a repudiation of two thirds of the national debt and the establishment of new indirect taxes. This probably did nothing for its popularity among the already stricken rentier bourgeoisie. The introduction of conscription could hardly have done it any good among the common people. In the military sphere, the Jourdan law of 19 fructidor An VI (5 September 1798) annually registered all the young men aged twenty, known as a class. They drew ballots to see who would actually depart, and, although Bonaparte later reintroduced the appalling practice of allowing the rich to buy exemption, replacement was not allowed. Yet the government would have been strong enough to weather the discontent if it did not also have to face the consequences of the coup at home and abroad. Since the Directory had a reasonably accurate picture of the extent of British involvement in the royalist conspiracy, its conditions for peace tightened and talks which had been going on for some months at Lille broke off one week after the coup. The war with Britain would thus continue and with it the slow process of building the Second Coalition. The Treaty of Campo Formio of 26 vendémiaire An VI (18 October) with Austria, which Bonaparte negotiated in defiance of the Directors who owed him too much, risked giving Britain continental allies again. It shamelessly handed over Venice to the Austrians and with it a base for the campaign of 1799, and achieved Austrian recognition for the annexation of Belgium and the left bank of the Rhine. Thus was created the temptation to adopt a forward policy in Germany and Switzerland and with it the risk of a new war. The problem was whether a government so alienated from the nation could call forth any new sacrifices. In the event, the regime could not and collapsed. The coup of the Year VI also ensured that it would receive little help from the politicians. The very success of the coup of fructidor thus created the conditions for the regime's downfall.

Chapter 9

Failed Consolidation

The price of the survival of the Republic was the subversion of the Constitution of the Year III. After fructidor, it was no longer a question of the survival of representative institutions or whether the will of the electorate would be respected. Since the voters had shown themselves sympathetic to counterrevolutionaries, so much the worse for them. The question for the future then was whether the Directory could solve the major problems confronting the nation in defiance of the electorate. As it turned out, it was largely successful. The purge of local administration, repression against priests and nobles and the restoration of peace on the continent permitted the government to impose a large degree of order at home. The financial reforms of the Year VI began the process of restoring state solvency. Yet the Second Directory was unable to stabilize itself or reach an accommodation with the nation. This was because the so-called coup of 22 floréal An VI (11 May 1798) alienated some politicians and convinced others the regime could not endure. The renewal of war in the spring and summer of 1799 required new sacrifices from the country which many were not willing to make. War revived internal subversion and since the regime had repressed, not won over, dissidence, this too contributed to instability. Finally, for all the relative success the Directory had in controlling its civilian administration, it failed to control the military. The attempt to do so alienated the constituency that had twice saved the thermidorean Convention and the Directory in fructidor. Thus the army allied itself with the disgruntled politicians to overthrow a regime which no longer had any strategically placed friends.

Saving the Republic . . . Again: the 22 Floréal Coup

The very scale of the fructidor coup created an enormous problem for the elections of the Year VI. Not only would the legislature have to be renewed by one third as the Constitution required, but the 198 deputies purged in the Year V would have to be replaced, bringing the total to be elected to 437. With nearly three fifths of the seats thus about to be contested, there was every danger that the royalists would repeat their successes of the previous two years and the Republic would face a crisis identical to the one it had just escaped. The solution to this problem was the passage of the law of 12 pluviôse An VI (31 January 1798) by which the outgoing legislature would pronounce on the validity of the elections of the incoming deputies. Although this had the effect of allowing a sizeable proportion of defeated deputies to validate the elections of their successful opponents, it served the practical purpose of avoiding the upheaval of fructidor while still eliminating enemies of the government.

Just as the law was passed, however, the spectre of a Jacobin victory began to overtake the fear of a royalist one. This probably had something to do with the accession of Merlin de Douai to the presidency of the Directory on 7 ventôse (25 February). From one of the movers of the Law of Suspects to one of the leading thermidoreans, Merlin became the national election manager in all but name. Although scarcely anyone knew it, he also had his own election agents. These were men who were ostensibly sent out to the provinces to investigate the implementation of the recently voted road tolls. They also received the mission to report on public opinion and to coordinate elections in the departments. Since government dispatches were always at the mercy of highway robbers, their reports are full of the vocabulary of road engineering applied to elections. But for all the complaints about appalling roads (unfavourable public opinion) or the difficulty of trying to find capable chief engineers (pliable candidates), it is doubtful whether the election agents did much good. There were only nine of them to cover ninety-eight departments and the five who submitted accounts spent only about 39,000 francs, mostly on campaign expenses or buying free meals for influential electors. Their real significance was that they inaugurated a century-long tradition of governments trying to influence the outcome of elections at public expense.

The Directory did not rely entirely on its own election agents, however. In dozens of manifestos, it warned the public against 'royalisme à cocarde blanche et royalisme à bonnet rouge'. Although royalists were certainly not beneath supporting their adversaries at the other extreme in order to undermine the moderates – Antraigues had advised just such a tactic as early as 1791 and Mallet du Pan renewed it after fructidor – the Directory only produced the flimsiest evidence that it did occur in the Year VI. In any case, the electorate does not appear to have been strongly influenced by such propaganda. Nor did the government limit itself to a campaign of shrill denunciation. It suppressed eleven Jacobin newspapers in Paris and the provinces, closed at least thirty-four clubs or 'constitutional circles' as they were called and declared a state of siege in Lyon (where the Jacobins were reported to have refashioned their old alliance with the 'workers and artisans'), Marseille, Saint-Etienne, and throughout the Belgian departments.

The scale and range of the repression suggests the Directory was genuinely apprehensive about the Jacobin revival but this was fairly limited all the same. Dozens of provincial clubs or constitutional circles were founded in the wake of fructidor and soon each of the twelve arrondissements of the capital had its own neighbourhood club. The constitutional circles were not much hampered by Article 362 of the Constitution which forbade affiliation partly because the new Minister of Police, Sotin, was sympathetic to them and partly because the press, particularly the much-persecuted *Journal des hommes libres*, kept the clubs in contact. But since there was no central club to coordinate their activities as there had been until the Year II, the Jacobins tended to reflect local concerns more than ever. In Paris, Jacobin writers advocated the democratization of the institutions of government, progressive taxation, rewards for army veterans financed from émigré property, the right of subsistence and the right to free education. While the provincial clubs generally supported these ideals, many of which had been proposed as early as 1790, they were often more immediately concerned with the problem of counterrevolution. In the Sarthe, for example, where the chouans dominated nearly half the department, the Le Mans constitutional circle sent out missionaries to the countryside to preach against 'superstition' and to establish new circles in each of the cantons. In the Haute-Loire, devastated by the rural White Terror, efforts focused on the appointment of democrats in the place of purged moderates, hunting out refractory priests, circulating anticlerical propaganda, mainly through the rural teachers, and a severe repression of those who hosted clandestine Masses. In the royalist Ardèche where the purge took on similar contours, the little circle of Montpézat demanded the expulsion 'from your midst of the returned émigrés, the refractory priests and the despots. . . . They are ferocious animals who wish to devour the Republic and annihilate its faithful supporters.'

Repression of the 'ferocious animals' took as prominent a place among the Jacobins' schemes for republican defence as it did for the Second Directory. They differed, however, on a number of fundamental issues. Jacobin apologists considered the Year II an era of popular government and so deplored 9 thermidor. They sympathized with Babeuf and his friends even if they thought his schemes chimerical. They insisted that authority should be accountable to the people on a more or less permanent basis. They denounced the regime's oligarchic tendencies and its allegiance to profiteers and war contractors and would have corrected these evils by a healthy dose of democracy. The ultimate danger was, therefore, that the Jacobins would bring the working people of the towns back into the political process with the attendant risk of terrorism and attacks on property. This was no mere figment. The constitutional circles with their professional and artisan membership recalled the earlier Jacobin clubs and fraternal societies. The *Réunion politique du Faubourg Antoine* in Paris, for example, was composed almost entirely of small manufacturers, shopkeepers and skilled and semiskilled craftsmen including the *sans-culotte* 'scourge' of the Vendée, Rossignol. Sizeable contingents were former members of the civil and revolutionary committees of the Year II, veterans of the revolutionary army, insurgents in germinal and prairial or even veterans of the Champ de Mars and 10 August, like Fournier l'Américain. It was ominous for such men to demand 'inflexible justice' for counter-revolutionaries and to denounce 'uncivic' employers, even if they thought of themselves as seconding the government.

In the event, the election results could not have satisfied anyone completely. The turnout was abysmally low in the primary assemblies, despite the Directory's exhortations to vote. About the same as the Year V in the Côtes-du-Nord, Meurthe and Colmar, it fell by 16 per cent in the Sarthe and by nearly half in Toulouse. Whatever the reason – priests encouraging people to vote in the Côtes-du-Nord, royalist abstentions in the Sarthe and Toulouse, Jacobin intimidation in the Côte-d'Or – one major element of the constitutional process continued to crumble from below. The electoral process was similarly undermined both in the primary and departmental assemblies. As usual, these were turbulent affairs ranging from pedantic challenges to procedure when one faction disliked a result, to occasionally calling in troops to restore order when too much furniture was destroyed over opponents' heads. What was new in the elections of the Year VI was the phenomenon of secessions when one faction split off and announced itself as the true assembly. Very rare in previous elections, they were originally promoted by Merlin as an electoral device but soon every faction saw its advantages. In the end, about one in six of the primary assemblies outside the Seine and twenty-seven of ninety-eight departmental assemblies were affected by secessions. With innumerable procedural appeals in assemblies that did not split, the legislature was faced with a colossal mess which was still being sorted out when the regime fell eighteen months later.

Nor could the results be considered entirely satisfactory from the Directory's point of view. If its commissioner in the Côte-d'Or managed to circulate an impressive pro-government packet of propaganda to the electors on the eve of their assembly which resulted in a compliant set of deputies, the central administration of the Sarthe would have no truck with royalists and encouraged the list of the constitutional circles which was entirely successful. The attempt to use the administration to return a pro-government majority, therefore, had mixed results. The elections were still favourable, however. Although the Jacobins registered the greatest gains, they still comprised less than one third of the deputies in both houses, so that the government could be as confident of having a majority as it was possible to be in a political system without organized parties. This still left the problem of what to do with the 178 deputies elected by the secessionist electoral assemblies. This was accomplished by simply excluding candidates who were perceived as the Directory's enemies. The pro-government press and its friends in the legislature began a campaign proclaiming the results 'execrable'. This was a gross exaggeration but it was enough to cite the names of some of the Paris electors – Santerre, Prieur de la Marne, Brutus Magnier who had been president of the military commission of Rennes in the Year II – or some of the names of the elected deputies – Lequinio, representative on mission who had threatened to shoot Vendean prisoners without trial, Bazon, president of Javogues's revolutionary tribunal at Mâcon, Robert Lindet of the Committee of Public Safety – to create the impression of a terrorist landslide. The result was the law of 22

floréal An VI (11 May 1798) which deprived 127 newly elected
deputies of their seats, 83 of whom are thought to have been
Jacobins. As Ballieul, the deputy of the legislative commission
applying the law of 12 pluviôse, reported, the elections which
produced a 'bad result' would be annulled and secessions which
'were only the product of caprice and cabal' would be rejected.
Hardy, one of the more unrestrained anti-Montagnards of 1793, put
it even more baldly: 'If a scoundrel presents himself here as a
deputy, you have the right to repel him; for it is a question not only
of the electoral mechanism but of its results.'

Deplorable as the so-called 'coup' of 22 floréal was from the point
of view of parliamentary government, it could be justified as a
device to fend off any challenges to the existing ruling group while
the process of governmental consolidation continued. As such, the
election by the post-fructidor legislature of Treilhard, a
distinguished if lacklustre jurist, for François de Neufchâteau who
drew the unlucky ball, was a natural complement to the law of 22
floréal. The Directors were thus the main beneficiaries of the
operation even if their role had been limited this time to private
conversations with their minions in the legislature and to supplying
the deputies with information from the ministries. Significantly, La
Révellière, the leading apologist, saw it as something far more than
excluding political opponents. According to him, 'The legislature
is only a constituted authority like the others', sharing only a part
of the sovereignty delegated to it by the nation, while the
government was better placed 'to protect the public welfare'
because it was better informed. Even the defenders of the
Constitution had to admit that government was impossible without
a stronger executive.

If floréal represented the rejection of a politics of movement and
a narrow defence of property to men in Paris, it represented
something quite different in the provinces. As usual, anti-
Jacobinism in the capital was interpreted as a relaxation of the
anticlerical legislation in the provinces. In the mountains of the
Ardèche, the refractories 'celebrated religious offices with as much
solemnity as before 18 fructidor. The processions of Ascension and
Fête-Dieu have attracted an extraordinary following . . .' At Is-sur-
Tille in the Côte-d'Or, the inhabitants broke the windows of the
former presbytery and ripped up the trees in the garden because,
they said, the new owner was responsible for a thunderstorm which
had harmed the crops. When soldiers tried to disperse Sunday

worshippers at Ecommoy in the Sarthe, they provoked a riot which quickly swelled to eight hundred people. Elsewhere, there was a wave of attacks on liberty trees and harassment of officials. Even in Paris, several churches were reported to be overflowing, mainly with women, and priests were appearing in public in clerical dress.

The Directory showed, however, that it was no more willing to encourage the clergy and its followers than it was the Jacobins. Unlike every other convulsion of the period, the aftermath of floréal inaugurated a policy of eliminating all opposition. The press law of 19 fructidor was renewed and shortly afterwards twelve conservative newspapers were suppressed while the *Journal des hommes libres* underwent half a dozen bans and name-changes by the end of the year. The constitutional circles withered away when they were not closed, too dispirited to offer any more than perfunctory protests. The Directory also promised rewards for those who denounced returned émigrés and it organized domiciliary visits in Paris. As an antidote to Catholicism, it also tightened the laws on the use of the revolutionary calendar and observance of the *décadi*. François de Neufchâteau, now returned to the Interior, prescribed the ceremonies of the *culte décadaire* in a famous circular whereby local officials read new laws to the assembled citizens, recounted military successes and celebrated civil marriages while everyone listened to patriotic hymns sung by school children. As with everything the Directory did, such official dechristianization had a limited success. The tedium of such ceremonies apart, its own officials sometimes even incited defiance. In the Nord where it was commonplace in the countryside, the justice of the peace of Quesnoy-sur-Deule told his fellow citizens, 'Amuse yourself on Sundays, no law prevents you. . . . Besides, what will happen to you if you're taken before the JP? I'll be there.' Elsewhere, there was greater success. After the arrest of some of the leading Jacobins of Dijon and a new round of searches for the hiding places of refractory priests, the commissioner of the Côte-d'Or reported, 'All the parties seem to be crushed from now on; there is only one remaining in this department, that of the law, that of the government.' But the social basis of the government's 'party' was extremely fragile. In the adjacent Saône-et-Loire, 'The urban proprietors whose wealth, leisure and education draw them to politics . . . desire peace . . . are tired of seeing authority in the hands of partisans of the Revolution . . . [but] they support the Republic as an inevitable evil.'

Expansion: Switzerland, Italy, Egypt

The Directory could thus draw on begrudging support so long as it could hold out the prospect of peace. It failed to do so because of its inability to finance itself from a ruined domestic economy, the temptations of an imperialist exploitation of the new conquests and the great influence of traders, financiers and war contractors in government circles. The result was the renewal of war, the disastrous expedition to Egypt, the formation of the Second Coalition and finally the renewal of domestic instability which led to the collapse of the Constitution itself.

For a war that began so frivolously in 1792, it proved stubbornly difficult to end. After Campo Formio, it should have been possible to end it but there were several reasons why it proved impossible. Like all the governments which preceded it, the Directory believed that France alone should not bear the costs of the implementation of the 'fraternité et secours' decree of 1792. Thus it appeared to be entirely reasonable to demand reparations, war contributions and local requisitions for the occupying armies from the newly liberated peoples. Besides, the penury of all French governments and the high costs of transport probably made such a policy inevitable. Every government from 1792 onwards also shared the far less defensible policy of profiting from the war to establish French economic hegemony. Although often justified as necessary to combat English economic supremacy, such policies as maintaining the assignat at artificially high levels in Belgium in 1792 or the Montagnard Convention's decision to strip the Rhineland of its advanced machinery, certainly crossed the line into naked exploitation. Such practices continued after thermidor and with military victory and territorial expansion, the Directory set about subjecting the economies of allied countries to the French. The law of 10 brumaire An V (31 October 1796) forbade the import of all products 'reputed to be of English origin'. Coupled with the refusal of a commercial treaty with the Batavian Republic whose merchants were natural competitors, this almost ruined the Dutch. The commercial treaty with the Cisalpine Republic, however, forbade English manufactures, provided a market for French and gave French ships exclusive carrying rights for the Cisalpine's mainly agricultural products.

Implementation of such policies proved to be a great deal more difficult because, as in everything else, there were several decision-making points and influential lobby groups within the apparatus of government. There was a running debate between Merlin and La Révellière on the one side and Reubell on the other over support for the 'sister republics' or the 'natural frontiers', a debate which turned out to be one of emphasis rather than principle. More serious was corruption in government. Barras had agents siphoning money and bribes into the master's pockets while Talleyrand was so blatant at soliciting bribes and consequently so unreliable that he was kept from the foreign policy meetings of the Directory. Both heaped up immense fortunes. The government's inability to pay these private entrepreneurs throughout the period produced innumerable abuses. It had already resulted in the scandal of the abbé d'Espagnac trying to buy influence in the Convention. Payment to his successors in devalued currency or in *biens nationaux* in the occupied territories which were difficult to sell was supplemented with authorization to take payment from captured foreign treasuries or from requisitions levied with military support. Generals often received their cut when padding their expenses was insufficient. For such men liberation of oppressed peoples was synonymous with swollen profits or massive wealth, and their activities, as well as the religious policy, more than offset the advantages the French brought with them of a cheap and rational administration. There was scarcely an occupied territory or sister republic which did not witness an anti-French rebellion due in part to the liberators' rapaciousness. Significantly, not one financier was ever convicted of malversation. A grand design of economic hegemony thus degenerated into another of semilegal pillage and most unfraternal resentment because the Directory was unable to control its own personnel.

Although the details of the story differ, the occupations of Switzerland and Rome in the winter–spring of the Year VI both illustrate the colliding *mélange* of government strategy, financial need, personal diplomacy and private greed which made up the Directory's foreign policy. Occupation of Switzerland and a forward policy in Italy would put pressure on the Austrians to settle at Rastadt, a satellite in Switzerland would link the Rhineland with northern Italy and Bonaparte recommended the seizure of the Swiss Alpine passes to secure the Paris–Milan route. There was also the reputedly fabulous treasury of the city of Berne, Swiss 'patriots' like Laharpe and Ochs demanding intervention against the patricians, the fact that numerous émigrés were there, Wickham's use of it as a base, and the advanced industries in Geneva. With so many temptations, it was only a matter of coordinating a series of apparently spontaneous insurrections and sending in troops to support the 'patriotic' side. Although Geneva was annexed (as was Mulhouse for good measure), the 'République helvétique', whose new constitution was vetted by Reubell, was treated better than the Batavian or Cisalpine in that the French civil commissioner, unfortunately named Rapinat, tried to forbid military requisitioning. This did not prevent a peasant rising in the Catholic cantons, the levying of 'war contributions' on the religious orders and the 'oligarchs' nor the officially sponsored looting of the city treasuries of Berne, Zurich and Bâle, among others. In any case a system of military requisitions was in place within the year because Paris could not supply its occupying troops and the yield from the treasuries was disappointingly meagre.

The result was much worse at Rome. Although the Directory had no wish to invade the papal states and its ambassador, Joseph Bonaparte, consistently advised the local 'patriots' against it, an antipapal insurrection broke out on 27 December 1797 in which General Duphot was killed. The Directory acted promptly. The Pope's apologies were refused. General Berthier, commander of the Army of Italy, was ordered to march on Rome, and to organize a republic while making it look as if this was the spontaneous demand of the people. The city capitulated on 10 February at the price of the usual exactions but Berthier, conforming to government instructions, kept the Roman Jacobins at arm's length. Subordinate French agents stirred them up, however, and they proclaimed the Republic. The Pope fled to Siena. The Directory sent in a civil commission which, once it had brought the soldiers' pillaging under control, imposed a constitution in which all positions, including the legislators, were nominated by the French government. Before the French had even established themselves, risings in both the city and the countryside had to be put down. The new republic was turned over to willing puppets. One dishonest company of war contractors succeeded another and the Directory itself had 640 cartons of paintings, books, manuscripts and jewellery looted from the Vatican shipped to Paris.

If the occupation of Rome was unplanned but lucrative, that of Switzerland was intended in part to provide money for the continuation of the war against the British. In the circumstances, a direct fight was not possible. With the destruction of much of the Dutch fleet at Camperdown (11 October 1797), with the fleet bottled up in Brest, Lorient and Toulon and with Spain an unwilling ally whose fleet was blockaded, it was impossible to mount an invasion of England, just as it was impossible for the British to attack France without a continental ally. After a tour of the Channel coast Bonaparte concluded that an invasion would have to be postponed and instead proposed an attack on Egypt. This would assure France of her share of the expected break-up of the Turkish Empire, restore commercial domination of the eastern Mediterranean, above all threaten some British trade routes to India, inspire the restive Indian princes to revolt and provide a base for an expedition to India through the Red Sea. A successful blow against the British would also restrain Austria and Russia both of whom were alarmed at the continued French expansion after Campo Formio.

The Egyptian expedition was a disappointment which was nearly a disaster. Bad luck and bad weather prevented Nelson from sighting the French transports at sea and thus from capturing a prize of incalculable value. Consequently Bonaparte easily captured Malta and landed peacefully near Alexandria on 1 July. Three weeks later, he crushed the Mamelukes at the Battle of the Pyramids and the French occupied Cairo the next day. On 1 August, however, Nelson finally found the French fleet at anchor at Aboukir Bay and, raking it with a devastating crossfire, destroyed or captured eleven of the thirteen ships of the line. However much Bonaparte tried to evade the blame for not ordering the fleet out of Egyptian waters, and however much his strange apings of Moslem customs have distracted subsequent biographers, the fact was that an army of 30,000 men, many of them veterans of the Army of Italy, were now totally isolated, without hope of relief or rescue.

War and the New Fiefdoms

The Egyptian expedition achieved none of its objects and the Battle of Aboukir Bay began the process of the formation of the Second Coalition which in turn led to the collapse of the Directory itself. Turkey declared war on France on 9 September. The Kingdom of

Naples, egged on by the Austrians and British and believing the sister republics vulnerable, occupied Rome on 27 November. The half-mad Tsar Paul, self-styled protector of the Knights of Malta, and intolerably vexed by the reception given to Polish 'patriots' in Paris, declared war on 23 December. For allowing Russian troops transit rights on its territory, France declared war on Austria the following March.

The immediate consequence of the renewal of war was the occupation of most of the rest of Italy. Troops under General Championnet reoccupied Rome on 13 December and moved on to Naples. He ignored the armistice with the Neapolitan government and, responding to the appeal of the local Jacobins, established another republic, the Parthenopean. While Championnet consolidated his fief and the soldiers helped themselves, Joubert, commander of the troops in the Cisalpine, and Eyman, ambassador to the court of Turin, organized the occupation of Piedmont on 5–6 December. Although the Directory was as worried as its officials on the spot that the king was intriguing with the Austrians, it never anticipated their solution of an occupation. Faced with a *fait accompli*, it gave the Piedmontese the choice of independence or annexation. Hoping that it would minimize the usual exploitation, and encouraged by the disappointed Jacobins, the population voted massively in favour of annexation in a rigged plebiscite. Finally, Tuscany was occupied in March 1799, the Pope captured and shipped off to Valence where he died in August.

Generals with their own foreign policy and greedy financiers and contractors clearly made the war more difficult to fight and finance. Such men had to be brought under control but the attempt to erode their satrapies reinforced the generals' long-held contempt for civilian government. The most blatant conflict of this sort erupted between Championnet and the civil commissioner, Failpoult. As a faithful servant of the Directory, Failpoult tried to halt military requisitions and pillaging in Naples and was as astonished as the Directory when Championnet proclaimed the Parthenopean Republic which effectively prevented the seizure of the Neapolitan treasury. With the precedent of Bonaparte creating a republic free of civilian control, Championnet expelled the civil commissioners and made himself the hero of the local Jacobins. The Directory replaced Failpoult and Championnet with General Macdonald who established some order and arrested some parasitic contractors. At bottom, the struggle between Failpoult and Championnet was a struggle over whether the government or the army could profit most from the war. Such struggles could take other dimensions as well. General Brune, a crony of Danton's in the Cordeliers days, operated a pro-Jacobin coup in the Cisalpine Republic on 19 October 1978 and had it ratified by hastily convoked primary assemblies in which even women and children were allowed to vote. The French commissioners protested, secured Brune's transfer to Holland and reversed the coup, much to the annoyance of Joubert, the new military commander. Joubert himself had been at loggerheads with the French minister to the Batavian Republic, Delacroix, while Masséna was accused of lining his pockets in Switzerland just as Macdonald was caught trying to start a personal art collection at Naples.

Revenge for Fructidor. The Countercoup of 30 Prairial

On the whole, the Directory failed to bring its agents abroad to heel but the attempt to do so meant that no generals could be found to support the triumvirate in the crisis of the Year VII. Relations with the politicians both in and outside the legislature were even more complex and this time led to subversion. Simply because 22 floréal had a fig leaf of legality, it was impossible to exclude every Jacobin or every critic of the Directory. The new deputy, Lucien Bonaparte, for example, quickly assumed the Jacobin line on the feeble state of government finances and the shady deals with the contractors. There were also about a hundred or so Jacobins remaining from the elections of the Years IV and V. Coupled with the reactionaries who had quietly camouflaged themselves among the government majority since fructidor, the opposition to the government was potentially impressive. Confounded with these groups were about two hundred newly elected commissioners, departmental and municipal administrators and judicial officials. These are usually thought to have been government toadies but until the parliamentary history of the regime is better known, such blanket condemnations are premature. After all, many of them were private citizens who aided the government, who could hardly live from stipends which were invariably in arrears and who passed muster after fructidor because they were antiroyalists and anticlericals; in other words because in the context of local politics they were Jacobins. Legislative support for the Directory was not necessarily automatic.

From time to time, the deputies showed their independence. There were complaints, for example, sometimes from former departmental commissioners, that the Directors had not followed their advice on new appointments in the inevitable local purges following floréal. Throughout the summer the deputies debated the issue of corruption in the ministries and the pay-offs made by war contractors. Although the indignation over these scandals continued to grow and so the frustration with a government apparently powerless to stop them, little was done for the moment. Finance could also be a source of tension. The rejection of a proposed salt tax in pluviôse–germinal An VII (February–March 1799) by the Elders after its passage by a narrow majority in the Five Hundred and the passage of taxes on doors and windows showed a curiously 'Jacobin' hostility to regressive taxes on the poor and a predisposition for others on exterior signs of wealth.

None of this suggested an imminent rebellion on the part of the legislature and might explain why the government did not feel it necessary to intervene as forcefully in the elections in germinal. Special agents were sent to only twenty departments and money to only half. Instead, the government relied on its local commissioners who, in the end, were ineffective. Almost everywhere, turnout in the primary assemblies reached record lows. After all, if the government was going to alter the results, there was no point in voting. Even so, the electors continued their policy of rejecting experienced politicians and the Directory's candidates. Less than one fifth of the legislators of the Year VII had sat in a national assembly before the Year IV, and of the 187 recommended candidates only a little over one third were elected. Contemporaries interpreted the results as a Jacobin victory. There is some truth in this even though only 21 Jacobins 'floréalized' the year before were reelected. But the elections are better conceived as a rejection of the existing ruling group and of the triumvirate in particular.

It is possible that the election results encouraged the old legislature to defy the Directory, a defiance that gathered force once the new deputies were in place. When Reubell drew the unlucky ball and resigned, the legislature chose Sieyès as his replacement on 27 floréal (16 May). Reubell's departure may have been prearranged to appease the regime's critics but if it was, it backfired. A few days later, there was a stormy debate on the financial question in which there were demands for an investigation of the Directors' sources of income. Furthermore, Sieyès had no intention of being tamed by office. As a well-known critic of the Constitution, he was seen by both Jacobins and moderates as a man of integrity and he had influential acquaintances including Bonaparte, Talleyrand, the journalist Roederer and the deputy Boulay de la Meurthe who agreed with him that the Constitution had to be revised to strengthen the executive. In the event, most of these men had few concrete ideas beyond cries for order, restoring finances and ending the war. Sieyès himself never developed much beyond the fierce hatred of nobles, priests and the populace which had made his reputation a decade earlier, and his criticism of the Treaty of Campo Formio for not expelling the Austrians from Italy completely was hardly a formula for an early peace. It is a reflection of how deep the alienation from the Directory was that these disillusioned thermidoreans and fructidoreans were able to acquire the influence they did.

The remaining Directors realized the threat and resolved not to cooperate with Sieyès and to whistle past the graveyard of a hostile legislature. Military reverses made this impossible. After the initial successes against Rome and Naples in December–January, Jourdan's thrust into the Danube plain was halted by the Austrians under the Archduke Charles at Stockbach near Lake Constance on 25 March. A typically undersupplied and demoralized French army had to retreat to the Rhine with two of its commanders under arrest for misconduct and two others – the future marshals Saint-Cyr and Bernadotte – alleging illness. The Archduke then struck through Switzerland. Masséna fought off a pincer attack at Zurich on 16 prairial (4 June). This prevented an invasion through Franche-Comté but French power collapsed ignominiously in Italy. Schérer's incompetence near Verona forced the Directory to order the evacuation of Naples and Rome but Macdonald's casual retreat north and then his personal decision to attack the Austro-Russian lines of communication on the Po split the French forces. Consequently, Moreau, Schérer's replacement, had to abandon first Milan and then Turin to the allied commander Suvarov who subsequently mauled Macdonald at Trebbia on 29 prairial–1 messidor (17–19 June). As they withdrew, a popular anti-French rebellion broke out in Piedmont and Lombardy. Except for a small enclave around Genoa, Italy was lost and Dauphiné and Provence were threatened. The spring campaign of the Year VII could not have illustrated better the folly of choosing military objectives with inadequate means and the danger of permitting generals to go their own way.

These difficulties were not generally perceived in Paris. In fact, the Republic was probably saved by the quarrelling which had broken out among the allies particularly over Suvarov's intended restoration of Piedmont to the House of Savoy, Austrian ambitions in Alsace and Lorraine and the inability of the British to launch a diversionary expedition in time. While the allies transferred troops and commanders among the various fronts, the factions in Paris jockeyed for position. No more than in the spring of 1793 did defeat abroad lead to unity at home. Instead, Jourdan blamed the Directory for his defeat. The defeats reinforced the conviction among the newly elected deputies and the Jacobin journalists and pamphleteers that the basic problem was corruption in government. The notion that foreign reverses were caused by an internal enemy was thus revived even if this time it was enlarged to include war contractors, financiers and corrupt politicians. The Jacobin offensive began with a legislative address warning the country of its perils and promising severe measures on 17 prairial (5 June). The first concrete step was the abrogation of the press law of 19 fructidor which was followed by a shower of denunciations from the newly liberated journalists. The second was the purge of the Directory. Although the differences between them were fundamental, Sieyès, his neo-moderates and the Jacobins all agreed that the 'radical' or 'corrupt' Directors had to go. In order to save himself, Barras stood aside and sacrificed his colleagues. Seizing on the pretext that his election was unconstitutional, the Councils removed Treilhard from the Directory on 29 prairial (16 June). La Révellière and Merlin tried to persuade him to resist and even spoke of appealing to the military, even though after two years of harassment there was no general to defend them. Treilhard had no heart for it anyway, and as soon as he heard of the decree, picked up his umbrella and strode out of the Luxembourg into the morning sun. La Révellière and Merlin were then subjected to an unbearable campaign demanding their resignation. Amidst a background of violent denunciations in the legislature, delegations from the moderates under Boulay de la Meurthe and from the Jacobins visited the besieged Directors, alternately threatening criminal proceedings if they did not resign, or promising immunity if they did. There were undignified shouting matches with Sieyès while Barras stomped about waving a sword. The final blow was the threat of military intervention. Joubert above all wanted the shabby honour of chasing out the lawyers, although Bernadotte was not far behind. Thus Italian politics and the failure of the spring campaign in Germany had direct repercussions at home. In the end, there was no need to appeal to a man on horseback since La Révellière and Merlin resigned on 30 prairial (18 June).

The Failure of the Jacobin Offensive

Thus the Constitution of the Year III entered its twilight phase, a victim, not of the royalists as it nearly was in fructidor, but of disillusioned and opportunist revolutionaries, passionate Jacobins and some vengeful generals. In fact, prairial was as close as the army ever got to exercising political power in the entire period, Bonaparte's coup a few months later notwithstanding. General Moulin, known only for an uninspired campaign against the chouans, became a Director, Bernadotte soon became Minister of War and Sieyès began grooming Joubert for great things. Sieyès got little beyond the appointment of the undistinguished Roger Ducos as Director. In fact, the 30 prairial appeared to be a Jacobin victory. Most of the new appointments were in the broad Jacobin mould including those of Gohier, the third Director and of Robert Lindet from the Great Committee of Public Safety as Minister of Finance. The three new Directors had been 'floréalized' the year before and four of the five were regicides. The ministries soon began to fill up with former terrorists as well, particularly War, Interior and Police.

The Jacobins pressed home their advantage in the country and the legislature as well. Although their provincial press never quite revived, the Jacobin press and pamphleteers in the capital did, along with their extensive royalist counterparts, so that readers were treated to a robust journalism they had not seen since 1792. Clubs in over two dozen provincial towns sprang to life. In Paris, the 'Society of the Friends of Liberty and Equality' was founded in direct descent from the Jacobin club of old. From the beginning, the cavernous hall of the former riding school where it met resounded with the strident and defiant speeches which were the Jacobins' hallmark. The club soon claimed 250 deputies and 3000 ordinary members which showed that fine oratory still had a great appeal in the capital. But the Jacobins offered more than rhetoric in that ominous summer of the Year VII for the atmosphere of renewal following 30 prairial quickly translated itself into legislative action. On 9 messidor (27 June) Jourdan persuaded the Five Hundred to call up simultaneously the five classes of conscripts specified in his earlier law. On 24 messidor (12 July) the legislature passed a new measure of internal proscription, the infamous 'Law of Hostages'. In some respects, this was a greater violation of civil rights than the Law of Suspects of 1793 since it recognized that the hostages would suffer even though they were personally innocent of the crimes committed by others. The law required authorities in any department declared to be in a state of disturbance or where troubles were imminent to seize hostages from among the relatives of émigrés, from former nobles and from the chouan bands. For every murder or kidnapping of an official, owner of *biens nationaux* or the parents, wife or children of a soldier, four hostages were to be deported. The hostages would also be held financially responsible for the pillages of the chouan or brigand bands. Finally, on 9 messidor (27 June), the legislature passed a forced loan, to help finance Jourdan's conscripts. In reality, this was a progressive income tax, exempting those with an annual income of less than 300 *livres*, rapidly doubling the incidence on incomes between 300 and 4000 *livres*, taking as much as three quarters of the annual revenue of the very wealthy and authorizing the total confiscation of purely 'speculative' fortunes. The 'forced loan' also had a political objective in that ex-nobles could be arbitrarily classed in a category above what their actual fortune justified, and the special tax juries which the law established could assess speculators and contractors on the basis of the moral certainty of their wealth, irrespective of the amount listed on the tax rolls.

Although these measures undoubtedly gave great satisfaction that the government was at last striking hard at its enemies in the nation's moment of peril, they were attenuated considerably by the Directory's shaky bureaucracy. In theory, conscription ought to have produced 402,000 young men but in fact only 248,000, or about 60 per cent, ever joined the colours. In some departments, draft-dodging reached breathtaking proportions. In the Ariège, for example, only 11 of 1319 young men joined their regiments, the rest never appearing at all or else stealing away at night from the columns marching to the rallying centres. Nor was the Ariège unique. Along the northern frontier extending into Normandy, in Gascony to the Spanish frontier, throughout the Massif Central and

finally along a band stretching through Lyon from the Alps to the
Hérault, there was considerable resistance. As in 1793 and the Year
III, many of the young men took to the forests and mountains
joining the brigand bands or the chouan die-hards. They were
encouraged too by counterrevolutionaries and refractory priests so
that the reappearance of the royalist bands in the interior was
certainly linked to the application of conscription. Aside from
simple resistance in a country not yet habituated to conscription,
the reason the government could do so little to combat 'the spirit
of subordination nourished by fanaticism' as one official put it, lay
with the elected municipalities. Fathers and employers had little
advantage in seeing the young men depart and they were as dilatory
at drawing up the lists of eligible conscripts as they were apathetic
about searching out draft-evaders. The post-fructidor departments
which were a good deal more zealous could do little with an
inadequate gendarmerie and no funds to equip conscripts.

The forced loan and the Law of Hostages failed in similar ways
for similar reasons. The press claimed the rich bribed the tax juries
who were in any case amateurs too poor to be subject to the tax.
Evasion and arbitrariness were evidently rife and there were
innumerable stories of workshops closing because of the tax. In
fact, the increasing unemployment probably had more to do with
the mild depression brought on by the overly rapid monetary
deflation of the previous year, but blaming the forced loan for it
hardly enhanced the government's popularity. By the time of the
brumaire coup, only about 10 million of the estimated 100 million
livres had been gathered. Overall taxes in the last three months of
the Year VII were down by one third over the corresponding period
of the previous year because of the lack of business confidence and
the depression.

The Law of Hostages ended by alienating large sectors of
opinion. Sieyès's Directory was slow to list which departments were
considered to be in a 'state of trouble' and there was considerable
infighting among the ministries over the law's application until
Fouché, in a new metamorphosis, became Police Minister on 29
July and the law was quietly forgotten.

Meanwhile, implementation was far from easy. Some
commissioners were hostile to it but even where they were not, they
had to rely on the inept and often hostile municipalities to suggest
names. In the Sarthe, there were only twenty-two 'hostages' most

of them women or ageing ex-nobles. Experience in the Vendée, Morbihan and Ille-et-Vilaine was almost identical. But where these measures were accompanied by a new round of harassment of priests, preventive arrests, police spying and fines of communes under the law of 10 vendémiaire An IV, hostility in the countryside grew. The chouan leaders who had never surrendered began to find recruits once again and to organize them into tighter units. As in 1791–3, measures of rigour against perceived internal enemies provoked a bloody response.

Meanwhile, the Jacobin offensive in Paris began to falter. The former terrorists were weeded out of the ministries before they even had time to get settled. The club itself was tossed out of the riding school on 8 thermidor (26 July) and finally closed three weeks later, a warning to the Jacobins not to pursue their campaign for the indictment of the deposed Directors and possibly a move to reassure the financiers with whom the government concluded a loan on the same day the club was closed. Five days later and after a vigorous anti-Jacobin speech by Sieyès, the Five Hundred rejected the indictment of the Directors by a narrow majority of three. The Jacobin press replied by accusing Barras and Sieyès of royalism and treason to the foreign enemy and there were certainly many clubbists in the provinces and local officials who believed the central government to be hopelessly corrupt.

Royalist Defeat

Although checked, the Jacobin offensive was thus far from over and the renewal of domestic counterrevolution and the allied offensive promised to win them more converts still. Royalist strategy in the Year VII revolved around the familiar combination of internal insurrection and foreign invasion. Although fructidor was a serious setback in the sense that many royalist sympathizers were purged from government, the Philanthropic Institutes were far from dead. In the course of the Year VI, they were reorganized with a central headquarters at Lyon which divided the Midi into four 'arrondissements'. Yet it is doubtful whether the Philanthropic Institutes were at all capable of carrying out a massacre of all the patriots on the same day, as some of the more alarmist government reports suggested. In the first place, various police and military agencies had discovered the general contours of the Institutes by the summer and there were a number of unsettling raids on arms caches, as well as some arrests, particularly at Bordeaux, Pau and in the Gers. In the second, the vast movement of royalist opinion throughout the Midi and the southwest was practically uncontrollable. Some bands, like that led by the Chevalier de Thermes which had terrorized the border between the Gers and the Haute-Garonne for years, were part of the coming insurrection but most others went their own way. This was especially true of the dozens of bands of leaderless draft-dodgers which sprang up as the Jourdan law of conscription was applied. These bands harassed municipal officers, pillaged buyers of *biens nationaux* and robbed merchants. The royalist leaders too had problems. Smuggling in arms from Spain was difficult, communications with Lyon and the princes were sporadic and there was no effective coordination with the chouans in the *Vendée militaire* and north of the Loire. Worse still, the leadership fell out, those of Bordeaux claiming to reorganize the Institute in Toulouse in accordance with new instructions from Lyon while those in Toulouse under Pourquery du Bourg, a former royal bodyguard and veteran of the *camp de Jalès* and Saillons conspiracies, insisted on giving orders to Bordeaux. Each could claim authorization from the princes. Whatever their differences, neither committee wanted the insurrection to start when it did. Royalists afterwards claimed that the premature rising was provoked by a counterfeit order from Louis XVIII written by a police spy but this is improbable since Toulouse was so badly defended. There were only 30 line troops in the entire Haute-Garonne and a mere 539 National Guards in the Ariège. More likely, the inappropriate timing can be attributed to a combination of the misplaced zeal of Rougé, former republican general turned royalist, and the pressure of his men, many of whom were conscripts due to leave shortly for the frontiers. Whatever the reason, Rougé's troops came pouring out of the hills of the Ariège on 19 thermidor (6 August), ten days ahead of schedule, shouting 'We're going to kill all the Huguenots' children, then their mothers, then their fathers, to be rid of them at last!' Many insurgents heard Mass before going into battle. The news of Rougé's rising set off major insurrections in the Gers and Ariège and minor ones in the Hérault, Lot-et-Garonne, Basses-Pyrénées and Aude so that as many as 32,000 rebels may have been involved. But all of this was to no avail. Although Rougé picked up support in the Haute-Garonne and as many as 16,000 royalists besieged Toulouse, the republicans counterattacked and, at Montréjeau on 3 fructidor (20 August), inflicted a devastating defeat. About 2000 rebels were killed, another 2000 in mopping-up operations and 1100 prisoners were taken. Although the government soon released many on the grounds that they were misled or drunk, hundreds languished in prison for months afterwards. Significantly enough, many of these were small farmers and labourers from the Garonne valley where bourgeois landholdings and acquisitions of *biens nationaux* were extensive. As always, for all its ability to appeal to nostalgia and anti-Protestantism, royalism in the Midi drew on material frustrations as well.

Bonaparte and Brumaire

Royalist morale was as high as it was before Montréjeau because of the continuing success of the allied advance. After the mid-summer reconsideration, the new plan was to direct a four-pronged advance through Provence, the Jura and Alsace with Austrian and Russian troops while an Anglo-Russian force would land in North Holland. This would either provoke a rising on behalf of the House of Orange or, at its most optimistic, roll through the Low Countries to Lille and on to Paris. There was one initial success. A French advance over the Alps was halted at Novi on 28 thermidor (15 August) and Joubert was killed, shot through the heart as he was leading his soldiers. This left only 35,000 troops to defend Provence but the Austrians contented themselves with siege warfare instead of following up so the Italian theatre quietened down. Meanwhile, Masséna, who had received sizeable reinforcements, inflicted a heavy defeat on the Austrians and Russians near Zurich on 3 vendémiaire (25 September). This in turn forced Suvarov's Russians, who had been marching north, to retreat east to the headwaters of the Rhine, with immense losses. Masséna's victory also made pointless anything more than a war of manoeuvre by the Archduke Charles against the Army of the Rhine. So Moreau held the defences of Mainz. It also spelled the end of the Anglo-Russian expedition in North Holland. This had landed on 27 August and quickly seized what remained of the Dutch fleet after Camperdown, but the 48,000 allied troops could do little in a difficult countryside of dykes and canals and the initially outnumbered French troops under Brune fought a steady defensive war. On 18 October an armistice was signed which permitted a humiliating allied withdrawal in return for the release of eight thousand prisoners of war held in England.

By the end of the campaigning season, the Directory was out of any serious danger from royalism at home or invasion from abroad. But the repercussions of the abortive risings and campaigns contributed further to the deterioration of political life. The Directory profited from circumstances to order the deportation of the publishers and journalists of forty-two royalist newspapers. Three more Jacobin newspapers were included which led to further accusations in the Five Hundred that Sieyès was plotting treason and preparing a coup to put Orléans or the Duke of Brunswick on the throne. With no club behind them and no force in the National Guard, some Jacobins approached Bernadotte to ask him to overthrow the government but legalistic scruples held him back for the moment. Thus even some staunch republicans looked to a general to save them. Jourdan next tried to detach Barras from Sieyès and when this failed, led his fellow Jacobins on 27 fructidor (13 September) in the Five Hundred to propose declaring *la patrie en danger*. If this simply meant mobilizing the National Guard and ordering local authorities into permanent session as the law of July 1792 prescribed, it could have been justified since the foreign advances had not yet been checked, the southwest was still troubled and the chouans in the west were showing signs of renewed activity. But in the context of shrill denunciations of treason against the Directors, and given the precedent of 1792, it could also be interpreted as a call to arms to overthrow the Constitution. As Lucien Bonaparte pointed out, if the Jacobins were really serious about defending the Republic, they would support the Directors rather than constantly challenging executive power. But as the deputies heard as a crowd of about eight hundred outside the legislature chanted 'Down with the thieves, the chouans and the traitors!', the Jacobins considered that power to be corrupt. In the event, the proposal was extremely inept. Sieyès used it as a pretext to remove Bernadotte as Minister of War and it lost on the second day of debate by 245 to 171, a significant vote of confidence in the government. The refusal of the Five Hundred to declare *la patrie en danger*, however, was immensely significant. The Jacobins' parliamentary support had dwindled still further since the failure to indict the deposed Directors, and they had lost the one general in a position of power to protect them against the coup they feared.

Moreover, the tumultuous debate, the ominous appeal to the galleries and the fact that they lost the vote without ceasing to be a force made any accusation that they were plotting a coup of their own all the more credible. Their *Ennemi des oppresseurs* fuelled these fears by its call for 'the mass of the French people and soldiers, tired of this constant oppression, to unite [and] rise up together, to give *la patrie* its independence'. Such irresponsible talk would be put to good use in brumaire.

The general who would do the job landed at Fréjus on 17 vendémiaire (9 October). At first, Sieyès had cast Joubert for this role but after his death at Novi, the plan to overthrow the Constitution was postponed. Negotiations were then opened with Moreau but he felt inadequate. Meanwhile, Bonaparte was ordered home from Egypt with his army. He never received the orders. Instead, he abandoned his army to its own devices as soon as he received old newspaper accounts from English naval officers of the disasters in the European theatre. Bonaparte's reception ought to have given the conspirators pause. Jacobins in the Five Hundred celebrated him as the sword of victory and peace and the author of the 'political regeneration' of Italy. The *Ennemi des tyrans* claimed his return confounded those who wished to surrender the territory of the Republic in a humiliating peace. The moderate *Messager du Soir* claimed his arrival 'could change something of the system of violence which has been established for some time. . . . Bonaparte has proved that it is possible to ally victory to moderation and patriotism to humanity.' Few probably thought much about this invitation to intervene in civilian politics. According to the police, the public saw it as 'an omen for the success of our armies, as a guarantee of prompt and striking victories . . .' His reception was everywhere ecstatic. Peasants in the foothills of the Alps flocked to see him and escort him along his way, just as they would do again in 1815. People in Lyon crowded around his hotel trying to catch a glimpse and actors quickly improvised a play entitled *Le Héros du Retour*. Part of this extraordinary reception was the widespread relief and ecstasy at Masséna's and Brune's victories and the hope that Bonaparte's providential return would finish off the foreign coalition. But part of it was also the focusing on the man of Toulon and vendémiaire and Campo Formio of the élan of 1792, of national defence and 'democracy', of the missionary spirit which brought 'liberty' to Europe once and would do it again. For although Frenchmen certainly wanted peace in 1799, the constant linking of

Bonaparte with military success showed that large sectors of opinion had lost none of their martial ardour. Most sinister of all, Bonaparte was popular in the army not only because of his successes but because officers and men had felt for years that civil society had let them down, that they were the last bastion of true revolutionary principles and that they might be obliged to regenerate the nation as a whole. But Bonaparte not only had a popular following of sorts, he had strong contacts among the intellectual and political elites. He was greatly admired by fellow members of the Institute. As the spiritual descendants of the Encyclopedists, these scientists, engineers and writers dreamed of an efficient government of talents, liberal without being participatory. One of his few public appearances before the coup was an address to them on the possibilities of a Suez canal and on Egyptian antiquities. Bonaparte was always able to attract some of the best minds in the country. The link with the Institute was also a link with the Sieyès faction and this was reinforced by his brothers. Joseph had kept his name before salon society throughout the summer and Lucien, who had played a prominent role against the Directors on 30 prairial and had proved himself one of the most able anti-Jacobin speakers in the Five Hundred afterwards, was already cooperating with Sieyès before Napoleon's arrival. The anti-Directoral coalition was thus already quite large and extensive. Within the legislature, it was composed of newcomers and moderates. Of the sixty-odd known legislators who supported the coup, about half entered national politics only under the Directory and, while most of the others had served in the Convention, only seven were regicides. Of the nineteen surviving members of the Committees of Public Safety and General Security of the Year II, less than one third ever served the Consulate or Empire, despite the spectacular exceptions of Jeanbon Saint-André, Carnot and David. Of the thirty-eight principal Jacobin speakers between 30 prairial and the coup, twenty-four never rallied. Thus the regime's claim to have reconciled the factions turns out to have been, as usual, a half-truth.

What drew the conspirators together was the conviction that the Constitution of the Year III had to be replaced by another giving more authority to the executive. They were so confident that they felt they could do it with an appearance of legality and a minimum of force. The conspiracy unfolded in the early morning of 18 brumaire (9 November) with the convocation of sympathetic

members of the Elders. They were then informed of a terrifying
Jacobin plot and voted two decrees, one transferring the entire
legislature to Saint-Cloud for the next day, where it would
presumably deliberate on the nation's peril in safety; the other
appointing Bonaparte commander of the Paris military district.
Barras, as always determined to be on the winning side, was
induced to resign and Moreau and his troops held Gohier and
Moulin under protective custody in the Luxembourg. The plan
came apart the next day, however. When the Councils met at Saint-
Cloud, the Five Hundred realized the Jacobin plot was a hoax and
immediately took an oath to defend the Constitution, a constitution
which, of course, many of them had violated on 18 fructidor and
22 floréal. With the Elders wavering, Bonaparte was persuaded to
retrieve the situation by addressing the deputies. He was no public
speaker and when he appeared before the Five Hundred, there
were cries of 'Down with the tyrant!' and 'Outlaw him!' In the
mêlée, he was jostled. Bonaparte's bumbling intervention thus
failed. While he beat a strategic retreat under Murat's protection,
Lucien, who was president of the Five Hundred, addressed the
Councils' guards outside claiming the jostling incident was an
assassination attempt, imploring them to disperse the
'représentants du poignard' inside and swearing he would stab his
own brother if he ever betrayed liberty. This proved decisive. With
the regular soldiers under Murat menacing them from behind, the
guards cleared out the deputies. That night, a rump of both houses
established a provisional Consulate of Sieyès, Roger Ducos and
Bonaparte. They also established two commissions composed of
their own members which would design a new constitution. Finally,
they deprived sixty-two members of the Five Hundred of their
seats. Like every other coup of the period, it had to have a purge.

Why the Constitution Failed

The Constitution of the Year III disintegrated amidst deception and
false hopes on the part of the conspirators and a hypocritical oath
on the part of the Five Hundred. No doubt this clumsy instrument
had to go sooner or later because, like the Constitution of 1791, it
contained no device for resolving an urgent clash between the
executive and the legislature except force. Thus it is beside the point
to say that brumaire was not 'necessary' because internal

counterrevolution and the threat of foreign invasion were in abeyance. Beside the point too that the Sieyès Directory had resolved the major issues of contention with the legislature once part of the post-prairial coalition refused to indict the deposed Directors and once it refused to declare *la patrie en danger*. For if the Constitution did not succumb to an immediate crisis, its failure was intimately bound up with a permanent crisis in the polity as a whole. This was the failure of the political nation to enact the role for which it had been cast. All of the major convulsions of the period can be traced to the fact that the politicians elected in 1792 refused to accept the verdicts of subsequent elections. The Montagnards showed the way by conniving at the expulsion of the Girondins and shelving the Constitution of 1793. Their thermidorean enemies followed suit with the 'two-thirds decree', with the purges of 18 fructidor and 22 floréal and with trying to rig the elections of the Year VI and Year VII. In their own minds, ignoring or defying the electorate was justified by the higher necessity of fighting off counterrevolution or the extremism which would lead to the same thing. Robespierre's arguments against the dechristianizers and the Hébertists in the Year II and those of the Directory against democratic Jacobins in the Year VI thus dovetailed and both consequently led to elitist justifications of government. Yet the electorate refused to accept government by the men of 1792 whenever it had the chance. In the Year IV, it reelected the minimum number of *conventionnels* it could by law and returned a little over one fifth of the regicides. The repudiation of these men continued in every subsequent election until by the Year VII, only 12 per cent of the *conventionnels* and 5 per cent of the regicides were left. The big landowners, wealthy farmers and urban rich who were directly responsible for choosing the deputies thus rejected governors who were too adventurist and too demanding. The ordinary first-degree voters reacted to violations of mandates and manipulation of results by not voting. This too showed itself early in the appalling turnout in the plebiscite of the Year III and also in subsequent elections where local studies indicate that turnout was lower in the Year VII than at any other time since 1790, lower in some cases than for the plebiscite. It is a dismal commentary on the state of the nation that more young men probably dodged the draft than bothered to vote.

Ordinary voters may have been apathetic, but on the whole the political nation was not. Of the 671 deputies sitting immediately after the floréal coup, three quarters had never sat in a national legislature before, but of these about two thirds had held appointed or elected positions at the local level. Of those elected in the Year VII, the vast majority as non-governmental candidates, just over half had never sat in a national legislature but nearly three quarters had local experience. The *conventionnels* and the regicides were replaced by men who resembled them socially and who were equally committed to republicanism in that many of them must have been vetted in the local versions of fructidor and floréal before ascending to national office. In many cases, this local experience went back to 1790, with an interruption perhaps in 1793–4, an experience which involved trying to implement the settlement of 1789, veering away from the rule of law in the crisis of 1792 and trying vainly to reestablish it after the Year II. In the present state of research, one can only wonder about the typicality of a man like Borie, a leader of the Third Estate in Rennes in 1788–9, president of the directory of the Ille-et-Vilaine in 1790–1, and first prefect of the department in the Year VIII. The common feature in the careers of such men was a willingness to cooperate with government which promised order on the basis of reasonable liberty and civil equality. The dilemma for them was that constitutional royalism was bound to be a prelude for counterrevolution and civil war so long as Louis XVIII stood by the Declaration of Verona. Jacobinism, with its aggressive foreign policy, unreflecting anticlericalism, populism and hostility to the rich was bound to lead in the same direction. It remained to be seen whether a strong executive under a general could extricate them from it.

Chapter 10

Consulate and Dictatorship

Like the 9 thermidor or 18–19 fructidor, the new regime following the 19 brumaire began by announcing itself as a government of moderation in the mould of the revolutionary tradition. The brumairians also stood for a stronger government even though no one really knew quite what that meant, and in fact the coup made central authority even weaker. For all the brave face they put upon it, Bonaparte and his fellow conspirators retained a strong sense of the fragility of the state for several years afterwards. They were also aware of how much the restoration of order at home depended upon a successful military record abroad. This was achieved within a year of the coup but restoring order also required compromising with the Church, in other words with the popular counter-revolution. Since this was a risk, even more authority was necessary. Thus a strong government, unaccountable to the legislature or to the nation, with broad appointive powers over the administrative and judicial hierarchies which is what the brumairians wanted, slid into personal dictatorship.

Bonaparte and Government

Bonaparte's ambition counted for less in this process than one might think. It is doubtful whether he was aiming at the dictatorship from the first let alone the throne. Many individuals like brother Lucien, Roederer, Talleyrand and Fouché suggested or were thought to have suggested this to him but he was cautious, partly because his ambition was of a more indefinable character. A belief that true immortality was to be remembered by posterity for great things in war and statecraft was the basis for his ambition; all else was means. Throughout his life, he remained a consummate opportunist, supremely capable of manipulating other men's hopes and fears through flattery, intimidation or force. Although he was generally a deist, antiaristocratic, anti-Jacobin, fearful of the common people and a progressive, he nonetheless used religion, heaped honours on family and friends, roused the masses (in 1814), reestablished slavery and reintroduced some of the most hated arbitrary features of the Old Regime government, because all of these exceptions to his general outlook suited the needs of the moment. For all his reputation as a warrior, he was not fundamentally a violent man. If violence served his ends, as with the deportation of the Jacobins in 1801, or the murder of the Duc d'Enghien in 1804, he had no qualms about using it, but if peace could do just as well to weaken his enemies, as with the Treaty of Amiens and the Concordat in 1802, so much the better. A man so able at using others inevitably had much contempt for his fellow men and his own knowledge of his superior gifts only contributed to it. He could work eighteen hours at a stretch, sleep at will, keep half a dozen secretaries busy, absorb vast amounts of information and distil it into crisp formulae and never allow one problem or decision to intrude upon another. He learned quickly. At first he knew little about government and so listened unperturbed to all sorts of unpleasant advice or criticism (so long as it was in private), but as he learned more and became enamoured of his own success, he did more on his own. For all that, it is doubtful whether the quality of government declined as he became more despotic. Doubtful too whether his own powers of organization, intuition and boundless energy ever left him. After all, he was only forty-four when he fell.

Above all, Bonaparte wanted to assert the authority of government by having it stand apart from the factions. At first, the provisional government appeared to be anti-Jacobin. On 22 brumaire (13 November), the Law of Hostages was repealed and Bonaparte made a great sensation by going to the Temple prison to receive the released hostages himself. The forced loan, or progressive income tax, was replaced by a modest surtax on existing taxes on the 28th. Four days later, Bonaparte met with a party of leading bankers, promising them a government of social defence and order. Unfortunately, they loaned the government only a quarter of what it requested and for some time, it had to survive with a series of *ad hoc* financial measures including lotteries and further loans. If these measures pleased the rich and well-born, the government did not mean to be dependent on them or anyone else. Bonaparte, with Fouché's cooperation, intervened personally to prevent Sieyès from ordering the arrest and deportation of dozens of Jacobins. The government also lifted the legal penalties on the relatives of émigrés – the first step towards closing the émigré list altogether. As Bonaparte said so often in this period, he meant his government to be one of reconciliation.

He also meant that government to be strong, but the personal twists he gave to the executive aspects of the Constitution of the Year VIII also gave it an immediately authoritarian character. Sieyès provided the basis of the Constitution, but to everyone's surprise he had no master plan ready. Instead, his friends had to listen to his ideas and these notes provided the essential working documents of the commissions appointed on the morrow of the coup from the old legislature. These provided for an extraordinarily sharp separation of powers, even among the legislative and executive branches of government, and a significant reduction of the role of elections. Thus there was to be a bicameral legislature. The Tribunate of 100 members would discuss government bills but could not vote on them, after which the Legislative Body of 300 would vote on bills but could not discuss them. Before promulgation, a bill would then be examined by a Senate of 60 members for its constitutionality. None of these bodies was elected directly. Instead, the Senate was to choose the members of the Tribunate and Legislative Body from a national list of 6000 'notabilities'. In a bizarre and complicated arrangement, all adult males in a 'communal arrondissement', irrespective of wealth, would elect a tenth of their number to a communal list. The 'communal notables' could elect a tenth of their number to a departmental list and departmental notables another tenth to form the national list. In Sieyès's convoluted reasoning, this evaded the weakness of democracy or of any representative system, of governors being inherently incapable of exercising sufficient power over the governed. As he put it, 'Confidence from below, authority from above'. Originally, Sieyès intended a 'Grand Elector' to choose legislators and officials from these lists and executive power to be exercised by two Consuls, one for foreign affairs, the other for internal. But Bonaparte, whether he feared being appointed 'Grand Elector' or not as is often said (he called the position 'a fatted pig'), had no intention of seeing government paralysed by an excessive balance among its institutions. He wanted a government that was above all effective and, not surprisingly, drew upon a military model for it. Thus Sieyès was intimidated into accepting the demise of the 'Grand Elector', and the appointment of Bonaparte as First Consul for ten years. The two other Consuls, Cambacérès and Lebrun, were both able men but by law had only advisory powers, after which, as Article 42 of the Constitution said, 'the decision of the First Consul shall suffice'. This clause put the entire executive authority of government in the hands of an immensely able, tireless and impatient man. At a stroke, Bonaparte acquired staggering powers of appointment in the local, national, military and civil spheres of government. In no sense were the Consuls or the ministers responsible to the legislature. Instead, they had control of budgetary proposals which would be passed as an annual financial law, and the right to initiate legislation, while the First Consul alone could propose amendments, not the legislature. In all of this, he would be aided by another of Sieyès's ideas, a Council of State. This remarkable body, which soon attracted some of the most able men in the country, prepared bills, often after considerable investigation and internal debate, and its members took turns defending them before the Tribunate and Legislative Body. It also acquired the powers of an administrative tribunal. As experience would show, Bonaparte's powers of appointment, his constitutional position and his own and his colleagues' abilities reduced the powers of the legislature still further.

In theory, the Constitution should have been handed to the Councils of the old legislature but undoubtedly, because this would have risked submitting the magnificent executive authority to amendment, Bonaparte decided at the last minute to put the Constitution to a plebiscite. The result was hardly an unqualified vote of confidence from the nation. About 1.5 million voted in favour, about 1500 against. The electoral apathy of the nation had not changed. About 400,000 more voted in the Year VIII than in the Year III but the turnout was still 400,000 fewer than in 1793. In fact, the process of depoliticization of the nation, and especially the cities, continued. From 50–60,000 in 1793–Year III, the turnout in Paris fell to 32,000, that is to 23 per cent. There were 2500 signatures on an antiroyalist petition in Marseille in the Year IV, 1200 voters in the Year VIII. Nearly 40 per cent voted in the elections of the Year VII in Toulouse, only 20 per cent in the plebiscite. In fact, however, the plebiscite was made to look like a ringing national approbation of brumaire by a colossal fraud. Lucien Bonaparte, now Minister of the Interior, possibly with his brother's knowledge, had officials add between 8000 and 14,000 affirmative voters to each department's total with the result that the

number of voters nationally was about double. The navy voted
under very dubious conditions while the soldiers' votes were simply
invented out of thin air since the army did not vote at all. Until very
recently, both contemporaries and historians believed the officially
announced results: 3,011,007 *yes*, 1562 *no*.

Continuing Disintegration

But fraud was not going to solve the problems of this extraordinarily
fragile regime. Many officials remained loyal to the Directory and
practised a prudent *attentisme*. The departments of the Pas-de-
Calais and Pyrénées-Orientales refused to publish the decrees of 19
brumaire while the administration of the Jura tried to raise its own
little army. Throughout the Midi, departments held the central
government at arm's length and avoided making commitments as
much as they could. The Jacobins were divided and dispirited.
Where those of Toulouse raised the call to arms against the coup
and the club had to be closed by General Lannes, the *Journal des
hommes libres* in Paris advised accepting the Constitution as the
lesser evil. This was probably wise if unheroic since the coup
encouraged anti-Jacobin sentiments, and here and there prominent
clubbists were mugged or meeting halls forcibly closed down. In
wide areas of the country, the coup was perceived as anti-Jacobin
and therefore many expected greater religious freedom. Priests in
Alsace and along the Pyrenees advised their parishioners to accept
the Constitution for this reason but in the civil war zones of the
west, where the priests had long ago given up on the Republic, the
royalist laity did not vote. Elsewhere, much of the country was
under the sway of the brigands and bands of draft-dodgers inherited
from the Directory. On the eve of the coup, for example, royalist
brigands, men 'habituated to crime' backed by 2500 deserters and
encouraged by defeats on the frontiers, had taken the field again
in the Vaucluse, attacking gendarmes, robbing a tax officer and
ripping open the chest of a married priest. There were murders of
officials and raids on tax offices in the Ardèche, Maine-et-Loire and
Bouches-du-Rhône, and threats against the owners and farmers of
biens nationaux followed by arson in the Hérault and Lot. Ex-
nobles were trying to recruit a royalist army in the forests of the
Seine-Inférieure, 'cavaliers royaux' were roaming the countryside
around Amiens and Abbeville in the Somme and bands of brigands

calling themselves the 'Armée rouge', probably in imitation of British soldiers, were trying to recruit draft-dodgers in the Indre-et-Loire. The situation was hardly any better after the coup. With authority in disarray and the military preparing for the spring campaign, it was possibly even worse. There were only two hundred soldiers in the Gard, five hundred in the Ardèche, recuperating from wounds and so poorly supplied, according to General Ferino, that they became 'the most impure' in the army, themselves a cause of 'brigandage and murder and an impediment to the direction of the present government'. Their ill-disciplined reprisals on innkeepers and farmers suspected of harbouring brigands simply added to the prevailing chaos. In fact, their desperate blows were powerless. In the first six months of the Year VIII in the Vaucluse alone, the brigands murdered seventy-nine people while the number of victims in the Year VIII in the Drôme was higher than it had been for the entire White Terror before fructidor. In one particularly ghastly incident in the Bouches-du-Rhône, they murdered the daughter of an official while her neighbours continued working in the fields. Officials' homes were burned in the Aveyron, there was a pitched battle with the National Guards of Pertuis in the Vaucluse, an invasion of Joyeuse in the Ardèche where the brigands disarmed the garrison and robbed tax offices, further robberies of the tax offices at Saint-Esprit in the Gard and Gamas in the Allier, as well as a hold-up of the Toulouse–Bordeaux stagecoach. A riot at Auterrive in the Haute-Garonne in which five hundred people liberated three recently arrested draft-dodgers showed that little had changed.

It would be another year before popular royalism in the Midi was brought under control, but the Consulate did have a quick success of a sort against the chouans. They should have risen at the same time as their counterparts in the southwest in the summer, but the usual lack of direction from the princes and the fatal decision to postpone the insurrection until the harvest meant that the last of the royalist insurrections of the Year VII was fatally isolated. The second chouannerie began well enough. On 22 vendémiaire (14 October) Bourmont's men surprised Le Mans and this provided the signal for similar occupations of Nantes, Saint-Brieuc, La Roche-Bernard, Redon and Locminé. Even the attacks of 1793 had not been so successful. But the chouans were not strong enough to hold these towns while Cadoudal failed to take Vannes and Frotté, and d'Autichamp failed in Normandy and southern Anjou. Unable to exploit initial successes, the chouans were also less numerous since conscription, which had helped them so much in the first war, was not applied in the Year VII in the west. As always, they were short of powder. The allied defeats on the frontiers and the abrogation of the Law of Hostages after the coup also sapped morale so that they agreed to an armistice with General Hédouville on 2 frimaire (23 November). The chouans also hoped, as did many émigrés including the Pretender for that matter, that Bonaparte would restore the monarchy.

Spurning Reconciliation

Bonaparte soon disillusioned royalist agents on the subject of a restoration. In fact, he meant to undercut royalist popular support by making concessions on the religious issue. The edicts of 7–9 nivôse (28–30 December) allowed Christians to worship on Sundays, thus interring the *culte décadaire*, and returned all churches which had not been sold to the communes. The oath of 19 fructidor An V on *haine à la royauté* was replaced by another requiring a simple oath of loyalty to the Constitution. On the same day, the use of the revolutionary calendar was made obligatory only for officials and teachers. This was not exactly full religious toleration, however, since the restrictions on outdoor religious ceremonies and bell-ringing remained in force, and guaranteeing the sales of churches and presbyteries was hardly satisfactory to much Catholic opinion. Catholic-royalist consciences were eased somewhat by a later decree limiting republican fêtes to 14 July and 22 September so that the regime no longer commemorated the execution of Louis XVI. The government also rescinded the laws depriving relatives of émigrés and former nobles of their civic rights. This was followed by a whole series of individual measures of reconciliation: ending the proscription of politicians proscribed in fructidor including Carnot and Barthélemy, lifting the police surveillance on the Jacobins proscribed after brumaire, releasing the priests still held on the islands of Ré and Oléron and offering an amnesty to the rank-and-file chouans. These measures gave some force to the words of the famous proclamation of 24 frimaire (15 December) presenting the Constitution to the nation: 'Citizens, the Revolution is established upon the principles which began it: It is ended.'

In the context, such declarations were little more than pious hopes. The early measures of the Consulate closely approximated the legal situation of the Year III and so there was as yet no reason to believe that its fate would turn out any better than that of the thermidorean Convention or First Directory. As in the Year III, the countryside went far beyond the legal limits on worship defined on 7–9 nivôse. A week later, a crowd convoked by the nocturnal ringing of bells by a carpenter invaded the church at Flogny in the Yonne, tossed the busts of national heroes into a joyous bonfire, restored statues of saints, chanted 'Down with the Republic, Vive le Roi, no more laws!', and hung a dog wearing a tricolour sash on the end of a ladder. Elsewhere in the Yonne, people started quietly working on the *décade* again and covering the statues of liberty with a cloth during Sunday worship. At Caen, there were funeral processions in the streets 'with all the signs and pomp of the Catholic cult' while there were rumours in the rural Seine and the Lot that religious toleration merely presaged the destruction of all republican institutions. It was now routine that there was yet another rash of destruction of liberty trees and republican emblems. Needless to say, the only priests who could be counted on to take the oath to the Constitution were the constitutionals. Few refractories bothered, many emerged from hiding or returned in droves from abroad. Nor were they much tamed. In the Morvan region of the Nièvre, seven of them preached against conscription and paying taxes. Another told the 'ignorant and coarse' peasants of Saurnt in the Ariège that the Revolution was a divine punishment 'for the sins of the people' and predicted 'the time when everything would return to good order'. Much of this sort of preaching was clearly welcome. A 'popular insurrection' installed the refractories in the church at La Canourgue in the Lozère where they proceeded to demand the return of *biens nationaux* and to reinstitute the Old Régime fees for baptisms and funerals. At Doziene in the Loire, a crowd of 'furies' interrupted a funeral service being conducted by a constitutional and dragged him out by the hair. Clerics who preached sedition or who refused the new oath were sought out by the gendarmerie and whenever possible imprisoned. Many could be forgiven for believing the regime had not changed substantially.

The parallel with the Year III was matched with the émigrés as well. Just as many refractories returned because they interpreted brumaire as anti-Jacobin, so did many laymen. 'They are returning

with all the trust and candour of innocence', one official reported
from the Bas-Rhin. Although the Constitution maintained the
émigré laws in all their force, the returnees were scarcely molested
because the government had decided to move away from the laws
altogether. On 25 pluviôse (3 March), a decree of the Council of
State closed the list from 4 nivôse (25 December) and Bonaparte
established a commission to speed the removal of names from the
general list. Magnanimous as this was intended to be, past
experience suggested that it was still a risk.

Centralization and the Rule of Experts

The government meant to minimize the risk and bring the country
under tighter control by reorganizing the basis of local government.
One of the reasons why royalists were able to threaten the Republic
as much as they did before fructidor was that they were able to
intimidate local officials or elect sympathizers to government posts.
The great ideal of 1790 that locally elected citizens would
participate in the execution of laws had also broken down because
amateurs with conflicts of interest easily were paralysed or deflected
from their obligations in time of trouble. The continuing difficulties
in collecting taxes or in organizing conscription, for example, could
be attributed in part to the nature of local government. The
repeated purgings after fructidor, the constant politicization, the
reluctance to serve, the electoral apathy which was little better than
in national elections, completed the sad breakdown of a noble
experiment.

The law of 28 pluviôse An VIII (7 February 1800) implicitly
recognized the failure of citizen participation in local government
and instead turned over all its operations in each department to a
prefect. He was to be appointed by the First Consul and responsible
only to the Minister of the Interior. Except in the Seine where
police was under its own prefect, he was to supervise all aspects of
local government including police, communal affairs, hospitals,
roads, forests, *biens nationaux*, communal finances, public works,
conscription, payment of taxes and so on. Below and subordinate
to the prefect were subprefects in charge of a new unit called an
arrondissement. These officials had no independent authority
and were merely the prefect's executors. The municipal cantons
of the Directory were replaced with the communes of 1790

administered by a mayor and council. Municipal councils were severely controlled by the superior organs of government. The prefect nominated the mayors in communes with less than five thousand people and could suspend or sack their mayors or councillors. In larger communes, the central government exercised this right directly. As with the national government, the ability of citizens to influence government through elections was much reduced. Each department or arrondissement had a council composed of notable citizens who were appointed at first and later elected but their functions were purely advisory and generally were limited to allocating the distribution of taxes among the arrondissements and communes.

Tocqueville rightly celebrated the institution of the prefects as completing the centralization of the Bourbons, a centralization which has scarcely altered to the present day. Yet the institution was a radical break with revolutionary practice. The commissioners of the Constituent and Legislative Assemblies and the representatives on mission of the Year II had limited terms of reference and, along with the commissioners of the Directory, they were supposed to cooperate with elected local bodies, even though practice often differed. While cooptation of experienced administrators became more of a habit after fructidor, the prefects differed essentially in that they were rarely local men and their careers entirely depended on the central government. This administrative reorganization had social consequences too. The lawyers who ran the departments and districts in 1790 and the country notaries who ran the municipal cantons after the Year III were often shunted into the department or arrondissement councils, replaced by men of a different and sometimes higher social standing. Of the initial appointments, roughly half were lawyers and/or politicians while nearly one quarter were recruited from the military or civilian administration. Nearly one quarter were nobles and the return of so many to local administration was probably a real innovation. Certainly the prefects' substantial salaries, between 8000 and 24,000 francs in addition to generous allowances, raised them well above the incomes of all but the wealthiest of the former administrators. Bonaparte's respect for expertise and social éclat thus showed itself from the beginning.

The regime showed its preference for experts in the fiscal sphere as well. Gaudin, who remained Minister of Finances until 1814, secured the passage of the law of 3 frimaire An VIII (24 November

1799) which turned over the collection of direct taxes in each department to a special directory. Its members and the local tax collectors were not bureaucrats in the modern sense, since they received a percentage of the taxes collected, posted bonds to assure their honesty and were often ordinary private businessmen and financiers in their other activities. Although this had a crusty Old Regime air about it, the system worked extremely well. For the first time in a decade, the bulk of the taxes of the Year IX were collected in the year they were assigned. By 1810, the administration had completed an extraordinarily meticulous land survey of about one quarter of the communes of France. The curious overlapping of private and public also showed in the organization of the Bank of France established on 24 pluviôse An VIII (13 February 1800). Among other things, it was to discount promissory notes held by tax collectors, make loans to the treasury and receive and manage some government assets. Yet it also issued 30,000 shares of 1000 francs each to the public, and the shareholders elected fifteen of their number, called 'regents', to the bank's governing council. As the regime became more authoritarian, so too did the organization of the bank. In 1803, the 200 biggest shareholders alone could elect regents. The Bank of France operated in the stratosphere of high finance since the denomination of its notes had to exceed 500 francs and it later opened branches only at Rouen and Lyon. More relevant to ordinary people was the law of 7 germinal An XI (28 March 1803) which established the so-called 'franc de germinal'. This regulated the silver content of the franc, fixed the value of silver to gold and set the denominations of the coins in circulation. Even so, ordinary people continued to use ancient and/or foreign coins along with the new and to ignore the decimal system of money for another couple of generations.

Eclectic and utilitarian in the recruitment of personnel, the Consulate also affected to ignore the political past of its servants. This appears to have been reasonably true in the case of the Council of State. Of the forty appointments in the Year VIII, nine were former *conventionnels* while ten had been imprisoned in the Year II. There was even a handful of federalists and veterans of the émigré armies who rallied to the regime. The reaction against professional politicians, which also manifested itself in the initial appointments to the prefectoral corps, showed here as well. Only twenty-three had been deputies and of the 112 appointments down to 1814, only forty-one had sat in the revolutionary legislatures, many of them, like the prefects, coming to national politics for the first time after the Year IV. Again, like the prefects, they were chosen less for their political background than for their expertise in legal, financial, educational or administrative areas which they had acquired in the royal or revolutionary bureaucracies.

By contrast, the appointments to the various branches of the legislature reflected the desire to reward the brumaire coalition. Sieyès was especially influential in drawing up the list of the first twenty-nine senators who were to coopt the rest. Bonaparte limited himself to vetoing men he felt were too young or radical. The first senators were conservative former deputies and ministers, members of the Institute, businessmen and military officers. From the beginning, lustre outweighed political or legal acumen and this in turn was to propel the Constitution towards dictatorship. The Senate chose the members of the Legislative Body and Tribunate largely from the world of politics. Less than one in ten of the legislators had never held a national post before, although the trend against regicides which had begun under the Directory continued. Only twelve of the members of the Legislative Body and a handful of tribunes and senators were regicides. The same was true in the Council of State, incidentally, where only six initial appointments were regicides. Whatever institution the Consulate established, it could largely do without overly prominent Jacobins.

Defeating the External and Internal Enemies

The brumaire coalition was riddled with factions based on personalities, differences of strategy and attitudes to the First Consul. What held it together was the conviction that the Directory had been too weak to defend the post-thermidorean property settlement from Jacobinism and popular royalism. In itself, the coup had done nothing to stave off these threats and none of the reforms in local government, finance and the Civil Code, which was already in the process of being drafted, could have any effect unless the war and internal subversion could be mastered. Furthermore, large areas of the country had in effect rejected the degree of religious toleration which the government was willing to offer. If it was to make its presence felt, it would have to do so by force.

Bonaparte realized from the beginning that there was an intimate connection between external and internal threats to the Republic.

Right after the coup, he had launched peace feelers to the allies but was rebuffed.

Despite Tsar Paul's withdrawal in disgust from the coalition, the British would not accept the continued occupation of Belgium and Holland, and after the successes of 1799 Austria could hardly accept a settlement in Italy based on Campo Formio. Since a spring campaign was certain, Bonaparte was determined to finish off the internal enemy partly to convince foreign opinion of the solidity of his government and partly because he needed the troops to fulfil the plan of campaign. Measures were taken to reorganize the gendarmerie and two special military commissions were established in the Rhône valley and the southwest to give summary justice to the 'brigands royaux'. Appropriately, Fouché, the Minister of Police, was the spokesman for the harsher measures against internal dissidence. 'Clemency is a virtue', he told local officials in language reminiscent of the Year II, 'but weakness is a vice . . . a crime when it is applied at the expense of the public security.'

Bonaparte judged military commissions useless against the chouans. When the armistice with them expired on 1 pluviôse (21 January), the republican armies in the west had been substantially reinforced and provided with a new commander, Brune, whose prestige and vigour were greater than Hédouville's. Bonaparte ordered Brune to abandon the towns to their own defences, shoot captured rebels without trial, and burn the most intransigent communes to the ground. The whole region was put under martial law. It is doubtful, however, whether measures worthy of Carrier and General Turreau were applied extensively, for the chouan bands were desperately short of powder. Only Cadoudal's bands in the Morbihan were well armed because the British had managed only one major supply operation in the west at the end of November. The others were in no position to undertake a protracted campaign. Consequently, aided by the crafty abbé Bernier, Stofflet's erstwhile advisor, Hédouville secured the surrender of d'Autichamp and Suzannet south of the Loire in return for exempting the priests from the oath to the Constitution. Then Bourmont in Maine, the Boisguy brothers' bands in Upper Brittany and finally Cadoudal in the Morbihan surrendered their weapons on the same terms. Frotté and his staff in Normandy were arrested and later shot despite a promise of safe conduct to the local negotiations issued by republican officers. The procedure was indescribably shabby but Bonaparte, who undoubtedly knew most of the details and who wanted an example, was exultant. Although the chouan die-hards gave trouble for some time, chouannerie was defeated yet again, a victim of poor coordination among the leaders and with the British and the émigrés; and fatally weakened against a regular army with greater fire power. Sentiments did not change but the popular counter-revolution was dead in the west until 1815. And Bonaparte had accomplished it by applying the old Jacobin formula of defeating the internal enemy first. Even as martial law was lifted on 1 floréal (21 April), veterans of the western campaigns were marching to join a special Army of Reserve centred on Dijon. Two weeks later, the First Consul left Paris to take them to Italy to defeat the foreigner.

The campaign was very nearly a disaster. In the first place, Moreau refused to allow the Army of the Rhine to play the major strategic role assigned to it and Bonaparte did not feel politically strong enough to force the issue, an indication that brumaire did not solve the problem of independent generals immediately. This probably made an all-out drive to Vienna impossible and certainly made northern Italy the main theatre. Consequently, Bonaparte moved the Army of Reserve through the Swiss Alpine passes, a surprise thrust into the Austrian rear immortalized in another of David's famous paintings, although in fact the First Consul travelled by donkey through the treacherous St Bernard Pass with his troops hauling artillery by hand over the snow and ice. By 13 prairial (2 June) he was in Milan but, despite a heroic resistance, Masséna was finally compelled to surrender Genoa two days later. Nor did Bonaparte anticipate the Austrian attack when it came at the village of Marengo near Alessandria on the morning of 25 prairial (14 June). With all his reserves desperately committed, it was only the arrival of fresh troops under Desaix that turned an apparent disaster into a stunning victory. The Battle of Marengo led to the French reoccupation of Piedmont and Lombardy and, along with Moreau's belated occupation of Ulm and Munich, to a truce with the Austrians. The talks which followed were abortive, however. When hostilities began again, Moreau resumed the drive on Vienna. On 3 December, he smashed the Austrians at Hohenlinden. This produced the Peace of Lunéville (8 February 1801) whose terms were essentially those of Campo Formio, so that the French restored their dominance over northern Italy and the left bank of the Rhine.

The foreign victories had immense consequences on the internal political situation. Marengo, for all that the Italian campaign was a gambler's throw, consolidated Bonaparte's prestige at home and put an end to the intrigues of the politicians around Sieyès who were disgruntled at the amount of power the First Consul had already acquired. Without a victory, he might not have survived. The public was overjoyed. The prefects reported spontaneous illuminations in Paris, Strasbourg, Lyon and Bordeaux. The peace with victory that so many had desired the previous autumn appeared to be imminent.

Some of the victorious troops were quickly assigned to repression of brigandage in the Midi and to mopping up the remnants of chouannerie in the west. The British, who had given Cadoudal considerable sums of money to put his die-hards on a permanent footing, now told him to postpone an insurrection indefinitely. They also stopped payments to Condé's army of émigrés and it had to disperse. In February 1801, no less than two hundred newly established brigades of gendarmes were scattered throughout the western departments. A series of amnesties proclaimed in the summer of the Year VIII in the Midi brought a mixed response, however, and the royalist murders, robberies and pillaging continued much as before. Authorities were able to make some gradual progress. Some of the prefects, notably those of the Drôme and Var, organized a system of spies which produced some spectacular catches. Mayors were able to inform military authorities which private citizens could be reliably armed. Within months of its foundation, therefore, the new administrative system was contributing effectively to the repression of popular royalism. Most decisive was the use of troops. With large numbers released from the Italian theatre, commanders were able to make use of the flying columns technique which had proved so effective in the west in the Year IV. From the late autumn, there were more and more reports of brigand bands being arrested or dispersed, fleeing their mountain hideouts, profiting from the amnesty on condition they denounce their comrades, of collective defections or even killing their own intransigent chiefs. The government managed to wrest the law of 18 pluviôse An IX (7 February 1801), from a legislature belatedly sensitive to civil rights, which was to try brigands by special judicial commissions without juries or possibility of appeal. At least two hundred brigands were shot by these commissions in the Midi and possibly as many in the west, not to mention hundreds of others killed in countless skirmishes. The establishment of a special National Guard unit at Marseille composed entirely of outsiders reduced vengeance killings in the city to about one every six months. The government's vigorous show of force encouraged the brigands' enemies, many of them undoubtedly local 'patriots' or terrorists, to take a stand, and in the Var, for example, no less than seventy-four communes were described as being 'in a state of insurrection against the brigands'. Without local cooperation, the capture and execution of such prizes as the brigand-priest 'Sans-Peur' in the Hérault would have been impossible. There were seventy-nine assassinations in the Vaucluse in the Year VIII, but only nine the next year. There was not a single incident of brigandage in the once-infested Basses-Alpes in the first six months of the Year IX. Even the refractory priests were intimidated and it was said many of them were too afraid to excommunicate the buyers of *biens nationaux*.

More Conspiracies

Repression showed the limits of the government's trumpeted policy of moderation and reconciliation. Its increasing success and the consolidation of the regime after Marengo and Hohenlinden drove the true believers and the die-hards, both Jacobin and royalist, into conspiracy. The extremist Jacobins attracted an array of insurrectionary veterans, former deputies, exasperated artists and Italian revolutionaries. In the cafés and backrooms it was difficult to distinguish their intoxicating talk about convoking the primary assemblies and imposing the Constitution of 1793, from genuine plots to kill the tyrant. One attempt, the 'Opéra Plot' in which the First Consul was to be stabbed during a performance, would not have got as far as it did if it had not been nourished by men in Bonaparte's entourage who hoped to embarrass Fouché. Another plot by a fireworks-maker, Chevalier, to set off a bomb on the street as Bonaparte rode by, was nipped in the bud. Fouché's informers were able to report most of the extremists' activities but they were less successful in penetrating the royalist organizations. In the spring, royalists had plotted to kidnap the First Consul on his way to his château at Malmaison but the discovery of Hyde de Neuville's agency appears to have put an end to these hopes. But the kidnapping of Senator Clément de Ris and the murder of the constitutional bishop of Finistère showed that the royalists were capable of reaching almost any public figure. They just failed to assassinate Bonaparte himself on 3 nivôse An IX (24 December 1800).

The 'affair of the rue Nicaise' was another element in driving the regime to dictatorship. It was the work of several of Cadoudal's most trusted associates, particularly Picot de Limoelan alias Beaumont, whose curriculum vitae in conspiracy stretched back to the La Rouerie affair in 1791, and Saint-Régent alias Pierrot who was a former chouan commander in the Ille-et-Vilaine. Royalist agents managed to smuggle Chevalier's plans for a shrapnel bomb out of prison and Fouché lost the trail altogether when the chouans murdered two of his informers. When the 'machine infernale' exploded with shards of glass and bits of iron on the rue Nicaise on the evening of 3 nivôse (24 December), somewhere between thirty-nine and seventy-eight people were killed or horribly injured. Bonaparte, who was on his way to the Opéra, was unharmed because the fuse had been lit too late. Saint-Régent and his domestic who turned him in were captured two months later and executed. Most of the important conspirators remained at large.

The 'affair of the rue Nicaise' propelled a shocked political nation into giving Bonaparte still more authority. At first everyone except Fouché was convinced that the outrage was the work of Jacobins. Bonaparte led the way denouncing 'anarchists', 'septembriseurs', 'men of blood', 'the hundred or so *misérables* who have slandered liberty by the crimes they have committed in its name', and so on. Two days later, he saw advantages in the situation. He told the Council of State, 'The action of the special tribunal would be too slow, too limited. A more striking vengeance is necessary for such an atrocious crime, a vengeance as rapid as lightning . . . [we must] profit from the occasion to purge them from the Republic . . .' 'A great example' against the chiefs would also dissolve the party, persuade 'workers' to return to work and 'attach the intermediate class to the Republic'. It was decided therefore to deport to the Seychelles and Cayenne 129 'Jacobins' culled from a prearranged list including Fournier l'Américain, the *sans-culotte* general Rossignol, Felix Lepelletier and René Vatar, former publisher of the *Journal des hommes libres*. Among the others were officers of the revolutionary army, officials of revolutionary committees, Parisians who had been with Fouché at Lyon who knew too much and Lyonnais whom Fouché knew all too well after the quarrels during the mission. In addition, there was a wave of arrests of former terrorists or revolutionaries in Toulouse, Mâcon and Turin. The deportations were not the first exceptional measures the Consulate had taken against political enemies – shooting suspected chouans without trial came earlier – but it was the first which directly associated the brumairians in what was certainly an illegal measure against innocent men. This illegality in turn established a precedent which permitted subsequent violations of the Constitution. Although the Tribunate promised to cooperate with new legislation beyond existing statutes on murder which would prevent such crimes 'or punish them with the necessary severity', a special law would have had to have been retroactive. Although Bonaparte doubted it, it might not have passed if the Jacobins were proved innocent. Despite considerable qualms, the Council of State was unanimous in supporting a mass deportation and referring the matter to the Senate which declared the act constitutional on 15 nivôse (5 January). This was the first *senatus consultum*, a device later used to subvert the Constitution altogether. As Bonaparte was aware, it made the brumairians his accomplices. There was perhaps a twinge of conscience when those involved in the Opéra and Chevalier plots were executed, perhaps another when Fouché finally proved the royalists were responsible for the affair. No one rescinded the deportation order. In the end, they all accepted Bonaparte's logic that the deportees were guilty for what they had been, not for what they had done. As he expressed it, '. . . in the absence of legal proofs it [the government] cannot proceed against these individuals. We transport them for their share in the September Massacres, the crime of 31 May, the Babeuf Conspiracy, and all that has happened since.' Cambacérès concurred, 'It would be misleading to speak of the crime of 3 nivôse as being the motive for this measure, which is one of general utility.'

Peace, Concordat . . .

Talleyrand had supported a dramatic measure because it would demonstrate the government's strength to the foreign powers. It certainly reduced still further the ability of the British to interfere in French affairs. Diplomatic and domestic problems also drove them towards a settlement. The erratic Tsar Paul, vexed at British insistence on retaining Malta, took the lead in forming the League of Armed Neutrality in which Sweden, Denmark and Prussia closed the Baltic to British shipping. Since Russian policy was veering towards France and since a bad harvest was made worse by the stoppage of grain imports in a traditional source of supply, a thoroughly war-weary public demanded peace. When Pitt's government fell over the issue of the repeal of civil disabilities on Irish Catholics, a new francophile government under Addington opened peace negotiations. British fortunes did improve during the year. On 23 March 1801 Paul was assassinated and a new government under his son, Alexander I, tilted Russian policy towards Britain again. Five days later the British fleet shelled the Danish fleet at Copenhagen and together with Paul's death, this broke the League of Armed Neutrality. Finally, a British expeditionary force arriving from the Mediterranean and another composed of Indian troops sent by Wellesley through the Red Sea combined with a Turkish army to defeat the French in Egypt. Despite these successes, however, the British continued peace negotiations. The talks resulted in the Peace of Amiens of 25 March 1802. France was to keep her continental conquests, although England did not recognize the sister republics. Of all the conquests in the Mediterranean, the Caribbean and the Indian Ocean, England was to keep only Ceylon and Trinidad. Malta would be restored to the Knights of St John as soon as the Order was strong enough to defend its fortifications. Neither side was entirely satisfied. The British were disappointed that there was no commercial treaty and Bonaparte considered the Peace of Amiens a device to curtail British economic and political influence. Still, Bonaparte's prestige within France was immense. As many had hoped, he brought peace with victory.

If Marengo was the starting point of a network of threads which led to peace abroad, and pacification of Jacobin and royalist dissidence at home and so to consolidation of the government, Marengo also contributed to the Concordat with the papacy. Already on the eve of the battle, Bonaparte had promised the assembled clergy of Milan that Catholicism would enjoy a full, extensive and inviolable freedom and, in a direct appeal to the papacy, claimed that 'France, having learned from its misfortunes, has at last opened her eyes; she has recognized that the Catholic religion is as an anchor which alone can . . . save her from the tempests'. This was hardly true but, as he made clear in this speech and in a long conversation with Roederer at Malmaison the following August, religion had its uses: 'How can there be order in the state without religion? Society cannot exist without inequality of fortunes and inequality of fortunes cannot exist without religion. When a man is dying of hunger beside another who is stuffing himself, he cannot accept this difference if there is not an authority who tells him: "God wishes it so . . ."' Social and political utility were inseparable. He told Thibaudeau, 'A religion is necessary for the people. . . . Fifty émigré bishops paid by England lead the French clergy today. It is necessary to destroy their influence. The authority of the Pope is necessary for that . . .' An accommodation with Rome would thus contribute to the pacification of the west and help assuage the religious discontent in the conquered territories and sister republics. Bonaparte's ultimate aim was thus comparable to that of the Legislative Assembly, the Convention and the Directory in that clerical legislation was directed at winning over the laity even though the means were radically different. Nor by the Year IX was Bonaparte alone in realizing that repression had failed to achieve it. Hoche and his fellow officers still serving in the west had urged the widest possible religious liberty. Some officials in the closing years of the Directory and some newly appointed prefects had also come to appreciate the sociological and political importance of popular religion. There was still considerable hostility to an accommodation with Rome from the 'Jacobin' generals, notably Brune and Bernadotte, from the Institute, the Council of State, the Tribunate and, depending on its form, from both Talleyrand and Fouché. Without Bonaparte's immense prestige and authority, it is doubtful whether the Concordat could have been concluded. Yet if Bonaparte meant to coopt the clergy, Thibeaudeau realized that the clergy's hostility would mean a 'war to the knife between them and the Revolution forever'. The alternative was a new round of persecutions which experience had shown to be incapable of mastering popular counterrevolution or 'good discipline and an effective police'. Thus a reconciliation with the Church required greater authoritarianism.

The papacy, for its part, was willing to go far. The saintly Pius VII scarcely resembled his intransigent predecessor and he brushed aside the pro-Austrian and royalist factions in the curia. French reminders that the great powers could not offer support and threats that Murat's troops occupying Tuscany might move on Rome had little influence. In fact, the curia was appalled at Bonaparte's demand for the simultaneous resignation of all the Old Regime bishops and it tried to save them for as long as possible. Thus in a curious way the papacy defended the Gallican principle of non-interference in the French Church while the government invited it. It was Louis XVIII's clumsy attempts to prevent an accommodation that finally convinced the papacy of the truth of Bonaparte's point that the émigré bishops were erecting the interests of the monarchy above those of religion. In the end, the papacy wanted a reconciliation, at the price of the bishops, of the ecclesiastical property sequestered in 1789 and even a declaration of Catholicism as the state religion. Instead, the Pope had to settle for a declaration of Catholicism as the religion of the majority of Frenchmen. He would even have to accept the constitutional bishops. Although Pius demanded they accept the condemnations of his predecessor and Bonaparte refused to accept even this mild form of retraction, the Concordat was signed on 15 July without their fate being settled. This left the way open for the government to reappoint them. The abbé Bernier who had rallied to the regime to become one of the negotiators of the Concordat assured Cardinal Consalvi, his Vatican counterpart, that the constitutional bishops had retracted when in fact they never did. As experience would show, this was only one of several deceptions practised on the papacy. But there was also justification in the papacy's hope that the Concordat was a mere beginning for the restoration of the Church.

... and Dictatorship

The Concordat provided the occasion for a sharp deterioration in the government's relations with the politicians. Until the beginning of the Year X, the government's record in getting its bills through the Tribunate and the Legislative Body was excellent by any standards. In part this was because the politicians were as anxious as anyone to cooperate in the process of reconstruction and in part because, as the tribune Chauvelin put it in the early days of the Consulate, the dangers to the Republic required 'the pressing need of union between the branches of government'. Greater stability through more authority, however, raised questions about whether the line between strong and arbitrary government had not already been passed. This would explain why opposition to the law of 18 pluviôse An IX establishing special tribunals against brigandage was so vigorously attacked when no one objected to the use of military commissions in the Midi and the west the previous summer or to the deportation of the 129 Jacobins without trial following the rue Nicaise Affair. Yet Bonaparte interpreted all public manifestations of opposition as subversive and saw himself in a special relationship with the nation. He stigmatized opposition orators in the Tribunate like Constant, Chenier and Daunou as 'ideologues' and 'metaphysicians'. Reacting to opposition to a bill (which was passed) which set time limits on debate, he said that the government aimed 'to destroy the spirit of faction'; to govern through parties was to become dependent on them, 'I am national'. Almost as soon as opposition appeared, all but thirteen newspapers in Paris were suppressed and this was later reduced to nine. Like so many of his contemporaries, he was incapable of conceiving of a loyal opposition or of politics as a process of reconciling interests through compromise. Like the Montagnards and the Second Directory too, his solution to the problem of faction was to eliminate it in the name of national unity. He described opponents to the special tribunals bill as 'vermin that have got under my skin. . . . They need not think that I will let myself be attacked like Louis XVI. I won't stand for it.' Thus when the legislature reconvened in November 1801, it was difficult to disentangle the politicians' anxieties over the government's authoritarianism from their objections to specific government proposals. Probably they were not sure themselves but Bonaparte had clearly misjudged their temper if he expected them to applaud unquestioningly the restoration of order at home and peace abroad.

Everyone expected the crisis to come over the Concordat and the Legislative Body threw down the gauntlet by electing Charles Dupuis, ex-priest and anti-Christian author, as its president and Grégoire, the embodiment of the constitutional church, to a vacant Senate seat. This persuaded Bonaparte not to submit the Concordat immediately so the crisis broke over other issues. The peace treaty with Naples provided tribunes with the occasion to denounce the obscurantism and brutality of Bourbon rule and they denounced the treaty with Russia because it referred to the French as 'subjects'. Meanwhile, the tribunes condemned the first titles of the Civil Code and rejected the first two by impressive margins. Bonaparte reacted by withdrawing all bills from parliamentary consideration. At first, he seems to have been willing to live with this stalemate but since the Constitution required the renewal of one fifth of the membership of the legislature in the Year X, he soon saw an opportunity to rid himself of his most galling opponents. The Constitution was silent on how the renewals were to proceed although most assumed it would be by lot. Instead, Bonaparte delegated to Cambacérès, the Second Consul, the shoddy business of cooperating with the Senate in designating which four fifths were to stay. The majority of senators, however queasy they were, seem to have gone along for no better reason than to end the legislative stalemate and out of fear that they were forestalling something worse. Thus in March 1802 they eliminated the same men they had appointed two years before. Among the eighty were the 'ideologues', Constant, Chenier, Daunou and Ginguene as well as friends of Sieyès and anticipated opponents of the Concordat.

With most opposition eliminated, Bonaparte secured the passage of a number of controversial measures which imposed his sense of hierarchy on the nation. The Legislative Body accepted the Concordat and Organic Articles on 8 April. A *senatus consultum* of 26 April granted an amnesty to all but about a thousand émigrés provided they took an oath of loyalty to the Constitution. This meant that they had to accept the sale of *biens nationaux* as definite. Although the government returned all unsold property except forests to them, they had to remain under police surveillance and controlled residence for ten years. The government was hardly caving in to counterrevolutionaries. A law on branding for forgers and certain classes of recidivists which had been withdrawn earlier in the session passed quickly. The Legion of Honour was created on 19 May. As we shall see, this reflected the increasing militarization of national life. The government tightened its control over the Bank of France and reestablished slavery in the colonies. Finally, the passage of the Treaty of Amiens by the Senate on 6 May provided the pretext for a further and decisive subversion of the Constitution. As a token of gratitude, the senators proposed to reelect Bonaparte for an additional period of ten years. The Council of State, with only a few members absenting themselves in protest, then drafted a proposal for a plebiscite asking the nation whether Bonaparte should be made Consul for Life. The Legislative Body approved, as did the Tribunate which presented its approbation in a particularly grovelling address.

The plebiscite was approved by a vote of 3,568,855 to 8374. While no one knows whether these results were altered as they were in the Year VIII, the vote was hardly free. As in the Year VIII, voters had to sign their names in a public register and some may have feared reprisals. Officials were certainly in this position as were priests, many of whom were seeking appointments. And if the official results were honest, the turnout of roughly 60 per cent was by far the largest of the period even though in the Côte-d'Or entire communes voted unanimously, as did some women and illiterates. Yet there were reasons why a large yes vote could be expected. With the return of peace, taxes were marginally lower than they had been in 1791. The demands for conscripts were dramatically lower than they had been in the year VII. Only 30,000 men were called up in each of the classes of the Years VIII and IX, that is less than 10 per cent of the numbers demanded under the Directory. With large numbers of soldiers demobilized, the families of the young could be grateful. Finally, the Concordat restored freedom of religious expression, the only kind of freedom large numbers of Frenchmen had shown they cared about, under a clergy who were not obviously the tools of others. It was significant that in the Ille-et-Vilaine, where religious troubles and chouannerie had been rife, the turnout quintupled. Paradoxically, the reestablishment of a dictatorship meant less government for most people.

Before the results of the plebiscite were even known, the Constitution of the Year X was drafted and later promulgated on 16 thermidor (3 August 1802). Combined with two other *senatus consulta* of 30 August and 20 December, this effectively organized the dictatorship. Bonaparte became Consul for Life with the ability to nominate his successor. The independence of the Senate, whose record was supine enough, was further reduced since the First Consul could nominate up to forty members. With fourteen vacancies still available, he could control the majority. In cooperation with the Senate, he could name the other eighty members nominated by departmental electoral colleges. These were new bodies which replaced Sieyès's excessively complicated and much-criticized indirect electoral lists. Instead, citizens chose members of electoral colleges from the list of the six hundred most heavily taxed men in the department. Since election to the college was also for life, the citizenry's participation in the institutions of the nation was an illusion. So too was that of the notables in the colleges since the First Consul could make up to twenty life appointments to the colleges from the list of the thirty most heavily taxed as well as choose the presidents of the colleges. The Legislative Body no longer ratified treaties of peace or alliance which the First Consul alone negotiated, and the Tribunate, already

divided into three permanent sections after the purge, had its
membership reduced to fifty. Neither had to meet regularly. In
theory, the Senate still had some feeble powers of appointment
over these bodies but the senators were given considerable reason
to be cooperative by the creation of 'senatoreries' in each appeal
court jurisdiction, that is a domain which offered sizeable revenues
to the favoured few who received them. Senators could also hold
other lucrative government jobs so there was an additional
incentive to be docile. If the original idea of a fief was a grant of
land or revenue in return for state service, a 'senatorerie' was a fief.
There was thus considerable irony in Bonaparte's constitutional
oath 'to oppose the return of feudal institutions'. In fact, the
Constitution meant nothing to him. 'The belief that a sheet of paper
can be of any value unless it is supported by force has been one of
the cardinal mistakes of the Revolution.' 'A constitution', he said,
'ought to be made so that it does not impede the action of
government and force it to violate it. . . . [A constitution's]
development is always subordinated to men and circumstances.'

The Process of Dictatorship

In order to understand how 'men and circumstances' had brought
the dictatorship about, it is necessary to question some of the
persistent myths about Bonaparte's rise to power. One of these is
that the Consulate was a 'military dictatorship'. The army was
critical, of course, in brumaire, at Marengo and Hohenlinden and
for defeating the chouans and 'brigands royaux'. But the army as
such did not take power in brumaire or afterwards. There was no
marked infusion of military personnel into civilian institutions. If
anything, the army was an obstacle on the road to dictatorship since
envious generals retained the same limited views of politics they
had held under the Directory. Nothing could better illustrate the
futility of the army's 'Jacobinism', however, than the so-called
'Libel Plot' of the spring of 1802 in which some officers on
Bernadotte's staff at Rennes circulated handbills denouncing the
Concordat and 'the tyrant'. The call to arms had almost no echo and
Fouché's police were soon on the trail of the 'plotters'. They were
equally quick to detect the inebriated threats of junior officers on
half-pay with too little to do in peacetime. Otherwise, officers were
allowed to mutter. Where opponents looked dangerous, as they did

in some of the regiments of the Army of the Rhine and the Army of Italy, the source of most of the hostile military votes, they were transferred to the expedition to Saint-Domingo.

Bonaparte himself claimed that 'France would never submit to a military government. . . . Any attempt of that kind is bound to fail, and to ruin the man who makes it. It is not as a General that I am governing France; it is because the nation believes that I possess the civil qualities [earlier defined as 'foresight, power of calculation, administrative ability, ready wit, eloquence . . . and above all knowledge of men] which go to make a ruler.' The dictatorship was thus the work of civilians but this can be misunderstood too. Bonapartist historians constantly claim that a grateful nation, sick of disorder and bloodshed, turned to a saviour. There is some truth in this. The joyous reception upon the return from Egypt and the plebiscites, however fraudulent or poorly administered they were, attest to a genuine popularity among some people. Yet the plebiscites played almost no role in establishing the dictatorship. The Constitution of the Year VIII was implemented when only the results from Paris were known and the Constitution of the Year X was drafted before the Senate had completed tabulating the results of the second plebiscite which, incidentally, merely asked approval for an amendment to the Constitution, not its subversion. Popular attitudes to the regime contributed to the dictatorship in so far as they were basically apathetic. The depoliticization of the nation which had begun in the Year II stifled the ability of one sector of opinion to influence government. The Concordat had much the same effect on Catholic and royalist opinion. With the return of the old priests and wide freedom of religious expression, there was no need to challenge the government. To borrow an expression of Tocqueville's, repression and cooptation removed the 'intermediary institutions' of popular opinion and action and so made government effective for the first time in nearly a decade.

Although the basis of Bonaparte's dictatorship was his constitutional right to pack assemblies, he scarcely had to use it to secure the regime. After the purge of the Year X, the Legislative Body never again rejected a government bill and opposition in the Tribunate was trivial until its unlamented abolition in August 1807. The Senate, whose membership became increasingly subsumed in the system of honours as the representation of the world of politics declined, gave everything the government asked of it until the senators tried to save themselves in the catastrophe of 1814. In short, Bonaparte did not usurp power, it was given to him by a fairly narrow political class who, strictly speaking, represented nobody because they had all been appointed. This was because, like the Directory before them, the brumairians fundamentally distrusted elections and parliamentary government. When Thibaudeau proposed a return to this system upon the conclusion of peace, his fellow councillors of state shuffled in embarrassed silence. Lanjuinais, whose whole career can be understood as a defence of parliamentary government, was the only senator to oppose the Constitution of the Year X. Indeed, the distrust of assemblies was so great that Cambacérès considered even the Council of State as a potential impediment to administration. This attitude in turn was a function of the sense of the fragility of the achievements of the Consulate. 'Hardly any institutions,' wrote Roederer in 1802, 'nor yet any formed or rooted habits.' As the councillor Defermon said regarding the settlement with the clergy who were still perceived as potentially hostile, 'All that will go very well so long as the Consul lives. The day after his death, we will all have to emigrate.' To men like this, the surrender to someone who was prepared to use power crudely, even brutally, was necessary since the country was only recently pacified, the Concordat's prospects of success were not yet certain and the peace had only been achieved through conquests in Italy and along the Rhine. This is what the Council of State meant when it approved the plebiscite on the Consulate for Life claiming that 'stability alone can avoid war and permit the enjoyment of the advantages of peace'.

Conspiracy and Empire

No one in governing circles was inhibited about exploiting an advantageous peace to the fullest and this in turn led to a new war with Britain. Not only did the dictatorship refuse a commercial treaty which the British thought a natural supplement to the Treaty of Amiens, tariffs against British and colonial products were actually raised. The expedition to Saint-Domingo, designed to reassert French authority, and plans to develop Louisiana, recently acquired from Spain, raised the spectre of unwanted competition in the Caribbean trade to Europe and in the contraband trade to the Spanish colonies. Developments on the continent aggravated these commercial quarrels. Bonaparte's refusal to evacuate

Holland, the annexation of Piedmont, the Act of Mediation of 19 February 1803 which left the Helvetic Republic with only a fig leaf of independence and renewed intrigues in Egypt and the Middle East generally with the implicit threat to India, encouraged all those in England who had doubted the wisdom of peace in the first place. The British press, still in its most licentious epoch, pilloried the dictator mercilessly and Bonaparte, who understood the value of propaganda better than the rulers of his time, was enraged when the government refused to curb it. Such aggressiveness in Europe, the Near East and America determined the British to hold on to Malta, which was an explicit violation of the Treaty of Amiens. They were also encouraged to reverse their previously conciliatory attitude because none of the other great powers was satisfied with French conduct either. Neither Prussia nor Austria was content with the new territorial settlement in Germany and the Hapsburgs risked losing a great deal of prestige since the settlement gave a majority in the Imperial electoral college to Protestants. Russia too was anxious about French designs on Turkey. Thus more essential issues underlay the agonizing negotiations over Malta: commercial supremacy over the oceans, Mediterranean hegemony and the European balance of power.

The renewal of hostilities led directly to Bonaparte's assumption of a crown. Ever since 1792, war had divided the nation but for once this did not happen. When the British began seizing French merchantmen, shortly after breaking diplomatic relations on 2 May 1803, a controlled press and the absence of political outlets created the impression of a unified national indignation at the piracy of the hereditary enemy. Public opinion, such as it was, thus rallied round the government of the invincible general. More importantly, the royalists' attempts to break the apparent consensus strengthened the dictatorship even further, as such efforts always had. This involved an ambitious conspiracy to kidnap the First Consul or failing that, kill him, as soon as a prince, presumably the Comte d'Artois, arrived in France. Cadoudal and an elite company of chouans slipped into Paris from England were to take charge of that operation while Pichegru would secure at least the neutrality of the army by approaching Moreau whom Bonaparte greatly resented for the victory at Hohenlinden. How much responsibility the British government shared in this plot has never been settled satisfactorily. Certainly the ministers had no objection in principle to assassinating a foreign head of state since Grenville dismissed a project to murder the Directors a few years before as impractical, not immoral. The Cadoudal plot also coincided with a plot by the British agent, Drake, to provoke an insurrection in the Rhineland. It is also hard to believe that ministers were entirely ignorant of their own junior officials' providing the royalists with money, documents, weapons and naval transport. In any case, there was never much chance of the plot succeeding. Despite Cadoudal's waiting in Paris for five months completely unknown to the police, no prince ever materialized. Moreau, if he promised Pichegru anything which is not clear, refused to lend himself to a conspiracy aimed at restoring Louis XVIII. Eventually, the police captured a minor royalist agent who confessed after having his fingers crushed under a musket hammer. In February–March 1804, Moreau, Cadoudal and Pichegru were arrested, along with dozens of other agents and chouans.

Although a dismal failure, the Cadoudal plot had momentous consequences. Bonaparte decided that the prince in question was the Duc d'Enghien, grandson of the Prince de Condé, who was residing in Baden. The unfortunate young man was kidnapped, dragged back to Paris and shot within hours of his arrival after a farcical appearance before a military tribunal. Although Enghien was captured on neutral territory and no connection with the Cadoudal plot was ever proven, Bonaparte never regretted the murder. It may have stunned his admirers then and since, it may have made him a regicide after a fashion, but it worked. It was the end of the cycle of royalist assassination plots. The same brutally opportunistic cast of mind operated with Moreau. His eventual banishment was a further warning to the other 'Jacobin' generals that plots of any sort were futile. Even the mysterious suicide of Pichegru, found in his cell apparently having garrotted himself, showed sceptics how unscrupulous the regime was prepared to be. Cadoudal died a martyr to royalist hagiographers but his plot seemed to show that only Bonaparte stood between a restoration and the preservation of what remained of the revolutionary achievement. It was a conclusion which the British government was already well primed to take in its own way after the rupture of the Treaty of Amiens. The ministry was now committed wholly to the Bourbons because only their restoration could also restore peace and the balance of power on the continent. The overthrow of Bonaparte's regime and the destruction of the conquests in 1814 were implicit in the events of 1804.

Most of the significance of this was lost in the spectacular elevation of Bonaparte to the imperial crown on 18 May 1804. The dictator's entourage, particularly Fouché, adopted the entirely specious argument that only the hereditary principle would eliminate assassination attempts. Everyone, the Tribunate, Legislative Body, Senate, Council of State and ministry, acquiesced with even less manoeuvring than that which preceded the Life Consulate because everyone hoped to advance himself in the regime. After all, if no one of note even resigned after the Enghien Affair – the decision to kidnap was collective at which a large number of ministers, councillors and senators were present – no one could be expected to protest the reintroduction of an institution many had sworn to die opposing. In the Tribunate, only Carnot, a man of principle in lost causes, voted against and promptly resigned. The nation dutifully voted in favour by 3,572,329 to 2569 even though the new constitution had already been adopted. 'The government of the Republic is confined to a hereditary emperor', it declared, and the Emperor was to take an oath to respect 'equality of rights, civil and political liberty [and] the irrevocability of the sales of *biens nationaux*'. Aside from organizing a court with pompous medieval titles and permitting the childless Napoleon to name his successor, government institutions changed little. Any possibility of opposition from the Senate was forestalled by permitting the Emperor to appoint an unlimited number of senators. The Senate also received the right to investigate arbitrary arrests and infringements of press freedom. Despite numerous violations of civil rights in the next ten years, the Senate never once used its power to declare that a *de facto* case existed.

The revolutionary era began with men hoping they could place limits on the actions of an arbitrary government. It ended with some of the very same men creating a government far more arbitrary and despotic than the monarchy of the Old Regime. Thus Napoleon's frequent claim that he found the crown in the gutter is only a typical half-truth. The political and intellectual elite picked it up first and embossed it for him in the interests of national stability. But even while Napoleon crowned himself at a gaudy ceremony presided over by Pius VII at Notre Dame on 2 December 1804, the development of the war was showing what a costly and calamitous risk the surrender to a dictator was proving to be.

Chapter 11

Napoleon and France

In 1802 Napoleon said that the aim of his reforms was to create institutions which would act as 'masses of granite' binding the nation together. The statement reflects how far the brumairians had travelled from the preoccupations of the Constituent Assembly which also thought of itself as reconstructing a nation out of chaos. Instead of a society based upon the free exercise of property and limiting the state by defining political and civil liberty, the men of the Consulate and Empire wanted to create a society based on order and hierarchy. Protecting property was as important to them as to the Constituents but the despotism they established ended by favouring the rich and heaping honours upon the wealthy and the exceptionally talented. Since the regime was at war from 1803 onwards, military values and military notions of hierarchy seeped into the system of rewards and honours, and even to a certain extent into religious and family life. The Consulate and Empire was not so much a military despotism, however, as a bureaucratic and professional machine which encountered remarkably little opposition. As the war dragged on, it became more arbitrary and more demanding. It is a measure of the success of the construction of the 'masses of granite' that it could only be toppled by the foreign invasion.

Honours and Titles

If a society can be characterized by the kinds of activities and people it rewards, then the Consulate and especially the Empire were military societies. This tendency showed itself from the beginning in the institution of the Legion of Honour founded in May 1802. Despite protests in the Tribunate that it was a violation of the principle of equality, the practice of recognizing civic contributions was not new whether these were in the form of the special uniforms for the conquerors of the Bastille or the 'civic crowns' or the declarations of merit of the Convention. But with its internal hierarchy of grand officers, commandants, officers and legionnaires, and its combative oath of defence of the Republic, it did resemble several of the military orders of the Old Regime. Once its members received decorations and a new oath shortly after the declaration of the Empire, the resemblance was even closer. The difference was that no one was excluded on the basis of religion or birth. But it was military merit which counted. Of the 38,000-odd creations between 1802 and 1814, only 4000 went to civilians, most of them to high officials.

The Legion of Honour was the first step towards the recreation of an aristocracy. There were others: the creation of senatoreries and of princely titles for the imperial families, and the resuscitation of the honorific title of 'marshal' for outstanding generals. Finally, Napoleon created imperial titles in March 1808, because, he said, he wanted to fuse the old and new elites and because he wished to forestall the restoration of the Old Regime nobility. None of the cluster of associations which formerly defined the old nobility in law and practice – legal privilege, exemptions, reserved office, venality, seigneuries, and so on – were revived with the new nobility. Only imperial titles were recognized, Old Regime titles were not. The Emperor, not office, was the source of titles and the sole criterion was state service much as it had been in eastern Europe a century before. The most distinctive criterion was that the holder of an imperial title had to be a man of defined wealth. Thus a duke had to have revenues of 200,000 francs, a count 30,000, a baron 15,000 and a chevalier 3000 which would suggest a minimum personal fortune ranging from 4 million francs to 50,000 francs. Money in itself did not imply a title since only a few businessmen and financiers, including only a minority of the Regents of the Bank of France, were ever ennobled. Instead, the imperial nobility practised an ideal of the Old Regime in that status determined wealth. Men whose personal fortunes were unimpressive received grants of property from the imperial domain or a share of the tribute from the conquered territories, and this in turn allowed them to build up substantial fortunes on their own account. Thus Marshal Davout, the descendant of an old but modest family of Burgundian nobles, acquired an annual income of close to 1.2 million francs, over three quarters of it derived from lands and revenues in Poland, Germany and Italy. Ney, the son of a barrel-maker, acquired a similarly fantastic fortune, equally dependent upon foreign sources. The spectacle of wealthy generals was not particularly new since Ney, Leclerc and Murat, among others, bought magnificent châteaux and their dependencies in the later Directory–early Consulate with money that was almost certainly derived from accepting 'gifts' from conquered towns and territories, but Napoleon transformed the practice of accepting personal tribute into an extravagant system of largesse. This generosity towards the marshals and their dependence on foreign sources of revenue gave them a direct material interest in maintaining the frontiers of the Empire at their greatest possible extent. However war-weary they are said to have become in 1814, it is no wonder that none of them 'betrayed' it until the military situation was hopeless.

The acquisition of an imperial title became in effect another honour marking a distinguished career. Napoleon created 3263 nobles between 1808 and 1814, the great bulk of them, understandably enough, in the first three years. Since state service in this period was above all military, it is not surprising that nearly 60 per cent were officers, the grade of the title neatly corresponding to the holder's military rank. The others were divided between the upper ranks of the civil service (councillors of state, prefects, bishops, etc., for 22 per cent) and notables (senators, members of electoral colleges and mayors, for 17 per cent). Service in the arts or culture or in economic life was scarcely rewarded at all. In social terms, the imperial nobility was drawn ovewhelmingly from the old Third Estate. Only 22 per cent were from the Old Regime nobility while 20 per cent were from the popular classes and 58 per cent were bourgeois, not, however, from the supposedly frustrated office-holding families of 1789 but from the more modest milieux of minor officialdom, law, medicine and petty industry. The recognized social elite of the country, therefore, had been drastically shaken and there was some truth in the regime's claim that it was open to men of energy and talent.

To acquire its talent in the future, the regime once again had recourse to a military model. The law of 11 floréal An X (1 May 1802) replaced the decentralized secondary schools of the Directory with 'lycées', of which there were only forty-five, that is fewer than one for every two departments. They implemented an eighteenth-century continental idea that the state should educate its future officials. Two thousand five hundred scholarships were even set aside for the sons of officers and civil servants. Both teachers and students were subject to a strict military discipline. Both wore uniforms, those of the teachers indicating their rank, both were subject to a graded series of punishments for violation of rules, the boys participated in military exercises for an hour a day and were subject to discipline by their older or brighter peers who were given military titles. The curriculum was actually narrower than that of the 'central schools' of the Directory since the lycées eliminated the study of modern languages to concentrate on Latin and mathematics. An arid environment and unexciting curriculum may have alienated some parents. The lack of religious education certainly did. Despite close state supervision and the fact that they were taxed, other secondary schools established by municipalities or the 'Frères des écoles chrétiennes', the Old Regime teaching order revived in 1802, attracted many more boys than the lycées did.

Napoleon allowed both girls' and primary education to languish since in his view women had no other destiny than marriage and there was no advantage to the state in educating the masses. Yet it was in these areas that some of the greater strides of the period were made. Whether it was through the restored religious orders who taught both boys and girls, by itinerant schoolmasters, by teachers hired on an occasional basis by the communes or by village savants, popular literacy continued to increase throughout the revolutionary and imperial epochs. Men's literacy increased from 37 per cent to 54 per cent and women's from 27 per cent to over 35 per cent. Despite the destruction of the Old Regime school system, literacy increased, possibly because schools had never been crucial in teaching it. The acquisition of literacy and basic arithmetic could be one of the most important skills parents could provide for their children. In the Mâconnais, for instance, it was the most important single factor ahead of parents' wealth or social position in effecting young people's transitions from a manual to a non-manual job. Often this was a modest career in government service although the imperial government had done nothing to encourage it.

The Crisis of the Concordat

In fact, the Empire meant to control popular opinions, not educate them, and its primary instrument was the Concordat and its accompanying police regulations. The Concordat recognized the right of the government to regulate the public exercise of religion and this provided the justification for the Organic Articles published on 18 germinal An X (8 April 1802). This was an extremely detailed law which restrained considerably the powers of the papacy in France. Despite protests from Rome, the government revived a number of measures taken from the old monarchy and added a few of its own. It gave the Church an almost military hierarchy. The publication of papal bulls, the convocation of national councils, the establishment of cathedral chapters and seminaries, and the creation of new parishes were all subject to government approval. The duties of archbishops, bishops and parish priests such as maintaining the faith, pay scales, residence, visitations, clerical garb and certain career requirements, were all specified. Diocesan and parish boundaries were fixed while below the bishops there were three thousand or so curés, ideally one per canton, who in turn were to supervise 'desservants' in the 'succursales' or communes. Desservants alone could be removed by the bishops and initially were unpaid. The clergy was also required to denounce all crimes, subversive or otherwise, to the police, as they had been expected to do in the Old Regime, and to preach obedience to the state, particularly to the conscription laws, a tendency reinforced by the publication of the *Imperial Catechism* in 1806. The Feast of the Assumption, 15 August, was even followed the next day by the celebration of Saint-Napoléon, once the story of this obscure martyr was unearthed.

The reconstruction of the Church was a long process which continued well beyond 1815. Portalis, the first Minister of Religion, intended to strike a reasonably fair balance between the former refractory and constitutional clergies, but in fact the application of the Concordat tended to benefit the refractory more. Thus a document which gave the state an enormous authority over the Church could be evaded and stretched in practice to suit the perceptions and biases of the refractory clergy. Bonaparte led the way by appointing twelve former constitutionals and sixteen refractories to the new episcopate and promoting thirty-one refractories and only one constitutional. In the dioceses, overt discrimination and circumstances combined to keep the constitutionals out. In the Bouches-du-Rhône, for example, less than one quarter of the curés and less than one third of the desservants were former constitutionals. In the diocese of Rouen, headed by the brother of the Second Consul, a little over one in ten of the cures and one in five of the succursales went to constitutionals. Of twenty-seven appointments to cures in the diocese between 1806 and 1818, only one went to a constitutional. In some regions of the country, the dislike for constitutionals was so great that even their parishes were suppressed on the pretext that they were too small. But such discrimination was only partly a question of bias against men the bishops considered schismatics. In the Mâconnais, 80 per cent of the cures had taken the oath but refractories received 35 per cent of the parishes in 1802 because so many constitutionals had retracted after the Terror. In the Morbihan, there were simply not enough constitutionals left as loss of vocation, dechristianization, marriage and the chouans had thinned their ranks considerably. In the diocese of Quimper, the bishop's policy was to appoint priests to their former parishes whether they were former constitutionals or not, but since the deportations of 1792 and 1797 had kept the corps of refractories better intact, four of five cures went to them. Throughout the west, a generally hostile laity often refused to accept constitutionals and noisily demonstrated against them, much as they had ten years before. Even the appointment of a constitutional bishop did not achieve the equity Portalis desired. Monseigneur Belmas in the Nord had to accept a generally refractory clergy because refusal of the oath had been very high in 1791. He had also to submit to an unedifying campaign against him from his subordinates until the prefect forbade all discussion of the past. It was a sad end to the constitutional church whose priests had been celebrated as part of a national regeneration in 1791 only to be despised and cast aside by the revolutionaries and royalists alike.

The Concordat was close to a restoration of the refractory church. Civil authority often tolerated violation of its spirit. So long as the clergy did not preach sedition, and few did even in 1814, the Consulate and Empire had coopted a major source of popular discontent. In the first appointments, the prefects simply insisted that those rare priests who had served actively in the royalist armies should not be given places. The bishops usually concurred because such men were too independent and often too violent. The prefects tolerated much in other spheres. Although it was strictly illegal, they ignored the humiliating retractions that were forced on the constitutionals in the dioceses of Aix, Bayeux, Bordeaux, Nancy, Rennes and elsewhere. They also tolerated ceremonies 'cleansing' parish churches which had been 'sullied' by the Mass of the constitutionals and they ignored collective re-baptisms and re-marriages. Bishops were eventually able to impose outdoor religious festivities. The government also permitted the return of the religious orders, at first those dedicated to teaching and hospitals, and ended by subsidizing foreign missions. The amount of money devoted to religious affairs mounted, desservants received a modest salary in 1804 because communes proved exceptionally niggardly in supporting them and, until the break with the Pope in 1809, seminarians were exempted from military service. Within a decade, poor-relief institutions were largely rechristianized and the period witnessed the beginning, or rather the revival, of paternalistic conceptions of poor-relief which were to continue in ever more elaborate forms for the next half-century. In Montpellier, for example, nursing sisters ensured that the hospital routine was governed by the traditional liturgy and calendar, the bishop chaired the hospital board and priests and pious laymen organized much private charity. When the Bourbons returned in 1814, the Church had gone far in restoring its influence over public life and even in regaining some of its former independence.

None of this was accomplished painlessly and there remained serious problems at the pastoral level. Revolutionary dechristianization had wrought such havoc in the Marne that only one third of the priests could be restored to their former parishes, 40 parishes had no priest at all as late as the Year XIII and since there had been so few ordinations in the 1790s, nearly 40 per cent of the parish clergy were aged over sixty. In the diocese of Rouen, the figure was 30 per cent, and in 1815 nearly half the parish clergy in the country were over sixty. In the Vendée, where the executions, drownings, massacres and deportations had been terrible, only a little over half the Old Regime clergy was available for service in 1801 and of these, over a third died in the next ten years and were only slowly replaced. In the nearby Vienne, nearly half the secular clergy had died or had disappeared without trace in 1801. The problem of ageing and replacement was as severe as it was because in most parts of the country, the newly established seminaries did not graduate enough priests – some parishes in the Var had to make do with Italian priests until the 1820s – but even where they did, as in the exceptional diocese of Vannes, it was accomplished at the price of an increasing ruralization which was not new, and an increasing plebeianization which, on the whole, was. A more rural and modest recruitment did not necessarily reflect on the Concordat clergy's abilities or the quality of pastoral care but it was certainly one of the roots of the antiurban antiliberal attitudes which turned the nineteenth-century church in on itself. Consider the attitude of the students in the seminary at Vannes to the better-off bourgeois, all the more remarkable since the town was one of the most backward in the country: they disdained 'the luxury and wealth of the cities which they could not share . . . and the success of the young gentlemen who, enriched by a better up-bringing, stole the prizes and applause from them in every class in society'.

The crisis of clerical recruitment may even have aided the restoration of Old Regime forms of popular piety in the sense that it made controlling these forms more difficult. Assertions from the clerical and government elite that the people were indifferent to religion on the eve of the Concordat have to be treated sceptically. The councillor of state, François de Nantes, observed, for example, that 'Avignon and Aix are the only towns where the priests have a great influence. There is no question of it at Marseille, and at Toulon, there is no priest and there are no services of any sort.' But lack of priests or clerical influence did not mean that popular piety had died out. Among the first lay organizations to be revived were the parish and trade confraternities and funeral societies, authorized or not, and with them an old debate among authorities about institutions which easily escaped official control. Nothing could better illustrate the government's desire to regulate what it could not suppress than the subprefect of Tarascon's opinion that confraternities should be contained within the archbishop's surveillance because they limited 'libertinage', added to 'the majesty of the cult' and gave 'a very great ascendancy to the priests'. But it was not always possible to channel popular religious feelings. Priests who boycotted pilgrimages to local shrines or feasts of patron saints because they usually degenerated into mass drinking bouts often had to restrain a quiet rage as the celebrations took place anyway. Country people showed a great deal of nostalgia for feast days suppressed under the Concordat. In the Côte-d'Or, a region not noted for its fervour, peasants 'daring to take the place of the the curés . . . filled the functions of the sacerdoce in the most scandalous manner . . . recited the prayers of the Mass [and] sang vespers . . .' to celebrate Nativity in 1807. There was little lay or religious authorities could do about this just as they could do nothing to eradicate the elaborate cult of the dead in Lower Brittany where people left biscuits out for drowned sailors at All Saints or warmed rocks, thought to be anchors for lost souls, in bonfires on St John the Baptist's day.

But if the Concordat unleashed a burst of popular religious sentiments thus giving people a freedom of expression under an authoritarian government which they had not enjoyed before, there were still signs at the individual level of a mutation in religious feeling. At Montpellier and no doubt elsewhere, for example, bequests to traditional charities and requests for Masses for the souls of the departed continued the slow decline which had begun over a half-century before. Whatever this means – a decline in religious sentiment as such, the transformation of the baroque and ostentatious ceremonies of old into a more private faith or a growing conviction that family members would care for the needs of the dead – at the very least, a different form of religious expression was emerging. More significant perhaps was the decline in the national birth rate, an indication that at least among men, a quiet defiance of traditional Catholic teaching on the family and reproduction was spreading. Knowledge and use of 'evil secrets' was not new but the revolutionary decades appear to have marked a decisive step.

Family, Law and Property

The Civil Code reflected many of the aspirations of the revolutionary period, the desire for a uniform system of law, for legal equality and for the protection of the individual and property; but in matters relating to the family it added a number of provisions which reflected the preoccupation with subordination and authority of the Consular period. The Code was above all concerned with the disposition of the property of households between and among generations. Consequently, it strengthened legal rights of the male head. Women could not be members of a family council, exercise wardship or be a legal witness to a birth, marriage or death. A married woman had few legal rights over community property and could not sell, alienate or mortgage even the property brought to the community by her own dowry. The Civil Code retained the principle of divorce enunciated during the revolutionary period but instead of the extremely liberal provisions of the law of 29

September 1792 which included incompatibility, it recognized only mutual consent, adultery, beatings and imprisonment as grounds, whereas desertion, which was frequent and which left many women destitute, was not. Furthermore, instead of the emphasis of the revolutionary period on reconciliation through *ad hoc* family and neighbourhood councils which unfortunately had never been an entire success, the Code introduced an appalling double standard. The husband could obtain a divorce for his wife's adultery but the wife could only do so if the husband brought his mistress into the household. A husband could even have his adulterous wife imprisoned for up to two years. In the event, divorce in both periods, whatever the method of obtaining it, was very rare. In Rouen, for example, they averaged 161 per year under the Convention, 71 under the Directory and 8 per year during the Empire, undoubtedly because marriages at the time were as much economic alliances among families as love matches. Couples also married fairly late in life so that men and women had relatively low expectations of emotional satisfaction. Nonetheless, the intention of Bonaparte, who presided over half the sessions of the commission which drew up the Code, and its draftors to impose a comparable subordination and hierarchy over the family as they were trying to impose on the nation as a whole is clear enough.

There were also few constraints over the disposition of private property, which, after all, was the ideal of all the revolutionary assemblies. Contracts always favoured men of property. Thus tenants had no legal security on the land they farmed beyond the stipulations of the lease, their personal property could be seized for arrears and they could be imprisoned. The law of 22 germinal An XI (12 April 1803) forbade attempts on the part of employers and employees to undertake actions in restraint of trade by conspiracies to lower salaries or by strikes to raise them, but provided much more severe penalties for workers than for employers. Workers were also obliged to carry a 'livret' or passbook to be held by the employer in which the details of the employee's work record were kept. The livret thus helped ensure a working man's docility. The Civil Code also increased the freedom of testators to dispose of their property. Where the Convention required an absolutely equal division of property among heirs, the Code permitted a testator to reserve anywhere between one quarter and one half of the property, depending upon the number of heirs, for a single heir. Thus the Code permitted a preference for eldest sons and the partial maintenance of family holdings. By law, proprietors could also create a 'majorat' or entail, forbidding the alienation of their property and allowing for its perpetual transmission through the family. Failing the invocation of these devices, however, property was to be divided equally among heirs. Although majorats were fairly rare, no one knows for certain whether testators followed a strategy of favouring particular heirs or not, even though nineteenth-century commentators were convinced that the Code was responsible for breaking up family holdings. This was misleading since several Old Regime provincial codes had permitted equal division and there is some evidence that even in provinces whose codes had tried to render it difficult, testators worked towards equal inheritance anyway.

How the Empire was Ruled: Conscription and Taxation

The Consulate and Empire established themselves by force but they did not always rule that way. On matters of conscription for instance, the government imposed itself on the nation through a combination of intimidation, guile and incentives. Throughout the revolutionary years, conscription and resistance to it had been one of the many elements linking popular royalism, chouannerie, brigandage and simple disobedience. The Consulate inherited all of these problems following the war crisis of the Year VII and the near failure of the levies of that year. It naturally used the same methods the Convention and Directory had to try to bring draft-dodging under control: patrols by the gendarmerie, encouraging denunciations, billeting troops on recalcitrant communes and sending mobile columns of soldiers on rapid searches through forests, wastelands and mountains. In themselves, these methods would not have been any more successful than in the past without several other steps. By law, the government made the communes responsible for their draft-dodgers and required them to provide substitutes for successful evaders. This must have done much to shatter the community and kinship links which made evasion possible. The government also took account of economic resources and regional attitudes to military service, and asked more of the frontier departments of the east and often considerably less from the west, the Midi and the annexed territories of the Rhineland. Thus in the Year IX, it demanded one conscript for every 860 people in the Haut-Rhin, one per 4930 in the Finistère, one per 1204 in the Lozère and one per 2208 in the four Rhine departments. Greater centralization, making prefects' careers depend upon fulfilling their departments' quotas, greater coordination between the prefects and the military authorities, assigning officers in each department to oversee conscription and offering cash rewards were among the administrative measures taken to secure obedience. The Concordat also helped in immeasurable ways since the clergy was expected to preach obedience to conscription from the beginning. One sign of the success of the Concordat was in the west, which met its deliberately reduced quotas without serious trouble when conscription was applied to the region in the Year XII for the first time since 1793. Above all, the Consulate demanded far less of the country than either the Montagnard Convention or the Directory had. In the five years between the Years VIII and XII, the government conscripted about 200,000 men, that is less than half the number required in the single levy of the Year VII, and less than one in five of every eligible young man. Military victory, the destruction of the royalist bands which conscription had helped produce and which in turn protected draft-dodgers, as well as the Concordat, permitted the government to align its administrative capacity to raise troops with the nation's willingness to submit. The contrasts with the revolutionary years were dramatic. The three major forced levies of the 1790s – February and August 1793 and the Year VII – all produced less than half the number of conscripts expected. Throughout the Consulate and up to 1808 (which therefore covers the early call-ups to fill the voids of the campaigns between 1805 and Tilsit, and an increase in the number of conscripts of nearly 50 per cent), well over 90 per cent of the young men actually joined their regiments. Punishment for evaders also appears to have become much more certain. As the administrative machinery tightened, the number of condemnations declined. Between the Years XII and XIII, punishments inflicted in the once brigandage-ridden Department of the Loire fell from 1597 to 836, in the Haute-Loire from 1066 to 562 and in the troubled Nord from 1270 to 501. The link with brigandage had been virtually broken. In 1809, there were a mere 18 stagecoach robberies in the entire Empire, in 1810, only 11; in 1809, 168 murders, in 1810, only 167.

Few Frenchmen accepted conscription with enthusiasm and evasion remained a problem to the end. In the west and the Massif Central, for example, young men carried talismans to recruiting centres to protect themselves from drawing the wrong number and parents gave their sons charms against death in battle. Self-mutilation, destruction or falsification of records, marrying aged widows to become the sole support of a family and bribery of officials and doctors were commonplace down to 1814 but this merely shifted the burden to the less cunning, for at no point during the Empire was anything like a majority of those eligible actually conscripted. For all the devastation of his wars, Napoleon conscripted about two million men between 1800 and 1814 or about 7 per cent of the total population; by contrast, the Third Republic conscripted four times as many between 1914 and 1919, or about 20 per cent of the population.

Draft-dodging remained a problem for the Empire because not even a dictatorship could override certain geographical facts and political attitudes. In the Hautes-Pyrénées where escaping over treacherous sheep-tracks and smugglers' trails to Spain was fairly easy for knowledgeable locals, 40 per cent of the conscripts evaded as late as 1809. In the Puy-de-Dôme, the prefect felt that it simply was not worth the effort to send gendarmes into the mountains to pursue the families of draft-dodgers when whole villages decamped with their meagre belongings to hideouts higher up. The scale of the government's demands was yet another element. After the amnesty of 1810, there were only 1250 deserters and draft-dodgers being sought in the Puy-de-Dôme from all the classes from 1806 onwards, but the next year there were another 1500. Even so, this did not approach the 4000 who evaded the call-up of the Year VII. This example suggests that administrative capacity was important too. Chouannerie which fed on anticonscription sentiments was latent in the Côtes-du-Nord until 1807 but the department met all of its quotas down to the end of the Empire. So too did the Var and the Nord where religious troubles, anticonscription and brigandage had gone hand in hand in the 1790s. Political factors were clearly important too. There were only 19 draft-dodgers in the nine separate levies in 'revolutionary' Finistère between 1809 and 1813, while the 'chouan' Morbihan next door had 900 in the five of 1813. In the levy of 1814, which was a disaster nationally, Finistère not only met its quota but provided 350 volunteers. In general terms, it would appear that well into 1813 resistance to conscription was less than it had been under the Consulate, let alone the Directory. It was only with the massive levies of over one million men following the catastrophe in Russia that officials became genuinely alarmed. By then, the conscription service was overwhelmed by the demands placed on it, national morale sagged, especially after the Battle of Leipzig in October 1813, and public opinion was shocked by the government's attempt to conscript married men or men who were the sole support of their families. Until then, the administration was strong enough and intimidating enough to prevent conscripts from voting with their feet, no matter what their feelings.

Aside from taxation which affected everyone, conscription was the most important institution linking state and nation. Its administration illustrates much about the attitudes of the men in power to their fellow countrymen. It was grossly unequal, thus demonstrating that the loss of equality accompanied the loss of liberty. Differentiating conscription demands by region may have shown an empirical good sense but it was still the case that the Ile-de-France was expected to surrender five young men for every one from Brittany. Such a flagrant regional inequality diminished over time as the regime became stronger and more informed about the demographic profile of each department but it never altered the opportunity for a rich man to pay someone to replace him. This particularly vicious amendment to the Jourdan law was passed in the first legislative session of the Consulate by the Tribunate and Legislative Body, by men who had all been appointed and who would never have to face direct popular election. Such was the result of Sieyès's constitution exercising authority from above. Bonaparte himself considered replacement a natural consequence of economic inequality. Thus 5–10 per cent of the conscripts managed to buy themselves out. That the poor had to be greatly tempted is suggested by the extraordinarily high price of a replacement – it rose from 1900 francs to 3600 francs in the Côte-d'Or between 1805 and 1811; that is, from more than six to more than nine times the annual income of an unskilled labourer. Conscription discriminated against the poor in informal ways as well. Among the wealthy families of Upper Normandy, there were not only more sons who had bought a replacement than there were officers, there was also a remarkably high number of merchants' sons who managed to get themselves places in such exempted professions as ships' carpenters. In fact, the authorities had to hush up a scandal involving more than two hundred families who had bribed exemptions of one sort or another lest it create an unfortunate impression among the common people.

Such partiality undoubtedly contributed to the increasing hostility to conscription which manifested itself as the regime collapsed in 1814. The same result occurred with taxation. With the renewal of war in 1803–4, the government had more recourse to indirect taxes, in other words to taxing consumers and the poor. Although the Directory revived these Old Regime devices, most notably the *octroi* (in effect tariffs on certain goods entering towns and cities), the Empire expanded them greatly. In the Year XII, the government regrouped taxes on tobacco, playing cards, coach seats and hallmarks into the *droits réunis* and extended them to alcoholic beverages. The *droits réunis* were exceptionally unpopular in the wine-growing districts since inspectors could snoop in wine cellars, prevent shipment of unstamped bottles and verify stocks of wholesalers and innkeepers. In 1806, the state reestablished taxes on salt which recalled the *gabelle* of the Old Regime, raised postal rates (which varied by distance at that time) by 50 per cent, and finally, in 1810, reestablished the state's tobacco monopoly. All of this was done in the name of sound finances which for many apologists in governing circles simply meant shifting the burden of taxation from property-holders to consumers. There were even some officials who claimed this regressive fiscal policy aided economic growth. In fact, it probably had the opposite effect as the state came to rely increasingly on indirect revenues and so reduced mass purchasing power. Thus, while the taxes on land rose only slowly until near the end, the yield of various indirect taxes increased by well over 50 per cent. The prospect of public hostility mattered little to Napoleon. As First Consul, he had rejected indirect taxes; as Emperor, he thundered, 'Don't I have my gendarmes, my prefects, my priests? If there is a rising, I'll have five or six rebels hanged and the rest will bend.'

No Economic Breakthrough

Increased tax revenues signified a genuine increase in economic activity and with it a real prosperity for some, at least down to the crisis of 1811. Between the cyclical phases of 1798–1802 and 1817–20, the price of wheat rose by 25 per cent, rye by 14 per cent, wine by 20 per cent and beef by 33 per cent. This certainly benefited most of those able to sell on the market, from large landowners to modest owner-occupiers. Contemporaries often remarked on the improvement in peasant dress, housing and diet at least in the cereal-growing regions of the north. The rise in living standards was probably slower in the viticultural districts of the Midi since the revenues of the taxes on alcohol increased by 240 per cent between 1806 and 1812, in itself a sufficient explanation for the unpopularity of the *droits réunis*. Agricultural workers too saw little real change in their incomes despite labour shortages caused by conscription, since their wages rose by only 20 per cent. In fact, the major beneficiaries were the big landowners whose rents rose by 50 per cent. Since the demand for land remained high, they were able to command high rents. Undoubtedly, this allowed them to reap most of the benefits of the abolition of the tithe and feudal dues for themselves. Tenants, as they had been doing since the closing years of the Old Regime and the 1790s, had to tighten their belts still further.

Stagnant real wages in the countryside and rising rents and prices were a sign that demographic pressures rather than any significant changes in production or productivity explain most of the evolution of the rural economy during the Empire. Despite much official encouragement, land-clearing and swamp drainage were disappointingly minimal. Yield ratios were not significantly different than they had been hundreds of years before. Labour productivity in the countryside remained well behind that of England and the gap was to open still wider after 1815. In other words, the big landowners did not reinvest their swollen rents back into agriculture and probably continued the habits of sumptuous display of their ancestors or, if they had been émigrés, spent their time trying to reconstitute their estates. Since small and medium-sized holders' margins were too small and since the urban sector of about one fifth of the population was no different than in the previous century, there were few demand pressures driving agriculture towards a genuine transformation. Despite the abolition of feudalism in the countryside, therefore, there was no 'capitalist' revolution in agriculture.

In fact, economic warfare and technical innovations were bringing about a severe structural crisis in both town and country. The prices of many traditional textiles fell by around 30 per cent which must have brought considerable misery to many northern towns and to a deindustrializing countryside. Lyon and Nîmes, their hinterlands and Piedmont were even worse off since the price of silk fell by 97 per cent. Consequently, wages in the textile industries overall dropped by 40 per cent. In part, this crisis was due to the wars and the blockades, whose effects were exceptionally serious after the traditional Spanish market was cut off, and in part to a swing away from silks among the upper classes. Above all, cottons were rapidly replacing traditional textiles because of the government's strategy of prohibiting the importation of British manufactured cottons. Behind the high protective wall, the cotton industry grew at a breathtaking pace throughout the region bounded by Ghent, Rouen, Paris and the northern and eastern frontiers. The population of Mulhouse, for example, grew by over 40 per cent between 1800 and 1810 thanks to cotton and calico printing. The number of cotton-spinning firms in Paris doubled between 1803 and 1806, tripled between 1806 and 1808 and nearly doubled again to 57 between 1808 and 1811. In 1807, there were 12,270 cotton workers in Paris, 7900 of whom worked for the giant Richard-Lenoir firm whose revenues were 24 million francs in 1810. But much of this was a forced and unstable growth due to war. The British blockade raised the price of raw cotton to levels considerably higher than those in London, sudden shortages threw the manufacturers into disarray and, understandably in the circumstances, the industry was plagued by shortages of skilled workers, speculation and undercapitalization. Richard-Lenoir could only survive the crisis of 1810–11 with government loans, and when the frontiers were thrown open in 1814 the industry nearly collapsed.

If there were signs in textiles and chemicals of the industrial revolution to come, most manufacturing remained artisanal. In 1791, there were only fifty firms in the capital which employed a hundred or more workers; during the Empire, there may well have been fewer, although the ratio of employer to employee was identical. Even Richard-Lenoir carried on an old practice of having about one tenth of its workers in a central place, the rest scattered in a cottage-industry pattern throughout the city and the country districts. With the restoration of a court, Paris soon found its old vocation as a world centre of the luxury trades, particularly jewellery, clocks, porcelains and fine furniture. Thus in part, the revival of Paris industry was due to government, from the largesse it distributed to its functionaries and clients, itself partly financed from tribute from abroad. The structure of manufacturing in the provincial centres followed a similar pattern. The economic growth which took place within these old structures was real enough, however. One estimate puts production 50 per cent higher in 1810 than the 1780s and while this seems high, there was a modest prosperity. It was modest indeed for many ordinary people. Building workers' wages, always a sensitive indicator, rose by 20–25 per cent between the Consulate and early Restoration while wages overall rose by 24 per cent, enough to keep ahead of the rise in food prices but this does not take account of the incidence of taxation or the rise in urban rents which was at least as high as those in land.

The countryside suffered severely from the structural crisis in textiles since peasants and rural artisans traditionally derived substantial proportions of their income from processing woollens, flax and hemp. A simultaneous crisis in landholding weakened another major prop. There had been so much poverty in the eighteenth century because of the pressures of rising population on stable agricultural resources and this problem continued into the Empire and beyond. The population rose from 27.9 million in 1789 to 30.2 million in 1814. Young men and women had reacted to such 'Malthusian' pressures in the past by marrying later in life, but on the eve of the Revolution the age at first marriage for women began slowly to drop while the decline for men was dramatic, because many hoped to avoid conscription. Another 'Malthusian' reaction, but utterly forbidden, was to adopt birth control. Some couples had begun to practise this before the Revolution in parts of Normandy, Languedoc and the Ile-de-France, but after 1790 it had become general and national. Depending upon region, the number of births per married woman fell between 13 per cent and 28 per cent between mid-century and the Restoration. No one is certain why birth control spread so rapidly but it undoubtedly had much to do with the economic catastrophes of the 1790s and the relaxation of traditional family morality. Interestingly, the regions where it was practised most were generally those with a high proportion of constitutional priests. This suggests that the destruction of the constitutional clergy from 1793 onwards and the difficulty of staffing the Concordat church in these regions led to a relaxation of clerical discipline and with it a more independent attitude to family planning. In any case, if the number of births per family fell, infant and child mortality fell even more from the 1780s onwards so that life expectancy rose dramatically. The healthy generations born in the 1780s were thus coming to maturity in the Consulate and Empire. Thus the reservoirs of men for Napoleon's armies, thus too the pressure to pay high rents.

The revolutionary land settlement did little to alleviate the population-resources problem. In fact, in some ways it accelerated the very long trend of French agrarian history of the urban conquest of the land. In the Nord, for example, the share of peasant property rose from 30 per cent to 42 per cent but that of the bourgeoisie rose from 16 per cent to 28.5 per cent, each group an unequal victor over a despoiled church and weakened nobility. Peasants did better in the region around Chartres since their share rose from an average of 33.6 per cent in eight villages in 1790 to 44.6 per cent in 1820 whereas the share of the bourgeoisie rose from 26.4 per cent to only 29.6 per cent. But demographic pressures had raised the number of proprietors overall by 30 per cent over the same period. The peasant majority had to make do with the lion's share of the property of less than 5 hectares whereas the urban minority came close to monopolizing the holdings larger than 10 hectares. Such a process was very old. The formation of large holdings by clearing and purchase and the pulverizing of the peasant remainder had begun in the sixteenth century at Lattes in the Hérault. By 1677, the number of estates greater than 40 hectares had doubled and the average size had increased from 66 hectares to 84 hectares. In 1820, there were 15 such estates, averaging 125 hectares. The nearby village of Manguio had 8 estates larger than 100 hectares occupying 37 per cent of the surface in 1770; by 1820, there were 16 large estates occupying considerably more. In other words, even for the owner-occupying peasantry, the abolition of the various feudal levies had done little to provide the extra margin of security necessary to preserve their holdings for the next generation. Although there are no figures available, there must have been as much, if not more, poverty in 1815 as in 1789.

The Notables, a Powerless Elite

On the other hand, everything indicates that the rich did well out of the Empire. Who were they? The question is vital because historians have found the significance of the entire period in the altered nature of the elite. According to classical historiography of which Lefebvre was the last great exponent, a thrusting, ambitious bourgeoisie threw aside a privileged aristocracy in 1789, and, after a momentary challenge in the Year II, eventually consolidated its power under the Empire. Recent research on both the Old Regime and Revolution has shaken the classic view considerably and specialists on the Empire have done the same. In order to understand the relation between power and socioeconomic prominence, it is necessary to answer three related questions. What was the composition of the social elite? What was the relation between the social and administrative elites? What was the place of the old nobility in the new elite?

The imperial administration itself provided the basis for analysis of the elite by drawing up lists of notables, that is the most highly taxed in each department. This was a requirement of the Constitution of the Year X which used wealth to define eligibility to the departmental electoral colleges. The lists of numbers of the electoral colleges themselves have sometimes been used as a shorthand to define the notables as a whole. This can be a misleading procedure since the electorate as a whole selected their membership from the lists of the wealthy. Nonetheless, the results are instructive. A massive count of the arrondissement college lists for which there was no wealth qualification, and the departmental college lists for which there was, breaks 66,735 notables in the Empire in 1810 into 24.5 per cent proprietors, 33.9 per cent administrators, 14.4 per cent liberal professions, 10.8 per cent tradesmen, 8.2 per cent owner-occupiers, and others 8.2 per cent. Whatever the faults of nomenclature and selection, the men at the top of the social pyramid in the Empire derived their income from land, state service and the professions rather than from industry and commerce. The use of the lists of notables as a whole only accentuates the landed, service and professional basis of the elite. Over 60 per cent of the notables of the Haute-Garonne described themselves as 'proprietors', 23 per cent were in the professions and only 13 per cent were businessmen. Nearly one third of the notables of the arrondissement of Toulouse, 12 of the 30 wealthiest in the Vaucluse and 9 of 30 in the Ardèche had bought *biens nationaux*. This gave them a stake in any regime which promised to preserve them, which for the moment was the Empire, because Louis XVIII was still on record as promising to reverse this aspect of the land settlement. It is an indication too that *biens nationaux* did not underpin the notables and since these lands had been acquired at auction, an indication that the buyers were already well off. Elsewhere, there was the same feeble representation from the world of commerce and industry: 30.5 per cent in the Var, 8.2 per cent in the Isère, 8.5 per cent in Mont-Blanc and so on. For all its emergence as a banking and industrial centre during the Empire, even Paris fitted this pattern. In the Seine in the Year IX, businessmen accounted for 7 per cent of the notables, 28 per cent of the notables of the right bank of the city in the more accurate lists of 1809 and 24 per cent of the members of the electoral college.

Furthermore, given the enormous upheavals of the period, there had been surprisingly little renewal of the elites. In the once turbulent Var, for example, no more and probably less than 15 per cent of the wealthiest men were new. In the Gard, two thirds of the wealthiest members of the elite had not suffered from the Revolution and the other third, who had emigrated, were patiently recouping their fortunes. Three quarters of the members of the electoral colleges in the widely scattered departments of the Côte-d'Or, Haute-Garonne, Nord, Seine-Inférieure and Yonne were exercising the same professions in 1810 as they had been in 1789. If anything, there had been a ruralization of the elite during the period. In the Var, the rich commercial and manufacturing bourgeoisie was smaller in the Year IX than it had been in 1789. This phenomenon was especially marked all along the Atlantic seaboard from Saint-Malo, through Nantes to Bordeaux where the devastations of the 1790s and the blockade after 1807 convinced many of the old merchant families to follow a time-honoured tradition and reorient their portfolios into land. Of course, no one should exaggerate this movement. Landed proprietors had to live by the laws of the agricultural market too even if they did try to shift most of the burden to their tenants. Many of them as well as functionaries also invested in business and held bonds and many men designated as 'proprietors' on the lists were businessmen who had retired late in life to a safe and easily administered investment. But all this had been true in the Old Regime too. The elite was landed before the Revolution, it was landed after.

The Old Regime nobility continued to occupy an important place within this elite. Estimating the extent of noble losses of the revolutionary period is a risky business because no one knows for certain how many nobles there were in 1789. The more there were, the less significant the losses. It is clear enough that the most spectacular onslaughts on them in the period – execution and emigration – affected only a minority. Of the victims and émigrés whose social origins were known, 1158 and 16,431 respectively were nobles in a group that may have numbered 100,000 in 1789. Even raising the numbers to account for those executed after the Terror (e.g., Quiberon), or guessing that the requisitions, forced loans, revolutionary taxes and so on were applied more vigorously to the nobles who did manage to stay aloof from politics, suggests that the nobility was severely damaged but not destroyed. A prudent *attentisme*, which after all was the reaction of the majority, may even have paid off. The sequestration laws and the discriminatory policies were applied unevenly, unaffected family members maintained estates through sham transfers or divorces; unsold lands were returned in 1800–2 and forests in 1814; there are stories dating from both the Empire and the Restoration that owners of *biens nationaux*, fearing a general restoration, sold property to their former owners at bargain prices; and in 1825, the law known as the *milliard des émigrés* partially indemnified émigrés for their losses which certainly allowed some nobles the opportunity to reconstitute their estates. In the Sarthe, a department of civil war and moderate emigration, this restoration was more or less complete by 1830 but reconstitution was less successful elsewhere. Nobles in the war-ravaged Nord lost about one third of their property between 1789 and 1804 while those in the comparatively peaceful Eure-et-Loir lost about one fifth between 1791 and 1828.

One careful estimate suggests that a typical provincial noble may have lost one fifth of his land and one third of his income as a result of the Revolution. Perhaps so, but the economic circumstances of the Empire permitted the old nobility to compensate for sharply increased taxes and the loss of feudal dues by raising rents on the lands that remained. Moreover, such an estimate does not take account of the possibility that the nobility was a smaller group after the Revolution, so that while some families were utterly ruined others managed to survive somehow. Figures for the 1830s, which appear to include the imperial nobility and the post-1815 creations, show that the Breton nobility was far less than half its size of the previous century, the nobility of Limoges had dropped by over half and only the Toulousain nobility was about the same.

If the Old Regime nobility declined in numbers – a trend which began in the seventeenth century, incidentally, not in 1793 – the survivors retained a prominent position at the top of the social heap. A survey of the 1000 biggest landowners in the country in the Year XI shows that 33.9 per cent were former nobles, 14.4 per cent were rentiers, 37 per cent were in the liberal professions and 13 per cent were manufacturers. This hints at a decline in the share of

landed wealth even though there are no comparable figures for the
Old Regime. The suspicion is confirmed by an examination of the
nobles of the Marais quarter in Paris. In 1749, nobles comprised one
third of those whose marriage contracts were over 50,000 *livres*,
over half of those over 100,000 and all of the millionaires. Although
the parlementaire nobility still comprised one third of the notables
in 1809 in the same district, their fortunes were commonly in the
15,000 francs to 20,000 francs range. It is doubtful whether any
could have financed the fabulous marriage contracts of their
ancestors since their fortunes, heavily invested in state bonds
before the Revolution, had been ruined as much by the inflation
and bankruptcies as by executions and confiscations. Still, nobles
were a wealthy group even if they had to share the top rungs with
non-titled rentiers, officials and bankers. In the rich and dynamic
first arrondissement, they comprised 81.2 per cent of those with
landed revenues over 60,000 francs, 36 per cent of those between
10,000 francs and 50,000 francs and 36.8 per cent of those with less
than 10,000 francs. Moreover, their share of private wealth was
disproportionately large. In the Paris of 1820, they filed 1.4 per cent
of the wills for 18.2 per cent of the value and among the largest
fortunes, 40 per cent of the wills for 70 per cent of the value. As
late as 1840, 10 of the 15 wealthiest men in the country were
descended from Old Regime nobles. Once again the pattern of
fortunes in Paris mirrored that of the nation. The lists of imperial
notables indicate that former nobles comprised between one sixth
and one quarter of the 600 most highly taxed, and their share was
exceptionally large. Among the 30 most highly taxed in Mont-
Blanc, 20 were nobles, in the Gard 16, in the Var 26, in the Hérault
21 and so on. As in the Old Regime, aristocrats were the wealthiest
single class.

What had gone irrevocably for the old aristocracy were the
partial fiscal immunities and the virtual occupational monopolies
they had enjoyed under the old monarchy. They became a part of
the ruling group, making contributions out of proportion to their
numbers but not as overwhelmingly as in the past. The notables as
a whole were only a part of the ruling group too. They were not a
ruling gentry in the contemporary English or American sense.
Wealth in itself only made one eligible for the electoral colleges
which met rarely and even then had trouble rounding up half their
number for their meetings. No wonder, since as the regime became
increasingly bureaucratic and despotic, representative institutions

of all sorts at the national and local level atrophied. For all his belief that wealthy men had a stake in the regime, Napoleon had no intention of giving any real power as such. They were an important reservoir of talent for the state apparatus, not much more.

The notables contributed to public life but did not entirely dominate it. Indeed the state had a powerful influence over the electoral colleges, not only formally through Napoleon's powers of appointment but because at least a third of their members were civil or military functionaries. The distinction between bureaucrat and illustrious citizen could be blurred, however, because these men were often related. In the Allier, for instance, about two dozen civic-minded families, continuously allying to each other through marriages to produce intricate family trees, emerged in 1790 to produce prefects, deputies, bureaucrats, local councillors and mayors in lush variety for the next hundred years. Curiously, only the Jacobins of the 1790s produced no prominent descendants. In the Ain, as well, a substantial proportion of the members of the electoral colleges had participated in local government during the Revolution and a clear majority among the lawyer-notables had done so.

Among the important institutions of state, notability was allied with 'capacité', which, incidentally, was the ideal the ruling class had of itself down to the 1870s. Of Napoleon's ministers, for example, about one third were ex-nobles, all, except Talleyrand, of fairly minor extraction. The rest derived from professional or military families but his most brilliant Minister of the Interior, the scientist-industrialist Chaptal, was of recent peasant stock. Among the generals, the percentage of former nobles steadily fell from 26.6 on 1 April 1802 to 20.1 on 1 April 1814, which refutes the frequently repeated comment that Napoleon increasingly favoured the nobles. Nor is it likely that he reconciled the counterrevolutionary aristocracy to his regime. Some 1353 generals served the Empire but only eight had fought in the émigré armies. It is also a cliché of the period that every soldier had a marshal's baton in his haversack. This is true enough in the cases of Ney and Gouvion Saint-Cyr who were born to very modest families or of Lannes, Brune and Suchet who rose from the voluntary and conscripted levies of 1791–3. The overwhelming proportion of generals, however, were born to commercial, civil service or military families who had already destined their sons to military careers before the Revolution. The elimination of ancestry requirements opened possibilities these men would never have had otherwise but real career mobility was still restricted to a relatively narrow elite. It was practically closed to the population as a whole. The pattern among the prefects was almost identical: no 'noble reaction' as such, recruitment mostly from bourgeois families, increasingly professional training, promotion following further experience, and close supervision by superiors. By the time one reached the upper echelons of the state apparatus, the civil and military personnel of the Empire were professionals.

The Mechanics of Repression and Opposition

Linking the old and new elites, bureaucratizing the administration, rewarding friends and loyal officials, currying the rich, making the principle of subordination a feature of every institution, mobilizing the young into the military were all characteristics of Napoleonic government. So was repression. As the war made increasing demands on the country and the administration became more professional, the regime became more dictatorial. Representative institutions counted for next to nothing. The Legislative Body met for only seventeen days in 1811. There was no session at all in 1812 and the first meeting of 1813 was notable only for the Emperor's brave speech and the grant of more money following the catastrophe in Russia. The enfeebled state of quasi-representative institutions was even more evident in the provinces. If the Côtes-du-Nord was at all typical, the sessions of the general councils became more perfunctory from 1807 onwards, declining to a mere three days in both 1812 and 1813, just long enough to vote an address of loyalty to the Emperor. Outside the government apparatus, there was no legal forum for opposition. The Paris press, cut to thirteen then to nine newspapers in 1800, was further reduced to four in 1811. From 1805, a system of prior censorship evolved and the government taxed newspaper profits heavily. Napoleon regularly dictated articles himself or told his ministers or editors what to write. From 1807, the provincial press had to take all its political articles from the official *Moniteur* and after 1810, there was to be only one newspaper per department. Prefects too tried their hands as journalists and the result was predictably boring and misleading. Writers too were subject to prior censorship and for those who felt they could get along with the regime, like Bernardin de Saint-Pierre, Monge or Sismondi, there were handsome pensions. For those who could not, like Mme de Staël, Necker's daughter, there was police harassment, seizure of works and eventually deportation. Finally, in addition to the continuing bureaucratization of government, the manipulation of public opinion, the system of rewards and exile for friends and enemies, the government introduced a system of administrative arrest in 1810 and designated prisons where internees could be held indefinitely without trial. The practice was not new and while there were comparatively few such prisoners, at least by modern standards – 810 in 1811, 289 in 1812 of whom 106 were political, 640 in 1814 of whom 320 were political – there were still far more than those held by *lettre de cachet* in 1789.

There was always opposition to the Empire, from elements in the Church after 1809, from royalists, from some of the common people and from malcontents in the military but it is doubtful whether that opposition was growing or was even very effective in undermining the 'masses of granite'. An examination of the sources and strength of opposition illustrates a great deal about how the imperial administration worked.

One of the tests of how strong the regime felt itself to be was how it handled the breach with the papacy. This was a crisis which did not have the consequences that might have been expected because Napoleon was able to divide the prelates and eventually to intimidate Pius VII himself into submission. The crisis began with the annexation of Rome and the papal states in 1809, ostensibly to bring these territories more firmly into the Continental System but ultimately because the self-proclaimed successor to Charlemagne and the Caesars could not resist possessing the ancient imperial capital. The Pope was arrested and interned in the northern Italian town of Savona. Pius's response was to forbid his former subjects to obey the new conquerors and to refuse to annul the marriage with Josephine or bless that with Marie-Louise. More seriously, he excommunicated Napoleon and refused to invest bishops. On learning of the excommunication decree, Napoleon dismissed the Pope as a 'raving madman' and claimed that Pius had excommunicated himself. This was very nearly true. Although thirteen cardinals refused to attend the wedding with Marie-Louise and although twenty-seven dioceses soon languished because the Pope refused to confer spiritual powers on new appointees, Napoleon was able to take advantage of the not yet extinguished traditions of Gallican liberties and the episcopate's desire for a compromise. An ecclesiastical commission, uneasy at the Pope's use of spiritual powers in a temporal dispute, claimed that a national council was a higher authority than the Pope himself. When the council itself finally met in June 1811, most of the councillors showed their good will by attending the baptism of the King of Rome and after some high-handed pressure, including the arrest of three bishops, the prelates finally agreed that a metropolitan could confer canonical institution if the papacy deferred for more than six months. This was no victory for Napoleon, however, since the council required that the Pope approve this decision and it was hardly forthcoming. Pius was then moved to Fontainebleau in June 1812 and six months later, Napoleon, turning on his usual charm, got the old man to accept the council's decision. Pius understood this as a secret negotiating document but, having learned nothing about the man who had produced the Organic Articles, was astonished when Napoleon immediately published it as a 'Concordat'. His protests were swept aside, he remained interned and cardinals who supported him were arrested. Only the defeat of 1814 averted the papacy's becoming an appendage of the Ministry of Religion.

The long quarrel with the Pope undoubtedly shocked Catholic opinion in regions directly outside French control, particularly in Spain, where it hardened opinion still more against the irreligious usurper. Within France itself, the consequences were considerably muted. Despite the dissolution of pro-papal religious orders like the Sulpicians in 1810 and the spectre of arrests of bishops and cathedral canons, many churchmen remained quiescent. In the archdiocese of Aix and Arles, for example, some clerics recalled the persecutions of the Year II and gave funeral orations for Louis XVI but such manifestations were rare. As late as 1814, priests in the old *Vendée militaire* preached obedience to the conscription laws and in the diocese of Rouen, clerics preached that desertion was against religion despite the fact the archbishop had refused to attend Marie-Louise's wedding. The catechism of the diocese of Quimper continued to refer to military service as a 'sacred duty' and the bishop circularized the priests to 'recall to their duty the cowards who evade their holy obligation to serve their country'. In this diocese which contained well over three hundred parish priests, only four were designated as enemies of the government. Whether the reason for this continued acquiescence was gratitude for the

Concordat or fear of the power of the imperial police, Napoleon could afford to treat the Pope with characteristic arrogance.

But the quarrels with the Pope did contribute towards giving a new direction to royalism. Of course, royalism never died out. As late as 1808, the police uprooted a vast network of safe houses, courier-drops and hideouts in Brittany which served to inform the British of naval dispositions in Lorient and Brest. This had been masterminded from Jersey since 1794, had informed on chouan operations and after their defeat became a classic spy operation run by émigrés and French royalists. After the police uprooted this remnant, genuine royalist activity, as opposed to a bucolic nostalgia and *attentisme*, risked dying out. Ferdinand de Bertier, a son of the intendant of Paris who had been murdered in 1789, took it upon himself to recast remaining royalist sentiment. His prayers told him that his only sign would be success and, undaunted by this rather Calvinist mark of religious favour, he founded yet another royalist secret society known as the 'Chevaliers de la Foi'. As a group, the Chevaliers are more interesting for their quixotic romanticism and what they reveal about royalist mentalities than for their political impact. Formed in 1809, the Chevaliers helped distribute the bull of excommunication, which the police would have preferred to suppress, and spread antigovernment propaganda generally, but they were no ordinary secret society. With its cells called *bannières* under the direction of a *sénéchal*, it reflected both a reviving sense of medieval chivalry and the flourishing antifreemasonry of royalist circles. Indeed the abbé Barruel, whose celebrated history of the Revolution explained the collapse of the Old Regime as a masonic plot, was an organizational consultant. Like the continental freemasons and the Philanthropic Institutes of the Directory, the Chevaliers were organized in circles with only the inner group knowing the true royalist purposes while the front organizations masked as public charities. There were also the same heady array of secret handshakes, signs and the menacing oaths as candidates were inducted from one organizational ring and one level of knowledge to the next. The Chevaliers soon claimed to have *bannières* in most of the cities and regions of the country and the claim may well be true but, as their blundering efforts in the crisis of 1814 showed, they were not a significant military organization. With the spectacular exception of recruiting the mayor of Bordeaux in 1813, they did not make any serious inroads into the military or the administration. Theirs was a salon royalism which served to

keep the memory of the Bourbons and the better days of the Old
Regime alive among the squirearchy, little more.

In so far as there was a popular movement during the Empire that
was also dissident, it was the Petite Eglise, the 'church' whose
members refused to recognize the Concordat. The numbers
involved even in its strongholds were never very large: perhaps 2000
lay followers in Rouen, perhaps as many in Lyon, at least 20,000
in Poitou where by far most of the followers lived and much smaller
numbers of adepts in pockets of Brittany, Normandy and the Midi.
But the influence of the Petite Eglise cannot be measured in
numbers alone for it was held in great respect by many laymen who
normally went to the Mass of the Concordat clergy. This was
because of the extraordinary clerics who refused the oath to the
Concordat and the compromises it involved, and because in many
ways the Petite Eglise continued the forms of religious dissidence
which had shown themselves under the Directory and so it
represented an authentic layman's form of religious expression.
Some of the individual priests certainly showed uncommon
courage. Charles Barbedette, curé of Grand-Luc in the Deux-
Sevrès, for example, refused all of the oaths of the 1790s, was never
captured and never emigrated. He also evaded the imperial police
because after a decade's experience he was an expert at disguises.
The abbé Grangeard, former curé of Souligné-sous-Vallon in the
Sarthe, had been deported to Jersey but returned in 1801 to preach
for the next twelve years until his arrest, celebrating clandestine
Mass at dawn in haylofts, private rooms and barns to followers who
often considered him a 'real' priest and martyr. Clerics like this
spoke to a laity which had not reconciled itself to the changes in
legal status of the Church. The popular hostility to the sales of *biens
nationaux*, to the constitutional clergy who were now incorporated
into the Condordat church, to the abolition of many of the Old
Regime parishes and above all to the suppression of the
innumerable feast days which had traditionally marked the passage
of the year thus continued. Popular religiosity had always laid great
emphasis on liturgy and ceremony as a way of somehow controlling
the unknown and the supernatural so that a strong nostalgia for
'true' religion persisted. The Petite Englise also shared another
characteristic of popular mentalities: a taste for prophecy.
Sometimes this was the work of laymen. In the Hautes-Alps, a man
known by no other name than 'Louis' who claimed to know the
esoteric languages of Latin and English and to have visited the New

World, hated Napoleon so much he refused to handle the coinage and predicted all manner of catastrophes including the fall of the usurper from 1812 on. In 1819, a certain Fleuriel from Alençon appeared in the Sarthe to announce that he was the angel of life come to combat Bonaparte, the angel of death, along with his minions, the king and the heretic pope. The world would end in flames in two years when Bonaparte returned. Much to the distress of the Petite Eglise clergy, their congregations were very sympathetic but the priests often prophesied too, especially about conscription. The abbé Grangeard regularly predicted that all the young men without exception would be conscripted, while in the Deux-Sevrès the areas of greatest resistance to conscription were those with the highest numbers of adherents to the Petite Eglise. This undoubtedly explains why the government found what would otherwise have been a movement of harmless millenarianism and hopeless nostalgia so threatening. Arrests of dissident priests usually coincided with renewed military efforts.

In the final analysis, however, the Petite Eglise was no threat. According to the prefect of the Seine-Inférieure, its followers were 'widows, men without education, illiterates . . . the most miserable class of the people . . .' This was not quite true, for among the laymen arrested in one of the periodic sweeps in Rouen were three flannel manufacturers and an apprentice printer, but the prefect was right enough to lay the emphasis on the poor and the powerless. Women were much more attracted to the Petite Eglise than men, and in the Auvergne the audience was almost entirely female. The prefect of the Deux-Sevrès claimed that it was only dangerous in his department because there were so many 'sharecroppers, small tenants and poor peasants who rent their land. The police have much less leverage over this class of men than over proprietors whose interests keep them obedient because they have something to lose.' The Petite Eglise was also weak because there was no national organization, no bishops and no seminaries. It was a concoction of local movements, as indicated by the bewildering variety of local names for them: 'illuminés' in Gascony, 'purs' in Languedoc, 'élus' in Perche, 'enfarinés' in Rouergue (so called because followers wore long hair whitened with flour), and so on. The Petite Eglise is significant for its great tenacity. The last 'Louiset' around Fougères in the Ille-et Vilaine only died in 1970 and there still is a little community of 'Blancs' near Charolles in the Saône-et-Loire which has lived without priests now for a century and a half.

With such popular and clerical dissidence as there was easily contained and with the politicians in the Legislative Body and Senate supine, the only potential threat to the regime was from the army. The general who took it upon himself to play this role was Claude-François Malet. Strictly speaking, neither of the Malet conspiracies was military since none of the officers involved had an active command. Indeed, Malet's first conspiracy in 1808 was something of an accident, since he was only in Paris because he was awaiting a hearing on charges that he was running illegal gambling casinos while stationed in Italy. He contacted a little circle of extremists and dreamers remaining from the Year II and together they hit on the old solution of a dictatorship which would prepare the country for a return to the Republic. The idea was to throw the government in disarray while Napoleon was at the Spanish front by means of a false *senatus consultum* deposing the Emperor and then appealing to the army and forming a provisional government. As always, however, word leaked out and the conspiracy dissolved. The police took Malet so lightly that he was only imprisoned as a mildly dangerous crank. Once Malet got himself transferred to a hospital prison where security was extremely lax, he began to plan the second conspiracy.

His means were essentially the same, except Malet hit upon the crafty device of claiming in the fake *senatus consultum* that Napoleon had been killed in Russia. Escaping from the hospital prison on the morning of 23 October 1812 with two other cashiered generals who were completely taken in, Malet managed to bamboozle the commander of the National Guard at the Popincourt armoury, whose men then proceeded to toss Pasquier, the Prefect of Police, and Savary, Minister of Police, into La Force prison (thus Savary's enduring nickname, Duc de la Force). Comte Frochot, prefect of the Seine, was also relieved of his post. All three of the highest officials in the Empire had been completely duped. It was only when Malet personally tried to use the counterfeit *senatus consultum* to take over the military police headquarters that a sceptical officer had an aide-de-camp grab him from behind and arrest him in turn. The whole adventure was over by 10 a.m.

The conspiracy, ludicrous as it was, nonetheless revealed much about the Empire and the opposition to it. Malet himself had no fixed ideas. He appears to have wanted to reintroduce the Constitution of the Year VIII which had done nothing to impede the tyranny he so deplored and there may have been an understanding with the Chevaliers de la Foi to recall the primary assemblies and let the Republic and the monarchy fight it out at the ballot box. The abbé Lafon, who drew up the inevitable proclamation deposing tyranny, was a member of the society, albeit a renegade. In 1808, a group including a few senators around General Servan, the former 'patriot' Minister of War in 1792, which had been discussing what to do if Napoleon were killed, probably knew of Malet's first adventure but were not directly involved. In other words, opposition to the Empire was fragmented. Even so, the government in 1812 was frightened. A secret military commission condemned fourteen men to death either as conspirators or for failing to do their duty, that is, for taking Malet seriously. The higher gullible officials were spared after one of Napoleon's interminable fits of temper but as the Emperor was quick to realize, almost no one reasoned that the *senatus consultum* had to have been fake because if he was dead, it should have proclaimed a regency for the King of Rome. Few, in short, had much loyalty to the Bonaparte dynasty. The affair also showed a weakness in the bureaucracy. Malet got as far as he did with his suborned National Guards because the military never informed the civil police of its movements in the capital. Although this was soon made good, it is doubtful whether anyone could have done anything about the combination of numbing credulity and habits of passive obedience which made the affair possible. After all, the existence of the dictatorship depended on such an outlook.

Chapter 12

The Fall of the Dictator

With the largest population in western Europe by far, with roughly 40 per cent of the men in the full vigour of adulthood, with the economy making a spectacular recovery from the disasters of the previous decade and with the state subject to a single will as it never had been in the Year II, France was well poised to support the great military adventures of the next few years.

The Strategy of Victory

But it was not enough to possess these men and resources, they had to be deployed and utilized. This is where Napoleon showed his greatest genius. As in the other spheres, he did not develop any great theoretical design but was a great practitioner of the doctrines worked out by the general staff after the losses in the Seven Years War. In particular, he was influenced by the writings of the Comte de Guibert who urged the formation of mass armies inspired by patriotism, led by a military genius and supported by the nation's economic resources; by his teacher, the Baron du Teil, whose brother wrote a celebrated artillery manual; and by the strategical conceptions of Frederick the Great who advocated lightning flank attacks on the enemy's lines of communication or base of operations. For all his incredible attention to detail in planning a campaign, Napoleon also realized that the ultimate aim of speed, flexibility and surprise was to dazzle and defeat the enemy on the battlefield and to demoralize his political superiors into capitulation. To achieve these aims, Napoleon reorganized the French army in the period of relative peace between 1800 and 1804. Instead of the separate armies of the republican period with the attendant problems of generals developing their own political and military ambitions, the army was reformed into seven separate corps, each one composed of a varying number of regiments of artillery, cavalry and infantry. This was the organizational basis of the *Grande*

Armée. It suited Napoleon's desire to dominate everything, of course, but it also allowed for unity of command and maximum flexibility. Each corps was a little army on its own so that while each had an assigned task in a campaign march, its role could be changed rapidly. Thus it was theoretically possible for a single corps in the same campaign to find itself guarding the flank of the main march, pinning the enemy while the other corps pivoted and reinforced it, or leading the frontal assault. Regiments could also be transferred easily from one corps to another and the whole protected by a heavy cavalry screen. Thus the enemy commander had little or no idea whether he was facing the main or a secondary concentration. Despite long and careful preparation before every campaign, the ability to improvise and deceive remained essential ingredients of Napoleonic warfare. The same conceptions governed battlefield tactics, for in Napoleon's mind, unlike those of his tradition-bound contemporaries, there was no difference between a war of manoeuvre and the crowning battle. All was subject to the concept of a knock-out blow. The ideal on the field was to manipulate the enemy into an unfavourable terrain through manoeuvre and deception, force him to commit his main forces and reserve to the main battle and then undertake an enveloping attack with uncommitted or reserve troops on the flank or rear which either would produce a devastating surprise effect on morale or force him to weaken his main battle line. Either way, the enemy's own impulsiveness began the process by which even a smaller French army could defeat the enemy's forces one by one. With the exceptions of Eylau and Auerstadt, the battles of Marengo, Ulm, Austerlitz, Jena, Friedland and Wagram thus produced enemy casualties at least three times greater than those of the French. Where the enemy refused to be enticed, as at Borodino and Leipzig, the result was a draw or even a numerical loss.

The ability to carry out an offensive war depended on certain qualities of the ordinary soldier which Napoleon inherited and developed from the Revolution. Many republican historians deny this, claiming that the imperial army was increasingly cut off from the nation. While the memoirs of soldiers like Coignet certainly show men who imbued the entire ethos of booty and glory that were the unreflecting mentality of the ideal *grognard*, the *Grande Armée* of 1805 was still composed of a sizeable majority of recent conscripts. Only one quarter were veterans of the revolutionary wars, roughly the same proportion of veterans, in other words, as were present at Valmy in 1792. Nor were training methods much different: a week's training at home base, a march to the front of 50–60 days to get in shape and receive equipment along the way and drilling during rest periods. Most of the training was received from veterans on the battlefield and so the methods of the *amalgame* of the Year II continued. The imperial soldier too shared many of the same qualities of enthusiasm, self-reliance and unending sacrifice as the volunteers of the Revolution. Since the soldier was assumed to be an upright citizen, he could be trusted to fend for himself without deserting, while the other European armies, composed of every conceivable ne'er-do-well including criminals and prisoners of war, had to be kept well supplied by expensive and lumbering baggage trains. The French soldiers thus travelled light with a week's rations at the most and their superiors were willing to pay the price of an alienated invaded population. When Napoleon was compelled to adopt an extensive supply system for the 1812 campaign in Russia, his army too proved to be almost as cumbersome as those of his enemies. Most of the famous marches of the *Grande Armée* can be explained, less by the supply system or lack of it, however, than by careful staff work. Lightning marches such as that from the Channel to the Danube in 1805 were in fact exceptional and the general rule was a methodical march. Leading such large numbers of men and materiel over an expanding or contracting front, arranging the transfer of regiments from one corps to another, scouting, and deceiving the enemy, the whole orchestrated to arrive at a predetermined point, speaks volumes about the quality of the NCOs, and junior and middling officers. Not much is known about these men as opposed to the marshals and generals who have been dissected from every angle but their sometimes reckless courage certainly set an example to their men. Between 1805 and 1815, 15,000 officers were killed, 35,000 wounded, the infantry officers alone suffering 34,700 casualties. The military schools could hardly cope. The *Ecole spéciale militaire* at Saint-Cyr graduated only 4000 officers during the period despite an accelerated programme of studies, so that after 1808 somewhere between a fifth and a quarter of the officers were commissioned directly from the ranks.

The Destruction of the Third Coalition

The Anglo-French war languished for over two years with neither side being able to harm the other much. Napoleon sold the Louisiana territory to the Americans for 80 million francs in the hopes of embroiling them with the British. It did indeed light the fuse which provoked the American attack on Upper and Lower Canada but only in 1812. In the meantime England had no continental allies as in previous wars and was able to bottle up the main French fleet at Brest and so keep control of the Channel approaches. For his part, Napoleon assembled a huge army christened the 'Army of England' around Boulogne and constructed hundreds of flat-bottommed boats and transports in the harbours from Antwerp to Le Havre. Contrary to his own statements, he undoubtedly meant to make the crossing if the opportunity presented itself, but both naval and diplomatic developments closed that option. He did achieve one success when Spain became a formal ally after the English clumsily attacked her treasure ships and so he increased his naval power. But this was wasted in a series of improvised and contradictory orders to his naval commanders. In March 1805 Admiral Villeneuve broke out of Toulon, slipped by Gibraltar and sailed to the West Indies, hoping to sow confusion among the British and then return home to protect the crossing. Nelson, believing Villeneuve had made for Egypt, turned east, discovered his mistake, chased him to Barbados and back across the Atlantic. Villeneuve believed he was too weak to relieve Brest, however, and set anchor at Cadiz where the British promptly blockaded him. The fleet would have been safe enough here but Napoleon ordered Villeneuve to break out and attack Naples. On 21 October, off Cape Trafalgar, Nelson trapped and split the allied fleet. Of thirty-three ships of the line, only nine escaped. Trafalgar not only closed the Channel-crossing option for good, it made possible subsequent British operations in Holland, Spain, Portugal and Naples. Without it, it is doubtful whether the 'Spanish ulcer' would have bled quite so much.

Meanwhile, the same aggressive exploitation of the peace which had so alarmed the English also alienated the continental powers. This was hardly an inevitable result. However much Napoleon was hated in European aristocratic circles as a revolutionary parvenu

and spiller of royal blood, none of the powers initially was inclined
or able to offer much beyond token resistance. Austria was
exhausted by her mauling in the 1799–1801 war, Prussia was kept
in breathless anticipation by waving French-occupied Hanover
before her, and Russia was a potential rival with England in the
Baltic and Mediterranean. Of the great power courts, only the
Russian went into mourning over the murder of the Duc d'Enghien.
(The embarrassing Gustave IV of Sweden ostentatiously adopted
the young prince's dog and paraded it through the smaller German
courts.) But when Napoleon rejected an offer of Russian mediation
which would have guaranteed the neutrality of the Italian states,
Holland, Switzerland, Germany and Turkey and so in effect
announced he had a free hand in these areas, Tsar Alexander
concluded an alliance with England. In the treaty signed in April
1805, Pitt promised generous subsidies and both agreed to work for
a restoration of the frontiers of 1791 and of the Bourbons. In short,
the British were committed to inflicting a more thorough defeat on
France and imposing a more drastic alteration of her government
than they had been ten years earlier. The proclamation of the
Empire finally goaded Austria into the alliance. The assumption of
the title 'Emperor', the coronation in the presence of the Pope and
crowning himself King of Italy at Milan in May 1805 showed the
Hapsburgs that Napoleon meant to claim a Roman, Carolingian
and Hohenstaufen legacy they considered their own. Unlike the
rickety Holy Roman Empire, this was a claim to universal dominion
which could be enforced. Thus the War of the Third Coalition was
no more a defence of France's 'natural frontiers' than any of the
other wars of the period, although the great historian Sorel claimed
otherwise. As Amiens showed, England was prepared to accept
French possession of Belgium and the Rhineland, albeit against the
better judgement of some of her leaders, but she could not accept
the combination of a bid for colonial empire and the domination of
central Europe and Italy as well. It was Napoleon's belief that the
'natural frontiers' were a mere springboard for far greater things
that also provoked the continent. Rolling back the 'natural
frontiers' was a measure of European defence.

At the end of August, well before Trafalgar but while there was
still a campaigning season, Napoleon wheeled the Army of England
to the Rhine and the upper Danube. On 20 October, a converging
manoeuvre surrounded the Austrian general Mack at Ulm who
surrendered 30,000 men in addition to 30,000 who had already been

captured as well as 60 guns. But there were still the Russians, the main Austrian force slowly retreating from Italy and the Tyrol under attack from Masséna and the possibility Prussia would join the allies. Napoleon, therefore, chased after the Russians but Kutusov refused to give battle, retreating to more secure lines of communication and to reinforcements in Poland and Silesia. The *Grande Armée* was also close to exhaustion because of the unrelenting marches, the miserable sleet and cold and short supplies. The more it extended itself the more it risked being caught between the Russians in the north and the Austrians from the Tyrol in the south. But by purposely feigning weakness while calling up troops under Bernadotte and Davout from near Vienna, Napoleon tempted the emperors Alexander and Francis to attack. On 2 December on the anniversary of his coronation, Napoleon achieved one of his most decisive victories at the Battle of Austerlitz. The Austrians and Russians suffered 15,000 casualties, lost 12,000 prisoners and 180 guns while the French suffered perhaps 9000 casualties. Ulm and Austerlitz shattered the Third Coalition.

The campaign of 1805 produced the Grand Empire, a series of institutions, territorial rearrangements and shufflings of sovereigns dependent on Napoleon alone. It was designed to reflect the new power relations following the victories, to reward family and favourites, and to reorganize European resources for the war against England. Thus, the Grand Empire was bound to carry the possibility of renewed conflict so long as England remained undefeated. This was shown from the beginning in the treatment of Prussia. Napoleon knew that Frederick William had intended to defect to the allies as soon as France's defeat was certain, so although the Treaty of Schonbrunn of 24 February 1806 did give her Hanover, she was forced to cede Neuchâtel (which was given to Berthier who became its Prince), Cleves and Berg (to Murat who become Grand Duke) and Ansbach (to Bavaria). As if possession of Hanover was not enough to embroil her with the English, she was also forced to close her ports to British commerce. Austria fared even worse. By the Treaty of Pressburg of 26 December 1805, she lost Venetia to the Kingdom of Italy and other German territories to Bavaria and Württemberg which became kingdoms in their own right. Later, on 12 July 1806, the Holy Roman Empire ceased to exist, replaced by the Confederation of the Rhine, a collection of states which promised troops to the *Grande Armée*. Napoleon's brother Louis became King of Holland, a move to spread largesse within the family and to tighten economic warfare against the British. As it had been under the Directory, Italy especially became a source of private profit. Principalities and dukedoms were showered upon favourites and marshals. Another brother, Joseph, became King of Naples after a short invasion and even his rapacious sisters received little territories. The rapid extensions of French power provided the occasion for a sharp deterioration in relations with Pius VII. When Napoleon seized some small papal lands, the Pope's forbearance, already strained over the Organic Articles and the application of the Concordat to Italy, was at an end. When Pius refused to close his ports to the British, Napoleon threatened him too, although the invasion only came three years later. Thus the victories of 1805 with the consequent tightening of the seacoasts and rearrangements in Germany and Italy carried with them the seeds of new conflicts.

Prussia was first to react. The British reacted to the occupation of Hanover and the closure of the Baltic ports by declaring war and seizing hundreds of Prussian merchant ships in British harbours. Her officials then revealed that Napoleon intended to return Hanover to George III in a proposed peace settlement. Napoleon also refused to satisfy Prussian ambitions for a North German Confederation of her own. All this was enough to encourage the war party at the Prussian court and preparations began in August. Despite its respectable size of 171,000, however, the Prussian army and its allies suffered from visible dry rot, with ancient muskets, outmoded concepts of a war of manoeuvre, a cumbersome system of supply and the deadening hand of an ageing leadership, many of whom were veterans of the Seven Years War. With no thought of awaiting Russian reinforcements and with a hopelessly confused and shifting campaign strategy, the Prussians stumbled into disaster. On 14 October 1806, Napoleon engaged the Prussian flank at Jena inflicting 10,000 casualties for 5000 of his own, while on the same day Davout withstood the main Prussian assaults at nearby Auerstadt, killing 10,000 as against 7000. In addition to the casualties, the two battles netted 25,000 prisoners and 200 guns. Nor was this all. The relentless and rapid pursuit accounted for at least another 100,000 prisoners and 1500 cannon as one fortress after another capitulated. The Prussian army had ceased to exist.

Yet the now weary *Grande Armée* could have no respite. The Prussian court, particularly influenced by Queen Louise, refused to sue for peace because there was still the promise of salvation from

Russia. Austria too might intervene and so long as England was available to finance future coalitions, Napoleon's overall position was risky. England and Russia would have to be defeated. To handle the first, Napoleon issued the Berlin Decrees in November 1806 blockading all commerce with Britain. The 'Continental System' was not new; the Directory had tried a blockade in 1799 and the Consulate and early Empire had tried to choke off British trade too. Despite the limited success of these measures, the Berlin Decrees were intended to be much more systematic, their ultimate aim being to ruin the British economy and its government's finances. Yet, since trade flowed around and through artificial barriers, Napoleon was drawn to increasingly strong measures and new conquests.

Circumstances also required that Russia be defeated as quickly as possible and so the *Grande Armée* pushed on into Poland, Murat occupying Warsaw on 28 November. The French arrival stimulated nationalist feelings among the aristocracy and bourgeoisie but there was never any question of restoring Polish independence, let alone freeing the serfs. Napoleon raised many hopes with his praise of the Polish nation and so raised many Polish battalions, but behind the backs of her leaders he was usually contemptuous, willing to sacrifice the Poles for future relations with the partitioning powers. More immediately, the advance against the retreating Russians slowed because of the appalling roads, winter rains, and food and clothing shortages. With discipline breaking down, Napoleon contemplated wintering along the line of the Vistula but the Russian manoeuvres and counterattacks tempted him into another knock-out blow. Yet he probably did not intend to give battle at Eylau on 8 February 1807 where the Russian artillery raked the French and only Murat's resplendent and daring cavalry charge saved the day. It was a severe check, Napoleon losing perhaps 25,000 men, the Russians and a Prussian remnant, 15,000, many of the wounded on both sides suffering horribly until they froze to death, their blood spreading over the falling snow. The Russians retreated, however, while the French used the rest of the winter to reequip and to integrate reinforcements. At last, on 14 June, the anniversary of Marengo, as he repeated to his refreshed troops, he achieved the great victory he had sought so long against the Russians. At the Battle of Friedland, he inflicted losses on the enemy nearly three times his own. Four days later, Tsar Alexander asked for an armistice.

On 25 June, the two emperors met on a covered barge decorated with their eagles on the Niemen River near Tilsit. For the next few days, Napoleon and Alexander privately settled the fate of Europe, each convinced his own charms and blandishments had seduced the other. On 7 July, their ministers signed the Treaty of Tilsit. Two days later, a separate treaty was signed with Prussia whose King, Frederick William, had been kept waiting in supplication at a nearby village. The treaties arranged yet another German settlement. The Confederation of the Rhine, already greatly enlarged after its initial proclamation, acquired a new member, the Kingdom of Westphalia, under younger brother Jerome, composed of parts of Hanover, some formerly Prussian territories and some central German states. Prussia, who lost half her population, was reduced to four small provinces, ceding all of her territory west of the Elbe, most of her Polish lands to a newly created Grand Duchy of Warsaw with the King of Saxony as ruler, and Danzig which became a free city under French occupation. Prussia would remain occupied until she paid a massive indemnity. She also agreed to join the Continental System. Alexander agreed to do the same and to influence Denmark and Sweden to follow. Undoubtedly, Alexander thought of this as little more than a revival of his father's anti-British League of Armed Neutrality of 1801, a device to extend Russian influence in the Baltic since the agreements also recognized Finland as his sphere whereas Napoleon thought it made Russia part of his 'system'. The war in 1812 thus grew out of this original misunderstanding. For his part, Napoleon abandoned Turkey to Russia who agreed to remove her garrisons from the Ionian Isles and Dalmatia, although, in fact, he had no intention of permitting Turkey to be dismembered totally. If he was not willing to concede the eastern Mediterranean to the British, why should he to the Russians? Finally, there was an understanding that Portugal would close its ports to the British. As with the Treaties of Lunéville and Amiens, the Tilsit agreements laid the basis for the next wars.

It had been almost two years since the *Grande Armée* had plunged from Boulogne to the Danube. France herself was now composed of 110 European departments and her influence and vassal states stretched from the Straits of Gibraltar to the Baltic, from the Atlantic to the Niemen. It had been achieved with dizzying speed, with the courage and patience of the thousands of ordinary soldiers and officers of the *Grande Armée* and with a centralized command system subject to a single will that had managed to defeat its enemies one by one. There was a heavy price to pay, of course. In the six major battles alone, over the two years, the *Grande Armée* had lost nearly 65,000 men out of an effective original strength of about 210,000. The losses were made good by calling up the classes of 1806 and 1807 early, and the class of 1808 no less than eighteen months before its time. Switzerland, Holland, Spain, Poland and Italy were also asked to contribute more or less willingly so that the strength of the army was perhaps 600,000, two thirds of whom were stationed between the Rhine and the Niemen. The effect of the Grand Empire was to Europeanize the *Grande Armée*. Although the demands for conscripts from France were nearly triple what they had been under the Consulate, the country appears to have accepted the situation well enough. Nor was the fiscal burden very great since most of the war had been financed from tribute, Germany alone contributing 560 million francs. The army itself was overwhelmed with loot of all sorts, the Prussian fortresses alone providing enormous stores, equipment, artillery and horses. A period of consolidation was necessary.

The Unstable Grand Empire

So long as the war with England continued, however, the Continental System had to be regulated, refined and expanded. Thus French economic hegemony over the continent tightened while the system's inherent dynamic required further expansion. For those countries already within it, this meant increasing resentment among the conquered and for those outside, the threat of conquest. Resistance to expansion also inspired resistance among those already conquered and thus gave the English another opportunity to subsidize continental allies. There was a straight logic, therefore, between the rising of the Portuguese and the Spanish, English intervention in the Iberian peninsula and the new war with Austria. The settlement following that war also contributed to the growing alienation of Russia. At a more minor level, the invasion of the papal states and arrest of the Pope, intended, among other things, to bring all Italy into the system, not only inflamed the Spanish rebels and Catholic Europe generally, but contributed directly to the renewal of conspiracy at home. Napoleon could have prevented the forging of many of the links in this logical chain but his increasing penchant for forceful solutions, which had always been present and which his very strength after Tilsit made quite understandable, resulted in the unravelling of the Grand Empire.

Although most of the continent joined the economic boycott after Tilsit, Portugal refused because so much of her trade was with England. Such defiance was intolerable. Napoleon secured transit rights through Spain by the Treaty of Fontainebleau of 27 October 1807 which bribed Godoy, the coarse parvenu who dominated the Bourbon court, with a morsel of Portugal for himself. Although the French army under Junot found the march difficult, as it always did in poor countries where there was little to forage, it was never put to the test because the Portuguese royal family fled to Brazil. Junot took Lisbon without a fight on 30 November. At the same time, Napoleon typically stretched his treaty rights to the point of beginning to occupy Spain as well. This was too much for the anti-Godoy factions who engineered his arrest and, amidst rioting by peasants, lackeys and army officers on 17–19 March 1808, Charles IV abdicated in favour of his son, Ferdinand VII. Sensing a great opportunity to regenerate Spain, Napoleon summoned the royal family to Bayonne where he intimidated Charles into surrendering his crown outright. The Bourbons were promptly interned, the crown handed to Joseph, Naples to Murat. Meanwhile, the departure of Ferdinand sparked a rising in Madrid on 2 May 1808. Although Murat hanged many of its leaders, the Spanish rebellion had begun.

The Spanish rising was quite unlike those the French had encountered in the Tyrol and Calabria or in their own Vendée fifteen years earlier. True, there was a strong religious element which was understandable in a country whose ostentatious and lush Christianity contrasted so much with the austerity of the Concordat. But the social forces were far more complex than the intemperate preachings of fanatical monks on a superstitious peasantry which was how the French characterized this revolt. There was plenty of that but these same peasants profoundly distrusted the 'rich' as potential collaborators; urban working people in Castile and elsewhere attacked Godoy's officials who did cooperate; and students donned red cockades. The juntas which sprang up all over the country in the summer of 1808 comprised the most diverse elements: cranky aristocrats, reactionary enemies of Godoy who had passed for a mild progressive, conservatives who joined only to keep order, idealistic middle-class professionals who hoped to impose a constitution on the absolute monarchy, and so on. All could agree that a government which brought about the disastrous alliance of 1804–8 which permitted the British to sever the vital trade with the Americas, desperately needed reforms. All too could focus on Ferdinand as the prince whom they mistakenly believed could bring this about. When he left for Bayonne, many hopes departed with him. But the juntas could scarcely agree on how this was to be done, nor did the provincial juntas show much inclination to help each other in military operations.

Even though the Portuguese also rose and even though much of the regular Spanish army went over to the rebels, there was so much bickering among the juntas, so much provincial feeling and so many conflicting social forces that the French could have dealt with the rebels piecemeal. Yet large contingents of the army were composed of Germans and Poles who could see little point in this war and they were poorly supplied and poorly commanded. As often happens to such an army fighting guerrilla bands, discipline broke down. The atrocities each side consequently inflicted on the other hardened the bitterness of the war. The major difference, however, was British intervention. British agents worked hard to force the juntas to work together and funnelled large quantities of arms and money to them. This was not substantially different from the policy they had pursued towards the Vendeans and chouans in the 1790s, but with the Spanish rebellion they finally realized the potential of exploiting internal subversion and landed an army of 30,000 under Wellington on 1 August 1808. Until the winter of 1812, Wellington conducted an essentially defensive war using Portugal as a base where his troops could be supplied by sea and so the war was inconclusive. But the British and their allies pinned down forces of the *Grande Armée* which rarely numbered less than 200,000 men and inflicted casualties which averaged about 40,000 per year. In a short stay at the end of 1808, Napoleon himself could not force a result. In fact, he had to hurry back to Paris to prepare for a new war. The Spanish rebellion had inspired the Austrians to take the field again.

Dealing with the Spanish rebellion required securing the eastern flank which meant appeasing Tsar Alexander. The meeting of the two emperors at Erfurt in September 1808 was a moderate diplomatic success for both sides even though relations had clearly cooled since Tilsit. Neither had been able to agree on the details of a plan to dismember the Ottoman Empire and the Tsar had to settle for a reduction of Prussian reparations, not the complete evacuation he wanted. But Napoleon only wanted to stall Alexander long enough to transfer much of the *Grande Armée* from Germany to Spain. With his usual makeshift diplomacy, Napoleon did achieve this, although it was ominous that Russia refused to intervene to stop Austrian rearmament.

Thus it was Russia's *de facto* neutrality which made the war of 1809 possible while Austria's war made it impossible to finish off Spain. Once again the inadequacies of his enemies played into Napoleon's hands. With only English money and some incomplete military reforms, the Austrian court whipped itself into a war fever without bothering to search for allies. The Austrians were certainly encouraged by the amount of popular support they had. Once the war began, peasants in the Austrian and Italian Tyrol, fearful of increased taxes and conscription, rose in the name of religion. Among the enemies were Bavarian and French officials, soldiers and the 'rich'. Once again, a popular movement was anti-French and counterrevolutionary.

Napoleon took the field with the usual improvisations: calling up the classes of 1809 and 1810 early and mobilizing troops from the Confederation of the Rhine, Holland, Italy and the Grand Duchy of Warsaw. This gave him roughly 300,000 men. It is doubtful, however, whether the international character of the army was as important in explaining the Emperor's difficulties as the Archduke Charles's inherent caution which saved him from falling into the typical Napoleonic traps. Thus Charles was able to inflict a serious check on Napoleon at Essling on 21 May where Lannes was killed, even though the Austrians had to evacuate Vienna. Napoleon did defeat him at the Battle of Wagram on 5–6 July but the French suffered too many casualties to undertake a pursuit and much of the Austrian army was able to retreat intact. In the end, however, neither Prussia nor Russia would help so Austria had to submit. By a new Treaty of Schonbrunn of 14 October, she had to pay out 75 million and surrender the area around Salzburg to Bavaria, Istria to the Grand Empire and Galicia to the Grand Duchy and Russia. The most significant aspect of the treaty was that it continued the alienation of Russia since Alexander hoped for more of Galicia and perhaps even a predominant influence in Poland. Napoleon's divorce of Josephine and remarriage to an Austrian princess, Marie-Louise, had the same effect. Alexander probably had no intention of allowing a Russian princess to marry Napoleon but he was certainly miffed when Napoleon abruptly broke off the talks and announced his engagement to Marie-Louise. Indeed, this had been the intention of the new Austrian Chancellor, Metternich, all along. Thus the birth of the long-desired heir, the King of Rome, on 20 March 1811, took place amidst new threats of war, and so did nothing to consolidate the regime.

Developments in the Continental System completed the break. The British replied to the Berlin Decrees of 1806 by issuing a series of Orders in Council restricting neutral shipping to the continent, forbidding some products altogether and subjecting merchantmen on the high seas to search. Napoleon retaliated by issuing the Milan Decrees of November–December 1807 declaring neutral shipping which complied with the Orders in Council to be lawful prizes. These measures certainly hurt the British economy particularly when the American government, outraged at the violation of freedom of the seas, imposed an embargo of its own. Manufacturing, cotton and shipping interests in the United States did not submit to the embargo for long, however, and by 1809–10 Anglo-American trade had resumed its former levels. Meanwhile, Britain found new trading partners in the Levant and, with the weakening ties between Spain and her South American colonies after 1804, began developing a commercial empire in Latin America which flourished for another century. By 1809–10, Britain had so frustrated the Continental System that overall exports and coal, iron and cotton production were at near-record highs. Problems remained, of course. The beginning of the independence movements in Latin America after 1808 disrupted trade, relations with the United States plummeted after 1810, the import of wood supplies from Lower Canada for the merchant navy could not compensate for the closure of Baltic sources and the country still had to import a significant amount of its grain despite land clearings and investments in livestock and leguminous crops which far surpassed the improvements of the previous century.

British success was thus one of the pressures which induced Napoleon to modify the Continental System. The blockade also reduced customs revenues from 60.6 million francs in 1807 to 11.6 million francs in 1809. Harvests and low prices made it difficult for landowners to pay their taxes. With war looming in 1809 and consequently the need for more revenues, a limited system of export licences was adopted which cleared the agricultural surpluses. In addition, by the Saint-Cloud decree of 3 July 1810, the system of licences was generalized but limited to French subjects, the ideal being that exports from the Empire should be paid in cash, taxable colonial goods or naval stores. By the Trianon and Fontainebleau decrees of 5 August and 18 October, import duties rose dramatically and a system was established to confiscate and sell or destroy contraband goods, mainly manufactured products like textiles, throughout the Empire and the vassal states. There is no doubt that these measures had a drastic effect on the British economy, since they coincided with the failure of many merchant houses and banks which had overstocked or speculated too wildly in South America. Transportation costs to European markets through the Baltic or the Black Sea to Vienna were also astronomical. Consequently, overseas trade in 1811 was lower than at any time since the war began, and because of the calamitous harvest of 1810 and the necessity to pay for the grain imports with gold, the pound fell. Shaking Britain's international finances by forcing a crisis in the balance of payments was thus not as foolish as is sometimes claimed, and without the war in Russia Britain's prospects were certainly bleak. This, however, was the problem. As in 1805, measures designed to weaken Britain had serious repercussions on the continent too. The boycott had already caused shortages of colonial goods such as sugar and coffee and a blaze of publicity and government encouragement for sugar beet and chicory had not filled the gap. After 1810, the seizures, sale or destruction of contraband ruined many merchants and made the imperial despotism all the more unbearable, even if the simultaneous burning of contraband on the market squares of European cities had a greater propaganda than economic effect. Granting licences only to French subjects exposed what Napoleon had believed all along, that France should be the prime beneficiary of the Empire. The reorientation of the system was a success of sorts. By granting licences Napoleon went into competition with the smugglers, and by the end of 1811 customs revenues rose to 105.9 million francs, and the confiscations may have produced a further 150 million francs. At the same time, in a neat reversion to the methods of the absolute monarchy, he forced corrupt officials to disgorge millions. With others, he contented himself with a percentage of their bribes. On the diplomatic plane, the offensive against contraband in 1810 led to the annexation of Holland and the Hanseatic towns which were major sources of smuggling into Germany. The consequent absorption of the Grand Duchy of

Oldenburg whose Grand Duke was the Tsar's brother-in-law was a further slight to the Russians. So too was the permission given to the Americans to apply for licences. This made sense from Napoleon's point of view in that it embroiled the Americans and British and fitted in with the new strategy of draining British reserves, but it made no sense at all from Alexander's. If France could trade with Britain, what prevented Russia from doing so? Unable to supply traditional markets with her major exports of grain and timber, Russia's balance of payments deficit soared, the rouble had to be devalued and there were consequent shortages of imported manufactured goods. With the economy in trouble and the big landowners complaining, Alexander finally retaliated in December 1810 by imposing heavy duties on imported luxury goods, which were mainly French, and by opening his ports to neutral and British shipping. The tightening of the economic war on Britain thus blew Russia out of the Continental System. Finally, Russia interpreted the Swedes' invitation to Marshal Bernadotte to become their Crown Prince in May 1811 as a hostile act, even though within a year Sweden proved she was no French puppet.

The purpose of Napoleon's attack on Russia was to bring her back into the Continental System. The issue too was the maintenance of French hegemony in Europe. If the Russians challenged it successfully, Prussia and Austria could be expected to spin out of the French alliance because all the European countries had an ambivalent attitude to the Continental System. The blockade protected home industries like textiles in Saxony and Silesia. On the other hand, the 'allies' resented the system of tribute and the prohibition of colonial goods. The risks of attacking Russia were therefore very great. In the event, the maintenance of the Bonaparte dynasty was also at risk.

A Classic Crisis of Misery

A considerable proportion of the nation's resources were devoted directly towards military expenditure. Very roughly, half of all spending on war between 1804 and 1814 was derived from French sources, the other half from tribute from the conquered territories. Until 1809 when costs of the war in Spain began to bite, the wars had been financed with no increases in taxation and no public borrowing. In 1810, a general economic crisis broke which made it increasingly difficult for Frenchmen to pay. This was followed in turn by the defeats in Russia and Germany and with them the unravelling of the system of tribute. The Empire was thus thrown back on to French sources at a time when the economy was either still recovering or had been plunged into yet another depression by the tightening British blockade. The inability of Frenchmen to pay in late 1813 had a role in the inability of the army to equip itself and explains much of the antifiscalism of many sectors of the population which was so prominent a feature of popular reactions in 1814.

In the first instance, the economic crisis was typical of so many that were to follow in the nineteenth century, a result of fast growth in a leading economic sector, in this case cotton and textiles generally, a relative overproduction and sudden contraction, the inability of smaller or weaker firms to meet their debts, followed by bankruptcies which shook the entire financial system. This crisis was more severe than others, however, because it was followed immediately by the very poor harvest of 1811, which, like those of the Old Regime, had disastrous effects on consumer purchasing power. This in turn rebounded on some parts of the manufacturing sector. The effects of this double crisis could still be seen in 1814.

After Tilsit and the years of relative peace which followed, the textile industry, particularly cotton and silk, prospered. Exports gradually recovered to their pre-1806 levels by 1811, discounting activity at the Bank of France came close to doubling and government bonds rose by about 20 points. But there was already an inherent difficulty in this renewed growth. While wages held their own in this period, the rise in the price of raw textiles exceeded the price of the finished product. In the case of cotton, this can be attributed to a combination of the British naval blockade and Napoleon's prohibitively high duties on English spun cotton. In the case of silk and wine, the Continental System forbade the central and eastern European countries to trade with England so that they could no longer pay for French exports whose price consequently fell. Nor did the government help this situation when it quadrupled the duties on raw cotton and sold contraband English cotton at auction. The only way for firms to survive, therefore, was to borrow, even though bankers were putting their money into increasingly fragile enterprises. The financial system itself had inherent weaknesses. Provincial and foreign financial houses were closely tied to their Parisian counterparts but those in turn had invested heavily in low-yield real estate which made it difficult for them to meet their obligations quickly should the need arise. This was an old habit but war jitters contributed to reinforcing it. The war and the blockade also led to a frenzied speculation in rare colonial products especially by merchants from Bordeaux, Nantes and Marseille, who, in the circumstances, could do no better than bid up prices in the Paris markets. The house of cards began to collapse with the Russian devaluation in September 1810 and the failure of several banking houses in Holland and Germany in which a number of Parisian bankers had invested heavily. In turn, they had to call in their loans which produced a disastrous depression. There were 270 bankruptcies in the Department of the Seine alone in 1810. Two thirds of the textile workers in Mulhouse were unemployed, only one in five of the country's cotton-spinning machines was in production and the hardship in the rural textile regions of Normandy was massive. The Midi was particularly hard hit. A 'cyclone' in June 1810 produced heavy flooding in the lower Rhône valley which killed half the mulberry leaves in the Bouches-du-Rhône and Gard and two thirds in the Vaucluse. As a result, half of the working population of Lyon was unemployed and even a year later, only one in five of the silk-weaving machines in Nîmes was operating while 20,000 were unemployed. Other industries were affected frightfully as well. The luxury or highly skilled trades in Paris suffered unemployment rates varying between 70 and 80 per cent, which indicates how severely affected the middle-class clientele was as well. Overall, the government estimated that two in five workers in Paris were out of work.

By the spring of 1811, the worst of the crisis was over. This was followed, however, by heavy storms in the Paris region and a long drought in the Midi. It was one of the worst harvests of the period. It was particularly poor in parts of Picardy, Normandy, Alsace, the Saône-Rhone valleys and in parts of the west and southwest, that is in regions which normally supplied neighbouring cities with their excess production. Thus, as always in a subsistence crisis, cities stretched their normal supply areas considerably. Prices were so high in the Haute-Saône, one of the traditional markets of Marseille, that its merchants ventured as far away as the Ile-de-France to find supplies. The coastal departments suffered terribly. Most of these were never self-sufficient so prices were always higher but the British blockade aggravated the distress. Prices rose by over 100 per cent in these regions between 1810 and 1812 while they rose by 50 per cent in the interior. The government responded as its predecessors always had by imposing a grain census and forcing those with a surplus to sell, by arrests of some of the more prominent speculators, by requiring bakers to keep a register of sales, by limiting acquisitions on markets to locals and bakers within the first hour of opening, by the creation of a special reserve for Paris, by subsidized sales to the poor who paid one third less for their bread than the well-off, and by public works in most of the large towns. There was one new element in the form of the millions of bowls of freely distributed so-called Rumford soups, a vegetable concoction, and the latest bread substitute praised by philanthropists as an earlier generation praised potato flour or rice. The government even revived the maximum in May 1812, a measure whose purpose was almost entirely demagogic since the prefects, who were allowed to set prices at the local level, used the law to supply their departments at the expense of neighbours. A prefect who set prices low thus suffered from those who set them high. Thibaudeau, prefect of the Bouches-du-Rhône, was proud of not having set a maximum at all even though he drew grain from the rest of Provence and the lower Rhône valley. The government in Paris was perfectly informed of these activities but did nothing about them which only underlines the public relations motive behind the operation. Such manipulation was effective, however. In several regions the common people were apparently delighted.

Until the harvest of 1812 was in, the amount of misery ordinary people suffered was almost unimaginable. Wages fell even for those who were employed and the number of pathetic articles held in pawn shops more than doubled. As always in a time of severe crisis, public and private charities were overwhelmed and, although there was a minor rash of machine-breaking in the Nord, the most common reaction for the poor was to beg. In classic fashion, this led to bands of vagabonds roaming the countryside. The prefects in the north and west, particularly in the textile districts, spoke of 'armies' of mendicants numbering in the thousands, besieging isolated farms and threatening arson if they were not fed or lodged. In some districts, the vagabonds crossed the line from threats to brigandage as soon as they began to arm or disguise themselves. Brigandage, which the government had brought under control by 1808, was more or less endemic in some regions from 1812 on. Elsewhere, there were attempts to control the movement or price of grain. For a regime which prided itself on maintaining order, there was a considerable amount of disorder in its closing years. According to the government's figures, there were 505 cases in 126 departments brought before the courts which were directly related to the economic crisis and this does not include the innumerable acts of petty thievery and violence which can only be measured by an examination of the actual trials. The repression was exceptionally severe. At Caen and Carentan and no doubt elsewhere, some of those who participated in grain riots were sentenced to death or forced labour.

The economic crisis of 1810–12 had few, if any, direct political effects. The rioters at Caen believed that the Emperor had been killed in Russia and that Marie-Louise had fled to Germany but this was not so much subversive as an additional problem for prefectoral authorities in repressing the disturbances. Many people attributed the unemployment of the winter of 1810 to the government's clumsily explained policy of demonetizing old coins which had been announced in August. But in the panic which swept the country as people unloaded old coins on reluctant merchants and tax officials, and tried to hoard newly minted francs, there were no cries for the overthrow of the Empire. The effects of the monetary, industrial and agricultural crisis were more indirect. Small savings which had been built up between 1806 and 1810 evaporated and tax revenues fell dramatically. But if the treasury suffered, there was still enough money to launch the enormously costly Russian campaign. Thus began the end.

Anatomy of Disaster

Napoleon was well aware of the staggering problems of mounting a Russian invasion. With the exception of parts of Spain, the French armies normally supplied themselves locally which would be impossible in the poorly developed and sparsely populated plains of western Russia. To operate on such an unprecedentedly vast theatre, Napoleon estimated he would need 600,000 men who would have to be equipped and supplied over long distances and poor roads, so that one of the largest armies Europe had seen in centuries would have to bring its own supplies with it. Consequently a year-long effort was put into organizing transport battalions and when the *Grande Armée* finally crossed into Russia, it resembled a small nation of soldiers with their attendant corps of bakers, cooks, shoemakers and tailors. Even the exact timing of the invasion was affected by the problem of supply – it was expected that by June the cavalry and transport horses and oxen would be able to acquire some supplies locally. But the *Grande Armée* was no longer the army of the *Grande Nation*. No less than a dozen nationalities from throughout the Empire were represented in its ranks. No European army had been so heterogeneously composed since the Crusades and it was almost as difficult to command. The Prussian and Austrian contingents were potentially unreliable: brother Jerome, King of Wesphalia, commanding 70,000 Germans proved to be obstinate and incompetent; stepson Eugène de Beauharnais, Viceroy of Italy, commanding 80,000 Bavarians and Italians was just adequate; several marshals refused direct orders or proved unable to take initiatives; and Napoleon himself was inexplicably indecisive and lethargic at critical moments.

Because it was the Napoleonic style and because of the problem of supply, Napoleon needed a quick victory. But whether because the Russian generals, Barclay de Tolly, Prince Bagration and later Prince Kutusov, deliberately sacrificed space for time to draw Napoleon away from his supply lines or because they stumbled on to the policy due to the very size and reputation of the *Grande Armée* intimidating them, the Russians refused to give battle and retreated. On three occasions between the crossing of the Niemen on 28 June and the capture of Smolensk on 17 August, Napoleon was almost able to manoeuvre one or the other of the two Russian corps into an encircling trap but each time they escaped. By the time the Russians had evacuated Smolensk, the campaign had already gone well over Napoleon's estimate of a mere twenty-four days. Consequently, supplies began to run short and discipline began to waver. Hot weather fatigued the troops, rains delayed transport convoys, the sick and wounded suffered horribly since medical services had been inadequately prepared, thousands of horses died because of fatigue or green fodder. By mid-August, the central army group commanded by Napoleon may have lost as many as 100,000 men from active service and a further 60,000 were lost by early October. This increasingly desperate situation certainly affected French tactics at the Battle of Borodino on 7 September. When Kutusov finally ceded to court and public opinion and made a stand, he faced an army which Napoleon himself estimated was too weak and depleted to execute Marshal Davout's proposal of an encircling manoeuvre around the Russian left. The battle thus consisted of an endless series of brutal frontal assaults and even though the Russian losses were immense, the main corps were able to withdraw, greatly tattered but intact, while the French losses were so great that no serious pursuit could be undertaken.

Borodino left the road open to Moscow, however, which the French entered on 14 September. As far as Napoleon was concerned, the war was over, since he had captured the enemy's ancient capital. But Alexander, whose sense of betrayal was by now boundless, rebuffed all peace feelers. Nor was there any reason why he should accept them. Napoleon offered no concessions and while the French situation weakened daily, the Russian was improving. The French had made no appeal to the serfs; instead, all levels of the Russian population had from the beginning worked themselves to a furore of hatred of the irreligious invader. Thousands of young men flocked to the national colours much as their French counterparts had in 1792. The Russian position was consequently improving while the French was greatly overextended. More and more troops had to be detached from active service for garrison duty and to protect the stretched lines of communication. Napoleon wasted a month in Moscow waiting for Alexander to come to his senses, as he saw it, even though the Russians' failed attempt to burn the holy city as they retreated ought to have convinced him of his enemy's determination. When he finally realized the Tsar would not negotiate he decided on a retreat, possibly intending to go only as far as Smolensk for the winter. But a number of circumstances forced a ragged and calamitous retreat into Germany. At first, the weather remained reasonably good; more disastrous was the decision to take the same road the *Grande Armée* had already traversed. Since the two enemy armies had already devastated the region, there were few supplies to scour, supply dumps were too far west and necessities too difficult to move over the poor and muddy roads. Men were numbed at the horrible sight of the decomposing bodies of their comrades on former battlefields or of the wounded who had been sent ahead but who had died because their escorts abandoned them. No one, not even Napoleon who was normally so cool under fire, dared face up to the disaster. He deluded himself that it would be possible to winter in Russia. His officers refused to abandon some artillery which the horses were too weak to haul only to abandon all of it when the horses died. Thousands of transport and cavalry horses were also slaughtered for food and the army's retreat was lit by the fires of abandoned baggage and munitions wagons. Starving men abandoned their guns and struggled along behind their more disciplined colleagues. The harassment from mounted Cossacks and civilian partisans also caused great damage. The weather began to close in almost as soon as the army reached Smolensk in November and all thoughts of wintering there had to be abandoned. There were far fewer stores than expected and the Russians had destroyed much-needed relief troops further west. With lines of communication severely threatened, Napoleon had to continue the retreat, made all the more desperate by the Russian capture of the supply depot at Minsk. The *Grande Armée* had to fight its way westward and in one particularly murderous engagement while crossing the Berezina river, it may have lost 20–30,000 troops. By the time it staggered into Poland and Prussia in January, it had lost 570,000 men, 370,000 through death in battle, sickness or frost and another 200,000 taken prisoner. The French had also lost over 200,000 trained horses and over 80 per cent of their artillery. The Russians' losses were almost as great so no headlong pursuit was possible, but their prospects took a decided turn for the better when the generals of Napoleon's Prussian and Austrian contingents, Yorck and Schwartzenburg, signed armistices with them, each treaty a prelude to their own sovereign's defection to the Anglo-Russian alliance.

Defeat and Abdication

Meanwhile, Napoleon had left his marshals to conduct the last stages of the retreat and returned to Paris on 18 December partly to put out his own version of events, where the catastrophe was quite misleadingly blamed on the weather, and partly to raise new armies. Amazingly enough, many of the losses in Russia were made good. By a whole series of expedients – calling up the classes of 1813 and 1814 in advance of their normal times, combing through those between 1808 and 1810 for more able-bodied men, conscripting National Guards, transferring naval gunners into the artillery and mounted gendarmes into the cavalry, removing regiments from Spain, and so on – an army growing to over half a million men was constituted. The country was also transformed into a vast arsenal to make uniforms, guns and cannon. Inevitably, there was a makeshift quality about these efforts. Young men arrived at rallying centres to find inadequate food or shelter or too few uniforms and the new armies were inexperienced, poorly trained and overly weighted with the young or with ageing veterans. But clearly a prefectoral corps and conscript organization which could put nearly 300,000 men into the field within four months of the Emperor's return, however haphazard their training and equipping had been, had suffered no perceptible decline from the disaster in Russia.

The campaign of 1813 showed that at least among the remaining soldiers and the recently conscripted young men, battle ardour too remained high. Yet the military odds against the Empire were mounting. Prussia, which had secretly rebuilt its army to a quarter of a million men, joined the alliance against Napoleon in March. The opening battles were still French successes. The French defeated combined Russian and Prussian forces at Lutzen (2 May) and Bautzen (20–21 May). But they were not able to follow up in classical Napoleonic fashion because of the shortage of horses and trained cavalrymen – this was the most devastating effect of the Russian campaign. The conscripts also tired easily after long marches and some of the marshals committed almost witless blunders. The allies' defeats had also weakened their forces, so quite unexpectedly, the combatants signed an armistice (2 June) as a prelude to arranging a final European settlement. Probably neither side was sincere in its public protestations for a general peace since the allies put forth the impossibly high demands of the dissolution of the Confederation of the Rhine and the Grand Duchy of Warsaw, the ceding of the Illyrian provinces to Austria and the restoration to Prussia of her pre-Jena frontiers. At the Congress of Prague, Napoleon played for time and tried to prevent Austria from joining the alliance by offering a few trivial slices of territory. But the interlude benefited the allies far more than the French whose resources were stretched to the limit. First Sweden then Austria joined the coalition against Napoleon so that when the fighting resumed again in mid-August, the allies were able to put close to a million well-equipped and fresh soldiers against the inexperienced and weary French. The effects were to show almost immediately. While Napoleon was able to inflict a serious defeat on the allies at Dresden (26–27 August), separate detachments on special missions under Marshals Oudinot, Vandarme and Macdonald were badly mauled. It was not possible, therefore, to envelop the allied armies and deal with each peacemeal as in 1805–6. Thus individual battles were not likely to bring the enemy to heel and produce the spectacular political results of Napoleon's earlier career. The best he could do was not lose. At the Battle of Leipzig (16–19 October), the so-called Battle of the Nations (more 'nations' fought in Russia the previous year), for example, the French were able to fight the allies to a draw with about equal numbers of casualties on both sides but were forced to retreat in the face of advancing allied reinforcements. This forced a withdrawal to the Rhine which in turn produced great dividends for the allies. The King of Bavaria had defected on the eve of the battle, Saxony was subsequently occupied and its king, Napoleon's only German ally, was a prisoner of war, while one by one the German princelings prudently switched sides. Furthermore, the entry of Austria into the war had opened a new front in Italy which pinned down Eugène's forces. The situation in Italy was rendered all the more difficult by Murat's defection in January, while in Spain, Wellington and his allies were advancing towards the Pyrenees against the French armies which had been depleted to reinforce the army in Germany.

As the vice tightened, Napoleon responded by a flurry of diplomatic activity and a renewed attempt to plumb the depths of French resources. The Pope was restored to Savona in the hope of rallying support in Italy but after some hesitation, the Spanish refused an offer of an end of hostilities in return for the release of Ferdinand VII. Among the main combatants, there was a confused round of negotiations at Frankfurt in which the astonished allies had to withdraw an offer of a general peace on the basis of France's 'frontiers of 1792' after Napoleon accepted it. Once again, neither side was sincere. Much of allied diplomacy was directed towards painting Napoleon as warmonger to both French and European public opinion and it is certain that the British, who were the paymasters of the coalition, would not have accepted the annexation of Belgium which the phrase 'frontiers of 1792' could have implied. Napoleon, for his part, probably only wanted to spin out negotiations while he organized yet another army for the approaching campaign. Napoleon was also facing considerable pressures at home for peace which manifested themselves in the Senate and Legislative Body which met towards the end of the year. Both were allowed to examine diplomatic documents to evaluate Napoleon's claim that he had done all he could to secure peace and while the Senate reported favourably, an unpublished report presented by Laine, an unknown Bordeaux lawyer, argued that

Napoleon had needlessly delayed replying to the allies and that a truly national effort against the impending invasion was only possible so long as Napoleon respected liberty, property and free institutions. This was too much and the Legislative Body was promptly dissolved. The Emperor would appeal to the nation directly.

For once, the nation's response was poor. In a crudely cynical move, the government tried to revive the sentiments of 1793 by ordering a *levée en masse* and sent out *commissaires* to whip up patriotic fervour and supervise the prefects' efforts to conscript more men and resources. Bonapartist and patriotic historians have consistently misunderstood this phase of the decline for they lay the blame for the failure of the *levée en masse* on the *commissaires* whose twenty-year average age difference over the representatives on mission of the Year II is supposed to have made them lacklustre and uninspiring. Yet the unspoken assumption behind this interpretation, that ardent Frenchmen only desired to be given a lead which was not forthcoming, masks a very real difference from the circumstances of 1793.

In 1814, France alone had lost about 562,500 soldiers through death, missing in action or prisoners of war. Overall, the Napoleonic wars cost her roughly 916,000 men. For the age cohort born between 1790 and 1795, this represented a loss rate of 38 per cent which is 14 per cent higher than the casualties inflicted on the generation of 1891–5 in the First World War, generally thought to be France's most devastating war. Furthermore, for certain parts of the country there was no recovery from the 1810–12 economic crisis. Although the harvest of 1812 was good and those of 1813 and 1814 were even abundant, times were hard, particularly in the Midi. Heavy frosts in the autumn of 1811 destroyed olive trees which in some regions were just coming into production after the disastrous winter of 1788–9. The recovery of the fair at Beaucaire in 1812, always a sensitive barometer of the economy of the Midi, was a partial illusion since merchants liquidated stocks at a loss to American buyers. Once the Anglo-American war began in June, even this market was lost. Much of the region's troubles can be attributed to the tightening British blockade. In 1812 and 1813, only twenty-four neutral ships entered Marseille, in 1814, a mere eight, while wine exports plummeted by over 2000 per cent. Freight and maritime insurance rates shot up. Shipbuilding and coastal fishing practically ceased. Misery was so great people could no longer afford soap, and in 1812 this industry employed only one tenth the number of people it had the year before. Roughly the same proportion of the population was inscribed on the indigent rolls.

With the tribute from the conquered territories lost, France was expected to finance the war entirely from her own resources at a time when large sectors of the economy were unable to do so. The land tax was raised by 30 per cent and then by 50 per cent, personal taxes by 50 per cent and then by 100 per cent and the various indirect taxes at rates varying between 10 per cent and 100 per cent. Even before this immense gouging, taxes of all sorts in the Côtes-du-Nord, and undoubtedly elsewhere, had risen by 42 per cent between the Year IX and 1813, more, in other words, than most incomes had. It is no wonder that as political control slackened with the allied advance, the country underwent a fiscal rebellion. Nor was there time to raise, equip and train a new army. From the beginning, recruiting ran into difficulties. Culling the classes of 1808–14 once again brought an excess of 24,000 men because of enthusiastic volunteers in some of the old revolutionary areas, but the call-up of the class of 1815 was not pursued with vigour and the levy of another 300,000 men from all the classes between 1800 and 1814 ran into enormous difficulties. The administrative system could scarcely keep track of individuals in the shower of levies, classes which had already been called up two and three times were resentful and many deserted. All the old tactics of garrisoning gendarmes and reprisals against families were deployed with mediocre results. In the west, the old link between conscription and violence was reforged as bands of deserters robbed stagecoaches and tax offices. At the end of January 1814, only 63,000 of the levy of 300,000 had been enrolled. Nor were there any weapons, since many of the arsenals in Germany were cut off by the allied advance. Altogether, it was estimated that 700,000 muskets had been lost in the previous two years. Finally, there were no reserves. At the cavalry depot at Versailles, for instance, there were only 7100 men available for service out of a theoretical complement of 18,600, but there were only 3600 horses.

The *levée en masse* of 1814 then failed because the imperial government had already accomplished much of what the Committee of Public Safety was trying to do in 1793. But the invaders of 1814 were very different from those of the previous generation. In 1793, the Austrians had restored as much of the Old Regime as they could along the occupied northern frontier, including the parlements and the tithe; in 1814, the allies proclaimed that their only enemy was Napoleon, not the French people. Not only did they not repeat the mistake of the Brunswick Manifesto, they did not even proclaim the restoration of the Bourbons as a war aim. This was not because of a wily instinct for propaganda but because there was no consensus about the shape of postwar French government. The British were convinced that only a Bourbon government could secure a lasting peace but were not willing to impose Louis XVIII; Tsar Alexander spoke vaguely about consulting the French nation on its future; Metternich, the Austrian minister, could see advantages in a regency under Marie-Louise so that France could be used as a counterweight in the coming dispute over Poland; and the stolid Prussians were prepared to follow an Austrian lead. More than anything else, it was Napoleon's stubborn insistence on fighting to the end against all odds which brought down the Bonaparte dynasty.

That he would not have the time to reconstitute and train his armies ought to have been clear to Napoleon once the allies decided on a winter campaign. In the event, the defensive line of the Rhine was easily breached and the allies poured into France from several points. From then on, a defeat was inevitable for however brilliant and successful Napoleon was in the half-dozen or so engagements and battles in which he took personal command, he had lost the ability to control the overall strategic situation. As late as February, the allies offered the French representative, Coulaincourt, at negotiations at Châtillon-sur-Seine the prewar frontiers of 1792 while Napoleon held out for the 'natural frontiers', that is, the Rhine, a counterproposal which was completely unacceptable and which Napoleon was quite unable to enforce. The failure of these talks produced the Treaty of Chaumont (1 March) whereby the allies, lubricated by considerable British subsidies, promised each other not to conclude a separate peace and to continue the war for twenty years if necessary. They gave Napoleon an ultimatum of a cease-fire and a settlement on the basis of the 1791 frontiers, which he, gambler to the last, rejected. Meanwhile, the vice was closing. By mid-March, the allies were in control of large areas of French territory on a line from Lyon to Nancy, and in the southwest Anglo-Spanish forces were threatening Bayonne and Toulouse. On 12 March, Lynch, mayor of Bordeaux who had been recruited into the Chevaliers de la Foi the year before and who was aided by conspirators, some of whom had been involved in the insurrection of the Year VII, turned over Bordeaux to Wellington. Bordeaux's noisy proclamation of the Bourbons was designed to convince the sceptical allies that there really was popular support for the former ruling house and no doubt it helped but, as always, military events were decisive. After the Battle of Arcis (20–21 March), Napoleon was forced to withdraw eastwards to the fortresses near the Marne, which exposed Paris to an allied attack. In the event the capital surrendered.

Characteristically, Napoleon was convinced he could fight on but almost no one else was. In Bonapartist historiography, this phase comprised the series of weaknesses and betrayals which brought the Empire down but these events are better conceived as the struggle for the nature of the successor regime. Napoleon's position was extremely weak. In the immediate vicinity of the fighting, he was outnumbered by well over two to one, not counting other troops available to the allies on short notice. Paris was also in no position to withstand a long siege. The only fortification was the incomplete *octroi* wall, good enough to protect against cavalry raids but useless against artillery. The only men capable of handling the city's artillery were the coastguards and polytechnic students since the naval gunners had been sent to the front. The only experienced troops were a handful of Young Guards and gendarmes. The National Guard, which had only been revived in January, soon reached an impressive number of 40,000 on paper but many were armed with only ancient hunting muskets and 3000 were armed only with pikes. Overall then, the city's forces were no match for the 145,000 allied troops rapidly massing near the northern and western barriers. Accordingly, Joseph, lieutenant-general of the Empire, authorized Marshal Marmont to open talks with the allied generals and then he, Marie-Louise, the King of Rome and some members of the government left the city. The next day, 31 March, Marmont arranged an armistice which permitted the withdrawal of his army to the south of Paris. A few hours later, 'the Cossacks', as Parisians called most allied troops, entered the city.

The marshals too finally lost their fighting spirit. In a celebrated interview at Fontainebleau, Ney, speaking for the four other marshals present, told Napoleon that the soldiers would no longer fight, a statement which was manifestly untrue since the ordinary soldiers with the Emperor were enthusiastically clamouring to march to relieve Paris. It was an ominous portent for the future. But Ney undoubtedly spoke for his colleagues. Napoleon had to give

up. At allied insistence, he abdicated both for himself and his
successors on 6 April.

The First Restoration

When the allied armies occupied Paris, they issued a declaration
under the name of the Austrian commander-in-chief, Schwartzenburg, refusing to deal with Napoleon or any member of his
family and inviting the Senate to form a provisional government.
For the first time in public at any rate, the allies proclaimed the
overthrow of the Empire as one of their aims. This probably made
a restoration of the Bourbons inevitable. The exclusion of a
Regency was suggested by Talleyrand who had arranged a
convenient tumult on the streets to keep himself in Paris when other
members of the government left. The establishment of the new
regime was a collective effort, however, and the basis of the new
constitution reflected the interests and concerns of the men who
made it. This was the work of the Senate which contributed five of
its number to the provisional government and twenty members to
a constitutional commission. That is, the body which took
responsibility for deposing Napoleon on 2 April was composed of
men from the old revolutionary legislatures, the dignitaries of the
Empire, imperial officials, officers and the like. Economically
speaking, land must have contributed greatly to their incomes since
many of them depended upon the revenues of the 'senatoreries', or
state domains turned over to them by the government. In social
terms, Napoleon was overthrown by an assembly of landowners
and functionaries. The conceptions of government of all these men
reflected their backgrounds as revolutionary and Napoleonic
politicians and officials. There would be a bicameral legislature
responsible for consenting to taxes, an independent judiciary,
equality of opportunity, an amnesty for all political opinions,
freedom of religion and the press, fiscal and legal equality,
irrevocable guarantees for owners of *biens nationaux*, and
recognition of both the Old Regime and imperial nobilities.
Although this was changed later, it was even said that Louis XVIII
was 'called' to the throne by 'the French people', in other words,
the nation, not the king, was sovereign. It should not be surprising
that the 'Charter' resembled the Constitution of 1791. It was on the
table for reference as the commissioners worked, although the

king's powers of appointment were much greater in 1814.

If the 'men of 1789' were to triumph, it was essential to get Louis XVI's brothers to accept the Charter. In the event, it was forced on them. When the Comte d'Artois arrived in Paris in early April in the uniform of the National Guard no less, the Senate was extremely reluctant to recognize his title of lieutenant-general until he accepted the Charter. Tsar Alexander also insisted that he recognize it. Thus the emergence of a parliamentary regime in France depended in part upon the most despotic of the European monarchs. With nowhere to turn, Artois conceded. As long ago as 1805, his brother the Pretender had interred the Declaration of Verona which had promised an integral restoration of the Old Regime and instead accepted the existing judicial, military and administrative structure but said nothing about a legislature with powers over taxation. Another declaration issued from his English residence at Hartwell on 1 February 1813 reiterated these points and expressed the hope that the issue of *biens nationaux* could be settled by 'transactions' among the present and former owners. Privately, he disliked the notion of the state paying Protestant ministers. In the circumstances of 1814 he too would have to bend and, recognizing reality with none of Artois's bad grace, he waited until the eve of his entry to Paris to publish the Declaration of Saint-Ouen on 3 May which accepted the principles of the Senate's project but not the actual document. A new commission set to work on a new charter which differed from the old only in that the Senate was replaced with a Chamber of Peers nominated by the king, the 'senatoreries' were abolished, and to be an elector for the Chamber of Deputies one had to pay 300 francs in taxes, to be eligible to be a deputy, 1000 francs. Of all the various electoral schemes of the entire period, this was the most restrictive. As experience would show, this put electoral power overwhelmingly in the hands of big landowners. Finally, the preamble to the Charter did not recognize national sovereignty; instead the Charter was said to be 'granted' by the king. Thus were planted the seeds of the revolution of 1830.

The fact that the Restoration was effected the way it was ensured that it would not be counterrevolutionary. None of the elements of opposition to the Empire – the clergy, the malcontents in the army, the intelligentsia or the royalists of the Chevaliers de la Foi – played a crucial role. Nor had the out-and-out reactionaries. In 1790, Artois and the émigrés had planned to effect the counterrevolution by a combination of military conspiracy and popular insurrection.

Yet in 1814, the officers had remained loyal almost to the last and many of the troops were Bonapartist. In fact there had been no great royalist upsurge. Even the royalists of Bordeaux were probably a minority. The council which succeeded the imperial administration is generally supposed to have represented the big merchants and viticulturalists who had suffered greatly from the blockade. But their limited programme of the rule of law and maintenance of the sales of *biens nationaux* was not such as to give them overwhelming support from within the city. They only assumed power when the prefect and most of the garrison had left. When the archbishop arranged a magnificent Te Deum to mark the entry of the British, many National Guardsmen and municipal councillors were visibly disgruntled. At its most optimistic, the little royalist Bordelais army never numbered more than 800 in a city of 70,000. Elsewhere, violent royalism was rare. An attempt to seize Rodez by the Chevaliers de la Foi in March had to be called off when only 200 'knights' showed up. There was a royalist riot at Marseille on 14 April in which Provençal-speaking crowds vainly attacked the prefecture. This showed that popular royalism still existed but such disturbances were almost unique. Even the old *Vendée militaire* and the chouans north of the Loire had not risen, an indication of just how effective the imperial government's policy of disarming the west had been. Instead, the young men had responded by trying to avoid conscription, and by the spring there were signs of a general breakdown of law and order as brigand bands roamed the countryside. But this was only a pale shadow of the great days of 1793.

There were even pro-Bonapartist demonstrations. Peasants in Lorraine, goaded beyond endurance by requisition or outright pillage, formed partisan units. One of them was actually led by a parish priest whose men showed considerable skill in guerrilla attacks. There are numerous examples of country people killing allied stragglers or observation troops, or picking up muskets from allied dead on the battlefield and turning them over to imperial soldiers or coming forward to help troops move heavy cannon through the muddy roads of Champagne. In mid-April, soldiers stationed in Clermont-Ferrand countered the prefect's reading of the deposition decree with cries of 'Vive l'Empereur!', while a crowd of cavalrymen led by junior officers broke down the door of the cathedral to harass a priest who had unfurled the white flag of the Bourbons. In the countryside of Auvergne, there were rumours that a restoration presaged the reimposition of the tithe and feudal dues, while later that summer in a few communes peasants paraded an effigy of the king on an ass. In Strasbourg, soldiers almost rebelled when they were told to wear the royalist white cockade. Almost everywhere there was a general refusal to pay taxes, and in some places there were antifiscal rebellions. In the Haute-Garonne, Gironde, Vendée, Seine-Inférieure, Pas-de-Calais and at Marseille, Rennes, Cahors, Chalon-sur-Saône and Limoges, officials of the *droits réunis* and the *octroi* were attacked and their registers burned. Royalist agents and a proclamation of the Prince de Condé had led people to believe that those taxes would be abolished or much reduced. In some regions like Anjou, people acted on this propaganda, reasoning that since the war was over no taxes at all were necessary – a remarkable example of the survival of medieval notions of fiscality. When Louis XVIII maintained the *droits réunis*, disappointment was sharp.

Given time, the restored Bourbons might have been able to assuage these fears, but from the top down experience soon showed that reconciling the servants and loyalists of the imperial and royalist regimes would be far from easy. As major instruments in overthrowing Napoleon, the senators did exceptionally well. Only 37 of the French senators were excluded from the 155-member Chamber of Peers, 12 because they were *conventionnels*, while 84 were included, each with a magnificent pension of 36,000 francs. To the end, they had known how to look after themselves. The continuity of personnel among the upper courts was also great but other institutions suffered more. Since it was so closely identified with the Emperor, it is not surprising that 40 per cent of the members of the Council of State were eliminated. There was no thoroughgoing purge of the prefectoral corps but 28 of 87 were fired outright because they had been revolutionaries or imperialist zealots, while of the 36 new appointments which the first Restoration made, one third were former émigrés. The number of nobles in the corps as a whole nearly doubled – a significant indication of whom the regime thought its friends were. Much of this was to be expected and the purges were not very great in comparison to those of the previous twenty-five years, but the voluble courtiers around the Comte d'Artois let it be known that this was only the beginning of a vast settling of accounts. Intelligent and indolent, Louis XVIII could not muzzle his dim and impetuous brother. Nor could he always control his ministers. When the remaining *biens nationaux* still in state hands were returned to their former owners, the minister defending the bill claimed that the émigrés had followed the 'right line' in the 1790s. This was an enormous blunder since it seemed to suggest that the government itself was not committed to the promises of the Charter and the Declaration of Saint-Ouen. The owners of *biens nationaux* and their descendants were certainly a significant constituency, a group in which the urban bourgeoisie was disproportionately represented so that the loyalty of this element of the ruling class was doubtful.

In the constitutional scheme of things, the common people counted for nothing so nothing was done to wean them from the shock of Napoleon's defeat. Thus the Emperor retained much of his popularity well after his abdication. The old Napoleonic bric-à-brac – playing cards, medallions, statuettes, broadsheets, dinner plates, and so on – continued to circulate with the addition of mawkish engravings of the Emperor confining the King of Rome to the care of the National Guard who supposedly represented the French people. Enterprising printers put out other drawings depicting a sleeping eagle with the caption, '*He* will return!' Indeed, there were rumours from the beginning of the Restoration that he already had returned or had escaped to raise an army in Turkey. The docks in the lower courts were jammed with unfortunate individuals being prosecuted for having shouted 'Vive l'Empereur!' within earshot of a gendarme. During the second Restoration especially, there were many who predicted that his third coming would be a prelude to the end of days or that he returned secretly and spoke only to those who really believed or to innocent children.

After the disasters of the 1812–13 campaigns, the army was closer to its civilian roots than it had been for some time and so imperial feeling ran high among officers and men as well. The government also contributed to it through a number of clumsy policies. New generals with émigré or chouan service were created at the rate of about three a month, many of the peasant captains of the west were given direct commissions and their followers given pensions. About six thousand men, mostly composed of Louis XVI's former bodyguards, émigrés from Condé's and the British mercenary regiments, chouan and Vendean officers, and well-heeled young men with connections were appointed to the Maison du Roi, a royal bodyguard designed to prevent another 10 August. If there was enough money for old friends and new, the necessity to pay off the Empire's debts required a rapid demobilization of former imperial soldiers who were dumped into a disorganized economy which had not yet made the transition to civilian production. For those who remained, pay was irregular and many thousands of officers were retired on half-pay. Many found it difficult to make the transition to the isolation and boredom of civilian life. Other soldiers were clearly angry. When the allies evacuated the country in June and the prisoners of war returned, many simply refused to believe the Emperor had gone. The thousands who returned from the abominable and deadly prison hulks in England were in no mood to consider the allies as liberators. The thousands of others who returned from the garrisons and fortresses of Germany, Holland and Belgium *knew* that no one had defeated them and believed that somehow Napoleon had been betrayed. Even defeat did not convince soldiers from Spain who marched through the streets of Grenoble shouting 'Vive l'Empereur! Vive le Roi de Rome!'

The Hundred Days

The insensitivity of the Bourbons to Napoleon's continuing popularity among the common people and the army created a fantastic opportunity. For a time, it appeared as if the old gambler would content himself with his fate. The Treaty of Fontainebleau gave Napoleon the island of Elba off the coast of Tuscany and certain Italian states to Marie-Louise. The powers also lived up to their policy of maintaining that Napoleon was the only enemy and the Treaty of Paris limited France to her Old Regime frontiers with significant adjustments. But fissures which had always existed in the anti-Napoleonic coalition, particularly over the disposition of Poland, quickly manifested themselves. The allies also refused all contacts between Napoleon and his son who was to lead a pariah's existence at the Hapsburg court until his sad death in 1832. Finally, the Bourbons refused the pension they were bound by treaty to pay. So as Napoleon busied himself with organizing his Lilliputian army and navy and throwing himself with characteristic energy into organizing public works of all sorts on Elba, his agents were able to report the division among the allies and the bad faith of the Bourbons. Most promising of all were stories of the massive discontent in the army and among the common people. Adventurer to the last, he escaped, eluding a small British naval squadron and landing on the French coast near Cannes on 1 March 1815 with a mere 1100 men. On 20 March, he was in Paris; as he had predicted, he had reconquered his kingdom without firing a shot. Louis XVIII had fled to Ghent. Soldiers had thrown down their arms at the sight of him. Ney melted despite his promise to bring him back to Paris in an iron cage, partly because his troops had begun to defect to the Emperor and partly because the old magic had mesmerized him too. It was symbolized by the poetic proclamations printed up on Elba and rapidly distributed: 'The eagle, with the national colours, will fly from steeple to steeple until it reaches the towers of Notre Dame.' Many of his old officials were ecstatic. His former postmaster, the Comte Lavallette, met him amidst a tumultuous crowd on the steps of the Tuileries: ' . . . he walked up slowly, his eyes closed and his hands outstretched, as a blind man walks, and showing his happiness by his smile alone.' On 12 June, Napoleon set out for Waterloo. The adventure was over.

The sudden flash of the Hundred Days lit up the many faces of France as they had been for the previous twenty-five years. Not only did the episode show the Empire's trumpeted claim to have united Frenchmen to have been utterly hollow, it nearly ignited the dialectic of revolution and counterrevolution of the 1790s. It also showed that Napoleon had been assimilated into ancient peasant beliefs of a just king protecting the people against a vexatious nobility. When that protection was removed, the result was panic. Thus as early as April 1814, officials in the Corrèze reported the anxieties of the countryside that the Restoration meant the revival of tithes and seigneurial dues. During the Hundred Days, peasants in the mountains of the Cantal were saying, 'Eh bien, if Bonaparte returns, we are certain not to pay the tithe and dues' while in the Puy-de-Dôme, peasants 'were overjoyed to be subjected no longer to the nobles who are already beginning to regard them as their vassals'. In the Tarn, the country people regarded his return 'as a grace from heaven which has saved them from oppression'. In the Nièvre, one former constitutional priest even denounced the pretensions of 'the noble caste'. In all of these assertions, it was less a question of fear of returned émigrés since the vast majority had returned home over a decade earlier, than the fear of a rapacious nobility once the government ceased to control them. Thus, the Napoleonic myth in the countryside showed how ancient beliefs of royalty tinged with divinity could become revolutionary in the appropriate circumstances. Napoleon's very presence thus stimulated revolution. When his army approached Grenoble on the night of 6 March, it was accompanied by at least 2000 peasants bearing torches to light the way and laying pine boughs before his horse. There were some who reminded him that 'liberty' had begun in these lonely mountains – they were referring to the agreement at Vizille in 1788. His proximity set off a revolt among the soldiers and working people of Grenoble and the commanding officer had to flee. Much the same happened at Lyon. The La Guillotière quarter where many silk weavers lived was particularly overjoyed and some shouted, 'A bas les prêtres! Mort aux royalistes!' Similar anticlerical and antiroyalist slogans were heard at Besançon, Bar-le-Duc, Rennes, Saumur and Strasbourg. Insurrections broke out in most of the Burgundian towns along the route while thousands lined the highway to celebrate his passage, sing the Marseillaise and plant liberty trees. Further afield, in the Corrèze, peasants removed the 'seigneurial' pew from a parish church and burnt it on the public square just as their ancestors had in 1790 and there were one or two incidents of presbyteries being attacked by armed crowds and the priests having to flee in terror. In the Isère, at least four châteaux were attacked by rural National Guards and a crowd of unruly Guards murdered the mayor of La Sône, who was also a silk manufacturer, because he tried to prevent them from raising the tricolour. Earlier, the inhabitants of the same commune shouting antiroyalist slogans, had attacked the employees of the *droits réunis*.

The Hundred Days revived antiseigneurial, anticlerical and antifiscal sentiments among the common people. It also revived Jacobinism among the small-town bourgeoisie. In Burgundy, Brittany, Dauphiné, the Lyonnais, Languedoc and elsewhere, 'patriots' formed 'federations' to 'defend liberty', 'maintain the rights of man menaced by the hereditary nobility...', and to 'terrify traitors, confound plots and vanquish the counterrevolution'. There was a good deal of talk about immobilizing the interior enemy, about the danger of moderation, and about the necessity of 'grandes mesures de salut public'. No more than in 1793 were the men who uttered these chilling statements wide-eyed individuals on the margin of society. As earlier, they were often provincial officials, small-town lawyers and ordinary working people. In Paris, the social composition of the 'fédérés' was much the same except students and officials played an even greater role. Recruitment for the special volunteer battalions often depended on the attitude of employers, as it had twenty years before. In one case, all sixty employees of a tobacco firm – a state monopoly – enrolled, and overall the battalions represented a fair cross-section of the world of work. Even so, they attracted less than one third of their desired complement, although whether this was because of popular apathy or because men preferred the army is not clear.

Napoleon must have been astonished at the extent of revolutionary feeling his return evoked. The two Elba proclamations he wrote himself appealed to the glory of the army, blamed his defeat in 1814 on the betrayal of Marshals Marmont and Augereau and claimed the throne in the name of a plebiscitary monarchy born of the Revolution. He scarcely alluded to social problems and to fears of the old privileged classes. Although he soon adjusted his language to suit the situation, as when he referred to himself in one speech as the 'father of the poor', his profound aversion to terrorism and disorder and the necessity to appease the broadest possible current of opinion, pushed him in a liberal direction. This was symbolized by the appointment of Carnot to the Interior. More importantly, he induced his old political enemy, Benjamin Constant, to draft a new constitution, called the 'Additional Act to the Constitutions of the Empire'. Aside from raising the electorate from 15,000 to 100,000 for the new lower house and instituting a more liberal press law, the 'Additional Act' was remarkably similar to the Bourbon Charter. No matter who reigned, France would be a constitutional, parliamentary monarchy, even though neither liberal royalist nor liberal imperialist trusted their respective monarchs. The Additional Act even spoke of the necessity of granting free institutions as a way of rallying the nation for its own defence, a proposition Napoleon had explicitly rejected in 1813. Not surprisingly, he considered this an expedient but the political situation in the spring of 1815 showed that he could not act without the support of the liberal bourgeoisie and the common people, that is, the major elements in the old revolutionary coalition. The results of the plebiscite on the Additional Act show this clearly. It was approved by 1,552,942 to 5740 with exceptionally large majorities in a broad band stretching from Lorraine southwestwards to the Charentes, that is in regions where the Revolution had always had strong support. In Paris, nearly half the positive votes came from officials, and in the provinces support came overwhelmingly from mayors and notaries who voted in far greater proportion than their fellow citizens. On the other hand, like all the elections of the period, only about one in five of the electors bothered to vote, with most of the large towns showing only half as much interest as the surrounding countryside. In so far as it is possible to generalize about a plebiscite with such a low turnout, Napoleon had lost significant support compared to the plebiscite of the Year X but Bonapartism was already showing its ability to appeal to the rural masses.

Contemporaries were quick to notice the parallels between the Hundred Days and the Revolution. As in the 1790s, a revolutionary upsurge evoked an equally powerful response of popular counterrevolution. In the west, the leaders from the great days of the Vendée or their descendants, d'Autichamp, Sapinaud, La Roche Jacquelin, etc., prepared to organize another explosion under the Duc de Bourbon. Their prospects were hardly encouraging. As always, they quarrelled about the timing of the rebellion, the men lacked arms, the gendarmerie stopped powder from getting into their hands and the fédérés in the towns and villages were mobilizing in their turn. The leaders were so demoralized that the Duc de Bourbon, who soon left the country, asked for terms from the imperial authorities. The men were less discouraged, however. Soon, the chouans in Brittany and Normandy, some of whom were beginning their third campaign, were roaming the countryside undertaking the familiar ambushes of troops, molesting mayors and buyers of *biens nationaux* and trying to besiege the towns. Although the western departments were exempted from the hated conscription which had so fuelled rural discontent in earlier risings, the government still had to leave 20,000 badly needed troops in the region to contain the situation. The 'internal enemy', therefore, aided the 'external enemy' at Waterloo.

The royalist response in the Midi was much more vicious. Lynch and his friends got a meagre response from the National Guard of Bordeaux and none at all from the garrison so that their small army soon capitulated. Headquarters at Toulouse under the Baron de Vitrolles quickly collapsed too, but elsewhere the overall commander, the Duc d'Angoulême, did manage to recruit large numbers of rural volunteers, called *miquelets*, from the Gard, Ardèche, Aveyron, Lozère and Haute-Loire. But the untrained *miquelets* and the single royalist regiment moving on Lyon were no match for the Bonapartist army especially since it was rapidly being reinforced by enthusiastic volunteers from the National Guards of the Saône-et-Loire, Ain, Côte-d'Or, Jura and Haute-Saône.

Consequently, Augoulême capitulated at La Pallud on 8 April. Unfortunately, the *miquelets* had been responsible for all sorts of excesses on their way to battle: killing Bonapartist prisoners, molesting Protestants who were overjoyed at Napoleon's return, raiding tax offices or pillaging the rich. As they returned home, there were numerous reprisals. In one particularly ugly incident in the Protestant village of Arpaillarques, they were fired on, a few were killed, the women, it was said, finishing them off with scissors and stripping and mutilating the bodies. After Waterloo, the response to this and other outrages was another round of the bloody White Terror in which hundreds of Protestants, fédérés and Bonapartists were assaulted or killed.

The legacy of the Hundred Days which most struck the generation of younger romantic writers was the image of the lonely figure stalking the rock of St Helena. For many ordinary Frenchmen there was another, of bloody violence and civil war.

Conclusion

In his most famous of insights, Tocqueville argued that the Empire was no mere episode in French history, that beneath the spectacular details of Napoleon's biography the period witnessed the completion of the millennial process of centralization. He claimed that centralization emasculated the Old Regime nobility and while this is questionable, it was certainly true of the imperial notables. Here was a dominant class that did not rule, nor was it bourgeois. It was an adjunct of the professional bureaucracy which paid less and less attention to it over time. Its members furnished their sons to the state while the state transformed its most illustrious servants into notables through generous salaries, grants and rewards. They were a heretogeneous group of financiers, bankers, merchants, functionaries, landowners, rentiers, military personnel and old and new aristocrats. Whatever their private values were – and most derived their incomes in one way or another from the market place – the regime paid little attention to them. Instead it celebrated military, not 'bourgeois', mores, rewarding entrepreneurial activities even less than had the so-called 'feudal' monarchy of Louis XV. The notables settled for a dictatorship and in return received a regressive fiscal system, an exemption from military service opportunity and a married property settlement that underpinned the social position of the rich paterfamilias until the First World War.

Centralization in its Napoleonic form represented the failure of an ideal so many had promoted at the beginning of the period. Many articulate Frenchmen in the 1780s had begun to conclude that the solution to the problem of rapacious royal despotism was not to reinforce corporate privileges which determined ministers had shown they knew how to subvert, but to impose a constitution based on contract theories of government and concepts of natural rights. This proved to be extremely difficult. If anyone had any illusions about the aristocracy, the events of the six weeks following the opening of the Estates-General showed that a majority of the representatives of the nobility was willing to concede fiscal privileges but that their constituents were a good deal less certain on questions of a liberal constitution and individual liberties, and rejected equality of rights without question. Opinion even within the non-privileged bourgeoisie, who had the most to gain from a programme of fiscal equality and equality of opportunity, was hesitant. Many clung to urban, corporate and individual privileges beyond the spring of 1789. Only the extraordinary events of the summer, including the general breakdown of government, the widespread violence and the fears of an aristocratic plot, permitted the patriots to overcome this natural caution and persuade the political nation to accept their views. They were remarkably successful. When counterrevolutionary plotters tried to revive corporatist or particularist appeals in 1790–1, they received almost no response and even in 1793 when it might have been expected, the federalists said next to nothing about provincial rights or decentralization.

Nonetheless, the extraordinary sentiment of national unity at the end of 1789 was something of an illusion. In the first place, the Revolution was largely an urban phenomenon. The demands for the most radical changes in 1789, the ones that most closely anticipated the actual reforms, originated in the larger towns and cities. Even within the cities, as the local elections of 1790 and the membership of the newly forming clubs showed, the revolutionary coalition appealed to particular groups. The nobility mostly remained aloof, as did the poor and the mobile. Instead, the revolutionaries were professional bourgeois and skilled and settled artisans. Their Manichaean rhetoric when they contested power among themselves suggested enormous struggles among vast numbers, but an examination of participation rates in the National Guard and the low electoral turnouts throughout the period show that they operated on a comparatively narrow base. In some cities in the Midi where sectarian strife and Old Regime lines of clientage were strong, that base was extremely fragile and it took the collective efforts of the patriots throughout the region to keep each other in power. Unfortunately the expeditions, plots and counterexpeditions also contributed to the extraordinary violence which continued in the Midi in one form or another from 1790 to the end of the decade.

Support could be even more narrow in the countryside. When it came to policy on property rights, the revolutionaries were inflexible, despite some theoretical musings from time to time which have overheated some historians' imaginations. There was, therefore, no assured place within the revolutionary galaxy for large numbers of people with little or no property to defend. Farmers, sharecroppers, labourers, the semiskilled or the unskilled, the poor and the marginal were left to make their own calculations of whether a revolution none had anticipated had left them better off than before. The Civil Constitution compounded the difficulty of this decision. As a rule of thumb, where the material benefits of the reforms of 1789–90 were spread widely enough, as they were likely to have been where peasant ownership was extensive, people tolerated a religious settlement they may have detested otherwise. But where Protestant communities which welcomed the Revolution were too impetuous or where substantial numbers, or critically placed individuals, had gained nothing or perhaps had even lost, the result was likely to have been a festering and debilitating round of disturbances which made the countryside impossible to govern.

The immense turmoil resistance and repression provoked had immense economic consequences. In the west, for instance, local textile production did not recover Old Regime levels until the 1830s. The war with Britain ruined the great Atlantic seaboard economy of the Old Regime and its attendant industries like shipbuilding, rope-making, sail-making and so on. If the woollen trade was at all typical, up to one third of the departments witnessed a shattering deindustrialization. The extensive deurbanization which was still evident as late as 1815 and the fact that there was no agricultural revolution (that is, no change in productivity, no overall change in land use and little new cropping) suggests continued, perhaps even greater, misery for the poor. A generation of economic competition was skipped. The gap between Britain and France in labour productivity growth was wider in 1815 than it had been in 1789. Although the performance of some sectors like cottons, chemicals and banking were impressive under the Empire, overall it seems perverse to speak of a capitalist breatkthrough in this period.

Repression and its failures had other consequences. An easy reflex from the beginning, it became a necessity in wartime. The war was supposed to be the occasion also to repress the internal enemy. In fact, the revolutionaries' analysis that the people were only misled by the self-serving machinations of nobles, foreign agents and priests proved to be dangerously wrong. Such ideas justified represssion but the war made repression more difficult and called for sacrifices from those who received nothing and who therefore resented any demands. Resistance, war, repression, resistance was a vicious circle which proved nearly impossible to break. The revolutionary dictatorship did not. It achieved great successes against the foreign and internal enemies, but even under the Terror there were signs of spreading discontent at the military levies, at dechristianization and at the requisitions and controlled prices. Meanwhile, the revolutionaries fell out among themselves over the direction and aims of repression. It was a debate which was played out on the floor of the Convention and in myriad forms in the provinces, but, whatever its exact contours, exemplary and pitiless repression created an atmosphere of mutual fear and hatred. Once the consensus which supported repression evaporated after thermidor, the discontents of the previous four years snapped the bonds among the revolutionaries and between them and much of the nation. In the thermidorean reaction, the revolutionary coalition imploded upon itself because some reckoned former colleagues had become crazed cutthroats. In the new purges, many of those willing or able to govern were pushed from sight as well as the ultraterrorists. Challenged from below and subverted from within, government scarcely existed in some regions.

With the failure of even an elitist form of representative institutions in fructidor, the political nation recognized the necessity for some form of authoritarian government. It was an assumption shared by all the brumairians who wished to institutionalize what the Directors stumbled upon of not allowing public opinion a decisive role in national politics. The ruling clique wanted a free hand to conclude the war on France's terms, that is a peace which could only be enforced through aggressive domination. It was willing to surrender itself to Bonaparte because the price of peace at home was an even more authoritarian government than they had anticipated. Since the Concordat restored so much of the refractory clergy, it also risked reopening the sores of the dozens of local chouanneries which had finally bled the last Directory towards its final convulsions. Governing circles viewed most clerics and their adherents as potential counterrevolutionaries, as men who were in league with the most unscrupulous reactionaries, who in turn were subsidized by the foreign enemy, notably England. Only a ruthless, centralized dictatorship could forestall the disorders which Bonaparte had so recently quelled.

In the end, therefore, the vast weight of ancient peasant France imposed itself upon the government, at the expense of many of the ideals of 1789. This too should be seen as the result of a popular movement, perhaps even as one of the most profound revolutions of the revolutionary epoch.

Bibliography

Abbreviations

AHR	*American Historical Review*
AHRF	*Annales historiques de la Révolution française*
Annales. ESC	*Annales. Economies Sociétés Civilisations*
BJRL	*Bulletin of the John Rylands Library*
CSS	*Congrès des sociétés savantes*
EHR	*English Historical Review*
ESR	*European Studies Review*
FHS	*French Historical Studies*
JMH	*Journal of Modern History*
P & P	*Past and Present*
RF	*La Révolution française*
RHMC	*Revue d'histoire moderne et contemporaire*

Books in French were published in Paris unless otherwise noted.

Chapter 1

There are countless general studies which cover all or part of the revolutionary period. Among the best and most recent in ascending order of difficulty are: G. Rudé, *Revolutionary Europe, 1783–1815* (London, 1964), Marxist; A. Goodwin, *The French Revolution* (London, 1953), liberal; M. J. Sydenham, *The French Revolution* (London, 1965), stressing adherence to the idea of national sovereignty as a destructive force; N. Hampson, *A Social History of the French Revolution* (London, 1963), emphasizing the rise of a popular movement and the role of the provinces; G. Lefebvre, *The French Revolution* (2 vols., London, 1962–4), Marxist, detailed, often cryptic; and finally, J. M. Roberts, *The French Revolution* (Oxford, 1978), reflects much recent revisionist writing. Almost all of these end in 1794–5 or 1799 which is itself a judgement; for the continuation of the story, see below under 'Directory' and 'Napoleon'. On the historiography of the Revolution, see G. Rudé, *Interpretations of the French Revolution* (London, 1961), A. Cobban, *Historians and the Causes of the French Revolution* (London, 1967) and especially J. McManners, 'The Historiography of the French Revolution' in A. Goodwin (ed.), *New Cambridge Modern History*, vol. 7.

Among the best treatments of the Old Regime in its European context are W. Doyle, *The Old European Order, 1660–1800* (Oxford, 1978) and O. Hufton, *Europe: Protest and Privilege, 1730–1789* (Glasgow, 1980). The starting point for relating the Old Regime to the Revolution is the excellent revisionist W. Doyle, *Origins of the French Revolution* (Oxford, 1981) which is really an extended dialogue with G. Lefebvre's classic statement of the bourgeois theory of the Revolution in his brilliant *The Coming of the French Revolution* (Princeton, 1947), as is A. Cobban's argumentative *The Social Interpretation of the French Revolution* (Cambridge, 1964).

The question of the relations between bourgeoisie and aristocracy is discussed in Doyle's 'Was there an Aristocratic Revolution in Pre-Revolutionary France?', *P & P*, 57 (1972), 97–122, and G. V. Taylor's two articles which attack the question of the form of wealth between the two groups: 'Types of Capitalism in Eighteenth-Century France', *EHR*, lxxix (1964), 478–97, and 'Noncapitalist Wealth and the Origins of the French Revolution', *AHR*, lxxii (1967), 469–96. On the question of office-holding directly, see P. Dawson, *Provincial Magistrates and Revolutionary Politics in France, 1789–1795* (Cambridge, Mass., 1972), J. Egret, 'L'aristocracie parlementaire française à la fin de l'ancien régime', *Review historique*, cviii (1952), 1–14, and the more general M. Reinhard, 'Elite et noblesse dans la seconde moitié du XVIIIe siècle', *RHMC*, iii (1956), 5–37. On the question of social mobility, see D. Bien, 'La réaction aristocratique avant 1789: l'exemple de l'armée', *Annales. ESC*, xxix (1974), 23–48, 505–34, and 'The Army in the French Enlightenment: Reform, Reaction and Revolution', *P & P*, 85 (1979), 68–98, both of which force considerable revision of the frustrated ambition theory, as does L. R. Berlanstein, *The Barristers of Toulouse in the Eighteenth Century (1740–1793)* (Baltimore, 1975), a model of one type of social history.

On the nobility, see the self-consciously revisionist G. Chaussinand-Nogaret, *La Noblesse au XVIIIe siècle. De la féodalité aux lumières* (1976) and the following classics: R. Forster, *The Nobility of Toulouse in the Eighteenth Century* (Baltimore, 1960), his 'The Provincial Noble: a Reappraisal', *AHR*, lxviii (1968), 681–91, and his *The House of Saulx-Tavannes* (Baltimore, 1971) and finally J. Meyer, *La noblesse bretonne au xviiie siècle* (2 vols., 1966). On another plane, P. Higonnet, *Class, Ideology and the Rights of Nobles During the French Revolution* (Oxford, 1981) has the merit of carrying the story down to 1799 but is often very odd. The question of noble privileges in taxation has not received the attention it merits but there is C. B. A. Behrens, 'Nobles, Privileges and Taxes in France at the End of the Ancien Régime', *Economic History Review*, xv (1962–3), 451–75, vigorously and effectively challenged by G. J. Cavanaugh in *FHS*, viii (1974), while the debate peters out in *ibid.*, ix (1976), 521–7, 681–92. Ms Behrens's assertion that the British paid more than the French is borne out in P. Mathias and P. K. O'Brien, 'Taxation in Britain and France, 1715–1810. A Comparison of the Social and

Economic Incidence of Taxes Collected for the Central Governments',
Journal of European Economic History, v (1976), 601–50, although to an
historian of France this is less interesting than the question of distribution
among groups and regions, a topic which is almost entirely neglected.

There is also far too little on the political and administrative history of
the century although there are signs of a renewal in W. Doyle, 'The
Parlements of France and the Breakdown of the Old Regime, 1771–1788',
FHS, vi (1969–70), 415–58; the allusive and brilliant D. Richet, *La France
moderne. L'Esprit des Institutions* (1973); J. Egret, *Louis XV et
l'opposition parlementaire* (1970); J. Bosher, *French Finances, 1770–1795:
From Business to Bureaucracy* (Cambridge, 1970); and the attempt to
rehabilitate Necker in R. D. Harris, *Necker, Reform Statesman of the
Ancien Regime* (Berkeley, 1979).

The essential introduction to the crisis of 1787–8 is J. Egret, *The French
Pre-Revolution, 1787–1788* (Chicago, 1977). On the first phase: A.
Goodwin, 'Calonne, the Assembly of French Notables of 1787 and the
Origins of the "Révolte Nobiliaire"', *EHR*, lxi (1946), 202–34, 329–77,
with attempts to supplement the story with perhaps too great a claim for
the notables' liberalism by V. Gruder, 'Paths to Political Consciousness:
the Assembly of Notables of 1787 and the "Pre-Revolution" in France',
FHS, xiii (1984), 323–55. On the role of the Paris parlement in the latter
part of the century, which stresses how unrepresentative of the nobility's
views the magistrates were, see B. F. Stone, *The Parlement of Paris, 1774–
1789* (Durham, NC, 1981).

It is becoming increasingly clear how socially heterogeneous the 'patriot
party' was. See, for example, the fine study by D. Wick, 'The Court
Nobility and the French Revolution: the Example of the Society of Thirty',
Eighteenth Century Studies, xiii (1980), 263–84; L. A. Hunt, *Revolution
and Urban Politics in Provincial France: Troyes, and Reims, 1786–1790*
(Stanford, 1978); and the bizarre but essential A. Cochin, *Les sociétés de
pensée et la Révolution en Bretagne, 1788–1789* (2 vols., 1925), as well as
his sketchy study of Burgundy in 'La campagne électorale de 1789 en
Bourgogne' in *Les Sociétés de pensée et la démocratie* (1921), 235–82. On
the influence of the patriots, M. Bouloiseau, 'La campagne électorale pour
les Etats-généraux de 1789. L'exemple d'Orléans', *Actes du 88ᵉ CSS.
Clermont-Ferrand 1963* (1964), 221–32. The question of the sociology of
the Enlightenment was first thoroughly investigated in D. Mornet's classic
Les origines intellectuelles de la Révolution française (1933) but has since
been renewed in the most exciting way by R. Darnton's *The Business of
Enlightenment. A Publishing History of the Encyclopédie (1775–1800)*
(Cambridge, Mass., 1979) and his 'The Encyclopédie Wars of
Prerevolutionary France', *AHR*, lxxviii (1973), 1331–52. What Turgot
meant to some reformers can be seen in D. Dakin, *Turgot and the Ancien
Régime in France* (London, 1939) and K. M. Baker, *Condorcet, from
Natural Philosophy to Social Mathematics* (Chicago, 1975), while the
question of diffusion of enlightenment to social classes is attacked more

directly in F. Furet (ed.), *Livre et société dans la France du XVIIIe siècle* (2 vols., 1965, 1970), R. Chartier, 'Culture, lumières, doléances: les cahiers de 1789', *RHMC*, xxviii (1981), 68–93 and A. Burguière, 'Société et culture à Reims à la fin du XVIIIe siècle: la diffusion des "Lumières" analysée à travers les cahiers de doléances', *Annales. ESC,* xxiii (1967), 303–39. On the whole, all of the recent authorities allow for a greater influence of the Enlightenment than Mornet or Lefebvre did but also show that it worked in unexpected ways on unexpected groups.

The social composition of the Estates-General is analysed in E. LeMay, 'La composition de l'Assemblée nationale constituante: les hommes de la continuité', *RHMC*, xxiv (1977), 340–63; of the clergy and much else in M. G. Hutt, 'The Role of the Curés in the Estates-General', *Journal of Ecclesiastical History*, vi (1955), 190–220 and his 'The Curés and the Third Estate: the Ideas of Reform in the Pamphlets of the French Lower Clergy in the Period 1787–1789', *ibid.*, viii (1957), 74–92, while R. F. Necheles, 'The Curés in the Estates-General of 1789', *JMH*, xlvi (1974), 425–44, emphasizes the patriot clergy. The composition of the nobility and its relation to region and life experience is thoroughly delineated in P. Higonnet and J. Murphy, 'Les députés de la noblesse aux Etats-généraux de 1789', *RHMC*, xx (1973), 230–43, and their 'Notes sur la composition de l'Assemblée Constituante', *AHRF*, xlvi (1973), 31–6.

For the differences in the Second and Third Estates, compare the figures in Chaussinand-Nogaret, *La Noblesse*, 201–26 with G. V. Taylor, 'Revolutionary and Nonrevolutionary Content in the *Cahiers* of 1789: an Interim Report', *FHS*, vii (1972), 479–502. An exciting angle on this issue, urbanization, ennobling office and state of opinion in the spring of 1789, is in G. Shapiro and P. Dawson, 'Social Mobility and Political Radicalism: the Case of the French Revolution of 1789', in W. O. Aydelotte, A. G. Bogue and R. W. Fogel (eds.), *The Dimensions of Quantitative Research in History* (Princeton, 1972), 159–91.

Chapter 2

There is no general social history of the countryside in the Old Regime or even the cities for that matter but the general themes of rural history enunciated in Marc Bloch's *French Rural History* (London, 1966) are still accepted. There are general syntheses of land-holding and social structure in G. Lefebvre, 'Répartition de la propriété et de l'exploitation foncière à la fin de l'Ancien Régime', in his *Etudes sur la Révolution française* (1954), 279–306, in C. E. Labrousse and F. Braudel (eds.), *Histoire économique et sociale de la France* (4 vols., 1970–6), t.ii, and G. Duby, *Histoire de la France rurale* (3 vols., 1975), t.ii. One of the best monographs in either language is T. J. A. Le Goff, *Vannes and Its Region: a Study of Town and Country in Eighteenth Century France* (Oxford, 1981). Le Goff shows how close urban and rural societies were in this period and there were similar dependencies even with large cities like Paris (D. Roche, *Le peuple de Paris. Essai sur la culture populaire au XVIIIe siècle* [1981], an indication that a misconception that wage-earners were the cutting edge of Revolution can affect research on an earlier era) or Lyon in M. Garden, *Lyon et les lyonnais au XVIIIe siècle* (Paris, n.d. [1975]).

Michel Morineau (*Les Faux-semblants d'un démarrage économique* [1971] and 'History and Tithes', *Journal of European Economic History*, x [1981], 437–80) almost single-handedly overturned Labroussian notions of economic growth (C. E. Labrousse, *Esquisse du mouvement des prix et des revenus en France au XVIIIe siècle* [1933]) although E. Le Roy Ladurie and J. Goy, *Tithe and Agrarian History* (Cambridge, 1982) allow for some growth and put the French experience in a continental perspective. Morineau's work on national and individual incomes ('Budgets populaires en France au XVIIIe siècle', *Rev. hist. écon. soc.*, 1 [1972], 203–37) puts O. Hufton's evocation of poverty, crimes, failure of charitable institutions and government bungling (*The Poor of Eighteenth Century France* [Oxford, 1974]) in its economic context. On subsistence questions, see S. Kaplan, *Bread, Politics and Political Economy in the Reign of Louis XV* (2 vols., The Hague, 1976) and his briefer but similar 'The Famine Plot Persuasion in Eighteenth Century France', *Trans. American Phil. Soc.* (1982). Opinion in Paris can also be followed through Ch.-L. Chassin (ed.), *Les élections et les cahiers de Paris en 1789* (4 vols., 1888), t.iii (for Hardy's notes), and G. Rudé, 'The Bread Riots of May 1775 in Paris and the Paris Region', in J. Kaplow (ed.), *New Perspectives on the French Revolution* (New York, 1965), 191–210.

The basic overview of the economic and social crisis of 1788 is still C. Schmidt, 'La crise industrielle de 1788 en France', *Revue historique*, xcvii (1908), 78–94, but the subject badly needs updating. Among the basic new contributions are L. Trenard, 'The Social Crisis in Lyons on the Eve of the French Revolution', in Kaplow's *New Perspectives*, 47–67; P. Dardel, 'Crises et faillites à Rouen et dans la Haute-Normandie', *Rev. hist. écon. soc.*, (1948–9), 53–71, M. Bouloiseau, 'Aspects sociaux de la crise cotonnière dans les campagnes rouennaises en 1788–1789', *Actes CSS*, lxxxi (1956), 403–28; O. Hufton, *Bayeux in the Late Eighteenth Century* (Oxford, 1967) and her 'Beggary, Vagabondage and the Law: an Aspect of the Problem of Poverty in Eighteenth Century France', *ESR*, ii (1972), 97–123; N. Castan, *Justice et répression en Languedoc à l'époque des lumières* (1980), while I. Cameron, *Crime and Repression in the Auvergne and the Guyenne, 1720–1790* (Cambridge, 1981) is tantalizing on the problem of the impact of the crisis on one of the major police institutions.

On the electoral process in the countryside, see J. Dupâquier, 'Structures sociales et cahiers de doléances. L'exemple du Vexin français', *AHRF*, xli (1968), 433–54, R. Robin, *La société française en 1789: Sémur-en-Auxois* (1970) and G. V. Taylor, 'Revolutionary and Nonrevolutionary Content in the *Cahiers* of 1789'.

The rumours, disturbances and eventually revolution in Paris can be followed in G. Rudé, *The Crowd in the French Revolution* (Oxford, 1959); J. Godechot, *The Taking of the Bastille, July 14th, 1789* (London, 1970) which not only illustrates the atmosphere of fear and mounting economic disorder but also the Crown's military dispositions, a subject further developed by examining morale and desertion in S. F. Scott, *The Response of the Royal Army to the French Revolution: the Role and Development of the Line Army during 1787–93* (Oxford, 1978), while J. Chagniot, 'Le Problème du maintien de l'ordre à Paris au XVIIIe siècle', *Bull. soc. hist. moderne*, no. 8 (1975), 32–45, completely revises received ideas about the structure of the French guards; P. Caron, 'La Tentative de Contre-révolution de juin-juillet 1789', *Revue d'histoire moderne*, vii (1906–7), 5–34, 649–78, is still a basic article for detecting the contours of the royal plot and popular fears about it. 'J.J.G.' (ed.), 'Documents inédits sur le mouvement populaire du 14 juillet 1789 et le supplice de M. de Launay, gouverneur de la Bastille et de Bertier de Sauvigni', *Revue historique*, i (1876), 497–508, shows the underside of the 'popular movement' in Paris.

The literature on the revolution in the provinces is immense. A vital starting point is L. A. Hunt, 'Committees and Communes: Local Politics and National Revolution in 1789', *Comparative Studies in Society and History*, xviii (1976), 321–46, which completely replaces D. Ligou, 'A propos de la révolution municipale', *Rev. hist. écon. soc.*, xxiv (1960), 146–77. The peasant revolution is the subject of one of the best history books written this century: G. Lefebvre, *The Great Fear of 1789: Rural Panic in Revolutionary France* (London, 1973). See also his thesis *Les Paysans du Nord pendant la Révolution française* (2 vols., 1924) and O. Hufton, 'The Seigneur and the Rural Community in Eighteenth-Century France: the Seigneurial Reaction: a Reappraisal', *Transactions of the Royal Historical Society*, 5th ser., xxix (1979), 21–39; A. Soboul, 'La Révolution française et "la féodalité". Notes sur le prélèvement féodal', *Revue historique*, ccxl (1968), 33–56; F. Sabatié, 'Stagnation démographique, réaction seigneuriale et mouvements révolutionnaires dans la région de Toulouse. Le cas de Buzet-sur-Tarn', *AHRF*, xliv (1971), 176–96; M. A. Pickford, 'The Panic of 1789 in Touraine', *EHR*, xxvi (1911), 703–18, and her 'The Panic of 1789 in Lower Dauphiné and in Provence', *ibid.*, xxix (1914), 276–301; R. Jouanne, 'Les Emeutes paysannes au Pays Bas-Normand', *Le Pays Bas-Normand*, 1 (1957), 2–85; Jean Girardot, 'L'Insurrection populaire de 1789 dans le bailliage d'Aumont', *Bull. Soc. d'Agriculture, Lettres, Sciences et Arts du département de la Haute-Saône* (1932), 18–57; H. Diné, *La Grande Peur dans la généralité de Poitiers* (1951). The narrative for the Mâconnais is based on interrogations and depositions in Archives départementales de Saône-et-Loire, B 1717–18 and F. Evrard, 'Les Paysans du Mâconnais et les brigandages de juillet 1789', *Ann. Bourgogne*, xix (1947), 1–39, 97–121. Lefebvre omitted P. Conard, *La Peur en Dauphiné (Juillet–Août 1789)* (1904) from his narrative. A. Aulard, *La Révolution française et la féodalité* (1919) is full of common sense. E. Le Roy Ladurie, 'Révoltes et contestations rurales en France de 1675 à 1788',

Annales. ESC, xxix (1974), 6–22, and A. Davies, 'The Origins of the French Peasant Revolution of 1789', *History*, n.s., xlix (1964), 24–41, provide different overviews.

The Night of 4 August has been renewed by J.-P. Hirsch (ed.), *La Nuit du 4 août* (1978) and P. Kessell, *La Nuit du 4 Août 1789* (1969) but the interpretation in this book is based largely on the entire text (Hirsch omits the vital part) of R. Hennequin (ed.), 'La nuit du 4 août 1789 racontée par le constituant Parisot', *RF*, lxxx (1927), 17–22 and then by Boullé's correspondence published in volumes xi–xiii (1889–92) of *Revue de la Révolution*. Both C. Kuhlmann, *Influence of the Breton Deputation and the Breton Club in the French Revolution (April–October, 1789)* (Lincoln, Nebraska, 1902) and A. Bouchard, *Le Club Breton* (1920) are still useful, while L. Desgraves (ed.), 'Correspondance des députés de la sénéchaussée d'Agen aux Etats Généraux et à l'Assemblée nationale (1789–1790)', *Receuil Trav. Soc. Acad. d'Agen, année 1967*, 3rd s., t.l (1966), 9–191, are interesting for their coolness. R. de Crévecoeur (ed.), *Journal d'Adrien Duquesnoy* (3 vols., 1894) shows the reactions of a deputy ('un délire, une ivresse') not in on the secret. For those who were like Parisot and Boullé, there was an explicit link with the Declaration of the Rights of Man, the most extensive discussion of which is in L. Gottschalk and M. Maddox, *Lafayette in the French Revolution Through the October Days* (Chicago, 1969). G. Chinard, *La Déclaration des droits de l'homme et du citoyen et ses antécédents américains* (Washington, 1945) shows, as do Gottschalk and Maddox, that there were greater links with American examples than Lefebvre allowed.

Both A. Mathiez, 'Etude critique sur les journées des 5 et 6 octobre 1789', *Revue historique*, lxvii (1898), 241–81, lxviii (1899), 258–94, lxix (1900), 41–66 and J. Egret, *La Révolution des notables. Mounier et les monarchiens* (1950) are vital to a study of the October Days.

Chapter 3

The period between October 1789 and June 1791 witnessed the installation of new institutions, considerable disturbance and the beginnings of both the counterrevolution and a growing radical movement in the large cities. Most of these are connected in complex ways and the route to understanding them begins with J. Godechot's magnificent *Les Institutions de la France sous la Révolution et l'Empire* (1968) and P. Sagnac, *La Législation civile de la Révolution* (1898).

Many local histories contain discussions of the workings and results of the new electoral system, although no one has attempted a synthesis. An exception, and this only on a narrow theme, is M. Edelstein, 'Vers une "sociologie électorale" de la Révolution française: la participation des citadins et campagnards (1789–1793)', *RHMC*, xxii (1975), 508–29. Otherwise, there is F. Mourlot, *La Fin de l'Ancien Régime dans la*

généralité de Caen (1787–1790) (1913); Ch. Jollivet, La Révolution dans
l'Ardèche (1788–1795) (Largentière, 1930); J. Bricaud, L'Administration
du département d'Ille-et-Vilaine au début de la Révolution (Rennes, 1965);
H. Pommeret, L'Esprit public dans le département des Côtes-du-Nord
pendant la Révolution, 1789–99 (Saint-Brieuc, 1921); P. Bois, Paysans de
l'Ouest (Le Mans, 1960); P. Thomas-Lacroix, 'Le Conseil général du
Morbihan sous la Révolution', Bull. Soc. polymathique du Morbihan, ci
(1974), 61–77; E. Appolis, 'La formation du département du Tarn', Bibl.
de la Rév. du Tarn (1938); M. Bruneau, Les Débuts de la Révolution dans
le Cher et l'Indre (1789–1791) (1913); M. Jusselin, L'Administration du
département d'Eure-et-Loir pendant la Révolution (Chartres, 1935); P.
Bertrand, 'L'Administration du district de Narbonne pendant la
Révolution, 1790–1795', Thèse de 3ᵉ cycle (Toulouse, 1973); J. Girardot,
Le Département de la Haute-Saône pendant la Révolution (2 vols., Vesoul,
1973); J. Viguier, Les Débuts de la Révolution en Provence (1894) on the
Bouches-du-Rhône, Var, Basses-Alpes; M. Agulhon, La vie sociale en
Provence intérieure au lendemain de la Révolution (1970); J. Sentou,
'Impôts et citoyens actifs à Toulouse au début de la Révolution', Annales
du Midi, lx (1948), 159–79; H. Millot, Le Comité permanent de Dijon
(juillet 1789–février 1790) (Dijon, n.d. [1925]); M. Wahl, Les Premières
Années de la Révolution à Lyon, 1788–1792 (1894); D. Ligou, Montauban
à la fin de l'ancien régime et aux débuts de la Révolution (1958).

Most of these also contain much material on the impact of other reforms
but these should first be tackled through general histories. For finances: M.
Marion, Histoire financière de la France (4 vols., 1914–21), R. Schnerb, Les
Contributions directes à l'époque de la Révolution dans le Puy-de-Dôme
(1933) and his 'La répartition des impôts directs à la fin de l'Ancien
régime', Revue d'histoire économique et sociale, xxxviii (1960), 129–45, and
especially the generally neglected L. de Cardinal, 'Le "citoyen" de 1791
payait-il plus ou moins d'impôts que le "sujet" de 1790?', Comité des
travaux historiques et scientifiques. Notices inventaires et documents, xxii
(1936), 61–110. Finally, S. E. Harris, The Assignats (Cambridge, Mass.,
1930).

On the Civil Constitution of the Clergy: J. McManners's elegant The
French Revolution and the Church (London, 1969) and his vibrant French
Ecclesiastical Society under the Ancien Regime: a Study of Angers
(Manchester, 1960); C. Langlois and T. Tackett, 'A l'épreuve de la
Révolution (1770–1830)' in F. Lebrun (ed.), Histoire des catholiques en
France du xvᵉ siècle à nos jours (1980) and their 'Ecclesiastical Structures
and Clerical Geography on the Eve of the French Revolution', FHS, xi
(1980), 352–70. Unlike many local studies which highlight the refractories,
Tackett's Priest and Parish in Eighteenth-Century France; a Social and
Political Study of the Curés in a Diocese of Dauphiné, 1750–1791
(Princeton, 1977) is a sensitive evocation of a region of high oath-taking.
Among older general studies, on the republican side there is A. Aulard,
Christianity and the French Revolution (London, 1927) and A. Mathiez,

Rome et le clergé français sous la Constituante (1911); on the Catholic, P. de la Gorce, *Histoire religieuse de la Révolution française* (5 vols., 1902–23) and A. Sicard, *Le clergé de France pendant la Révolution* (3 vols., 1912–17). Among the best regional studies there is E. Sevestre, *Les Problèmes religieux de la Révolution et de l'Empire en Normandie, 1787–1815*, vol. ii, *La Constitution civile du clergé, 1791–95* (1924); M. Giraud, *Essai sur l'histoire religieuse de la Sarthe de 1789 à l'An IV* (1920); A. Lallié, *Le Diocèse de Nantes pendant la Révolution* (Nantes, 1893); C. Port, *La Vendée angevine* (2 vols., 1888); J. Peter and C. Poulet, *Histoire religieuse du département du Nord pendant la Révolution* (2 vols., Lille, 1930); G. Richard, 'L'Application de la Constitution civile du clergé dans le département du Nord (juin 1791 à septembre 1792)', *Revue d'histoire moderne*, xii (1909), 229–56; R. Reuss, *La Constitution civile du clergé et la crise religieuse en Alsace (1790–1795)* (2 vols., Strasbourg, 1922); R. Pallnat de Besset, 'La résistance à la Constitution civile du clergé dans le district de Montbrison', *Les Amitiés foréziennes et vellares*, v (1926), 305–10, 398–410; E. Sol, *Eglise constitutionnelle et église réfractaire* (1930); F. Barry, *Etienne Delcher, évêque constitutionel de la Haute-Loire. Etude religieuse sur la Révolution* (1925); R. Fage, *Le Diocèse de Corrèze pendant la Révolution* (Tulle, 1890); F. Brideux, *Histoire religieuse du départment de Seine-et-Marne pendant la Révolution* (2 vols., Melun, 1953); Marquis de Roux, *Histoire religieuse de la Révolution à Poitiers et dans la Vienne* (Poitiers, 1952).

On the fall of the seigneurial regime: S. Herbert, *The Fall of Feudalism in France* (London, 1921); G. R. Ikni, 'La terre de Lierville de 1715 à la Restauration' and J.-N. Luc, 'Le rachat des droits féodaux dans le département de la Charente-Inférieure (1789–1793)' both in A. Soboul (ed.), *Contributions à l'histoire paysanne de la révolution française* (1977); and M. Giraud, *La Révolution et la propriété foncière* (1959).

On troubles in general, S. F. Scott, 'Problems of Law and Order during 1790, the "Peaceful" Year of the French Revolution', *AHR*, lxxx (1975), 859–88. The risings of 1790–1, however, are much neglected relative to those of 1789. The only synthesis is A. Ado, *The Peasant Movement in France during the Great Bourgeois Revolution of the End of the Eighteenth Century* (Moscow, 1971), in Russian. Until the promised translation appears, one must make do with J. Boutier, 'Les révoltes paysannes en Aquitaine (décembre 1789–mars 1790)', *Annales. ESC*, xxxiv (1979), 760–86; H. Sée, 'Les troubles agraires en Haute-Bretagne, 1790–91', *Bull. d'hist. écon. de la Révolution* (1920–1), 231–373; M. Ozouf, 'Du mai de liberté à l'arbre de la liberté: symbolisme révolutionnaire et tradition paysanne', *Ethnologie française*, n.s., v (1975), 9–32; G. Bussière, *Etudes historiques sur la Révolution en Périgord* (3 vols., ? – 1903), vol. 3; E. Lapeyre, *Les Insurrections du Lot en 1790* (Cahors, 1892); and E. Sol, *La Révolution en Quercey* (4 vols., 1930–2), vol. 2. The narrative here has also been supplemented by the enormous documentation in the *Archives parlementaires*, and by Arch. nat., D XXIX (Comité des rapports) and D

XXIX bis (Comité des recherches). The best overview on the *biens nationaux* is still G. Lefebvre, 'La vente des biens nationaux' in his *Etudes sur la Révolution française* (1963), 307–37.

On the counterrevolution, J. Godechot's *The Counter-Revolution: Doctrine and Action, 1789–1804* (New York, 1971) is somewhat outdated but is the only synthesis, while E. Vingtrinier, *La Contre-révolution, première période 1789–1791* (2 vols., 1924–5) deftly portrays the links between the émigrés, the powers and the conspiracies. On these latter, see E. Daudet, *Histoire des conspirations royalistes du Midi sous la Révolution (1790–1793)*(1881); Comte d'Espinchal, *La Coalition d'Auvergne (Avril 1791)* (Riom, 1899); H. Martineau, 'La coalition de Poitou et la préparation de la guerre de Vendée', *Revue du Bas-Poitou*, xxiv (1911), 360–7; A. Goodwin, 'Counterrevolution in Brittany: the royalist conspiracy of the Marquis de la Rouerie, 1791–3', *BJRL*, xxxix (1957), 326–55; C. de Parrel, 'La coalition de Basse-Normandie, 1791', *Bull. Soc. Hist. de Normandie* (1951), 249–57, 271–97; and G. Lewis, *The Second Vendée: the Continuity of Counterrevolution in the Department of the Gard, 1789–1815* (Oxford, 1978). Lewis points the way to a social interpretation as does J. N. Hood in his articles 'Protestant-Catholic Relations and the Roots of the First Popular Counterrevolutionary Movement in France', *JMH*, xliii (1971), 245–75, 'Revival and Mutation of Old Rivalries in Revolutionary France', *P & P*, 82 (1979), 82–115, and 'Permanence des conflits traditionnels sous la Révolution: l'exemple du Gard', *RHMC*, xxiv (1977), 603–40. An analytic overview is the highly suggestive C. Lucas, 'The Problem of the Midi in the French Revolution', *Trans. Roy. Hist. Soc.*, 5th ser., xxviii (1978), 1–25. For the incredibly complex struggles in Avignon and the Comtat generally, see the allusive P. Charpenne, *Les grandes épisodes de la Révolution dans Avignon et le Comtat* (4 vols., Avignon, 1901), and the too brief J. Barrual, *La contre-révolution en Provence et dans le Comtat* (Cavaillon, 1928). It is possible to get some idea of the social forces in play in the Midi in 1790–1 through A. Segond, 'Les foules révolutionnaires à Avignon (1789–1791)', *Provence historique*, xix (1969), 307–28, and above all through the articles by P. Arches in 'Etude sociale d'un bataillon contre-révolutionnaire de la garde nationale de Montauban', *Actes du 80ᵉ CSS. Lille 1955* (1955), 163–9, 'Aspects sociaux de quelques gardes nationales au début de la Révolution', *Actes du 81ᵉ CSS. Rouen-Caen 1956* (1956), 443–56 (Nancy, Aurillac and Marseille), and 'La garde nationale de Tarbes au début de la Révolution (juillet 1789–juillet 1790)', *Actes du 82ᵉ CSS* (1958), 69–77.

Radicalism in Paris in this period is not well served. Fortunately, J. Censer, *Prelude to Power. The Parisian Radical Press, 1789–1791* (Baltimore, 1976) fills a gap while R. B. Rose, *The Making of the Sans-culottes* (Manchester, 1983) carries the story through 1792 showing, *inter alia*, that *sans-culotte* ideology did not merely spring out of the circumstances of 1793–4 but was inculcated by local politicians who, whatever else they were, were not artisans. For the provinces, see M.

Kennedy, *The Jacobin Clubs in the French Revolution* (Princeton, 1981).

Chapter 4

There is no general study in English of the crisis which eventually brought about the fall of the monarchy but A. Mathiez, *Le Dix Août* (1916) and M. Reinhard, *La chute de la monarchie* (1969) more than compensate. Reinhard is especially good on Varennes and its relation to 10 August. See also G. Martin, 'La fuite à Varennes et l'impression dans le Sud-Ouest', *RF*, lxxxii (1929), 113–32.

Events in Paris are studied in A. Mathiez, *Le Club des Cordeliers pendant la crise de Varennes et le massacre du Champ de Mars* (1919) and F. Braesch, 'Les Pétitions du Champ de Mars', *RH*, cxlii–iv (1923), 192–209, 1–39, 180–97. G. A. Kelly, 'Bailly and the Champ de Mars Massacre', *JMH*, lii (1980), on demand supplements is a convenient summary while H. B. Applewhite, 'Political Legitimacy in Revolutionary France 1788–1791', *Jl Interdis. Hist.*, ix (1978), 245–73, studies evolving opinion among deputies.

The effect of Varennes on the provincial clubs was crucial. Kennedy's *Jacobin Clubs* explains the little support the Feuillants got, but both H. Chobaut, 'La pétition du club de Montpellier en faveur de la République', *AHRF*, iv (1927), 547–63, and R. Marx, *Recherches sur la vie politique de l'Alsace prérévolutionnaire et révolutionnaire* (1966) are important studies of exceptional clubs. See also P. Nicolle, *Histoire de Vire pendant la Révolution (1789–1800)* (Vire, 1923) and G. Maintenant, 'Les Jacobins d'Alençon (mai 1791–mars 1793)', *Soc. arch. de l'Orne*, xciv (1976), 79–104, 107–47, for echoes in two small Norman towns.

The impact of the ecclesiastical crisis in the provinces has been reconstructed through the local studies cited in the previous chapter, the papers of the *Comité ecclésiastique* (AN, D XIX 22) and the *Archives parlementaires* which also contain numerous petitions and addresses from clubs and from Paris sections, which also demonstrate a rising ride of war fever in the nation and its links to frustration over use of the veto. I. Bourdin, *Les Sociétés populaires à Paris pendant la Révolution* (1937) is generally disappointing on this period. M. Kennedy, 'The Jacobin Clubs and the Press: "Phase Two"', *FHS*, xiii (1984), 474–99, examines one aspect of the clubs' activities in this period.

On the economic crisis and the disturbances of 1792 see: Ch. Lorain (ed.), *Les subsistances en céréales dans le district de Chaumont de 1788 à l'An V* (2 vols., Chaumont-Paris, 1911–12); G. Lefebvre (ed.), *Documents relatifs à l'histoire des subsistances dans le district de Bergues pendant la Révolution (1788-an V)* (2 vols., Lille-Paris, 1914–21); G. Ikni, 'L'Arrêt de bateaux de grains sur l'Oise et l'Aisne, février 1792', *Annales historiques compiegnoises*, no. 5 (1979), 13–36; M. Vovelle, 'Les Campagnes à l'assaut des villes sous la Révolution' on the troubles of the Beauce in his *Villes et campagnes au 18ᵉ siècle (Chartres et la Beauce)* (1980), 227–76; his 'Les troubles sociaux en Provence, 1750–1792', *Actes du 93ᵉ CSS. Tours 1968* (1971), 325–72; and his 'Formes de politisation de la société rurale en Provence sous la Révolution française: entre jacobinisme et contre-révolution au village', *Ann. Bretagne*, lxxxix (1982), 187–204; F. Rouvière, *Histoire de la Révolution française dans le département du Gard* (4 vols., Nîmes, 1887–9), ii; F. Evrard, 'Les subsistances en céréales dans le département de l'Eure de 1788 à l'an V', *Com. Recherche et Publication des documents rélatifs . . . à la Révolution. Bulletin* (1908), 1–96; E. Campagnac, 'Un prêtre communiste; le curé Petit-Jean', *RF*, xlv (1904), 426–45; D. Hunt, 'The People and Pierre Dolivier: Popular Uprisings in the Seine-et-Oise Department (1791–1792)', *FHS*, xi (1979–80), 184–214; the *Archives parlementaires* and the papers of the 'Commission extraordinaire des douze' in AN, D XL.

On the unfolding political crisis in Paris and relations among the agitators, see F. A. Aulard (ed.), *Mémoires secrets de Fournier l'Américain* (1890); F. A. Aulard (ed.), *Mémoires de Chaumette sur la Révolution du 10 août 1792* (1893); J. Pollio and A. Marcel, *Le Bataillon du 10 août* (1881); J. Savina, *Les volontaires du Finistère et la prise des Tuileries (10 août 1792) (Journal d'un volontaire)* (Quimper, 1909); and J.-P. Cointet, 'Le bataillon des Filles Saint-Thomas et le 10 août', *AHRF*, xxxvii (1965), 450–67, while C. J. Mitchell, 'Political Divisions within the Legislative Assembly of 1791', *FHS*, xiii (1984), 356–89, convincingly revises our outlook on high politics.

For the aftermath, see the two classics F. Braesch, *La Commune du 10 Août* (1911) and P. Caron, *Les Massacres de Septembre* (1935) while J.-P. Bertaud (ed.), *Valmy* (1970) shows the 'nation-in-arms' view of 1792 to be very much alive, but Ch.-L. Chassin (ed.), *La Préparation de la guerre de Vendée, 1789–1793* (3 vols., 1892) and A. Du Chatellier, *Histoire de la Révolution dans les départements de l'ancien Bretagne* (6 vols., Paris-Nantes, 1836) are an antidote.

Chapter 5

M. Sydenham, *The Girondins* (London, 1961) first showed the Girondins were not a party but A. Patrick, *The Men of the First French Republic. Political Alignments in the National Convention of 1792* (Baltimore, 1972) tried to give alignments more consistency. One can follow the debate between the authors in *JMH*, xliii (1971), 287–93, 294–7. T. A. Di Padova, 'The Girondins and the Question of Revolutionary Government', *FHS*, ix (1976), 432–50, argues for Girondin hostility to revolutionary government by ignoring some critical details.

On the king's trial, there is the agreeable D. P. Jordan, *The King's Trial. The French Revolution vs Louis XVI* (Berkeley, 1979), M. Walzer (ed.), *Regicide and Revolution* (London, 1974) and A. Soboul (ed.), *Le Procès de Louis XVI* (1966).

There is still too little on the economic crisis of 1793 beyond A. Mathiez, *La vie chère et le mouvement social sous la Terreur* (2 vols., 1927), S. Peterson, 'L'approvisionnement de Paris en farine et en pain pendant la Convention girondine', *AHRF*, lv (1984), 366–85, and R. B. Rose, *The Enragés: Socialists of the French Revolution?* (New York, 1965).

By contrast, the material on the war of the Vendée is overwhelming. One can make a start with the boring but succinct G. Walter, *La Guerre de Vendée* (1963); the partisan-republican L. Dubreuil, *Histoire des insurrections de l'Ouest* (2 vols., 1926–30); the conservative E. Gabory, *La Révolution et la Vendée* (3 vols., 1941); and the massive Ch.-L. Chassin, *La Vendée patriote 1793–1800* (4 vols., 1893–5). An attempt to write retrospective sociology appears in C. Tilly, *The Vendée* (Cambridge, Mass., 1964) while an analysis of such literature was attempted by H. Mitchell, 'The Vendée and Counter-revolution: a Review Essay', *FHS*, v (1968), 405–29. On troubles elsewhere see J. Richard, 'La levée de 300,000 hommes et les troubles de mars 1793 en Bourgogne', *Ann. Bourgogne*, xxxiii (1961), 213–51.

Two very different overviews of federalism appear in M. Sydenham, 'The Republican Revolt of 1793: a Plea for Less Localized Studies', *FHS*, xii (1981), 120–38, and B. Edmonds, '"Federalism" and the Urban Revolution in France in 1793', *JMH*, lv (1983), 22–53. One of the best of local studies also chillingly conveys the atmosphere of fear of Jacobinism: C. Riffaterre, *Le Mouvement Anti-Jacobin et Anti-Parisien de Lyon et dans le Rhône-et-Loire en 1793* (2 vols., Lyon, 1912–28). Also on Lyon, see A. Grand, 'Le Club des Jacobins de la Croix-Rousse', *B. Soc. Lit., hist., arch. Lyon*, v (1913), 178–90; S. Charléty, 'La journée du 29 mai 1793 à Lyon', *RF*, xxxix (1898), 340–74, 385–426; and B. Edmonds, 'A Study in Popular Anti-Jacobinism: the Career of Denis Monnet', *FHS*, xiii (1983), 215–51.

A. Forrest, *Society and Politics in Revolutionary Bordeaux* (Oxford, 1975) believes federalism was a reflection of a bourgeoisie avid for profits but this is not what emerges from W. H. Scott, *Terror and Repression in Revolutionary Marseilles* (London, 1973) or from G. Guibal, *Le Mouvement fédéraliste en Provence en 1793* (1908). There were social forces in play certainly, as is clear in J. Brelot, 'L'Insurrection fédéraliste dans le Jura en 1793', *Bull. Féd. des Soc. sav. de Franche-Comté* (1955), 73–102, and in M. Crook, 'Federalism and the French Revolution: the Revolt of Toulon in 1793', *History*, lxv (1980), 383–97.

Federalism wore quite a different face in Normandy, however. See P. Nicolle, 'Le mouvement fédéraliste dans l'Orne en 1793', *AHRF*, xii (1935), 482–512, xiv (1937), 215–33, xv (1938), 12–53, 289–313, 385–410; J. Grall, 'Le Fédéralisme (Eure et Calvados)', *Bull. Soc. Antiquaires de Normandie*, lv (1961), 135–53; and A. Goodwin, 'The Federalist Movement in Caen During the French Revolution', *BJRL*, xlii (1959–60), 313–44.

The crisis in Paris can be followed in great detail in the *Archives parlementaires*, in A. M. Boursier, 'L'émeute parisienne du 10 mars 1793', *AHRF*, xliv (1972), 204–30, H. Calvet, 'Les origines du comité de l'Evêché', *AHRF*, v (1928), 430–41, and the outdated H. Wallon, *La Révolution du 31 mai et le fédéralisme en 1793* (2 vols., 1886).

Chapter 6

Much of the interpretation of the Terror as a conflict between a popular *sans-culotte* movement and bourgeois revolutionary government was fixed by A. Soboul, *Les Sans-culottes parisiens de l'An II* (1958), only part of which is available in English in separate translations entitled *The Parisian sans-culottes and the French Revolution* (Oxford, 1964) and *The Sans-Culottes* (New York, 1972). Although G. Williams, *Artisans and Sans-culottes* (London, 1968) and the extended reviews by Palmer (*FHS*, i [1960], 445–69) and by Bergeron, Furet and Mazauric (in Kaplow's *New Perspectives*) provide an excellent overview. The conflict was particularly sharp through institutions but less so socially, as is clear from R. C. Cobb, *The Police and the People. French Popular Protest, 1789–1820* (Oxford, 1970). While even in Paris, *sectionnaires* even in apparently militant sections showed great hesitancy and tried to avoid committing themselves. See M. Slavin, *The French Revolution in Miniature. Section Droits de l'Homme, 1789–1795* (Princeton, 1984). The correlation between humble social position and militancy breaks down for the provinces: see the neglected classic C. Brinton, *The Jacobins* (New York, 1930); R. C. Cobb, 'La Commission temporaire de la Commune-Affranchie' in his *Terreur et subsistances* (1965); A. Soboul and W. Markov (eds.), *Die Sansculotten von Paris* (Berlin, 1957) with French translations; M. T. Lagasquié, 'Recherches sur le personnel terroriste toulousain', *AHRF*, xliii (1971), 248–64; and M. Lyons, 'The Jacobin Elite of Toulouse', *ESR*, vii (1977), 259–84. Nor was the conflict always so sharp even in Paris: see R. B. Rose, 'Nursery of Sans-culottes: the Société patriotique of the Luxembourg Section, 1792–1795', *BJRL*, lxiv (1981), 218–45, and R. M. Andrews, 'Réflexions sur la Conjuration des Egaux', *Annales. ESC*, xxix (1974), 73–106.

On popular ideology itself, in addition to the translations of Soboul, see also his 'Religious Sentiment and Popular Cults during the Revolution: Patriot Saints and Martyrs of Liberty' in Kaplow (ed.), *New Perspectives*, 338–50, and R. Cobb, 'The Revolutionary Mentality in France', *History*, n.s., xlii (1957), 181–6.

On clubs in general in this period see H. Chobaut, 'Le nombre des sociétés populaires du Sud-Est', *AHRF*, iii (1926), 450–5, the letter from L. de Cardenal in *ibid.*, iv (1927), 77–9 and his *La Provence pendant la Révolution. Histoire des clubs jacobins (1789–1795)* (1929).

On the maximum and agrarian problems in general see G. Lefebvre (ed.), *Questions agraires au temps de la Terreur* (La Roche-sur-Yon, 1954) and R. B. Rose, 'The "Red Scare" of the 1790s: the French Revolution and the "Agrarian Law"', *P & P*, 103 (1984), 113–30 which show the hopes some groups had in this period. Experience was considerably grimmer. See P. M. Jones, 'La République au village in the Southern Massif Central, 1789–1799', *Hist. Jl,* xxiii (1980), 783–812. In addition to the collections of documents on subsistence cited earlier, see F. Mourlot, *Receuil des documents d'ordre économique . . . district d'Alençon, 1788–An IV* (3 vols., Alençon, 1907–10); J. Adher (ed.), *Le comité des subsistances de Toulouse (12 août 1793–3 mars 1795)* (Toulouse, 1912); P. Caron (ed.), 'Une enquête sur la récolte de 1792', *Bull. com. écon. Rév. fr.* (1913), 161–84; his 'Rapports de Grivel et Siret . . . sur les subsistances et le maximum', *ibid.* (1907), 67–231; G. Lefebvre (ed.), 'L'Application du maximum général dans le district de Bergues (sources, méthodes, histoire)', *ibid.* (1913), 415–46; C. Riffaterre (ed.), 'Les revendications économiques et sociales des assemblées primaires de 1793', *ibid.* (1906), 321–80. On the application in various regions see R. Legrand, 'La loi du Maximum en Basse-Picardie. Essai sur la réglementation économique', *Bull. Soc. Antiquaires de Picardie* (1946), 1–33; A. Richard, 'L'Application du 1er Maximum dans les Basses-Pyrénées', *Ann. révolutionnaires*, xiii (1921), 207–14; A. Dernier, 'Enquêtes agricoles de 1792 et 1793 dans la Vienne', *Bull. Soc. Antiquaires de l'Ouest*, 4e sér., viii (1965), 311–19; H. Carré, 'Essai sur les lois de Maximum dans le département de la Vienne', *ibid.* (1935), 700–15; Ch. Carrière, 'Le problème des grains et farines à Marseille pendant la période du Maximum', *Actes du 82e CSS* (1958), 161–84; P. Bécamps, 'La question des grains et la boulangerie à Bordeaux de 1792 à 1793', *Actes du 83e CSS. Aix-Marseille 1958* (1959), 261–76; E. Colet, 'Situation économique de Toulon pendant la rébellion de 1793', *Actes du 87e CSS. Poitiers 1962* (1963), 269–98; and his 'Situation économique de Toulon pendant la rébellion (juillet–août 1793)', *Provence historique*, xii (1962), 79–92; and H. Calvet, *L'Accaparement à Paris sous la Terreur. Essai sur l'application de la loi du 26 juillet 1793* (1933).

The account of the important *journées* of 4–5 September was derived largely from traditional sources like Soboul and Rudé but also from W. Markov (ed.), *Jacques Roux. Scripta et Acta* (Berlin, 1969), the *Archives parlementaires*, and A. Aulard (ed.), *La Société des Jacobins* (6 vols., 1889–97), t.v which Soboul precipitately dismissed as inaccurate, and so with it the fact that the idea of a demonstration originated in the Jacobin club and not, as he would have it, with the *sans-culottes*.

The study of dechristianization has been completely renewed by M. Vovelle, *Religion et révolution. La déchristianisation de l'An II* (1976) but see also the critique of G. Cholvy in *AHRF*, 233 (1978), 451–64, and Vovelle's reply in *ibid.*, 465–70. This number of the *AHRF* also contains essays on dechristianization in the Puy-de-Dôme, Oise, and the 'west' (i.e., Normandy). See also S. Bianchi, 'Les curés rouges dans la Révolution française', *AHRF*, liv (1982), 349–92, and the special issue of the *AHRF*, lv (1983) on Couthon. R. C. Cobb, 'Les débuts de la déchristianisation à

Dieppe', *ibid.*, xxviii (1956), 191–209; M. Dommanget, *La déchristianisation à Beauvais et dans l'Oise* (1918); E. Campagnac, 'Les débuts de la déchristianisation dans le Cher', *Ann. révolutionnaires*, iv (1911), 626–37, v (1912), 41–9, 206–11, 358–73, 511–20; H. Forestier, 'Les campagnes de l'Auxerrois et la déchristianisation', *Ann. Bourgogne*, xix (1947), 185–206; and his 'Le culte laical, un aspect spécifiquement auxerrois de la résistance des paroisses rurales à la déchristianisation', *ibid.*, xxiv (1952), 105–10.

On the question of resistance to dechristianization in addition to the local studies cited earlier, see G. Cholvy, 'Résistance populaire et clandestinité sous la Révolution française: la bordure orientale et méridionale du Massif central face à la persécution religieuse', *Revue du Vivarais* (1979), 175–90, F. Birdeux, *Histoire religieuse . . . Seine-et-Marne* and J. Charrier, *Histoire religieuse du département de la Nièvre pendant la Révolution* (2 vols., 1926).

The starting point for any study of repression is D. Greer, *The Incidence of the Terror during the French Revolution: a Statistical Interpretation* (Cambridge, Mass., 1935), a classic which has withstood critics like R. Louie, 'The Incidence of the Terror: a Critique of a Statistical Interpretation', *FHS*, iii (1964), 379–89, or statistically minded historians who misuse his tables (see Hunt, Lansky and Hanson below) because no one seems to realize that many of the victims of the revolutionary courts were executed outside their native departments. One of the curious effects of Greer's book was to reduce the emphasis on represssion in the Terror. M. Reinhard, for instance, gives it only one sentence in his *Nouvelle histoire de Paris. La Révolution, 1789–1799* (1971) and many historians sympathetic to the Jacobins manage to find other atrocities in history far worse than those of the Year II. This, however, is to miss what the Terror meant to contemporaries. See Scott's *Terror and Repression in Revolutionary Marseilles* and the dull B. Pocquet du Haut-Jussé, *Terreur et terroristes à Rennes, 1792–1795* (Mayenne, 1974).

To appreciate the impact of the Terror fully, it should be studied in its local context. Lyon is particularly well served. See E. Herriot, *Lyon n'est plus* (4 vols., 1937–40); D. Longfellow, 'Silk Weavers and the Social Struggle in Lyons during the French Revolution', *FHS*, xii (1981), 1–40; M. Séve, 'Sur la pratique jacobine: la mission de Couthon à Lyon', *AHRF*, lv (1983), 510–43; A. Solomon de la Chapelle, *Histoire des Tribunaux révolutionnaires de Lyon et de Feurs* (Lyon, 1879); and L. Madelin, *Fouché, 1759–1820* (n.d.).

On Marseille, Scott's *Terror and Repression* and P. Gaffarel, 'La Terreur à Marseille (Proconsulat de Barras et de Fréron)', *Ann. Provence*, 10ᵉ année (1913), 158–88, 229–62. On Orange, the unsatisfactory S. Bonnel, *Les 332 victimes de la commission populaire d'Orange* (2 vols, Carpentras, 1888); on Nantes and the west generally, Gaston Martin, *Carrier et sa mission à Nantes* (1924); E. Lockroy (ed.), *Une mission en Vendée, 1793* (1893); and Cl. Petitfrère, 'Blancs et bleus. Essai de sociologie historique du militantisme en Anjou (1791–1793)', *Bull. hist. écon. soc. Rév. fr.*

(1977), 19–34; on the north, L. Jacob, *Joseph Lebon* (1933) and G. Sangnier, *La terreur dans le district de Saint-Pol, 10 août 1792–9 thermidor An II* (2 vols., Blangermont, 1938). Above all, the Terror and its bureaucratic tendencies were tempered by geography, social structure and personalities which even an uninhibited representative could do little about, as is shown in the fine study by C. Lucas, *The Structure of the Terror. The Example of Javogues and the Loire* (Oxford, 1973).

The classic general study of the revolutionary committees is J. B. Sirich, *The Revolutionary Committees in the Departments of France, 1793–4* (Cambridge, Mass., 1943) which should be supplemented by L. Jacob, *Les suspects pendant la Révolution, 1793–1794* (1952); N. Bazin, 'Les suspects dans le district de Dijon', *Ann. Bourgogne*, xli (1969), 63–74; M. Lyons, *Revolution in Toulouse: an Essay on Provincial Terrorism* (Berne-Las Vegas, 1978); J. Godechot, 'Le comité de surveillance révolutionnaire de Nancy (2 avril 1793–1er germinal An III)', *RF*, lxxx (1927), 249–62, 295–311; R. C. Cobb, 'Un comité révolutionnaire du Forez. Le comité de surveillance de Bonnet-la-Montagne (Loire) (11 frimaire–28 fructidor An II)', *AHRF*, xxix (1957), 265–315; A. Richard, 'Le comité de surveillance et les suspects à Dax', *ibid.*, vii (1930), 24–40; G. Hardy, 'Le comité révolutionnaire de Sauçoins', *Ann. révolutionnaires*, v (1912), 492–510; M. Fabre, 'Uzès révolutionnaire. L'application de la loi des suspects en l'An II', *Mém. Acad. Nîmes*, 7th ser., xl (1922–3), 121–50; E. Poupé, 'Le comité de surveillance de la Roquebrussance (Var)', *Bull. hist. et philologique* (1907); J.-L. Rigal, 'Comité de surveillance de Saint-Geniez-d'Olt', *Archives historiques de Rouergue*, xvi (1942), 1–616; and P. Bécamps, 'Le comité de surveillance de Sainte-Foy-la-Grande, 1793–1794', *Rev. hist. Bordeaux*, n.s., viii (1959), 119–32.

The major book on the revolutionary armies is R. C. Cobb, *Les armées révolutionnaires* (2 vols., 1961–3).

The high politics of the Terror has attracted much attention, much of it influenced by Mathiez who was determined to prove Danton corrupt. Even when Mathiez's influence was still great, not everyone was convinced, as is shown in R. R. Palmer, *Twelve Who Ruled The Year of the Terror in the French Revolution* (Princeton, 1941), a general study very sympathetic to men whom the author saw as democrats under siege (note the date of publication) which in turn had a great influence on L. Gershoy, *Bertrand Barère, a Reluctant Terrorist* (Princeton, 1962). Some French scholars have tried to renew the question of corruption directly. See A. Lestapis, *La 'Conspiration de Batz' (1793–1794)* (1969) and M. Eudes, 'Une interprétation "non-mathiézienne" de l'affaire de la compagnie des indes', *AHRF*, lii (1981), 239–61. But the most dispassionate and clear in either language is the work of N. Hampson, 'François Chabot and his Plot', *Transactions of the Royal Historical Society*, 5th ser., xxvi (1976), 1–14, *The Life and Opinions of Maximilien Robespierre* (London, 1974) and *Danton* (London, 1978).

The interpretation here of the laws of ventôse which is bound to be controversial is taken from the text of the laws themselves partly printed in J. H. Stewart (ed.), *A Documentary Survey of the French Revolution* (New York, 1951) and a comparison of the full French texts in the *Moniteur*, as well as Saint-Just's accompanying speech which emphasizes repression as much as distributive justice. Contemporaries grasped the repressive intent in the provinces according to R. Schnerb, 'Les lois de ventôse et leur application dans le Puy-de-Dôme', *AHRF*, xi (1934), 403–34.

The atmosphere of crisis and the collapse of revolutionary government can be followed in M. Lyons, 'The 9 Thermidor: Motives and Effects', *ESR*, v (1975), 123–46; A. Mathiez, *The Fall of Robespierre and Other Essays* (New York, 1968); J. M. Thompson, *Robespierre* (2 vols., Oxford, 1939) and his *Robespierre and the French Revolution* (New York, 1962); G. Lefebvre, 'Sur la loi du 22 prairial An II' in his *Etudes*, 108–37; M. Eudes, 'La loi de prairial', *AHRF*, lv (1983), 544–59; the handy R. Bienvenu (ed.), *The Ninth of Thermidor: the Fall of Robespierre* (New York, 1968); and for the *journée* itself G. Walter, *La conjuration du neuf thermidor, 24 juillet 1794* (1974); Soboul's *Sans-culottes parisiens*; and P. Saint-Clair Deville, *La Commune de l'An II* (1946).

Chapters 7, 8, 9

The period 1794–9 quite logically forms a thematic unity as most of the general books on the subject recognize: G. Lefebvre, *The Thermidoreans* (New York, 1964) and his *The Directory* (New York, 1964); Lefebvre's studies were his lecture notes published forty years ago on subjects for which he had little taste. There have been several attempts since to deal with the period more sympathetically, notably by M. Sydenham, *The First French Republic, 1792–1804* (London, 1974) which blames the thermidoreans' and directorals' dogmatism for the failure to reestablish order. Sydenham's focus on high politics perhaps underestimates the extent of uncompromising royalism abroad and in the provinces. M. Lyons, *France Under the Directory* (London, 1975) provides a handy survey of all aspects of national life in a rather loose analytical frame. One could say the same of D. Woronoff, *The Thermidorean Régime and the Directory, 1794–1799* (1984) while A. Soboul, *Le Directoire et le Consulat* (1967) is entirely derivative. C. H. Church, 'In Search of the Directory' in J. F. Bosher (ed.), *French Government and Society, 1500–1850. Essays in Memory of Alfred Cobban* (London, 1973) is an important historiographical essay, while A. Goodwin, 'The French Executive Directory: a Revaluation', *History*, xxii (1937), 201–18, is a defence of its legislative achievements.

In addition to the appropriate local studies cited above for chs. 3 and 6 and those below, one can follow the winding down of the repression in J. Sirich, 'The Revolutionary Committees After Thermidor', *JMH*, xxvi

(1954), 329–39; M. Fabre, 'La réaction thermidorienne et la liquidation de la Terreur à Uzès', *Mém. Acad. Nîmes*, 7th ser., xli (1922–3), 65–85; P. Vaillaudet, 'Après le 9 thermidor. Les débuts de la Terreur blanche en Vaucluse', *AHRF*, v (1928), 109–27, and his 'Le procès des juges de la Commission révolutionnaire d'Orange, *ibid*., vi (1929), 137–63; F. Courcelle, 'La réaction thermidorienne dans le district de Melun', *ibid*., vii (1930), 113–28, 252–61, 329–50, 443–53; A. Richard, 'La réaction thermidorienne à Lescar (Basses-Pyrénées)', *Ann. révolutionnaires*, xii (1920), 130–5; and R. C. Cobb, 'Note sur la répression contre le personnel sans-culotte, de 1795 à 1801' in his *Terreur et subsistances*, 179–201, which is as much about the bureaucratization of the police as what happened to the *sans-culottes*. The failure to revive after thermidor shows that the Montagnards had dealt a mortal blow to the 'popular movement' in Paris. See the basic K. D. Tonnesson, *La défaite des sans-culottes. Mouvement populaire et réaction bourgeoise en l'An III* (Oslo, 1959) which also contains an exhaustive account of the *journées* of germinal and prairial, although R. Cobb and G. Rudé, 'The Last Popular Movement of the Revolution in Paris: the Journées of Germinal and of Prairial of Year III' in Kaplow's *New Perspectives* is clear and distinct. Cobb resumed the enquiry into the fate of the radicals and showed in his excellent *The Police and the People* that 'bourgeois reaction' is hardly a sufficient description. In fact, weakness is the continuing theme down to the deportations of 1801 as R. B. Rose, *Gracchus Babeuf; the First Revolutionary Communist* (London, 1978) and I. Woloch, *Jacobin Legacy: the Democratic Movement Under the Directory* (Princeton, 1970) show in different ways.

The 'other' popular movement in this period is described in F. Gendron, *La jeunesse dorée* (Québec, 1979) although the author's attempt to make these toughs into the motor of the thermidorean reaction is ludicrous. It does have the merit of updating H. Zivy, *Le 13 vendémiaire an IV* (1898). See also H. Mitchell, 'Vendémiaire, a Revaluation', *JMH*, xxx (1958), 191–202.

As Cobb shows, economic ruin was one reason for the collapse of the *sans-culottes* and he has done much to explore the social contours of the crisis of the Years III–IV. See chapters VIII–XI in his *Terreur et subsistances* and his more general 'Quelques aspects de la crise de l'An III en France', *Bull. Soc. hist. mod.* (1966), 2–5. Other studies include G. Leroy, *La famine à Melun en l'An III* (Melun, 1902) and J. R. Harkins, 'The Dissolution of the Maximums and Trade Controls in the Department of the Somme', *FHS*, vi (1970), 333–49. The consequences of the crisis for the cities can be followed in J. Dupâquier, *La population française au XVIIᵉ et XVIIIᵉ siècles* (1979), R. Cobb, *Death in Paris* (London, 1978), O. Hufton, *Bayeux*, and via the essays in M. Reinhard (ed.), *Contributions à l'histoire démographique de la révolution française* (2 vols., 1962–5). The explanations for the crisis are much more complex than a class-motivated attempt to restore a free market economy and in fact there is no comprehensive one. A starting point, but only that, is R. G. Hawtrey, 'The

Collapse of the French Assignats', *Economic Jl*, xxviii (1918), 300–14.

Economic and administrative collapse went hand in hand as the following local studies and the correspondence of the national agent of the district of Mâcon (AD, Saône-et-Loire, 2L 616) show. Thus French history in this period became more local than ever and it is a pity historians have so neglected it. Among the rare studies are the classic M. Reinhard, *Le département de la Sarthe sous le régime directoral* (Saint-Brieuc, 1935); P. Clémondot, *Le département de la Meurthe à l'époque du Directoire* (Nancy, 1966), a study of an uneventful department; E. Delacambre, *La période du directoire dans la Haute-Loire* (3 vols., Aubenas-Rodez, 1940–3); G. Sangnier, *Le district de Saint-Pol de Thermidor à Brumaire* (2 vols., Blangermont, 1946); G. Caudrillier, 'Bordeaux sous le Directoire', *RF*, lxx (1917), 19–54; J. Beyssi, 'Le parti jacobin à Toulouse sous le Directoire', *AHRF*, xxii (1950), 28–54, 108–33; J. Brelot, *La vie politique en Côte-d'or sous le Directoire* (Dijon, 1932); and C. Bloch, 'Le recrutement du personnel municipal dans le Loiret pour l'An IV', *RF*, xli (1904), 153–67.

Most of these studies illustrate a mounting, if diffuse, resistance whether in the form of religious revival spearheaded by women as in O. Hufton, 'Women in Revolution, 1789–1796', *P & P*, 52 (1971), 90–108, or with a more material base as shown in S. Aberdam, 'La Révolution et la lutte des métayers [dans le Gers]', *Etudes rurales*, 59 (1975), 73–91. Of course, such a distinction is usually too sharp. See G. Brégail, 'L'Insurrection de l'An IV dans le Gers', *Bull. Soc. arch. Gers*, x (1909), 235–50, 277–87 and his 'Une insurrection des bordiers...', *ibid.* (1901), 172–7.

This could slide into more overt and continuous antirevolutionary activity. Cobb began to discuss it in his *Police and People* and expanded it greatly in his *Reactions to the French Revolution* (London, 1972). It has been treated more systematically by C. Lucas in 'Violence thermidorienne et société traditionnelle. L'exemple du Forez', *Cahiers d'histoire* (1979), 21–43, his 'The First Directory and the Rule of Law', *FHS*, x (1977), 231–60, and 'Themes in Southern Violence after 9 Thermidor' in Lucas and G. Lewis (eds.), *Beyond the Terror. Essays in French Regional and Social History, 1794–1815* (Cambridge, 1983), 152–95, while G. Lewis tries to uncover the links with royalist conspirators in his 'Political Brigandage and Popular Disaffection in the South-East of France, 1795–1805' in *ibid.*, 195–231. There were also links between individual murders and prison massacres as the above and the following show: R. Fuoc, *La Réaction thermidorienne à Lyon* (Lyon, 1957); G. Martinet, 'Les débuts de la réaction thermidorienne à Marseille. L'émeute du 5 vendémiaire An III', *Actes du 90ᵉ CSS. Nice 1965* (3 vols., 1965), i, 149–66; E. Poupé, 'Le département du Var, 1790–An VIII', *Mem. Soc. d'études sci. et arch. de Draguignan*, xxxviii (1933), 5–553; R. Palluat de Besset, 'Les compagnons de Jésus dans le district de Montbrison', *Les Amitiés*, vi (1927), 240–52, 332–41; E. Perrin, 'La terreur blanche à Lyon sous le Directoire. L'assassinat de Pancrace d'Istria', *Revue du Lyonnais*, 5 (1922), 113–23 and his 'La journée du 1ᵉʳ prairial An IV et la destitution

du général Montchoisy', *ibid.*, 13 (1924), 75–102, 245–52, focus on the
murder gangs. The *Mémoire historique sur la réaction royale et sur les
massacres du Midi par le citoyen Fréron* (1824) and Chénier's two reports
to the Convention dated 6 messidor An III and 29 vendémiaire An IV
(Bibliothèque nationale Le[38] 1507 and Le[38] 1725) are still worth reading.

On brigandage, the only general survey is the inadequate and confused
M. Marion, *Le Brigandage pendant la Révolution* (1934). For the criminal
type, M. Vovelle, 'From Beggary to Brigandage: the Wanderers in the
Beauce During the French Revolution' in Kaplow's *New Perspectives*, 287–
304, and R. C. Cobb, *Paris and its Provinces* (London, 1975), 287–304. For
the more political, C. Joelivet, *L'agitation contre-révolutionnaire dans
l'Ardèche sous le Directoire* (Lyon, 1930); F. Saurel, *Les brigands royaux
dans l'Hérault et autres départements du Midi sous la République et le
Consulat* (Montpellier, 1893); P. Gaffarel, 'La bande d'Aubagne sous la
Révolution', *Ann. Provence*, 2nd ser., xvii (1920), 5–16, 75–92; E.
Lamouzèle, 'Un épisode des menées royalistes en l'an IV dans le canton
de Cintegabelle (Haute-Garonne)', *Rev. Pyrénées*, xviii (1906), 261–74; A.
Pons-Devier, 'Le banditisme sous le Directoire', *Rev. hist. arch. Béarn et
Pays-Basque*, 2nd ser., xi (1928), 24–30, 91–100, 129–38; C. Faure,
'L'affaire Dominique Allier', *Bull. Soc. Lit., hist., arch. Lyon*, xv (1937–
9), 117–39; M. Riou, 'Les chouans du Tanargue: de la clandestinité à la
guerre populaire (1795–1799)', *Revue du Vivarais* (1979), 191–224; R.
Maltby, 'Le brigandage dans la Drôme, 1795–1805', *Bull. arch. stat.
Drôme*, lxxix (1973), 116–34, and his 'Protestants, insurgés, et sans-
culottes dans la Drôme, 1792–An II', *ibid.* (1974), 209–21; and finally, E.
Poupé, *L'affaire des brigands d'Aups (brumaire an IX)* (Draguignan, 1906)
(BN, Lk[7] 36000). On desertion specifically: J.-P. Bertaud, 'Aperçus sur
l'insoumission et la désertion à l'époque révolutionnaire', *Bull. hist. écon.
soc. Rév. fr.*, 1 (1970), 17–48, and G. Dubois, 'Les résistances à la
conscription et les appels royalistes à la désertion dans la Seine-Inférieure',
Bull. Soc. Libre d'émulation . . . Seine-Inférieure (1942).

On the so-called religious revival see C. Ledré, *Le diocèse de Rouen et
la législation religieuse de 1795 à 1800* (1939), R. Patry, *Le régime de la
liberté des cultes dans le Calvados* (1921), A. Latreille, *L'opposition
religieuse au Concordat, de 1792 à 1803* (1910) and A. Durand, 'Le culte
catholique dans le Gard sous la Convention', *Mém. Acad. Nîmes*, 7th ser.,
xxxi (1922–3), 30–63.

In fact much of the material on brigandage, popular religion, desertion
and so on under the thermidorean Convention and the Directory remains
unpublished. Consequently, I have made extensive use of the
correspondence in Arch. nat. F[7] 4268, 7267–75, F[19] 1005–6, AF III 46–7,
93–4, BB[3] 7 (lists of executed brigands), BB[18] 174 (Bouches-du-Rhône),
BB[18] 720–7 (Saône-et-Loire), BB[18] 888 (Vaucluse – on murder gangs).

The risings in the west are still subject to a huge literature since popular
counterrevolution reached its apogee in this period. The best include C.
Chassin, *Les pacifications de l'Ouest, 1794–1801* (3 vols., 1896–9) and M.

G. Hutt, *Chouannerie and Counter-Revolution. Puisaye, the Princes and the British Government in the 1790s* (2 vols., Cambridge, 1983) which contains the best analysis of the controversial Quiberon expedition available. For the sociology of counterrevolution in the west see my *The Chouans. The Social Origins of Popular Counter-Revolution in Upper Brittany, 1770–1796* (Oxford, 1982), and (with T. J. A. Le Goff) 'The Revolution and the Rural Community in Eighteenth Century Brittany', *P & P*, 62 (1974), 96–119.

There are few attempts to explain regional patterns of political options. Le Goff and I have tried in 'The Social Origins of Counter-Revolution in Western France', *P & P*, 99 (1983), 65–87, and in 'Religion and Rural Revolt in the French Revolution: an Overview' in J. M. Bak and G. Benecke (eds.), *Religion and Rural Revolt* (Manchester, 1984), 123–45. So has Colin Lucas, 'The Problem of the Midi in the French Revolution', *Transactions of the Royal Historical Society*, 5th ser., xxviii (1978), 1–25 which tends to emphasize the earlier period.

Elections undermined the Constitution and so there are a number of important studies. See A. Lajusan, 'Le plébiscite de l'An III', *RF*, lx (1911), 5–37; P. Vaillandet, 'Le plébiscite de l'An III en Vaucluse', *AHRF*, ix (1932), 501–16; J. Suratteau, 'Les élections de l'An IV', *AHRF*, xxiii (1951), 374–93; xxiv (1952), 32–62; his 'Les élections de l'An V aux Conseils du Directoire', *ibid.*, xxx (1958), 21–63; and his *Les élections de l'An VI et le coup d'état du 22 floréal* (1971). Suratteau's works have been very influential but since he does not explain how his categories of allegiances were derived and, as J. Bourdon ('Les élections de la Côte-d'Or en 1792 et 1795', *Ann. Bourgogne*, xxix [1957], 189–94) points out, does not appreciate the significance of the low turnouts and shifting composition of the interminable electoral assemblies, his work must be treated with caution. But see the maps drawn from the results (Lyons, *Directory*, 220–2) or the figures in L. Hunt, 'The Political Geography of Revolutionary France', *Jl Interdis. Hist.*, xiv (1984), 535–59. She is much more successful with D. Lansky and P. Hanson in 'The Failure of the Liberal Republic in France, 1795–1799: the Road to Brumaire', *JMH*, li (1979), 734–59, an important study of the deputies of the Directory.

For political history of the period, A. Meynier, *Les coups d'état du Directoire* (3 vols., 1928) is indispensable but since he did not believe in the foreign conspiracy it is also necessary to consult G. Caudrillier, *L'Association royaliste de l'Institut philanthropique à Bordeaux* (1908), W. Fryer, *Republic or Restoration in France, 1794–7* (Manchester, 1965) and the especially comprehensive H. Mitchell, *The Underground War Against Revolutionary France: the Missions of William Wickham, 1794–1800* (Oxford, 1965). See also A. Bernard, 'Le 18 fructidor à Marseille et dans les Bouches-du-Rhône', *RF*, xli (1901), 193–215.

On foreign relations, the basic introduction is R. R. Palmer, *The Age of Democratic Revolution* (2 vols., Princeton, 1959–64), vol. 2. Palmer was quite optimistic about the French impact but few others are so sure. See

J. Godechot, *La Grande nation* (2 vols., 1956), the special issue of the
AHRF, xlix (1977) on Italy during the Directory and Empire, the essays
in R. Devleeshouwer (ed.), *Occupants-Occupés, 1792–1815* (Brussels,
1969), S. Schama, *Patriots and Liberators: Revolution in the Netherlands,
1780–1813* (London, 1977) and T. C. W. Blanning, *French Revolution in
Germany: Occupation and Resistance in the Rhineland, 1792–1802* (Oxford,
1983).

There is no recent comprehensive study of the crisis of the Year VII.
Most studies go back to the still serviceable and unjustly criticized A.
Vandal, *L'Avènement de Bonaparte* (2 vols., 1907). For the exterior crisis,
see A. B. Rodger, *The War of the Second Condition, 1798 to 1801. A
Strategic Commentary* (Oxford, 1964) and S. T. Ross, 'The Military
Strategy of the Directory: the Campaigns of 1799', *FHS* (1967), 170–87.
For the internal, A. Ollivier, *Le Dix-huit brumaire, 9 novembre 1799*
(1959) is pure unanalytical narrative; J. Lacouture, *Le Mouvement
royaliste dans le Sud-ouest (1797–1800)* (Hossegor, 1932), a neglected
classic; T. de Hansy, *Contribution à l'histoire de l'insurrection royaliste de
thermidor An VII (Août 1799) dans l'Ariège* (Foix, 1936); P. Dieuzade,
'L'Insurrection royaliste de l'An VII', *Rev. Gascogne*, n.s., xxii (1927),
199–210, and Arch. nat. F^7 7602–3.

Chapters 10, 11, 12

Among the biographies from the most basic to the most complex are: M.
G. Hutt, *Napoleon* (London, 1965), F. Markham, *Napoleon and the
Awakening of Europe* (London, 1954) and his *Napoleon* (New York,
1963), J. M. Thompson, *Napoleon Bonaparte; His Rise and Fall* (Oxford,
1963) and the masterpiece, G. Lefebvre, *Napoleon* (2 vols., New York,
1969). P. Geyl, *Napoleon, For and Against* (New Haven, 1963) is a
thorough examination of two centuries of biographical writing by an author
who was himself against. Two recent treatments are L. Bergeron, *France
under Napoleon* (Princeton, 1981) which certainly exaggerates the amount
of opposition, virtually ignores the impact of foreign affairs and war but
is excellent on the notables; and J. Tulard, *Le Grand Empire, 1804–1815*
(1982) which is a genuine overview, not another biography. There are two
fascinating collections of documents: M. G. Hutt (ed.), *Napoleon* (New
York, 1972) and J. C. Herold, *The Mind of Napoleon* (New York, 1975).

The best military studies are the lush and detailed D. Chandler, *The
Campaigns of Napoleon* (London, 1966) and the delightful and compact
G. Rothenberg, *The Art of Warfare in the Age of Napoleon* (Bloomington,
1978).

All modern authorities agree that Napoleon's myth not only predated
St Helena but also the Consulate. See J. Lucas-Dubreton, *Le culte de
Napoléon* (1960), J. Adhéman and N. Villa (eds.), *La légende
napoléonienne, 1796–1900* (1969), the BN exposition catalogue, and J.

Tulard, *Le mythe de Napoléon* (1971). But as Tulard shows (*L'Anti-Napoléon, La légende noire de l'Empereur* [1965]), there was also a countermyth.

To appreciate fully the reforms of the Consulate, it is necessary to appreciate the state of the country. There are two classic sources: F. Rocquain (ed.), *L'Etat de la France au 18 brumaire* (1874) and F.-A. Aulard (ed.), *L'Etat de la France en l'An VIII et l'An IX* (1897). Lest it be thought these exaggerate the disintegration (some of it the product of the coup), see Arch. nat. AF III 47 (the 'rapports décadaires' to the Directors), F^7 7603, 7704–8, which includes material on the repression of brigandage down to the Year IX. See also C. Langlois, 'Complots, propagandes et répression policière en Bretagne sous l'Empire (1806–1807)', *Ann. Bretagne* (1971–2), 369–421. J. Tulard continues this theme into the Empire with 'Quelques aspects du brigandage sous l'Empire', *Rev. Inst. Napoléon*, xcviii (1966), 31–6.

C. Langlois shows how fragile the early Consulate was as well as the fraud in the plebiscite in 'Le plébiscite de l'An VIII ou le coup d'état du 18 pluviôse An VIII', *AHRF*, xliv (1972), 43–65, 231–46, 390–415. For the reforms themselves F. Ponteil, *Napoléon Ier et l'organisation autoritaire de la France* (1956) only complements Godechot's *Les Institutions*. R. Holtman, *The Napoleonic Revolution* (Baton Rouge and London, 1967) is handy and agreeable. But as is clear from I. Collins, *Napoleon and his Parliaments, 1800–1815* (London, 1979) and J. Vidalenc, 'L'opposition sous le Consulat et l'Empire', *AHRF*, xl (1968), 472–88, the reforms cannot be understood except in their political context. The basic book here is Thibaudeau's memoirs translated as *Bonaparte and the Consulate* (London, 1908) which should be supplemented with Roederer's *Journal* (1909). These show how the etablishment of the dictatorship was hardly a usurpation. On specific crises, see M. J. Sydenham, 'The Crime of 3 Nivôse' in Bosher (ed.), *French Government and Society*, 295–320; E. d'Hauterive, *La Contre-police royaliste en 1800* (1931); P. Sagnac, 'Le Consulat à vie', *Rév. études napoléoniennes*, xxiv (1925), 133–54, 193–211; G. Caudrillier, 'Le complot de l'An XII', *Rev. historique*, lxxxiv (1900), 278–86, lxxv (1901), 257–85, lxxviii (1902), 45–71; G. de Cadoudal, *Georges Cadoudal et la chouannerie* (1889) and N. Gaukert, *Conspirateurs au temps de Napoléon Ier* (1962). Jean Thiry's books (*Le Sénat de Napoléon* [1931], *Le coup d'état du 18 brumaire* [1947], *Marengo* [1949], *L'Aube du Consulat* [1948], *La machine infernale* [1952], *Le Concordat et le Consulat à vie* [1959], *L'Avènement de Napoléon* [1959]) have the merit of quoting extensively from contemporary sources and memoirs. See also G. de Bertier de Sauvigny, *Le comte Ferdinand de Bertier (1782–1864) et l'énigme de la Congrégation* (1949) for opposition in the later period.

On the administrative system see the valuable and provocative E. Whitcomb, 'Napoleon's Prefects', *AHR*, lxx (1974), 1089–1118, and the detailed C. Durand, *Etudes sur le Conseil d'Etat napoléonien* (1949). C. Church, *Revolution and Red Tape: the French Ministerial Bureaucracy,*

1770–1850 (1981), by trying to make the opposite case, confirms the older view of the claims of the imperial bureaucracy to being a genuine innovation. Bureaucracy is best studied in the provinces yet there are too few good local histories of this period. An exception is R. Durand, *Le Département des Côtes-du-Nord sous le Consulat et l'Empire (1800–1815)* (2 vols., 1926). Others are not up to this standard. See L. Benaerts, *Le régime consulaire en Bretagne* (1914), P. Viard, *L'Administration préfectorale dans le département de la Côte-d'Or sous le Consulat et le premier Empire* (1914), J. F. Soulet, *Les premiers préfets des Hautes-Pyrénées, 1800–1814* (1965) and M. Rebouillat, 'L'établissement de l'administration préfectorale dans le département de Saône-et-Loire: les deux premiers préfets', *RHMC*, xvii (1970), 860–79.

On the Concordat and its application see Boulay de la Meurthe, *Histoire de la négociation du Concordat* (1921); S. Delacroix, *La réorganisation de l'Eglise de France après le Concordat (1801–1809)* (1962); C. Langlois and T. Le Goff, 'Les vaincus de la Révolution. Jalons pour une sociologie des prêtres mariés' in A. Soboul (ed.), *Voies nouvelles pour l'histoire de la Révolution française* (1978); J. Godel, *Le diocèse de Grenoble et la Restauration concordataire (1802–1809)* (1968); L. Lévy-Schneider, *L'Application du Concordat par un prélat d'Ancien Régime. Mgr Champion de Cicé, Archévêque d'Aix et d'Arles* (1921); C. Ledré, *La réorganisation d'un diocèse français au lendemain de la Révolution. Le Cardinal Cambacérès, archévêque de Rouen* (1943); C. Langlois, *Le diocèse de Vannes au XIXe siècle, 1800–1830* (1974); J. Valette, 'Le clergé du diocèse de Poitiers en 1802', *AHRF*, lv (1983), 137–54; G. Clause, 'La mise en application du Concordat de 1801 dans la Marne', *Actes du 82e CSS* (1958), 293–306; J.-L. Le Floc'h, 'L'Organisation du clergé dans le nouveau diocèse de Quimper en l'année 1803', *Bull. Soc. arch. du Finistère*, civ (1976), 209–37; and on the 'restoration' of piety, the sensitive C. Jones, *Charity and bienfaisance. The Treatment of the Poor in the Montpellier Region, 1740–1815* (Cambridge, 1982).

On clerical and popular opposition to the Concordat, C. Latreille, *Après le Concordat. L'opposition de 1803 à nos jours* (1910), the remarkably detailed A. Billaud, *La Petite Eglise dans la Vendée et les Deux-Sèvres (1800–1830)* (1961), A. Pioger, 'Un apôtre de la Petite Eglise dans le Maine, L'abbé Grangeard, 1753–1832', *Bull. Soc. Ag., Sci. et Arts Sarthe*, 3rd ser., xvi (1955–6), 58–93, E. Dermenghem, 'La Petite Eglise dans les Hautes-Alpes de 1801 à nos jours', *Bull. Soc. Etudes Hautes-Alpes*, xlix (1957), 115–47, and C. Brun, 'Les blancs ou anticoncordataires du Charollais', *Ann. Bourgogne* (1929), 215–35.

Declining draft evasion is a measure of successful bureaucratization. One can follow this improvement in the classic G. Vallée, *La conscription dans le département de la Charente, 1798–1807* (1937) which covers much of the national scene too; A. Forrest, 'Conscription and Crime in Rural France during the Directory and the Consulate', in Lucas and Lewis (eds.), *Beyond the Terror*, 92–120; L. Ogès, 'La conscription et l'esprit public dans le Finistère sous le Consulat et l'Empire', *Mém. Soc. hist. arch. Bretagne*, xlii (1962), 105–28; A. Maury, 'Réfractaires et déserteurs dans le Puy-de-Dôme sous le Directoire, le Consulat et l'Empire', *Rev. Auvergne*, lxxii (1958), 113–33; J. Vidalenc, 'La désertion dans le département du Calvados sous le premier Empire', *RHMC*, vi (1960), 60–72, and his 'L'Attitudes des notables de la Seine-Inférieure en face de la conscription de 1811', *Rev. Inst. hist. mil.*, xxx (1970), 233–43; M. Lantier, 'L'opposition de la conscription de 1808 à 1815 dans le département de la Manche (d'après le *Journal de la Manche*)', *Rev. Manche*, ii (1960), 23–47; and J. Waquet, 'L'insoumission et la désertion sous le Consulat et le premier Empire vues à travers les états d'arrestations', *Actes du 93ᵉ CSS, Tours 1968* (1971), t. 2, 373–80.

On the economy and its vicissitudes, the central study is A. Chabert, *Essai sur le mouvement des revenus et de l'activité économique en France de 1798 à 1820* (1949). In addition see C. Rollet, 'L'effet des crises économiques du début du XIXᵉ siècle sur la population', *RHMC*, xvii (1970), 391–410; P. Butel, 'Crise et mutation de l'activité économique à Bordeaux sous le Consulat et l'Empire', *ibid.*, 540–58; J. Vidalenc, 'L'agriculture dans les départements normands à la fin du Premier Empire', *Ann. Normandie*, vii (1957), 179–201 and his 'La vie économique des départements méditerranéens pendant l'Empire', *RHMC*, i (1954), 165–98; R. Dugrand, *Villes et campagnes en Bas-Languedoc* (1963); M. Vovelle, 'Propriété et exploitation dans quelques communes beauceronnes de la fin du 18ᵉ et au début du 19ᵉ siècle' in his *Villes et campagnes*, 215–26; G. Lefebvre, *Paysans du Nord*; R. Laurant, 'La lutte pour l'individualisme agraire dans la France du premier Empire', *Ann. Bourgogne*, xxii (1950), 81–401; G. Thuillier, 'La crise monétaire de l'automne 1810', *Rev. hist.*, ccxxxviii (1967), 51–84; L. Bergeron, *Banquiers, négociants et manufacturiers parisiens du Directoire à l'Empire* (1978); J. Tulard, *Nouvelle histoire de Paris. Le Consulat et l'Empire, 1800–1815* (n.d.).

On economic policy, E. Heckscher, *The Continental System* (Oxford, 1922), updated and corrected in F. Crouzet, *L'économie britannique et le blocus continental (1806–1813)* (2 vols., 1958) and his 'Wars, Blockade, and Economic Change in Europe, 1792–1815', *Jl Econ. Hist.*, xxiv (1964), 567–88. G. Ellis, *Napoleon's Continental Blockade. The Case of Alsace* (1981) argues for a coherent market strategy which had permanent effects.

On the nature of the elite, it is best to start with R. Forster, 'The Survival of the Nobility during the French Revolution', *P & P*, 37 (1967), 71–86, where the argument for a decisive decline is deployed, challenged by Cobban in *ibid.*, 39 (1968), 169–70, with a rejoinder on 171–2. T. Beck, 'The French Revolution and the Nobility. A Reconsideration', *Jl Soc. Hist.*, xv (1981), 219–33, is interesting despite methodological problems. G. Ellis, 'Rhine and Loire, Napoleonic Elites and Social Order' in Lucas and Lewis (eds.), *Beyond the Terror*, 232–67, is a fine introduction to studies of the notables. Alas, this subject is more confusing than it need be because local studies do not appear to be conducted according to a standardized questionnaire. G. Chaussinand-Nogaret, L. Bergeron and R. Forster, 'Les notables du "Grand Empire" en 1810', *Annales. ESC*, xxvi (1971), 1052–75, is really about members of the electoral colleges in five departments, while M. Agulhon, 'Les notables du Var sous le Consulat', *RHMC*, xvii (1970), 720–5, A. Palluel-Guiliard, 'Les notables dans les Alpes du Nord sous le premier Empire', *ibid.*, 740–57, are about the 600 most highly taxed while J.-M. Levy, 'Les notables de l'Ain sous le Consulat et l'Empire', *ibid.*, 726–40, is about both. The close to a dozen departmental monographs with the overall title *Grands Notables du Premier Empire* (1978–) are very uneven and quite understandardized. This makes regional comparisons very difficult. See also P. Bouyoux, 'Les "Six Cents plus imposés" du département de la Haute-Garonne en l'An X', *Ann. Midi*, lxx (1958), 317–27. On their incomes, A.-M. Boursier and A. Soboul, 'La grande propriété foncière à l'époque napoléonienne', *AHRF*, liii (1981), 405–18. On the imperial nobility and the system of honours generally see J. Tulard, *Napoléon et la noblesse d'Empire* (1979).

On life-chances and promotions into various institutions see G. Rougeron, 'Le personnel du département de l'Allier sous la Révolution française (1790–An VII)', *Notre Bourbonnais*, 8th ser., 188 (1974), 129–33, 150–5, 172–7, 189–90, Whitcomb's 'Napoleon's Prefects', and his *Napoleon's Diplomatic Service* (Durham, NC, 1979) which, not surprisingly, was very blue-blooded, and G. Six, *Les généraux de la Révolution et de l'Empire* (1947).

On the fall, the most exciting, although strictly a political narrative, is still H. Houssaye, *1814* (1888) and *1815* (3 vols., 1889–1905). On public opinion such as it was, J. Regnault, 'L'Empereur et l'opinion publique, 1813–1814', *Rev. hist. de l'Armée*, xiii (1957), 29–50 and J. Vidalenc, 'L'opinion publique dans le département de la Seine-Inférieure à la fin du Premier Empire', *Rev. Soc. savantes Haute-Normandie*, 15 (1959), 69–82. On the military losses controversy, J. Houdaille, 'Le problème des pertes de guerre', *RHMC*, xvii (1970), 411–23 and E. Whitcomb, 'Napoleon's Invasion of Russia: a Study of Statistics and Prejudice', *Laurentian University R.*, iv (1972), 47–62. On the economy, in addition to Chabert, *Prix et revenus*, see J. Vidalenc, 'La crise des subsistances et les troubles de 1812 dans le Calvados', *Actes du 89e CSS. Dijon 1959* (1960), 321–64; P. Viard, 'Les subsistances en Ille-et-Vilaine sous le Consulat et l'Empire', *Ann. Bretagne*, xxii (1917), 328–511, 471–88, xxiii (1918), 131–54; M. Lantier, 'La crise alimentaire de 1812 dans la Manche', *Rev. Manche*, iii (1961), 130–47; J. Tulard, 'Du Paris impérial au Paris de 1830 d'après les bulletins de police', *Bull. soc. histoire Paris et Ile-de-France*, xcvi (1969), 157–75; and Cobb, *Police and People*.

On the final crisis, see the very patriotic F. Ponteil, *La chute de Napoléon Ier* (1943); J. Thiry, *La chute de Napoléon Ier* (2 vols., 1938–9); E. Gallo, *Les Cent-Jours* (1924); K. Tonneson, 'Les fédérés de Paris pendant les Cent-Jours', *AHRF*, liv (1982), 393–415; F. Bluche, *Le Plébiscite des Cent Jours* (1974); J. P. T. Bury, 'The End of the Napoleonic Senate',

Cambridge Hist. Jl, ix (1949), 165–89; P. Mansel, *Louis XVIII* (London, 1981); and Arch. nat. F^7 9081–2, 9639–40.

Index

Index